Global Perspectives on Reforming the Criminal Justice System

Michael Pittaro
American Military University, USA

IGI Global
PUBLISHER of TIMELY KNOWLEDGE

A volume in the Advances in Criminology, Criminal Justice, and Penology (ACCJP) Book Series

Published in the United States of America by
IGI Global
Information Science Reference (an imprint of IGI Global)
701 E. Chocolate Avenue
Hershey PA, USA 17033
Tel: 717-533-8845
Fax: 717-533-8661
E-mail: cust@igi-global.com
Web site: http://www.igi-global.com

Library of Congress Cataloging-in-Publication Data

Names: Pittaro, Michael, editor.
Title: Global perspectives on reforming the criminal justice system / Michael Pittaro, editor.
Description: Hershey : Information Science Reference, 2021. | Includes bibliographical references and index. | Summary: "This book aims to provide relevant theoretical frameworks and the latest empirical research findings in the area of criminal justice reform on a global scale offering a variety of chapters written for criminal justice professionals, scholars, students, community advocates, and elected officials who want to improve and widen their understanding of the strategic role of scientific research in addressing crime prevention, commission, rehabilitation, and recidivism"-- Provided by publisher.
Identifiers: LCCN 2021004889 (print) | LCCN 2021004890 (ebook) | ISBN 9781799868842 (hardcover) | ISBN 9781799868859 (paperback) | ISBN 9781799868866 (ebook)
Subjects: LCSH: Criminal justice, Administration of. | Law enforcement. | Crime prevention. | Police-community relations.
Classification: LCC HV7419 .G567 2021 (print) | LCC HV7419 (ebook) | DDC 364--dc23
LC record available at https://lccn.loc.gov/2021004889
LC ebook record available at https://lccn.loc.gov/2021004890

This book is published in the IGI Global book series Advances in Criminology, Criminal Justice, and Penology (ACCJP) (ISSN: pending; eISSN: pending)

British Cataloguing in Publication Data
A Cataloguing in Publication record for this book is available from the British Library.

Advances in Criminology, Criminal Justice, and Penology (ACCJP) Book Series

Liam J. Leonard
Arden University, UK

ISSN:pending
EISSN:pending

Mission

Criminology has never been more relevant. Violence, serial murder, crime and victimization continue to remain an unfortunate staple of society. Crime is a key issue globally, nationally, and regionally. Law enforcement personnel within the criminal justice system must keep pace with ever changing modes of crime. As officials work to predict and prevent crimes, as well as apprehend offenders, they will need to devise new tools and strategies to preserve the safety of society and ensure proper justice is served.

The **Advances in Criminology, Criminal Justice, and Penology (ACCJP)** Book Series explores emerging research behind crime control strategies, crime motivation, new methods and the utilization of technology for committing illegal acts, criminal justice and reform strategies, and the effects of crime on society and its victims. The publications contained within this series are valuable resources for government officials, law enforcement officers, corrections officers, prison management, criminologists, sociologists, psychologists, forensic scientists, security specialists, academicians, researchers, and students seeking current research on international crime.

Coverage

- Serial Killers
- Victimology
- Fraud
- Hacking
- Criminal Rehabilitation
- Law
- Hate Crimes
- Criminology
- Criminal Justice Systems
- Restorative Justice

IGI Global is currently accepting manuscripts for publication within this series. To submit a proposal for a volume in this series, please contact our Acquisition Editors at Acquisitions@igi-global.com or visit: http://www.igi-global.com/publish/.

The Advances in Criminology, Criminal Justice, and Penology (ACCJP) Book Series (ISSN pending) is published by IGI Global, 701 E. Chocolate Avenue, Hershey, PA 17033-1240, USA, www.igi-global.com. This series is composed of titles available for purchase individually; each title is edited to be contextually exclusive from any other title within the series. For pricing and ordering information please visit http://www.igi-global.com/book-series/advances-criminology-criminal-justice-penology/212650. Postmaster: Send all address changes to above address.

Titles in this Series

For a list of additional titles in this series, please visit: www.igi-global.com/book-series/advances-criminology-criminal-justice-penology/212650

Interventions, Training, and Technologies for Improved Police Well-Being and Performance
Eamonn Patrick Arble (Department of Psychology, Eastern Michigan University, USA) and Bengt B. Arnetz (College of Human Medicine, Michigan State University USA)
Information Science Reference • © 2021 • 278pp • H/C (ISBN: 9781799868200) • US $195.00

Invisible Victims and the Pursuit of Justice Analyzing Frequently Victimized Yet Rarely Discussed Populations
Raleigh Blasdell (North Central College, USA) Laura Krieger-Sample (Southeast Missouri State University, USA) and Michelle Kilburn (Southeast Missouri State University USA)
Information Science Reference • © 2021 • 474pp • H/C (ISBN: 9781799873488) • US $195.00

Global Perspectives on People, Process, and Practice in Criminal Justice
Liam J. Leonard (Northern Arizona University, USA)
Information Science Reference • © 2021 • 282pp • H/C (ISBN: 9781799866466) • US $195.00

Combating the Exploitation of Children in Cyberspace Emerging Research and Opportunities
Hossam Nabil Elshenraki (Dubai Police Academy, UAE)
Information Science Reference • © 2021 • 165pp • H/C (ISBN: 9781799823605) • US $160.00

Encyclopedia of Criminal Activities and the Deep Web
Mehdi Khosrow-Pour D.B.A. (Information Resources Management Association, USA)
Information Science Reference • © 2020 • 1162pp • H/C (ISBN: 9781522597155) • US $2,450.00

Handbook of Research on Trends and Issues in Crime Prevention, Rehabilitation, and Victim Support
Augusto Balloni (Italian Society of Victimology, Italy) and Raffaella Sette (University of Bologna, Italy)
Information Science Reference • © 2020 • 553pp • H/C (ISBN: 9781799812869) • US $245.00

Global Perspectives on Victimization Analysis and Prevention
Johnson Oluwole Ayodele (Lagos State University, Nigeria)
Information Science Reference • © 2020 • 272pp • H/C (ISBN: 9781799811121) • US $195.00

Handbook of Research on Mass Shootings and Multiple Victim Violence
Gordon A. Crews (University of Texas Rio Grande Valley, USA)
Information Science Reference • © 2020 • 531pp • H/C (ISBN: 9781799801139) • US $265.00

IGI Global
PUBLISHER of TIMELY KNOWLEDGE

701 East Chocolate Avenue, Hershey, PA 17033, USA
Tel: 717-533-8845 x100 • Fax: 717-533-8661
E-Mail: cust@igi-global.com • www.igi-global.com

Table of Contents

Detailed Table of Contents

To prevent and control crime using the community-oriented policing model, law enforcement agencies must develop positive relationships and partnerships with the communities they serve. Unfortunately, several obstacles impede the development and maintenance of police-community partnerships, particularly excessive force and other forms of misconduct, and negative coverage of law enforcement by the media. To restore public trust in the police, agencies must implement competency-based interviews and assessments during the hiring process; develop a recruitment plan to attract more diverse applicants; provide regular crisis intervention, de-escalation, and implicit bias training to all officers; and evaluate and make any necessary improvements to existing use-of-force and disciplinary policies. Future research should continue to evaluate the impact of community policing on crime rates, the impact of body-worn cameras on misconduct, and the correlation between higher education and misconduct.

This chapter addresses the voices of Black individuals and their communities urging police officers to be trustworthy and transparent, and urging them to be intentional in building relationships in the Black community. Qualified immunity, fraternal order of police, and law enforcement bill of rights discussions have emerged from recent incidents that add to the Black community's mistrust in the police. This chapter discusses how officers fail to recognize past and current issues where officers are unapologetic, and which, in turn, contributes to making it difficult to see police transparency and legitimacy. The chapter also addresses the partial education officers receive on Black culture and, more importantly, officers' lack of knowledge about cultural humility with self-reflection. Global positive social change and using a conceptual communication framework are the foundation for building and strengthening police relationships in the Black community to improve police strategies.

The Nigerian police force is an institution established to protect the lives and properties of residents. Some of her duties include tackling armed robbery, banditry, recovery of stolen assets, investigation of cases, and settling violence-related issues among persons. Just like every other institution, her operations are premised on certain ethical codes and conduct which guarantees checks and balances in her relationship with ordinary citizens. Maximum productivity can be achieved by the Nigerian police if only they display ethical behaviour in the discharge of their lawful duties to the public. Growing unethical work behaviour among Nigerian police officers has drawn attention to the various despicable and condemnable acts perpetrated by some personnel. This study makes a scholarly attempt to investigate the trend of the unethical work behaviour in the Nigerian police force. Using content analysis, the findings suggest that

correctional facilities and probation-parole departments. However, this evidence-based approach in reducing recidivism is moot if correctional leadership is not supportive of rehabilitative programs for offenders. The efficacy and success of these programs are dependent on effective leadership along with professionals and paraprofessionals that are specifically credentialed or licensed and have the qualities and skillsets to provide these types of rehabilitative measures.

Tough-on-crime policies and strategies, such as mandatory minimum and determinate sentencing laws and more severe punishments for juveniles, sex offenders, and drug offenders, have caused a substantial increase in the U.S. incarceration rate. Mass incarceration has generated several negative consequences, including racial bias and disparities, economic and social costs, and prison overcrowding. As such, the use of community corrections programs as an alternative form of sentencing has significantly increased. To effectively reduce crime and recidivism, community corrections programs must 1) utilize a validated risk and needs assessment when determining program placement; 2) provide participants with comprehensive, evidence-based services, including substance abuse and mental health treatment; 3) focus on modifying participants' behavior through treatment goal setting and the use of graduated incentives and sanctions; and 4) strive to hire and retain qualified staff, provide both initial and ongoing training, and monitor treatment staff with regular clinical supervision.

Today, every prison around the world requires a correctional programme so that rehabilitation and reintegration of offenders can be done successfully. Correctional reforms is a serious issue and has been taken seriously even internationally. In India, many attempts have been made to improve the condition of prisons and prisoners, but little changes have been seen at the root-level. There is a scope of modifications in the correctional reforms to meet the present-day needs of the criminal justice system. The chapter will give an overview of the correctional reforms in Indian prisons and after reviewing the existing literature will attempt to identify the limitations of the correctional programs which need to be addressed for effective rehabilitation and reformation of prisoners. Lastly, the chapter will conclude with a number of suggestions and with a comprehensive model for rehabilitation.

Globally, at least half of the released prisoner population will return to incarceration before the end of their first year in society. Going against generally accepted notions, deliberation should be given to the existence of transience in habitual recidivists' or habitual convicted criminal offenders' (HCCOs') life course. The HCCO is habitually, chronically, or serially recidivistic (above the average recorded number of arrests and imprisonment, i.e., anything above or equal to five). Furthermore, transience can

Homelessness and related community ailments have plagued society for a number of years, and governments have found it difficult to get these under control. The sheer number of homeless with mental health afflictions and problematic substance use problems leaves no doubt about the need for a stronger, more urgent government response. Community ailments such as these have led to increased crime rates and incarcerations and overcrowded prisons without a lasting solution in sight. This chapter uses the transformative justice model, with the expectation it produces better results than current models, by examining the source of homelessness, mental health afflictions, and problematic substance use and their bi-directional relationship with crime. This inter-jurisdictional study compares the current situations in the state of California and the province of Ontario, which have a high percent of homeless populations. It proves that special attention to vulnerable populations such as racialized groups, the socioeconomically disadvantaged, and youth is warranted.

Trafficking of persons, primarily women and children, is one of the growing social dilemmas concerning global society today. Not only is human trafficking a highly sensitive and polarizing subject, but it is also considered a common norm in many countries. Many women recruited into commercial sex work are coerced into the profession exploiting their financial and economic condition but continue to work in the profession to survive through easy money. The chapter focuses on a theoretical framework for understanding the victimization of female sex workers. It also reflects various lacuna in the present criminal justice system and law enforcement mechanism in criminalizing victims within the sex work industry. The chapter narrates the voices of commercial sex workers in India over the prejudices and criminalization by various laws and regulations towards their consensual sex work. The chapter recommends sensitization training and awareness amongst various stakeholders of the criminal justice system.

Preface

Calls for criminal justice reform across the world have grown louder in recent years and yet, few laws have been enacted and even fewer policies, procedures, and programs have been implemented to address the disparate treatment of certain members of our global society, namely the impoverished and those of color who are disproportionately represented at every stage of the criminal justice system from arrest to conviction to punishment. Criminal justice reform efforts and initiatives are not confined solely to the United States, but rather extends globally to nearly every country in which inequity and inequality between social classes exists.

For those of us, like myself, who have served as criminal justice practitioners, educators, and researchers, we must do more. We must be better. These issues are not new but rather extend back to the earliest days of policing and sentencing. The criminal justice system is not beyond repair, but it is flawed. For change to occur, we must change the deep-seated culture of this vast system, which is no easy task, but it is possible. To be successful, criminal justice practitioners and scholars worldwide must come together to share and disseminate information and innovative ideas as to what we need to achieve as a global society. This requires using our collective critical thinking skills and, in my opinion, assistance from not just those as criminal justice practitioners and/or scholars, but the active recruitment of sociologists, legal experts, psychologist, politicians, community advocates, coaches, teachers, parents, and the list goes on and on. It reminds me of the saying, "it takes an entire village to raise a child." Well, that holds true here. To effectively reform the criminal justice system, we must actively engage individuals from other professions who can share their expertise with the decisionmakers.

Global Perspectives on Reforming the Criminal Justice System is unique because it is the first of its kind in providing scholarly international perspectives on reforming the criminal justice system in one comprehensive volume. I believe that it is the first of many books on this topic because this book is intended to generate an international dialogue pertaining to the complex issues that we face in regard to policing, sentencing, and imprisoning individuals who, even though they hail from various parts of the world, share more similarities than differences. They are often comprised of disenfranchised, marginalized members of society. Racial, ethnic, and social class disparity are evident at every stage of the criminal justice system. Therefore, we must confront the reality that discrimination, intolerance, and biasness are deeply embedded within the criminal justice system, and that must change. The chapters within this book provide a great start point to creating positive change.

In short, *Global Perspectives on Reforming the Criminal Justice System* provides in-depth and current research about the criminal justice system around the world, its many inadequacies, and why it urgently needs reformation. Offering a fully fleshed outline of the current system, this book details the newest research and is incredibly important to fully understand the flaws of the criminal justice system across the globe. The goals of this book are to improve and advance the criminal justice system by addressing the glaring weaknesses within the system and discuss potential reforms including decreasing the prison population (decarceration) and improving police/community relations. Highlighting topics that include accountability, community-oriented policing, ethics, and mass incarceration, this book is ideal for law enforcement officers, trainers/educators, government officials, policymakers, correctional officers, court officials, professionals, researchers, academicians, and students in the fields of criminal justice, criminology, sociology, psychology, addictions, mental health, social work, public policy, and public administration.

The chapters are divided into four sections. Section 1 is comprised of Chapters 1 – 6, which focus on police reform. Section 2 is comprised of Chapters 7-11, which focus on prison reform. Section 3 is comprised of Chapters 12 – 14, which focus on legal reform, and finally, Section 4, which is comprised of Chapters 15-17, focuses on victim reform. A detailed breakdown of each chapter is described below.

Chapter 1, "Body-Worn Cameras: Panacea or Distraction for Increased Police Use of Force Accountability?" provides a great opening to any discussion pertaining to police reform. The police hold a unique and distinctive status compared to any other occupation in society, with their authority to use force. With such responsibility, communities expect law enforcement to be held accountable when force is applied. One of the many proposed solutions embraced by authorities and the public to decrease the number of force encounters is body-worn cameras (BWCs). The purpose of this chapter is to examine BWCs as a measure of reducing force by law enforcement, explore the technology as an enhancement to transparency within the context of police-community relations, and offer recommendations for adoption rooted in best practices. For the public, it is imperative to recognize BWCs as just one part of improving law enforcement oversight as opposed to providing an all-encompassing solution that will completely resolve issues of transparency.

Chapter 2, "School to Prison Pipeline: The Role of School Resource Officers (SRO)," focuses on a specific policing assignment, which could have a positive influence on the school to prison pipeline that we often reference in relation to K-12 schooling. Juvenile crime rates are plummeting, and the number of youths in juvenile detention centers has dropped; however, school discipline polices are moving in the opposite direction. In recent years, the lines between the school system and the juvenile justice system have become indistinct. There are several trends in K-12 education contributing to the school-to-prison pipeline such as declining school funding, re-segregation of schools by race and class, under-representation of students of color in advanced placement, over-representation of student of color in special education, creation and expansion of zero-tolerance policies, tracking, increased presents of SROs, No Child Left Behind (NCLB), standardized testing, and rising drop-out rates. However, the focus here is the expansion and increased reliance on "zero-tolerance policies and the use of the SRO to enforce those policies which play an immediate and integral role in feeding the school-to-prison pipeline.

Chapter 3, "Improving Police-Community Relations in the USA," highlights the importance of improving police- community relations, and even though it addresses police-community relations in the United States, it could easily be applied to policing in other countries. To prevent and control crime using the community-oriented policing model, law enforcement agencies must develop positive relationships and partnerships with the communities they serve. Unfortunately, several obstacles impede the development and maintenance of police–community partnerships, particularly excessive force and other forms of misconduct, and negative coverage of law enforcement by the media. To restore public trust in the police, agencies must implement competency-based interviews and assessments during the hiring process; develop a recruitment plan to attract more diverse applicants; provide regular crisis intervention, de-escalation, and implicit bias training to all officers; and evaluate and make any necessary improvements to existing use-of-force and disciplinary policies. Future research should continue to evaluate the impact of community policing on crime rates, the impact of body-worn cameras on misconduct, and the correlation between higher education and misconduct.

Chapter 4, "Policing Strategies and Approaches to Improving Community Relations: Black Citizens' Perceptions of Law Enforcement Efforts to Intentionally Strengthen Relationships," addresses the voices of Black individuals and their communities urging police officers to be trustworthy and transparent, and urging them to be intentional in building relationships in the Black community. Qualified immunity, Fraternal Order of Police, and law enforcement bill of rights discussions have emerged from recent incidents that add to the Black community's mistrust in the police. This chapter discusses how officers fail to recognize past and current issues where officers are unapologetic, and which, in turn, contributes to making it difficult to see police transparency and legitimacy. The chapter also addresses the partial education officers receive on Black culture and, more importantly, officers' lack of knowledge about cultural humility with self-reflection. Global positive social change and using a conceptual communication framework, are the foundation for building and strengthening police relationships in the Black community to improve police strategies.

Chapter 5, is "An Assessment of Unethical Work Behavior Among Police Personnel in Nigeria." The Nigerian Police Force is an institution established to protect the lives and properties of residents. Some of her duties includes tackling armed robbery, banditry, recovery of stolen assets, investigation of cases and settling violence related issues among persons. Just like every other institution, her operations are premised on certain ethical codes and conduct which guarantees checks and balances in her relationship with ordinary citizens. Maximum productivity can be achieved by the Nigerian Police if only they display ethical behaviour in the discharge of their lawful duties to the public. Growing unethical work behaviour among Nigerian police officers in recent time has drawn our attention to the various despicable and condemnable acts perpetrated by some personnel. This study makes a scholarly attempt to investigate the trend of the unethical work behaviour in the Nigerian Police Force. Using content analysis, the findings suggest that only handful of Nigerian Police officers display professionalism and ethical behaviour in the discharge of their duties.

Chapter 6 is "Reform the Police and End the Violence: What Works Between Community Policing and State Police in North Central Nigeria." Policing in Nigeria has never been this challenging. Aside from accusations of violence and brutality, the police are widely regarded as ineffective and inefficient. While insecurity surges across the country, regional security networks are springing up in an uncoordinated manner, raising questions about ownership and control. This further gave rise to agitations for either community policing and state police from the political class, civil societies, and traditional institutions. This chapter situates police violence within the context of the popular #EndSARS# protest and reviews issues surrounding police reforms in Nigeria. Within the context of the challenging insecurity in the north central region, the chapter looks at the merits and demerits of community police and state police to determine what works and makes recommendations on the appropriate policing strategy in the region.

Chapter 7 is "The Five Rs of Prison Reform With Ethnoracially Diverse Offenders: A Clinical Forensic Psychological Perspective." There are various barriers associated with successful reentry into society for individuals released from prison. Reuniting with family members, rehabilitation efforts, employment, and housing are just some examples of obstacles individuals face when released into the community. Additionally, the costs stemming from the number of people incarcerated, length of stay in prison, racial disparities, and the mental status of offenders create an increased risk for post-release readjustment complications. This book chapter focuses on what we call the Pentagonal Post-Release Risk Assessment Framework, or the 5 R's, which includes consideration for risk association of recidivism, reunification, rehabilitation, reintegration, and racism. For individuals released back into the community, it is imperative to consider the 5 R's. Neglecting one or more of the 5 R's may perpetuate a cycle of reoffending.

Chapter 8 is "Recidivism and Cognitive Behavioral Therapies: The Efficacy of Correctional Programming." Recidivism of criminal offenders has become a national problem in the United States. New criminal activity along with technical violations of conditions of probation or parole are the results of deficiencies in cognitive behaviorisms. Numerous studies have revealed that weaknesses in cognitive behavior are a common denominator among offenders. These studies have led to the development and implementation of treatment strategies that, when administered to criminal offenders, have proven to be effective in reducing recidivism. Therapeutic programs grounded in evidence-based practices are widely used throughout correctional facilities and probation – parole departments. However, this evidence-based approach in reducing recidivism is moot if correctional leadership is not supportive of rehabilitative programs for offenders. The efficacy and success of these programs are dependent on effective leadership along with professionals and paraprofessionals that are specifically credentialed or licensed and have the qualities and skillsets to provide these types of rehabilitative measures.

Chapter 9 is "The Potential of Community Corrections to Reduce Mass Incarceration in the USA." Tough-on-crime policies and strategies, such as mandatory minimum and determinate sentencing laws and more severe punishments for juveniles, sex offenders, and drug offenders, have caused a substantial increase in the U.S. incarceration rate. Mass incarceration has generated several negative consequences, including racial bias and disparities, economic and social costs, and prison overcrowding. As such, the use of community corrections programs as an alternative form of sentencing has significantly increased. To effectively reduce crime and recidivism, community corrections programs must: 1) utilize a validated risk and needs assessment when determining program placement; 2) provide participants with comprehensive, evidence-based services, including substance abuse and mental health treatment; 3) focus on modifying participants' behavior through treatment goal setting and the use of graduated incentives and sanctions; and 4) strive to hire and retain qualified staff, provide both initial and ongoing training, and monitor treatment staff with regular clinical supervision.

Chapter 10 is "Overview of Correctional Reform in India: A 'Different' Approach to Offender Rehabilitation." Today, every prison around the world requires a correctional programme so that rehabilitation and reintegration of offenders can be done successfully into society. Correctional reforms are a serious issue and have been taken seriously even internationally. In India, many attempts have been made to improve the condition of prisons and prisoners but little changes have been seen at the root- level. There is a scope of modifications in the correctional reforms to meet the present-day needs of the criminal justice system. The present chapter will give an overview of the correctional reforms in Indian prisons and after reviewing the existing literature, will attempt to identify the limitations of the correctional programs which need to be addressed for effective rehabilitation and reformation of prisoners. Lastly, the chapter will conclude with a number of suggestions and with a comprehensive model for rehabilitation.

Chapter 11 is "The Transient State of Habitual Convicted Criminal Offenders." Globally, at least half of the released prisoner population will return to incarceration before the end of their first year in society. Going against generally accepted notions, deliberation should be given to the existence of transience in habitual recidivists' or habitual convicted criminal offenders'(HCCOs') life course. The HCCO are habitually, chronically, or serially recidivistic (above the average recorded number of arrests and imprisonment, i.e. anything above or equal to five). Furthermore, transience can be considered as junctures of socio-cognitive unsteadiness, impermanence and inconstancy that leads to the uncoupling of positive bonds within human and environmental relationships. Accordingly, this chapter discusses two outlooks of the transient state of HCCO: the habitual prisoner revolving door syndrome and habitual transient life course disconnect. Finally, this work concludes by promoting the reentry and rehabilitation of convicted criminal offenders based on conditions of productive law-abiding citizenship.

In Chapter 12, "Procedural Justice and the Power of the Judge in the Courtroom: A Comparison Between Africa and the West," the author conducts a critical analysis and comparison of laws and practices that legitimise discretionary power in the courtroom from a selection of global north and south jurisdictions. The specific offence of contempt of court in facie curiae is the central focus, where the use of full judicial autonomy, summary and arbitrary hearings have survived now well into the twenty-first century. The research conducted shows that there is a global problem with significant overreach of power by members of the judiciary in nearly all jurisdictions investigated. In some cases, this could be viewed as being extreme enough in its overreach to justify being described as abuse of power. Further evidence is presented showing little by way of accountability being held against those judges who misuse their discretionary powers in the courtroom. Recommendations are that there should be reform or development of practice through both judicial training and proportionate disciplinary action where overreach is proven to have occurred in order to minimise future overreaches of power.

Chapter 13 is "Culture, Ethnicity, and Hate Crimes: A Comparative Analysis of Preventive Laws Between India and the USA." Traditionally, India is a multilingual, multi religious and multicultural country. Ingression of different races in India since ancient period has brought in different personal laws. Similar to India US also has a multiracial, religious, linguistic and cultural society. The country also has similar experiences of hate crimes especially from the perspectives of racial violence. This chapter aims to research on the hate crime preventive laws in the US and India to find out best solutions from both the jurisdictions.

Chapter 14 is:Charge Sheet to Charging: A Comparative Analysis of Case Management by Police and Prosecution Between India and UK With Special Reference to Cybercrime." Police and prosecution are the two essential elements in criminal justice system especially for justice delivery to the victims as well as for the accused. Cybercrimes targeting women had remained a menace for the victims, police, and prosecution for over a decade now in India and UK. . This chapter aims to research on the comparative analysis of relationship of police and prosecution for case management with special reference to cybercrimes against women cases between UK and India to find out positive solutions for restitution of justice in such cases.

Chapter 15 is "Homelessness, Mental Health Afflictions, Problematic Substance Use, and Associated Criminality: A Transformative Justice Resolution." Homelessness and related community ailments have plagued society for a number of years and governments have found it difficult to get these under control. The sheer number of homeless with mental health afflictions and problematic substance use problems leaves no doubt about the need for a stronger, more urgent government response. Community ailments such as these have led to increased crime rates and incarcerations, and overcrowded prisons without a lasting solution in sight. This chapter uses the transformative justice model, with the expectation it produces better results than current models, by examining the source of homelessness, mental health afflictions and problematic substance use and their bi-directional relationship with crime. This inter-jurisdictional study compares the current situations in the state of California and the province of Ontario which have a high percent of homeless populations. It proves that special attention to vulnerable populations such as racialized groups, the socioeconomically disadvantaged and youth is warranted.

Chapter 16 is "From Victim to Criminality: Understanding Sex Trafficking Within the Walls of Sex Work – Victimization of Victims of Commercial Sexual Exploitation." Trafficking of persons, primarily women, and children, is one of the growing social dilemmas concerning global society today. Not only is human trafficking a highly sensitive and polarizing subject, but it is also considered a common norm in many countries. Many Women recruited into commercial sex work are coerced into the profession exploiting their financial and economic condition but continue to work in the profession to survive through easy money. The chapter focuses on a theoretical framework for understanding the victimization of female sex workers. It also reflects various lacuna in the present criminal justice system and law enforcement mechanism in criminalizing victims within the sex work industry. The chapter narrates the voices of commercial sex workers in India over the prejudices and criminalization by various laws and regulations towards their consensual sex work. The chapter recommends sensitization training and awareness amongst various stakeholders of the criminal justice system.

Chapter 17 is "Centers for the Investigative Interviewing of Children in Turkey." Conducting interviews with witnesses and suspects is a core function of policing across the world. Child sexual abuse is broadly described as any sexual activity involving a child where consent is not or cannot be given. Child sexual abuse differs from other types of childhood victimization in that there is usually no witness apart from the victim and the accused and often no physical evidence. This chapter aims to summarize the components that play important role during the investigative interviewing of children. In addition to that, the role of the interviewers, interview aids, cognitive interview, risks of repeated interviewing of children, and effects of child sexual abuse on child will be outlined. This book chapter will also give information about the child interviewing centers that are still being used actively in Turkey.

Global Perspectives on Reforming the Criminal Justice System is undoubtedly a book that will appeal to a wide, diverse audience of readers, and will have undoubtedly contributed to advancing and improving the scientific literature on criminal justice reform initiatives from a global perspective.

Acknowledgment

We live in a global society and as such, we must acknowledge that crime transcends all international borders whether it be in the physical world or the cyber world, therefore, we must continue to communicate, collaborate, and cooperate on a global scale on all matters related to crime and justice, particularly criminal justice reform. Criminal justice practitioners and researchers throughout the world must learn from one another and share information and intelligence in order to tackle some of the world's most pressing issues related to crime and justice.

The world is a much better place thanks to the criminal justice subject matter experts from across the world who contributed to this book. I would like to thank each of you for your unwavering commitment and dedication to advancing the criminal justice profession by addressing the concerns that call for the most attention in law enforcement, the courts, and corrections. Without the education and vast experiences of the contributing authors, this book would not exist.

I especially want to thank Lindsay Wertman, managing director with IGI-Global. Lindsay was my "go-to" person for every question that I had and every challenge that I faced. I sincerely appreciate you and the enthusiasm you've shown in walking me through every single stage of the publication process.

I would be remiss if I didn't thank all the professors that I had the pleasure of learning from throughout my undergraduate, graduate, and doctoral years.

And finally, I must acknowledge my beautiful, intelligent, supportive, and understanding wife, Christina. I'm incredibly fortunate to have you in my life.

Chapter 1
Body-Worn Cameras: Panacea or Distraction for Increased Police Use of Force Accountability?

Scott Thomas Duncan
Bloomsburg University of Pennsylvania, USA

Hannah Geczi
University of Cincinnati, USA

ABSTRACT

Police hold a unique and distinctive status compared to any other occupation in society with their authority to use force. With such responsibility, communities expect law enforcement to be held accountable when force is applied. One of the many proposed solutions embraced by authorities and the public to decrease the number of force encounters is body-worn cameras (BWCs). The purpose of this chapter is to examine BWCs as a measure of reducing force by law enforcement, explore the technology as an enhancement to transparency within the context of police-community relations, and offer recommendations for adoption rooted in best practices. For the public, it is imperative to recognize BWCs as just one part of improving law enforcement oversight as opposed to providing an all-encompassing solution that will completely resolve issues of transparency.

INTRODUCTION

On July 2, 2017, a police officer in Fort Collins, Colorado encountered a male subject grasping a knife and walking on the sidewalk. The individual matched the description of a person previously reported to authorities as experiencing a mental health crisis and wanting to kill members of his family (Hindi, 2017). After activating a body-worn camera (BWC), the officer exited a patrol car and immediately gave verbal instructions for the man to drop the knife. For more than two minutes, the camera recorded video and audio of the tense and developing situation.

During the incident, the officer is seen backpedaling to increase the distance between the two, while the armed man repeatedly verbalized that he wanted to die. After a second unit arrived at the scene, the

DOI: 10.4018/978-1-7998-6884-2.ch001

armed man charged the officers, resulting in a fatal police shooting. The BWC imagery and audio were later released to the public and showed that the first officer responding can be heard ordering the man to drop the knife more than 40 times (2017). The recording was crucial to understanding the incident as it offered compelling evidence that corroborated officer accounts, and aided authorities in ruling the encounter as a justifiable use of lethal force.

Tragically in October of 2019, a BWC documented another fatal police shooting that occurred in Fort Worth, Texas. This incident involved police investigating an open door at a house and shooting a Black resident who was inside their own bedroom after an officer mistook the resident for a burglar (Ortiz, 2019). After viewing the related video and audio, a grand jury indicted the now former officer who was involved in the shooting for murder. In contrast to the Colorado and Texas cases, BWC footage does not always provide sufficient clarity regarding the justification for police in using force. Body cameras are far from the panacea some had hoped in providing sufficient oversight of law enforcement. The mission of this chapter is to examine BWCs as a measure of reducing force by law enforcement, explore the technology as an enhancement to transparency within the context of police-community relations, and offer recommendations for adoption rooted in best practices.

BACKGROUND

Police hold a unique and distinctive status compared to any other occupation in society, with their authority to use force. Despite impressions from present-day media coverage, this power is infrequently evoked yet highlighted as a central concern surrounding police and their existence. Much of the controversy related to this element of policing is concentrated on police brutality and the application of deadly force (Klinger, 2004; Saulnier et al., 2019). Exacerbating the collective unease are concerns of police tactics prompting hostile confrontations and the long-standing conflict between the authorities and racial minorities. Although proven to be effective in reducing crime, strategies for more police-initiated contacts with the public, commonly referred to as proactive policing, have had adverse consequences, especially for minority populations who tend to be the subjects of these frequent stops and encounters (National Academies of Sciences, Engineering, and Medicine, 2018).

In terms of force responses by law enforcement, the pressing national issues of disparate and discriminatory policing are also evident in statistics of lethal shootings. For example, *The Washington Post* estimates that 4,931 individuals have been killed by on-duty police officers between 2015 and 2019. With the data collected, numbers show that Black decedents are killed by police at a disproportionate rate as compared to whites. In general, these fatal incidents are costly to both police agencies and their relationship with larger society (Micucci & Gomme, 2005). As a byproduct of highly publicized officer-involved shootings, the nation's police organizations have collectively paid for the unjust actions of others. Further, the current police-civilian relationship has suffered from controversial applications of fatal force, resulting in high tensions and low levels of trust towards the authorities (Culhane et al., 2016; Zamoff, 2019).

One of the many proposed solutions embraced by authorities and the public to address the issues surrounding use of force is body-worn cameras (BWCs). Initial interests in applying this technology to policing began in the early 2000s, but dramatically increased after the controversial death of Michael Brown in Ferguson, Missouri (Zamoff, 2019). The Ferguson shooting in 2014 was a catalytic event that amplified reform in the transparency of police actions through the use of cameras. With its characteristics of high mobility and a real-time view into contacts with citizens, body cameras offer a "solution" to make police more visible than ever (Ariel et al., 2015; Lum et al., 2020).

By 2016, Nix, Todak, and Tregle (2020) estimated that one-half of US law enforcement agencies have adopted the use of BWCs. Support for this reform not only existed within state-level and local jurisdictions but also received high praise from the federal government, civil rights advocacy groups, and professional police organizations across the nation (White et al., 2018). Though the technology was advertised and implemented to increase oversight of police, Ready and Young (2020) noted that false accusations by community members against law enforcement have plummeted. With its exponential growth in the field and widespread popularity as an accountability mechanism, Lum et al. (2019), deems BWCs the most rapidly implemented technology in contemporary policing.

LITERATURE REVIEW

Despite public calls for the increased use of BWCs, the results of peer-reviewed studies of the efficacy for this technology are inconclusive (Gaub & White, 2020). In addition, existing quantitative research has been criticized for ineffectual methodologies that limit the validity of findings (McCamman & Culhane, 2017; Smykla et al., 2015). Primarily, published studies examining BWCs elucidate one or more of the following themes: ethical issues involving recording police interactions, effectiveness in reducing use of force, and perceptions of the technology by community members and law enforcement practitioners.

Recording Police Interactions

Recording interactions between police and community members through body-camera technology can be viewed as a double-edged sword that satisfies public outcry for more transparency yet propounds a list of imperfections. With its mobility compared to any other advancements in police recording (i.e., dashboard cameras), these devices can offer positives in terms of documenting use of force. Encounters of this nature do not always occur in the public eye as officers tend to operate and make decisions in low visibility environments, which raises societal concerns in how authority is exercised by officials. Not only does video documentation offered by BWCs bring to light the discretionary decisions made by police, but also adds context and improved accuracy to narratives and recollections of events (Gonzalez & Cochran, 2017; Lawrence et al., 2019). Although this conveys perceptions of increased accountability, Mateescu et al. (2016) believe this measure is counterproductive. Considering its initial purpose to increase oversight, body-camera footage is criticized for producing a biased lens directed towards surveilling civilians rather than officers.

Other concerns of recording interactions include invasion of privacy and the potentially sensitive material it captures. Body cameras offer insight to the traumatic side of police work and depict subjects in some of their most vulnerable states (Todak & Gaub, 2019). When they are activated, there is not always a clear distinction between public and private entities in which one has a reasonable expectation of privacy. Most agencies do not require notice or consent prior to recording; therefore, the presence of body-worn cameras could be deemed intrusive by subjects, victims, and witnesses (Merola et al., 2016; Mateescu et al., 2016). Regardless of where or how long the devices are recording, produced footage can store a plethora of private and undisclosed information about individuals that they may not want to be available for public viewing.

Additionally, Adams and Mastracci (2017) questioned whether increased use of BWCs could further hinder sexual assault victims from reporting. The authors feared that documenting encounters with a traumatized victim creates additional barriers that deter involving representatives from the criminal justice system. Miller and Toliver (2014) expressed similar reservations in that some of the subject matter captured may be sensitive and potentially compromise the positive relationships necessary for effective law enforcement. Therefore, it is critical that police agencies develop protocols to protect confidential information in calls of sensitive nature (e.g., domestic violence and sexual assault cases) and consider the potential consequences of recording.

Use of Force Reductions

Another recurrent theme evident in the body of research on police BWCs is the technology's effectiveness in reducing use of force. In the world's first randomized control trial of body-worn cameras, known as the Rialto Study, Ariel et al. (2015) hypothesized a deterrent or civilizing effect on both sides of a police-community encounter. As cameras are utilized to deter socially unacceptable behaviors, it prompts a sense of self-awareness or a modification of one's conduct precipitated by knowledge that they are being monitored. With cameras acting as a neutral third witness to these contacts, the authors suggest that the awareness of being observed is a prerequisite to effective deterrence as video documentation increases the likelihood of detection and prosecution.

Building upon this point in a subsequent study, Ariel et al. (2016) asserted that this response rests on the conditions that officers wear and activate the devices, while civilians are cognizant of being recorded. Therefore, initial analyses of body-camera technology proposed that its increased presence in practice may discourage violence and elicit more reputable conduct from both parties. The results of Ariel et al.'s (2015) study seemingly support the theoretical deterrent effect of BWCs, as force responses and complaints against officers decreased under experimental conditions. However, the authors acknowledged the device's limited influence on behavior as its capacity to discourage certain actions is not apparent in every encounter.

Despite the promising preliminary findings of early research and the concurrent rising popularity in advocating for police body-worn cameras, evidence to conclude successful outcomes have been mixed in subsequent peer-reviewed studies (Ariel et al., 2015; Lum et al., 2015; Ariel et al., 2016). For example, some experiments analyzing the impact of BWCs on policing found that use of force decreased with the presence of cameras (Ariel et al., 2015; Jennings et al., 2015; Braga et al., 2017). Other studies revealed no significant differences between officers equipped and non-equipped with the devices (Ariel, 2016; Yokum et al., 2019). Contrary to these trends, Ariel et al. (2016) and Ariel et al. (2017) observed increases in force responses and assaults on police officers, respectively.

Beyond initial implementation periods of the technology, researchers have also sought to evaluate the potential persistent effects of body-worn cameras on police practices (Sutherland et al., 2017; Koslicki et al., 2020). In a follow-up study to the pioneering work of Ariel and colleagues, Sutherland et al. (2017) provide evidence against post-implementation fade out effects in Rialto and suggest that personnel do not become accustomed to this form of surveillance overtime. The observations of Koslicki et al. (2020) infer a contrasting argument that body cameras have a short-lived effect on officer conduct that weakens with more routine use. Considering the ambivalence in the extant research on this emerging technology, both in the course of and post- adoption, Lum et al. (2019) and Malm (2019) draw comparable conclusions in that the available research lacks both clear and consistent answers regarding the efficacy of police body cameras.

To further explain these variant effects, specifically in the context of police instances of force, White (2019) notes that agency context and background can serve as moderators in the relationship between BWCs and certain police outcomes. In essence, each organization has their own starting point that may enhance or diminish the effects of the technology in practice. It is plausible that troubled departments plagued with officer misconduct experience significant differences after implementation because these conditions engender ample opportunities for improvement. Conversely, agencies characterized as highly professionalized institutions may not experience an appreciable difference due to the levels of training, supervision, accountability processes, etc., that are instilled in the work environment (White, 2019; Gaub & White, 2020). In addition to the aforementioned organizational factors, Lum et al. (2020) regards departmental policies, specifically the amount of discretion allotted to officers in activation, as a significant impediment to the device's overall success in diminishing use of force responses by authorities.

Inconsistencies are also rooted in research design and methodology. Criticisms of existing quantitative research include the use of weak designs, variation in units of analyses or methods of randomization, and inconsistent definitions of outcomes (e.g., use of force), which may limit the validity of findings (Lawrence et al., 2019; McCamman & Culhane, 2017; Smykla et al., 2015). Further, researchers have voiced trepidation of the Hawthorne Effect. In terms of studies on BWCs, this threat to internal validity raises questions as to whether the intervention or participants' knowledge of being scrutinized in a research setting drives the observed outcomes (Ready & Young, 2015; Ariel et al., 2015; Koslicki et al., 2020).

Beyond the United States, body-camera programs have also been piloted and carried out all over the globe. Compared to the available peer-reviewed literature on this topic in American policing, international empirical studies are scant (Mitchell, 2018; Lum, 2019). Despite this shortcoming in the research, studies conducted in Australia, Canada, Latin America, the UK, and other countries have disclosed the device's impact on policing from a global perspective (Clare et al., 2019; Toronto Police Service, 2016; Mitchell et al., 2018; Henstock & Ariel, 2017; Owens & Finn, 2018). Similar to the observations of American peer-reviewed research, these studies of body-worn cameras document a range of effects including increases, reductions, and null effects on police outcomes, such as use of force, civilian complaints, and assaults against officers. Although these findings add to the perplexity of BWC effectiveness, Mitchell et al. (2018) suggest that the impact of this intervention on policing is not reliant on time and place. As countries operate under disparate social and political contexts, global studies still replicate the trend of inconclusive findings found in American-based empirical research.

POLICE AND COMMUNITY MEMBER PERCEPTIONS

Perceptions: Law Enforcement

With the contemporary challenges of police use of force, BWCs offer a sense of protection to both police and civilians. Nonetheless, the initial response by some officers to police BWCs was predictably unfavorable in that the quasi-military structure of law enforcement agencies tends to resist innovation and change. Associating the technology with invasive spying intended to identify violators of minor departmental policies, officers were critical of what they considered unnecessary micromanagement and efforts to limit discretion (Ariel, 2016). In contrast to this incipient response and as departments initiated

BWC pilot programs, officers began recognizing the value that recordings provide—specifically in terms of evidence and the perceived deterrent effect on citizen misconduct (Smykala et al., 2015; Sacharoff & Lustbader, 2017). In demonstrating this transition to general support, police unions in Pennsylvania recently and strongly advocated revising state legislation to enable law enforcement agencies to adopt BWCs (Metrick, 2019b).

Although these entities are an important collaborator in the implementation process, Bies (2017) also recognized the capacity of police unions to potentially counteract the desired outcomes of increased transparency and accountability in present-day reform efforts as they advocate for the interests of their members. While general support for the devices exist, police labor unions have previously challenged the legal authority of law enforcement agencies in adopting BWCs. In 2017, the Seattle Police Officer's Guild filed an unfair labor practices complaint against then mayor Ed Murray, after the mayor's office issued an executive order mandating the city's officers employ BWCs while on-duty (Browning, 2017). The union argued that membership was not against the technology, but rather the issue was subject to collective bargaining.

For local and state law enforcement agencies, statutes and collective bargaining practices vary, and disagreements are either negotiated or settled by applicable court rulings. In Florida, Meck (2018) surmised that based on that state's court rulings, authorities in the Sunshine State are authorized to implement BWC programs without collective bargaining. In contrast, tangential issues pertaining to Florida police management's use of collected data on officers (e.g., assessment of job performance, internal disciplinary hearings, training, etc.) do require collective bargaining to resolve.

Though overall acceptance by law enforcement for cameras has increased in the past decade, support varies by department. After the Minneapolis death of George Floyd even law enforcement practitioners, long opposed to the full BWC adoption, became more open-minded including Pinellas County (FL) Sheriff Bob Gualtieri. In a recent interview, the sheriff admitted to reconsidering BWCs in that persistent constituent feedback and the potential that the devices offer for law enforcement to reduce liability and increase accountability have contributed to his current interest in equipping some of the agency's 3,000 personnel with cameras (Varn, 2020). Interestingly, an internal opinion study that queried 544 of Sheriff Gualtieri's deputies found that only 45% supported general BWC adoption, while 58% of respondents preferred a recording system that activated only when a deputy's firearm was removed from their holster if such technology was mandated (2020).

In another opinion survey that included questions about police cameras, Graham et al. (2019) examined a small subset of their respondents who reported being employed as law enforcement officers (n = 45). From the group, 66% approved of BWCs for police, but only about 12% reported they felt very strongly that police must secure and utilize the technology immediately. Police officer responses contrasted with opinions of other community members in that the latter emphasized immediate adoption of the technology as essential. The authors theorized that police practitioners are more knowledgeable of the complexities of camera adoption (e.g., legal privacies, long and short-term costs, etc.), and are therefore more reluctant to voice full support without adequate clarifications and provisions guiding usage (2019).

Finally, and from a public relations perspective, law enforcement agencies have realized how powerful messages from BWCs can resonate with community members. Specifically, imagery generated by BWCs can promote goodwill by police departments in showing enduring moments and depicting the oft unreported compassion displayed by law enforcement officers. For instance, a police officer in Utah, responding to a check the welfare call of an elderly woman afflicted with blindness, ended the exchange by complying with the woman's request to sing a song acapella (Powell, 2017). Similar camera recordings of officer compassion were released by the Carrollton (TX) Police Department (Murphy, 2016) and the Gwinnett County (GA) Sheriff's Office (Dahler, 2020) both resulting in viral videos portraying police in a positive light.

Perceptions: Public

Accordant with practitioner sentiments, citizen perceptions of body cameras have been predominately positive as well, with endorsement across political and racial divides (Crow et al., 2017; Gonzalez and Cochran, 2017). As advocates for this reform to address controversial incidents of lethal force, the public had generally high yet somewhat unrealistic expectations regarding the impact of these devices. Studies of public perceptions reveal that beliefs of increased transparency, improved relationships, and strengthened levels of trust had a significant influence on increased communal support (Miethe et al., 2019; Sousa et al., 2018).

Despite the widespread approval of these devices as a proposed solution to handle issues surrounding use of force, Sousa et al. (2018) found that attitudes towards the technology's purported ability to reduce or control these occurrences did not have a profound impact on overall support. Although cameras were embraced by the public to enhance accountability, Taylor and Lee (2019) acknowledge a significant power imbalance that exists with the use of these devices. Counteracting public outcry for more transparency in police actions, this incongruity favors the authorities as they exercise almost complete control over ownership, storage, and distribution of footage. Their discretionary power in activation and the ability to select evidentiary value of footage also generates concerns regarding the modification, manipulation, and falsification of documented narratives and undermine the initial premise of BWCs.

To better understand BWC opinions in diverse communities, Graham et al. (2019) employed a random sampling approach and surveyed 1,000 African Americans to gauge support for specific police reforms including the adoption of camera technology. The authors found that only less than 5% of the sample completely opposed BWCs, while two in three respondents indicated definitive support for police using the technology. In addition, participants from all reported socioeconomic and sociopolitical categories approved of the use of BWCs, and only showed variance in degree of support. For instance, young adults with limited economic means and residing in high crime areas, were less favorable to BWCs as compared to other demographic groups, but still offered majority support. The authors concluded that the results verify consensus among African Americans for police reforms including camera adoption (2019).

Beyond general public support, BWC footage has demonstrated usefulness in criminal defense as well. For example, the recordings of DUI arrests are typically viewed by defense attorneys in preparing for criminal proceedings. The expectation of public access to available camera footage to corroborate prosecutorial evidence has also been elevated. Recently, Flaherty (2020) reported that an Arkansas lawmaker had publicly criticized the Little Rock Police Department for violating internal retention policies and deleting video recordings associated with the arrest of a dozen protestors before defense attorneys could file discovery motions and view the imagery. Interestingly, an attorney from those cases lamented being restricted to preparing client defenses using only written reports, testimony, and other traditional forms of evidence (2020)—ironically describing the foundational basis used in criminal convictions for the past two hundred years.

LEGISLATION

Federal

In the US, no comprehensive legislation exists mandating BWCs for federal law enforcement officers. Predominantly, camera adoption efforts have focused on state and local police, which account for a far greater percentage of officers, and where more notable lethal encounters have occurred. Subsequently, federal efforts have focused on funding like in 2015, when President Obama's administration issued $23 million in grants to local and state law enforcement agencies for the purchase and development of BWCs (Van Ness, 2020).

Nonetheless, uniformed officers at the federal level have not been exempted from discussions centering on BWC adoption. In November 2018, Representatives Don Beyer (VA) and Eleanor Holmes Norton (DC) introduced a bill that would require all federal officers be equipped with the technology, but the effort stalled until June 2020, when it was included in House of Representatives legislation on police reform. In general, National Park Service rangers are the only federal law enforcement agency employing widespread use of body cameras (Jackman, 2020).

Previously, representatives from federal agencies have argued that BWC mandates could reveal tactics, compromise officer safety, as well as expose and thereby endanger witnesses or victims cooperating during investigations. Interestingly, federal officials reluctant to adopt BWCs have caused friction with municipal police administrators who support the technology. For instance, after an officer with the Atlanta Police Department shot an individual while working on a federal task force, federal administrators refused to allow Atlanta officers to participate in future collaborative efforts while wearing the recording technology. Atlanta's chief of police and other local chiefs responded by withdrawing all personnel from federally operated task forces (2020).

State

Despite limited activity at the federal level, numerous states have explored laws requiring BWC technology for police officers. In 2019, representatives from Maine, Mississippi, North Carolina, and Illinois considered legislation that would require all law enforcement agencies in each state to employ BWCs (Van Ness, 2020). Other states including New Mexico (Maxwell, 2020) and New Jersey (Thompson, 2020) assessed and then passed similar proposals in 2020. With Maine's efforts, legislators recognized that the issue is highly complex in terms of financing, adoption, and legal considerations. After consulting with legal and law enforcement experts, state officials favored a cautious approach in enacting mandates that best protect the public and authorities, while balancing financial feasibility (Van Ness, 2020).

Nevada and South Carolina were the first to have existing statutes requiring all law enforcement agencies in their jurisdictions to use BWCs, but neither state is currently in compliance with their mandates. In Nevada, a law was passed in 2015 that required state police to use the technology, followed by a second in 2017 that expanded the approach to include all law enforcement agencies within the state. Purchase and use of the technology were to be supported by increased taxes generated from 911 surcharges, but the Federal Communications Commission characterized Nevada's tax plan as a misappropriation of funds, slowing the BWC adoption. Most recently, state officials reportedly are unsure the number of law enforcement agencies following the required deployment of cameras (2020).

South Carolina's efforts to mandate comprehensive use of BWCs also experienced challenges trying to finance the effort. Similar to Nevada, South Carolina passed legislation requiring statewide adoption of BWCs in 2015, with one primary difference: laws would be effective after the state had fully funded programs that allowed law enforcement agencies to purchase and maintain the equipment. Considering that almost 300 such law enforcement agencies exist in South Carolina, providing adequate funding to support widespread camera technology is a monumental endeavor, and one that remains unachieved (2020). Further and following South Carolina's plan, New Jersey legislators mandated BWCs for all law enforcement officers in the state that takes effect contingent upon suitable funding for the initiative (Thompson, 2020). New Jersey's governor then immediately established working groups to devise funding and implementation strategies.

In some states, existing open record and privacy statutes need to be revised before BWCs can be utilized by law enforcement. According to 2018 research published by the National Conference of State Legislators, 23 states and the District of Columbia treated BWC recordings under open record statutes that address the type of footage released. For instance, authorities in Oklahoma may redact video footage that depicts violence or the death of a person, unless the involved individual's harm was caused by law enforcement. Texas law restricts released BWC footage to that which is being used or could be used as evidence in criminal proceedings. Both Texas and North Dakota may exempt records taken in private places from public release under applicable open records laws (NCSL, 2018).

As a two-party consent state, states like the Pennsylvania faced another formidable obstacle to BWC adoption. In 2017, Pennsylvania's governor signed Act 22 that amended the state's wiretapping act to permit police officers to use audio and video recording devices without obtaining prior consent from all parties. The legislation also categorized video footage as not a public record, thereby exempting mandated disclosures that would have applied under Pennsylvania's Right to Know statute.

Interestingly, the Pennsylvania law was opposed by the American Civil Liberties Union (ACLU) for several reasons including lack of public access to data, placing unreasonable costs on the public applying to obtain BWC data ($125 court filing), and the failing to require a data retention schedule for law enforcement agencies to follow (McKelvey, 2017). The ACLU argued that the new legislation reduces BWCs as an accountability tool to protect the public from government authorities, and instead allowed police to use the technology unabated for public surveillance and evidence gathering (i.e., using BWC data in conjunction with facial recognition technology). Likewise, Vermont's ACLU advocated for privacy protections for community members, as well as directions detailing appropriate use by law enforcement as legislators considered camera adoption statutes in that state (State of Vermont, 2020).

The ACLU's concern over consequences for police in failing to properly use camera technology was previously a point of contention in Tennessee. In 2018, three Memphis officers were charged with violating internal policies after being accused of intentionally deactivating their BWCs during a vehicular pursuit that ended in the lethal police shooting of twenty-five-year-old Martavious Banks (Lou & Griggs, 2019). A fourth supervisor was also disciplined for not activating their recording upon arrival at the incident scene.

Tennessee law allows a district attorney to criminally charge an officer with a misdemeanor for manipulating BWCs, but in 2019 and subsequent to the Memphis cases, two state lawmakers proposed to increase the sanction to a Class E felony—punishable by up to two years in prison. The goal was to deter police officers from deactivating BWCs to obstruct justice, but critics posited that language should be included to allow for the instances of accidental camera deactivation (2019). In any event, the public has a low tolerance for police departments offering excuses as to why footage of a critical incident is unavailable after the extensive financial resources and time are invested in equipping officers with BWCs. Thus, it is reasonable to expect future legislation addressing officer misconduct in an effort to ensure availability of collected video and audio data.

MISCONCEPTIONS AND CHALLENGES

Several misconceptions reside in arguments advocating BWCs as definitive solution that ensures police accountability. First, it is falsely presumed that equipping officers with body-worn cameras will present the public with comprehensive accounts of police instances of force. As with any technology, these devices are not 100 percent foolproof and encounter risks for deficiencies and malfunctions in practice. Circumstances, such as the physicality of certain police actions (e.g., scuffles and foot pursuits) and the placement of cameras, also act as barriers that can limit quality of the recordings and capacity of BWCs to document critical moments in force responses (Merola et al., 2016).

The Carmel (IN) Police Department, comprised of 128 sworn officers, was in the process of outfitting all uniformed personnel with BWCs, when a lethal force incident involving one of the agency's officers went unrecorded. During the summer of 2020 case, the involved officer was running with a rifle prior to the firearm's discharge, and inadvertently knocked the camera from his uniform (Lange, 2018). Agency administrators and prosecutors were limited to evaluating the recording produced while the camera was attached, along with faint audio of the shooting captured by the dislodged device. In sum, critical footage of the shooting essential for the full transparency demanded by community members was not captured.

Unfortunately, there are no empirical studies regarding the frequency of BWCs being knocked from officer uniforms during scuffles, foot pursuits, or other physical activity, but anecdotal evidence exists in that it does occur (Schindler, 2020). After a fatal shooting in Florida resulted in questions about BWC's becoming unattached, a spokesperson for the Jacksonville County Sheriff's Office responded to media inquiries that their department does not track such information. In 2019, the Aurora (CO) Police Department announced that the agency was considering another camera vendor after BWCs for three officers all became dislodged during an altercation with Elijah McClain, who died later at a nearby hospital (Gilha, 2019).

BWC manufacturers work to reduce these malfunctions in both strengthening the bond of the equipment to officer uniforms, as well as modifying the positioning of the camera. The adherence of the camera to the uninform has limitations in that the technology is designed to tear-away, preventing assailants from grabbing and pulling an officer by their camera. The most effective camera mount for an officer can vary depending on what type of uniform is worn. Some BWC designs are mounted externally on the officer's uniform, while others are mounted within the attire. With the latter, some BWCs feature holders that are fastened inside the officer's uniform—designed to reduce accidental and contact-based dislodgements (Lange, 2018).

Peer-reviewed research have also expressed concerns over the biased lens of body camera footage (Mateescu et al., 2016; Taylor & Lee, 2019; Bellin & Pemberton, 2019). Although one may assume the use of BWCs would facilitate determinations of appropriate and necessary applications of force, these one-sided accounts are often incomplete and lack context. Such incomplete accounts can lead to subjective and biased interpretations of police-civilian interactions.

Second, the number of and disparate nature of law enforcement in the US makes universal implementation of BWCs implausible. Organizational characteristics, such as location (i.e., urban vs. rural areas), number of personnel, and access to sufficient financial resources, are significant factors that contribute to the large variation in the adoption rates across the nation's law enforcement agencies. When these devices are adopted, differing aspects of the implementation process, such as policy and availability of cameras to all personnel, can also broaden the divide in universal use of BWCs in law enforcement (Police Executive Research Forum, 2018). Regarding policy challenges, a recent study by the National Conference of State Legislators found that only 19 states and the District of Columbia required law enforcement agencies to have written policies before deploying camera technology (2018).

The swift and urgent call for universal adoption of body-worn camera programs across the US was met with an extravagant price tag for police departments. On average, the financial cost for a single camera ranges between $800 and $1,200. Considering hardware, software, etc., agencies can spend a median cost of $4,000 per year for these programs, with maximum costs reaching over $1.3 million (Police Executive Research Forum, 2018). Several law enforcement agencies have halted BWC programs due to unanticipated expenses related to maintenance, data storage, and other issues. Police departments in Arlington, VA and Madison, WI discontinued BWC adoption programs after pilot programs revealed what authorities considered untenable annual costs (Kindy, 2019).

Regrettably, many smaller agencies investigated the costs, and chose not to pursue BWC adoption. A recent survey of municipal police departments in Central Pennsylvania revealed only 13.6% reported use of the camera technology (Metrick, 2019a). The Highspire (PA) Police department, a small Pennsylvania agency consisting of five-full time and a few part-time officers, has a BWC policy ready for when the agency begins using the technology, but lack of financial resources has left the initiative in limbo (2019a). The department's chief reported that several cameras were previously donated but are now obsolete as administrators attempt to secure the funding necessary to maintain the program in the long-term.

Of all associated expenses, Miller and Toliver (2014) found that police leadership commonly noted that issues related to data storage (e.g., video length, retention period, location security, personnel, training, technical assistance, etc.) were one of the most expensive aspects of implementation. Considering the experience of a large urban agency like the New York City Police Department (NYPD) illustrates the financial challenges involved in maintaining data for a BWC program. NYPD began extensive deployment of BWCs prior to 2017 and has since filmed over 8 million officer-community member interactions, generating approximately 130,000 new recordings per week. NYPD officials estimate that 22,000 (63%) of sworn personnel are equipped with BWCs, including all patrol officers and those assigned to specialized units (Southall, 2020). Strictly in terms of data storage expenses, authorities estimate spending an exorbitant $144,000 annually by fiscal year 2024 (Geringer-Sameth, 2020).

Overall, inadequate funding hampers law enforcement BWC adoption, and has resulted in some agencies being creative to pay for the technology. In a 2018 study, only 13 states and the District of Columbia were found to provide funding to local law enforcement agencies wanting to adopt BWC technology with North Carolina and Texas offering matching grant funds, while Massachusetts offered a competitive grants program for potential applicants (NCSL, 2018). Officials in Everett, Washington were able to secure federal funding to defray BWC program expenses and equip all 150 uniformed officers in the city's police department at a total cost of $1.46 million over five years (Watanbe, 2020). Similarly, the Carlisle (PA) Police Department became one of Pennsylvania's first law enforcement agencies with BWCs after securing a federal grant in 2015 (Metrick, 2019a).

Third, releasing BWC footage of use of force incidents to the public is not an absolute. In the 2018 study, California, Georgia, Illinois, Nevada, New Hampshire, Pennsylvania, and Oregon had created exceptions to applicable wiring tapping laws that allow discretionary release of BWC content from police officers during the discharge of duties. (NCSL, 2018). In 2017, the non-profit Leadership Conference on Civil and Human Rights examined the use of BWCs by 75 large city/county police departments in the US and found only a handful had policies allowing filmed community members to view collected data. Researchers cautioned that law enforcement adoption of camera technology does not automatically result in the anticipated transparency that the public desires (Upturn & LCCHR, 2017).

Open Records Acts may also represent an obstacle to the release of BWC recordings, and some states have offered remedies. For example, Georgia officials may release recordings if an individual believes it is relevant to pending criminal or civil court proceedings. South Carolina law offers authorities similar discretion to release but restricts the applicant to being either the recorded individual, a criminal defendant whose case pertains to the video, or a civil litigant and owner of property damaged as part of the filmed incident (NCSI, 2018). In Pennsylvania, each police department is permitted discretion in determining whether or not to release BWC footage to interested community members. If a release request is initially denied by an agency, an appeal can be filed with the applicable district attorney's office for additional consideration (Metrick, 2019b).

As the dominant owners of the technology and its produced contents, police departments have significant influence in what footage is disclosed. Pressures from community members and/or advocacy groups, as well as administrator views on organizational transparency also carry weight in the public availability of footage. When there is limited access to video depictions of encounters, Culhane et al. (2016) asserted that there are serious consequences on perceived legitimacy and justification of police responses. Additionally, any resistance or delay in producing video depictions of controversial incidents can fracture community relations, especially in minority communities.

Finally, not all law enforcement agencies have personnel with technical expertise available to assist in BWC implementation and maintenance. Larger agencies typically have advantages in support through access to local government information technology professionals. In contrast, small police departments may have inadequate technical support in-house, and either rely on a technologically savvy sworn officer or on outsourced assistance (Metrick, 2019b). Making a poor purchasing decision with BWCs can not only cause immediate headaches for officers, supervisors, and the public but also may cost a department long-term with unanticipated expenditures.

One such unexpected potential cost for local, state, and federal governments, but an unfortunate reality of the 21st Century, is the threat of cyberattacks. Simply storing BWC or any official records on private agency networks is inadequate as global hackers target government systems in the US. Stored BWC data from the Lawrenceville (GA) Police Department was virtually compromised in July 2019 with the intruders demanding a ransom. The Georgia Department of Public Safety confirmed that along with Lawrenceville, Henry County (GA) and the Blackshear (GA) Police Department's computer networks were also targeted (Thomas, 2019). At the Stuart (FL) Police Department, official data were compromised by an external entity in 2019. Not only did the intrusion violate privacy rights for individuals who police were building investigations against, but at least six narcotics cases had to be dismissed due to the agency's inability to access video evidence and other records needed to prosecute (Badcock & Altman, 2020).

Purging data from BWCs can be an overlooked necessity for law enforcement. Retention schedules of 90-120 days for police recordings not involving active criminal investigations are common, but it is ambiguous if agencies actually abide by these policies. Further, it is unclear how many agencies have personnel technologically skilled to use best practices in removing data from devices. In July of 2020, an antiquated BWC used by military police was purchased online and found to have recordings of what appeared to be search warrants and other law enforcement activity still present on the device. Allegedly, the recovered footage was from a camera manufactured in 2013 and depicted US Army personnel assigned to Fort Huachuca in Arizona. If accurate, this lack of properly purging data and subsequent public release of footage violates the rights of those shown and is extremely concerning (Canales, 2020).

RECOMMENDATIONS AND BEST PRACTICES

To perform effectively, law enforcement agencies require general adherence to directions given by officers. In environments of widespread non-compliance by community members, police quickly become overwhelmed and are rendered ineffective (Tyler, 2004). With significant levels of mistrust of police by the public, especially by persons of Color, the use of BWCs has become an expected action in fulfilling community expectations of accountability. Nevertheless, it is important to recognize BWCs as an integral part of efforts to improve law enforcement and the criminal justice system, and not an isolated practice that will resolve all issue of transparency (Graham et al., 2019).

Support: Officer, Constituent, and Financial

Effective BWC programs require planning and integration of best practices. Essential first steps are to obtain external and internal stakeholder buy-in for the technology. Sandhu (2017) determined that officers tend to hold a more strategic outlook on cameras, rather than viewing them an asset for improved accountability. To that end, footage can be used by authorities to provide justification for courses of action, especially in force responses, and act as a safeguard against frivolous complaints by civilians. In light of these opinions toward BWCs, Ready and Young (2015) contend that police personnel, as primary employers of this technology, play an instrumental role in its value, efficacy, and long-term sustainability in practice. Subsequently, sworn personnel should be involved in the many aspects of BWC integration including testing, feedback, and policy recommendations.

In terms of external police stakeholders, community members should play visible roles in BWC programs. Graham et al. (2019) posited that police leaders that proactively adopt cameras tend to be viewed as taking preemptive and favorable steps to strengthen agency accountability among Black residents. In contrast, law enforcement professionals that continue to oppose this technology could be viewed as being duplicitous and hiding illegal and unethical practices from the public. As a result, such agencies are more susceptible to accusations of misconduct that challenge overall police legitimacy. Further and employing Routine Activities Theory, the authors speculated that cameras may be perceived by minority residents as an effective protection deterring their victimization by police.

Further, financial support is essential for police to adopt BWCs. As discussed previously, Nevada officials recognized the financial burden that mandating universal adoption of cameras in that state would create, and though it was unsuccessful, should be applauded for their innovation in attempting to use cell phone taxes to fund BWCs. States like South Carolina and New Jersey have similar legislation requiring BWCs, but efforts to finance such costly initiatives remain works in progress. Government agencies and other involved organizations will need to cooperatively solve this financial dilemma for widespread camera adoption. In essence, any police reform effort lacks comprehension if funding for BWC programs is omitted.

Moreover, the financial resources necessary for BWC programs go beyond simply purchasing the technology but are inclusive of data storage and security as well. Lack of security can quickly undermine public trust as was demonstrated in 2018. At the annual and immensely popular DEF CON conference in Las Vegas, a security consultant presented on operational vulnerabilities that left four different police BWCs susceptible to remote digital attacks (Newman, 2018). The researcher found that the tested cameras lacked data encryption that could allow video deletion, and that imagery could be downloaded, manipulated using software, and then reuploaded later leaving no evidence of intrusion. The consultant noted that adding a digital signature to videos and enhancing encryption would significantly hamper the tested cyberattack methods.

After the shocking presentation on BWC vulnerabilities, manufacturers were quick to respond to the potential for security breaches and worked independently to develop patches to correct security flaws (2018). This is promising in that legitimate concerns that go unaddressed about integrity of police camera recordings significantly hamper public transparency. With jurors equating video evidence as almost irrefutable, concerns about BWC video integrity should always be taken seriously. Moreover, it is essential that legislative and implementation efforts for BWC technology emphasize proper security protocols to address data integrity.

Reasonable Access

An area of continued contention between the public and police has been over access to BWC footage. To address the fundamentally biased authority over BWC footage and advance the goals of this technological reform, Morton (2018) and Sacharoff and Lustbader (2017) similarly posited that the decision to permit community members access to video documentation should not be controlled by police officials, but rather an independent agency. Further, Sacharoff and Lustbader (2017) suggested that the addition of third-party accountability entities could enhance perceptions of fairness in the criminal justice system with its focus on neutrality. From a researcher perspective, the authors also highlight the potential value of these agencies as they could be utilized to critically analyze BWC footage and draw generalized observations for future improvements in police practices.

In establishing guidance pertaining to BWC release, the Pennsylvania District Attorneys Association (PDDA) recommended state-compliant practices including that each agency must appoint a media access officer to address release requests. The organization cautioned that the public release of footage related to active criminal investigations could violate ethical rules and potentially taint jury pools (2018). As such, the media access officer should work collaboratively with prosecutors before disseminating imagery to avoid issues that would hinder a defendant's right in obtaining a fair trial.

Suitable Guidance

Another strategy to effectively involve external constituents is to encourage feedback in initial policy development as well as with continued use of the technology. Nationally, the US Department of Justice, the American Civil Liberties Union, and the Police Executive Research Forum (PERF) have issued resources to guide law enforcement agencies implementing BWCs. With the latter organization, PERF has issued comprehensive protocols addressing not only camera issuance, but also recording, data storage, release of footage, training, and evaluation (Miller & Tolliver, 2014). A simple but necessary clarification from PERF was prioritizing the issuances of BWCs to personnel with the most public contacts and forbidding officers from using non-departmental issued equipment that could hinder investigations through lack of data ownership—the limited access could thereby reduce public confidence in the integrity of the recordings.

In addition, PERF recommended other essentials for BWC adoption. In recording, it is essential that officers document in agency reports that a BWC was activated consistent with organizational policy. This serves not only to reinforce sound BWC practices in law enforcement, but also makes attorneys aware that footage of the interaction should be available for civil and/or criminal court proceedings. This seemingly minor inclusion serves as an important notice to prosecutors that the defense may need to be provided with exculpatory materials consistent with due process. Further, officers should provide written documentation whenever discretion was used in deciding not to record part of an incident (e.g., necessary to protect the privacy of a victim or witness, maintain the confidentiality of an undercover operation, etc.). This incorporation provides supervisors notice about missing footage and emphasizes individual accountability (2014).

State agency resources on BWCs can also provide law enforcement agencies with useful guidance. Similarly, state law enforcement authorities in Maryland, Delaware, and Virginia, among others, have disseminated model BWC policies for agencies within their respective jurisdictions (PDAA, 2018). Minnesota and California post model policies online that are available for public inspection. Vermont's model camera policy details 7 specific instances when recordings by officers should be made including during all investigative stops (CJTC, 2020). Police departments in South Carolina are required to submit BWC policies to the state's Law Enforcement Training Council for review and approval.

As part of the state's revised statute to encourage law enforcement adoption of BWCs, the Pennsylvania Commission on Crime and Delinquency (PCCD) disseminated a 6-page model policy specifying standards for the technology's operation, storage, dissemination, and disciplinary actions for misuse (PCCD, 2018). Likewise, Pennsylvania agencies can access the Pennsylvania District Attorneys Association's (PDAA) best practices for BWCs and a model policy to act as a resource for law enforcement agencies in that state considering adoption of the technology.

Interestingly, the PDAA offered rationale along with guidance. For instance, the organization asserted that video documentation for murder prosecutions be retained until the individual has no more appeals and is no longer under the control of a criminal justice agency—essentially recommending that the footage be retained indefinitely (2018). Further, the Pennsylvania Law Enforcement Accreditation Commission revised their required agency standards to incorporate policies and procedures concerning BWCs (PALEAC, 2020). Currently, over 120 law enforcement agencies in Pennsylvania voluntarily participate in LEAC's accreditation program and are recognized as meeting high levels of professional standards that include professional approval of BWC policies.

Agency policies should clearly prohibit tampering with BWCs by personnel and incorporate audit procedures to randomly inspect footage for organizational accountability. At the scene of lethal force, involved officers should immediately provide BWCs to supervisors to best ensure chain-of-custody and data integrity. The Los Angeles Police Department demonstrated the necessity of audits recently when supervisors inspecting random BWCs watched an officer who appeared to be fondling a corpse (Holcombe, 2019). The shocking footage was evidently obtained after the officer had tried to deactivate the equipment, but a delay buffer lasting approximately 120 seconds nonetheless captured the incident.

Training

As previously discussed, continued design improvements are important to reduce instances where BWCs become dislodged or are otherwise unable to provide quality recordings of encounters. In addition, providing field officers with extensive training is imperative to successful camera programs. To remind officers not to forget to activate BWCs when required, agencies should invest in training as would accompany any other piece of valued equipment. In Connecticut, a goal with officer BWC instruction is to create muscle memory emphasizing the repeated act of activating a camera (Lindsay, 2019).

For example, the repeated act of wearing a seat belt while operating a vehicle instills a positive association for the safe driver. The safe operator always buckles their seat belt before driving. Without the safety strap properly in place, the safe driver will feel different—a sensation that will continue until the seat belt is correctly buckled. Similarly, the repeated practice of appropriately activating a police officer BWC can also become second nature on calls. Although efforts to remind officers to turn-on cameras seems mundane, these exercises are essential in building public trust. Agencies with cameras that have to explain to community members why an encounter was not recorded due to user-error in forgetting to activate the technology will be barraged by criticism and demands for improved transparency.

CONCLUSION

The adoption of body-worn cameras in policing is unlike any other reform in the profession. Despite the initial limited knowledge on its efficacy, this technology was quickly embraced by practitioners and the public to address one of the most controversial aspects of this field, use of force. Compelled by controversial recorded lethal force encounters, elected officials in nearly every state have considered legislation requiring universal adoption of BWCs. In addition, researchers have turned body cameras into a rapidly growing area of criminal justice research and produced a significant amount knowledge on the topic and its implications for policing.

Although early studies on the efficacy of these devices demonstrated positive results, similar replications in later works have revealed mixed findings. Overall, the wide range of outcomes evident in the body of peer-reviewed literature suggest that this technology is merely a reactive device with limited impact that will not completely reform police and their organizational environment (Koslicki, 2019). BWC initiatives tend to target current tactics utilized by officers, while fundamental practices and values of the organizational culture remain untouched. In essence, BWCs are not a panacea for law enforcement agency change, but rather agency contexts shape the technology and its impact in practice (Lum et al., 2019).

In addition to the lack of significant declines of force with police embracing body camera use, numerous other misconceptions exist regarding the technology. Despite public perceptions, universal BWC adoption by police has not occurred, and due to financial challenges and the disparate nature of US law enforcement, it is unlikely. With use of force incidents typically involving struggles and foot pursuits, the technology is prone to becoming dislodged, resulting in incomplete video and/or audio recordings. Further, when BWC data are collected, there is no guarantee that recordings will be released to the public, as law enforcement agencies typically act as gatekeepers for the information.

Undeterred by these outcomes, one facet that has remained consistent is the predominantly positive perceptions of BWC use in policing. While the rapid trend of adoption continues to gain traction with instances of lethal force at the forefront of collective attention and the present-day animosity towards police, body-worn cameras are evolving into a necessary and essential component of the police uniform. For effective camera adoption programs, law enforcement agencies must garner support from not only officers wearing the technology, but also from the public and other external constituencies including district attorneys, public defenders, the judiciary, civil rights advocacy groups, and professional organizations. Providing the public with reasonable access to BWC data, either through police collaborating with a third-party reviewer for initial inquiries, or at least having available appeal mechanisms established are sensible provisions to encourage openness.

Moreover, camera adoption programs should incorporate best practices and reflect model policies that detail use and misuse, as well as establish procedures for data retention, audits, release, and security. Any police reform measure that incorporates increased use of BWCs without a complimentary funding mechanism, should be viewed as incomplete. As more collective trust is placed on video documentation and its ability to unveil detrimental flaws in police practices, such as controversial instances of force, the reluctance to aptly implement BWCs and/or conceal program details may further hinder the perceived legitimacy of law enforcement within society.

ACKNOWLEDGMENT

This research received no specific grant from any funding agency in the public, commercial, or not-for-profit sectors, but the research was supported by Bloomsburg University of Pennsylvania.

The authors dedicate this work to our late friend and colleague, Dr. Robert Moschgat, who never failed to inspire us.

REFERENCES

Adams, I., & Mastracci, S. (2017). Visibility is a trap: The ethics of police body-worn cameras and control. *Administrative Theory & Praxis*, *39*(4), 313–328. doi:10.1080/10841806.2017.1381482

Ariel, B. (2017). Police body cameras in large police departments. *The Journal of Criminal Law & Criminology*, *106*(4), 729–768.

Ariel, B., Farrar, W., & Sutherland, A. (2015). The effect of police body-worn cameras on use of force and citizens' complaints against the police: A randomized controlled trial. *Journal of Quantitative Criminology*, *31*(3), 509–535. doi:10.100710940-014-9236-3

Ariel, B., Sutherland, A., Henstock, D., Young, J., Drover, P., Sykes, J., Megicks, S., & Henderson, R. (2016). Report: increases in police use of force in the presence of body-worn cameras are driven by officer discretion: A protocol- based subgroup analysis of ten randomized experiments. *Journal of Experimental Criminology*, *12*(3), 453–463. doi:10.100711292-016-9261-3

Badcock, M., & Altmann, E. (2020 February 21). Police evidence lost in Stuart hack attack; six suspected drug dealers walk free. *WPTV West Palm Beach News*. https://www.wptv.com/news/local-news/stuart/police-evidence-lost-in-stuart-hack-attack-six-suspected-drug-dealers-walk-free

Bellin, J., & Pemberton, S. (2019). Policing the admissibility of body camera evidence. *Fordham Law Review*, *87*(4), 1425–1457.

Bies, K. J. (2017). Let the sunshine in: Illuminating the powerful role police unions play in shielding officer misconduct. [vi]. *Stanford Law & Policy Review*, *28*(1), 109.

Braga, A., Coldren, J. R., Sousa, W., Rodriguez, D., & Alper, O. (2017). The benefits of body-worn cameras: New findings from a randomized controlled trial at the Las Vegas Metropolitan Police Department. *National Institute of Justice.* https://www.ncjrs.gov/pdffiles1/nij/grants/251416.pdf

Brown, P. (2017 July 25). Seattle police union challenges new body camera requirement. *KUOW: Puget Sound Public Radio.* https://www.kuow.org/stories/seattle-police-union-challenges-new-body-camera-requirement

Canales, K. (2020 July 8). People are buying used police body cameras on eBay and other sites and discovering unencrypted footage of officers searching homes. *Business Insider.* https://www.businessinsider.com/used-police-body-cameras-sold-ebay-footage-surveillance-2020-7

Clare, J., Henstock, D., McComb, C., Newland, R., & Barnes, G. C. (2019). The results of a randomized controlled trial of police body-worn video in Australia. *Journal of Experimental Criminology.* Advance online publication. doi:10.100711292-019-09387-w

Criminal Justice Training Council (CJTC). (2020). LEAB model body-worn camera policy. *State of Vermont Online.* https://vcjc.vermont.gov/content/leab-model-body-worn-camera-policy

Crow, M. S., Snyder, J. A., Crichlow, V. J., & Smykla, J. O. (2017). Community perceptions of police body-worn cameras: The impact of views on fairness, fear, performance, and privacy. *Criminal Justice and Behavior*, *44*(4), 589–610. doi:10.1177/0093854816688037

Culhane, S. E., Boman, J. H. IV, & Schweitzer, K. (2016). Public perceptions of the justifiability of police shootings: The role of body cameras in a pre- and post-Ferguson experiment. *Police Quarterly*, *19*(3), 251–274. doi:10.1177/1098611116651403

Dahler, D. (2020 March 9). Heart-warming birthday treat captured on police body cam. *CBS News.* https://www.cbsnews.com/news/body-cameras-capture-georgia-officers-act-of-kindness-2020-03-09/

Flaherty, J. (2020 December 1). Lawyer irked by deletion of Little Rock police footage. *Arkansas Democrat Gazette.* https://www.arkansasonline.com/news/2020/dec/01/lawyer-irked-by-deletion-of-police-footage/?news

Gaub, J., & White, M. (2020). Open to interpretation: Confronting the challenges of understanding the current state of body-worn camera research. *American Journal of Criminal Justice*, *45*(5), 899–913. doi:10.100712103-020-09518-4

Geringer-Sameth, E. (2020 February 27). Initial report shows benefits and challenges of NYPD body camera program for police watchdog. *Gotham Gazette.* https://www.gothamgazette.com/city/9167-initial-report-shows-benefits-and-challenges-of-nypd-body-camera-program-for-watchdog-agency

Gliha, L. (2019 October 25). Aurora PD says body cameras recorded but fell off during altercation with man who later died. *Fox 31 News, Denver*. https://kdvr.com/news/problem-solvers/family-of-man-who-died-after-altercation-with-aurora-first-responders-says-body-camera-footage-disgusting/

Gonzales, A. R., & Cochran, D. Q. (2017). Police-worn body cameras: An antidote to the "Ferguson Effect"? *Missouri Law Review*, *82*(2), 299–337.

Graham, A., McManus, H., Cullen, F., Burton, V. Jr, & Jonson, C. (2019). Videos don't lie: African Americans support for body-worn cameras. *Criminal Justice Review*, *44*(3), 1–20. doi:10.1177/0734016819846229

Henstock, D., & Ariel, B. (2017). Testing the effects of police body-worn cameras on use of force during arrests: A randomised controlled trial in a large British police force. *European Journal of Criminology*, *14*(6), 720–750. doi:10.1177/1477370816686120

Hindi, S. (2017 November 21). Body camera video: Officers asked suspect to drop knife more than 40 times. *The Coloradoan*. https://www.coloradoan.com/story/news/2017/11/21/police-body-camera-video-fatal-shooting-jeremy-holmes/884711001/

Holcombe, M. (2019 December 4). LAPD officer allegedly caught fondling corpse. *CNN*. https://www.cnn.com/2019/12/04/us/lapd-officer-fondle-corpse/index.html

Jackman, T. (2020 July 2). Federal body camera bill, inspired by Park Police killing of Bijan Ghaisar, included in House police reform package. *The Washington Post*. https://www.washingtonpost.com/crime-law/2020/06/09/federal-body-camera-bill-inspired-by-park-police-killing-bijan-ghaisar-included-house-police-reform-package/

Jennings, W. G., Lynch, M. D., & Fridell, L. A. (2015). Evaluating the impact of police officer body-worn cameras (BWCs) on response-to-resistance and serious external complaints: Evidence from the Orlando police department (OPD) experience utilizing a randomized controlled experiment. *Journal of Criminal Justice*, *43*(6), 480–486. doi:10.1016/j.jcrimjus.2015.10.003

Kindy, K. (2019, January 21). Some U.S. police departments dump body-warn camera programs amid high costs. *The Washington Post*. https://www.washingtonpost.com/national/some-us-police-departments-dump-body-camera-programs-amid-high-costs/2019/01/21/991f0e66-03ad-11e9-b6a9-0aa5c2fcc9e4_story.html

Klinger, D. (2004). *Into the kill zone*. Jossey-Bass, Inc.

Koslicki, W. M. (2019). Accountability or efficiency? Body-worn cameras as replicative technology. *Criminal Justice Review (Atlanta, Ga.)*, *44*(3), 356–368. doi:10.1177/0734016819856079

Koslicki, W. M., Makin, D. A., & Willits, D. (2020). When no one is watching: Evaluating the impact of body-worn cameras on use of force incidents. *Policing and Society*, *30*(5), 1–14. doi:10.1080/10439463.2020.1765778

Lange, K. (2019 October 19). A Carmel police body camera fell off at a critical moment. It's not all that rare. *Indianapolis Star*. https://www.indystar.com/story/news/local/hamilton-county/carmel/2020/10/19/carmel-police-axon-body-camera-fell-off-critical-moment/5941701002/

Lawrence, D. S., McClure, D., Malm, A., Lynch, M., & La Vigne, N. (2019). Activation of body-worn cameras: Variation by officer, over time, and by policing activity. *Criminal Justice Review*, *44*(3), 339–355. doi:10.1177/0734016819846228

Lindsay, R. (2019 July 8). Behind the body camera: The ethics, adoption, and impact of recording police interactions. *WNPR, Connecticut Public Radio Online*. https://www.wnpr.org/post/behind-body-camera-ethics-adoption-and-impact-recording-police-interactions

Lou, M., & Griggs, B. (2019 February 27). A proposed Tennessee law would make it a felony for police officers to disable their body cams. *CNN*. https://www.cnn.com/2019/02/27/us/tennessee-body-cam-felony-trnd/index.html

Lum, C., Koper, C., Merola, L., Scherer, A., & Reioux, A. (2015). Existing and ongoing body worn camera research: knowledge gaps and opportunities. *Laura and John Arnold Foundation*. https://www.arnoldfoundation.org/wp-content/uploads/Phase-I-Report-Nov-28-2015-FINAL.pdf

Lum, C., Koper, C. S., Wilson, D. B., Stoltz, M., Goodier, M., Eggins, E., Higginson, A., & Mazerolle, L. (2020). Body-worn cameras' effects on police officers and citizen behavior: A systematic review. *Campbell Systematic Review, 16*(3).

Lum, C., Stoltz, M., Koper, C. S., & Scherer, J. A. (2019). Research on body-worn cameras: What we know, what we need to know. *Criminology & Public Policy*, *18*(1), 93–118. doi:10.1111/1745-9133.12412

Malm, A. (2019). Promise of police body-worn cameras. *Criminology & Public Policy*, *18*(1), 119–130. doi:10.1111/1745-9133.12420

Mateescu, A., Rosenblat, A., & Boyd, D. (2016). Dreams of accountability guaranteed surveillance: The promises and costs of body-worn cameras. *Surveillance & Society*, *14*(1), 122–127. doi:10.24908s.v14i1.6282

Maxwell, N. (2020 July 15). Body cameras: What is different and what is the same. *Alamogordo Daily News*. https://www.alamogordonews.com/story/news/local/community/2020/07/15/local-law-enforcement-and-new-body-cam-rules/5441740002/

McCamman, M., & Culhane, S. (2017). Police body cameras and us: Public perceptions of the justification of the police use of force in the body camera era. *Translational Issues in Psychological Science*, *3*(2), 167–175. doi:10.1037/tps0000117

McKelvey, W. (2017 May 10). PA Senate approves police body camera bill the ACLU says restricts public access. *Penn Live Patriot News*. https://www.pennlive.com/politics/2017/05/police_body_cameras.html

Meck, S. (2018). Focusing the lens of justice: The implementation of police body cameras is a management right, not a mandatory subject of collective bargaining. *The Florida Bar Journal*, *92*(4), 42–47.

Merola, L., Lum, C., Koper, C. S., & Scherer, A. (2016). *Body worn cameras and the courts: A national survey of state prosecutors (Report for the Laura and John Arnold Foundation)*. Center for Evidence-Based Crime Policy, George Mason University. https://bja.ojp.gov/sites/g/files/xyckuh186/files/media/document/bwcprosecutors.pdf

Metrick, B. (2019a July 1). Find out if your town's police officers wear body cameras: check here. *Penn-Live Patriot News*. https://www.pennlive.com/news/2019/07/does-your-local-police-department-have-body-cameras.html

Metrick, B. (2019b July 1). Police body cameras can help officers and suspects, so why don't more departments have them? *Penn-Live Patriot News*. https://www.pennlive.com/news/2019/07/why-dont-more-police-departments-have-body-cams-cost-is-the-biggest-but-not-the-only-reason.html

Micucci, A. J., & Gomme, I. M. (2005). American police and subcultural support for the use of excessive force. *Journal of Criminal Justice*, *33*(5), 487–500. doi:10.1016/j.jcrimjus.2005.06.002

Miethe, T. D., Lieberman, J. D., Heen, M. S. J., & Sousa, W. H. (2019). Public attitudes about body-worn cameras in police work: A national study of the sources of their contextual variability. *Criminal Justice Review*, *44*(3), 263–283. doi:10.1177/0734016819846241

Miller, L., & Toliver, J. (2014). Implementing a body-worn camera program: recommendations and lessons learned. *US Department of Justice Online, Police Executive Research Forum*. https://www.justice.gov/iso/opa/resources/472014912134715246869.pdf

Mitchell, R. J., Ariel, B., Firpo, M. E., Fraiman, R., Castillo, F., Hyatt, J. M., Weinborn, C., & Brants Sabo, H. (2018). Measuring the effect of body-worn cameras on complaints in Latin America: The case of traffic police in Uruguay. *Policing*, *41*(4), 510–524. doi:10.1108/PIJPSM-01-2018-0004

Morton, D. (2018). Improving police transparency and accountability in violent encounters with African Americans. *Journal of African American Studies*, *22*(1), 125–138. doi:10.100712111-018-9396-6

Murphy, E. (2016 October 14). Body cam catches groomsmen's dance practice after police respond to noise complaint. *ABC News*. https://abcnews.go.com/Lifestyle/body-cam-catches-groomsmens-dance-practice-police-respond/story?id=42810933

National Academies of Sciences, Engineering, and Medicine. (2018). Proactive policing: Effects on crime and communities. *The National Academies Press*. https://www.nap.edu/resource/24928/Race.pdf

National Conference of State Legislators (NCSL). (2018). Body-worn-camera data. *NCSL Online*. https://www.ncsl.org/research/civil-and-criminal-justice/body-worn-cameras-interactive-graphic.aspx#/

Newman, L. (2018 August 11). Police bodycams can be hacked to doctor footage. *Wired*. https://www.wired.com/story/police-body-camera-vulnerabilities/

Nix, J., Todak, N., & Tregle, B. (2020). Understanding body-worn-camera diffusion in U.S. policing. *Police Quarterly*, *23*(3), 396–422. doi:10.1177/1098611120917937

Ortiz, R. (2019 December 20). Fort Worth police officer who fatally shot Atatiana Jefferson indicted on murder charge. *NBC News*. https://www.nbcnews.com/news/us-news/fort-worth-police-officer-who-fatally-shot-atatiana-jefferson-indicted-n1105916

Owens, C., & Finn, W. (2018). Body-worn video through the lens of a cluster randomized controlled trial in London: Implications for future research. *Policing. Journal of Policy Practice*, *12*(1), 77–82.

Pennsylvania Commission on Crime and Delinquency (PCCD). (2020). Body-worn camera policy recommendations. *Pennsylvania Commission on Crime and Delinquency Online*. https://www.pccd.pa.gov/criminaljustice/advisory_boards/Documents/BWC%20Policy%20Recommendations%20Commission%20Approved.pdf

Pennsylvania District Attorneys Association (PDAA). (2018). Pennsylvania district attorneys issue best practices on body-worn cameras. *Pennsylvania District Attorneys Association Online*. https://www.pdaa.org/pennsylvania-district-attorneys-issue-best-practices-on-body-worn-cameras/

Pennsylvania Law Enforcement Accreditation Commission (PALEAC). (2020). LEAC Standards Manual. *LEAC Online*. https://pcpa.memberclicks.net/assets/docs/AccreditationDocuments/Standards%20Manual%20AUGUST%202020%20FINAL.pdf

Police Executive Research Forum. (2018). Cost and benefits of body-worn camera deployments. *Police Executive Research Forum Online*. https://www.policeforum.org/assets/BWCCostBenefit.pdf

Powell, T. (2017 June 27). Body-worn camera captures heart-warming moment police officer serenades elderly blind woman. *Evening Standard*. https://www.standard.co.uk/news/world/heartwarming-moment-police-officer-serenades-elderly-blind-woman-caught-on-bodycam-a3574226.html

Ready, J., & Young, J. (2015). The impact of on-officer video cameras on police-citizen contacts: Findings from a controlled experiment in Mesa, AZ. *Journal of Experimental Criminology*, *11*(3), 445–458. doi:10.100711292-015-9237-8

Ready, J., & Young, J. (2020 October 1). The unfulfilled potential of police body cameras in the Era of Black lives matter. *Slate*. https://slate.com/technology/2020/10/black-lives-matter-police-body-cameras.html

Sacharoff, L., & Lustbader, S. (2017). Who should own police body camera videos? *Washington University Law Review*, *95*(2), 269.

Sandhu, A. (2017). 'I'm glad that was on camera': A case study of police officers' perceptions of cameras. *Policing and Society*, *29*(2), 223–235. doi:10.1080/10439463.2017.1285917

Saulnier, A., Burke, K. C., & Bottoms, B. L. (2019). The effects of body-worn camera footage and eyewitness race on jurors' perceptions of police use of force. *Behavioral Sciences & the Law*, *37*(6), 732–750. doi:10.1002/bsl.2443 PMID:31997421

Schindler, A. (2020 December 3). JSO: Dislodged police body cameras "'non-issue;'" public concerned about transparency. *ABC First Coast News*. https://www.firstcoastnews.com/article/news/local/dislodged-body-worn-cameras-hinder-transparency-but-are-not-tracked-by-jso/77-666a8644-0191-4c90-b40c-5a18d6f7c90e

Smykla, J. O., Crow, M. S., Crichlow, V. J., & Snyder, J. A. (2015). Police body-worn cameras: Perceptions of law enforcement leadership. *American Journal of Criminal Justice*, *41*(3), 424–443. doi:10.100712103-015-9316-4

Sousa, W. H., Miethe, T. D., & Sakiyama, M. (2018). Inconsistencies in public opinion of body-worn cameras on police: Transparency, trust, and improved Police–Citizen relationships. *Policing. Journal of Policy Practice*, *12*(1), 100–108.

Southall, A. (2020 November 30). Police body cameras cited as 'powerful tool' against stop-and-frisk abuses. *The New York Times*. https://www.nytimes.com/2020/11/30/nyregion/nypd-body-cameras.html

State of Vermont. (2020 June 23). Testimony provided to the house government operations and judiciary committees on S.B. 219 and S.B. 119. *State of Vermont Online*. https://legislature.vermont.gov/Documents/2020/WorkGroups/House%20Government%22Operations/Bills/S.219/Written%20Testimony/S.219~James%20Lyall~ACLU-VT%20Written%20Testimony~6-24-2020.pdf

Sutherland, A., Ariel, B., Farrar, W., & De Anda, R. (2017). Post-experimental follow-ups—Fade-out versus persistence effects: The Rialto police body-worn camera experiment four years on. *Journal of Criminal Justice*, *53*, 110–116. doi:10.1016/j.jcrimjus.2017.09.008

Taylor, E., & Lee, M. (2019). Off the record? Arrestee concerns about the manipulation, modification, and misrepresentation of police body-worn camera footage. *Surveillance & Society*, *17*(3/4), 473–483. doi:10.24908s.v17i3/4.6550

Thomas, T. (2019 July 10). Lawrenceville police latest victims of cyberattack. *WSB-TV Atlanta News Online*. https://www.wsbtv.com/news/local/gwinnett-county/lawrenceville-police-the-latest-victims-of-cyber-attack/968533646/

Thompson, A. (2020 December 2). All cops to wear cameras in NJ. *New Jersey Today*. https://njtoday.net/2020/12/02/all-cops-to-wear-cameras-in-nj/

Todak, N., & Gaub, J. E. (2019). Predictors of police body-worn camera acceptance: Digging deeper into officers' perceptions. *Policing*, *43*(2), 299–313. doi:10.1108/PIJPSM-06-2019-0085

Toronto Police Service. (2016). Body-worn cameras: A report on the findings of the pilot project to test the value and feasibility of body-worn cameras for police officers in Toronto. *US Department of Justice, Bureau of Justice Administration Online*. https://bja.ojp.gov/sites/g/files/xyckuh186/files/media/document/tps-body-worn-camera-pilot-project-evaluation.pdf

Tyler, T. R. (2004). Enhancing police legitimacy. *The Annals of the American Academy of Political and Social Science*, *593*(1), 84–99. doi:10.1177/0002716203262627

Upturn and Leadership Conference on Civil and Human Rights (LCCHR). (2017). The body-worn camera scorecard. *Upturn and the Leadership Conference on Civil and Human Rights Online*. https://www.bwcscorecard.org/static/pdfs/LCCHR%20and%20Upturn%20-%20BWC%20Scorecard%20v.3.04.pdf

Van Ness, L. (2020 January 14). Body cameras may not be the easy answer everyone was looking for. *The Pew Charitable Trusts*. https://www.pewtrusts.org/en/research-and-analysis/blogs/stateline/2020/01/14/body-cameras-may-not-be-the-easy-answer-everyone-was-looking-for

Varn, K. (2020 August 12). Once reluctant, Pinellas sheriff exploring body cameras for deputies. *Tampa Bay Times*. https://www.tampabay.com/news/crime/2020/08/12/once-reluctant-pinellas-sheriff-exploring-body-cameras-for-deputies/

Watanbe, B. (2020 November 24). Critics wary as Everett OKs body camera program for police. *The Herald.* https://www.heraldnet.com/news/critics-wary-as-everett-oks-body-camera-program-for-police/

White, M. D. (2019). Translating the story on body-worn cameras. *Criminology & Public Policy, 18*(1), 89–91. doi:10.1111/1745-9133.12421

White, M. D., Todak, N., & Gaub, J. E. (2018). Examining body-worn camera integration and acceptance among police officers, citizens, and external stakeholders. *Criminology & Public Policy, 17*(3), 649–677. doi:10.1111/1745-9133.12376

Yokum, D., Ravishankar, A., & Coppock, A. (2019). A randomized control trial evaluating the effects of police body-worn cameras. *Proceedings of the National Academy of Sciences - PNAS, 116*(21), 10329-10332. 10.1073/pnas.1814773116

Zamoff, M. (2019). Assessing the impact of police body camera evidence on the litigation of excessive force cases. *Georgia Law Review (Athens, Ga.), 54*(1), 1–60.

ADDITIONAL READING

Bureau of Justice Assistance. (2020, August 27). Body-Worn Camera Toolkit. https://bja.ojp.gov/program/bwc

Gaub, J., & White, M. (2020). Open to interpretation: Confronting the challenges of understanding the current state of body-worn camera research. *American Journal of Criminal Justice, 45*(5), 899–913. doi:10.100712103-020-09518-4

Miller, L., & Toliver, J. (2014). Implementing a body-worn camera program: recommendations and lessons learned. *US Department of Justice Online, Police Executive Research Forum.* https://www.justice.gov/iso/opa/resources/472014912134715246869.pdf

Police Executive Research Forum. (2018). Cost and benefits of body-worn camera deployments. *Police Executive Research Forum Online.* https://www.policeforum.org/assets/BWCCostBenefit.pdf

KEY TERMS AND DEFINITIONS

Body-Worn Camera (BWC): Technology worn by law enforcement that captures video and audio interactions between police officers and the public.

Officer-Involved Shooting: An incident in which lethal force is either intentionally or unintentionally applied by a police officer via firearm.

Police Brutality: An excessive or unnecessary use of force by police officers in their encounters with civilians. These instances do not always involve deadly force, but rather encompass a variety of civil rights violations. Examples of this concept include a range of physical and nonphysical means, such as the intentional use of racial stereotypes by police, physical and/or verbal assaults, coercion, and intimidation.

Proactive Policing: A broad range of crime prevention tactics utilized by law enforcement to address agents of crime and deviance and deter criminal activity prior to its occurrence. The proactive element of these prevention strategies leaves officers to act on their own initiative and may allow for more discretion in responses to crime. These efforts can take various forms that include, but are not limited to stop and frisks, hotspots policing, focused deterrence tactics, and problem-oriented policing.

Records Retention Schedule: An agency's plan for retaining and discarding collected data. Records created from BWC video and audio files require retention schedules that conform to applicable federal and state laws, as well as local ordinances.

Routine Activities Theory: Developed in 1979 by Lawrence Cohen and Marcus Felson, this theoretical explanation emphasizes the contributions of intersecting space and time to criminality. Specifically, the theory posits that crime is likely to occur when the presence of an appealing or suitable victim, a motivated offender, and the lack of capable guardianship exists simultaneously. In contrast, prevention efforts should focus on reducing any or all of these three conditions to diminish the frequency of criminal offenses.

Two-Party Consent: Some states require consent from all the parties involved prior to communications being recorded. This adds complexity to police BWCs in that law enforcement interacting with community members often don't have time to secure permissions while managing the dynamics of encounters.

Chapter 2
School-to-Prison Pipeline:
The Role of School Resource Officers (SRO)

Sheri Jenkins Keenan
University of Memphis, USA

Jeffrey P. Rush
Department of Anthropology, Sociology, and Criminology, Troy University, USA

ABSTRACT

Juvenile crime rates have declined steadily since 1994 (Nelson & Lind, 2015) and the number of youths in juvenile detention centers has dropped (Annie E. Casey Foundation, 2011; Hockenberry, 2014; Nelson & Lind, 2015; Smith, 1998); however, school discipline polices are moving in the other direction (Nelson & Lind, 2015). In recent years, the lines between the public school system and the juvenile justice system have become indistinct. There are several trends in K-12 education contributing to the school-to-prison pipeline such as declining school funding, resegregation of schools by race and class, under-representation of students of color in advanced placement, over-representation of student of color in special education, the creation and expansion of "zero-tolerance" policies, tracking, increased presence of SROs, No Child Left Behind (NCLB), standardized testing, and rising drop-out rates (Heitzeg et al., 2009). However, the focus here is the expansion and increased reliance on "zero-tolerance" policies and the use of the SRO to enforce those policies which play an immediate and integral role in feeding the school-to-prison pipeline.

INTRODUCTION

Juvenile crime rates have declined steadily since 1994 (Nelson & Lind, 2015) and the number of youths in juvenile detention centers has dropped (Annie e. Casey Foundation, 2011; Hockenberry, 2014; Nelson & Lind, 2015; Smith, 1998); however, school discipline polices are moving in the other direction (Nelson & Lind, 2015). In recent years, the lines between the school system and the juvenile justice system have become indistinct. The school-to-prison pipeline refers to this growing pattern of seamlessly moving juveniles out of the school and into the juvenile justice system. There are several trends in K-12 education

DOI: 10.4018/978-1-7998-6884-2.ch002

contributing to the school-to-prison pipeline such as declining school funding, resegregation of schools by race and class, under-representation of students of color in advanced placement, over-representation of student of color in special education, creation, and expansion of 'zero-tolerance" policies, tracking, increased presents of SROs, No Child Left Behind (NCLB), standardized testing, and rising drop-out rates Heitzeg et al., (2009). However, the focus here is the expansion and increased reliance on "zero-tolerance" policies and the use of the SRO to enforce those policies which play an immediate and integral role in feeding the school-to-prison pipeline.

The school resource officer (SRO) program began in the United States in the early 1950s. However, the program did not gain popularity until the mid-1990s in response to the rise in the number of public-school shootings. Currently, no one knows exactly how many SROs there are in the United States because they are not required to register with any national database, police departments are not required to report how many officers work as SROs, and school systems are not required to report how many SROs they use. The National Association of School Resources Officers (NASRO), (2021), estimates that approximately 40% of all K-12, public and private, are served by SROs. The most recent available data on the number of SROs comes from a 2018 report by the National Center for Education Statistics (NCES): U.S. Department of Education. The Center (Musu et al., 2019) reported that 42% of public schools were being served by at least one SRO, at least one day a week during the 2015-2016 academic year. Many SROs serve more than one school and some schools have more than one officer; therefore, we cannot reliably extrapolate the number of SROs there really are.

The National Association of School Resource Officers (NASRO) is the national association for SROs dedicated to making schools safer by providing high quality training to SROs. In addition, each state has been divided into regions; ten regions. Each region has its own board and provides trainings and conferences to its members.

THE SCHOOL RESOURCE OFFICER (SRO)

School resource officers (SROs) are sworn law enforcement officers who are deployed by a police department/sheriff's department in a community-oriented policing assignment to work in collaboration with one or more schools (Coon & Travis, 2012). SROs are responsible for safety and crime prevention in schools.

NASRO (2021) recommends that law enforcement agencies utilize a rigorous selection process when selecting officers for SRO assignments and that officers received at least 40 hours of specialized training, beyond basic law enforcement training/academy, in school policing before being assigned.

According to NASRO (2021), the goals of a well-founded SRO program include:

- providing safe learning environment,
- providing valuable resources to school staff members,
- fostering positive relationships with youth, and
- developing strategies to resolve problems affecting youth and protecting all students.

Finally, NASRO considers it a best practice to use what they call a "triad concept" (2021) to define the three main roles of school resource officers: educator (i.e., guest lecturer), informal counselor/mentor, and law enforcement officer.

School Resource Officer (SRO) vs. School-Based Law Enforcement (SBLE)

Another approach to providing school districts with law enforcement services is the school-based law enforcing or SBLE. Sometime these two terms: SRO and SBLE, are used synonymously; however, there is a clear distinction between them. The major distinction between the two approaches is related to the organizational structure of the department. Contrary to SROs, School-Based Law Enforcement (SBLE) officers are employees of the school district's school-based police department. SBLE agencies are under the direct control of the school district rather than the local or county governments. These departments follow the traditional organizational structure of a police department, but are ultimately accountable to the school district superintendent, board of trustees, school boards, etc. (McKenna et al., 2016). For example, SBLE officers in school district police departments report to the Chief of Police of the school district police department, who then reports to the district Superintendent.

SBLE agencies are responsible for serving the entire school district, but most of their focus does tend to be geared toward middle and high schools. Texas has approximately 200 school-based law enforcement department across the state (Texas Commission on Law Enforcement, 2021) and school districts across the nation have adopted their own school-based police departments. All 25 of the nation's largest school district have sworn police officers in at least some of their schools; 10 run their own police forces (Diliberti, et al., 2019). Nationwide more than half of all public schools have sworn law enforcement officers (Diliberti, et al., 2019)

In the case of SROs, there is a memorandum of understanding or contract between the school district and the local police department to assign a certain number of officers to the school district and individual schools during the academic year. During the summer months, these officers may return to their normal function under the police department (McKenna et al., 2016). There are some SRO programs that choose to host summer programs/camps for at risk youth in their communities.

Funding for SROs or SBLE comes from city, county, school districts, federal grants, or thought shared cost agreements (Javdani, 2019). Because SROs and SBLE are employed by different agencies and not required to register with a centralized database, we are not sure how many their truly and know very little about their demographic characteristic other than they are likely to be male (85.2%), white (67%) with the median age of the officer being 40; the average of national law enforcement demographics (Banks et al., 2019).

THE ROLE OF LAW ENFORCEMENT IN SCHOOLS

After the expansion of law enforcement in the school setting, research began to look at the role, utilization, and issues of having law enforcement officers in school (Clark, 2011; Coon & Travis, 2012; Finn et al., 2005; Kennedy, 2001; McDaniel, 2001; McKenna et al., 2016). The most accepted implementation model for law enforcement officers in schools is the "triad model." This model provides law enforcement three main roles: enforcement, education, and mentoring.

Enforcement consists of crime prevention, law, discipline, and apprehension of violators. Officers typically patrol the school grounds, investigate incidents, handle students' misconduct, and ensure the school day goes uninterrupted (Lawrence, 2007; McKenna et al., 2016). Coon and Travis (2012) and McDaniel (2001) found that officers spend more time in this enforcement role more than the other two:

education and mentoring. McDaniel (2001) estimated a little more than half of the officer's time is spent in the enforcement role.

Education consists of law enforcement officers teaching students in the classroom on topics like drugs, alcohol, crime prevention, law, and criminal justice/juvenile justice system (Weiler & Cray, 2011). Coon and Travis (2012) found that almost 42 percent (41.6%) of the officers reported teaching Drug Abuse Resistance Education or DARE, 27% (26.6%) reported teaching about alcohol awareness, and 28% reported teaching crime prevention.

Mentoring consists of law enforcement officers assisting students and families with law related issues; behavior and discipline (Weiler & Cray, 2011). Coon and Travis (2012) found that 83.8% of law enforcement officers working in high schools reported providing some guidance or mentoring to students and their families; 89.5% for those working in junior high.

HISTORY OF SCHOOL RESOURCE OFFICERS (SRO)

The first recorded school resource officer (SRO) was assigned to a school in Liverpool, England in 1951 (Bond, 2001). In the United States, the first SRO was assigned to a school in Flint, Michigan in the mid to late 1950s (Black, 2009; Canady et al., 2012; McKenna et al., 2014; Weiler & Cray, 2011); however, the program did not gain popularity until the 1990s in response to the rise in school shootings (e.g., events associated with Columbine High School, Marjory Stoneman Doulas High School, and Santa Fe High Schools (Blad et al., 2018; McCurdy, et al., 2019; Weiler & Cray, 2011). The program was titled the "Police-School Liaison Program" and school and police administrators' early opinion of the program was very positive; other states followed with a similar strategy. McDaniel (2001) credited the police chief in Miami, Florida with coining the term "School Resource Officer (SRO) in the early 1960s. The RSO program did not take off until the 1990s in response to increased numbers of school shootings, the federal Gun-Free Schools Act of 1994, and the public schools creating expansive "zero-tolerance" policies (Trump, 1998).

The early days of the SRO program in the United States involved placing plainclothes police officers in the middle and elementary schools to foster a relationship between the local police department and the youth; this continues to be one of the goals of the program (Nelson and Lind, 2015). Since the 1970s, the role of the SRO shifted from mentorship to crime prevention and law enforcement (Nelson & Lind, 2015).

In the 1980s and early 1990s SROs facilitated crime prevention programs such as Drug Abuse Resistance Education (D.A.R.E.) and Gang Resistance Education and Training (G.R.E.A.T.), and the use of SROs assigned to schools was limited; only about 1% of U.S. schools had an SRO (Hunt et al., 2019; National Institute of Education, 1978). However, by the late 1990s SROs presence in schools increased to 22% (Heaviside et al., 1998), by 2004 to 36%, by 2008 to 40% (Na & Gottfredson, 2013), and by 2016 to 48% (Hunt et al., 2019). Today, SROs are the main enforcers and interpreters of the states' school disturbance laws (Nelson & Lind, 2015).

There are several reasons for the increase presence of SROs in schools. One reason might be the public's perceptions of an increase in juvenile crime; increased number of school shootings and increase in juvenile community violence spilling over into local schools. In addition, the federal government began to pass legislation in response to the public's fear of juvenile crime. For example, the Gun Free Act of 1994 gave schools the authority to have a "zero-tolerance" policy towards weapons on school grounds. Over time, this policy was broadened to include drugs and alcohol. The Act of 1994 removed the arbitrary nature of school policies and put formal disciplinary standards into place. SROs became the most obvious individuals that could enforce the new policies. Similarly, at the federal level a large amount of funding for SROs was created in the Office of Community Oriented Policing Services (COPS) (U.S. Department of Justice, Office of Community Oriented Policing Services, 2021). The COPS office helped with defining, implementing, and standardizing community-oriented policing, which included placing large numbers of officers on school grounds (Patterson, 2007). In addition, COPS created the Cops in Schools (CIS) grant program, which awarded over $750 million for the hiring of more than 6,500 SROs (Na & Gottfredson, 2013); the program helped fund over 13k SROs in schools across the U.S (Reaves, 2010). Finally, states have provided funding for the hiring and training of SROs.

There are several controversial issues related to SROs. First, there have been several incidents in the United in which SROs are reported to have used excessive force. For example, in May 2017, an SRO with the Dallas Independent School district (ISD) allegedly handcuffed and tasered a 7-year-old special needs student and, in that same week (Crunden, 2017), another SRO at Dallas ISD reportedly body-slammed and pepper sprayed a 12-year-old female student on campus (Crunden, 2017). There have also been additional high-profile incidents over the past few years echoing the excessive force concerns related to SROs role in the schools.

- In October 2015, an SRO body slamming a 16-year-old girl at her desk in Spring Valley High School, South Carolina (Stelloh & Connor, 2015).
- In October 2015, an SRO was filmed choking a 14-year-old while trying to break up a fight at Round Rock High School, Texas (Boyer & Uchida, 2015).
- In 2015, an SRO at Tolman High School, Rhode Island body-slammed a 14-year-old, leading to protest (Staff, Journal, 2015).
- In August 2015, SRO handcuffed an 8-year-old boy and a 9-year-old girl, both with special needs in Kentucky (Stolberg, 2015).

In addition, another criticism of SROs in schools pertains to the rate of juvenile arrests. Petteruti (2011) indicates that school referrals to the juvenile justice system have increased with the presence of SROs. A high percentage of those referrals were for minor offenses that could have been handled by the administration but because there was an SRO the juvenile was "pushed out" to the juvenile justice system. This concern has attracted attention and there are studies indicating that the use of the SRO and juvenile justice system for minor offenses contributes to the school-to-prison pipeline (Petteruti, 2011).

Duxbury and Bennell (2019) concluded that for every dollar invested in SRO programs, a minimum of $11.13 of social and economic value was created. The report lists numerous benefits of the program, including:

- Prevention or minimization of property damage in the school and surrounding areas.
- Prevention of student injuries and even death due to violence, drug overdoses, etc.
- Reduction of the need for schools to call 911.
- Reduction of the likelihood that a student will get a criminal record.
- Increase of the likelihood that students (particularly those with mental health issues) will get the help they need from the social service and health care systems.
- Increase in feelings of safety among students and staff.

EFFECTIVENESS OF USING SROS IN PUBLIC SCHOOLS

School crime and violence include things like fighting, bullying, property damage, illegal drugs, and the rare school shooting. Although school shootings are highly publicized, only 3% of youth homicides occur at school (Musu-Gillette et al., 2018). Nevertheless, concern over the safety of students, faculty, and staff in our nation's schools continues to grow. There are two reasons for this. First, the highly publicized, all be it rare, media coverage of mass school shootings such as the events at Columbine High School (1999), Sandy Hook Elementary School (2012), and Stoneman Douglas High School (2018). Second, the growing recognition that effective teaching and learning can only happen in a safe and positive school environment. The solution to this growing concern has been the increase use of SROs.

Research finding on the effectiveness of using SROs in K-12 public schools are mixed. When looking specifically at reductions in school crime/violence, victimization, SROs training, increase rates of arrest, and rising litigation we find the following.

School Crime/Violence

Crawford and Burns (2015), used data from the 2006 School Survey on Crime and Safety (SSOCS) to assess the impact of protective measures, polices, and school/neighborhood characteristics on school violence. They concluded that the use of SROs in controlling school violence were mixed and often counterproductive. They found that while some prior research suggested that SROs have a mitigating effect on crime and violence, their study showed this was dependent upon grade level and the type of crime or violence the school is trying to address. Na and Gottfredson (2013), found that increased use of SROs resulted in more crime involving drugs and weapons and a higher percentage of non-serious crime being reported to the police. Swartz et al., (2016) using data from the 2010 SSOCS examined whether the presence of SROs and their level of involvement in place management activities was associated with an increase or a deduction in the reporting of serous violence within schools. Their findings found SROs can contribute to higher incidence of school crime and did not support the notion that SROs are acting as effective place managers. In a later study, Crawford and Burns (2016), they found that minority schools often face higher levels of reported violence and have a heavier law enforcement presence than white schools. They suggested this was counterproductive in reducing school violence and influenced incarceration trends, contributing to the school-to-prison pipeline.

Victimization

Conflicting findings make it difficult to determine what works to prevent school violence, crime, and victimization. For example, Burrow and Apel (2008), found that students in schools with SROs were more likely to be victims of theft. In contrast, Jennings et al. (2011), found that SROs appear to be an effective crime prevention approach. Their findings suggest that SROs were promising in mitigating and confronting problems regarding bullying, racial tensions, student disrespect, and gangs in high schools. Finally, Johnson (1999) found that crime and school suspension decreased in middle and high schools where SRO were assigned.

Student victimization by the school and or school district for the sake of "school safety" and discipline is not recognized as a problem, but it does contribute to student alienation and aggression (Hyman & Perone, 1998). Included in this type of victimization are metal detectors, overuse of RSOs, enhanced school security, strip searches, use of undercover agents, corporal punishment, exclusionary discipline, and psychological maltreatment (Hyman & Perone, 1998). Psychological maltreatment includes verbal assaults: sarcasm, ridicule, name calling, denigrating statements, sexual exploitation, negative role models, exposing children to systematic bias and prejudice, and subjecting youth to institutional practices that are clearly harmful to basic human needs (Hyman & Perone, 1998): denying youth proper food for overdue lunch accounts.

Training

According to the NASRO (2021), the SROs' "best practice" is to employ the triad model: educator, informal counselor/mentor, and law enforcement officer. This three-pronged approach requires that the SRO possess a skill set unique to both law enforcement and K-12 educators. It should allow the SRO to protect the community and the campus while supporting the education mission of the school in which they serve (NASRO, 2021). From a law enforcement standpoint there is an underlying crime prevention strategy at play here as well: community policing. Initial training and continuing education in all these areas are vital to the SRO. Like most of the research on SROs, research on SROs education and training is also mixed.

Rural areas across the U.S. typically have fewer resources: smaller school budgets, small to mid-size police departments with limited training funds, fewer access points to health, human and social services which can all affect the nature and extent of training SRO receive (Hunt et al., 2019). Inconsistency in SROs training throughout the U.S, i.e., SRO specialized training, professional association memberships, experience, and duties, are of concern.

For example, Hunt et al. (2019) study found that rural SROs were significantly different than urban SROs in terms of race, education, and several areas of training. The rural groups consisted of 87% white, with fewer college graduates (65%) and a higher proportion attended several basic SRO training courses, while a higher percentage of urban SROs completed implicit bias trainings. The study found that most of the rural SROs' time was spend in law enforcement related activities, followed by role model/informal counseling, acting as a public safety liaison and educational related actives.

Ruddell and May's (2011) research in Kentucky comparing the characteristics and task of rural and urban SROs and found them to be almost identical. For example, both groups were in their mid to late 40s. Both had almost two decades of law enforcement experience; an average of about 5 years as SROs. Both groups had similar amounts of education; average of two years post-secondary education. Generally, both spent almost identical amount of time between the three areas of the triad model: educator, informal counselor/mentor, and law enforcement officer.

Ruddell and May (2011) did find two significant differences between the two groups. The first, was urban officers were more likely to be members of professional associations and participate in the extra training these associations provided. Second, urban SROs were more likely to have SRO, NASRO and advanced NASRO training where rural SROs had only attending SRO training. Furthermore, they found that rural areas did have fewer resources compared to their urban counterparts. Finally, SROs in rural school district reported feeling more supported by school administrators.

Increase in the Rate of Arrest

Exclusionary discipline encompasses any type of school disciplinary action that removes or excludes a student from the classroom. Disparities in the use of exclusionary discipline can lead to a school-to-prison pipeline for some of the most vulnerable student population (American Psychological Association, 2021). For example, Hunt et al., (2019) found that students were arrested in 61% of the cases by SROs; thus, accelerating the school to prion pipeline. They recommended that schools should use more proactive strategies such as school wide positive behavior intervention and support to prevent challenging behavior in schools in lieu of SROs.

Similarly, Theriot (2009) found that the presence of an SRO gives a 197.7% increase in the rate of arrests per one hundred students (Theriot, 2009). Theriot (2009) also found that larger percentage of student at school with an SRO had economic disadvantage compared to schools without an SRO; there were 216 more arrest at schools with an SRO than at comparison schools. The most common charge at SRO schools was disorder conduct (Theriot, 2009).

In addition, Gottfredson et al., (2020) study assessed the effects of placing SROs in K-12. They found that the increased use of SROs increased the number of arrest and exclusionary disciplinary actions. These negative effects were more frequently found for students with special needs. Gottfredson et al., (2020) suggest that increasing SROs does not improve school safety and that by increasing exclusionary disciplinary action increases criminalization, i.e., school-to-prison pipeline.

Furthermore, data from the Government Accountability Office (GAO) (2018), found that among six different area of disciplinary action: out of school suspension, in-school suspensions, *referrals to law enforcement*, expulsions, corporal punishment, and *school-related arrest*, African American youths; boys and girls, were the only student groups overrepresented in all six areas. Similarly, data from the United States Department of Education Office for Civil Rights (2018) found that African American girls are suspended at higher rates than girls of any other race or ethnicity and most boys.

Finally, Hirschfield's (2009) multilevel multivariate logistic model study found that students who were arrested during their 9th or 10th grade year were six to eight times more likely to drop out of high school and were 3.5 times more likely to drop out in that year; even minor brushes with the law, SROs, seem to produce negative educational opportunities for youth of color by weakening participate in school, social mobility, and limited potential of educational advancement.

This disparity in school discipline is of great concern because of the correlation between school discipline and involvement in the juvenile justice system, i.e., school-to-prison pipeline. Ramey's (2016) study found that student who experience even just one suspension were twice as likely to be involved in the juvenile justice system. Mowen and Brent's (2016) study found students who received harsh punitive discipline were four times more likely to report being arrested in the future.

Litigation

There is research regarding litigation and SROs. For example, Chan et al. (2019) sought to determine whether the courts had found SROs to be acting within the parameters of their job/followed appropriate procedures. An analysis of 44 cases that comprised 98 allegations against SROs were examined. They found that the courts have largely (83%) ruled in favor of SROs (Hunt et al., 2019). The 17% of cases ruling in favor of the parents included examples of improper search and seizure, unacceptable use of force, and improper notification of rights.

The School-to-Prison Pipeline

The school-to-prison pipeline starts in the classroom. When combined with "zero-tolerance policies", a teacher's decision to refer students for punishment can mean they are pushed out of the classroom and much more likely to be introduced into the juvenile justice system, via SROs. Current policies have increased the risk of youths being suspended, expelled, and arrested at school; also contributing to the high rates of school dropouts. Risk of entry into the school-to-prison pipeline disproportionately impacts the students who are poor, have disabilities, LGBTQ, and are of color (Advancement Project, 2005; Children's Defense Fund, 2007; Hunt el al., 2019; NAACP, 2005; Wald & Losen, 2003). The tendency towards criminalization and incarceration has bled into the schools, and with each new academic year, this legal net ensnares younger and younger children. Behavior that once resulted in a trip to the principal's office now is grounds for a trip to jail, via SROs (Heitzeg, 2009).

The American Civil Liberties Union (2008) defines the school-to-prison pipelines as "the policies and practices that push school children, especially the most at-risk children, out of classrooms and into the juvenile and criminal justice systems (p.1)."

HISTORY OF THE SCHOOL-TO-PRISON PIPELINE AND ZERO-TOLERANCE POLICIES

During the late 1980s and throughout the 1990s, the media's representation of violence, gang violence, and crack cocaine use among youth; especially youth of color, generated a public "moral panic" (McCorkle & Miethe, 1998). Terms like "super-predator" were coined and they were to come of age by 2010; urban, black and brown, and violent (Templeton, 1998).

Zero-Tolerance was a term taken from the "war on drugs" and "get tough on drugs and crime," policies of the 1980s where law enforcement agencies swiftly and harshly responded to drug offenders. This led to a tripling in the national prison population; the United States leads the world in its incarceration rate. As mentioned before, the misguided "super predator" theory branded youth as criminal and zero-tolerance policies were created and initiated in school systems in numerous states.

The Gun Free Schools Act of 1994 provided the initial inducement for "zero-tolerance" policies. The 1994 Act had two mandates for all schools that received federal funding. First it mandated that all schools have policies to expel for a calendar year any student who brings a firearm to school. Second, that schools report student to local law enforcement. Subsequent amendments to the Act and changes at the state and local school district level have broadened the Act's focus on firearms to apply to many other kinds of weapons.

Schools have now adopted "zero-tolerance" policies for a variety of behavior issues beyond weapons: alcohol and drugs, threatening behavior, fighting, tardiness, and disorderly conduct (Heitzeg, 2009). Finally, there is mounting evidence that these policies contribute to the school-to-prison pipeline. For example, according to the Advancement Project (2005), "Zero-tolerance" has engendered a number of problems: denial of education through increased suspension and expulsion rates, referrals to inadequate alternative schools, lower test scores, higher dropout rates, and racial profiling of student (12)." Consella (2003) found that *once many of these youths are in "the system", they never get back on the academic track. Sometimes, schools refuse to readmit them, and even if these students do return to school, they are often labeled and targeted for close monitoring by school staff and police. Consequently, many become demoralized, drop out, and fall deeper and deeper into the juvenile or criminal justice system. Those who do drop out find that their [school] discipline and juvenile or criminal records haunt them when they apply to college or for a scholarships or government grants or try to enlist in the military or find employment. In some places, a criminal record may prevent them or their families from residing in publicly subsidized housing (p. 64).*

When a school allows, or more often requires, the SRO to arrest a student (or the school refers a student to law enforcement or juvenile court) as a form of discipline, they are turning the student over to the juvenile justice system. This "pushing out" of the youth makes it much easier for youth to get a juvenile record. This process does happen way more at schools with SROs. A report by the Justice Policy Institute (Nelson & Lind, 2015) found that, even controlling for a school's district's poverty level, schools with SRO had five times as many arrests for "disorderly conduct" as schools without SROs.

CONCLUSION

The research on SROs is inconclusive about whether their presence on school grounds improves safety, reduces crime, violence, victimization, and reduces the likelihood of a school shooting. However, we do know that there is an association with SROs and students being arrested at higher rates, having increased rates of exclusionary discipline, out of school suspensions, and expulsions.

Similarly, we know that overuse of suspension, expulsion, and other harsh disciplinary polices increases the likelihood that youth will enter the juvenile justice system; thus, increasing the likelihood of future involvement with the adult criminal justice system. They are linked with lower ratings for overall "positive" school climate, lower academic performance among students, lower school wide academic performance, and an increased likelihood of school dropout. Decades of social science research documents the devastation to youth, families, and communities.

"Zero-tolerance" policies represent the most immediate and direct conduit for the school to prison pipeline (Heitzeg et al., 2009). Short of repealing "zero-tolerance" legislation, policy makers and school systems could take steps to alleviate some of the surrounding legal issues and disparities (Heitzeg et al., 2009). Finally, school systems need to revise their policies regarding suspension and expulsion and offer more meaningful alternatives. They must examine their lust for punishment and invest in education rather than incarceration for youth, but especially for youth of color and students with disabilities.

REFERENCES

Advancement Project. (2005). Education on lockdown: The school to jailhouse track. Washington, DC: Author.

American Psychological Association Services, Inc. (2021). *The pathway from Exclusionary discipline to the school to prison pipeline.* https://www.apa.org/advocacy/health-disparities/discipline-facts.pdf

Annie E. Casey Foundation. (2011). *No place for kids: The case for reducing juvenile incarceration*. Author.

Banks, D., Hendrix, J., Hickman, M., & Kychelhahn, T. (2019). National sources of law enforcement employment data. U.S. Department of Justice, Office of Justice Programs. Bureau of justice Statistics. NCJ 249681.

Black, S. (2009). Security and the SRO. *The American School Board Journal, 196*(6), 30–31.

Blad, E., Kim, H. Y., Decker, S, Manzo, K. K., Maxwell, L. A., & Peerle, H. (2018). School shootings of 2018: What's behind the numbers? *Education Week*.

Bond, B. (2001). Principals and SROs: Defining roles. *Principal Leadership, 1*(8), 52–55.

Boyer, A., & Uchida, A. (2015). Incident between round Rock pd officers and student caught on camera. *KEYE TV*. https://cbsaustin.com/news/local/incident-between-round-rock-pd-officer-and-student-caught-on-camera

Burrow, J. D., & Apel, R. (2008). Youth behavior, school structure, and student risk of victimization. *Justice Quarterly, 25*(2), 349–380. doi:10.1080/07418820802025181

Canady, M., James, B., & Nease, J. (2012). *To protect and educate: The school resources officer and the prevention of violence in schools*. National Association of School Resource Officers.

Children's Defense Fund. (2007). *America's cradle to prison pipeline*. CDF.

Clark, S. (2011). The role of law enforcement in schools: The Virginia experience a practitioner report. *Directions for Youth Development, 129*(129), 89–101. doi:10.1002/yd.389 PMID:21491575

Consella, R. (2003). Punishing dangerousness through preventive detention: Illustrating the institutional link between school and prison. *New Directions for Youth Development: Deconstructing the School-to-Prison Pipeline*, 63-65.

Coon, J. K., & Travis, L. F. III. (2012). The role of police in public schools: A comparison of principal and police reports of activities in schools. *Police Practice and Research, 13*(1), 15–30. doi:10.1080/15614263.2011.589570

Crawford, C. & Burns, R. (2015). *Preventing school violence: Assessing armed guardians, school policy, and context*. Academic Press.

Crawford, C., & Burns, R. (2016). Reducing school violence considering school characteristics and the impact of law enforcement, school security, and environmental factors. *Policing, 39*(3), 455–477. doi:10.1108/PIJPSM-05-2016-0061

Crunden, E. A. (2017). Dallas school police tased a 7-year-old, and then boy slammed a 12-year-old the next day. *ThinkProgress*. https://archive.thinkprogress.org/dallas-police-schools-violence-kids-fd6cd565a8c0/

Diliberti, M., Jackson, M., Correa, S., & Padgett, Z. (2019). *Crime, Violence, Discipline, and Safety in U.S. Public Schools: Findings from the School Survey on Crime and Safety: 2017–18 (NCES 2019-061). U.S. Department of Education*. National Center for Education Statistics. https://nces.ed.gov/pubsearch

Duxbury, L., & Bennell, C. (2019). *Police in schools: An evidence-based look at the use of school resource officers*. Routledge. doi:10.4324/9780429243905

Finn, P., Shively, M., McDevitt, J., Lassiter, W., & Rich, T. (2005). *Comparison of program activities and lessons learned among 19 school resource officer (SRO) programs*. United States Department of Justice.

Gottfredson, D. C., Crosse, S., Tang, Z., Bauer, E. L., Harmon, M. A., Hagen, C. A., & Greene, A. D. (2020). Effects of school resource officers on school crime and responses to school crime. *Criminology & Public Policy*, *19*(3), 905–940. doi:10.1111/1745-9133.12512

Heaviside, S., Rowand, C., William, C., & Farris, E. (1998). Violence and discipline problems in U.S. public schools: 1996-97. Department of Education, national Center for Education Statistics., NCES 98-030.

Heitzeg, N. A. (2009). Education or incarceration: Zero tolerance policies and the school to prison pipeline. *The Forum of Public Policy*. https://eric.ed.gov/?id=EJ870076

Hirschfield, P. (2009). another way out: The impact of juvenile arrest on high school dropout. *Sociology of Education*, *82*(4), 368–393. doi:10.1177/003804070908200404

Hockenberry, S. (2014). *Juvenile in residential placement, 2011. U.S. Department of Justice. Office of Justice Programs.* Office of Juvenile Justice and Delinquency Prevention. https://ojjdp.ojp.gov/sites/g/files/xyckuh176/files/pubs/246826.pdf

Hunt, V. H., Taylor, M. A., Fitzgerald, B., Button, E. D., & Kerr, B. (2019). An examination of the characteristics and perceptions of school resource officers in rural and urban Oklahoma schools. *Journal of Rural Social Sciences*, *34*(2), 1–25.

Hyman, I. A., & Perone, D. C. (1998). The other side of school violence: Educator policies and practices that may contribute to student misbehavior. *Journal of School Psychology*, *36*(1), 7–27. doi:10.1016/S0022-4405(97)87007-0

Jennings, W. G., Khey, D. N., Maskaly, J., & Donner, C. M. (2011). Evaluating the relationship between law enforcement and school security measures and violent crime in schools. *Journal of Police Crisis Negotiations*, *11*(2), 109–124. doi:10.1080/15332586.2011.581511

Johnson, L. M. (1999). School Violence: The effectiveness of a school resource officer program in a southern city. *Journal of Criminal Justice*, *27*(2), 173–192. doi:10.1016/S0047-2352(98)00049-X

Kennedy, M. (2001). Teachers with a badge. *Security and Safety*, *4*, 36–38.

Lawrence, R. (2007). *School crime and juvenile justice*. Oxford University Press.

McCorkle, R. C., & Miethe, T. D. (1998). The political and organizational response to gangs: An examination of a moral panic in Nevada. *Justice Quarterly*, *15*(1), 41–64. doi:10.1080/07418829800093631

McCurdy, B. L., Empson, D. N., Knoster, T., Fluke, S. M., & Grant, C. A. (2019). School resource officers and schoolwide PBIS: Considerations for training. *Revisiting School Failure: Alternative Education for Children and Youth*, *4*(63), 317–324. doi:10.1080/1045988X.2019.1605970

McDaniel, J. (2001). *School resource officer: What we know, what we think we know, what we need to know.* https://files.nc.gov/ncdps/div/JJ/whatweknow.pdf

McKenna, J.M., Martinez-Prather, K., & Bowman, S. W. (2014). The role of school-based law enforcement officer and how these roles are established: A qualitative study. *Criminal Justice Policy Review, 27*(4), 420–443. doi:10.1177/0887403414551001

Mowen, T., & Brent, J. (2016). School discipline as a turning point: The cumulative effect of suspension on arrest. *Journal of Research in Crime and Delinquency, 53*(5), 628–653. doi:10.1177/0022427816643135

Musu, L., Zhang, A., Wang, K., Zhang, J., & Oudekerk, B. A. (2019). *Indicators of school crime and safety: 2018 (NCES 2019-047/NCJ 252571)*. National Center for Education Statistics. U.S. Department of Education, and Bureau of Justice Statics, Office of Justice Programs, U.S. Department of Justice.

Musu-Gillette, L., Zhang, A., Wang, K., Zhang, J., Kemp, J., Diliberti, M., & Oudekerk, B. A. (2018). *Indicators of school crime and safety: 2017 (NCES 2018-036/NCJ 251413)*. Washington, DC: National Center for Education Statistics, U.S. Department of Education, and Bureau of justice Statistics, Office of Justice Programs, U.S. Department of Justice.

Na, C., & Gottfredson, D. C. (2013). Police officers in schools: Effects on school crime and the processing of offending behaviors. *Justice Quarterly, 30*(4), 619–650. doi:10.1080/07418825.2011.615754

NAACP. (2005). *Interrupting the school to prison pipeline*. Washington, DC: NAACP.

National Association of School Resource Officers. (2021). https://www.nasro.org/faq/

National Institute of Education. (1978). *Violent schools – Safe schools: The safe school study report to congress*. U.S. Government Printing Office.

Nelson, L., & Lind, D. (2015). *The school to prison pipeline, explained*. The Policy Institute. https://www.justicepolicy.org/news/8775

Patterson, G. (2007). The role of police officers in elementary and secondary schools: Implications for police-school social work collaboration. *School Social Work Journal, 31*(2), 82–99.

Petteruti, A. (2011). *Education under arrest: The case against schools*. Justice Policy Institute.

Ramey, D. M. (2016). The influence of early school punishment and therapy/medication on social control experience during young adulthood. *Criminology, 54*(1), 113–141. doi:10.1111/1745-9125.12095

Reaves, B. (2010). *Local police departments, 2007*. U.S. Department of Justice, Bureau of Justice Studies, Office of Justice Programs. https://www.bjs.gov/content/pub/pdf/lpd07.pdf

Ruddell, R., & May, D. C. (2011). Challenging our perceptions of rural policing: An examination of school resource officers in rural and urban Kentucky schools. *Journal of Anthropology and Sociology, 1*(1), 1–14.

Smith, B. (1998). Children in custody: 20-year trends in juvenile detention, correctional, and shelter facilities. *Crime and Delinquency, 44*(4), 526–543. doi:10.1177/0011128798044004004

Staff, J. (2015). *State police to probe 'takedown' of student by officer that led to protest, arrests at Pawtucket school*. https://www.providencejournal.com/article/20151015/NEWS/151019570

Stelloh, T., & Conner, T. (2015). Video shows cop body-slamming high school girl in S.C. classroom. *NBC News*. https://www.nbcnews.com/news/us-news/video-apprears-show-cop-body-slamming-student-s-f-classroom-n451896

Stolberg, S. G. (2015). A.C.L.U. sues over handcuffing of boy, 8, and girl, 9, in Kentucky school. *The New York Times*. https://www.nytimes.com/2015/08/04/us/aclu-sues-over-handcuffing-of-boy-8-and-girl-9-in-kentucky-school.html

Swartz, K., Osborne, D. L., Dawson-Edwards, C., & Higgins, G. E. (2016). Policing schools: Examining the impact of place management activities on school violence. *American Journal of Criminal Justice*, *41*(3), 465–483. doi:10.100712103-015-9306-6

Templeton, R. (1998). *Super scapegoating: Teen 'super predators' hype set state for draconian legislation*. FAIR.

Texas Commission on Law Enforcement. (2013). *Contract information for Texas indecent school district police department.* Author.

The American Civil Liberties Union. (2008). *Locating the school-to-prison pipeline*. https://www.aclu.org/node/29079%C2%A0

Tillyer, M. S., Fisher, B. S., & Wilcox, P. (2011). The effects of school crime prevention on students' violent victimization, risk perception, and fear of crime: A multilevel opportunity perspective. *Justice Quarterly*, *28*(2), 249–277. doi:10.1080/07418825.2010.493526

Trump, K. S. (1998). Keeping the peace: What you should know about staffing a school security department. *The American School Board Journal*, *185*(3), 31–35.

U.S. Department of Education office for Civil Rights. (2018). *Civil rights data collections: School climate and safety. Data Snapshot: School Discipline*. https://www2.ed.gov/about/offices/list/ocr/docs/school-climate-and-safety.pdf

U.S. Department of Justice, Office of Community Oriented Policing Services (COPS). (2021). *Supporting Safe Schools*. https://cops.usdoj.gov/supportingsafeschools

U.S. Government Accountability Office. (2018). *K-12 education: Discipline disparities for black students, boys, and students with disabilities*. Report to Congressional Requesters. https://www.gao.gov/products/gao-18-258

Wald, S., & Losen, D. (2003). *Defining and re-directing a school to prison pipeline*. Harvard Civil Rights Project.

Wald, S., Spohn, C., & MeLone, M. (2007). *The color of justice: Race, ethnicity, and crime in America* (4th ed.). Belmont, CA: Wadsworth.

Weiler, S., & Cray, M. (2011). Police at school: A brief history and current status of school resources officers. *The Clearing House: A Journal of Educational Strategies, Issues and Ideas*, *84*(4), 160–163. doi:10.1080/00098655.2011.564986

Chapter 3
Improving Police–Community Relations in the USA

Marty Allen Hatfield
Liberty University, USA

ABSTRACT

To prevent and control crime using the community-oriented policing model, law enforcement agencies must develop positive relationships and partnerships with the communities they serve. Unfortunately, several obstacles impede the development and maintenance of police-community partnerships, particularly excessive force and other forms of misconduct, and negative coverage of law enforcement by the media. To restore public trust in the police, agencies must implement competency-based interviews and assessments during the hiring process; develop a recruitment plan to attract more diverse applicants; provide regular crisis intervention, de-escalation, and implicit bias training to all officers; and evaluate and make any necessary improvements to existing use-of-force and disciplinary policies. Future research should continue to evaluate the impact of community policing on crime rates, the impact of body-worn cameras on misconduct, and the correlation between higher education and misconduct.

INTRODUCTION

Because traditional, reactive policing strategies and policies have been relatively unsuccessful at preventing and controlling criminal behavior, criminal justice practitioners, researchers, and policymakers have developed and implemented a variety of innovative policing models, including community-oriented policing. The community-oriented policing model asserts that the development and maintenance of positive relationships and partnerships between the police and the communities they serve is the key to effective policing. Unfortunately, several factors often negatively affect police–community relations and impede the development of such partnerships.

There are five primary purposes of this chapter. First, the chapter provides a brief history of law enforcement in the U.S. Second, it highlights the specific components of the community-oriented policing model; its benefits, limitations, and challenges; and theoretical perspectives of community policing. Third, the chapter discusses the potential benefits of positive police–community relations, as well as the

DOI: 10.4018/978-1-7998-6884-2.ch003

factors that impede the development of partnerships between law enforcement agencies and community members and organizations. Fourth, the chapter recommends solutions that may assist police agencies in reducing excessive force and other types of misconduct, which may ultimately aid in the restoration of the community's trust and willingness to partner with police. Finally, the chapter provides recommendations for future research regarding police misconduct.

A BRIEF HISTORY OF LAW ENFORCEMENT

One of the earliest formal policing models can be traced to London in 1829 (Walsh & Vito, 2019). The English Parliament introduced and passed the Metropolitan Police Act, creating the first full-time, uniformed law enforcement agency consisting of approximately 3,000 officers (Walsh & Vito, 2019). Sir Robert Peel, who was serving as the Home Secretary of England during this time, was responsible for the administration and oversight of the new agency (Walsh & Vito, 2019). The mission and operational standards of the new agency were outlined in Peel's *Principles of Law Enforcement*, which were issued to all incoming police officers (Walsh & Vito, 2019). Several of these principles focused on the relationship between police officers and the communities they served. For example, Peel argued that the ability of police officers to successfully perform their jobs was dependent upon public approval of their actions and behaviors (Walsh & Vito, 2019). Similarly, Peel asserted that law enforcement agencies must secure and maintain the trust of community members to maintain public safety (Walsh & Vito, 2019). Furthermore, officers must constantly demonstrate absolute impartiality when enforcing the law and dealing with the public to secure public approval, respect, and cooperation (Walsh & Vito, 2019).

In the early 19th century, several factors created social disorder and fear among citizens, prompting the creation of America's earliest police agencies in New York City, Chicago, Cincinnati, New Orleans, Philadelphia, Boston, Baltimore, Kansas City, and St. Louis (Walsh & Vito, 2019). Policing in the U.S. can be broken into four primary phases. The first phase, known as the political era of policing, began in the 1840s and lasted until the beginning of the 20th century (Walsh & Vito, 2019). During the political era, police departments were controlled by local political entities and focused heavily on maintaining public order through a watchman style of policing (Walsh & Vito, 2019). However, beginning in the early 20th century, police administrators sought to increase the professionalization of the police by eliminating political control and corruption (Walsh & Vito, 2019). This marked the beginning of the reform era of policing. During this period, reformers and administrators advocated for: 1) the elimination of political interference; 2) clearly defined duties and responsibilities; 3) constant supervision of officers and administrators; 4) strong executive leadership; 5) comprehensive training for officers; and 6) selection of officers based on merit and qualifications (Walsh & Vito, 2019). Police tactics during the reform era focused heavily on random motorized patrols, response to calls for service, after-the-occurrence crime investigations, and other reactive measures. In addition, a hierarchical structure defined by rank, policy, standards, and the specialization of tasks was introduced (Walsh & Vito, 2019). This hierarchy is still prevalent in most contemporary law enforcement agencies.

The 1980s marked the beginning of the community problem-solving policing era. Under this paradigm, police officers focused on community safety, stabilization, and problem-solving, which was facilitated by the creation of a positive relationship between law enforcement and the communities they serve (Walsh & Vito, 2019). The basic premise of community policing is that law enforcement agencies must understand community members to identify and develop responses to their problems (Walsh & Vito, 2019).

This is particularly important given the fact that police officers are responsible for meeting the needs of diverse communities and community members. The final phase of policing in the U.S., which began in 1994 and continues today, is known as the strategic policing era (Walsh & Vito, 2019). During this time, law enforcement agencies focused on the prevention, control, and reduction of crime through the development of data-driven strategies and policies (Walsh & Vito, 2019). Innovative policing strategies, including intelligence-led policing, have been popular during the strategic era.

COMMUNITY-ORIENTED POLICING

Components of Community-Oriented Policing

As indicated above, the community problem-solving policing era ushered in the community-oriented policing model. This model emphasizes the importance of bolstering confidence in the police, particularly within minority communities, and increasing the willingness of community members to participate in crime control and prevention initiatives (Wehrman & De Angelis, 2011). A large body of research has focused on outlining the specific components of community policing strategies and programs. Earlier studies have identified nine critical elements of the community-oriented policing model: 1) philosophy; 2) personalized; 3) policing; 4) patrols; 5) permanent; 6) place; 7) proactive; 8) partnership; and 9) problem-solving (Adams et al., 2002; Trojanowicz & Bucqueroux, 1994). Based on these elements, there are three features that separate community policing from traditional policing models. First, both the police and the community members are responsible for crime control and prevention (Adams et al., 2002).

Second, community policing focuses on proactive prevention, rather than reactive strategies like responding to calls for service (Adams et al., 2002). Under the community policing model, officers not only seek to address community problems before they occur, but also continuously search for alternatives to arrest and incarceration, such as pre-arrest diversion programs (Adams et al., 2002). Third, the community policing model provides law enforcement officers with increased discretion (Adams et al., 2012). When dealing with the community, officers must be given greater flexibility to handle problems effectively, rather than being subject to strict rules and procedures (Adams et al., 2002). A subsequent study expanded on this research and identified four primary dimensions of community policing. The ideas and beliefs about what police officers should do are included in the philosophical dimensions of community policing (Reisig, 2010). For example, the community policing model welcomes input from community members and civic organizations regarding strategies and policies that affect the community (Reisig, 2010).

Alternatively, the strategic dimension of community policing includes two specific actions of the police: 1) a reduction in the use of squad car patrols and the development and utilization of alternative strategies (e.g., foot patrol); and 2) long-term assignments to specific beats within the community (Reisig, 2010; Walsh & Vito, 2019). The tactical dimension of community policing refers to the practices and behaviors of police officers (Reisig, 2010). Under the community policing model, law enforcement agencies must develop problem-solving partnerships with community residents, as well as other service providers in the area including, but not limited to, professional associations, business associations, volunteer organizations, daycare centers, ethnic associations, and parent–teacher associations (Walsh & Vito, 2019). Finally, the organizational dimension of community policing refers to the alternation of traditional bureaucratic and paramilitary structures within law enforcement agencies to open communication, collaboration, and information sharing (Reisig, 2010).

Advantages of Community Policing

There are many advantages of the community policing model. In the late 1980s, a police department in Madison, Wisconsin, implemented the Quality Policing program, which focused on several internal processes, including problem-solving, citizen interaction, and the development of goals of service (Wycoff & Skogan, 1994). Researchers concluded that the program had a significant impact on officer job satisfaction and police perceptions of the community. However, there were no significant changes in crime rates or fear of crime (Wycoff & Skogan, 1994). In a subsequent meta-analysis, Skogan (1994) analyzed data from six jurisdictions where community policing strategies had been implemented in Baltimore, Birmingham, Houston, Madison, Newark, and Oakland. The author concluded that community policing resulted in lower fear of crime, victimization rates, crime rates, and drug availability, as well as improvements in community perceptions of the police (Skogan, 1994).

Adams et al. (2002) developed a survey that included questions regarding support for community policing, job satisfaction, and perceived effectiveness of community policing strategies. The survey was administered to police departments in Asheville, Greensboro, Lumberton, Morehead, and Whiteville, as well as the Forsyth County Sheriff's Department. These agencies, which are all located in North Carolina, were chosen for the study because they represented a wide range of community sizes and had implemented some form of community policing at least one year prior to the study. The authors concluded that, when compared to more traditional officers, community police officers: 1) are more accepting of innovative policing strategies; 2) believe that community policing strategies are effective at reducing crime; 3) are more supportive of community policing initiatives; and 4) are more positive about their jobs (Adams et al., 2002). A study by Pelfrey (2004) found evidence supporting the assertion that community policing programs increase job satisfaction and concluded that such satisfaction frequently increases productivity and performance. Another study found that community policing strategies and programs in Chicago generated improvements in community problems and quality of life (Somerville, 2009).

Lombardo and Donner (2018) confirmed the benefits of community policing in Chicago. Using a variety of bivariate and multivariate methods, the authors examined data from the Community Survey of the Project on Human Development in Chicago Neighborhoods (PHDCN) and the CAPS Prototype Survey to assess the impact of the Chicago Alternative Policing Strategy (CAPS), which focused on community mobilization and was the nation's largest community policing program. The study found that community policing increases informal social control and, more importantly, general satisfaction with the police is a crucial element of crime control and prevention (Lombardo & Donner, 2018). Tillyer (2018) merged data from the National Incident-Based Reporting System (NIBRS) with information from the Law Enforcement Management and Administrative Statistics survey and found that community policing strategies increase arrest rates for violent crimes. Finally, researchers have found that community policing reduces use-of-force incidents, particularly in communities experiencing high violent crime rates (McCarthy et al., 2019).

Limitations and Challenges of Community Policing

Several studies have also highlighted many limitations and challenges of community policing. Kerley and Benson (2000) used data from a comprehensive study conducted from 1987 to 1989 to examine the impact of community policing strategies on community processes. The authors concluded that community policing strategies had little measurable impact on community processes, crime rates, and fear of crime (Kerley & Benson, 2000). A subsequent study confirmed that community policing initiatives are not systematically linked to crime control and prevention and/or community development (Somerville, 2009). Additionally, Somerville (2009) asserted that community policing initiatives are often harmful to communities because they fail to consider local community conditions, as well as the state of local police agencies, which are often plagued with corruption and despised by community members. In addition, the implementation of community policing initiatives requires several organizational and role changes that are often problematic for police agencies (Adams et al., 2002). According to Adams et al. (2002), the implementation of community policing requires two primary changes.

First, law enforcement agencies must move resources away from reactive crime-control strategies toward proactive collaboration and information-sharing efforts, greater officer discretion and freedom, and problem-solving. Specifically, community policing requires agencies to "move away from a top-down, paramilitary style of management and toward a more participatory style, where officers from different ranks have input in the development and implementation of community policing in their departments" (p. 402). Second, community policing requires the duties and responsibilities of police officers to change significantly. Officers are expected to organize community watches and/or work with other city agencies, rather than focusing on duties associated with crime control. However, altering the traditions and culture of law enforcement is an arduous task. Often, police administrators are resistant to losing power to subordinate officers and believe that community policing initiatives cause interference from external agencies (Adams et al., 2002).

The implementation of community policing is particularly difficult for smaller police agencies. Earlier studies have asserted that the successful implementation of community policing requires the availability of slack resources, which are financial resources and technical expertise beyond what the agency requires for its ongoing operations (Morabito, 2010). Smaller agencies usually possess fewer slack resources than larger agencies (Morabito, 2010). Furthermore, smaller agencies typically have lower turnover and hiring rates than larger agencies; therefore, the infusion of innovative ideas and acceptance of innovative policing strategies are rare phenomena in smaller agencies (Morabito, 2010). The implementation and success of community policing requires an organizational commitment from officers of all ranks, but several factors can decrease this commitment, which can negatively impact community policing efforts. For example, Perez et al. (2017) found that officers who reported higher levels of feedback from supervisors, higher peer cohesion, and lower job-related stress possessed greater organizational commitment. In addition to these organizational and job characteristics, several individual-level factors reduce organizational commitment, including gender, age, education, and experience (Perez et al., 2017).

The success of community policing also depends on citizen support. Similar to organizational commitment, demographic characteristics may negatively affect citizen support. For example, earlier studies have found that African Americans often view law enforcement less favorably than do Whites (Lee et al., 2019). Furthermore, researchers have found that community members with higher education levels are more likely to support community policing initiatives (Lee et al., 2019). Finally, individuals of lower socioeconomic status are less likely to have positive views of the police (Lee et al., 2019). Citizen support may also be negatively influenced by community characteristics. Prominent levels of social and physical disorder within a community often result in the collapse of social control systems, which increases the likelihood of criminal behavior (Lee et al., 2019). When this occurs, perceptions of crime and disorder and the opinions of the police in general may be negatively impacted (Lee et al., 2019). Finally, public perceptions of the police, as well as encounters with law enforcement, influence attitudes toward officers (Lee et al., 2019).

Theoretical Perspectives on Community Policing

Community policing programs and strategies can be examined from a variety of theoretical perspectives, including social disorganization theory. Social disorganization theory posits that impoverished neighborhoods that experience high levels of instability are less likely to possess high levels of social organization (Reisig, 2010). Socially disorganized communities share a lack of harmony among residents, as well as the inability to maintain internal social control mechanisms (Reisig, 2010). Because of these factors, impoverished and disorganized communities often experience higher rates of crime and delinquency (Reisig, 2010). Community policing allows police officers to collaborate with neighborhood organizations and community members, which strengthens social controls, reduces crime rates, and improves quality of life for residents (Reisig, 2010). Another theory used to analyze community policing is the broken windows theory, which asserts that, if one element of a system is damaged or destroyed, the entire system will eventually collapse (Cerda et al., 2009; Gau & Pratt, 2010; Walsh & Vito, 2019; Xu et al., 2005; Yang, 2010).

In other words, a single crime or instance of disorder can ultimately result in the decay of an entire community and an increase in more serious, persistent criminal behavior (Gau & Pratt, 2010). Using the broken windows theory, Chappell et al. (2011), examined the impact of social and physical disorder on quality of life. The authors concluded that both physical and social disorder result in reduced quality of life, which breaks down informal social controls and increases the likelihood of crime and delinquency. A subsequent study found that community policing and other broken windows policing strategies were effective at reducing criminal behavior and disorder when police agencies focused on problem-solving, developed partnerships with community members and organizations, and targeted disorder in specific locations (Welsh et al., 2015). Jenkins (2016) added to these findings and asserted that broken windows policing strategies, like community policing, are effective when they receive support from officers. Ren et al. (2019) used the broken windows theory to evaluate citizen engagement in crime prevention, which is a critical element of community policing. The study concluded that community policing efforts increased collective efficacy, which increased engagement in crime prevention (Ren et al., 2019).

BENEFITS OF POLICE–COMMUNITY RELATIONS

Like the community policing model, there are several benefits of positive police–community relations. Earlier studies highlight the importance of collective efficacy when evaluating the benefits of these relationships. Collective efficacy is defined as the capacity of community members to protect themselves against criminal behavior, which is accomplished through the development and achievement of common goals and interests (Walsh & Vito, 2019). Collective efficacy can be increased by creating effective community partnerships. Such partnerships are effective because they: 1) accomplish what individual community members alone cannot; 2) prevent the duplication of community and law enforcement efforts; 3) enhance the power of advocacy; 4) increase recognition and visibility for community policing; 5) provide a systematic approach to crime problems; and 6) provide opportunities for new, collaborative projects between the police and community members (Walsh & Vito, 2019). Most importantly, however, by increasing collective efficacy, the development of partnerships between the police and the public creates safer communities (Walsh & Vito, 2019).

Police departments can also enhance community safety by fostering legitimacy, which consists of both instrumental and normative aspects (Brunson, 2015; Hinds & Murphy, 2007). From the instrumental perspective, police legitimacy is influenced by instrumental evaluations of police performance, risk, and perceptions/judgements regarding distributive justice (Hinds & Murphy, 2007). Law enforcement agencies can increase this form of legitimacy by effectively controlling criminal behavior, deterring those who break the law, and fairly distributing services across the communities they serve (Hinds & Murphy, 2007). The normative aspects of legitimacy are influenced by a variety of other factors, particularly procedural justice. Procedural justice exists when: 1) community members are offered an opportunity to actively participate in discussions with the police; 2) police decision-making is neutral and objective; and 3) community members are treated with dignity and respect (Hinds & Murphy, 2007). Legitimacy is important because community members are more likely to voluntarily obey the law and respect the police when they believe in the morality of the law and the legitimacy of the agency enforcing the law (Brewer & Grabosky, 2014; Walsh & Vito, 2019).

FACTORS THAT INFLUENCE POLICE–COMMUNITY RELATIONS

When positive relationships exist between law enforcement and the public, community members are more likely to report crimes and provide intelligence to the police, serve as witnesses, and participate in jury trials. However, several factors can negatively impact police–community relations. Researchers have analyzed the influence of race and other demographic factors on the development of police–community relations in minority communities where perceived legitimacy and procedural justice are low. Weitzer et al. (2008) collected data from residents of a majority-Black section of Washington, D.C. The authors concluded that: 1) Blacks were more likely than Whites to perceive police misconduct in Washington; 2) less-educated respondents were more likely than well-educated individuals to perceive misconduct; and 3) views of the police were influenced by experimental and situational factors (Weitzer et al., 2008). In a subsequent study, Wehrman and De Angelis (2011) found that Blacks were more willing than Whites to actively participate in community policing initiatives. However, the authors also concluded that relations are strained and citizens' willingness to work with the police is reduced in areas with higher levels of concentrated disadvantage, which is often more prevalent in minority communities.

A lack of public trust and confidence in the police can also obstruct the development of effective partnerships between law enforcement and the community. Saunders and Kilmer (2019) indicated that trust and confidence in the police dropped to 52% in 2015, the lowest level since the infamous 1993 beating of Rodney King by officers with the Los Angeles Police Department. By 2016, approximately 39% of non-Whites were confident in law enforcement, while 62% of Whites were confident. The authors also concluded that certain policing strategies (e.g., zero-tolerance policies and/or excessive use of stop-and-frisk) further damage the relationship between the police and community members (Saunders & Kilmer, 2019).

Other factors that may negatively influence police–community relations are power struggles, as well as conflicting interests and demands. The process of collaborating typically involves interactions between individuals from diverse backgrounds and organizations (Mangan et al., 2018). These individuals often face multiple levels of governance and are accountable for a variety of agendas and standards that can be conflicting (Mangan et al., 2018). Furthermore, like most bureaucratic agencies, power frequently remains vested in police departments, and agencies are often reluctant to release power to community members (Mangan et al., 2018). True collaboration cannot occur unless power relations are balanced (Mangan et al., 2018). Not surprisingly, police misconduct can also negatively impact police–community relations by increasing fear and distrust among community members. As indicated above, those who fear and/or distrust the police may refrain from reporting criminal activity. Furthermore, victims of misconduct may demonstrate their lack of trust in law enforcement and the criminal justice system by engaging in crime (Lumsden, 2017). Researchers have also found that police–community relations can be damaged by the Ferguson Effect, which refers to the excessive scrutiny of law enforcement by the public and negative publicity in the media (Walsh & Vito, 2019).

Chermak et al. (2006) examined the impact of a high-profile police misconduct trial on attitudes toward law enforcement officers and the services they provide. The authors concluded that news consumption of the trial had no significant effects on public attitudes toward police officers and services, but media coverage was found to alter evaluations of the guilt of the officers involved in the case among numerous community members. Likewise, residents who followed the case in the media were more likely to believe that the officer was guilty. A later study analyzed the impact of racial profiling on attitudes regarding profiling (Graziano et al., 2010). The study found that the media's framing of an incident impacts public perceptions more than the incident itself does (Graziano et al., 2010). Negative publicity often leads to alienation, dissatisfaction, and non-cooperation from the public, as well as decreased motivation and perceptions of self-legitimacy among police officers (Hinds & Murphy, 2007; Nix & Wolfe, 2015; Sunshine & Tyler, 2003).

SOLUTIONS AND RECOMMENDATIONS

Recruitment and Retention

The rotten apple theory argues that police misconduct is perpetrated by isolated officers within a department or unit who are able to evade detection during the recruitment, screening, and hiring process. From the perspective of this theory, police misconduct can be minimized by implementing effective standards and procedures that prevent the recruitment of individuals who are prone to deviance and misconduct. Most police agencies have a complex hiring process that consists of several stages, including a written test, criminal records check, background investigation, physical examination, and physical agility test (Miller, 2004). While these hiring procedures have remained fairly consistent since the 1970s, they are ineffective at identifying pre-existing mental health and/or emotional problems that increase the risk of misconduct (Hassell, 2016). As such, agencies should consider implementing competency-based interviews and assessments during the screening and selection process. Key competencies that should be assessed include, but are not limited to, communication skills, teamwork, respect for diversity, problem-solving, service delivery, and leadership skills.

A study conducted by Hong (2017) found that increased ethnic representativeness was associated with a substantial decrease in citizen complaints and police misconduct. Similarly, researchers have found that female officers are less likely than their male counterparts to receive citizen complaints (Hassell, 2016). Agencies should develop and implement a comprehensive recruitment plan to attract more diverse candidate pools that include women, racial and ethnic minorities, and individuals from the LGBTQ+ community. As part of the recruitment plan, agencies should enlist the help of social media and their own officers to recruit qualified candidates. Previous studies have also found that more experienced officers are less likely to engage in acts of corruption and misconduct than are less experienced officers (Hassell, 2016). Therefore, agencies should provide competitive salaries and benefits, training opportunities, and educational incentives to promote career growth and retain experienced officers.

Training

Effective training may also decrease the prevalence of police corruption and misconduct. The Police Executive Research Forum (PERF, 2016) reported that 990 fatal officer-involved shootings occurred in 2015. Of these shootings, approximately 25% of the subjects displayed signs of mental illness (PERF, 2016). Police agencies should partner with local mental health agencies to provide crisis intervention training to assist officers in identifying and responding to individuals with mental health disorders. Agencies should also consider creating crisis intervention teams consisting of police officers and mental health practitioners that can quickly and effectively respond to cases involving subjects with mental health disorders or similar issues. Police officers also frequently experience a phenomenon known as split-second syndrome, which occurs when officers are placed in high-stress situations (Walsh & Vito, 2019). The emotions experienced during these circumstances may cause officers to act in a manner that causes harm to themselves or others. As such, de-escalation strategies and tactics should be a primary focus of law enforcement training programs.

By using de-escalation strategies and tactics, officers are able to use warnings and verbal persuasion before resorting to lethal or non-lethal force (U.S. Commission on Civil Rights, 2018). Additionally, effective de-escalation requires the prohibition of neck holds and head strikes with hard objects, except where lethal force is necessary (U.S. Commission on Civil Rights, 2018). This may help decrease the number of cases of excessive force, as well as the number of complaints filed against officers. De-escalation techniques are particularly helpful when dealing with subjects who are experiencing a crisis due to mental health issues and/or substance use disorders (PERF, 2016). Police officers should also receive training in less lethal tools, including stun guns, pepper spray, and batons. Finally, officers should receive annual implicit bias training. Such training may help officers recognize implicit racial biases so they can avoid acting on them.

Effective Policies and Procedures

Unlike the rotten apple theory, the rotten barrel theory asserts that ineffective policies and procedures cause widespread corruption within many police departments and must be enhanced to decrease the prevalence of misconduct. While the need to use force cannot be eliminated from every encounter that police officers have with community members, agencies and administrators can optimize the practice by developing and implementing effective use-of-force policies. Effective policies should require the use of force to meet five primary criteria. Primarily, use of force must be proportionate (PERF, 2016).

In other words, officers should use only the level of force necessary to mitigate a threat. Second, there must be a legal basis for the use of force (PERF, 2016). Third, officers must be required to explain why they chose a particular course of action and why other actions were not taken (PERF, 2016). Fourth, the level of force chosen by an officer must be required to carry out their lawful duty (PERF, 2016).

Finally, use-of-force policies must reflect values of fairness, respect, and human dignity (PERF, 2016). Effective policies should also emphasize the importance of providing first aid to individuals who have been injured as a result of uses of force (PERF, 2016). In addition, agencies should adopt a formal policy that makes it clear that de-escalation strategies and techniques are preferred over the use of lethal and non-lethal force. Agencies should also implement effective policies and procedures for sanctioning officers who engage in excessive force and other forms of misconduct. Effective disciplinary policies must possess the following characteristics: 1) intervention at the lowest management level possible; 2) fair and consistent application of sanctions; 3) completion deadlines for internal investigations and sanctions; and 4) transparency (Stephens, 2011). Policies should also include a range of sanctions including, but not limited to, oral and written reprimands, loss of annual leave in lieu of suspension, demotion in rank, and removal from service.

Agencies should also develop and implement an early warning system to assist administrators with identifying problematic officers based on a variety of warning signs, including citizen complaints, use-of-force incidents, allegations of misconduct, a disproportionate number of resisting-arrest incidents, and firearm discharges (Walsh & Vito, 2019). Finally, agencies should consider including the use of civilian review boards in their disciplinary policies and procedures. A civilian review board consists of a group of citizens that is responsible for reviewing complaints filed against police officers. Board members are also usually responsible for providing recommendations to agencies regarding disciplinary action, as well as policy and training (U.S. Commission on Civil Rights, 2018). Public or semi-public hearings for misconduct cases may also assist in increasing accountability, legitimacy, and/or community trust. Overall, an agency's policies and procedures should reflect a zero-tolerance approach toward misconduct. Leadership staff must ensure that established policies, rules, and regulations are followed by sworn officers and civilian employees alike.

Building Community Partnerships

Police agencies must take proactive steps to restore the community's trust in law enforcement and other elements of the U.S. criminal justice system. This can be accomplished, in part, through community collaboration, which occurs when police agencies, community members, organizations, and other stakeholders agree to work together toward the goal of public safety. To facilitate this process, stakeholders should develop and continuously update a community profile (Walsh & Vito, 2019). This profile should include several vital pieces of information, including a list of community organizations and government agencies; a description of the community's population by race, gender, and age; and information regarding criminal and gang activity (Walsh & Vito, 2019). Police agencies should also work to develop partnerships with community members, local businesses, community organizations, schools, substance abuse and mental health treatment facilities, religious institutions, and the media. To further build collaboration and trust, agencies should be as transparent as possible with community stakeholders following incidents of excessive force and should consider providing periodic reports to the public regarding the dispositions of misconduct cases (PERF, 2016).

FUTURE RESEARCH DIRECTIONS

There are several areas that should be addressed by future research on police misconduct. First, earlier studies evaluating the impact of community policing programs and strategies suffer from several limitations. For example, most studies focus on a single agency and/or community (Adams et al., 2002). Future work should collect and analyze data from agencies and communities of varying size and geographic location. Second, future research should analyze the impact of community-oriented policing on quality of life, crime rates, victimization, and fear of crime when combined with other policing strategies, including intelligence-led policing and problem-oriented policing. Third, research regarding the impact of body worn cameras (BWCs) on police behavior has produced inconsistent results. Regardless of their effectiveness, the use of BWCs continues to increase, and future studies should seek to determine the impact of cameras on the use of excessive force and other types of misconduct. Finally, few studies have analyzed the impact of higher education on misconduct, and those that have also produced inconsistent results. Such future work may suggest the need for police agencies to revise educational requirements for potential job applicants.

CONCLUSION

Although community-oriented policing is a complex matter, the primary difference between community policing and other policing models is the former's emphasis on the development and maintenance of positive relationships and partnerships between the police and the communities they serve. While this chapter has identified several factors that obstruct the development of healthy police–community relationships and partnerships, the most frequently cited factor is the Ferguson Effect, which occurs when corruption, misconduct, and excessive negative coverage of law enforcement by the media increases community distrust and hostility toward the police.

Furthermore, agencies must take five steps to decrease the prevalence of misconduct and restore the public's trust in law enforcement. First, they must utilize competency-based interviews and assessments during the hiring process. Second, comprehensive recruitment plans must be developed to attract diverse applicants, including women and minorities. Third, officers must be provided with regular crisis intervention, de-escalation, and implicit bias training. Fourth, administrators must evaluate existing use-of-force policies and make any necessary improvements. These policies should emphasize the importance of proportionality when applying force and make it clear that de-escalation techniques and strategies are preferred over the use of lethal and non-lethal force. Fifth, agencies must develop and implement effective disciplinary policies and procedures to sanction officers involved in confirmed cases of misconduct. Ultimately, administrators are responsible for ensuring that sanctions are applied fairly and consistently in all misconduct cases. Future research regarding community policing and misconduct should: 1) continue to evaluate the impact of community policing on crime and victimization rates, particularly when community policing strategies are used concurrently with other policing models; 2) evaluate the impact of BWCs on misconduct and police–community encounters; and 3) determine the correlation between higher education and misconduct.

REFERENCES

Adams, R. E., Rohe, W. M., & Arcury, T. A. (2002). Implementing community-oriented policing: Organizational change and street officer attitudes. *Crime and Delinquency*, *48*(3), 399–430. doi:10.1177/001112870204800300З

Brewer, R., & Grabosky, P. (2014). The unraveling of public security in the United States: The dark side of police–community co-production. *American Journal of Criminal Justice*, *39*(1), 139–154. doi:10.100712103-012-9194-y

Brunson, R. K. (2015). Focused deterrence and improved police–community relations: Unpacking the proverbial "black box.". *Criminology & Public Policy*, *14*(3), 507–514. doi:10.1111/1745-9133.12141

Cerda, M., Tracy, M., Messner, S. F., Vlahov, D., Tardiff, K., & Galea, S. (2009). Misdemeanor policing, physical disorder, and gun-related homicide: A spatial analytic test of "broken-windows" theory. *Epidemiology (Cambridge, Mass.)*, *20*(4), 533–541. doi:10.1097/EDE.0b013e3181a48a99 PMID:19525689

Chappell, A. T., Monk-Turner, E., & Payne, B. K. (2011). Broken windows or window breakers: The influence of physical and social disorder on quality of life. *Justice Quarterly*, *28*(3), 522–540. doi:10.1080/07418825.2010.526129

Chermak, S., McGarrell, E., & Gruenewald, J. (2006). Media coverage of police misconduct and attitudes toward police. *Policing*, *29*(2), 261–281. doi:10.1108/13639510610667664

Gau, J. M., & Pratt, T. C. (2010). Revisiting broken windows theory: Examining the sources of the discriminant validity of perceived disorder and crime. *Journal of Criminal Justice*, *38*(4), 758–766. doi:10.1016/j.jcrimjus.2010.05.002

Graziano, L., Schuck, A., & Martin, C. (2010). Police misconduct, media coverage, and public perceptions of racial profiling: An experiment. *Justice Quarterly*, *34*(2), 52–76. doi:10.1080/07418820902763046

Hassell, K. D. (2016). Reducing police misconduct. In R. J. Burke (Ed.), *Stress in policing: Sources, consequences, and interventions* (pp. 220–236). Routledge. doi:10.4324/9781315611075-13

Hinds, L., & Murphy, K. (2007). Public satisfaction with police: Using procedural justice to improve police legitimacy. *Australian and New Zealand Journal of Criminology*, *40*(1), 27–42. doi:10.1375/acri.40.1.27

Hong, S. (2017). Does increasing ethnic representativeness reduce police misconduct? *Public Administration Review*, *77*(2), 195–205. doi:10.1111/puar.12629

Jenkins, M. J. (2016). Police support for community problem-solving and broken windows policing. *American Journal of Criminal Justice*, *41*(2), 220–235. doi:10.100712103-015-9302-x

Kerley, K. R., & Benson, M. L. (2000). Does community-oriented policing help build stronger communities? *Police Quarterly*, *3*(1), 46–69. doi:10.1177/1098611100003001002

Lee, H. D., Kim, D., Woo, Y., & Reyns, B. W. (2019). Determinants of citizen support for community-oriented policing. *Police Practice and Research*, *20*(1), 34–47. doi:10.1080/15614263.2017.1396459

Lombardo, R. M., & Donner, C. M. (2018). Can community policing increase residents' informal social control? Testing the impact of the Chicago Alternative Policing Strategy. *Police Practice and Research*, *19*(5), 427–442. doi:10.1080/15614263.2017.1405265

Lumsden, E. (2017). How much is police brutality costing America? *University of Hawai'i Law Review*, *41*(1), 142–202.

Mangan, A., Thomas, R., Davies, A., & Gasper, R. (2018). The challenges of police–community collaboration: Identity manoeuvres and power struggles in a neighborhood-based meeting. *Public Management Review*, *20*(9), 1353–1373. doi:10.1080/14719037.2017.1383718

McCarthy, M. M., Porter, L. E., Townsley, M., & Alpert, G. P. (2019). The effect of community-oriented policing on police use of force: Does community matter? *Policing*, *42*(4), 556–570. doi:10.1108/PIJPSM-10-2018-0148

Miller, L. (2004). Good cop–bad cop: Problem officers, law enforcement culture, and strategies for success. *Journal of Police and Criminal Psychology*, *19*(2), 30–48. doi:10.1007/BF02813871

Morabito, M. S. (2010). Understanding community policing as an innovation: Patterns of adoption. *Crime and Delinquency*, *56*(4), 564–587. doi:10.1177/0011128707311643

Nix, J., & Wolfe, S. E. (2015). The impact of negative publicity on police self-legitimacy. *Justice Quarterly*, *34*(1), 84–108. doi:10.1080/07418825.2015.1102954

Pelfrey, W. V. Jr. (2004). The inchoate nature of community policing: Differences between community policing and traditional police officers. *Justice Quarterly*, *21*(3), 579–601. doi:10.1080/07418820400095911

Perez, N. M., Bromley, M., & Cochran, J. (2017). Organizational commitment among sheriffs' deputies during the shift to community-oriented policing. *Policing*, *40*(2), 321–355. doi:10.1108/PIJPSM-04-2016-0051

Police Executive Research Forum (PERF). (2016). *Guiding principles on use of force.* https://www.policeforum.org/assets/30%20guiding%20principles.pdf

Reisig, M. D. (2010). Community and problem-oriented policing. *Crime and Justice*, *39*(1), 1–53. doi:10.1086/652384

Ren, L., Zhao, J., & He, N. (2019). Broken windows theory and citizen engagement. *Justice Quarterly*, *36*(1), 1–30. doi:10.1080/07418825.2017.1374434

Saunders, J., & Kilmer, B. (2019). Changing the narrative: Police–community partnerships and racial reconciliation. *Justice Quarterly*, 1–25. doi:10.1080/07418825.2019.1568520

Skogan, W. G. (1994). The impact of community policing on neighborhood residents: A cross-site analysis. In D. P. Rosenbaum (Ed.), *The challenge of community policing: Testing the promises* (pp. 167–181). Sage. doi:10.4135/9781483327006.n9

Somerville, P. (2009). Understanding community policing. *Policing*, *32*(2), 261–277. doi:10.1108/13639510910958172

Stephens, D. W. (2011). *Police discipline: A case for change*. National Institute of Justice.

Sunshine, J., & Tyler, T. R. (2003). The role of procedural justice and legitimacy in shaping public support for policing. *Law & Society Review*, *37*(3), 513–547. doi:10.1111/1540-5893.3703002

Tillyer, R. (2018). Assessing the impact of community-oriented policing on arrest. *Justice Quarterly*, *35*(3), 526–555. doi:10.1080/07418825.2017.1327609

Trojanowicz, R. C., & Bucqueroux, B. (1994). Community policing: How to get started (1st ed.). Anderson.

U.S. Commission on Civil Rights. (2018). *Police use of force: An examination of modern policing practices*. https://www.usccr.gov/pubs/2018/11-15-Police-Force.pdf

Walsh, W. F., & Vito, G. F. (2019). *Police leadership and administration: A 21st-century strategic approach*. Routledge.

Wehrman, M. M., & De Angelis, J. (2011). Citizen willingness to participate in police–community partnerships: Exploring the influence of race and neighborhood context. *Police Quarterly*, *14*(1), 48–69. doi:10.1177/1098611110393134

Weitzer, R., Tuch, S. A., & Skogan, W. G. (2008). Police–community relations in a majority-black city. *Journal of Research in Crime and Delinquency*, *45*(4), 398–428. doi:10.1177/0022427808322617

Welsh, B. C., Braga, A. A., & Bruinsma, G. J. (2015). Reimagining broken windows: From theory to policy. *Journal of Research in Crime and Delinquency*, *52*(4), 447–463. doi:10.1177/0022427815581399

Wycoff, M. A., & Skogan, W. G. (1994). Community policing in Madison: An analysis of implementation and impact. In D. P. Rosenbaum (Ed.), *The challenge of community policing: Testing the promises* (pp. 75–91). Sage. doi:10.4135/9781483327006.n4

Xu, Y., Fiedler, M. L., & Flaming, K. H. (2005). Discovering the impact of community policing: The broken windows thesis, collective efficacy, and citizens' judgment. *Journal of Research in Crime and Delinquency, 42*(2), 147–186.

Yang, S.-M. (2010). Assessing the spatial-temporal relationship between disorder and violence. *Journal of Quantitative Criminology*, *26*(1), 139–163. doi:10.100710940-009-9085-7

ADDITIONAL READING

Chanin, J. (2017). Early stages of pattern or practice police misconduct reform: An examination of the Department of Justice's investigation and negotiation processes. *Police Quarterly*, *20*(3), 250–274. doi:10.1177/1098611117709268

Donner, C. M., Fridell, L. A., & Jennings, W. G. (2016). The relationship between self-control and police misconduct: A multi-agency study of first-line police supervisors. *Criminal Justice and Behavior*, *43*(7), 841–862. doi:10.1177/0093854815626751

Greene, J. R. (1989). Police officer job satisfaction and community perceptions: Implications for community-oriented policing. *Journal of Research in Crime and Delinquency*, *26*(2), 168–183. doi:10.1177/0022427889026002004

Huff, J., White, M. D., & Decker, S. H. (2018). Organizational correlates of police deviance: A statewide analysis of misconduct in Arizona, 2000–2011. *Policing*, *41*(4), 465–481. doi:10.1108/PIJPSM-08-2017-0092

Lum, C., Stoltz, M., Koper, C. S., & Scherer, J. A. (2019). Research on body-worn cameras: What we know, what we need to know. *Criminology & Public Policy*, *18*(1), 93–118. doi:10.1111/1745-9133.12412

Maguire, E. R., Nix, J., & Campbell, B. A. (2017). A war on cops? The effects of Ferguson on the number of U.S. police officers murdered in the line of duty. *Justice Quarterly*, *34*(5), 739–758. doi:10.1080/07418825.2016.1236205

Manis, J., Archbold, C. A., & Hassell, K. D. (2008). Exploring the impact of police officer education level on allegations of police misconduct. *International Journal of Police Science & Management*, *10*(4), 509–523. doi:10.1350/ijps.2008.10.4.102

O'Connor Shelley, T., Hogan, M. J., Unnithan, N. P., & Stretesky, P. B. (2013). Public opinion and satisfaction with state law enforcement. *Policing*, *36*(3), 526–542. doi:10.1108/PIJPSM-03-2012-0027

Owens, E., Weisburd, D., Amendola, K. L., & Alpert, G. P. (2018). Can you build a better cop? Experimental evidence on supervision, training, and policing in the community. *Criminology & Public Policy*, *17*(1), 41–87. doi:10.1111/1745-9133.12337

Pyrooz, D. C., Decker, S. H., Wolfe, S. E., & Shjarback, J. A. (2016). Was there a Ferguson Effect on crime rates in large U.S. cities? *Journal of Criminal Justice*, *46*, 1–8. doi:10.1016/j.jcrimjus.2016.01.001

Yuan, Y., & McNeeley, S. (2017). Social ties, collective efficacy, and crime-specific fear in Seattle neighborhoods. *An International Journal of Evidence-Based Research, Policy & Practice*, *12*(1), 90–112.

KEY TERMS AND DEFINITIONS

Broken Windows Theory: A criminological theory that asserts that signs of crime and disorder create an environment that fosters additional crime and disorder.

Collective Efficacy: The ability of community members to control the behavior of other individuals within the community.

Community-Oriented Policing: An innovative policing model that emphasizes the importance of positive relations and partnerships between law enforcement officers and the communities they serve.

Ferguson Effect: An increase in crime rates due to community members' distrust and hostility toward police, caused by corruption, misconduct, and excessive negative coverage of law enforcement by the media.

Rotten Apple Theory: A theory of police corruption that argues that brutality and other forms of misconduct are perpetrated by a small number of isolated individuals within a department or unit who are able to evade detection during the recruiting, screening, and hiring process.

Rotten Barrel Theory: A theory of police corruption that argues that misconduct is widespread in an agency, department, and/or unit due to weak and ineffective policies and practices that promote misconduct.

Social Disorganization Theory: A criminological theory that postulates those factors of social disorganization, including low socioeconomic status, racial heterogeneity, unemployment, and deteriorating infrastructures, increase criminal behavior.

Chapter 4
Policing Strategies and Approaches to Improving Community Relations:
Black Citizens' Perceptions of Law Enforcement Efforts to Intentionally Strengthen Relationships

Christopher Lee Bush
Allen County Community College, USA

ABSTRACT

This chapter addresses the voices of Black individuals and their communities urging police officers to be trustworthy and transparent, and urging them to be intentional in building relationships in the Black community. Qualified immunity, fraternal order of police, and law enforcement bill of rights discussions have emerged from recent incidents that add to the Black community's mistrust in the police. This chapter discusses how officers fail to recognize past and current issues where officers are unapologetic, and which, in turn, contributes to making it difficult to see police transparency and legitimacy. The chapter also addresses the partial education officers receive on Black culture and, more importantly, officers' lack of knowledge about cultural humility with self-reflection. Global positive social change and using a conceptual communication framework are the foundation for building and strengthening police relationships in the Black community to improve police strategies.

INTRODUCTION

Community policing became more prevalent in the 1970s, after law enforcement began to take another approach from what was known as the "professional" model. The shift began to progress with officers being more engaged with the local citizens during the 1980's throughout the 90s (Patterson, 1995). This phenomenon would later saturate throughout the country where cities and states would adopt the

DOI: 10.4018/978-1-7998-6884-2.ch004

philosophy of implementing effective strategies to establish better relationships in communities while also addressing crimes (Cooley et. al, 2019). One demographic group that the early adoption of police community positively impacted was a community in Topeka, KS in the 1980's. Topeka police department utilized a strategy to engage with youth by disseminating Kansas City Chiefs football cards. This effective method installed by the Chief reflect to Peterson (1995) discussed about historical foundation of policing known as "beats" where Peel idea goal for implementing strategies where the officers would become known by the community and the community know the officers.

Ray (2014) stated that establishing relationships with youth at school and in the community extends beyond traditional policing. Police departments are at the forefront of becoming more engaged with bettering community policing. Efforts that officers are being encouraged to add with developing better strategies is establishing effective interventions with Black communities (Wahl, 2017) The phenomenon, that Topeka Police implemented over 30 years allowed the community and the police to work together to repair any lost communication along with plans to be in place. There are a several strategies that law enforcement can target a primary one emphasized by Higgins, et al, (2020) are police efforts to build relationships in the Black community. to solve problems before tensions escalated to the news.

Community policing goes beyond developing relationships with Blacks in their communities but ensures that law enforcement is improving public safety in areas where crimes may be high (Cooley et. al, 2019). Cooley et al (2019) stated that officers building relationships cannot just be the only focus, but officers maintain their skills to solving crimes. Two or more things can be done at once where all individuals engaged are benefiting where officers are addressing crime related issues and building relationships. Ray (2014) stated that having officers in dual roles in the schools and in the community can strengthen relationships. In addition, to the roles that officers was engaged with in the community patrolling developing relationships with youth and families, Topeka also had had officers engaged in school programs that also served the community where the school was located.

Members of the Black community in Topeka had confidence in the police and trusted that when they were engaged in incidents that involved work to protect the community, it was legitimate. The unfortunate efforts that is not present today is the Black community's eagerness to help police officers when they are seeking help. Being helpful was a testament to the community relationship that had been established and saturated the Black community, and schools (Ray, 2014).

All the ingredients' where police strategies were used for establishing a true relationship were in place 30 years ago in the capital city of Kansas, with the Topeka Police Department. The engaged efforts were a practice that Patterson (1995) stated that those who are practicing and implementing community policing need study their history to take on lessons from the past. The relationships between communities and police officers demonstrated a level of respect for each other when old principals from the early 80s and 90s was established. The Topeka Police department demonstrated efforts proved that in predominately black neighborhoods their strategies worked. These aspects of police work were not an emerging factor that divided the Black community and police relationships from evolving. The exact opposite has emerged after the 90s. The past 20 years community policing have been an area that police have worked on to increase their trust, transparency demonstrate their legitimacy (Wahl, 2017). Today, from across the nation since the awakening of incidents of police shooting in predominately Black communities, there has been a pushed for law enforcement and other disciplines to address the issue by implementing more profound police strategies that involve community policing, police awareness, education, and trainings to bridge the gap with Black communities Armstead (2019).

BACKGROUND

Police officers have expressed to the community across the nation that they are taking steps to be more transparent and trusting with Black communities (Wahl, 2017). The words and news conference don't align to what officers are sharing. This is creating more of a deterrence to improving community relations. Summer 2020, the shooting, and murder of George Floyd by an on-duty officer has push national and news has exacerbated tensions between police and members of the Black community (McFarland et al., 2018). At present spring 2021, several nation new stories have emerged with others continuing to rise to the forefront. These stories involve, police body worn camera delayed video release, false reports given to families, and inconsistent policies from the AG offices. Such incidents display police questionable transparency, extends to the Black community efforts to trust, alters the relationship building. This ongoing problem of community policing in the Black communities, which persists, is impacting individuals personally and indirectly (Bush, 2020b). The emergence and inception of police body worn cameras (BWC's) has contributed to community and police relationships where the community look for accountability, and transparency regarding police release videos. The BWCs intent was to establish trust to the community. Now that BWC is at the forefront of police engaged interventions, this could be a step that officers implement into their strategy to build increase transparency and to establish trust in the Black community. Bush (2020b) suggest that video does not need to be shared immediately with the community but should be shared with the family in a timely manner. Officers addressing this critical breakdown in the community can be additional approach to improving relationships. This sensitive topic will remain exploratory despite any considerations for changes in the future, with some law enforcement incidents appearing to continue to occur where the Black community do not see any reprimands, or where police departments and their officers are not held accountable for their questionable acts. It will take a systematic change from top officials such as legislation and city council to improve police and Black community relationships throughout the country (Armstead, 2019; Bush, 2020b).

Police departments that are making efforts to address and strengthen their police strategies and approaches to improve relationships have been informed by individuals other that members from the Black communities but from all diverse ethnic backgrounds to show more concern to be engaged in the Black communities since the death of George Floyd. These individuals that are not from the Black community have questioned police law enforcement current trainings, practices and education and requesting for better police strategies to be implemented (Patel, 2020). An area where the Black community is asking for police to develop more realistic strategies is to incorporate guidelines, policies and procedures that address officers who have demonstrated bad acts. Bush (2020b) suggested that officers who are not being held accountable within their department fueled more unrest. It is vital that while officers are addressing strategies that are in real time because of incidents that is being broadcast, that they also address incidents that are get looked over to be handled by police leadership with officers who commit unethical acts that should be discipline

Many individuals from all platforms have stepped up and defended the communities they come from are urging change for officers to be intentional in understanding the Black community is hurting (Birzer & Nolan 2002). Birzer and Nolan (2002) indicated that the lack of police officers establishing relationships with Black individual impacts the entire community nationwide. These concerns have extended to scholars, police disciplines to develop effective police strategies around community policing to enhance what is in place and what new community policing efforts could be implemented (Cooley, 2019). There must be good faith intentions from law enforcement wanting to establish community policing to build trust, ensure safety, and provide transparency to improve their conduct with the Black community. Multiple strategies with evaluated approaches must be in place for police to consider while building an effective community relations.

While police departments are working to engage in strengthen relationship with the Black community, officers need to have systems in place to continue their efforts of community building after several weeks or months have passed of incidents that have paralyzed the community nationally or from local incidents (Wahl). Bush (2020b) suggest that if an officer is in the community and has established some form of relationship, they should be able to have conversations about what they are seeing to help members of the community have a better or different perspective of what they are seeing.

Police integrity is on the line and has been questioned and appears to be growing. Doane and Cumberland (2018) stated this has become a consistent problem here in our backyard and across the nation issue with police–minority relations putting the country on edge. The Black community witnesses' actual events playing before their very eyes, which appear to be happening rapidly. Police officers focus to integrate better trainings, education and practices can help minimize and remove the stigmatism of Black members of the community having no trust in them, and the questioning of their transparency (Birzer & Nolan 2002).

FOCUS OF THE CHAPTER

The chapter will address how positive social change across police departments, locally and statewide, can be diffused to law enforcement to start developing relationships with the Black community. More importantly this chapter will provide insight to police strategies and approaches to improve in areas that have emerged as issues, controversies, and problems. With recent and current incidents around the nation involving police shootings of Black males and females, the unrest and division continue to widen the gap of distancing police and community relationships instead of bridging it. This chapter will discuss the principles that can contribute to police reform and provide key steps for police officers to produce better relationships to build trust, transparency, and the legitimacy of work ethic. These three impacted factors that have been fractured in the black community can be repaired (Wahl, 2017).

The chapter exposes three areas of policing that have hampered the Black community which have further widen the gap with the community (Cooley et al.). These three weaknesses of the police also are areas that can be turned to strength that benefits police to help with build positive police strategies. In this chapter, an examination of the Black community voice will speak to the poor communication efforts of police before incidents and during times of unrest, and how, after the incidents, newsworthy media tension has dissipated. The chapter discusses how police can be intentional with building relationships in the B lack community. The chapter also provides insight about how relationships in the Black community continue to be met with opposition from law enforcement, that include qualified immunity, Fraternal Order of Police, and Law Enforcement Bill of Rights.

The chapter discusses what illuminates the problems around police and Black communities' relationships, issues surrounding the problem that are barriers, and solutions where police officers can begin to establish strategies to improve relationships in the Black the community. The chapter extend some scholarship by briefly providing an overview of two communication theories, the diffusion of innovation theory (DIT) and policy feedback theory (PFT), providing a conceptual framework both can follow to take steps to establish trust, transparency, and the legitimacy of police work. Upon closing the gap with relationships amongst police and Black communities, the chapter concludes by addressing global perspectives on reforming the criminal justice system that can help create social change.

ISSUES

Police Destruction of Legitimacy, Trust, and Transparency With Black Communities

Voices of Black citizens from around the world are urging police officers to be intentional in establishing long-lasting community relationships with the Black community Wahl (2017). Police officers need to assure Black communities that they are taking steps to increase effective community policing, fix the distrust and questioning of their legitimacy, share more information, and reverse previously lacking communication and transparency. The efforts of police revised community policing and new established community policing programs can no longer wait where Black communities are ready to start the relationship-building. Adedoyin et al., (2018); Bent-Goodley and Smith, (2017) and other scholars have stated that if policies and careful attention to how effective communication with communities is not addressed, distrust will continue to spread into the community and prevent the community from establishing a relationship with law enforcement.

The Black community's perceptions of police trust, transparency, and legitimacy have been questionable nationwide (Gau & Brunson, 2015). Steps to be taken for law enforcement to show Black communities that they are addressing these controversial issues must look at what is being asked, requested, and shared. Officers examining their past and current ways of communicating that has caused concerned and unrest can be revised not to repeat the same problem from past incidents (Adedoyin et al., 2018).

Gau and Brunson (2020) stated that with all the Black population has been through and continues to endure, they still are able to identify and show some respect for the qualities and values of police work. The incidents that have spurred out of control because officer's poor assessments of making preconceived assumptions have led to innocent lives being lost have pushed the Black community to lose some respect when officers arrived after a call has been made. The Black community's perception is that law enforcement is not able to establish relationships with the Black community because of Black individuals lower socioeconomic status (Armstead, 2019). However, Camille et al., (2019) suggest, minorities that have lower socioeconomic status value non-threatening behavior, empathy, and fair handling of police situations in procedural justice. In fact, Black individuals who have been engaged in highly contested interventions with police officers in their communities recognize that they need police and actually want increased police presence in their neighborhoods (Camille et al., 2019). The Black community is frustrated by the perception that they do not support the police and, when they question problems that occur, that they do not want their presence in the community (Gau &Brunson, 2020).

CONTRIBUTING INFLUENCES FROM LAW ENFORCEMENT DISRUPTING POLICE AND BLACK COMMUNITY RELATIONSHIPS

Qualified immunity (QI) has taken precedence in discussions in Black communities this summer. Mandery (1994) defined *QI* "is doctrine that protects officials acting in the course of their duties from liability for all violations of civil rights under 42 U.S.C. sec. 1983(1) except those that are determined to violate "clearly established" principles of law. (2) Because claims of qualified immunity are evaluated under an objective standard, qualified immunity protection extends to some public officials who knowingly violate the civil rights of a citizen. Also, because the doctrine excuses public officials from liability for some behavior that violates citizens' civil rights, it is a social insurance scheme that protects civil rights violators from the consequences of uncertainty in the law".

In 2020 with George Floyd's murder in Minneapolis by a Minnesota police officer, along with the killing of Breonna Taylor in Louisville, Kentucky. This doctrine has exacerbated tensions surrounding these two incidents moved the country to seeking to learn and know more about what qualified immunity is and why it exists. Commentators have recognized that qualified immunity hinders community–police relationships and police accountability efforts in America (Carlos, 2019). The Black community has been informed by local news, and other reliable sources such as from Senator Corey Booker, and Vice President Kamala Harris that k officers had some layer of protection. This controversial topic reemerged to the forefront and began to saturate throughout the country through media, and social media, causing an uproar from the Black community emerged requesting clarification on how such a doctrine excused officers' misconduct (Pelura, 2020).

The controversy that contributes to police and Black community relationships is that the members of the community expressed that having this doctrine in place gives officers the green light to engage in unethical acts, corruption, misconduct, and mistreatment of African Americans, which has intensified and continues to strain the relationship between them (Doane & Cumberland, 2018). For law enforcement to continue to address police strategies to improve relationships their intensions to make efforts to meet the community request must be demonstrated (Schwartz, 2020)

QI was implemented in 1982 when the Supreme Court ruled that government officials were entitled to QI from civil rights lawsuits if their actions did not violate "clearly established" rights (Mandery, 1994). When officers are given discretion to make quick choices, where their life may be in danger and need some form of protection, they solely rely on knowing they have this doctrine in their defense. Romanicci et al. (2020), stated that since its inception, there have been questions about the doctrine. QI has spread across the news because of law enforcement's questionable acts, where misconduct has been present widening the gap between police and Black communities.

The Black community, since learning what QI is, has seen support from the highest level of Congress pushing to amend QI (Schwartz, 2020). Senator and Vice President-Elect Kamala Harris and Senator Corey Booker have come onboard pushing for change to this court-issued standard, led by Representative Karen Bass (Jackson, 2020). In addition, Schwartz (2020) stated that courts, scholars, and advocacy any many others have come on board to do away with QI.

In June, Colorado governor Jared Polis signed into law Senate Bill 20-217, known as the Law Enforcement Integrity and Accountability Act. The act addresses 8 significant areas, whereas the QI one listed states that officers can now be sued if citizens civil rights have been violated. Colorado governor and other elected state officials became the biggest champion of addressing QI and listening to Coloradoans urge to look at QI, where they passed legislation to remove the aspects of qualified immunity immediately after the George Floyd killing. Like Colorado, Virginia, Indiana, Michigan, and many others are making efforts to change QI rather than eliminating or reforming some of the language that has been passed by the supreme courts in 1982. These precedents have shown the Black community that the efforts of the state officials are drawing one step closer to holding officers accountable for their actions, which will move toward establishing transparency, trust, and legitimacy of their work details (Schwartz, 2020).

Police officers building relationships will take some efforts of joint relationships, with the community being invited by prominent members of their community, and city and state official positions (Schwartz, 2020). QI has hit home, whereas some local officers have opened to discuss what qualified immunity is to have discussion to help the community understand its purpose. More efforts need to address QI and what can be done need to be in place with local community members in Black communities (Kamalu & Onveozili, 2018). Police are listening but will need to take a stance to adopt making some adjustments or eliminating the QI to strengthen their relationships with Black communities and others (Schwartz, 2020).

The longer QI stays in effect, the longer police officers know they have some sort of protection and may act in ways knowing that their misconduct will be overlooked, given immunity, to have unethical acts and potential charges against them to be eliminated (Reinwald, 2020). This is a wedge that subtracts and divides relationships as opposed to adding and multiplying, for Black communities and police to establish relationships (Bush, 2020a). To extend building trusting relationships with community policing, this is a tier that police can implement as police strategy to demonstrate they are increasing their transparency to hold themselves accountable to unjustifiable acts (Kamalu & Onveozili, 2018).

The Fraternal Order of Police (FOP) is another contributing issue emerging controversial discussion; however, can be addressed to increase police strategies and police relations. FOP defined is A fraternal organization consisting of sworn law enforcement officers in the United States. The organization attempts to improve the working conditions of law enforcement officers and the safety of those they serve through education, legislation, information, community involvement, and employee representation.

As incidents started to surge over the past 4–5 years and caught the nation's attention, individuals have questioned the ethics of leadership procedures of police officers' unions, known as the Fraternal Order Police. "The FOP unions are known to have membership over 355, 000 and continues to grow. It has been identified as one of the nation's largest police association, where over 2000 chapters are saturated throughout the country" (Jackman, 2016). Over the past 20 years, police departments throughout the country have demonstrated efforts to become more racially diverse. However, the problem Jackman (2016) states is that the FOP seems committed to putting White men in charge. The Black community is met with members of the chapters being heavily represented with no leadership where Black men or women are in FOP leadership positions. The data points to these chapters being operated and run by White officers even in geographical areas where the demographic is predominantly individuals of color (Jackman, 2016). An example, Jackman (2016) showed that Baltimore's police department is 44% Black, but its FOP has never had a Black leader. He also stated that the Washington, DC, FOP chapter board is mainly White, although the demographic makeup of the Metropolitan Police Department is predominately Black male and females.

Black members of the Baltimore police force stressed that they had great concerns when the FOP endorsed President Trump in 2015 when he was running for president (Jackman, 2016). The Black officers expressed that they have to form their own Black community in some capacity, when the FOP endorsed Trump, that the FOP should adhere to those whom they personally support other than collective support as a union. The reason this message was shared was because of some of the remarks made by President Trump were divisive among Blacks and other minorities. The Black officers feared his remarks would put more strain on the police's and Black communities' relationships. Black officers who supported their colleagues and were ready to speak on their behalf have seen their own setbacks internally, as a small Black community (Jackman, 2016). Systemically this sends a message to the Black community that FOP sets the tone for division among Black officers in their membership, further justifying the FOP and its officers' efforts to engage in their communities.

Learning who the FOP body members are, which differ throughout the nation (e.g., retired police officers, officers' wives, and ex-police officers) has made the Black community furious, because they see these individuals as the same offices who inflicted the pain and have no concern for their well-being. The main controversy around FOPs, issues that the Black community is discovering, is that some of the terminology in police and FOP contracts appears to protect officers (Schwartz, 2020). This is perceived by the community as qualified immunity from an internal process as special privileged. When the Black community is aware that officers can remove disciplinary actions from their personal files after certain time periods; after confirmed police misconduct, officers can advance in other departmental positions; not being interviewed for several days after incidents (Bush2020a). Johnson (2020) stated that it is a national problem where officers move from department to department, and their histories do not follow them, whereas from how police FOP contracts are written to provide this protection.

Members of the Black community urges police officer to take a realistic approach to engaging in relationship by providing information that is relevant to help the communities to understand the FOP process. Police department can remove the controversial dilemma around the perception of FOP to be rectified, through education the public about FOPs. In addition, a strategy that police need to implement is employing union members that s that demonstrate they are working towards inclusiveness and putting forth a diverse group of officers in leadership positions of the FOP locally and nationally. Police FOPs operations can extend education to Black communities ensuring that the premise of the FOP do not protect members of the FOP from misconduct and other but describes how it benefits them where the community from a member. Addressing these maters can be another step closer to bridging the gap with police and community relationships. Bush (2020a) describes as a concern where the members of the community have shared to justify a direct link to supporting the lack of legitimacy, transparency, and trust. The FOP contract, and body of members further drives division with the Black community. It is imperative that police unions be allies in efforts to reform the criminal justice system, and be held accountable (Wear, 2015).

The Law Enforcement Bill of Rights (LEBOR or LEBoR), much like the QI, LEBoR is another layer that the Black community has discovered since the recent unrest in the nation. *LEBor* is defined as Intended to protect American law enforcement personnel from investigation and prosecution arising from conduct during the official performance of their duties and provide them with privileges based on due process beyond those normally provided to other citizens. The LEBoR came into effect after officers in Maryland addressed legislators in 1973. This law that was implemented was reviewed as one of the first in the nation that provided a shield in the workplace, providing protections for police officers far beyond those afforded to other government employees.

Currently, there is a leading group of lawmakers in Maryland calling for a full repeal of the statute because of what they have witnessed that is causing disruption in their state and local Black communities (Wiggins, 2020). Wiggins (2020) described the LEBoR as an impediment to accountability and transparency. The LEBoR, for over 40 years, community members, and citizens from around the country are saying the LEBoR is the knockout punch that provides growth to qualified immunity.

One of the major rights granted was discussed above, about the FOP contract language that disrupts Black communities' trust in the police, which the LEBoR includes giving officers a formal waiting period before they have "to cooperate with internal inquiries into police conduct. It also ensures that only fellow officers, not civilians, investigate police" (Wiggins, 2020, para. 11). The concern that moves the community to voice their opinions is that many of them are employees of the city and state and do not have the same privileges officers due under the LEBoR. As Wiggins (2020) stated, several members of the panel have gone on record calling for police offices to adhere to the same statute that covers other government employees who are under investigation. The Black community are not alone feeling the impact of the LEBoR, Hispanics, other minorities and some Whites also have emphasized how the LEBoR is an emerging problem. The Black community know that they now have leverage with state officials removing the LEBoR just as they are doing with QI so that it does not continue to hamper relationships with individuals in the community (Schwartz, 2020). Because of the unrest today with police and Black citizens who predominantly make up some communities, now is the time to look at making changes to the LEBoR. Jason C. Buckel (R-Allegany) suggested that the phrase 'bill of rights' be stripped from the law to remove what he called a perception that police officers are being given special treatment" (Wiggins, 2020). This problem and controversial topic impedes any citizen review board trying to question the unethical acts, given the protection of officers from being questioned for a period.

Currently, 15 states are protected under the LEBoR; however, the heated discussion that has emerged focuses on how the FOP is able to adopt some of the language into contracts to protect police officers that are not in one of the 15 protected states. Some state community Black leaders has begun to demand transparency about the FOP contract language and has discovered the language embedded in the contracts. Bush (2020b) research demonstrated that participants asking, why police and other law enforcement agencies go out of their way to hide or protect officers from incidents that have been shared by the media of police officers' misconduct that has went viral. In addition, since 2015, 15 states have enacted legislation to codify their own variations of LEBoR.

Law enforcement adopting and applying these practices into their professions creates what Romanucci et al. (2020) called a one-sided approach to QI, the bill of rights, and for FOP local chapters. The Black community perceives these acts as a direct message, telling officers that they can shoot first, commit police misconduct, and deal with the consequences later, when they will be exonerated. To establish efforts to increase police strategies in multiple areas, law enforcement needs to examine QI, FOP chapters, and the LEBoRs must be revised or entirely abolished, to have any sustainable police stratagies and approaches to improve relationship while building bridges to an effective Black and police relationship. This must take precedence, or the efforts to develop and implement new strategies for community policing with Black communities will fail.

PROBLEMS

The problems that are addressed are discussed like the issues that emerge to the forefront as major weakness that officers endure, however can be addressed with positive attributes that can impact bring about positive impacts to policing strategies and approaches to improving community relationships. The following four areas can help extend to addressing the underlying problems with police strategies:

- Police officers overlook the past and ignore present problems with building relationships
- Police social distancing themselves from the Black communities.
- Police Officers' Partial Education on Black Culture
- Cultural Humility: Looking What Police Officers Need for Self-Reflection, to be Culture-Competent

These four problems are areas that police can address around communication, transparency: trust, building relationships, education, training, and awareness. However, the problem is the strategies have been repeated over the years, and when some level of revision has taken place to do more, it has not changed for the better with the Black community.

Across the nation, community programs have some guided policies for community policing programs with evidence-based practices and best practices; but many are programs are just placeholders developed by professionals and others who have no understanding of what interventions should be implemented to establish relationships. Efforts must take place now to address the questions and concerns that the black community is expressing need to be in place. It is vital that law enforcement agencies take a stronger look at their work, and, to have accountability, the agencies need to advance their policing efforts and criminal justice practices (Adedoyin et al., 2018).

POLICE OFFICERS OVERLOOKING THE PAST AND IGNORING THE PRESENT PROBLEM OF RELATIONSHIPS WITH THE BLACK COMMUNITY

Police department efforts to implement community policing has been long established, even more since the 2014 shooting of Michael Brown. There is no one defined definition for community policing, however each program has some of the same similar expectations, however, take on a shape of its on depending on the police department approach. As departments continue to sharpen their engagements in the community, past and current incidents cannot go unnoticed. This ongoing problem impedes police strategies implementation goals (Wahl, 2017).

Police departments must do much more then talk and attempt to try implement strategies to address issues around trust, transparency and their legitimacy around respectfully acknowledging that past injustice incidence, and present issues has happened with no resolvable solutions to keep the same from happening in the future (Armstead, 2019). The problem over the years have been officers have struggled to engage black community voices who have suggested ideas for programs that can work such as Afrocentricity (Adedoyin et al., 2018). *Afrocentricity* is defined as culturally grounded social work practice-based model that affirms, codifies, and integrates common cultural experiences, values, and interpretations that cut across people of African descent. This applies that Afrocentricity would be utilized from a perspective of within Black experiences and not from Eurocentric perspective-developed resources. Bent-Goodley and Smith (2017) stated that they have seen what has been applied around the country by programs with community policing programs, and they applaud those efforts, but indicate that "nothing has been discussed those grounds the experience and the response in an African-centered perspective" (Bent-Goodley & Smith, 2017). Community policing programs need to be entrenched with trying to connect with the Black communities by honoring the past and present to create long-lasting future relationships, the programs must be centered around a cultural perspective. To help start this implementation, community policy can apply the African-centered theory "to frame the response within the Black experience and not from a Eurocentric perspective" (Bent-Goodley & Smith, 2017). Policies are inadequate and unrealistic, with outdated community programs for officers to establish relationships and without any genuine, intentional efforts. The police must show that they are speaking to the losses the Black community has endured or to build trust with the Black community, where they can see officers are working toward transparency.

There is no one-size-fits-all community policing program to fix the recent incidents where police have driven the Black community away from wanting to collaborate with them in any capacity. However, a foundation to start community policing off in the right direction is to make sure officers know and accept what has transpired in the past and what is present, so they can adapt to having programs such as the Afrocentric help guide their practice (Bent-Goodley & Smith, 2017). The outdated and unrealistic community policing approaches called out by the Black community will not work if it does not have a voice in helping to rebuild the community policing programs.

The past must be recognized, and present incidents must be discussed, acknowledging the wrongdoing, starting with a sincere apology. The incidents have grown to a number that is too large to account for where Black citizens see the challenges that exist between them and police officers, keeping them from building relationships, including a history of mistrust, racial bias, and perceptions of each other formed by past and present incidents (Bent-Goodley & Smith, 2017).

Adedoyin et al. (2018), suggested that it is extremely important that both the community and the police turn the distance poor relations around to build momentum, where both can be intentional in addressing the problems and finally improve relations between the Black community and the police.

POLICE SOCIAL DISTANCE AND RELATIONSHIPS WITH BLACK COMMUNITIES

An additional problem that has circulated in the Black community is police abstinence unless a crime has taken place in the Black Community to have them present (Harrisburg, 2016). In 2020, social distancing became a relevant term everyone became familiar with the nation was forced to implement in their lives because of the COVID-19 pandemic. The Black community has expressed that social distance has been long in place with them when it comes to police being present in the Black community. Harrisburg (2016, para 2) defines *social distance* as "the perceived closeness, or lack thereof, one has with the police. Social distance decreases with an increase in informal interactions." The Black community has adopted this term when officers have not been visual in their community and practicing their social distance, which further creates what Harrisburg (2016) describes as the lower confidence community members have in the police when there is a lack of presence officers in the community, especially for the Black community. The Black community is urging law enforcement to be intentional in building relationships with them (Harrisburg, 2016). Police Departments strategy to address the problem need to start with decreasing the social distance that has been present for years. Research has demonstrated that even in other settings where the officer did have engagement with Black citizens. Harrisburg (2016) suggested that the community felt there was no connectedness, whereas they expressed to build rapport, it needed to start with them being in their community before having any events outside the community. Harrisburg (2016) found that greater social distance did play a key role that diminished the relationships of Black communities and police. Also pointed out by Harrisburg (2016) that race became no longer a downward spiral if the social distance gap is closed. Reducing social distance is a mandate that can reflect the steps to which officers should pay close attention in modern policing, which will move toward the goal of securing high public confidence (Lee et al., 2015).

Police relationships with the community imply groups of individuals establishing levels of comfort with existing in the same space and corresponding among each other in close and distant circumstances. The problem that Blacks communities see that keeps police from establishing relationships with them is that the police devalue their Black culture and assume there is nothing they have in common to develop healthy relationships. Even when community programs are put in place, the community feels they are developed with intentions only to meet agency goals and not to truly engage with the community (Bent-

Goodley & Smith, 2017). It further promotes social distance when only a few offices engage in community policing programs and, from a community perspective, are forced to do so. The steps to start building bridges cannot happen if there are no strategic action plans for intervention and working interchangeably (Bent-Goodley & Smith, 2017). Conversation has grown where it is documented that community policing has established some noteworthy strategies to show positive attributes but will take strong efforts to minimize the struggle police departments have with implementing the strategies. The Black community is more apt to develop a positive attitude when it can join the police or personally know a police officer. The public attitude is a direct determinant of legitimacy in police presence and in activities to establish trust and transparency (Bent-Goodley & Smith, 2017). Police officers find it challenging to live in poor or underserved communities, which has been suggested to build rapport (Allen & Michaux 2013). A different approach to recruit individuals from the community can help minimize this concern.

POLICE OFFICERS' PARTIAL EDUCATION ON BLACK CULTURE

Educational courses and training have been developed for police officers over the years, and the education courses and trainings have increased in the past 5–7 years, to build police officers capacity and their awareness about minorities. The committee selected by President Obama in 2015 for 21st century policing discussed how education, training and awareness is lacking and need more attention. There still appear to be problems with officers who are going through training and course work, where officers are not grasping what they learn that carry over into their interventions with Black citizens, and more importantly, when they arrive in Black communities. The problem is that many of the trainings, and education are developed or taught from police and not outside sources. As stated, prior in the chapter implementing such trainings that is engages the Black community perspective can be advantageous to police departments when implementing strategies to understand Black cultures. When officer continues to build their own programs or repeat what they have learned from others that are not of the Black culture is that it further gives the Black community a perception that there are no real intentions to take the courses or training seriously (Bent-Goodley & Smith 2017). This is evident because of the repeated misconduct in officers' interactions and interventions with the Black community. When officers arrive to engage with Black citizens,' it appears that any training they may have received on Black culture for intervention is not present. Bent-Goodley and Smith (2017) suggest that officers while attending any educational platforms or training on Black culture, they first must also have express and acknowledge that they are truly starting to understand Black culture. To help build effective strategies to improve relations officers must adhere to be aware that they are willing to learn about themselves and forgo their own personal biases that stop them from accepting Black and other cultures they encounter. Antrobus et al. (2015, p. 1), emphasized that "community norms and beliefs of police can affect peoples' perceptions of procedural justice and their obligations to obey. Antobus et al. (2015) stated that is vital whereas, if officers do the same for Black community norms, beliefs, and cultural practices, they will have better interactions when going into Black communities or general interventions with Black citizens. Furthermore, an additional problem that will persist is if officers only taking a course, module, and several weeks of in-class learning about other cultures one time is not the solution that will address the problem (Bush, 2020a). These opportunities should be an ongoing goal and process long as they are employed, if working with the community directly or indirectly.

CULTURAL HUMILITY: WHAT POLICE OFFICERS NEED FOR SELF-REFLECTION, TO BE CULTURE-COMPETENT

One can master the learning behind other cultures; the question is what you do with the knowledge once received. The National Institutes of Health (NIH) defines *cultural humility* as "a lifelong process of self-reflection and self-critique whereby the individual not only learns about another's culture, but one starts with an examination of her/his own beliefs and cultural identities" (Surfin, 2019, para 2). If officers are quick to stand up and be proud of themselves individually or collectively as a unit and if they understand Black culture but are unaware of their own cultural biases, then they simply cannot say they are culturally competent and have cultural awareness. Officers must commit to examining themselves first, before engaging in training on ethical studies that pertain to the Black population. It is vital that this is a mandate, as the Black community can assess this when interventions take place where the White officer bias emerge, or they appear to assume what they believe because of their own teachings that prevent them from seeing things from a Black culture perspective. The Black community believes that when an officer checks the box on having cultural humility, it is not only a true step outside of having a humble and respectful attitude toward individuals of other cultures, but it will push officers to examine themselves and challenge their own cultural biases.

Over the past years and most recent since 2020 traumatic incidents that have shaken the nation, has given motivation for the Black community to take immediate action instill into officers the importance of getting them to start thinking about their own values, beliefs, and social position. For them to take a true evaluation of themselves they must examine within the context of the present moment and past incidences (Surfin, 2019). Taking the opportunity to examine and take the temperature of the feelings, how they reflect on incidents like George Floyd, Breonna Taylor, and other incidents from a personal standpoint, removing themselves from work duties can help officers to take another stance from the shoes of others in the Black community. Surfin states that "in order to practice true cultural humility, a person must also be aware of and sensitive to historic realities like legacies of violence and oppression against certain groups of people" (2019, Section 3 Cultural humility requires historical awareness, para. 1). Officers truly reflecting on recognizing the failures of the past and present issues to help with removing their own bias can contribute to building a better future that is founded in practices of cultural humility (Surfin, 2019).

In the past and currently the practices in place around culture humility is lacking where efforts must start with the department chief, ensuring that officers who are hired look at themselves and remove anything in their life that can be a problem with them being in the community where they are engaged with interacting with members in the Black community. This can be a preventative practice, helping with minimizing or removing any problems with any future incidents that do not alarm local or national media attention.

Implementing these practices before hiring can be a step in the right the direction, building some Black community trust toward police efforts in legitimacy and being transparent. Law enforcement views on procedural justice is a method of reinforcing the community sense of social identification and solidarity with police. Bradford et al. (2015) says that officers need to see it the same from the community perspective.

SOLUTION AND RECOMMENDATIONS

Global Social Change for Communities and Police Relationships

For there to be a global shift, positive social change will have to be addressed, starting within a community that can diffuse throughout the city, upward to the states, and across state borders and saturate globally Bush, (2020a). Likewise, this diffusion can also take place starting from the top down, and even those who feel they are in the middle can call for change to take place. This can be done by implementing theories centered around communication.

Once police have built better rapport with citizens of their community, they can have conversations to rectify past and current problems. Researchers, including Hemmer (2017), Lee (2016), and Whitten (2017), have contended that police departments can reduce any future barriers when implementing such strategies. Therefore, after a plan has been put in place to start these conversations, it is imperative that a collective effort be embraced by both the community and the police. This will ultimately improve community trust in the police and will ensure the police are accountable and transparent in sharing needed information. More communication may minimize skepticism the community may develop by allowing members to be engaged in the conversation early on. To achieve such a goal, the police would need to provide education and training on what can be shared and what information needs to be secured so that the community would have a better understanding (Bush, 2020a).

Two Communication Theories to Build Police and Black Community Relationships

There has been a lack of communication where the Black community has reached out to establish some sort of rapport only to be met with opposition. They expressed that law enforcement has echoed the same message and used this to their defense. In defense of the police perspective, this stands to be true, due to recent events in the past five years (2015–2020) and especially in the two years, with all the unrest and continued social injustice. It is vital that the one thing that drives relationships to start is simple communication where this allows parties to establish trust over time, open by being transparent, and have honest dialogues that can contribute to legitimate efforts of everyone in the circle. There are several models, frameworks, and theories that professional entities, groups, and others can apply to help stimulate conversation to move through processes to assess, look at capacity, make plans, implement, and evaluate in different approaches.

A conceptual Framework using to theories, The Diffusion of Innovation Theory (DIT) and the Policy Feedback Theory (PFT) were chosen to be incorporate in this chapter to demonstrate how communication will be the driver to establish a joint effort for police and the Black community can start closing the gap. A *conceptual framework is* an analytical tool with several variations and contexts. It is used to make conceptual distinctions and organize ideas. Strong conceptual frameworks capture something real and do this in a way that is easy to remember and apply. The DIT and PFT was used in Bush (2020a) dissertation providing a roadmap for all key players. The two theoretical frameworks can be utilized as conceptual framework model to aid and assist both the Black community and law enforcement.

Two theoretical frameworks that can be utilized to strengthen both the Black community and law enforcement. One is the *diffusion of innovation* (*DIT*), developed by Everett Rogers, which encompasses a social system in which innovation is communicated by the process of diffusion (Geary, 2016). The main tenet is having a collaborative, integrated process engaging several sectors of the community that can infuse positive change over time.

Geary (2016) describes how five major constructs are diffused throughout the community that spreads in the capacity of new ideas, innovation, adopters, communication channels, time and through a social system. More importantly Geary (2016) states that this theory has been used in tested in other law enforcement efforts to break from stagnant programing that has helped policed departments with changes. The DIT, have several players that consist of Innovators whom can represent the Black Community and members of the police department; second by Early Adopters- whom can be represented by the Black Community/Police, CJ disciplines, and some city officials, thirdly, the Early Majority-Whom can be represented by retired police officers, and city officials, fourth by Late Adopters, Law Enforcement Administration-Leadership, and Lasty Laggards-Government State Officials, Legislators and Senators. The fundamental purpose of the DIT regarding communication demonstrates how start with a few people who have creative ideas for better development of relationships, new ideas that began to spread to small group of others and over time reach those that in the beginning didn't have a vested interest that overtime come on board to implement new or revised programs.

The second theory, with which it can be combined, is the *policy feedback theory* (*PFT*) developed in the 1970s; historical institutionalism sought to explore the effects of policies while considering their context (Mettler & Sorelle, 2014). This theory allows for all the involved individuals to come to the table and be engaged in policy conversations examine old policies and discussing what new policies can be implemented. The caveat of the PFT is the initially focusing policies. This theory has a process that individuals follow for communication. It starts with identifying the policy; second, policy formation; third, policy approval, fourth, policy implementation, and the last feedback process being policy evaluation. It is similar to the DIT following process where communication take place but adding the DIT to develop a conceptual model allowed for individuals other than policy makers to be at the table along with allowing for time for new ideas, old and new policies to be examine through effective communication and bouncing back in forth reaching others over time to adopt the change being discussed. The figure below is the conceptual framework the demonstrate how the two-theory work interchangeably. Disseminating this model into an environment to help drive communication where there has been a breakdown can be a driving force to help stimulate effective communications and build strengthen relationships where the Black Community and Police can begin to close the gap and build a bridge to addressing the underlying issues and problems in community policing. The conceptual framework served as an underpinning in Bush (2020a) study that answered one of three research questions What can policy makers do to improve communication and transparency in your community?

CONCLUSION

Black Communities and Law Officers Building and Crossing Bridges Together

Lack of communication is a universal problem that contributes to failed relationships. When this is not present with police officers and the Black community, it illuminates the distrust the community has toward law enforcement. This is one of the factors that creates a gap in police relationships with the Black community that is affected by police transparency, their trust, and the legitimacy of their work. Sadly, little work has been started after the recent incidents that have sparked unrest, not just by the

Figure 1. Visual renderings of key processes in the diffusion of innovation and policy feedback theory
Note. Updated version adapted from Bush (2020a).

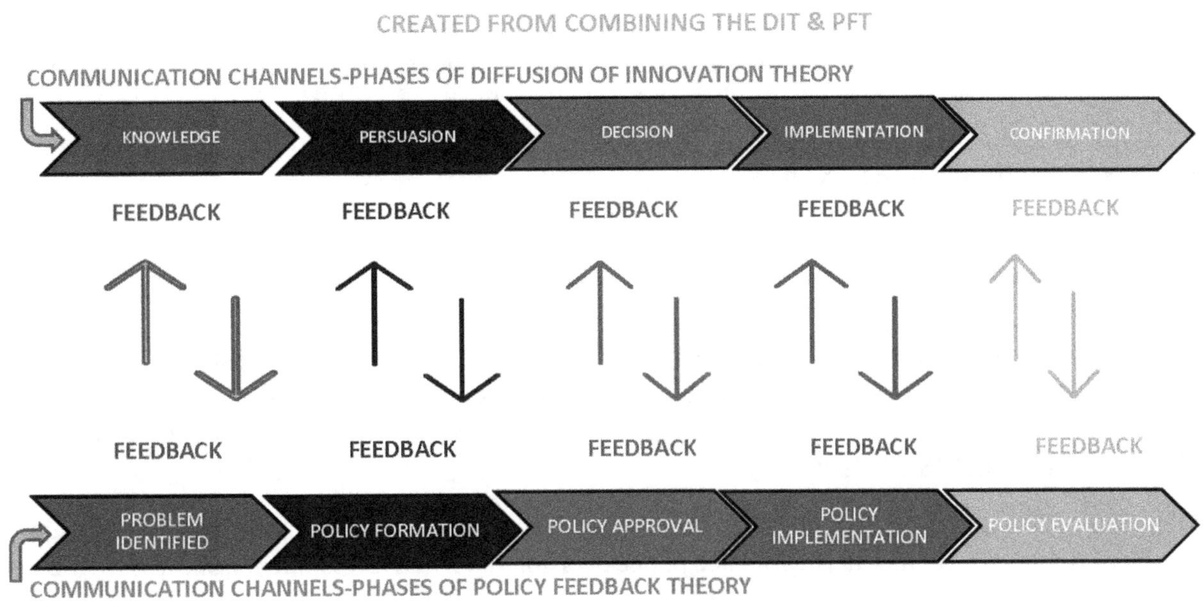

Black community but from a nation of individuals of all ethnic backgrounds who have said they can no longer allow themselves to be silent. There is a great need to build trust between the Black community and law enforcement. This issue goes both ways because of the mistrust on both sides; it will take joint efforts to bridge the gap (Bent-Goodley & Smith, 2017).

Police officers and their leaders in some parts of the country have also stepped up and recognized that there is a problem and that they have some work to do. Building this bridge cannot just rest on the shoulders of Black communities but will take a collective effort with everyone having some insight to restore old relationships. The accepted responsibility with both the Black community and police officers is that once they pledge to work with each other, they understand, as they are intertwined in the work, that they all win and lose together (Bent-Goodley & Smith, 2017). The same principles that the Black community and police officers felt worked over 30 years ago, which created a bridge where both the Black communities and police built together, is one that they all need to revisit and bring back into place to reach new heights, looking toward the future, turning corners, recognizing past failed relationships, and addressing present current incidents to prevent true Black and community relationships.

Future Research

Much has been discussed regarding how the Black community urges police officers to be intentional in building rapport and relationships with their community. The same can also be said regarding some responsibility of other city and state officials also to build relationships with their community. The theme that emerges from what is preventing police officers from having real, sustainable relationships is not showing any emotional ties, no connectedness, avoiding the community when national or local incidents are in the media, not listening or seeing what is really happening. The Black community is urging for officers to truly see the problem, look at the misconduct, and hold themselves accountable and call out what is wrong. They are urging that the police take out the earplugs and listen to Black community voices, calling for trust, transparency, and legitimacy of communication when it comes to being engaged with their community. Little research has had been published on Black police officers who grew up in the Black community they serve and what the impact on their relationships with friends, family members and the general Black members who live there. In addition, further research can extend to looking how Black officers' perceptions of relationship with their colleagues after local, and national news stories have emerged around police misconduct.

REFERENCES

Adedoyin, C., Robinson, M., Clayton, D. M., Moore, S., Jones-Eversley, S., Crosby, S., & Boamah, D. A. (2018). A synergy of contemporary activism to address police maltreatment of Black males: An intersectional analysis. *Journal of Human Behavior in the Social Environment*, *28*(8), 1078–1090. doi: 10.1080/10911359.2018.1513886

Allen, T. T., & Parker, M. M. (2013). Police officers and their perceived relationship with urban communities: Does living in the community influence police decisions? *Social Development Issues*, *35*(3), 82–95.

Antrobus, E., Bradford, B., Murphy, K., & Sargeant, E. (2015). Community Norms, Procedural Justice, and the Public's Perceptions of Police Legitimacy. *Journal of Contemporary Criminal Justice*, *31*(2), 151–170. doi:10.1177/1043986214568840

Armstead, D. R. (2019). Attitudes of black Americans towards police misconduct in an urban area (Order No. 13858102). Available from Dissertations & Theses @ Walden University; ProQuest Dissertations & Theses Global. *Social Sciences*, ▪▪▪, 2315248494.

Bent-Goodley, T., & Smith, C. M. (2017). An African-centered approach to community policing. *Journal of Human Behavior in the Social Environment*, *27*(1/2), 92–99. doi:10.1080/10911359.2016.1266856

Birzer, M. L., & Nolan, R. E. (2002). Learning strategies of selected urban police related to community policing. *Policing*, *25*(2), 242. http://dx.doi.org.ezp.waldenulibrary.org/10.1108/13639510210429356

Bonesteel, M. (2020, June 10). Athletes' petition calls for congress to end qualified immunity for police. *The Washington Post*. https://www.washingtonpost.com/sports/2020/06/10/athletes-petition-calls-congress-end-qualified-immunity-police/

Bradford, B., Hohl, K., Jackson, J., & MacQueen, S. (2015). Obeying the Rules of the Road: Procedural Justice, Social Identity, and Normative Compliance. *Journal of Contemporary Criminal Justice*, *31*(2), 171–191. doi:10.1177/1043986214568833

Bush, C. L. (2020a). *Public perceptions of delays in the release of police body-worn camera footage* (Publication No. 8442) [Doctoral dissertation, Walden University]. Walden Dissertations and Doctoral Studies. https://scholarworks.waldenu.edu/dissertations/8442

Bush, C. L. (2020b). Public perceptions of delays in the release of police body-worn camera footage. *Journal of Social Change*, *13*(1), 1–17. doi:10.5590/JOSC.2020.13.1.01

Carlos, H. (2019). Disqualifying immunity: How qualified immunity exacerbates police misconduct and why congress must destroy it. *Southern University Law Review. Southern University and A & M College. School of Law*, *46*(2), 283. doi:10.2139srn.3334586

Cooley, W., Bemiller, M., Jefferis, E., & Penix, R. (2019). Neighborhood by neighborhood: Community policing in a rust belt city. *Policing, 42*(2), 226-239. http://dx.doi.org.ezp.waldenulibrary.org/10.1108/PIJPSM-01-2018-0002

DeVan, K. (2016, September 22). Harrisburg Researchers Suggest Community Policing to Build Trust in Police States News Services. *Penn State News*. https:/link.gale.com

Doane, E., & Cumberland, D. M. (2018). Community policing: Using needs assessment to gain understanding before implementing. *Performance Improvement Quarterly*, *31*(2), 165–187. doi:10.1002/piq.21264

Gau, J. M., & Brunson, R. K. (2015). Procedural Injustice, Lost Legitimacy, and Self-Help: Young Males' Adaptations to Perceived Unfairness in Urban Policing Tactics. *Journal of Contemporary Criminal Justice*, *31*(2), 132–150. doi:10.1177/1043986214568841

Geary, P. (2016). *The Right to Remain Silent: Police department adoption and deployment of social media* (Dissertation). Retrieved from ProQuest Dissertations & Theses Global. (UMI No. 10147470)

Hemmer, J. W. (2017). *Exploring police beliefs in community-oriented policing and community trust: A multiple case study* (Dissertation). ProQuest Dissertations & Theses Global. (1965399982)

Higgins, E. M., Overstreet, S., Coffey, B., & Fisher, B. W. (2020). "Bridging the gap": School resource officers as bridge builders in the community policing era. *Journal of Crime and Justice*, *43*(4), 433–448. doi:10.1080/0735648X.2019.1704837

Jackman, T. (2016, September 16). Fraternal Order of Police union endorses Trump. *The Washington Post*. https://www.washingtonpost.com/news/true-crime/wp/2016/09/16/fraternal-order-of-police-union-endorses-trump/

Jackson, J. L., Sr. (2020, June 18). Police reform was never going to be easy—but now's the time. *The Washington Informer, 55*(36), 26. https://www.washingtoninformer.com/jesse-jackson-police-reform-was-never-going-to-be-easy-but-nows-the-time/

Johnson, K. (2020, June 10). Union: 'We don't want to protect bad cops'. *USA Today*, p. 3A. https:link.gale.com/apps/doc/A626234671/OVIC?u+minn4020&xid=4df20ec9

Kamalu, N. C., & Onveozili, E. C. (2018). A critical analysis of the 'broken windows' policing in New York city and its impact: Implications for the criminal justice system and the African American community. *African Journal of Criminology and Justice Studies: AJCJS*, *11*(1), 71–94.

Kocorowski, J. (2020, August 29). *Melvin Gordon Reacts to Jacob Blake Shooting: 'It Just Shocked Me'*. https://www.si.com/college/wisconsin/football/melvin-gordon-kenosha-jacob-blake-Jake

Lee, J., Lim, H., & Lee, H. (2015). Differential social distance and confidence in the police. *International Journal of Police Science & Management*, *17*(3), 147–154. doi:10.1177/1461355715596305

Lee, T. (2016). Tennessee citizens police academies: Program and participant characteristics. *American Journal of Criminal Justice, 41*(2), 236–254.

Liederbach, J., Fritsch, E. J., Carter, D. L., & Bannister, A. (2008). Exploring the limits of collaboration in community policing: A direct comparison of police and citizen views. *Policing, 31*(2), 271-291. doi:http://dx.doi.org.ezp.waldenulibrary.org/10.1108/13639510810878721

Mandery, E. J. (1994). Qualified immunity or absolute impunity? the moral hazards of extending qualified immunity to lower-level public officials. *Harvard Journal of Law & Public Policy, 17*(2), 479. https://ezp.waldenulibrary.org

McFarland, M. J., Taylor, J., McFarland, C. A. S., & Friedman, K. L. (2018). Perceived unfair treatment by police, race, and telomere length: A Nashville community-based sample of Black and white men. *Journal of Health and Social Behavior, 59*(4), 585–600. doi:10.1177/0022146518811144 PMID:30417689

McMenamin, D. (2020, August 25) *LeBron James says Black community 'terrified' of police conduct.* https://www.espn.com/nba/story/_/id/29735483/lebron-james-says-Black-community-terrified-result-police-conduct-Dave

Mettler, S., & Sorelle, M. (2014). Policy feedback theory. In P. A. Sabatier & C. M. Weible (Eds.), *Theories of the policy process* (3rd ed., pp. 151–181). Westview Press.

Patel, C. (2020). Tackling police racism. *The World Today*, *76*(4), 12–15.

Patterson, J. (1995). Community policing: Learning the lessons of history. *FBI Law Enforcement Bulletin*, *64*(11), 5.

Pelura, G. (2020). Note: Section 1983 & Qualified Immunity: Qualifying the death of due process and Americas Most Vulnerable Classes since 1871. Can it Be Fixed. *William & Mary Journal of Race, Gender, and Social Justice, 26*, 749. https: advance-lexis.com.ezp.waldenulibary.org

Pontes, C. (2017). Can bad police officers be kept off the streets? giving control back to the police chiefs. *Journal of California Law Enforcement*, *51*(2), 15–20. https://ezp.waldenulibrary.org/login?qurl=https%3A%2F%2Fwww.proquest.com%2Ftrade-journals%2Fcan-bad-police-officers-be-kept-off-streets%2Fdocview%2F1937605636%2Fse-2%3Faccountid%3D14872

Quinn, R. C., & Hope, C. E., & Cryer-Couper, Q. R. (2019). Neighborhood cohesion and procedural justice in policing among Black adults: The moderating role of cultural race-related stress. *Journal of Community Psychology*. Advance online publication. doi:10/1002/jcop.22251

Ray, J. M. (Ed.). (2014). *Rethinking community policing*. LFB Scholarly Publishing.

Reinwald, C. H. (2020). A one-two punch: How qualified immunity's double dose of reasonableness dooms excessive force claims in the fourth circuit. *North Carolina Law Review*, *98*(3), 665–687. https://scholarship.law.unc.edu/nclr/vol98/iss3/7

Romanucci, A., Raveendran, B., & Burton, C. (2020, September). Confronting Qualified Immunity and the 'Reasonable 'Officer Standard. *Trial (Boston, Mass.)*, *56*(9), 24. https: links.gale.com

Schwartz, J. C. (2020). After Qualified Immunity. *Columbia Law Review*, *120*(2), 309–388.

Surfin, J. (2019). *3 things to know: Cultural humility*. Hogg Foundation for Mental Health. https://hogg.utexas.edu/3-things-to-know-cultural-humility

Wahl, R. (2017). No justice, no peace? The police, people of color, and the paradox of protecting human rights. *Human Rights Quarterly, 39*(4), 811-831. http://dx.doi.org.ezp.waldenulibrary.org/10.1353/hrq.2017.0050

Wear, M. (2015, September 18). Hold police fraternities accountable. *USA Today*, p. 9A.

Whitten, E. L. (2017). *A case study of the effects the current community policing models have on rural police leaders in the south-central United States* (Dissertation). ProQuest Dissertations & Theses Global. (1874980994)

Wiggins, O. (2020, October 1). As decision nears on reform proposals, Maryland lawmakers struggle over police "Bill of Rights." *The Washington Post*.

KEY TERMS AND DEFINITIONS

Conceptual Framework: An analytical tool with several variations and contexts. It is used to make conceptual distinctions and organize ideas. Strong conceptual frameworks capture something real and do this in a way that is easy to remember and apply.

Fraternal Order of Police (FOP): A fraternal organization consisting of sworn law enforcement officers in the United States. The organization attempts to improve the working conditions of law enforcement officers and the safety of those they serve through education, legislation, information, community involvement, and employee representation.

Law Enforcement Officers' Bill of Rights (LEOBR or LEOBoR): Intended to protect American law enforcement personnel from investigation and prosecution arising from conduct during the official performance of their duties and provide them with privileges based on due process beyond those normally provided to other citizens.

Chapter 5
An Assessment of Unethical Work Behavior Among Police Personnel in Nigeria

Olugbemiga Samuel AFOLABI
Obafemi Awolowo University, Ile Ife, Nigeria & Osun State University, Osogbo, Nigeria

Adeyeye Adebowale
Osun State University Osogbo, Nigeria

Olumide Omodunbi
https://orcid.org/0000-0003-3432-2940
Osun State University Osogbo, Nigeria

ABSTRACT

The Nigerian police force is an institution established to protect the lives and properties of residents. Some of her duties include tackling armed robbery, banditry, recovery of stolen assets, investigation of cases, and settling violence-related issues among persons. Just like every other institution, her operations are premised on certain ethical codes and conduct which guarantees checks and balances in her relationship with ordinary citizens. Maximum productivity can be achieved by the Nigerian police if only they display ethical behaviour in the discharge of their lawful duties to the public. Growing unethical work behaviour among Nigerian police officers has drawn attention to the various despicable and condemnable acts perpetrated by some personnel. This study makes a scholarly attempt to investigate the trend of the unethical work behaviour in the Nigerian police force. Using content analysis, the findings suggest that only a handful of Nigerian police officers display professionalism and ethical behaviour in the discharge of their duties.

DOI: 10.4018/978-1-7998-6884-2.ch005

INTRODUCTION

Policing has existed for decades in human history. Policing has derived its importance from the dire need of individuals to be protected lawfully from another individual and its relevance to achieving security has continued to sustain its value through the years. Historically, policing has been traced to the reign of Roman Emperor Augustus when highly trained Praetorian Guards protected the palace and the emperor. They were responsible to the emperor and certain rules guided their operations. (Dempsey & Frost, 2008). Iwarimie-Jaja (2010) opined that in Nigeria, indigenous policing existed before colonial rule. Men of stature and strength who had native intelligence performed the duty of a policing in local communities in the most effective way.

In modern times, policing has increasingly gained more importance as crime rates continue to increase in developing countries. This is not to say that the developed world is entirely free of crime. However, the forces of poverty, inequality, and poor governance has greatly contributed to increased crime rate, which calls for more organised and effective policing (Ojukwu, 2016). Policing refers to professional work conducted by a police officer whose primary duty is to enforce the laws through means that are within legal jurisdiction. It is expected that police officers respect human rights in the discharge of their duties. Adherence to ethical codes by the police ordinarily would lead to respect for human rights and professionalism. Ethics in this regard, therefore, means abiding be a clear set of rules, respect for other people, fairness, and honesty. Ethical behaviour simply means the display of these values by individuals in relationship with others (Dibie, 2014).

The Nigerian Police force was established in 1930 and was later enshrined in section 194 of the 1979 constitution (BBC, 2009). Since then, the role of a Nigerian police officer has been the enforcement of law, maintenance of internal peace and security, and protection of lives and properties. Recently, tension between the populace and the Nigerian police force has increased because of negligence of constitutional duties by the Nigerian police officers. It seems the police have wandered away from their primary assignments toward harassing, killing, and extorting those they have sworn an oath to protect. As noted by David et al. (2015), there is growing concern among the Nigerian populace regarding unprofessional activities and behaviour of Nigerian police officers which includes pay offs on the roads, bribery, extortion, and false accusations on ordinary citizens. These have further damaged public trust in the Nigerian Police force so that the citizens see police officers as enemies.

Ladapo (2011) also observed that those of low socioeconomic status are always in constant fear of extortion when they come across police officers. For many years, the relationship between the Nigerian police force and the populace has been poor due to a lengthy history of unethical conduct and unprofessional acts of the NPF. What are the unethical work behaviors among the Nigerian Police officers? Are there internal and external contributing factors to the rising trend of these behaviors? What should be done to curtail these behaviors? This chapter seeks to provide answers to these questions. To achieve this, the chapter employs an analytical and empirical review method in assessing the unethical work behaviour among the Nigeria police force. The paper relies on secondary data sourced from journals, newspapers, and internet.

THEORETICAL FRAMEWORK

This chapter relies on deontological ethics theory. The major proponent of the theory is Immanuel Kant. Kant proposed that all human actions within an organisation had consequences that can be right or wrong. Thus, actions are judged as ethical or unethical based on duty, or intentions of an actor. Kant spoke of two kinds of imperatives. These are the hypothetical and categorical imperatives. Hypothetical imperatives are conditional. For example, "if you want to achieve X, you should do Y." Categorical imperatives are unconditional in that they must be obeyed under any conditions. For example, "You should do Y." The categorical imperative is much more required for performing a duty which is objectively practical according to law. To Kant, every action has a maxim. Maxim refers to a rule or principle. So, people should act that the maxim of their will could always hold at the same time as principle establishing universal law. Kant attempted to provide a universal law that is true under any circumstance for everyone. This theory emphasises universal morality. The principle of this theory can be summed up by the phrase "treat others as you would like to be treated." According to Kantian ethics, if an action passes the test of categorical imperative, the action is ethical.

This theory rules out certain practices such as theft, coercion, extortion, and misuse of power in government as well as within the private business organisations. This theory gives credence to the popular dissatisfaction in unethical work behaviour of some Nigerian police officers. There are certain principles that guide the operations of the NPF which are purposely neglected for personal gain. The categorical imperative condemns such behaviours, which are detrimental to the reputation of the institution. Their actions can also be judged ethical or unethical based on established code of conduct.

Overview of the Nigeria Police Force

The Nigerian Police Force (NPF) is a product of colonial government born out of thirty members of consular guard in 1861 in Lagos Colony, which later transitioned into an armed paramilitary organization called the Hausa constabulary in 1879. Later, in 1897, Lagos Police was formed while, in 1894, the Niger coast constabulary was formed in Calabar (Ikogho, 2006). By the early 1900s, the Royal Niger Company had two police forces: Northern and Southern Police force. They operated differently until April 1930 when they were merged into the modern Nigeria Police Force we all know today (Chukwuma, 2014). Ojukwu (2016) noted that the Nigerian Police Force is ruled by a Nigerian Police Council comprising of president of the nation as the chairperson, the Governor of each state, the chairperson of the police service commission, and the inspector General of Police. Furthermore, Ojukwu (2016) observed that the force covers 5,000 villages; 5,515 Police stations; 115 Police decisions; 123 area commands; 37 commands, and the police headquarters in Abuja. Each state has a commissioner of police representing the inspector general of police. The organisational structure of the police force is shown below:

- **Force headquarters**
- **Zonal headquarters**
- **State Commands headquarters**
- **Divisional Police headquarters**
- **Police station**
- **Police post**
- **Village post**

Chiemelle (2014) noted that the force is divided into administration, an anti-fraud section, a central criminal registry, a special anti-robbery squad, an x-squad, general investigation, unit, special fraud unit, legal section, forensic science laboratory, Interpol liaison, homicide, anti-human trafficking, special branch, and the CID investigation division Kaduna annex.

The Nigerian Police Force's code of conduct outlines what ethical rules of conduct each police officer must follow. The code represents an accountability mechanism that applies to all officers.

The essence of this code is to help police officers determine what is right or wrong in all their actions while on and off duty. The code consists of the following.

- Primary responsibilities of police officers
- Mode of performance of duty
- Use of discretion
- Use of force
- Personal professional capabilities
- Cooperation with other police officers and agencies
- Confidentiality
- Integrity

A police officer operates as part of the state's machinery in that the officers are empowered to enforce state laws in the best conceivable way without comprising the fundamental human rights of its people. The police are to act within the law to protect lives and properties, maintain peace, safeguard the rights of persons, and respond crime. They also conduct stop and search operations as a proactive approach to preventing crime.

In the discharge of their primary duties, police officers will act in an acceptable and ethical manner. They will perform such duties impartially and evaluate events objectively. This means all residents will be treated equally. Officers will not be influenced by personal feelings, animosities nor accept any bribes in the discharge of their duties. They will also conduct themselves in an appropriate manner and exude professionalism to inspire confidence and respect for the position of public trust they hold. They will also strive to seek maximum cooperation from the public through a friendly, civil relationship. Police officers will also use their discretion in solving complicated matters within the law. The use of force will only be necessary if after negotiation and persuasion, offenders are unwilling to yield to law. Police officers will be careful not to inflict cruel injuries on persons in using force as that might lead to inhumane treatment.

Police officers will make concerted efforts to improve their professional capacity by learning more about effective policing. It could be in form of pursuing an advanced degree aimed at acquiring a prominent level of knowledge and competence that is essential for efficient performance of their duties. Police officers will also collaborate with other specialized agencies, non-governmental organisations, and civil-society groups in pursuit of justice. They will also assist other police officers in enforcing state laws. Secret information given to police officers by an individual in the process of investigation will be kept confidential. To safeguard the life of the individual who has provided the information, safeguarding the individual's identity is paramount.

A police officer will not engage in corrupt acts such as extortion, bribery, intimidation, and harassment. The officer will earn respect from the public through his ethical work behaviour and encourage others not to accept gifts and favours that could be interpreted as seeking to cause them to refrain from doing their job honestly.

From the foregoing, the public expectations of an ideal police officer include:

- Storing and keeping track of information that was obtained.
- Becoming an expert at conducting stops and frisks, making arrests, conducting searches, and participating in covert operations all within the ambits of the law.
- The officer must be well rounded and comprehensive. They must understand the multifaceted communication course, and the barriers that often exist within the process and within society.
- The officer must be properly schooled in the field of making field enquiries, interviewing, and interrogating individuals, and in doing so, protect the constitutional rights of victims, suspects, and witnesses.

UNETHICAL WORK BEHAVIOUR AMONG THE NIGERIAN POLICE FORCE

It is of our opinion that the police do not respect their uniform and the code of conduct despite the many training programs intended to improve the development of officers upon selection and training (Davis, 2015). Akubo (2015) noted that the character of Nigerian Police Force has been associated with brutality, extra-judicial killings, unlawful detention of suspects, demanding payment for bail, search, and arrest without warrants, mounting of illegal roadblocks for the purpose of extorting money, use of alcohol and other drugs, harassment, and intimidation of political opponents of ruling parties. They have been targets of uncomplimentary headlines in many dailies for many inconceivable aberrations to duty.

It is unethical for a police officer to arrest an individual perceived to be involved in a crime without a warrant. This means it is not within the law for a police officer to arrest a person without evidence of an offence. It has been revealed that Nigerian police officers have arrested innocent individuals by relying on guesswork, or with the intention of forcefully demanding a sum of money before they are released. Odey (2017) noted that police often raid businesses, marketplaces, restaurants, and conduct illegal mass arrests. Illegal arrests and detention without trial are regarded as a violation of fundamental human right to personal liberty and dignity as stated in the section 35(6) of the 1999 constitution of Nigeria. Police officers have continued to unlawfully arrest and detain people despite the provision of law against unlawful arrest and detention. Odey noted further that many poor helpless citizens are often easily implicated by police officers and made to remain in jail because they could not afford to pay illegal bail charges. In recent times, a few lawyers have been able to challenge the bail irregularities. Even though the words, “bail is free” has been written in front of all police stations, police officers are seen negotiating bail charges in front of the notice.

The “end SARS” campaign was a response to extrajudicial killings and murder perpetrated by the SARS, a section of the Nigeria police force. Nigerian youths took to the streets and utilized the social media in calling for an end to police brutality in the country. The SARS operatives are known for stopping young people on the streets and demanding to go through their phones. Mere ownership of an iPhone is enough to make one a suspect. Some who refuse to grant the police access to their phones have been reportedly tortured and killed (Allwell, 2020). Human rights watch groups (2018) also attest that Nigerian citizens have been killed indiscriminately by the police. For example, Ebun Timilehin, a nine-year-old girl was killed by a stray bullet triggered by a SARS operative in Lagos in an unsuccessful attempt to extort money from a commercial bus driver at the checkpoint. In March 2019, SARS operatives, in an attempt to arrest one of the boys of a major music producer, killed a man named Kolade Johnson. Kolade was said to be watching a football match in a cinema remarkably close to his area at Mangoro, Ikeja, Lagos.

On March 20, 2019, a commercial motorcyclist named Ademola Moshood, was shot dead by a police officer for refusing to part with money being extorted for a bribe. On March 13, 2018, a police officer was sentenced to three-year jail term for shooting a commercial motorcyclist for not providing the money for a bribe (Omilona, 2019). It should be noted that "police order 237" statutorily permits the police to shoot at suspects attempting to evade arrests, however, today, the provision has been abused by killing suspects who have not attempted to evade arrest (Police Act, 2004).

Corruption is prevalent within the Nigerian police department. A prospective officer is introduced to the culture of corruption in the force at the point of application. The officer must tip someone to get an employment form. Desperate job seekers even pay between 30,000 and 40,000 naira (financial currency in Nigeria) to enter the Nigeria police training colleges (Okonkwo, 2004). Human rights watch groups (2010) claim that bribery and extortion are major forms of corruption among the police. According to its report, instead of ensuring road worthiness and checking vehicle licenses, the police extort money from private and commercial drivers. Often, commercial drivers do not want to be delayed by the police at checkpoints, knowing the intention of police, and they quickly give out a minimum of 50 naira to allow free passage. Punch newspaper (2012) claimed that police officers once arrested a driver of an ambulance in Lagos who did not commit an offence but was not allowed to leave until he paid a bribe. They go as far as making false accusations against the detained individuals for personal gain. The Democratic Socialist Movement (2010) noted that bribery and extortion occur frequently between police officers and members of the public. Corruption in the Nigeria police force continues to compromise public confidence and trust.

Regrettably, the chain of corruption stems from the top to the bottom of the police force (Human Rights Watch Group, 2010). Hills (2012) observed that there has been a succession of corrupt senior leaders in the Nigeria police force. Daniel (2013) confirmed that Tafa Balogun, a former Inspector General, was convicted in 2005 for accepting bribes and money laundering. Sunday Ehindero, the immediate successor of Tafa Balogun also tolerated a system of policing that depended on bribes, exploitation, and intimidation. He was arrested while attempting to flee the office with the sum of two hundred million naira as payment for electoral malpractice during the 2007 presidential election. Given this situation, it is clear that corrupt leadership in NPF has provided enabling grounds for officers at grassroots and local levels to perpetrate unethical practices. Adebule (2019) noted that police who should protect lives and properties are caught up in the act of smoking Indian hemp while on duty along with using heroin and cannabis, as well as drinking of alcohol in both hidden and public places. They often leave their checkpoints and other strategic spots to extort money, after which they go to alcohol drinking establishments to spend the bribery money.

FACTORS CONTRIBUTING TO UNETHICAL WORK BEHAVIOUR AMONG THE POLICE

Uncontrolled emotions and reactions to events in the discharge of duty has contributed to unethical work behaviour among the police. The police are armed with guns and assault rifles, which are naturally intimidating to the public. In fact, Susan (1999) argued that assault rifles should not be carried in the public by the police because of their unchecked emotions and unprofessional reactions to tense situations. While it is important to recognize that police officers are also humans, and that they can also get angry, anger in the discharge of their civic duties could lead to unprofessional acts. Oluwafefihan (2019) noted that most police officers have trouble controlling their own emotions while attempting to maintain order, provide service and controlling crime.

Poor remuneration is another major contributing factor to an increasing trend of unethical work behaviour among the police. Umeagbalasi and Ijeoma (2013) observed that overall welfare packages and necessary structures needed by the police for the effective discharge of their duties are grossly inadequate. While politicians and senior public officers plunder the wealth with impunity, the miserable salary, and emoluments of police officers to all intents and purposes is simply unacceptable. Amos, Francis and Les (2011) gave credence to the foregoing by noting that police recruits in Nigeria are the lowest paid in Africa. A police recruit earns an annual salary of 108,233.00 naira. Even the next rank earns maximum of 48,619.16 naira annually. The pay is not even enough to cater for basic lifestyle needs. It is believed that this complex web of system-induced problems has led police officers to engage in unethical acts of extortion and bribery to supplement their incomes.

CONCLUSION AND RECOMMENDATIONS

This chapter assessed the unethical work behaviour among police officers in Nigeria. A scholarly review revealed that there has been a lengthy culture of unethical work behaviour among the police engaging in acts of extortion, bribery, illegal roadblocks, and falsification of evidence for personal gains, favouritism, and inability to control anger and emotions, and false accusations, which have damaged public confidence in the police institution in Nigeria. This chapter also revealed that the various unethical acts are motivated by internal and external forces which has contributed to a deep-seated, complex culture in Nigerian policing. While it is easy to attribute police unethical work behaviour to poor living conditions and a meager salary, one should not forget that there are other Nigerians who are struggling to survive, yet do not engage in crime, but rather adhere to Nigerian law. We can therefore say that upholding personal and institutional integrity and professionalism requires more of reformed mind. The recurring unethical acts among the police requires drastic measures, which if not taken, will lead the country further down the wrong path in the not too-distant future. In response, we offer the following recommendations.

- Periodic training and retraining of police officers on professional conduct and ethics to aid better public service delivery.
- Implementation and execution of stern punishment for officers caught in unprofessional conduct on and off duty which could take the form of dismissal from the police, suspension, as the case may be. This will be done without favouritism to deter other police officer from engaging in similar or other unprofessional acts.
- General overhauling of the entire police system, giving priority to infrastructural enhancement and boost in housing, transportation, health, and other benefits for proper performance of duty.
- The Nigeria government should consider the suggestion of former US Assistant Attorney General, Laurie O. Robinson who recommended taking the guns away from vulnerable and dangerous police officers whenever they are engaged in civil matters; and codify the international tactics that would save lives in citizen's encounter with the Nigeria police.

- Develop recognition awards for stellar police service and ensure that promotions are only given to honest and hardworking police officers to encourage ethical work behaviour among the police.
- Engage police officers in remedial and advanced training programs that focus on police – citizen relationships similar to that of community policing initiatives.

REFERENCES

Akubo, A. (2015). Institutional Decay and Corrupt/Unethical Practices: Problems and Prospects for the Police Force in Nigeria. *IOSR Journal of Humanities and Social Science*, *20*(8), 66–72.

Alao, B., & Adeyemi, O. (2019). Ethics and governance of the Nigeria police force: A study of the Lagos state police command (2015-2016). *Global Scientific Journal*, *7*(2).

Allwell, R. (2020). *End SARS: The Movement against Police Brutality in Nigeria* (Vol. 33). Harvard Law School.

Aremu, A., Pakes, F., & Johnston, L. (2011). The moderating effect of emotional intelligence on the reduction of corruption in the Nigerian Police. *Police Practice and Research*, *12*(3), 195–208. doi:10.1080/15614263.2010.536724

Chiemelie, E. (2014). *Nigerian Police since 1960. THISDAY Newspaper.*

Daniels, F. A. (2012). A Historical Survey of Amalgamation of the Northern and Southern police departments of Nigeria in 1930. *European Scientific Journal*, *8*(18), 205–217.

Davis, R. C., Ortiz, C. W., Euler, S., & Kuykendall, L. (2015). Revisiting "Measuring What Matters": Developing a Suite of Standardized Performance Measures for Policing. *Police Quarterly*, *18*(4), 469–495. doi:10.1177/1098611115598990

Dempsy, J. S., & Forst, L. (2008). An Introduction to Policing (4th ed.). Academic Press.

Dibie, R. (2007). Ethical Leadership, Social Responsibility and Corruption in Nigeria. *International Review of Politics and Development*, *5*(1), 1–42.

Dibie, R. (2014). *Public Administration Theory, Analysis and Application*. Babcock University Press.

Esfahani, A., & Shahbazi, G. (2014). Workplace bullying in nursing: The case of Azerbaijan Province, Iran. *Iranian Journal of Nursing and Midwifery Research*, *19*(4), 409–415. http://ijnmr.mui.ac.ir/index.php/ijnm PMID:25183984

Gill, H., Meyer, J. P., Lee, K., Shin, K. H., & Yoon, C. Y. (2011). Affective and continuance commitment and their relations with deviant workplace behaviors in Korea. *Asia Pacific Journal of Management*, *28*(3), 595–607. doi:10.100710490-009-9165-0

Hills, A. (2012). Lost in translation: Why Nigeria's police don't implement democratic reforms. *The Royal Institute of International Affairs*, *88*(4), 740–755. doi:10.1111/j.1468-2346.2012.01099.x

Human Rights Watch. (2010). *Everyone's in on the Game Corruption and Human Rights Abuses by the Nigeria Police Force*. Available: http://www.hrw.org

Human Rights Watch. (2018). *Rest in Pieces: Police Torture and Deaths in Custody*. https://www.refworld.org/docid/45d2f62c2.html

Ibietan, J., & Joshua, S. (2013). Ethics in the Nigerian Public Sector: A Discourse. *The Public Administration and Social Policies Review V, 1*(10).

Ikogho, J. (2006). *Police Companion and Public Guide*. Law View Consult.

Iwarimie-Jaja, D. (2010). *Police and Policing in the Nigeria Political system*. Portharcourt: Pearl Publishers.

Ladapo, O. A. (2011). Effective investigations, a pivot to efficient criminal justice administration: Challenges in Nigeria. *African Journal of Criminology and Justice Studies*, *5*(1 &2), 79–94.

Odey, R. (2017). *Corruption, harassment, and injustice. Unlawful conduct of the Nigerian police towards civilians*. GRIN Verlag. https://www.grin.com/document/354593

Ojukwu, E. C. (2016). *Discovering the police: An excursion into police personality, powers, performance, and prudence*. Kraft Books Limited.

Oluwafifehan, O. (2019). *Protest against SARS in Nigeria*. Credit/opinionnigeria.com.

Omilana, T. (2019). Police abuse of power and limits of punishments. 17th April 2021: Twitter/NGR Senate. Police Act Cap., LFN 2004.

The Nigeria Police Force. (n.d.). Retrieved from www.npf.gov.ng

Umeagbolesi & Ijeoma. (2013). Institutional decay and corrupt/unethical practices: Problems and prospects for the police force in Nigeria. *IOSR Journal of Humanities and Social Science.*, *20*(8), 66–72.

KEY TERMS AND DEFINITIONS

Ethical Work Behaviour: Denotes acceptable patterns of action established in the code of conduct of an organisation which are required of every employee. These principles are meant to promote and sustain peaceful co-existence among employees in the workplace and aid professionalism in rendering service. Ethical behaviour refers to standard moral expectations necessary for building the reputation of individuals. Organisations are wary of those with a bad reputation. Therefore, those who do not follow the ethical rules at work are subject to disciplinary action (Hearst newspaper, 2018). Is it ethical to pay bribe to obtain a business contract? Is it ethical to do personal business on the organisation's time? Is it ethical for police officers to keep a suspect behind bars beyond 24 hours? It is obvious that despite one's initial inclination in response to these questions, the major point of it all is to remind organizations to operate in accordance with high ethical and moral standards.

Ethics: Refers to a moral standard used in determining what is right or wrong within a group, organization, and society. It has its roots in the Greek word, "ethikos," meaning custom (Ibietan & Joshua, 2013). Dibie (2007) provided a similar understanding of ethics in that it is similar to morality. To Dibie

(2007), it is a philosophical concept which is used in determining the proper course of action. To Ojokwu (2016), it also means adhering to a set of rules guiding the conduct of members of a profession. To Ojokwu (2016), the Nigerian Police Force (NPF) has set of rules which guides their actions, reactions, and response to events in the discharge of their duties. These rules are called ethics.

Unethical Work Behaviour: Refers to discretionary behaviour that tends to be damaging to the organisation as well as its members. It intends to violate appropriate norms and policies at workplace. Such behaviours include sexual harassment, lying, theft, and an unnecessary delay in attending to customers (Gill, Meyer, Lee, Shin, & Yoon, 2011; Reid & Ramarajan, 2016). Many executives, administrators and social scientists see unethical behavior as a cancer working on the fabric of society in too many of today's organizations and beyond. The crises of unethical behavior involve employees at all levels of the organization. For example, some local government officials in Nigeria have been tipped off before an impending raid, and it has been reported that some police officers drink alcohol during work hours, which can obviously affect their work behaviours and actions (Eshfani & Shabee, 2014).

Chapter 6
Reform the Police and End the Violence:
What Works Between Community Policing and State Police in North Central Nigeria

Daskyes Yohanna Gulleng
University of Jos, Nigeria

ABSTRACT

Policing in Nigeria has never been this challenging. Aside from accusations of violence and brutality, the police are widely regarded as ineffective and inefficient. While insecurity surges across the country, regional security networks are springing up in an uncoordinated manner, raising questions about ownership and control. This further gave rise to agitations for either community policing and state police from the political class, civil societies, and traditional institutions. This chapter situates police violence in the context of the popular #EndSARS# protest and reviews issues surrounding police reforms in Nigeria. Within the context of the challenging insecurity in the north central region, the chapter looks at the merits and demerits of community police and state police to determine what works and makes recommendations on the appropriate policing strategy in the region.

INTRODUCTION

From ancient times, policing has been part of every society and a necessary ingredient for order maintenance. Its absence could lead to increased crime rates and a needless loss of lives and property. This underscores the critical roles the police play in maintaining law and order and in crime prevention and internal security. However, there are variations in the nature and pattern of policing depending on the historical experience and institutional preferences of each political community (Swhartz, 2015). Police actions and conducts reflect the political and economic character of the society and what those in power are willing or able to tolerate or condone (Oladipo, 2013). Similarly, Alderson argued that when the society is adjudged to be corrupt, it deserves, and gets corrupt police; when it is under a totalitarian leadership, it

DOI: 10.4018/978-1-7998-6884-2.ch006

gets distrustful police while violent societies get violent police. A tolerant society on the other hand gets tolerant police and wise societies get restrained and legitimate police (as cited in Alemika, 2018, p.14).

In Nigeria, policing has never been this challenging. Aside from accusations of violence and brutality which have historical antecedence, it is highly regarded as ineffective, inefficient, and corrupt. This is not an isolated case for the police but a reflection of Nigeria's failing security architecture and state craft. While insecurity surges across the country, regional security networks are springing up in an uncoordinated manner, raising questions about ownership and control. In the North Central part of the country where attacks and kidnappings of farmers and herders are common occurrences, the police are facing more daunting tasks of securing lives as their professionalism is continuously being put to test.

At the center of this chapter are issues relating to police violence and the search for a policing strategy considered more effective in crime control and internal security. In specific terms, the chapter examines the extent of police violence towards its citizens and how reform policies have fared over time. Focusing on the North Central Nigeria, the chapter contextualizes the manner in which the police manage emerging and changing security challenge in the region. It also seeks to bring to light the unending debate about community policing and state police from the political class, civil societies, the police and traditional institutions with a view to recommending the most appropriate strategy for better policing in the country.

BACKGROUND

The history of policing in Nigeria can be traced to the colonial period when the British authorities imposed various aspects of their cultures and traditions including politics and economy on captured territories as a way of expanding their influence and dominance (Audu, 2016). During this period, the British colonial government established the police force and employed them as constabulary and para-military forces for colonial wars and punitive expeditions. In many areas, the police engaged in the brutal subjugation of communities and the suppression of resistance to colonial rule (Jonson, 2013). This orientation affected the psyche of the Nigeria Police Force (NPF) and it continued through the period of transition from military rule to democratic rule (Alemika & Chukwuma, 2000).

In 1992 for example, a unit of the NPF was created known as the Special Anti-Robbery Squad (SARS) to respond to increasing rates of violent crimes. The mandate of officers in the unit included arrest, investigation and prosecution of suspected armed robbers, murderers, kidnappers, hired assassins and other suspected violent criminals. Initially, they were to operate undercover with plain clothes and plain vehicles without any security or government insignia and never to carry arms in public. However, officers began to deviate from their original mandate of covert operation to mounting of roadblocks, extortion of money from citizens and started carrying arms in public (Malumfashi 2020). Today, activities of SARS have further complicated policing in Nigeria as members of the squad constantly harass and abuse citizens while pretending to be investigating armed robbery suspects(Paquette, 2020). Violence has therefore come to be associated with policing practice as their activities are rife with accounts and cases of brutality characterized by physical assault, harassment, illegal arrest, and detention (Lar, 2018). Their excesses have also been displayed during crime control operations, ranging from crowd control, demonstration, and protest management to harassment at checkpoints (Network on Police Reform in Nigeria, NOPRIN 2010; Lar, 2018).

Recent developments further indicate that the police have become more punitive as they are now being used by authorities to silence condescending voices. On a daily basis, the media is awash with reports of violence and abuse between the police and civilians with a high casualty rate. In 2018, 2,331 victims were reportedly killed in 350 lethal incidents involving the police and other security operatives (Ukoji, Ayodokun, & Eze 2019). The police and other security agencies have also been reported to have killed more Nigerians than Covid-19 while enforcing the lockdown directives by the government (BBC, April 2020). As of 16th April 2020, the report indicated that law enforcers have killed 18 people in Nigeria since lockdowns began on 30 March. The Council on Foreign Relation's Nigeria, a Nigerian based security tracker which catalogues, and maps out political violence based on weekly surveys of the country and international press reports that police killed three Shiite protestors in Kaduna on August 22nd, while on August 23rd, two State Security Service operatives and twenty-one IPOB members were killed during a clash in Enugu East, Enugu (Nigeria Security Tracker, 2020). These are indications that the Nigeria police have become so adamant to change even in this 21st century as they remain stuck to a traditional and reactive approach to maintain law and order. Their posture creates what Peytona, Sierra-Arévaloc and Randd, (2019) describe as 'public distrust' that is likely to escalate into contests for dominance.

Method of Data Collection

The chapter relied on both primary and secondary data sources with a focus on the North Central region of Nigeria. The choice was informed by the perennial ethno-religious and communal violence being experienced in the region and the frequency at which security forces, particularly the police who are often deployed as major stakeholders have contacts with citizens. The region comprises of six (6) states: Benue, Kogi, Kwara, Nasarawa, Niger, Plateau and Abuja the Federal Capital Territory. Out of these states, Plateau and Benue have been tagged hot spot States due to the magnitude of the violence and the casualties involved. Data collection was restricted to these two (2) States.

Primary sources of data were collected through Semi-Structured Interviews conducted with Civil Society activists and prominent citizens to get their views on the preferred policing strategy and how they could be best implemented to reduce the spate of violence and kidnapping in the region. To determine the reaction of the police to the security challenges, interviews were conducted with state Commissioners of Police (CPs), Area Commanders and Divisional Police Officers. Secondary data were collected from current reports and literature on police brutality in Nigeria. It is also important to note that Nigerian Mainstream Newspapers report most of the incidences of police violence and as such, publications between 2018 and 2020 on police violence were consulted. Again, there are expert reports documented by research-based organizations or agencies on security forces brutality including Amnesty International, Nigeria Security Trackers, Human Rights Watch. These reports served as major sources of data.

COMMUNITY POLICING, STATE POLICE AND ISSUES OF POLICE REFORMS IN NIGERIA

Community Policing Philosophy and Frameworks

Literature on policing is replete with definitions of community policing (Alemika & Chukwuma, 2000; Baker, 2002, 2008; Groenwald &Peake, 2004; Casey, 2010). In their 1998 publication, Harvard scholars Trojanowicz and Bucqueroux extensively addressed this issue and laid the foundation for better and broader understanding. According to them, community policing is:

a philosophical and an organizational strategy that promotes a new partnership between the people and their police. It is based on the premise that both the police and the community must work together as equal partners to identify, prioritize and solve contemporary problems such as crime, fear of crime, social and physical disorder, and overall neighbourhood decay, with the goal of improving the overall quality of life in an area (Trojanowicz & Bucqueroux, 1998, p. 6).

Here, community policing is seen as a strategy which is focused on the ideals of citizen-oriented police work with emphasis on services instead of a police-centred approach. The philosophy is that community members would have the opportunity to partner with the police by sharing intelligence and other information relating to the breakdown of law and order. It requires that police listen to citizens, take seriously how citizens perceive problems and issues, and seek to solve problems which have been identified (Peytona, Sierra-Arévaloc, & Randd, 2019; Paez & Dierenfeldtb, 2020).

Community policing has been categorized it into two complementary components: community partnership and problem solving (Bureau of Justice Assistance,1994). The community partnership component is the establishment and maintenance of mutual trust between the police and the communities they serve. The assumption is that the police cannot effectively maintain law and order without cooperation with the community members. As such, they are encouraged to come forth with relevant information through available neighborhood groups as well as other social agencies. Through partnership, the police become an integral part of the community culture. It helps in defining and reshaping future priorities of police forces into community change agents to collaborate with citizens to reduce crime at the neighborhood level (Siegel, 2008; Bureau of Justice Assistance, 1995). Community partnership recognizes the value of activities that contribute to the orderliness and well-being of the community. These may include but not limited to helping accident or crime victims, providing emergency medical services, helping resolve domestic and neighborhood conflicts. Others include working with residents and local businesses to improve neighborhood conditions, controlling automobile and pedestrian traffic, providing emergency social services and referrals to those at risk, protecting the exercise of constitutional rights and providing a model of citizenship (Bureau of Justice Assistance, 1994). As the police provide these services, they develop trust between them and the community and open the door for greater access to valuable information which helps in the prevention of crimes and engenders support for needed crime-control measures.

The problem- solving component of community policing is a proactive form of policing which identifies and responds to potential problems before they occur (Siegel, 2008). It goes beyond crime prevention to include other problems the community may face such as the application of appropriate resources and making right choices for the betterment of the community (US Bureau of Justice, 1994). This component suggests that there are underlying conditions that create problems which need to be addressed collectively between the police and the community. Such problems may include the characteristics of the offenders and potential victims, the social setting in which these people interact, the physical environments, and the way the public deals with these conditions (US Bureau of Justice, 1994).

Benefits and Barriers to Community Policing

Community policing has been found to be beneficial to both the police and community members. First, it brings the police closer to the people and strengthens internal coherence of local communities (Muller, 2020). In some sense, community members are expected to constantly hold meetings with the police to filter and screen the problems of the community while the police respond to their concerns (Manning,

2003). This helps to improve police-community relationships and community perceptions of the police. It also increases community capacity to deal with issues. More importantly, community policing contributes significantly to changing police officers' attitudes and behaviors towards citizens (Coquilhat, 2008). For community members, it leads to increasing perceptions of safety and reduces crime especially now that people are living in constant fear of attacks and kidnapping in the North Central region of Nigeria.

Promising as community policing is, there are barriers. The barriers range from implementation challenges which are mostly tied to scarcity of resources, funding and lack of trained officers who do not have experience in community involvement or empowerment. In Nigeria for example, the government is systemically corrupt and lacks internal management of available resources. Resources allocated for mobilization, deployment and training of manpower may end up in private pockets. Without adequate labor and training, it is unlikely that police will realize the full potential of community policing (Skogan, 2006). Resistant police culture to change constitute another major barrier. Traditionally, the police are 'formally trained to enforce laws and not to build relationships with the community. The involvement of public officials and the introducing ideas of solidarity or brotherhood are seen as soft policing or 'social work' and 'just politics' (Skogan, 2006). This raises fear of potential loss of autonomy and the 'tough-minded' status of the police (Coquilhat, 2008). Another barrier to community policing is lack of trust between the police and community members. The historical and present realities of community mistrust in law enforcement may affect the effectiveness of community policing if not well addressed. Citizens who live in deprived areas of a country are more likely to be hostile to government and especially to the police, which they see as a symbol of an insensitive and irresponsive government (Ikuteyijo, 2009; Okey Ordu, & Nnam, 2017). Other barriers common to Nigeria include Godfatherism, selective enforcement of the law based on either religion, ethnicity, or one's social status.

State Police Debate and the Politics of Implementation in North Central Nigeria

State police is a policing structure where state governments employ officers for the purpose of law enforcement. It is a situation where policing and all its operations and logistics are controlled by other governments than the national or federal government (Agwanwo, 2014; Aremu, 2014). The structure is supposedly made up of officers who understand the language, geography, and the peculiar security challenge of the people they police. It is also meant to provide quality policing service to the people and to enforce all criminal and crime related laws made by the state legislature for order maintenance (Alemika, 2018). The views of respondents and opinions in documented reports, literature and newspapers on state police can be categorised into two: Those in support for state police and those opposed to it.

Arguments in Support of State Police

Advocates of state police believe that the society has undergone social, economic, and political changes. Thus, as it is obtainable in advanced democracies, there is need for a policing structure that will conform to these changes. In Nigeria for example, the federal system of government which is managed alongside state and the local unit requires that the units be given the constitutional right to provide security for lives and property of people within their territory or circle of influence. Without a coercive power, a state no matter how big or rich is just like any other organized society. It may be able to bark but it certainly cannot bite. This opinion was shared by Owen (2018) who identified three key issues as the basis for state police. First, the belief that locally recruited police forces are more likely to relate better with the public and can respond promptly to community distress calls than federal police because they are drawn from within the state and are familiar with community terrains. Secondly, inability of the Federal Government to properly fund and equip the police force aside payment of salaries. This indirectly shifts the burden of funding to state governments who ironically do not have control over them. The third approach is the issue of a one size-fits-all where the federal laws are foisted on states on the basis of a centralized policing system regardless of peculiarity of the states (Owen, 2018).

With reference to the constitution, supporters of state police argue that the police are agents of the state, established for the maintenance of order and enforcement of law (1999 Constitution as amended). State governors continue to express their frustration regarding this arrangement stating that they have been operating without coercive powers to direct commissioners of police in charge of their states with respect to maintenance of public safety and order. A civil society expert responded to the question on whether state police will work in the north central region as follows:

the continuous agitation for state police is in response to the centralised policing system that is grossly ineffective. The police are unable to protect citizens and most of the burden of policing rests with the states and local governments with no iota of control over the police by these levels of government. For many communities, they resort to community level measures for protection. Using vigilantes have been more effective, in the face of non-implementation of recommendations on police reform (Interview with an CSO activist,2021).

This view was also shared by one of the governors in the North Central region when he argued that:

We (governors) are all frustrated. I am frustrated in my state; many governors are frustrated in their states; we are called chief security officers only in name; we have no control over the army and the police. We are almost helpless. We do not have a say in police operations, yet we fund some of their operations in our states (Alike, 2020.n.p).

The governors further observed that despite their influence in their states, they cannot ask the commissioner of police to do something, and it will be done immediately. The commissioner would first seek for clearance with the Inspector-General of Police. A governor argued that "we are not in control of the police, I don't determine who gets posted to my state as Commissioner of Police and if I give him directives, he can decide to flout the directives. So, we are all frustrated" (Alike, 2020.n.p).

Another reason put forward for the creation of state police is the over concentration of responsibilities on the federal government. With lots of issues to contend with, the federal government of Nigeria is already overburdened with other challenges leaving subsidy on security and other operations of the police in the hands of states. A governor lamented the negligence of the federal government in taking care of the welfare of the police when he argued that in a federal system, it is ironical that the police chief is asking states to prepare to pay salaries of community police officers when they are struggling to pay salaries of workers in their states (This day, 2020). The implication here is that if states would be required to pay salaries of community policemen, then there is no difference in the states establishing their own police which they can easily control.

The last argument in support of state police is that the concept of centralized management of most police organizations has often served to isolate police from the communities they serve. Nigeria is too large for its security matters to be over centralized. In a country that is usually bogged down by administrative bottlenecks, a lot of time is wasted on simple matter like deployment of troops to quell insurrection. The efficacy of local community security groups like the VGN and Neighborhood Watch has led credence to the belief by many that security is a local problem and only those who understand the terrain can manage it.

Arguments Against State Police

Arguments against state police also lies with the 1999 constitution of Nigeria which recognises only the federal police and constitutionally empowers the federal government to have absolute control on policing in all the states. This structure has been maintained right from inception of colonial domination in Nigeria (Onyeozili, 2005, p. 39). Thus, because the police were freely utilized to oppress political opponents and rig elections, state police would further be used for all sorts of abuses such as criminalization, 'gangsterism', 'commodification',' warlordism', terrorism radicalization, ignorance and abuse of basic human rights (Wisler & Onwudinwe, 2007). A respondent particularly argued that:

The clamor for state police has been there for quite some time since the return of democracy in 1999. It is born out of the current structure of federal policing and long years of neglect by the government in funding the police. As such, agitators are saying that if the federal government can no longer operate the police and reach every nook and cranny in Nigeria, state police can be considered an option. But because Nigeria is a very delicate society; a multilingual, multiethnic society. Attempts to involve in state policing, will be abused by the political, traditional, and religious powers that be, I recommend that the region go for community policing which will work better even though it is at the trial stage (Interview with a DPO, 2021).

Similarly, because state police is synonymous with indigenes police, it is largely unrepresentative and could be unaccountable to the generality of the people who live within the state jurisdiction. This would violate some of the key principles of democratic policing and threaten human rights, personal security, and national cohesion (Alemika, 2018). Yet again to be considered is the problem of conflict of interest and challenges that are likely to be the fallout of multiple security agents. Although the federal police in its present structure is guilty of most, if not all allegations leveled against local police, the issue is whether Nigeria should face the challenge of a single police instead of having to fight many battles at the same time. It is equally doubtful whether Nigerian politicians have the temperament to resolve amicably the jurisdictional problems that are likely to arise from operation of multiple police forces. Considering the issues raised, what may work well amid these security challenges is a mixture of both state police and community policing. While states have more control, the citizens are placed at the centre of the policing agenda.

Analysis of Police Reforms in Nigeria (1999-2020)

After years of military rule and dictatorship, the coming of a new democratically elected government in 1999 saw the need for the reform of the police which had hitherto been affected by military mentality. Former president Olusegun Obasanjo introduced police reform at the beginning of the transition to democracy by first focusing on personnel issues when he ordered the massive recruitment of 40,000 police officers annually for five years, without raising the budget (HRW 2010; Hills, 2012). This created an impression that the inadequacies of policing in Nigeria was due to a shortage of personnel. Even though it formed a part of the problem, significant aspects of the reform regarding human rights, accountability and efficiency were neglected.

Between 2006 and 2012, four presidential committees were constituted to study and recommend measures for the reform of the Nigeria Police Force. The first committee was constituted in 2006 by Obasanjo while the second was the Mohammadu D. Yusuf committee of 2008 by former President Yar'adua. The Parry Osayande committee constituted in 2012 was the third with a mandate to consider the factors militating against the effectiveness of the police, focusing on the issue of conditions of service, including welfare. The fourth committee was established by a civil society coalition under the coordination of Center for Law Enforcement Education in Nigeria (CLEEN) Foundation in the same year (2012) with the aim of reproducing a report from the civil society perspective. More recently, President Mohammed Buhari repealed the old Police Act of 2004 and signed into law a new one called the Police Act 2020. The 2004 Act had a broad objective of the prevention and detection of crime, the apprehension of offenders, the preservation of law and order and the protection of life and property of citizens. This only emphasised the enforcement of all laws and regulations alongside other military duties within and without Nigeria as may be required by them. It is silent on professionalism, respect for human rights, and other key components of democratic policing. The amended 2020 Act however seeks to achieve the following objective:

1. provide for a police force that is more responsive to the general public and has entrenched in its operations the values of fairness, justice and equity;
2. reposition the police force to uphold and safeguard the fundamental rights of every person in Nigeria in its operations.
3. bring about a positive change in the Police Force by ensuring that its functions are performed in a manner sensitive to the needs and well-being of the general public.
4. Empower the police force to effectively prevent crimes without threatening the liberty and privacy of persons in Nigeria.
5. Strengthen the police force in the performance of its functions including safety and security of all persons, communities, and property in Nigeria.
6. Ensure that the police perform its functions by creating the enabling environment to foster cooperation and partnership between it and the communities it serves to effectively prevent, reduce, and eradicate crimes.
7. Develop professionalism in the police force by providing relevant training in all police formations in Nigeria for enhanced performance and
8. respect for rights of victims of crime and an understanding of their needs.

This was seen as another major step towards the reform of the police. Embedded in the act are critical issues that have over the years been agitated by Nigerians whether as politicians, commentators, or analysts as the case may be.

In trying to know whether these reforms and amendments had impact on policing in Nigeria, respondents reported a fundamental problem with implementation. A police officer observed that the problem of police reform in Nigeria is the issue of implementation. According to him, "no one would have been talking about reform by now if the previous numerous recommendations were implemented" (Interview with a CSP in Benue). Attempts at implementing any of the recommendations have always been superficial and without a fundamental change and sustainable effect (Hills, 2008). At best, the ideas have mostly remained on paper even as politician's lash on such findings to create concepts that give them popularity when seeking for elective positions. They keep emphasizing the importance of reforming the security environment to deliver more protection in several areas, but in the public opinion and everyday experience, there are no relevant and sustainable positive effects or at best only few (Muller, 2020). This explains why the reforms have not had any significant impact on policing in Nigeria. Apart from the fact that officers are still involved in the abuse of the rights of citizens with lots of members of the public becoming victims by the day, corruption of senior officers has also been widely reported (Akinrujomu 2016; Ojukwu, 2016; Agbiboa, 2013; NOPRIN,2010). Table 1 is the brief summary of the major findings of the committee by Civil Society Organisations (CSOs).

Table 1. Major Findings of the CSOs panel on Police Reforms in Nigeria

Factors Affecting Effective Performance by NPF	Scope and Standard of Training	Causes of Collapse of Public Confidence in the NPF	Other Issues Covered by the Panel
Mission statement of the NPF in the Police Act does not capture the expectation of the new kind of police Nigeria requires	The current regulatory framework in the Police Act is a major obstacle to effective training and development of the NPF.	Incivility, cruelty, gross abuse of human rights, unkempt appearance of officers, stinking police stations and dilapidated barracks	Failure of the government to implement previous recommendations on creation of State police.
Lack of operational autonomy and politicization of appointment of the NPF leadership.	NPF training curriculum is highly undeveloped, with critical gaps in democratic policing.	Dilapidated and decayed training institutions and facilities.	Poor funding of the NPF, incomplete release of budgeted funds and late release of funds.
Over-centralisation of the NPF structure and, Corruption.	Training institutions and facilities available for police training in varying states of dilapidation and decay.	Insensitivity to victims of gender crimes such as domestic violence and rape.	No system of rewarding police officers for outstanding community service.

Source: CSO Panel Report on Police Reform, 2012

Another issue of interest to this paper is the finding related to the nature and manner in which the leadership of the police is appointed. Apart from the fact that the process is shrouded in politics and ethnicity, the president wields the power to hire and fire at any time thereby affecting the stability and performance of the police. For instance, in the twenty years of democratic rule since 1999, Nigeria has had 16 Inspectors General of Police (IGPs), a ratio of one in every two years (NPF,2020). Also, even though the appointment of the NPF leadership is determined largely by seniority and representation, the process is influenced by nepotism, political patronage and regime interests and preferences. From 1999 -2020, the pattern of appointment reflects the region from which the president or the vice president of the country is coming from as presented in table 2 below.

Further insight to the table reveals that when the IGP is not from the same region with the president, it is most likely to come from the region of the vice president. The case of Yaradua and Goodluck is a typical example. While Yaradua was from North West, the IGP came from the South; the region where the president came from. Similarly, when Geoduck who was from the South South became the president, the IGP was from the North West; the region the vice president came from. Under the current president, all the IGPs came from the North where the president is from. This has implications for policing as it does not show any evidence of independence and excellence in performance aside control.

Table 2. Geopolitical Regions of Presidents/Vice Presidents and their IGPs from 1999-date

Tenure/ Year	President	Region	Vice President	Region	IGPs/Year	Region
1999-2007	Olusegun Obasanjo	South-West	Atiku Abubakar	North-East	Musiliu Smith (1999-2002)	South West
					Mustapha Balogun (2002-2005)	South West
					Sunday Ehindero (2005-2007)	South West
2007-2010	Umaru Yar'adua	North West	Goodluck Jonathan	South South	Mike Nbama Okiro (2007-2009)	South-South
					Ogbona Onovo(2009-2010)	South South
2010-2015	Goodluck Jonathan	South-South	Namadi Sambo	North West	Hafiz Ringim (2010-2012)	North West
					Mohammed Abubakar (2012-2014)	North West
					Suleiman Abba/2014-2015	North West
2015-date	Muhammadu Buhari	North West	Yemi Osinbajo	South West	Solomon Arase/2015-2016	South South
					Ibrahim Kpotun Idris/ 2019-2019	North Central
					Mohammed Abubakar Adama (2019-2021)	North Central
					Usman Alkali Baba (2021-date	North East

Source: Nigeria Police Force ICT Department, 2020

Police Violence and the #End SARS Protest

The use of violence to suppress condescending voices by the police during colonialism created the type of law enforcement practice we have in North Central Nigeria today. The Human Rights Watch (HRW) argued that the British government established colonial police for the purpose of protecting its economic and political interests. "The police accomplished this objective through the often-brutal subjugation of indigenous communities that resisted colonial occupation. The use of violence, repression, and excessive use of force by the police has characterized law enforcement in Nigeria ever since" (HRW, 2010, p. 14). This kind of orientation has had impact on the psyche of the Nigeria police including public perception. Citizens feel that the police force have rather been attacking them than their primary duty of protecting lives and property. There are local reports of incidences where officers of the police force compelled motorists to stop at checkpoints and then threaten and sometimes shoot at those who refuse to pay bribe of as low as fifty naira (Oloyede & Elega, 2020).

Over time, SARS unit has been implicated in widespread human rights abuses, extrajudicial killings, torture, arbitrary arrests, unlawful detention and extortion (Amnesty International, 2020). In 2016, the Amnesty International reported the detention of 130 detainees living in overcrowded cells and being regularly subjected to methods of torture including hanging, starvations, beatings, shootings, and mock executions in various centres at the Federal Capital Territory (AI, 2016). The report specifically notes that people in SARS custody were:

subjected to a variety of methods of torture including hanging, mock execution, beating, punching, and kicking, burning with cigarettes, waterboarding, near-asphyxiation with plastic bags, forcing detainees to assume stressful bodily positions and sexual violence (AI, 2020).

The international human rights body further presented evidence for years that the unit's officers have repeatedly committed heinous violations, including extrajudicial executions, torture, and rape. Between January 2017 and May 2020, 82 cases of abuse by SARS were documented (Onubogu, 2020). These evidence underscores the extent to which this unit of the police has become violent, brutal, and abusive towards the citizens it is expected to protect. Responding to the continued abuse, a campaign was initiated popularly known as the #EndSARS #ReformPoliceNG' which began in 2016 but gathered more social media attention in December 2017 following the sharing of videos and testimonies of perceived victims of the SARS. This movement was able to successfully bring to light police abuses and other human rights violations. It also raised the level of social awareness which serves as rallying point for the collective war on the evils of policing believed to have been perpetrated by the police. The #EndSARS# protest climaxed in October 2020 after a video that showed the aftermath of a killing, allegedly by SARS officers, of a young man went viral.

Despite research findings suggesting that young individuals are at increased risk of offending and victimization, thereby creating higher chances of youth police encounter and arrest (Paez & Dierenfeldt, 2020; Brown, Murphy, 2015; Snyder & Sickmund, 2006), there are sociopolitical variations. In Nigeria for example, the youth have been targeted by SARS with little or no evidence of their involvement in crime. In most instances, the only evidence the police hold against them is their owning a laptop or smartphone, thereby accusing them of involvement in cybercrime or other online fraudsters and when arrested, they demand excessive bail fees to let them go.

Nationwide protests began on October 8, 2020, calling on the authorities to abolish the abusive unit. They handed down five major demands expected to be met by the government. These demands were as follows:

1. The immediate release of all arrested protesters
2. Justice for all deceased victims of police brutality and appropriate compensation for their families
3. Setting up an independent body to oversee the investigation and prosecution of all reports of police misconduct
4. In line with police act, psychological evaluation and retaining (to be confirmed by an independent body) of all disbanded SARS officers before they can be redeployed
5. Increase police salary so that they are adequately compensated for protecting lives and property of citizens.

However, at the initial mobilization of the police, they started shooting tear gas, water cannons, and live rounds at protesters, killing and wounding many. The Human Rights Watch (2020) was quoted as saying that:

People exercising their right to protest and calling for an end to police brutality are themselves being brutalized and harassed by those who should protect them. This underscores the importance of the protesters' demands and the culture of impunity across the policing system, which is in dire need of reform (HRW, 2020).

Other reasons that triggered the protest were the continued human rights abuses committed by SARS officers, lack of accountability for their actions on the side of the government and leadership of the police and the obsolete Police Act. For example, citizens phones have been seized without a warrant, while others have been arrested for tattoos or dreadlocks(Campbell, 2020). The act, which was adopted in 1943, leaves broad discretionary powers in the hands of police officers. It allows officers to perform warrantless searches and make arrests based on mere suspicion of guilt or even an intent to commit an offence. In summary, the #End SARS protest was adjudged to be one of the most coordinated agitations organized by Nigerian youth. The issues articulated were germane as they presented the picture of a police officer that is undemocratic, uncivil, and unfriendly towards citizens. At the end, it yielded some results as the authorities responded by disbanding the unit. Although government was able to contend the protest, the public is waiting to see what will come out of it.

Prospects for Community Policing in North Central Nigeria

In the past, African communities had ubiquitous community self-rule where informal policing constituted a net contributor to local safety with the state appearing very distant to local residents, and sometimes inhospitable (Wisler & Onwudiwe, 2007). The case of Nigeria was not different as community settings had traditional rulers and their cabinet, town union and opinion leaders as well as youth leaders and community security committee members. Community members met regularly to discuss their welfare, crime related problems and then work out modalities on how to combat those challenges (Okey-Ordu & Nnam, 2017). This kind of setting was considered an effective mechanism for social control. However, things have changed over time alongside the nature of community settlements and the shifting characteristics of crime and violence that have had significant impact on self and formal policing around the world. Policing strategies that worked in the past are not always effective today and the desired goal of an enhanced sense of safety, security, and well-being, has not been achieved.

Communities across North Central Nigeria for example are experiencing serious security challenges ranging from perennial, escalated, and expanded night attacks between farmers and herders, ethnoreligious and communal clashes as well as kidnappings and other violent crimes (Azad, Crawford, & Kaila, 2018. Responding to the nature of internal security challenge in the region, a Divisional Police Officer (DPO) observed that the north central region of Nigeria is characterized by

violent crimes in form of bandit attack, kidnapping and movement of nomadic herders alongside destruction of farm produce and other mischief against indigenous farmers without the federal government tackling the issue through the enactment of laws that can restrict such indiscriminate movement/mischief by pastoralists that are alleged to be armed with dangerous weapons and are into all sorts of criminal activities (Interview with DPO, 2021)

These attacks have prompted some states in the region to establish pseudo policing structures for enforcement of laws against grazing. They exist alongside federal police but lack the powers to detain suspects in cells and to bear lethal arms as there is no constitutional or legal framework for their operation (Alemika, 2018). The International Crisis Group (2018) also reported the emergence and resilience of ethnic related community vigilantes in the region backed by ethnic and communal leaders, including politicians, traditional rulers due to inadequate government protection and insistence on a right to self-defense.

In Plateau, Nassarawa and Benue States where kidnapping, farmer's herders clashes and bandits attack are frequent, policing has been redefined. Several statutory and non-statutory organisations have come up with strategies to close the gap by providing services that seek to ensure and maintain law, order, and security (Lar, 2018). Such informal security groups with varying names under the umbrella of Vigilante Groups of Nigeria (VGN) include but not limited to Livestock Guards and Agro Rangers in Benue state, Operation Rainbow, Night Watch Network and Neighbourhood Watch in Plateau state. These groups involved in policing their communities automatically become stakeholders as they meet regularly to discuss their welfare, crime related problems, police-community relationships, and then work out modalities on how to combat crime to the barest minimum. By implication, community members equally pull their resources together with that of the conventional police in the fight against crime and criminals.

As part of the reform process, governors in the region have already set the structure and modalities for its take off. What is left is the allocation of resources for full implementation. More recently, there is a renewed call on the NPF to strengthen synergy with State Governments in the recruitment and training of Community Police to provide adequate security at the grassroots level. They are also calling for the resuscitation of peace and security committees at the Local Government levels for quick decision on security and crime prevention. A respondent observed thus:

Community policing has commenced in earnest in North Central Nigeria. Youths and other volunteers from various parts of all the local governments have been subjected to rudimentary police trainings. They are to work side by side with the commissioner of police in collaboration with Divisional Police Officers (DPO) across the state. Although VGN exist on their own, they work hand in hand with the police. They are some of the principal organisations drawn from the communities. (DPO, Bukuru Police Division, Jos South, Plateau State)

Commenting on the modalities of recruitment, the DPO stated that "we select youths from various organisations including market unions, labour unions, youth groups, civil liberty organisations and any other individual willing to volunteer his/her services in providing security."

What Works Between State Police and Community Police in Northcentral Nigeria

From all indications, community policing appears to be the model that could work for the North Central region of Nigeria. It is an example of a multilayered policing structure with less elaborate hierarchy of command. The already existing localised policing structure in the region fits into this arrangement as it provides an opportunity for intelligence gathering and information sharing regarding any form of crime in the communities between the police and community members. This has been emphasised by Alemika (2018) who observed that a multi-layered police and policing system is what is needed in Nigeria in view of its complexities in terms of ethnic composition and population size. Such a system will help in addressing the scale of security challenge being witnessed today as it provides opportunity for regulation and oversight and to check the level of force and scale of arms and ammunitions in circulation. It also gives room for proper supervision, training and curricula, professional and operational standards.

Although calls for state police have intensified in recent times, there are political, sentimental, or even regional undertones beneath. Such calls could also be from state executives who are frustrated with bureaucratic bottlenecks involved in the deployment of the federal police when there is security emergency. State police will however be difficult to work in a region that is characterized as multi-ethnic, multi-cultural and multi-religious like North Central Nigeria. The tendency for state executives to abuse it is remarkably high especially in this era of politicking where access to political power is seen as license to impunity.

SOLUTIONS AND RECOMMENDATIONS

In Nigeria, the argument about state or community police is rooted in the politics and plurality of ethnicity, religion, and region. Supporters of one political party, religion, or region or even membership of one ethnic group have demonstrated their support for a given policing structure or the other because it fits their interest at a given point in time. Once there is a shift in leadership and political power, the support changes because each regime sees the operation of the police in their present structure as protecting their interest. This also explains why there is no security of tenure for IGPs in Nigeria once there is change in government. The habit of removing IGPs at will, make the position one of the most unstable leadership positions in the country, and perhaps accounts for the ad hoc, short term approach that has come to define the NPF (CSO Report on Police Reform, 2012).

One crucial point to note however is that the effectiveness of policing anywhere in the world is not dependent on whether the police is decentralized. It is also not dependent on whether government introduces state police or community policing, but the strategies adopted in controlling crime. Good and effective policing strategy are embedded in intelligence gathering, professionalism, funding, training, welfare, procedural justice, or what Tyler (1990) regard as legitimate policing. In other words, there is no correlation between centralised or decentralised police forces and efficiency, legitimacy, and accountability. What affects their capabilities and dysfunction are the political, social, and economic contexts in which the society and police organization are structured (Alemika, 2018; Owen, 2018; Tyler, 1990; Tyler & Fagan, 2008). For example, a country like the United States of America which is today seen as a model to most countries has a decentralized policing structure but frequently witnessing turbulent policing challenge in terms of political, racial and segregated policing. The case of George Floyd is one out of many cases the country has had to grapple with.

For effective police reform and improved performance, the following recommendations should be put into consideration.

1. **The organizational structure of the police should be reviewed to take care of the key ingredients of community policing such as partnership, problem solving, complexities of rural communities in terms of social, cultural, and environmental variations.** The command structure of the NPF is highly centralized thereby disempowering state and community-level commands. This hinders service delivery, create bottlenecks, and distance citizens from "their" police (Okenyodo, 2016).
2. **The process of making appointments into leadership positions needs to be fully defined, opened, competitive and transparent**. The IGP should be an officer who can confidently communicate the vision, mission, and strategic plan of the NPF to different audiences such as citizens, legislatures, the executive, criminal justice circles within and across jurisdiction to attract grants from development partners.
3. **The nature and pattern of recruitment of the police should be standardized and made independent.** Literature on recruitment indicate difficulties of hiring qualified police officers due to increased demand for police officers and the general decline in law enforcement applicants (Sarre

& Langos, 2014, Ford, 2008, Gulleng, 2016). In Nigeria, the pool of applicants that apply every year do not reflect the desire for career building opportunity but a manifestation of the deteriorating level of unemployment where any income generating platform is rushed at (Gulleng, 2016). The process is also fraught with political interference as senior politicians struggle for slots for their candidates whether they meet the requirement or not. At the end, even the rejected members of the society whose family members feel tired of them think that their place is in the police.

4. **Funding and general police welfare needs to improve**. Funding involves logistics, housing and all modes of operations of the police force. Unfortunately, the NPF is widely believed to have suffered the worst neglect by successive governments. Aside from poor remuneration, policemen are accommodated in poorly maintained and overcrowded barracks. Most of these barracks were designed by the British colonialists and have remained that way since independence without any efforts at modernization (Ndubuisi & Obayemi, 2019).
5. **The police need to be equipped with modern crime fighting equipment**. The NPF lack sophisticated and modern equipment to combat complicated crimes as there are cases where police claimed that Arm Robbers, bandits, and criminal gangs possessed superior weapons than they. As such, they end up retreating from crime scenes.
6. **Training and retraining of officers are also crucial**. There is no way a country would run a police force without training and advanced training in modern policing strategies in line with international best practices. The six months training the police cadet undergo at the point of recruitment is grossly inadequate. Apart from physical fitness training, there are other components of the training that should expose them to human rights issues and appropriate pattern of behavior for various situations. This is hardly done and hence, cases of brutality and accidental discharge continue to be recorded by various organs of the police.
7. **Finally, there is need for the implementation of reports of reform committees especially those that have to do with democratic policing**. It serves no purpose when a reform committee would be set by the government and findings and recommendations would be made without implementation. Government should stop playing politics with issues of policing as the image they project to the public is directly or indirectly the image of every regime.

FUTURE RESEARCH DIRECTIONS

Policing in today's world has changed from physical carrying of arms and operation show of force to a technology driven approach. It has also moved away from reactive approach to proactive or what is regarded as preventive policing. Societies that have remained adamant to change in view of emerging dimensions of crime and insecurity will continue face challenges. While the current debate for community policing or state police may be appropriate in a heavily pluralized society like Nigeria, such models can only work with a police organisation that is schooled in human rights and basic democratic principles. A reformed police whether state or community police is that which is legitimate, procedural, and professional in its activities of investigation, arrest, and other engagements with citizens. It is that type of police that is well equipped with modern working tools and has the requisite community network for intelligence gathering. That is the picture of police every Nigerian wish to see on the streets, which is the future research direction for researchers.

CONCLUSION

In 2016, a report published by the International Police Science Association showed that policing in Nigeria is the worst in the world. This was even before the peak of police brutality which resulted in the massive protest code named #ENDSARS#. Indications are that the situations have gotten worse than it was in 2016. This is partly due to the unwillingness of successive governments and regimes to implement series of recommendations put forward by several presidential panels and committees on police reforms in the country since 1999. In most instances, findings and recommendations of the panels are treated with levity due largely to politics and regime interest. Although informal community policing had been in existence in North Central Nigeria, in form of militias and other security networks, it is time to formalise the process with the appropriate legal framework to enable them function effectively. Also, the current security challenges being experienced across the country have given credence to the call for drastic police reforms including specialised training in human rights and democratic policing as well as funding. The problem now lies with the implementation which largely depends on governance and leadership. Police reform goes beyond bill repealing or sponsoring to include good governance on the part of the political leadership and the willingness of the police to demonstrate legitimate power and procedural approach in managing these challenges. Government should be seen to be matching words with action in its effort at investigating and prosecuting police officers found culpable of brutalizing and violating the rights of citizens in the course of their work. Above all, funding and training of police officers should guide the leadership of the police as it is the only means through which the NPF would compete with their peers in meeting global standard best practice when it comes to policing.

REFERENCES

Agbiboa, D. E. (2013). Corruption and economic crime in Nigeria: Social and economic perspectives. *African Security Review*, *22*(1), 47–66. doi:10.1080/10246029.2012.736869

Agwanwo, D. E. (2014). State policing and police efficiency in Nigeria. *Research on Humanities and Social Sciences*, *4*(5), 165–173.

Akinyemi, A. (2016). *Police seizes 19 vehicles from ex-IG Solomon Arase*. https://www.naij.com/1019651-scandal-nigeria-police-force-seizes-19-vehicles-ex-ig-solomonarase.html

Alemika, E. E. (2018). The constraints of rights-based policing in Africa. In E.E. M. R. Alemika & S. Howell (Eds.), *Policing reform in Africa: moving towards a rights-based approach in a climate of terrorism, insurgency, and serious violent crime* (pp. 14–43). APCOF.

Alemika, E. E. (2018). Why has police reform failed to produce reformed police in Nigeria? In O. Owen (Ed.), Police reform in Nigeria: The devolution debate. Monograph Series No.30, CLEEN Foundation.

Alemika, E. E., & Chukwuma, I. (2000). *Police-community violence in Nigeria*. Centre for Law Enforcement Education and National Human Rights Commission.

Alike, E. (2020, December 1). Insecurity: Governors are frustrated, almost helpless. *This Day*. https://www.thisdaylive.com/index.php/2020/12/01

Amnesty International. (2020). *Nigeria: Time to end impunity, torture and other Violations by special anti-robbery squad (SARS).* https://www.justice.gov/eoir/page/file/1290111/download

Aremu, O. (2014). *Policing and terrorism: Challenges and issues in intelligence.* Stirling-Horden Publishers.

Audu, A. M. (2016). *Community policing: Exploring the police/community relationship for crime control in Nigeria.* https://livrepository.liverpool.ac.uk/3002254/1/200817963

Azad, A., Crawford, E., & Kaila, H. (2018). *Conflict and violence in Nigeria: Results from the north east, north central, and south south zones.* Washington, DC: World Bank Group.

Baker, B. (2002). Living with non-state policing in South Africa: The issues and dilemmas. *The Journal of Modern African Studies*, *1*(40), 29–53. doi:10.1017/S0022278X01003809

Baker, B. (2008). Community policing in Freetown, Sierra Leone: Foreign import or local solution? *Journal of Intervention and State Building*, *2*(1), 23-42.

BBC News Africa. (2020). *Coronavirus: Security forces kill more Nigerians than Covid-19.* https://www.bbc.com/news/world-africa-52317196

Brown, R., Novak, K., & Frank, J. (2009). Identifying variation in police officer behavior between juveniles and adults. *Journal of Criminal Justice*, *37*(2), 200–208. doi:10.1016/j.jcrimjus.2009.02.004

Bureau of Justice Assistance. (1994). *Understanding community policing: A framework for action monograph (NCJ 148457).* US Department of Justice.

Campbell, J. (2020). *Nigerians cry out against police brutality.* Council on Foreign Affairs.

Casey, J. (2010). Implementing community policing in different countries and cultures. *Pakistan Journal of Criminology*, *4*(2), 55–70.

Constitution of the Federal Republic of Nigeria. (1999). Federal Government of Nigeria.

Coquilhat, J. (2008). *Community Policing: An international Literature Review.* New Zealand Police.

Ford, H. (2008). *Evaluating the operational effectiveness of west African female police officers' participation in peace support operations: The case of Ghana and Nigeria.* Kofi Anan International Peace keeping Training centre (KAIPTC) Occasional paper.

Groenwald, H., & Peake, G. (2004). *Police reform through community-based policing: Philosophy and guidelines for implementation.* New York: Safer World and International Police Academy.

Gulleng, D.Y. (2016). Police recruitment patterns and professionalism: Implications for effective crime prevention and control in Nigeria. *African Journal of Modern Society*, *4*(2), 57-80.

Hills, A. (2008). The dialectic of police reform in Nigeria. *The Journal of Modern African Studies*, *46*(2), 215–334. doi:10.1017/S0022278X08003200

Hills, A. (2012). Lost in translation: Why Nigeria's police don't implement democratic reforms. *International Affairs*, *88*(4), 739–755. doi:10.1111/j.1468-2346.2012.01099.x

Human Rights Watch. (2010). *Everyone is on the Game. Corruption and human right abuses by the Nigeria police force.* https://www.hrw.org/sites/default/files/reports/nigeria0810webwcover.pdf

Human Rights Watch. (2020). *Crackdown on police brutality protests.* Author.

Ikuteyijo, L. O. (2009). The challenges of community policing in Nigeria. *International Journal of Police Science & Management, 11*(3), 285–293. doi:10.1350/ijps.2009.11.3.130

International Crisis Group. (2018). *Stopping Nigeria's spiraling farmer-herder conflict.* https://www.crisisgroup.org/africa/west-africa/nigeria/262

Johnson, I. (2013). Policing in contemporary Nigeria: Issues and challenges. *African Journal for the Psychological Study of Social Issues, 16*(1), 71–77.

Lar, J. (2018). Policing actors, plural processes, and hybridization: Histories of everyday policing practice in central Nigeria. *Stability, 7*(1), 1–15. doi:10.5334ta.605

Laswell, H. D. (1950). *World politics and personal insecurity.* Free Press.

Malumfashi, S. (2020). Nigeria's SARS: A brief History of the anti-robbery squad. *Aljazeera.* Available at https://www.aljazeera.com/features/2020/10/22/sars-a-brief-history-of-a-rogue-unit

Manning, P. (2003). *Policing contingencies.* The University of Chicago Press. doi:10.7208/chicago/9780226503523.001.0001

Mawby, R. I. (1990). *Comparative policing issues: The British and American experience in international perspective.* Unwin Hyman Ltd.

Müller, N. (2020). *Nigeria's police work between international reform ideas and national security arrangements* (PRIF Working Papers, 48). Frankfurt am Main: Hessische Stiftung Friedens-und Konfliktforschung. https://nbnresolving.org/urn:nbn:de:0168-ssoar-69033-6

Murphy, K. (2015). Does procedural justice matter to youth? Comparing adults' and youths' willingness to collaborate with police. *Policing and Society, 25*(1), 53–76. doi:10.1080/10439463.2013.802786

Nadozie, E. (2017, December 23). How I founded SARS in the Police- RTD CP Medinda. *Vanguard.* https://www.vanguardngr.com/2017/12/founded-sars-police-rtd-cp-midenda/

Ndubuisi. J. M., and Olumide, K.O (2020). Assessment of the role of the Nigerian police force in the promotion and protection of human rights in Nigeria. *Annual Survey of International Comparative Law, 23*(1), 19-30.

Network on Police Reform in Nigeria. (2010). Criminal force: Torture, abuse, and extrajudicial killings by the Nigeria police force. New York: Open Society Justice Initiative.

Nigeria Police Force (2020). *ICT Department.* NPF.

Nigerian Security Tracker –Council on Foreign Relations weekly update. (n.d.). https://www.cfr.org/nigeria/nigeria-security-tracker/p29483

Ojukwu, E. C. S. (2016). *Discovering the police: An excursion into police personality, powers, performance, and prudence.* Kraft Books Limited.

Okenyodo, O. (2016). Governance, accountability, and security in Nigeria. *Africa Security Brief, 31.*

Okey Ordu, G. E., & Nnam, M. U. (2017). Community policing in Nigeria: A critical analysis of current developments. *International Journal of Criminal Justice Sciences, 12*(1), 83–97.

Okocha, C. (2020, August 26). Govs will not be responsible for funding of community policing, Says Akeredolu. *This Day.* https://www.thisdaylive.com/index.php/2020/08/26/

Oladipo, S. B. (2013). Ethnicity and marginalization within the Nigerian state: A case study of the Nigeria police force. *Research on Humanities and Social Sciences, 3*(1), 79–85.

Oloyede, F., & Elega, A. A. (2019) Exploring hashtag activism in Nigeria: A case of #Endsars campaign. In *Conference Proceeding: 5th In Communication and Media Studies (CRPC 2018).* https:// crcp.emu.edu.tr/Documents/Books/CRCP%202018%20Proceeding%20Book%20-%20Approved%20One

Olusegun, O. J. (2016). Community policing in south-west Nigeria: Finding a nexus between the police and the people. *Journal of Education and Practice, 7*(23), 29–35.

Onyeozili, E. C. (2005, April). Obstacles to effective policing in Nigeria. *African Journal of Criminology and Justice Studies, 1*(1).

Oriola, T. (2020, October 20). General Buratai: Leave the army out of #EndSARS protest. *Premium Times.* https://opinion.premiumtimesng.com

Owen, O. (2018). Police reform in Nigeria: The devolution debate. Monograph Series. No 30, CLEEN Foundation.

Paez, R. A., & Dierenfeldtb, R. (2020). Community policing and youth offending: A comparison of large and small jurisdictions in the United States. *International Journal of Adolescence and Youth, 1*(25), 140–153. doi:10.1080/02673843.2019.1601115

SO Panel. (2012). *Police Reform in Nigeria.* Civic Society Final Report.

Peyton, K., Sierra-Arévalo, M., & Rand, D. (2019). A field experiment on community policing and police legitimacy. *Proceedings of the National Academy of Sciences of the United States of America, 116*(40), 19894–19898. doi:10.1073/pnas.1910157116 PMID:31527240

Peyton, K., Sierra-Arévalo, M., & Rand, D. G. (2019). A field experiment on community policing and police legitimacy. *Proceedings of the National Academy of Sciences of the United States of America, 116*(40), 19894–19898. doi:10.1073/pnas.1910157116 PMID:31527240

Rosenbaum, D. P., & Lurigio, A. J. (1994). Inside look at community policing reform: Definitions, organizational changes, and evaluation findings. *Crime and Delinquency, 3*(40), 299–314. doi:10.1177/0011128794040003001

Sarre, R., & Langos, C. (2014). Policing young people: Can the notion of police legitimacy play a role? *Journal of the Institute of Justice & International Studies, 13*, 1–10.

Schwartsz, M. (2015). *Policing and (in)security in fragile and conflict affected settings: A review of perspectives on policing in sub-Saharan Africa.* Knowledge Platform Security and Rule of Law, Global Centre on Cooperative Security.

Siegel, L. J. (2008). *Criminology: The core*. Thomas Higher Education.

Skogan, W. (2006). Advocate - The promise of community policing. In D. Weisburd & A. Braga (Eds.), *Police Innovations: Contrasting Perspectives* (pp. 27–43). Cambridge University Press. http://www.ncjrs.gov/policing/use139.htm

Snyder, H., & Sickmund, M. (2006). *Juvenile offenders and victims: 2006 national report. office of juvenile justice and delinquency prevention*. U.S. Department of Justice.

Thisday. (2020). *Akeredolu: Amotekun will not be subsumed under FG's community policing*. Academic Press.

Trojanowicz & Bucqueroux. (1998). *Community policing: How to get started* (2nd ed.). Alderson Publishing Co.

Tyler, T. R. (1990). *Why people obey the law*. Yale University Press.

Tyler, T. R., & Fagan, J. (2008). Why do people cooperate with the police? *Ohio State Journal of Criminal Law*, *6*, 231–275.

Ukoji, V., Ayodokun, A., & Eze, V. (2019). *Nigeria watch: Eighth report on violence in Nigeria.* IFRA-Nigeria Working Paper Series, No 59.

Webb, V. J., & Katz, C. M. (1998). Citizen ratings of the importance of community policing activities. In *Community Policing: Contemporary Readings*. Waveland Press.

Wisler, D.& Onwudiwe, I.D. (2007). *Community policing: A comparative view*. Academic Press.

ADDITIONAL READING

Ahire, P. T. (1991). *Imperial Policing: The Emergence and Role of the Police in Colonial Nigeria, 1860–1960*. Open University Press.

Alemika, E. E., & Chukwuma, I. (2000). *Police-Community Violence in Nigeria*. Centre for Law Enforcement Education and National Human Rights Commission.

Alemika, E. E. O. (1988). Policing and Perceptions of Police in Nigeria. *Policy Studies*, *11*(4), 161–176.

Amnesty International. (2020). *We Dried Our Tears': Addressing the Toll on Children of Northeast Nigeria's Conflict*. Amnesty International.

Arase, S. E. (2018) "Strengthening Internal Security Frameworks and Community Policing in Nigeria: Models, Policy Options and Strategies." Inaugural lecture, delivered at the National Institute of Policy and Strategic Studies, Kuru-Jos, Nigeria. 19 February 2018. Available at https://www.nipsskuru.gov.ng/images/reports/Inaugurallecture-on-Strengthening-Internal-Security-Framework.pdf

Gascón, L. D., & Roussell, A. (2019). *The Limits of Community Policing: Civilian Power and Police Accountability in Black and Brown Los Angeles*. New York University Press.

Ndubuisi. J. M., and Olumide, K.O (2020). Assessment of the role of the Nigerian police force in the promotion and protection of human rights in Nigeria. *Annual Survey of International Comparative law* (23)1, 19-30.

Onyeozili, C. E., Agozino, B., Agu, A., & Ibe, P. (2021). *Community policing in Nigeria: Rationale, Principles and Practice*. Virginia Tech Publishing.

Trojanowicz, R., & Bucqueroux, B. (1998). *Community Policing: How to Get Started* (2nd ed.). Alderson Publishing Co.

KEY TERMS AND DEFINITIONS

#End SARS#: Movement initiated by youth to protest against police brutality in Nigeria.

Community: An aggregate of people sharing common geographical, social, and cultural pattern of life with relatively interdependent means of livelihood.

Community Police: Formal policing approach involving the police and community members aimed at crime control in communities.

Police: Formal or informal force organized by the community for the maintenance of law and order.

Reform: Improvement or correction of what is wrong or what is being done wrongly by an individual, organization, or a country for the better.

State Police: Functional policing structure by states and local governments different from the federal police in federal system of government.

Violence: The deliberate or intentional use of physical force to abuse or injure oneself or another person in the name of possession of superior power.

Chapter 7
The Five Rs of Prison Reform With Ethnoracially Diverse Offenders:
A Clinical Forensic Psychological Perspective

Jessica Mueller-Coyne
San Diego State University, USA

Ronn Johnson
Creighton University, USA

Valene Gresham
Chicago School of Professional Psychology, USA

ABSTRACT

There are various barriers associated with successful reentry into society for individuals released from prison. Reuniting with family members, rehabilitation efforts, employment, and housing are just some examples of obstacles individuals face when released into the community. Additionally, the costs stemming from the number of people incarcerated, length of stay in prison, racial disparities, and the mental status of offenders create an increased risk for post-release readjustment complications. This chapter focuses on what we call the Pentagonal Post-Release Risk Assessment Framework, or the 5 Rs, which include consideration for risk association of recidivism, reunification, rehabilitation, reintegration, and racism. For individuals released back into the community, it is imperative to consider the 5 Rs. Neglecting one or more of the 5 Rs may perpetuate a cycle of reoffending.

DOI: 10.4018/978-1-7998-6884-2.ch007

INTRODUCTION

There is a confluence of psychosocial and forensically relevant challenges encountered by post-release inmates (Coates, 2015; Cortes & Rogers, 2010; Dandurand et al., 2008; Taliaferro et al., 2016). It is not uncommon for them to experience obstacles that lead to them reoffending as they attempt to reconnect with significant others, gain meaningful employment, and essentially reintegrate into mainstream society (Esparza Flores, 2018; Morenoff & Harding, 2014; Taliaferro et al., 2016).

Reengagement or reunification after a lengthy incarceration is a psychosocial barrier that offenders must prepare for in advance of release in order to maximize re-entry into the community. Globally, the prison population is estimated at around 11 million, with rates of incarceration at 698 per 100,000 population in the United States (Walmsley, 2016). The United States has the highest incarceration rate in the world approaching 1.5 million people imprisoned (Bureau of Justice Statistics [BJS], 2017). The imprisonment rate of African American males was 5.8 times higher than that of white males. It is estimated about 48% of people in prison have mental health difficulties and 29% of those inmates were diagnosed with a serious psychiatric disorder (Hagan et al., 2018; Lurigio et al., 2004). By default, correctional facilities are the largest health care centers for mental disorders in the United States.

Collectively, the clinical forensic costs stemming from the number of people incarcerated, length of stay, racial disparities, and the mental status of offenders create an increased risk for post-release readjustment complications (Bahr et al., 2004; Walters, 2011). Although various forms of outside relational contacts while in prison do permit them to remain somewhat aware of evolving dynamics of a personal and world nature, their psychocultural rhythm is disrupted and distorted by an incarceration that allows only pockets of exposure to their previous life course. Since their old decision-making instincts are dysfunctional, offenders are often less likely to muster the capacity to reverse unwanted relational circumstances that can further stall reunification efforts (Franke et al., 2019; Tremblay & Sutherland, 2017). Further, upon release they are often psychologically and emotionally out of sync with significant others which can result in relational turbulence and other unwanted consequences.

Offenders are not a monolithic group as their ethnoracial and psychological circumstances are diverse (Cain & Parker, 2020). For example, pre-incarceration relational problems are not unusual and are unlikely to be mitigated simply as a byproduct of being in prison (Sanchez-Meier et al., 2002). Job options and employability obstacles also further exacerbate their ability to successfully reintegrate into their families, much less a non-offending community (Schaeffer & Borduin, 1999); efforts must be made to reverse some of these unwanted psychosocial trends.

A desirable post-release readjustment outcome must derive from an intrinsic motivation to heed the lessons learned or those that must be learned in order to achieve desired psychosocial adaptations. These are intrapersonal prerequisites for offenders in order to stop repeat behaviors from their past criminogenic histories that previously led to incarceration. The evidence is clear: rehabilitation of offenders for reentry is an intractable problem that nonetheless must be addressed.

It is important to adhere to empirically derived metrics that identify issues that could prove detrimental to an offender's readjustment. While the evidenced-based principles for post-release inmates may appear clear to some, there are five vital factors that should be captured: Recidivism, Rehabilitation, Reunification, Reintegration, and Racism. These post-release adjustment factors will hereafter be referred to as the Five Rs. The Five R's form the basis of the *Pentagonal Post-Release Risk Assessment Framework*. Each element of the Five Rs functions as a way to profile an offender prior to their release by understanding

Figure 1. Pentagonal Post-Release Risk Assessment Framework

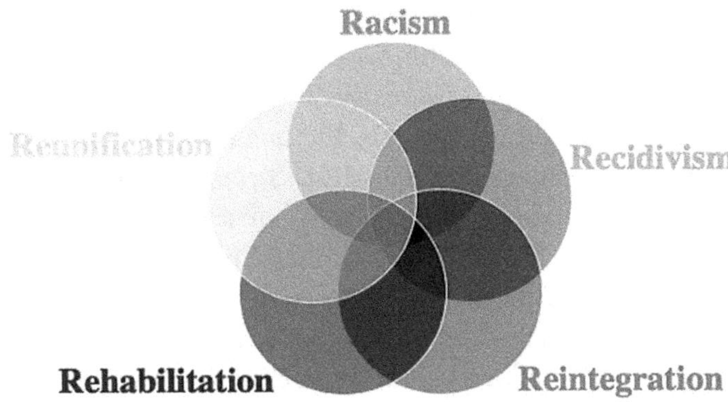

issues believed to be specifically relevant for understanding their risks. This chapter examines in detail the components of the *Pentagonal Post-Release Risk Assessment Framework*.

Racism

The authors' first objective is to address racism and racial disparities across the criminal justice system. Racism is embedded in the justice system, affecting all areas, and barriers exist across reintegration, rehabilitation, recidivism, and reunification. As an element of the *Pentagonal Post-release Risk Assessment Framework*, racism also plays a significant role in understanding barriers to ethnoracially diverse offenders' pre- and post-release adjustments. Structural or systemic racism is reflected in normal and embedded discriminatory ways of functioning within an institution like the criminal justice system. For example, in contrast to whites, African American defendants are 3.6 percentage points more likely to be required to post a monetary bail. This finding stands even when controlling for the aggravating nature of the crime, previous felonies, and the prior criminal record of the defendant (Starr & Rehavi, 2013). Even though white defendants have increased risk for being rearrested during the pretrial period, African Americans are detained at higher rates during the pretrial period. This finding reflects a racial bias in bond decisions against African Americans (Abrams et al., 2012). The narrative around sentencing is mostly about undeniable racial disparities. For example, Everett and Wojtkiewicz (2002) found that African Americans, Latinx, and Native Americans experience more severe sentences than whites. On death rows throughout the U.S. today, 41% of inmates are black and 13% are Hispanic (Banner, 2002; Garland, 2010).

Another glaring example of racial disparity may be observed in prison healthcare. COVID-19 is a global health crisis that has resulted in the deaths of millions and surprisingly the highest rates were found in the United States. Racial overcrowding in prisons is a recurring problem and it is generally acknowledged that the spread of the COVID-19 virus is associated with a mixture of human contact factors. Most notably, prison conditions (e.g., overcrowding, poor ventilation and substandard levels of healthcare) are predictable contributors of respiratory outbreaks in prisons (Centers for Disease Control and Prevention [CDC], 2019; Kinner et al., 2020). There are logistic problems in prisons punctuated by preexisting overcrowding which restrict availability of space required to prevent infections based on recommended isolation and quarantine preventive measures. African Americans and Latinx are more vulnerable to the COVID-19 pandemic (Solis et al., 2020) due to overrepresentation in the prison system as well as overcrowding. At the time this chapter went to print, a more transmissible variant of COVID-19 was just emerging that poses an increased healthcare danger for ethnoracially diverse offenders.

Race predicts psychological dispositions toward the law (Dowler & Sparks, 2008). Recurring exposure to negative race-based incidents creates a sequela of lifelong psychological symptoms. (Brown, 2013; Feagin, 1991; Loo, 1993; Nagata & Cheng, 2003). In the U.S., cross-generational histories of every racial group record repetitive incidents of trauma perpetrated by abuse of legal authority, ethnoracial policing, or gross evasion of justice (U.S. Department of Justice, 2015). Police misconduct was not investigated or went undisciplined. Awareness of racial trauma through police actions has grown through social media posts of mobile phone videos (Ready & Young, 2015; Reardon, 2013). These videos allow for third-party assessment of previously undocumented interactions, yielding three consequences. First, the videos provide evidence to courts and the community. Two weeks after the videotaped beating of Rodney King by members of the Los Angeles Police Department, confidence in the city's police department plummeted to 31% for Latino residents and 14% for African Americans (Weitzer, 2002). Second, videos prompt swift protests and reignite unhealed emotions from previous intergenerational racial trauma triggered by perceived law enforcement misconduct. Third, the videos facilitate a vicarious form of racial trauma. Low rates of conviction or departmental discipline erode trust in police. Better hiring, screening, and training for cross-racial and intergenerational concerns is needed to break the racial trauma cycle. (Carbado & Rock, 2016; Palmater, 2016). However, it is important to consider the vast difference in policies and practices in these departments across counties, states, and countries.

Past and present violations of core police relational tenets fuel criticism (Najdowski et al., 2015). Historical and contemporary police misconduct is experienced through the lens of U.S. ethnoracial history, creating lasting psychological effects (Hall et al., 2016). Yet, the cycle of racial trauma has not been adequately acknowledged or researched (Kahn, et al., 2016). Law enforcement structure must reflect a comprehensive psychohistorical understanding of the relationship between police and ethnoracial communities (Westcott, 2015). The lack of police accountability, cross-cultural credibility, perceived legitimacy, procedural justice, and desired civilian responses result in recurring racially traumatizing incidents (Alexander, 2010; Bonilla-Silva, 2001; Du Bois, 2003; Feagin, 2006; Marable, 1999; Rios, 2011).

Details of hostile police experiences are passed down through generations, worldwide. (Franklin, 2011; Nagata, 1990a, 1993, 1998). The continuing traumatic plight of Aboriginal people is analogous to Native American experiences. (Barta, 2008; Brave Heart et al., 2011; Culhane, 2003; Ellinghaus, 2006; Murphy, 2011). Irreversible distrust between Native Americans and authority was driven by centuries of racial trauma including marginalization, exploitation, theft, violence, racism, and genocide (Helgesen, 2011; Perry, 2009). Per capita, more Native Americans die due to police involvement than any other group (Hutson et al., 2007; Miller et al., 2017; Woodward, 2016). Despite being sovereign nations, a considerable number of tribes are under the legal authority of local non-tribal policing agencies. Over 80% of the deadly encounters between Native Americans and law enforcement involved non-tribal police (Chin et al., 2016). Native Americans have the longest history of exposure to racial trauma in the U.S. Native Americans were forcibly removed from their legal properties because of the Indian Removal Act (1830). An estimated 4,000 Native Americans died on the brutal march to what is now known as Oklahoma. Black slaves owned by Cherokees also walked in the Trail of Tears. Roughly 60,000 people were relocated by President Andrew Jackson under horrible weather. The elderly and disabled who were unable to continue the nearly 1000-mile trek were shot or left to die (Johnson, 2014). It is important to note that this is the experience of just one tribe of many and numerous people were forced to abandon their culture. The psychological impact of removal from their land, mistreatment along the way, and witnessing horrible deaths is echoed by trauma from contemporary police actions.

As a consequence of exposure to various forms of racism, rehabilitation efforts must be devoted to building racial resiliency in offenders. This would include developing the psychocultural skills awareness of race conscious behavior, personal adaptive skills, and how to secure appropriate access to a network of support (Jew et al., 1999; Mrazak & Mrazak, 1987). For offenders, resilience can function as a core construct that must also include microaggressions (i.e., navigating regular exposure to racist experiences) (Sue et al., 2007). From a clinical forensic perspective this could involve the use of cognitive approaches for gaining access to supportive networks, job resources as well as other appropriate ways of managing post-release stress (Singh et al., 2006).

Recidivism

Recidivism, also known as repeat offending, is a measurement of the effectiveness of prison system and post-release offender management programs (Ministry of Justice, 2017). The rate of recidivism for state prisoners was 83% over a nine-year study period while it was 39.8% for nonviolent and about 64% for violent federal prisoners over an eight-year period (Alper & Durose, 2018). About 44% of the incarcerated return to prison before the end of their first year out of prison. Globally, two-year post release recidivism rates vary between 26% and 63%; comparing rates across countries remains problematic (Yukhnenko et al., 2019) likely due to available resources, social services, and cultural approaches. High risk offenders in particular fail quickly post release from prison, which is attributed to a lack of preparation for release.

Throughout history, it is clear that the criminal justice system has been especially punitive against poor uneducated minorities. People of color are disproportionately incarcerated and reincarcerated post release. One study looked at 8-year recidivism rates among 21,462 incarcerated Black and White men and women and it was found that Black men were incarcerated more often and more quickly compared to the other race and gender groups despite having lower risk scores on nearly all of the risk variables considered (Ropes Berry et al., 2018). Understanding factors associated with an offender's risk of recidivism is vital to preparing someone for release and is a key part of the *Pentagonal Post-Release Risk Assessment.*

Social Factors

Getting released from prison is a very vulnerable time for offenders. A criminal conviction of any kind limits employment opportunities, public housing assistance, access to social services (Coates, 2015) and voting. Barriers to meeting basic needs for survival including lack of employment, stable housing, financial resources, and prosocial support can increase the possibility of being rearrested (Cortes & Rogers, 2010; Dickson et al., 2013). One study found that post-release employment was the most influential factor impacting recidivism regardless of race and education (Klinker Lockwood et al., 2016).

In conjunction with recent reform measures, an approach to reducing recidivism and assisting ex-offenders re-entering society successfully is prison education and re-entry programming. Many states have responded by offering adult education, adult postsecondary education, career, and technical education, and special education (Taliaferro et al., 2016).

Mental Health and Recidivism

Many offenders and ex-offenders have serious mental illnesses and incarceration is known to further exacerbate mental health symptoms (World Health Organization [WHO], n.d.). In some countries, individuals with serious mental health disorders are incarcerated inappropriately due to a lack of community mental health services. According to Bensen (2003), starting in the late 1950s and 1960s, new psychotropic drugs and the community health movement dramatically reduced the number of people in state mental hospitals in the US. However, in the 1980s many of the mentally ill who had left the mental hospitals in the previous two decades started to enter the criminal justice system (Benson, 2003). Prisons have essentially become de facto mental health hospitals despite not being built for this purpose (Benson, 2003). In 2011-2012, individuals with a serious psychological distress made up about 14% of prisons in state and federal facilities and about 26% in local jails as opposed to about 5% of the general population (BJS, 2017). Females in prison (20%) or jail (32%) were more likely than males in prison (14%) or jail (26%) to have symptoms that met the threshold for a serious psychological distress in the past 30 days (BJS, 2017).

A study comparing recidivism rates of individuals in a reentry program and individuals who received services through the Department of Mental Health and Addiction Services (DMHAS) found that 14.1% of those in the reentry program were rearrested within 6 months of discharge compared to 28.3% of those receiving services from the DMHAS (Kesten et al., 2012). Findings from this Connecticut-based study also found that individuals who were younger, who had a mental illness and who had a co-occurring substance use disorder were at the highest risk of recidivism (Kesten et al., 2012).

Rehabilitation

Rehabilitation programs include motivational programs, cognitive skills programs, sexual offending programs, violent offender programs, substance abuse programs and can also include educational and religious and spiritual services. Innovative rehabilitation efforts include growing a garden (Timler et al., 2019), dog programs (Renck Jalongo, 2019; Romero et al., 2018), and yoga (Muirhead & Fortune, 2016). In Martinson's 1974 study of prison rehabilitation programs, he concluded that offender treatment was largely ineffective and "nothing works". Since then, researchers have rigorously investigated several ways corrections-based programs can impact offender behavior in a prosocial manner. A growing body of research has focused on re-establishing offenders as active citizens and determining "what works." With regard to the *Pentagonal Post-Release Risk Assessment,* understanding the rehabilitative needs of an individual as well as their motivation to change is essential and should be considered throughout an offender's sentence and release into the community.

Many offenders do not have the necessary skills to be successful in the community. Released offenders may have poor interpersonal skills, low levels of formal education, illiteracy or innumeracy, or a lack of planning and financial management skills (Dandurand et al., 2008) as well as a host of psychological consequences of incarceration include hypervigilance, interpersonal distrust, suspicion, alienation, social withdrawal, and isolation which impacts individuals' post-prison in areas such as employment and parenting (Hanley, 2002). Limited practical support is available for offenders planning for release (Criminal Justice Joint Inspection [CJJI], 2017).

Rehabilitation programs typically focus on reducing the risk of reoffending. While not necessarily the primary focus of this chapter, there are two important rehabilitation models to highlight: Risk Needs

Responsivity (RNR) model and Good Lives Model (GLM). The RNR model was developed in Canada in the 1980's (see Bonta & Andrews, 2007) and is used to match the level of service to the offender's risk to reoffend, assess needs and target them in treatment, maximize the offender's ability to learn by tailoring intervention to the individual (Bonta & Andrews, 2007). GLM, created by Ward and colleagues (2002), is a strengths-based approach for offender rehabilitation that focuses on their interests, abilities, and aspirations. A number of GLM programs have been developed and implemented for forensic settings.

A variety of programs have been shown to be effective in reducing reoffending, but it is also important to consider that some people attend rehabilitation programs and reoffend. Rehabilitation programs are just one piece of the complex psychosocial puzzle. Generally, program efficacy does not provide us with information about how programs help some but not others (Maruna, 2001) and what further factors override rehabilitation and skill development. Treatment failures can be attributed to a lack of evidence-based treatment programs or an inappropriate match between offender characteristics/ presenting problem(s) and available/ offered programming (McMurran, 2002). Dickson et al. (2013) notes that in their study of high- risk offenders, some offenders entered treatment with high-quality plans that did not change throughout the course of treatment while others started program with poor plans, or no plans and it was unclear as to who had input into their offender program plans. Day et al. (2006) posited treatment failure may occur when interventions are offered but are not responsive to or fail to meet the needs of the individual at that time. This suggests that it is important to continue to review treatment plans, goals, and needs to reduce reoffending. For example, if an individual is required to attend a program but they have a major mental illness and are unsure how to obtain their medication once released from prison, the priority may need to be that they receive assistance getting their medication so that they can be successful in attending their program.

Prisoners who attend programs based on requirements of themselves and the prison in the short term are unlikely to comply considerably in the long term, but programs prisoners perceive to be legitimate which includes the maintenance of adequate living conditions, having opportunities to undertake meaningful work, having some choice about how to utilize rehabilitative opportunities and generate positive, collaborative relationships (Robinson & McNeill, 2008). Low engagement in rehabilitation programs may be demonstrated by "poor attendance, dropping out, a poor relationship with facilitators, and a reluctance to fully participate in the programs" (Howells, 2004). A person who is ready for treatment is motivated, able to respond, finds the treatment relevant and meaningful and has the capacity to enter a treatment program (Ward et al., 2004). Understanding an offender's readiness and motivation for engaging in and completing a treatment program aids in understanding and addressing risk post-release.

Therapeutic Communities

The prison climate can be quite complex given institutional demands, safety concerns, and rehabilitation needs. From the perspective of prisoners even when officers have good intentions, the climate of the institution and cynicism can wear them down (Bullock & Bunce, 2020) reducing the likelihood of prisoners attending programs or implementing changes while in prison. It can be challenging for corrections staff and prisoners to make relationships work and have a positive atmosphere in which rehabilitation needs could be met (Bullock & Bunce, 2020). However, Petersilia (2003) notes that for prison reform to be realized, it is important to alter the in-prison experience. Blagden et al. (2016) notes the importance of understanding the daily interaction between prisoners and prison staff as these contacts can undermine or support prisoner engagement with rehabilitation since positive attitudes about change can promote change in offender behavior. Harding (2016) provides support for social climate and communities as being an important part of rehabilitation and reduced recidivism rates. Part of understanding social climate is therapeutic communities. Therapeutic communities are a "method of organizing the social structure of a treatment setting to cultivate and take advantage of natural social relationships" (Filstead & Rossi, 1973, p. 10). In a systematic review on therapeutic community interventions aimed at reducing re-arrest, re-incarceration or drug misuse following release from prison, 75% of the studies reviewed reported effectiveness in reducing rates of re-incarceration (Galassi et al.,2015).

Reintegration

Prison reintegration continues to be studied by researchers particularly as it relates to barriers of successful reintegration and reunification, sociological analysis of minority problems, perception of public safety and the overwhelming lack of financial support, employment opportunities, and social support. Released offenders may not know how to use newer technology as they were left back in time while the world continued to move forward (Esparza Flores, 2018). Some may not know how to obtain or manage bank accounts, use a credit card, or how to pay basic bills (Esparza Flores, 2018). In addition to these tangible deficits in the reintegration process, there continues to be a challenge in addressing the solutions while an offender is incarcerated and when they are released to the community. Correctional organizations should consider reintegrative needs noted in the *Pentagonal Post-Release Risk Assessment* as they are crucial to survival and reducing recidivism.

Employment and Financial Resources

Lack of employment and financial resources is a complex issue in offender reintegration. The lack of financial resources is a huge barrier as it impedes the former inmates' ability to engage their basic needs which can immediately trigger a relapse in recovery, over-reliance on social supports, increase in symptoms of anxiety and depression, feeling trapped, helplessness, hopelessness, and a propensity to re-engage in anti-social behavior such as stealing and selling drugs. The American Psychological Association conducted a longitudinal study of Americans from 2007 until 2010 which revealed that the primary source of stress in America is money while work was the second major source of stress (APA, 2011). This statistic speaks volumes as it was conducted on the general population without controlling for extenuating circumstances such as criminal history.

While many employers have developed a reputation for hiring former inmates, the subject of offender related employment continues to draw attention to the reality that convicted felons are less likely to be hired for a job than individuals without criminal backgrounds. Additionally, convicted offenders tend to be less competitive for jobs because they typically have less education and training. Research has proven that correctional based educational programs and job training skills are more likely to yield successful results in community reintegration. However, the research around attitudes of offender employers appears unstable and is outdated. In a research study conducted through the use of a 300-employer survey by Albright and Denq (1996), it was noted that white collar ex-offenders experienced a difficult time securing employment commensurate with their experience and training as their crime as they often offended against an employer or company. In the same study of 300 employers in the Dallas, Texas and Houston, Texas, the category 'type of offense' attracted the largest response of written comments on their survey. Moreover, twenty-one respondents indicated that their decision to hire an ex-offender was likely based on the type of crime and circumstances around their behavior. At the time of the study 64%-88% of employers would not hire former inmates who committed crimes such as murder, robbery, arson, sexual offenses against a child, injury to a child or sexual assault. Only 12% expressed willingness to hire a former inmate. This number increased to 32% when the inmate had a college degree. Seven years later, Hlavka et al (2016) conducted a qualitative study of inmate interviews in Milwaukee, WI which noted that potential employers were about half as likely to hire applicants with a criminal record and the likelihood of a job callback for black applicants with a criminal record was about 5%. It was argued that the likelihood of securing employment remains so low that it is no surprise that young black men with criminal records have specifically been excluded from the job market (Hlavka et al., 2016).

In addition, former inmates struggle with chronic mental health and medical conditions which would make them more difficult to employ and many have limited community and social supports (Davis et al., 2018) which interfere with their general stability. The length of incarceration contributes significantly to the barriers to securing employment as well. Not only does a long prison sentence create large gaps of employment in one's work history, but it also creates large technology gaps that affect their job prospects.

Research has demonstrated gainful employment is a critical component to successful reintegration. Access to employment has been proven to decrease recidivism by increasing bonds and association with law abiding citizens. It allows offenders to demonstrate active involvement in their community by increasing their sense of belonging, which places a stake in their conformity and social capital. It also provides productive and responsible ways to spend time which is valuable for one's pride, self-esteem, and sense of purpose and self-worth (Davis et al, 2018).

Housing

Housing remains a major barrier to the reintegration of former inmates into the community. Prior to being released from prison, inmates are required to provide an address that demonstrates proof of stability after prison. In a study of qualitative interviews on the subject of inmate housing and stigma conducted by Keene et al. (2018) Doug stated, "You know being on parole, if you don't have an address, they basically lock you back up." Housing is seen as a fundamental necessity to the participation and achievement of successful reintegration yet the acquisition of fair, safe, and affordable housing is often not within reach. The limitations to acquiring stable housing exist far beyond affordability and continue to pose ongoing restrictions when accessing basic needs as a convicted offender. In some states, property owners have the right to use background checks as a screening tool to deny someone a lease, which further habituates the reintegration crisis for former inmates. These exclusionary policies, while often perceived as a measure taken for public safety, are justifiable reasons to deny housing and can dually act as a barrier to housing for convicted offenders. The reliance on these screening measures requires that formerly incarcerated individuals expose otherwise private information which as a result turns their past into a present circumstance that not only limit their ability to achieve stable housing but can potentially activate stigma and discrimination during their housing search (Keene et al, 2018).

Prior to release from prison, inmates are often provided with limited options for housing and the limitations increase as the housing becomes increasingly specific to their crime. For example, state regulations can determine if and where a former inmate is allowed to assume residency if he has been convicted of a sex offense, has a drug addiction, has severe medical conditions, and/or chronic mental health issues. These specialized residential facilities are often located in marginalized locations and considered undesirable and criminalized. As such, inmates are at higher risk for recidivism as the protective measures that were once taken by the inmate to survive these dangerous areas become increasingly likely to resume (i.e., selling drugs, gang activity and carrying a concealed weapon). "Residence in spaces that are associated with the criminal justice system, such as halfway houses, may represent a source of spatial stigma to potential employers, family members, and former prisoners themselves. Additionally, the challenges that formerly incarcerated individuals face in accessing decent affordable housing may restrict them to the most disadvantaged and stigmatized neighborhoods, the streets, or homeless shelters (Keene et al, 2018, p. 801)."

Without housing, or more specifically a viable address, inmates cannot move forward with accessing other resources to assist in meeting basic needs such as searching for a job, applying for medical care, governmental financial assistance, filing income taxes, applying for school, and other basic life resources. In some cases, housing is a requirement for family reunification as well. Housing is more than just a symbol of tangible stability. It can also be seen as a marker for economic self-sufficiency, independence, pride, and safety.

Physical Appearance

"They drink and smoke, they have tattoos, and they use slang. And their teeth are rotten. That's how people think women who've been in prison look" (Former prisoner) – Moran (2012). One's physical appearance represents a unique barrier to reintegration as it exposes both implicit and explicit bias regarding the offender population. Moran (2012) painted an image of a female inmate as he noted that missing teeth, along with tattoos, smoking, and swearing 'mark' individuals as a former inmate which triggers an immediate feeling of exposure for the ex-offender. This concept suggests that offenders are likely to face ongoing discrimination and prejudges based on physical features, habits, and markers of prison experience that were obtained while incarcerated.

Sometimes a part of survival, tattoos become a part of the story that is told about life in prison. They can signal gang affiliation, serving as a mode of protection during a prison sentence, and work as a symbolic cover to hide the years of damage done to the body. Regardless of their purpose, tattoos continue to pose a problem for successful reintegration. Sadly, research to date has concluded that a bias against tattoos does exist, particularly when obtaining a job is the primary goal. Researchers discovered that those with tattoos are perceived as less suitable for employment (Tews, 2020 as cited in Timming et al., 2017). Employers likely prefer non-tattooed employees as they are perceived to present a more clean-cut aesthetic. Hotels and other businesses continue to recruit employees whose appearance mirrors the image that a company would like to portray as many organizations believe that employee image is correlated to customer satisfaction (Tews, 2020 as cited in Efthymiou, 2018 & Adelman et al., 1994; Söderlund & Julander, 2009). While some research can qualify that the bias decreases with service line jobs, most of the research conducted does not account for minority perception or bias.

Gender Considerations

Reintegration may be particularly challenging for women of color. Richie (2001) found African American women are more likely to report lack of access to programs and services in their disenfranchised communities. As a result, women of color who return home from prison often report feelings of marginalization in the context of an economically distressed neighborhood, making successful reintegration more difficult. Some welfare reform acts preclude anyone convicted of drug-related or felony offenses from receiving government benefits or student loans for themselves or their families. These acts have had a large effect on African American and Hispanic mothers as they are more likely to struggle with poverty and are disproportionately represented in the welfare system. Excluding these individuals from aid categories can reduce opportunities for education for mothers and their children. In total, 48% of women affected by such reforms are black or Hispanic, further complicating successful reintegration for women of a minority race (Allard, 2002). While much has changed over the last two decades and some states have lifted bans against released offenders receiving government assistance, some have not.

Reunification

Released offenders have reported that the first 30 days post-release is harder than serving time in prison (Skinner-Osei & Stepteau- Watson, 2018). There are several barriers to family unification post incarceration. One study found that having prior convictions, living with a mental illness, being single or divorced, or reporting institutional barriers to family contact were all associated with experiencing a sharper decline in family contact or support over the course of an incarceration and release from prison (Mowen & Visher, 2016). Subjective reports from prisoners have highlighted the influence of being separated from loved ones while incarcerated resulting in inconsistent, unreliable social support and limited family visits. Institutional transfers and far-removed prison locations often made family contact difficult as well (Hlavka et al., 2015). It is also important to consider that individuals might also be returning to family members that are engaged in criminal behavior, or to families that are angry or hurt due to their criminal behavior and prison sentence (Phillips & Spencer, 2013).

Literature highlights the traumatic impact of parental incarceration on children but does not address how incarcerated parents are affected (Skinner-Osei & Stepteau- Watson, 2018). While serving a prison sentence, individuals may feel increasingly removed and or isolated from their family. Reentry success is closely tied to feeling accepted in society, which often begins with acceptance from family (Hlavka et al., 2015). Social and emotional support have been found to impact success of entry of men and women from various backgrounds (Hlavka et al., 2015). De Claire et al. (2019) examined intimate partner relationships between inmates and partners on the outside and found that supporting increased communication and maintaining a belief in the future were important components for the couples. Many facilities require prisoner's family members to pay for phone calls, which is often a significant expense and a barrier for many families to maintain communication on a regular basis. Visitation while incarcerated is noted to be important in familial relationships and increases the likelihood of success in reunification upon release (De Claire & Dixon, 2015; Hairston, 2007). In one study, visitation while in prison was associated with a reduction in recidivism rates by 13% (Minnesota Dept. of Corrections, 2011). Prison visits reduced depressive symptoms in female and adolescent prisoners and reduced recidivism upon release (De Claire & Dixon, 2015).

Developing or strengthening relationships with children is a core concern for both men and women. In a sample of prior male offenders, economic insecurity associated with unemployment and housing difficulties is found to be a barrier to family reunification (Western & Smith, 2018). Housing patterns are closely associated with parent-child relationships following incarceration; released offenders living in shelters or homeless had less contact with their families compared to those with more stable housing (Western & Smith, 2018). There are several barriers and challenges for mothers in trying to regain custody of their children upon release from prison. Stone et al. (2017) note that poverty, homelessness, abuse, and lack of access to service hinders reunification of mothers and children. Most incarcerated mothers are primary caregivers who plan to continue their parental responsibility upon release. Researchers have noted a lack of post-release programs to address barriers to mothers' reunification with their children and suggested that these programs should apply to all women post-release, regardless of sentence length or remand status (Baldry, 2010). Of note, an Australian study demonstrated that the profile of an incarcerated mother has changed little over the last 50 years and the available policies and programs remain inadequate (Stone et al., 2017). Collaborative services and gender-responsive policies and programs are necessary to support for incarcerated women (Stone et al., 2017).

Research has shown what has been helpful in promoting and maintaining positive relationships during and post incarceration as well as areas for improvement. One study notes that individuals who completed parenting classes, had more frequent visits from family members, and Black females experienced positive changes in family relationships while individuals who were single or divorced, had prior convictions or mental health issues reported negative changes in their family relationships (Moven & Visher, 2016). It has been recommended that jails and prisons document which inmates have formal reunification plans, prioritize their placement in available services, and ensure adequate visitation facilities to accommodate children and families (D'Andrade & Valdez, 2012). Improved communication and relationships between agencies are critical to ensure accessible visitation facilities and increase the quality of communication between social workers and incarcerated parents (D'Andrade & Valdez, 2012). McKay et al. (2016) notes that we must focus future research and intervention efforts on supporting family ties in communities affected by incarceration. Further strategies to support the maintenance of family relationships during incarceration and healthy family reunification post release are needed.

CONCLUSION

Addressing racism, rehabilitation, recidivism, reunification, and reintegration are pivotal to address in the context of prison reform. Prison reform is vital for ensuring the human rights of offenders are protected and increasing the likelihood of success upon release (United Nations Office on Drugs and Crime, n.d.). In terms of prison reform, reducing the use of prisons does not directly address some of the challenges that are often correlated with incarceration, such as low education, a lack of employment, poverty, and addiction. Supporting and improving the process of reintegration can help society become a better and safer place (Esparza Florez, 2018).

As noted by van Zyl Smit (2018), the outcomes of recognizing that prisoners have a positive human right to be given opportunities for rehabilitation are still to be explored. Prison sentences will have to be planned to provide prisoners with programs that can meet their individual needs and allow them to rehabilitate themselves. Attention should also be paid to prisoners' rights to contact their families as this is considered essential for their rehabilitation (van Zyl Smit, 2018).

Historically, while the racial inequities embedded in prisons are observed in other institutions, the carceral state sustains it in the most substantial way. Racism, rehabilitation, recidivism, reunification, and reintegration function as clinical forensic anchors for offenders even though addressing them comes about with a rather high cost. Still, the desired outcome for prison reform is premised on the assumption that a pragmatic vision of criminal justice is capable of ameliorating pressing problems confronting the nation. The opposite is certainly true, passive indifference or intentional indifference to the issues presented by post-release offenders is shortsighted with respect to meeting 21st Century prison reform efforts.

ACKNOWLEDGMENT

The authors would like to thank and acknowledge Sarah Robinson, Psy.D. for providing professional copy editing for this chapter. This research received no specific grant from any funding agency in the public, commercial, or not-for-profit sectors.

REFERENCES

Abrams, D. S., Bertrand, M., & Mullainathan, S. (2012). Do judges vary in their treatment of race? *The Journal of Legal Studies*, *41*(2), 347–383. doi:10.1086/666006

Albright, S. & Denq, F. (1996). Employer attitudes toward hiring ex-offenders. *Prison Journal, 76*(2).

Alexander, M. (2010). *The new Jim Crow: Mass incarcerations in the age of color blindness*. New Press.

Allard, P. (2002). *Life sentences: Denying welfare benefits to women convicted of drug offenses*. The Sentencing Project.

Alper, M., & Durose, M. R. (2018). *2018 update on prison recidivism: A 9-year follow-up period (2005-2014)*. US. Department of Justice NCJ 250975. https://www.bjs.gov/content/pub/pdf/18upr9yfup0514.pdf

Aurand, A., Emmanuel, D., Yentel, D., Errico, E., & Pang, M. (2017). *Out of reach 2017: The high cost of housing*. National Low Income Housing Coalition. Retrieved from http://nlihc.org/sites/default/files/oor/OOR_2017.pdf

Bahr, S. J., Armstrong, A. H., Gibbs, B. G., Harris, P. E., & Fisher, J. K. (2005). The reentry process: How parolees adjust to release from prison. *Fathering*, *3*(3), 243–265. doi:10.3149/fth.0303.243

Baldry, E. (2010). Women in transition: From prison to . . .. *Current Issues in Criminal Justice*, *22*(2), 253–267. doi:10.1080/10345329.2010.12035885

Banner, S. (2002). *The death penalty: An American history*. Harvard University Press.

Barta, T. (2008). Sorry, and not sorry, in Australia: How the apology to the Stolen Generations buried a history of genocide. *Journal of Genocide Research*, *10*(2), 201–214. doi:10.1080/14623520802065438

Bensen, E. (2003). Rehabilitate or punish? Psychologists are not only providing treatment to prisoners; they're also contributing to debate over the nature of prison itself. *APA Monitor*, *34*(7). https://www.apa.org/monitor/julaug03/rehab

Blagden, N., Winder, B., & Hames, C. (2016). "They Treat Us Like Human Beings"-Experiencing a Therapeutic Sex Offenders Prison: Impact on Prisoners and Staff and Implications for Treatment. *International Journal of Offender Therapy and Comparative Criminology*, *60*(4), 371–296. doi:10.1177/0306624X14553227 PMID:25305193

Bonilla-Silva, E. (2001). *White supremacy and racism in the post-civil rights era*. Lynne Rienner Publishers.

Bonta, J., & Andrews, D. A. (2007). *Risk-Need-Responsivity Model for offender assessment and rehabilitation.* Retrieved from https://www.publicsafety.gc.ca/cnt/rsrcs/pblctns/rsk-nd-rspnsvty/rsk-nd-rspnsvty-eng.pdf

Brave Heart, M. Y. H., Chase, J., Elkins, J., & Altschul, D. B. (2011). Historical trauma among indigenous peoples of the Americas: Concepts, research, and clinical considerations. *Journal of Psychoactive Drugs, 43*(4), 282–290. doi:10.1080/02791072.2011.628913 PMID:22400458

Brown, L. S. (2013). Treating the effects of psychological trauma. In G. Koocher, J. C. Norcross, & B. Greene (Eds.), *Psychologists' desk reference* (pp. 290–293). doi:10.1093/med:psych/9780199845491.003.0060

Bullock, K., & Bunce, A. (2020). 'The prison don't talk to you about getting out of prison' "On why prisons in England and Wales fail to rehabilitate prisoners. *Criminology & Criminal Justice, 20*(1), 111–127. doi:10.1177/1748895818800743

Bureau of Justice (BJS). (2017). *Mental health problems of prison and jail inmates.* Bureau of Justice Statistics Special Report. Retrieved from https://www.bjs.gov/content/pub/pdf/mhppji.pdf

Cain, B. E., & Parker, B. (2020). The Uncertain Future of Felon Disenfranchisement. *Mo. L. Rev., 84.* Available at: https://scholarship.law.missouri.edu/mlr/vol84/iss4/4

Carbado, D. W., & Rock, P. (2016). What exposes African Americans to police violence? *Harvard Civil Rights-Civil Liberties Law Review, 51*(1), 159–187.

Centers for Disease Control and Prevention. (2020). *Interim guidance on management of coronavirus disease 2019 (COVID-19) in correctional and detention facilities*. https://www.cdc.gov/coronavirus/2019-ncov/community/correction-detention/ guidance-correctional-detention.html

Chin, R. J., Schroedel, J., & Rowen, L. (2016). *Whose lives matter? The media's failure to cover police shootings of Native Americans.* Paper presented at the 58th Annual Conference of the Western Social Science Association Western Association of Social Science, Reno, NV.

Coates, T. N. (2015). The black family in the age of mass incarceration. *Atlantic (Boston, Mass.), 316*(3), 82.

Cortes, K., & Rogers, S. (2010). *Reentry Housing Options: The Policymakers' Guide*. Council of State Governments.

Criminal Justice Joint Inspection (CJJI). (2017). *An inspection of through the gate resettlement services for prisoners serving 12 months or more.* https://www.justiceinspectorates.gov.uk/cjji/wp-content/ uploads/sites/2/2017/06/Through-the-Gate-phase-2-report.pdf

Culhane, D. (2003). Their spirits live within us: Aboriginal women in Downtown Eastside Vancouver emerging into visibility. *American Indian Quarterly, 27*(3/4), 593–606. doi:10.1353/aiq.2004.0073

D'Andrade, A. C., & Valdez, M. (2012). Reunifying from behind bars: A quantitative study of the relationship between parental incarceration, service use, and foster care reunification. *Social Work in Public Health, 27*(6), 616–636. doi:10.1080/19371918.2012.713294 PMID:22963161

Dandurand, Y., Christian, J., Murdoch, D., Brown, R. E., & Chin, V. (2008). *Conditional Release Violations, Suspensions and Revocations – A Comparative Analysis.* Vancouver: ICCLR. http://www.icclr.law.ubc.ca/files/books/Condition al%20Release%20Violations%20Final_English.pdf

Davis, C., Bahr, S. J., & Ward, C. (2012). The process of offender reintegration: Perceptions of what helps prisoners reenter society. *Criminology & Criminal Justice, 13*(4), 446–469. doi:10.1177/1748895812454748

Day, A., Bryan, J., Davey, L., & Casey, S. (2006). The process of change in offender rehabilitation programmes. *Psychology, Crime & Law, 12*(5), 473–487. doi:10.1080/10683160500151209

De Claire, K., & Dixon, L. (2015). The effects of prison visits from family members on prisoners' well-being, prison rule-breaking, and recidivism: A review of research since 1991. *Journal of Trauma Violence, and Abuse, 18*(2), 185–199. doi:10.1177/1524838015603209 PMID:26330175

De Claire, L., Dixon, L., & Larkin, M. (2019). How prisoners and their partners experience the maintenance of their relationship during a prison sentence. *Journal of Community & Applied Social Psychology, 30*(3), 293–306. Advance online publication. doi:10.1002/casp.2445

Dickson, S. R., Polaschek, D. L. L., & Casey, A. R. (2013). Can the quality of high-risk violent prisoners' release plans predict recidivism following intensive rehabilitation? A comparison with risk assessment instruments. *Psychology, Crime & Law, 19*(4), 371–389. doi:10.1080/1068316X.2011.640634

Dodge, M., & Pogrebin, M. (2001). Collateral costs of imprisonment for women: Complications of reintegration. *The Prison Journal, 81*(1), 42–54. doi:10.1177/0032885501081001004

Dowler, K., & Sparks, R. (2008). Victimization, contact with police, and neighborhood conditions: Reconsidering African American and Hispanic attitudes toward the police. *Police Practice and Research, 9*(5), 395–415. doi:10.1080/15614260801980760

Du Bois, W. E. B. (2003). *Darkwater: Voices from within the veil.* Humanity Books.

Ellinghaus, K. (2006). Indigenous assimilation and absorption in the United States and Australia. *Pacific Historical Review, 75*(4), 563–585. doi:10.1525/phr.2006.75.4.563

Esparza Flores, N. (2018). Contributing Factors to Mass Incarceration and Recidivism. *Themis: Research Journal of Justice Studies and Forensic Science, 6*(4). Retrieved from https://scholarworks.sjsu.edu/themis/vol6/iss1/4

Everett, R. S., & Wojtkiewicz, R. A. (2002). Difference, Disparity, and Race/Ethnic Bias in Federal Sentencing. *Journal of Quantitative Criminology, 18*(2), 189–211. doi:10.1023/A:1015258732676

Feagin, J. R. (1991). The continuing significance of race: Antiblack discrimination in public places. *American Sociological Review, 56*(1), 101–116. doi:10.2307/2095676

Feagin, J. R. (2006). *Systemic racism: A theory of oppression.* Routledge.

Franke, I., Vogel, T., Eher, R., & Dudeck, M. (2019). Prison mental healthcare: Recent developments and future challenges. *Current Opinion in Psychiatry, 32*(4), 342–347. doi:10.1097/YCO.0000000000000504 PMID:30855296

Franklin, J. H. (2011). *From slavery to freedom: A history of African Americans*. McGraw-Hill/Connect Learn Succeed.

Galassi, A., Mpofu, E., & Athanasou, J. (2015). Therapeutic Community Treatment of an Inmate Population with Substance Use Disorders: Post-Release Trends in Re-Arrest, Re-Incarceration, and Drug Misuse Relapse. *International Journal of Environmental Research and Public Health*, *12*(6), 7059–7072. doi:10.3390/ijerph120607059 PMID:26103591

Garland, D. (2010). *Peculiar institution: American death penalty in an age of abolition*. Oxford University Press.

Hagan, B. O., Wang, E. A., Aminawung, J. A., Albizu-Garcia, C. E., Zaller, N., Nyamu, S., Shavit, S., Deluca, J., & Fox, A. D. (2018). History of Solitary Confinement Is Associated with Post-Traumatic Stress Disorder Symptoms among Individuals Recently Released from Prison. *Journal of Urban Health*, *95*(2), 141–148. doi:10.100711524-017-0138-1 PMID:28281161

Hairston, C. F. (2007). *Focus on Children with Incarcerated Parents: An Overview of the Research Literature*. Annie E. Casey Foundation.

Helgesen, E. (2011). Allotment of justice: How U. S. policy in Indian country perpetuates the victimization of American Indians. *University of Florida Journal of Law and Public Policy*, *22*(3), 441–472.

Hlavka, H., Wheelock, D., & Jones, R. (2015). Ex-offender accounts of successful re-entry from prison. *Journal of Offender Rehabilitation*, *54*(6), 426–428. doi:10.1080/10509674.2015.1057630

Hlavka, H. R., Wheelock, D., & Cossyleon, J. E. (2016). Narratives of commitment: Looking for Work with a criminal record. *The Sociological Quarterly*, *56*(2), 213–236. doi:10.1111/tsq.12086

Howells, K. (2004). Anger and Its Links to Violent Offending. *Psychiatry, Psychology and Law*, *11*(2), 189–196. doi:10.1375/pplt.2004.11.2.189

Hutson, H. R., Rice, P. L. Jr, Chana, J. K., Kyriacou, D. N., Chang, Y., & Miller, R. M. (2007). A review of police pursuit fatalities in the United States from 1982–2004. *Prehospital Emergency Care*, *11*(3), 278–283. doi:10.1080/10903120701385414 PMID:17613900

Jew, C. L., Green, K. E., & Kroger, J. (1999). Development and validation of a measure of resiliency. *Measurement & Evaluation in Counseling & Development*, *32*(2), 75–89. doi:10.1080/07481756.1999.12068973

Johnson, R. (2014). Ethnoracial factors in the U.S. prison system: Forensic psychological realities of correctional officers. In Color Behind Bars (vol. 2). Praeger.

Kahn, K. B., & Martin, K. D. (2016). Policing and race: Disparate treatment, perceptions, and policy responses. *Social Issues and Policy Review*, *10*(1), 82–121. doi:10.1111ipr.12019

Keene, D. E., Smoyer, A. B., & Blankenship, K. M. (2018). Stigma, housing, and identity after prison. *The Sociological Review*, *66*(4), 799–815. doi:10.1177/0038026118777447 PMID:32855574

Kesten, K. L., Leavitt-Smith, E., Rau, D. R., Shelton, D., Zhnag, W., Wagner, J., & Trestman, R. L. (2012). Recidivism rates among mentally ill inmates: Impact of the Connecticut Offender Reentry Program. *Journal of Correctional Health Care*, *18*(1), 20–28. doi:10.1177/1078345811421117 PMID:22095006

Kinner, S. A., Young, J. T., Snow, K., Southalan, L., Lopez-Acuña, D., Ferreira-Borges, C., & O'Moore, E. (2020). Prisons and custodial settings are part of a comprehensive response to COVID-19. *The Lancet. Public Health*, *5*(4), e188–e189. doi:10.1016/S2468-2667(20)30058-X PMID:32197116

Klinker-Lockwood, S., Nally, J. M., & Ho, T. (2016). Race, education, employment, and recidivism among offenders in the United States: An exploration of complex issues in the Indianapolis metropolitan area. *International Journal of Criminal Justice Sciences*, *11*(1), 57–74.

Loo, C. (1993). An integrative-sequential model of treatment for PTSD: A case study of the Japanese American internment and redress. *Clinical Psychology Review*, *13*, 89–117. doi:10.1016/0272-7358(93)90036-L

Lurigio, A. J., Rollins, A., & Fallon, J. (2004). The effects of serious mental illness on offender reentry. *Federal Probation*, *68*(2), 45–52.

Marable, M. (1999). *Black Liberation in Conservative America*. South End Press.

Martinson, R. (1974). What works? Questions and answers about prison reform. *The Public Interest*, *35*, 22–54.

Maruna, S. (2001). *Making good: How ex-convicts reform and rebuild their lives*. American Psychological Association. doi:10.1037/10430-000

McKay, T., Comfort, M., Lindquist, C., & Bir, A. (2016). If family matters: Supporting family relationships during incarceration and reentry. *Criminology & Public Policy*, *15*(2), 529–542. doi:10.1111/1745-9133.12209

McMurran, M. (2002). *Motivating offenders to change: a guide to enhancing engagement in therapy*. Wiley. doi:10.1002/9780470713471

Miller, T. R., Lawrence, B. A., Carlson, N. N., Hendrie, D., Randall, S., Rockett, I. R. H., & Spicer, R. S. (2017). Perils of police action: A cautionary tale from U.S. data sets. *Injury Prevention*, *23*(1), 27–32. doi:10.1136/injuryprev-2016-042023 PMID:27457242

Ministry of Justice. (2017). *Prison performance statistics 2016 to 2017*. Retrieved from https://www.gov.uk/government/statistics/prison-performance-statistics-2016-to-2017

Minnesota Dept. of Corrections. (2011). *Effects of prison visitation on offender recidivism*. St. Paul, MN: Author. Retrieved from doc.state.mn.us/pages/files/large-files/Publications/11-11MNPrisonVisitationStudy.pdf

Moran, D. (2012). Prisoner reintegration and the stigma of prison time inscribed on the body. *Punishment & Society*, *14*(5), 564–583. doi:10.1177/1462474512464008

Morenoff, J. D., & Harding, D. J. (2014). Incarceration, prison reentry, and communities. *Annual Review of Sociology*, *40*(1), 411–429. doi:10.1146/annurev-soc-071811-145511 PMID:25400321

Mowen, T. J., & Visher, C. A. (2016). Changing the ties that bind: How incarceration impacts family relationships. *Criminology & Public Policy*, *15*(2), 503–528. doi:10.1111/1745-9133.12207

Mrazek, P. J., & Mrazek, D. A. (1987). Resilience in child maltreatment victims: A conceptual exploration. *Child Abuse & Neglect*, *11*(3), 357–366. doi:10.1016/0145-2134(87)90009-3 PMID:3676892

Muirhead, J., & Fortune, C. (2016). Yoga in prisons: A review of the literature. *Aggression and Violent Behavior*, *28*, 57–63. doi:10.1016/j.avb.2016.03.013

Murphy, F. (2011). Archives of sorrow: An exploration of Australia's Stolen Generations and their journey into the past. *History and Anthropology*, *22*(4), 481–495. doi:10.1080/02757206.2011.626775

Nagata, D. K. (1993). *Legacy of injustice: Exploring the cross-generational impact of the Japanese American internment*. Plenum Press. doi:10.1007/978-1-4899-1118-6

Nagata, D. K. (1998). Intergenerational effects of the Japanese American internment. In Y. Danieli (Ed.), *International handbook of multigenerational legacies of trauma* (pp. 125–139). Plenum Press. doi:10.1007/978-1-4757-5567-1_8

Nagata, D. K., & Cheng, W. J. Y. (2003). Intergenerational communication of race-related trauma by Japanese American former internees. *The American Journal of Orthopsychiatry*, *73*(3), 266–278. doi:10.1037/0002-9432.73.3.266 PMID:12921207

Nagata, D. K., Trierweiler, S. J., & Talbot, R. (1999). Long-term effects of internment during early childhood on third-generation Japanese Americans. *The American Journal of Orthopsychiatry*, *69*(1), 19–29. doi:10.1037/h0080378 PMID:9990433

Najdowski, C. J., Bottoms, B. L., & Goff, P. A. (2015). Stereotype threat and racial differences in citizens' experiences of police encounters. *Law and Human Behavior*, *39*(5), 463–477. doi:10.1037/lhb0000140 PMID:26030449

Palmater, P. (2016). Shining light on the dark places: Addressing police racism and sexualized violence against indigenous women and girls in the National Inquiry. *Canadian Journal of Women and the Law*, *28*(2), 253–284. doi:10.3138/cjwl.28.2.253

Perry, B. (2009). Impacts of disparate policing in Indian country. *Policing and Society*, *19*(3), 263–281. doi:10.1080/10439460902871348

Petersilia, J. (2003). *When prisoners come home: parole and prisoner reentry*. Oxford University Press.

Phillips, L. A., & Spencer, W. M. (2013). The challenges of re-entry from prison to society. *Journal of Current Issues in Crime, Law, and Law Enforcement*, *6*(2), 123–133.

Ready, J. T., & Young, J. T. N. (2015). The impact of on-officer video cameras on police–citizen contacts: Findings from a controlled experiment in Mesa, AZ. *Journal of Experimental Criminology*, *11*(3), 445–458. doi:10.100711292-015-9237-8

Reardon, C. M. (2013). Cell phone, police recording and the intersection of the first and fourth amendments. *Duke Law Journal*, *63*(3), 735–779.

Richie, B. (2001). Challenges incarcerated women face as they return to their communities: Findings from life history interviews. *Crime and Delinquency*, *47*(3), 368–389. doi:10.1177/0011128701047003005

Rios, V. M. (2011). *Punished: Policing the Lives of Black and Latino Boys*. NYU Press.

Robinson, G., & McNeill, F. (2008). Exploring the dynamics of compliance with community penalties. *Theoretical Criminology*, *12*(4), 431–449. doi:10.1177/1362480608097151

Ropes Berry, K., Kennedy, C., Lloyd, M., Veeh, C. A., & Tripodi, S. J. (2020). The Intersectional Effects of Race and Gender on Time to Reincarceration. *Justice Quarterly*, *37*(1), 132–160. doi:10.1080/07418825.2018.1524508

Sanchez-Meier, S., Johnston, F. E., & Vanhasselt, V. B. (2002). Multi-Family Group Therapy for Families of Incarcerated Felons. *Justice Quarterly*, *37*(1), 132–160. doi:10.1300/J189v01n02_04

Schaeffer, C. M., & Borduin, C. M. (1999). Mother-adolescent-sibling conflict in families of juvenile felons. *The Journal of Genetic Psychology*, *160*(1), 115–118. doi:10.1080/00221329909595386 PMID:10048216

Singh, A.A., Chung, Y. B., & Dean, J.K. (2006). Acculturation Level and Internalized Homophobia of Asian American Lesbian and Bisexual Women. *Journal of LGBTQ Issues in Counseling, 1*(2), 3-19. doi:10.1300/J462v01n02_02

Skinner-Osei, P., & Stepteau-Watson, D. (2018). A qualitative analysis of African American fathers' struggle with re-entry, recidivism, and reunification after participation in re-entry programs. *Journal of Human Behavior in the Social Environment*, *28*(2), 240–255. doi:10.1080/10911359.2017.1402724

Solis, J., Franco-Paredes, C., Henao-Martınez, A. F., Krsak, M., & Zimmer, S. M. (2020). Structural Vulnerability in the United States Revealed in Three Waves of Novel Coronavirus Disease (COVID-19). *The American Journal of Tropical Medicine and Hygiene*. Advance online publication. doi:10.4269/ajtmh.20-0391 PMID:32383432

Starr, S. B., & Rehavi, M. M. (2013). Mandatory sentencing and racial disparity: Assessing the role of prosecutors and the effects of booker. *The Yale Law Journal*, *123*(1), 2–80.

Stone, U., Liddell, M., & Matinovic, M. (2017). Incarcerated mothers: Issues and barriers of regaining custody of children. *The Prison Journal*, *97*(3), 296–317. doi:10.1177/0032885517703957

Sue, D. W., Capodilupo, C. M., Torino, G. C., Bucceri, J. M., Holder, A. M. B., Nadal, K. L., & Esquilin, M. (2007). Racial microaggressions in everyday life: Implications for clinical practice. *The American Psychologist*, *62*(4), 271–286. doi:10.1037/0003-066X.62.4.271 PMID:17516773

Taliferro, W., Pham, D., & Cielinski, A. (2016). *A look at trends, gaps, and opportunities in correctional education and training*. Retrieved from https://www.clasp.org/sites/default/files/public/resources-and-publications/publication-1/2016.10.27_fromincarcerationtoreentry.pdf

Tews, M. J., & Stafford, K. (2020). Tattoos and perceptions of employment suitability in the hospitality industry. *Journal of Human Resources in Hospitality & Tourism*, *19*(2), 148–167. doi:10.1080/15332845.2020.1702865

Timler, K., Brown, H., & Varcoe, C. (2019). Growing connection beyond prison walls: How a prison garden fosters rehabilitation and healing for incarcerated men. *Journal of Offender Rehabilitation*, *58*(5), 444–463. doi:10.1080/10509674.2019.1615598

Tremblay, M., & Sutherland, J. (2017). The effectiveness of parenting programs for incarcerated mothers: A systematic review. *Journal of Child and Family Studies*, *26*(12), 3247–3265. doi:10.100710826-017-0900-8

van Zyl Smit, D. (2018). Rehabilitation as a dominant idea in European prison law: Problems and prospects. *Romania Journal of Sociological Studies. New Series*, *1*, 9–18.

Walmsley, R. (2016). *World Prison Population List* (11th ed.). International Centre for Prison Studies, Kings College. https://www.prisonstudies.org/sites/default/files/resources/downloads/world_ prison_population_list_11th_edition_0.pdf

Walters, G. (2011). Predicting recidivism with the psychological inventory of criminal thinking styles and Level of Service Inventory-Revised: Screening Version. *Law and Human Behavior*, *35*(3), 211–220. doi:10.100710979-010-9231-7 PMID:20464628

Ward, T. (2002). The management of risk and the design of good lives. *Australian Psychologist*, *37*(3), 172–179. doi:10.1080/00050060210001706846

Ward, T., Day, A., Howells, K., & Birgden, A. (2004). The multifactor offender readiness model. *Aggression and Violent Behavior*, *9*(6), 645–673. doi:10.1016/j.avb.2003.08.001

Weitzer, R., & Tuch, S. A. (2004). Race and perception of police misconduct. *Social Problems*, *51*(3), 305–325. doi:10.1525p.2004.51.3.305

Westcott, K. (2015). Race, criminalization, and historical trauma in the United States: Making the case for a new justice framework. *Traumatology*, *21*(4), 273–284. doi:10.1037/trm0000048

Western, B., & Smith, N. (2018). Formerly Incarcerated Parents and Their Children. *Demography*, *55*(3), 823–847. doi:10.100713524-018-0677-4 PMID:29770923

Woodward, S. (2016). The police killings no one is talking about. *In These Times*. Retrieved from: https://www.inthesetimes.com/features/native_american_police_killings_native_lives_matter.html

World Health Organization (WHO). (n.d.). *Mental health and prisons: Information sheet.* Retrieved from https://www.who.int/mental_health/policy/mh_in_prison.pdf

YukhnenkoD.SridharS.FazelS. (2019). A systematic review of criminal recidivism rates worldwide: 3-year update. *Welcome Open Research, 4*(28), doi:10.12688/wellcomeopenres.14970.2

ADDITIONAL READING

Ahalt, C., Haney, C., Ekhaugen, K., & Williams, B. (2020). Role of a US–Norway Exchange in Placing Health and Well-Being at the Center of US Prison Reform. *American Journal of Public Health, 110*(S1), S27–S29. Advance online publication. doi:10.2105/AJPH.2019.305444 PMID:31967893

Craig, L. A., Dixon, L., & Gannon, T. A. (2013). *What Works in Offender Rehabilitation: An Evidence-Based Approach to Assessment and Treatment*. John Wiley & Sons, Ltd., doi:10.1002/9781118320655

Polaschek, D. L. L., Day, A., & Hollin, C. R. (2019). *The Wiley International handbook of correctional psychology*. John Wiley & Sons, Ltd., doi:10.1002/9781119139980

Van Voorhis, P., & Salisbury, E. J. (2016). *Correctional Counseling and Rehabilitation* (9th ed.). Routledge., doi:10.4324/9781315668079

Ward, T., & Fortune, C. (2018). *Dynamic Risk Factors: What role should they play in the explanation, assessment, and rehabilitation of offenders?* Routledge. doi:10.4324/9781315266039

Wilson, A., & Koons-Witt, B. (2020). "They Still Know I'm Their Momma": Incarcerated Mothers' Perceptions of Reunification and Resuming a Caregiver Role. *Feminist Criminology*. Advance online publication. doi:10.1177/1557085120983468

KEY TERMS AND DEFINITIONS

Ethnoracially Diverse: A range of groups that include BIPOCS (Black, Indigenous, and People of Color), AIANPi (American Indiana, Alaska Native, Pacific Islander), Asian and Latinx.

Racism: A personal or institutional action that disproportionately negatively affects historically oppressed groups based on their perception of their experience or evidence. The consequences of the actions of the person or institution may be perceived as prejudicial, discriminatory, differential based on membership of one's racial or ethnic group.

Recidivism: A relapse in reoffending behavior.

Rehabilitation: The process of educating offenders and building skills in an effort to reduce reoffending and make offenders more successful upon release into the community. Rehabilitation programs include, but are not limited to, motivational programs, cognitive skills programs, sexual offending programs, violent offender programs, substance abuse programs, education, and religious and spiritual services.

Reintegration: The process of transitioning an offender from a correctional environment into the community.

Reunification: The process of reuniting an offender with their family post release from prison or jail.

What Works: A movement focused on re-establishing offenders as active citizens. This includes rehabilitation programs and opportunities for interventions and change in an effort to affect offender behavior in a prosocial manner.

Chapter 8
Recidivism and Cognitive Behavioral Therapies:
The Efficacy of Correctional Programming

Sheryl L. Pelletier
Saint Leo University, USA

Mary J. Flanegan
Saint Leo University, USA

Derek M. Moore
Saint Leo University, USA

ABSTRACT

Recidivism of criminal offenders has become a national problem in the United States. New criminal activity along with technical violations of conditions of probation or parole are the results of deficiencies in cognitive behaviorisms. Numerous studies have revealed that weaknesses in cognitive behavior are a common denominator among offenders. These studies have led to the development and implementation of treatment strategies that, when administered to criminal offenders, have proven to be effective in reducing recidivism. Therapeutic programs grounded in evidence-based practices are widely used throughout correctional facilities and probation-parole departments. However, this evidence-based approach in reducing recidivism is moot if correctional leadership is not supportive of rehabilitative programs for offenders. The efficacy and success of these programs are dependent on effective leadership along with professionals and paraprofessionals that are specifically credentialed or licensed and have the qualities and skillsets to provide these types of rehabilitative measures.

DOI: 10.4018/978-1-7998-6884-2.ch008

INTRODUCTION

Reducing and preventing criminal recidivism has been and continues to be the overarching goal of the criminal justice system. The correctional ideology that epitomized the benefits of rehabilitation was prevalent in the United States before the 1970s when mainstream society demanded that local, state, and federal governments implement stronger and harsher punishments regardless of crime classification. These demands shifted the correctional pendulum back to punishment and retribution for criminal convictions while eliminating rehabilitation through treatment and vocational training. As a result of societal change, state and federal statutory authorities implemented strategies designed to harshly punish those who committed misdemeanor or felony crimes, thereby ensuring societal retribution for criminal behavior. The federal Truth in Sentencing Act of 1994, which provided states with the financial means to build more prisons, enabled states to enact harsher sentences using convictions requiring incarceration. To qualify for federal funds, states enacted statutes requiring mandatory minimum sentences for a broad spectrum of violent and non-violent criminal acts. Many states also passed some variation of a "three strikes" rule, which mandated increased prison time or life without the opportunity for parole for three instances of criminal activity in the same crime category. The harsh punitive legislative and judicial actions satisfied mainstream society while causing the prison population to explode, thereby facilitating severe prison overcrowding. This overcrowding led to a plethora of problems that are slowly being addressed by the affected states. Prison overcrowding also led to the advent of private prisons run by corporations contracted by various states (Eisenberg, 2016; Blumstein, 2012; Ayre, 1995).

Late in the 20th century, mental health professionals began to utilize cognitive behavior therapies to mitigate behavioral issues of those individuals that had been diagnosed with mental health issues that affected their cognitive behaviors. These therapies were implemented in residential facilities and non-residential outpatient programs (Feucht & Holt, 2016). Given the success of the cognitive-behavioral intervention programs and treatments in the mental health field, criminal justice professionals adopted, adapted, and implemented these program ideations to promote positive change in offender populations. As a result, these cognitive-behavioral programs implemented by correctional facilities and community corrections providers are a way to reduce recidivism among juvenile and adult offenders. They have replaced ineffective programs that did nothing to mitigate recidivism.

The rehabilitation of offenders using evidence-based practices involves the implementation and utilization of effective cognitive-behavioral therapeutic programs. Although many cognitive-behavioral intervention programs have the same overall goal of modifying behavior and mitigating negative thought processes, not all programs are designed the same. Cognitive-behavioral therapies (CBT) and programs seek to change the learned dysfunctional thinking of offenders that leads to criminal behavior (Lizama et al., 2014). The variety of available programs for cognitive-behavioral intervention run the gamut from individual journaling to role-playing in group programs or individual therapy sessions. In a correctional setting, programs that involve groups of offenders are widely used as they are more cost-effective, more expedient, and can influence a reasonably substantial number of offenders at the same time (Gendreau & Smith, 2012). Cognitive-behavioral interventions or programs are more than appropriate in prison and probation or parole settings. The main goal of prison, probation, or parole is not only to hold individuals accountable for their unruly behavior but to reduce the recidivism rates of offenders. This goal is accomplished by teaching, modeling pro-social behaviors, and providing knowledge on mitigating dysfunctional and destructive thought patterns that control behavior. A regime of successful treatment practices drives the concept of cognitive-behavioral therapies based on empirical evidence that restructures the dysfunctional or criminological thinking of offenders using intensive short-term programs (Lizama et al., 2014). To ensure that offenders are placed in the program that will provide them the most benefit, an evaluation of the propensity to commit further criminal activity must be conducted. These evaluations look at the real risks to re-offend that an offender will face, the met and unmet needs that are realized or anticipated, and finally, these evaluations look at the responsivity of an offender to treatment or how well a program will be received by an offender based on individual characteristics (Marlow 2020; Cohen & Whetzel, 2014). To this end, the Risk, Needs, and Responsivity (RNR) assessment, along with several of the widely used cognitive-behavioral therapies, are discussed in the following sections.

Effective correctional leadership and the hiring of professional program facilitators or the selection of corrective staff program facilitators are critical to developing and implementing a successful cognitive-behavioral program. With the pendulum swing in correctional ideology, there have been ongoing issues in finding the right people to improve penal conditions vital to establishing and maintaining prison reform, leading to an overall reduction in recidivism. Jacobs & Olitsky (2004) assert that the need for competent, motivated, energetic, humanistic, mature, and innovative leaders in offender treatment and rehabilitation is imperative. Proactive and effective leadership are the deciding factors in any organization's success or failure, including state and federal correctional enterprises. Correctional administrators and managers must believe in the effectiveness, benefits, and efficacy of intervention strategies to mitigate offenders' dysfunctional thinking and actions. Organizational leadership and organizational dynamics directly affect staff motivation when implementing cognitive-behavioral therapeutic programs and directly affecting the program outcomes (Glick & Prince, 2016; Latessa, 2012; Lizama et al., 2014).

Facilitators for cognitive behavioral therapies can be categorized as either professionals or paraprofessionals. Individuals who are classified as professionals must, in most cases, possess advanced college degrees and certifications in psychiatry, psychology, or social work. These individuals must also be licensed nationally or in the state where they are practicing their skills. Paraprofessionals are those individuals chosen to facilitate cognitive-behavioral therapies from the ranks of correctional staff at each facility or probation – parole office. No one component ensures program success. Instead, leadership, program selection, accurate professional assessment of individual responsivity, and facilitator selection are integrally connected aspects that work together to ensure the success of any cognitive-behavioral program used to reduce recidivism.

CORRECTIONAL LEADERSHIP: FINDING THE RIGHT PEOPLE

Proactive and effective leadership in the correctional field has been an ongoing issue in finding the right people to improve correctional conditions vital to establishing and maintaining prison reform while reducing recidivism. Problems within correctional settings stem from corrupt leaders and leaders who do not understand the full effect and benefits of creating change to reduce recidivism. Jacobs and Olitsky (2004) discussed the importance of influential leaders who possess the skill set required to utilize court interventions as opportunities to improve the prison's physical plant and administration. The authors asserted the need for these leaders to be competent, motivated, energetic, humanistic, mature, and innovative in treating offenders. Leadership is not a new concept. Leadership is involved in many aspects of different organizations where success or failure depends on those who possess the right qualities and have developed an instinct to create change. Many private organizations often place the right leaders in the correct positions to take charge and make the necessary changes to foster better organizational results. These organizations pride themselves on their ability to recruit the right people and develop leaders who can help refine and shape policies through a creative approach that elicits the best results.

Skillful leaders who are charismatic, proactive, and effectively influence others that impact an organization's results. Correctional settings offer a unique opportunity to provide inmates with the best resources and staff to reduce recidivism. Through intervention programs and organizational commitment, stakeholders can propose and implement evidence-based programs that offer a shared investment in helping the organization achieve the desired goals. These goals are not made without the most qualified staff in place, setting the tone for overall organizational success. Glick and Prince (2016) analyzed the importance of evidence-based program implementation and staff development to succeed in the correctional setting. They noted the consideration of staff development as a critical aspect to assess how organizations work to build the performance and competencies of their workforce. Staff development is often overlooked in some cases; however, staff development remains an essential component to better treatment interventions and outcomes within the correctional setting.

Leaders rely on the organizational commitment that allows them to serve their clients and better foster change. Correctional settings are another place where leaders have a responsibility to be motivated and find the attraction to stimulate staff abilities to impact offenders. Through organizational commitment, leaders within the correctional settings must share an emotional attachment to the organization. Organizations often look for transformational leaders who share common interests and a vision that motivates positive and productive work-related behavior, exhibit a drive for self-development, and identify individual peers and subordinates (Wei, Lee, & Kwan, 2016). Leaders that display an emotional commitment to the organization often report a higher level of job satisfaction and bond to the organization's members. These aspects of organizational commitment provide a solid foundation for the leader as better overall results are often achieved when the leaders adopt a stronger emotional attachment. Conversely, leaders who possess a mindset that does not support the organization or promote change within the organization cannot produce quality results, have no place in a correctional setting, and are counterproductive to reduce recidivism.

The qualities and skillset of staff members involved in correctional intervention programs are essential to the success of recidivism outcomes. Practical applications are dependent on the people who drive the necessary changes that significantly impact the people involved in the process. Qualifications should be clear and consistent with the selected program (Glick & Price, 2016). Identifying the standards within the organization can promote and sell the requirements necessary to hire the best practitioners for the intended intervention programs. The challenges placed on correctional institutions and the agencies involved in making changes to interventions can be daunting. Diversity in offenders has increased in correctional settings, demanding that stakeholders carefully select the most qualified individuals to lead the charge in the complex environment they operate. Today's correctional organizations and departments must identify and establish influential leaders who can handle today's correctional climate tasks that offer complexity on the social, political, and legal aspects in which they operate.

Leadership must provide some skill or special qualifications that coincide with intervention programs. Latessa (2004) addressed the need for strong leadership to be involved in the everyday process. Leaders should embody the role model approach and be directly involved in the day-to-day implementation and operations of intervention programs. The right qualifications come with knowing the expectations of intervention programs. Such skills can benefit the offender in these intervention programs that might need more work than others. Selecting the right staff capable of implementing cognitive-behavioral programs should carefully be screened for traits that promote effective program implementation and group management (Glick & Price, 2016). Addressing the specific qualifications that leaders should look for in staff selection goes well beyond education requirements. The fit for the organization should also be discussed and carefully considered when looking for the right staff in the selection process.

When it comes to selecting the right staff members for behavioral intervention programs, other factors to be considered should be the traits and characteristics of those individuals. Leaders must embrace qualities that are conducive to the intervention programs in the correctional setting. Attributes such as a propensity for objectivity, empathy, the capacity to effectively manage the dual role of the group facilitator, excellent communications skills, and the ability to affirm and reinforce pro-social behaviors are just a few that blend an adaptive criterion that should be considered (Glick & Price, 2016). Traits can be challenging to assess compared with staff qualifications, as most characteristics are not shown right away and could be hidden during the initial screening process. The selection of staff with innate traits is hard to quantify over time and left up to interpretation in the appropriate range of the right staff members.

Enhanced intrinsic motivation is a skill set necessary to incorporate positive change in offenders. Miller and Rollnick (2002) determined that for lasting change to occur in evidence-based practices, the staff member must have intrinsic motivation to elicit change on an emotional level. The feelings of change can be discovered by the strong influence of the interpersonal interactions between staff members and offenders. To promote growth and positive behavior in offenders' evolution, the use of motivational factors instead of persuasion has been shown to dramatically influence the effectiveness of program techniques in initiating and motivating positive, pro-social offender behavior over time. It is incumbent upon correctional leaders and all stakeholders to establish specific criteria when selecting staff and program facilitators. The criteria used must reflect the organization's commitment to offender rehabilitation and reducing recidivism. Staff qualities and skillsets offer the best insight into the development and implementation of effective correctional intervention programs. Leaders must look for suitable candidates that fit well within their organization to ensure they are getting the biggest bang for their buck and address the needs of rehabilitative strategies.

Leadership qualities and traits not only stem from just education. Correctional leaders, supervisory staff, and staff members selected to facilitate intervention programs must be educated in criminology, penal law, sociology of organizations, and understand psychology as a means of understanding human behavior in a correctional setting. The interventionist approach to rehabilitation takes a team of well-qualified individuals looking to achieve the fundamental goals of rehabilitation and reducing recidivism. These goals must include a desire to change the mitigation of future offending while reinforcing better behaviors. Leadership qualities must embody a breadth of vision that stems from a mindset of change and interpersonal relationships with their peer groups. It takes a well-balanced team to tackle cognitive-behavioral, including influential correctional leaders, to inspire their subordinates to pursue behavioral changes in offenders through intervention methods.

The community plays an integral part in the rehabilitation process. Stakeholders such as lawyers, interest groups, volunteer groups, legislators, and families willing to positively impact offenders' rehabilitative success are essential to community development. Correctional institutions must look to remove the ideation of the command-and-control approach as the authoritarian approach to rehabilitation. The foundation of intervention methods should look to the staff members and stakeholders to apply the same intervention strategies that effectively reduce recidivism. The community is safer when good leadership is involved in correctional intervention programs that allow offenders to get treated by the right people. Excellent leadership qualities enable staff members to approach intervention methods with the right people in correctional institutions. Hiring the right people allows for effective intervention programs that carefully consider the individual offender's needs and help them become better members of the community upon release from the prison system.

RNR AND CBT PROGRAMS

An individual offender's need for cognitive-behavioral rehabilitation is based on an evaluation utilizing the risk, needs, and responsivity (RNR) platform. The RNR identifies an offender's future risk of committing new crimes, including technical violations of probation or parole, by identifying the criminogenic characteristics that apply to that offender. Criminogenic characteristics have been identified as antisocial behaviors, personality, attitudes, and peers or acquaintances coupled with legal or illegal substance abuse, poor educational performance, unstable or no employment, deviant recreational activities along a dysfunctional home environment (Andrews, 2012). Once an offender has been assessed using one of the many commercially available assessment tools, they will be placed into one or more CBT programs that address the specific needs of that offender. A variety of approaches are used to provide offenders with the knowledge and skills needed to effectuate behavioral change. Cognitive-behavioral treatments and programs seek to change the learned dysfunctional thinking of offenders that leads to criminal behavior (Lizama et al., 2014).

The risk analysis or assessment results then help identify what that offender needs cognitive interventions to mitigate the probability of committing future criminal deviance. Finally, the responsivity aspect of RNR determines what barriers are present that will impede the effectiveness. The delivery method of cognitive-behavioral programs must be appropriate to the learning ability of the targeted program participants. For instance, if an offender dropped out of formal schooling during grade school or junior high, it would be counterproductive to mandate that offenders participate in a program that reaches its program goals through journaling. In a correctional setting, either incarceration or probation and parole, group programs are widely utilized as it is believed to be more practical, cost-effective, and able to influence many offenders at the same time. Typically, individual psychotherapy strategies are only used for offenders that also exhibit other mental health needs (Gendreau & Smith, 2012).

Risk, Needs, and Responsivity (RNR)

The risk, needs, and responsivity (RNR) framework of offender evaluation is a multifaceted tool that allows the evaluator to assess all aspects of an offender's life to determine what is needed and which order the services should be provided an issue to address first. The development of RNR reflects the shift in societal ideation in offender treatment from retribution and punishment to rehabilitation and reformation. RNR is based on the premise of humane treatment of offenders and addressing the totality of circumstances and issues present in an offender's life (Andrews, 2006; Andrews, 2012). Due to the complex nature of criminal behavior and the needs of individual offenders, most effective programs have been designed with the idea that attention needs to be paid to a wide range of offender social skills such as stress management, decision-making skills, problems solving skills, communication skills, and skills to assist in the development of an individual's self-control (Gundersen & Svartdal, 2006; Glick & Prince, 2016).

Overall, 15 principles comprise the RNR framework. The first three are principles that guide the remaining principles and are identified as respect the person, psychological theories about crime and criminals, and providing enhancement of crime prevention strategies and services. The 12 remaining principles define the parameters in which the RNR framework operates to identify the risks, the needs, and the responsivity of each offender, along with addressing how correctional organizations should adapt to and utilize services that are available to rehabilitate an offender's way of thinking along with mitigating the possibility of future criminality (Andrews, 2012).

Moral Reconation Therapy

Moral Reconation Therapy or MRT revolves around the assumption that offenders cannot behave and think in a manner that reflects pro-social ideations resulting in having a low moral compass that negatively affects moral reasoning. The MRT cognitive behavioral program aims to increase an offender's reason using structured book exercises and homework assignments. MRT focuses on seven fundamental issues in the realm of treatment: confronting attitudes, behavior, and beliefs, assessing the aspects and parameters of current relationships, identify and reinforcing positive attributes or habits, enhancing an offender's concept of self, forming a positive identity, developing increased moral reasoning along with decreasing deviance while increasing tolerance and lastly, patience regarding instances of frustration (Arvidson, 2019). It is recommended that the number of offenders should be limited to no more than 15 participants per class, that each class should meet a minimum of one time per week but no more than two times per week for a total of 16 sessions, and that each class session is no more than two hours (Lizama et al., 2014; Glick & Prince, 2016).

Reasoning and Rehabilitation

The Reasoning and Rehabilitation (R&R) model of CBT appears to have been adapted from a cognitive program developed for school-age children. R&R seeks to instill and enhance self-control, cognition, social perspectives, and problem-solving by using three principles: thinking before acting, recognizing that words and actions have consequences that affect themselves and others, and displaying pro-social behaviors and attitudes in all situations encountered. R&R accomplishes the program goals through role-playing, discussion groups, puzzle development, game playing, and watching or listening to program-specific audio-visual materials. For this program, class size is limited to no more than eight participants in a classroom setting. A typical R&R program covers 35 sessions over a timeframe of 12 weeks (Lizama et al., 2014; Glick & Prince, 2016). While this program was initially longer in duration, studies proved that the longer the program, the higher the offender's recidivism rate. Accordingly, a shorter version of the R&R program was designed and became R&R2 (Arvidson, 2019).

Thinking for a Change

The Thinking for a Change (T4C) program seeks to change offenders' thinking and behavior patterns who exhibit enduring and acute behaviors that go against the grain of mainstream societal ideations of acceptable behavior. Three main goals have been identified with this particular program: developing appropriate social skills, cognitive restructuring, and developing pro-social problem-solving skills. Each of the three goals encompasses detailed and in-depth tools to identify behaviors that place offenders at risk of committing criminal acts, learn social skills that are pro-social, and identify problems while using appropriate methods for problem resolution. As a result, offenders who have deficits in social skills are provided with the skills necessary to make pro-social decisions and work through decisions without resorting to criminal behavior (Arvidson, 2019). T4C is comprised of 25 lessons that are presented interactively to groups of no more than 12 participants. It is recommended that each class be taught over 11 weeks and involve two sessions per week for one or two hours (Lizama et al., 2014; Glick & Prince, 2016).

COGNITIVE BEHAVIORAL THERAPY FACILITATORS

The success of any cognitive-behavioral therapy (CBT) program is dependent on several factors: effective leadership and the selection of program facilitators. These program facilitators may or may not be licensed social workers, psychologists, or psychiatrists. Consequentially, facilitators fall into two categories: professionals or specialized higher educational degrees and licensing and paraprofessionals with only program-specific training and are not required to have a state license to deliver therapeutic programs. Paraprofessionals or individuals who serve as program facilitators without a higher education degree need to be trained in the various cognitive behavioral modification techniques and program specifics. Before correctional staff can facilitate programs that address the skills required of the offender, they, themselves, must possess the skills, qualities, and enthusiasm necessary to accomplish the program goals effectively. Facilitator training is accomplished through program-specific training, which may last up to several months. Some basic skills that are essential for an effective facilitator are objectivity, empathy, the ability to handle multiple roles in a group setting, the ability to disapprove of and deal with negative behavior while maintaining other relationships within a group setting, provide affirmation of positive pro-social behaviors, holding individuals accountable, good communication skills, flexibility, expressiveness, cultural sensitivity, and the ability to model positive behaviors (Glick & Prince, 2016). These facilitator skills tend to be qualities found commonly in many people and do not necessarily have to be taught.

Group facilitators must be flexible in their methods of interacting and teaching cognitive-behavioral interventions while at the same time recognizing the variances in group dynamics and remaining true to the program design, thereby proving the integrity of the program. Throughout a CBT program, the facilitator must maintain objectivity while keeping the group's members motivated and focused on the program objectives. The parameters of each CBT program mandate that program facilitators also perform duties as group moderators and challengers. The responsibilities of the group moderator encompass keeping the program moving on an even keel and ensuring the participation of all group members. Facilitators must also tactfully challenge group participants on inappropriate remarks or behaviors without alienating any participants. A large part of program success is acknowledgment and celebration by facilitators for group progress. This acknowledgment and celebration help reinforce program lessons' messages, thereby effectively changing thinking patterns and unruly behavior (Glick & Prince, 2016).

Paraprofessional cognitive-behavioral interventionists or program facilitators are trained in cognitive therapeutic techniques that relate to specific programs. This program-specific training leaves a gap in the therapeutic knowledge of correctional staff or paraprofessionals regarding behavioral motivators that may be better addressed by someone specializing in social work, psychology, or psychiatry. Programs designed to address offenders' dysfunctional cognitive behaviors require that the professional or paraprofessional utilize evidence-based techniques to change a person's thought process in the hopes of changing their behavior. Outside of the criminal justice profession, this type of work is done by professional clinical workers who have achieved at least a bachelor's degree in fields of study such as social work or psychology. However, most organizations require a graduate degree in one of the three previously mentioned schools of study from an educational institution accredited by the Council on Social Work Education (Social Work Licensing Requirements, 2020).

Additionally, prospective behavioral therapists or interventionists are required, depending on their state, to undergo 1,000 hours or more of supervised practice before being able to practice alone. Following the conclusion of their education and internship, prospective therapeutic provider candidates must take an examination administered by the Association of Social Work Board to gain their licensure. Finally, paraprofessionals in the correctional setting must undergo training and be certified facilitators based on program mandates and the requirements established by each state. This training lasts between several weeks to several months, and there is no internship requirement. However, some departments may require a period of shadowing an experienced CBT facilitator and may additionally require periodic refresher classes.

PROFESSIONAL STANDARDS AND LIABILITY

CBT facilitators working with offender populations, either those currently incarcerated or on some form of community supervision, must recognize and acknowledge that offenders are human beings that deserve to be treated with the dignity, respect, and humanity afforded non-criminal populations. Social exclusion and labeling of offenders are counterproductive to the rehabilitation of this population and counterproductive with CBT goals (Millar & Burke, 2012). Providing services to inmate and offender populations, delivery of CBT strategies must be conducted to not further alienate these individuals through the use of language that is not easily understood or projecting an attitude that being unknowledgeable of program concepts is a character defect. The use of advanced language and the projection of a demeaning attitude have the potential of rendering any program progress moot. Professional licensing or certification must be maintained to ensure program standards, program stability, and professional accountability to provide program integrity. When correctional departments, facilities, and community supervision agencies utilize correctional or supervision staff as program facilitators or behavioral interventionists, these individuals must balance the duality of their diverse roles.

Paraprofessional CBT Facilitators

Paraprofessionals are those individuals who have received certification or specialized training in program delivery without the benefit of formal higher education. There are several advantages in utilizing correctional or community corrections staff to facilitate or provide offender instruction. First, there is no shortage of staff members that can be chosen to provide instruction. Choosing existing staff to promote CBT programs is cost-effective for shrinking departmental budgets, staff members have a better understanding of offender interactions and capacity for learning, and staff members will not be susceptible to the games that offenders play to manipulate or control the learning environment. The prison employees must be educated in the programs and services being offered. However, they need to be aware of the theory behind the specific program and the complex dynamics of how to work in two separate but distinct social systems, both in and out of prison (Caldwell, 1956).

As with all things in life, there are some drawbacks to utilizing correctional or community corrections staff as facilitators in CBT delivery. Correctional staff is only required to have a high school education or equivalency, whereas; community corrections personnel must have a bachelor's degree. Many of the correctional and community corrections staff do not believe in the rehabilitative benefits of CBT programs. They think that offenders are not capable of redemption or becoming productive members of society. Additionally, there may be a lack of staff motivation to provide CBT strategies to offenders. There is an unspoken perception among many correctional staff members that offenders, those incarcerated, and those on the streets do not deserve to be provided the tools to be successful.

Professional CBT Facilitators

Licensed psychologists are held to a higher performance standard and have several ethical standards that govern their behavior. Some of the ethical standards or principles of providing treatment to criminal offenders are the justice principle, the responsibility principle, and the nonmaleficence principle (Allan, 2012). The justice principle dictates that the psychologist must ensure the fair and impartial treatment of the offender. As such, they must avoid any bias about the offender or the job they are performing. The responsibility principle holds that practitioners need to be held to a higher level of accountability not only to their organization but also to their profession, the clients, and society. Finally, the nonmaleficence principle mandates that the medical principle of 'do no harm' be followed. Psychologists are tasked with acknowledging their personal and professional limitations of knowledge and not exceeding those limitations. In addition, professional interventionists or facilitators must avoid any action that would cause harm to other people and avoid any situation that presents a foreseeable risk of damage to others. One strong rationale for licensing is to ensure that the public is not harmed by incompetent or unethical practitioners (Hogan, 1983b). The licensure requirements lead to a higher level of fidelity within any program or service provided, along with possibly lowering any inadvertent negative consequence(s).

As with paraprofessional CBT facilitators, there are drawbacks in using individuals who are considered professionals due to their education and board certification licensing requirements. Professional CBT providers may present information in a manner that is not understood by the offender population, which can render the program ineffective. The hiring of professional therapists to provide program services is not feasible for many corrections and community corrections departments. Professional CBT program providers are at a greater risk than paraprofessional CBT program providers of being manipulated and taken advantage of by the offender populations. Finally, professional CBT program providers who are unused to working with this unique population may be intimidated because their clientele are criminals, many of whom have committed violent crimes.

OFFENDER GROUPS

Offender groups are comprised of individuals who share commonalities but at the same time are individuals. When assembled in a group of two or more, offender group dynamics are an intrinsic component of any institutional program. These offenders have their unique ways of interacting in the correctional setting. The selection of group participants for a CBT program must be completed with care to avoid group interaction complications because of gang affiliation, religious ideologies, and criminal offense convictions. These group dynamics will evolve throughout the CBT program. CBT programs that have been implemented in the field of corrections utilize evidence-based practices which have, through empirical evidence, been proven effective in reducing recidivism and increasing the safety of civilian and prison communities (Glick & Prince, 2016; Lizama et al., 2014).

Offenders, like societal members, while having common characteristics and traits, are individuals with distinct personalities. The melding of these personalities ebbs and flows throughout the program and as the group develops. The beginning of therapy needs to be done slowly with special care taken regarding the group's needs and the facilitator's methods in getting to those needs. The inmate cannot be asked questions right away to share their feeling and experiences with people they have never met in their lives. The therapist's role is to build a sense of community within the group with the primary objective of safety (Ritter et al., 1987). As the program group develops, there are four stages the group will progress through: the initial stage where group members, including the facilitator, become acquainted with each other; the transitioning stage where group members display anxiety or stress while starting to take risks that pertain to the information and skills that are being learned; the working stage where group members begin to believe in the power of the program and the ability to change their thinking and behavior; and the final stage where offenders realize that the end of the program is near and they begin to feel separation anxiety or sadness along with uncertainty in their ability to utilize their newfound knowledge and skills outside the safety of the program environment (Prince & Glick, 2016).

Any discussion of offender participants in CBT programs would be remiss if treatment strategies for special needs offenders were not addressed. Special needs offenders fall into several categories: mental health issues, developmental delays, substance abuse, aggressiveness, or complete resistance. Approximately one out of every ten adults in prison's general population have some form of a substance abuse issue, and one in five has some variation of a mental health problem (NADCP, 2020). The offenders that fall into these categories may best be provided cognitive-behavioral interventions by professional therapists as group programs may be too overwhelming for them. It is perhaps best that mental health needs, substance abuse issues, and developmental delays be addressed before offenders that fall into these categories are placed in programs that seek to change cognitive behavior. Resistant offenders and aggressive offenders require an extraordinary amount of patience and time to impart the knowledge and skillsets in CBT programs. Resistant and aggressive offenders may benefit from other available programs before participating in a CBT program that depends on group cohesiveness (Glick & Prince, 2016).

SOLUTIONS AND RECOMMENDATIONS

The information presented herein is not made to point out deficiencies within state and federal correctional facilities and programs but merely to provide an analysis of potential issues concerning the fidelity of cognitive-behavioral programs. To determine the overall efficacy of an individual program, a comprehensive evaluation needs to be accomplished. This evaluation needs to contain leadership's overall position and endorsement of cognitive-behavioral intervention programs, the facilitator's active and enthusiastic involvement in programs, and the role of offenders within the programs.

For programs to be truly effective, management needs to become active participants in the recruitment and training of facilitators. Whether the facilitators are paraprofessionals or technically trained, strict adherence to program guidelines and qualifications is imperative. Ideally, program facilitators would all be licensed social workers or psychologists; however, this may not be possible depending on the individual jurisdictions. When licensure of facilitators is not possible, consistent continuing education needs to be a priority. Additionally, routine procedural review needs to be put into place to ensure that the facilitators remain active stakeholders in the process of cognitive-behavioral therapy programming. Unfortunately, like most new programs, there will be resistance. With those individuals, management needs to make additional efforts to convey the ultimate goals of the programs to them in a manner to which they can relate. Allow them to be active participants in program design and roll-out in the agency, and they will develop a sense of ownership in the success of the programs.

FUTURE RESEARCH DIRECTIONS

There is no one size fits all approach to reducing recidivism. Programs such as those referenced herein are a proven and effective tool in lowering future criminality. There is always room for improvement, and future studies must be undertaken relative to the causal effect of poor leadership and dispassionate and unskilled facilitators. As society changes, so too must our approach to the care and treatment of offenders. Cognitive-behavioral therapy programs have consistently assisted offenders in reducing future criminality. Given the evidence of the positive results of these programs, it is essential to conduct studies to determine if the leadership and skill levels of facilitators are casually connected to program efficacy.

We are currently living in a time where criminal justice reform is at the forefront of conversation in society. The country is primed and ready for innovative new ideas and ways to improve already successful programs. Our correctional institutions are inundated with special needs offenders with issues such as mental health, developmental delays, substance abuse, aggressiveness, etc. Research needs to be done to determine the appropriate way to deal with these special populations and provide them with the best possible outcome. If we can find a link between program efficacy and program leadership and administration, specific steps can be taken to design functional and cost probative measures to decrease recidivism further.

CONCLUSION

The ideation of rehabilitating offenders for successful reentry into civilian communities and neighborhoods is slowly replacing the harsh punitive ideation of the correctional philosophy prevalent in the latter half of the 20th century. Society realizes that harsher, longer prison sentences do not deter criminal activity, nor do these types of punitive actions increase public safety. This realization and prison overcrowding, budgetary constraints, and empirical research studies have influenced the criminal justice field to implement programs designed to change offenders' dysfunctional thinking patterns and behaviors. Program selection must involve input from all stakeholders. Program implementation must follow the protocols established in the different program designs as these protocols are established on evidence-based practices and are imperative for program success. The societal benefits of implementing cognitive-behavioral interventions or therapeutic programs are many and varied. A successful behavioral intervention program will increase neighborhood safety along with safety inside a correctional institution. It can be argued that cognitive-behavioral intervention programs that are provided to offenders serving long incarceration sentences will increase the overall safety of facility staff and other offenders. Therefore, these types of programs should be made available at all prisons regardless of the facility security rating.

Effective leadership enhances not only the teaching environment but the learning environment as well. Organizational leadership and quality assurance of programs will promote a sense of trust and integrity in the institutional setting and within an offender's community upon their release from custody. Staff members who are equipped with the proper education and ideal traits are beneficial to intervention programs. Leaders must address their hiring needs when it comes to finding the right individuals to lead these programs. Understanding the need for the right leadership can effectively promote and increase the chances of reducing recidivism. Stakeholders play a role in how well these interventions play out with determining the need for the most qualified individuals to fill these roles. Identifying the right staff members for implementation in treatment programs is critical to the success of reducing recidivism. Treatment programs should know and respect the qualified individuals leading treatment programs to familiarize themselves with human behavior and other sociological factors that contribute to offenders' success. Leadership starts at the top of any organization, and everyone in the organization must understand and embrace the goals that stakeholders want to achieve. Goals set the tone for who they wish to see inside their organizations and help ensure the right candidate is considered when implementing intervention programs effectively.

Cognitive-behavioral therapy has become recognized as a viable mitigation strategy as it relates to criminal recidivism. A plethora of studies has provided empirical evidence as to the efficacy of the various CBT programs. However, as with any program, the result is only as good as the providers or facilitators of the program. By treating high-risk offenders with CBT programs, the criminal justice system is mitigating the commission of future criminal acts, ensuring public safety, and helping to rebuild communities by establishing the means to regain trust, cooperation, and unity of all community members and stakeholders. Not every offender needs treatment or programs; however, most offenders would benefit from some form of intervention to mitigate the circumstances that led to criminal behavior. To identify the offenders that would benefit from a CBT program, prison counselors or case managers, and community supervision personnel need to conduct a risk, needs, and responsivity (RNR) assessment on every offender to ascertain which programs best suit their individual needs. It cannot be stressed enough that the RNR assessments are vitally important to the rehabilitation of offenders if recidivism is to be effectively reduced without imposing long, harsh prison or supervision sentences. The utilization of RNR and the implementation of CBT programs reflect the shift in correctional ideology from punishment and retribution to providing various forms of treatment to mitigate future criminality.

Criminality is not confined to one group of offenders. Instead, there are many categories and subcategories of those who participate in criminal activity and other socially deviant behaviors. Therefore, it stands to reason that any single program developed and implemented to address individuals' dysfunctional cognitive-behavioral thoughts and behaviors will not be effective for the entire offender population. The basic premise of offender-neutral cognitive-behavioral programs and interventions works well for offender populations that have not been identified as special subcategories, such as females, sex offenders, substance abusers, or those who are developmentally challenged in some manner. However, to address the needs specific to these special offender populations, mitigation strategies for criminal and deviant behavior must be interwoven into the fabric of the generic cognitive-behavioral programs and interventions. To not address the unique needs of these groups does a disservice to the offender, has the potential to skew outcomes, and increases the probability that the community will suffer through continued criminal activity and increased recidivism.

Essentially, two distinct sets of group dynamics affect the outcomes of programs designed to rehabilitate offender thinking, thereby reducing recidivism, and improving offender behavior: correctional staff dynamic and offender dynamics. Effective leadership enhances both the teaching and learning environments and will positively impact the effectiveness of the CBT programs. To ensure that effective programming is being implemented within a facility or probation and parole office, CBT program facilitators must be carefully selected and model the behavior that reflects the desired outcomes identified in the program design. Correctional organizations and communities must work together to reinforce an offender's positive and pro-social thoughts, words, and actions. The structured learning environment of correctional CBT programs promotes trust and respect among peers and others while teaching offenders the basic tenets of community listening, learning, changing, and serving. To continue moving forward with the rehabilitation of offenders, the punishment mindset of correctional officials and staff must be mitigated through education and careful selection of those who are hired to ensure the safety of the community and the safety of offenders. For a recidivism reduction program to be successful, care needs to be taken regarding the skills, training, and enthusiasm of all criminal justice professionals involved in the mission of any cognitive-behavioral therapy or treatment program. Cognitive-behavioral therapies can and do work to reduce recidivism; however, the effectiveness of these programs is directly impacted by the quality of organizational leadership and the program facilitators.

ACKNOWLEDGEMENT

The authors of this book chapter express their appreciation and gratitude to Saint Leo University and their professors for the excellent education which they have provided to us over the years. The authors are alumni of the Saint Leo University Master of Science in Criminal Justice program and current students in the inaugural Doctorate in Criminal Justice program at Saint Leo University. Additionally, the authors are thankful for the opportunities provided that enable individuals with diverse backgrounds to work collaboratively on projects that combine diversity and experience to pursue a common goal.

REFERENCES

Allen, A. (2012). Ethics in correctional and forensic psychology: Getting the balance right. *Australian Psychologist*, *48*(1), 47–56. doi:10.1111/j.1742-9544.2012.00079.x

Andrews, D. A. (2006). Enhancing adherence to risk-need-responsivity: Making quality a matter of policy. *Criminology & Public Policy*, *5*(3), 595–602. doi:10.1111/j.1745-9133.2006.00394.x

Andrews, D. A. (2012). The risk-need-responsivity (RNR) model of correctional assessment and treatment. In J. A. Dvoskin, J. L. Skeem, R. W. Novaco, & K. S. Douglas (Eds.), *Using Social Science to Reduce Violent Offending* (pp. 127–156). Oxford University Press, Inc.

Arvidson, J. (2019). The utility and efficacy of cognitive behavioral interventions in the arena of corrections. An overview and appeal to the field of probation. *Forensic Scholars Today, 4*(4), 1-11. https://1q5krviw73e3rlh854lufacx-wpengine.netdna-ssl.com/wp-content/uploads/2019/04/FST-4.4-Utility-and-Efficacy-of-Cognitive-Behavioral-Interventions.pdf

Ayer, R. V. (1995). The prison crisis: An essay on social and political foundations of criminal justice policy. *Public Administration Quarterly*, *19*(1), 42–50. http://www.jstor.org/stable/40861644

Blumstein, A. (2012). Crime and incarceration in the United States. In A. Dvoskin, J. L. Skeem, R. W. Novaco, & K. S. Douglas (Eds.), *Using social science to reduce violent offending* (pp. 3–30). Oxford University Press, Inc.

Caldwell, M. (1956). Group Dynamics in the Prison Community. *Journal of Criminal Law and Criminology*, *46*(5), 648–657. doi:10.2307/1139377

Cohen, T. H., & Whetzel, J. (2014). The neglected "R" – responsivity and the federal offender. *Federal Probation Journal, 78*(2), 11 – 18. https://www.uscourts.gov/federal-probation-journal

Feucht, T., & Holt, T. (2016, September). Does cognitive behavioral therapy work in criminal justice? A new analysis from crimesolutions.gov (Report No. NCJ249825). *National Institute of Justice Journal, 277*, 10–17. http://nij.gov/journals/277/pages/crimesolutions-cbt.aspx

Gendreau, P., & Smith, P. (2012). Assessment and treatment strategies for correctional institutions. In J. A. Dvoskin, R. Skeem, W. Novaco, & K. S. Douglas (Eds.), Using social science to reduce violent offending (pp. 157 – 177). Oxford University Press, Inc.

Glick, B., & Prince, R. (2016). *Implementing successful cognitive behavioral interventions*. Civic Research Institute.

Gundersen, K., & Svartdal, F. (2006). Aggression Replacement Training in Norway: Outcome evaluation of 11 Norwegian student projects. *Scandinavian Journal of Educational Research, 50*(1), 63–81. doi:10.1080/00313830500372059

Hogan, D. (1983a). The effectiveness of licensing: History, evidence, and recommendations. *Law and Human Behavior*, *7*(213), 117–138. doi:10.1007/BF01044517

Hogan, D. (1983b). Professional regulation: An introduction to the issue. *Law and Human Behavior*, *7*(213), 99–101. doi:10.1007/BF01044515

Jacobs, J. B., & Olitsky, E. (2004). Leadership and correctional reform. *Pace Law Review*, *24*(2), 477–496. https://digitalcommons.pace.edu

Latessa, E. J. (2004). The challenge of change: Correctional programs and evidence-based practices. *Criminology & Public Policy*, *3*(4), 546–560. doi:10.1111/j.1745-9133.2004.tb00061.x

Lizama, J., Matthews, V., & Reyes, S. (2014). What works? Short-term, in custody treatment programs [Policy Brief]. *Center for Public Policy*. http://cpp.fullerton.edu/pdf/What%20Works.pdf

Marlowe, D. B. (2020). The most carefully studied, yet least understood terms in the criminal justice lexicon: Risk, need, and responsivity. *Policy Research Associates, Inc.* https://www.prainc.com/risk-need-responsivity

Millar, M., & Burke, L. (2012, July). Thinking beyond 'utility': Some comments on probation practice and training. *Howard Journal of Criminal Justice*, *51*(3), 317–330. doi:10.1111/j.1468-2311.2012.00711.x

Miller, W., & Rollnick, S. (2002). *Motivational interviewing: Preparing people for change*. Guilford Press.

National Association of Drug Court Professionals (NADCP). (2020). *Treatment Courts*. https://www.nadcp.org

Ritter, K., West, J., & Trotzer, J. (1987). Comparing family counseling and group counseling: An interview with George Gazda, James Hansen, and Alan Hovestadt. *Journal of Counseling and Development, 65*(6), 295–300. doi:10.1002/j.1556-6676.1987.tb01289.x

Social Work Licensing Requirements. (2020). *Educational Requirements for a Social Work License*. https://socialworklicensure.org/articles/social-work-license-requirements/

Wei, F., Lee, J., & Kwan, H. K. (2016). Impact of active constructive leadership and passive corrective leadership on collective organizational commitment. *Leadership and Organizational Development Journal, 37*(7), 822 – 842. https://psycnet.apa.org/record/2016-57029-001

ADDITIONAL READING

Becker, J. V., & Stinson, J. D. (2012). Extending rehabilitative principles to violent sexual offenders. In J. A. Dvoskin, J. L. Skeem, R. W. Novaco, & K. S. Douglas (Eds.), *Using social science to reduce violent offending* (pp. 223–261). Oxford University Press.

Bogestad, A. J., Kettler, R. J., & Hagan, M. P. (2010). Evaluation of a cognitive intervention program for juvenile offenders. *International Journal of Offender Therapy and Comparative Criminology, 54*(4), 552–565. doi:10.1177/0306624X09337211 PMID:19494167

Bouffard, J., Cooper, M., & Bergseth, K. (2016). The effectiveness of various restorative justice interventions on recidivism outcomes among juvenile offenders. *Youth Violence and Juvenile Violence*, 1-16. doi:10.1177/1541204016647428

Ferguson, L. M., & Wormith, J. S. (2012). A meta-analysis of moral reconation therapy. *International Journal of Offender Therapy and Comparative Criminology*, 1–31. http://ijo.sagepub.com/content/early/2012/06/26/0306624X12447771 PMID:22744908

Gobeil, R., Blanchette, K., & Stewart, L. (2016). A meta-analytic review of correctional interventions for women offenders. Gender-neutral versus gender-informed approaches. *Criminal Justice and Behavior, 43*(3), 302–322. doi:10.1177/0093854815621100

Hollin, C. R. (2012). A short history of corrections: The rise, fall, and resurrection of rehabilitation through treatment. In J. A. Dvoskin, J. L. Skeem, R. W. Novaco, & K. S. Douglas (Eds.), *Using social science to reduce violent offending* (pp. 31–48). Oxford University Press.

Latessa, E. (n.d.). *Designing more effective correctional programs using evidence-based practices*. Paper presented at the 151st International Training Course. https://www.unafei.or.jp/publications/pdf/RS_No88/No88_10VE_Latessa_Designing.pdf

KEY TERMS AND DEFINITIONS

Behavior: The physical or mental reactions of an individual because of an internal or external stimulus.

Cognitive-Behavioral Therapies: Programs designed to help clients discover and change the thought processes that lead to maladaptive behavior by emphasizing personal accountability.

Corrections: Any period of incarceration or supervision under the authority of a federal or state corrections department.

Facilitator: Any person with the training and desire to work together to understand common objectives in the rehabilitation of offenders.

Leader: Any person in a supervisory role who demonstrates the qualities of respect, courage, integrity, commitment, and the ability to influence others while administering their job duties.

Licensure: A certification granted through a professional governing board based on an individual's knowledge, skills, and abilities.

Offender: Any person convicted of a misdemeanor or felony offense currently incarcerated in a state or federal institution or placed on parole or probation.

Recidivism: The rate at which an offender re-offends immediately following his/her release from the custody of a local or state correctional program.

Rehabilitation: The process of changing an offender's thought processes and behavior in a way that allows for positive decision-making.

RNR (Risk, Needs, Responsivity): Assessment tools used to evaluate criminogenic needs of offenders to assist in the placement of the appropriate rehabilitative programming.

Chapter 9
The Potential of Community Corrections to Reduce Mass Incarceration in the USA

Marty Allen Hatfield
Liberty University, USA

ABSTRACT

Tough-on-crime policies and strategies, such as mandatory minimum and determinate sentencing laws and more severe punishments for juveniles, sex offenders, and drug offenders, have caused a substantial increase in the U.S. incarceration rate. Mass incarceration has generated several negative consequences, including racial bias and disparities, economic and social costs, and prison overcrowding. As such, the use of community corrections programs as an alternative form of sentencing has significantly increased. To effectively reduce crime and recidivism, community corrections programs must 1) utilize a validated risk and needs assessment when determining program placement; 2) provide participants with comprehensive, evidence-based services, including substance abuse and mental health treatment; 3) focus on modifying participants' behavior through treatment goal setting and the use of graduated incentives and sanctions; and 4) strive to hire and retain qualified staff, provide both initial and ongoing training, and monitor treatment staff with regular clinical supervision.

INTRODUCTION

With more than 1.8 million people incarcerated in federal and state prisons and local jails, the U.S. has the highest incarceration rate in the world (Kang-Brown et al., 2021). America's mass incarceration problem is the result of severe sentencing laws, including mandatory minimum, determinate, and three-strikes sentencing, as well as more severe punishments for juveniles, sex offenders, and drug offenders. Because of the ineffectiveness of the traditional corrections model, policymakers, practitioners, and researchers have advocated for the development and implementation of community corrections programs. These programs are responsible for the supervision of individuals who are not incarcerated but fall under the authority of the criminal justice system (Vera Institute of Justice, 2013). Most individuals under the su-

DOI: 10.4018/978-1-7998-6884-2.ch009

pervision of a community corrections program fall into one of the following five categories: 1) individuals on pretrial release with active court cases; 2) individuals with open court cases who have been placed in a diversion program or specialty court and who will not be sentenced if they successfully complete the program; 3) offenders who have been found guilty of their charges and are sentenced to some form of supervision, such as probation; 4) offenders who have been released from prison or jail but remain under supervision through parole and/or probation; or 5) individuals released from prison to finish the remainder of their sentence in a work release or related program (Vera Institute of Justice, 2013).

Unfortunately, if administered incorrectly, community corrections programs will generate little positive change and may increase crime and recidivism rates in some cases. There are three primary purposes of this chapter. First and foremost, the chapter provides a summary of the following seven correctional theories: 1) retribution; 2) deterrence; 3) incapacitation; 4) restorative justice; 5) rehabilitation; 6) reentry; and 7) early intervention. Second, the chapter discusses the factors that led to the departure from the theory of rehabilitation in the 1970s, as well as the advantages and disadvantages of institutional corrections in the U.S. Third, the chapter outlines the elements of effective community corrections programs and discusses the advantages and disadvantages of such programs. Recommendations for future research are also provided.

BACKGROUND

Seven Correctional Theories

Researchers have identified seven primary theories that have helped shape the American correctional system. The first is the theory of retribution, also frequently referred to as the theory of just desserts. Advocates of the theory of retribution assert that criminal justice practitioners lack the necessary experience and authority to figure out why an individual commits a crime or to attempt to rehabilitate an individual (Cullen & Jonson, 2016). Rather, the primary purpose of the U.S. correctional system is to get even with offenders. The retribution theory of corrections focuses on the crime, rather than the criminal. The second correctional theory is the theory of deterrence, which includes two primary types of deterrence. First, *specific deterrence* argues that individuals who commit crime can be deterred from future criminal behavior through punishment (Nagin, 2013). Second, *general deterrence* suggests that members of the public will be deterred from criminal behavior when they witness others being apprehended and punished (Nagin, 2013).

The deterrence theory of corrections argues that certain, swift, and severe sanctions deter individuals from crime (Loughran et al., 2012). One primary benefit of deterrence-based correctional policies and strategies is that they do, to some extent, control and prevent crime and enhance public safety. This is primarily due to the fact that offenders are unable to endanger the public while incarcerated. However, the deterrence theory assumes that offenders are rational actors who are capable of considering the consequences of their actions (Lee, 2017). However, Wright (2010) found that half of all state prisoners were under the influence of drugs or alcohol during their offenses. Therefore, punishment and/or the threat of punishment would likely have a minimal deterrent effect on these individuals due to their impaired capacity to consider the outcome of their actions (Wright, 2010). Like the theory of retribution, the deterrence correctional theory focuses on the crime rather than the individual.

The third correctional theory is the theory of incapacitation, which includes collective incapacitation and selective incapacitation. *Collective incapacitation* is the use of traditional sentencing policies (e.g., mandatory minimum sentences) to incapacitate individuals who fall within certain categories, such as those who commit murder (Cullen & Jonson, 2016). Alternatively, *selective incapacitation* occurs when criminal justice practitioners consider individual factors, such as the number of previous offenses, when sentencing offenders (Cullen & Jonson, 2016). Similar to the deterrence theory, there is one primary benefit of the theory of incapacitation: it prevents incarcerated individuals from threatening the general public. However, research suggests that incapacitation often leads to the recruitment of younger replacements, particularly within bureaucratic criminal organizations (Blumstein, 2011). These replacements often represent a far greater threat to public safety than the individuals they replace. Furthermore, incapacitation does very little to address an offender's reentry. Offenders often recommit crimes upon their release and are returned to the criminal justice system, a phenomenon known as the revolving door effect.

The fourth correctional theory is the theory of restorative justice, which consists of three primary components. First, the restorative justice theory argues that crime causes harm to the offender, their victims, and the community (Cullen & Jonson, 2016). Second, advocates of restorative justice argue that the U.S. correctional system should heavily focus on reversing the harm caused by criminal acts (Cullen & Jonson, 2016). Finally, harm is reversed by restoring the offender, victims, and the community to their states before the harm was inflicted (Cullen & Jonson, 2016). Unlike the retribution, deterrence, and incapacitation theories, restorative justice focuses on the criminal through offender reintegration. The fifth correctional theory is the theory of rehabilitation, which is the primary function of community corrections programs. Unlike the previous correctional theories, the rehabilitation theory argues that individuals engage in crime because of individual factors. Thus, criminal behavior can be controlled by interventions that are effective at altering these influences (Cullen & Jonson, 2016). For example, if substance abuse issues cause an individual to engage in crime, reoffending can be reduced through effective substance abuse treatment. Like the restorative justice model, the rehabilitative model focuses on the criminal rather than the crime.

The sixth correctional theory is the theory of reentry, which also focuses on the offender. Reentry is a general term that encompasses "all institutional and community-based programming dedicated to assisting individuals with mental illness to re-integrate into the community following release from incarceration or hospitalization, including efforts to prevent further criminal justice system involvement" (DeMatteo et al., 2013, p. 68). More than 713,000 offenders were released from prison in 2006, which is an average of nearly 2,000 individuals per day (Sabol & Couture, 2008). Many released prisoners have difficulty adjusting to life outside of prison. Prison reentry programs are designed to assist newly released offenders in their transition back into society. Unfortunately, there are several problems with reentry programs. For example, released offenders often have contact with law enforcement shortly after reentry, which often results in reincarceration (Cullen & Jonson, 2016). In fact, in a study of U.S. parolees, two-thirds were rearrested within three years of release and 52% were reincarcerated (Langan & Levin, 2002). Additionally, despite their potential benefits, reentry programs are not easy to sell to politicians because they lack vengefulness and are often seen as being soft on crime (Siegfried, 2001). Finally, successful reentry is often hindered by a lack of treatment and mental health services before and after release (Cullen & Jonson, 2016).

The final correctional theory is the theory of early intervention. This theory emphasizes the importance of intervening with youths who are at a greater risk of engaging in crime, such as children from a single parent home or those who have a history of substance abuse. Researchers have found that the following five intervention programs are particularly effective at preventing criminal behavior: 1) Nurse Home Visitation Program; 2) High/Scope Perry Preschool Program; 3) Functional Family Therapy (FFT); 4) Seattle Social Development Project; and 5) Multisystemic Therapy (Cullen & Jonson, 2016).

Advantages and Disadvantages of Institutional Corrections

During the Progressive Era, which occurred in the early 1900s, rehabilitation served as the dominant theory of corrections (Cullen & Jonson, 2016). However, policymakers, researchers, criminal justice practitioners, and the public began to question the effectiveness of rehabilitation less than a decade later. This attack against rehabilitative efforts was fueled, in part, by an essay published by Robert Martinson in 1974. In his essay, Martinson (1974) argued that nothing works when attempting to rehabilitate offenders. As such, the U.S. developed and implemented numerous get-tough crime policies and strategies that caused a substantial increase in the U.S. incarceration rate. First, transformed drug laws and policies have significantly contributed to increased incarceration rates. The war on drugs campaign began with the passage of the Anti-Drug Abuse Act of 1986, which established a five-year mandatory minimum sentence for 100 grams of heroin, 500 grams of cocaine, and/or 5 grams of crack cocaine (Cadora, 2014). Additionally, the law introduced a five-year mandatory minimum sentence for possession of crack cocaine, even if there is no intent to sell (Gottschalk, 2016).

In 1980, the number of individuals incarcerated in federal prisons for drug-related offenses was approximately 4,700, which was a little over 21% of the total number of incarcerated individuals (The Sentencing Project, 2020). By 1990, the number of individuals incarcerated for drug offenses was more than 30,000, which was more than 50% of the prison population (The Sentencing Project, 2020). In addition, Congress began to explore the possibility of longer prison sentences in the mid-1970s, which ultimately resulted in the passage of the Comprehensive Crime Control Act of 1984 and the establishment of mandatory minimum sentences (Gottschalk, 2016). Furthermore, the passage of the Violent Crime Control and Law Enforcement Act in 1994 by the Clinton Administration permitted a life-without-parole sentence for any person with two prior criminal convictions (Gottschalk, 2016). The rise in the incarceration rate was also fueled by a series of laws directed toward juveniles and sex offenders in the 1990s. As shown in Table 1, the number of individuals incarcerated in U.S. prisons increased approximately 52.3% from 1980 to 1985, 53.6% from 1985 to 1990, and 46.7% from 1990 to 1995 (The Sentencing Project, 2020).

As shown in Table 2, the U.S. has the highest incarceration rate in the world, with more than 2.1 million people incarcerated in its prisons and jails in 2019 (The Sentencing Project, 2020). Furthermore, as shown in Table 3, the U.S. incarceration rate is approximately 660 per 100,000 residents, a rate higher than those of Spain, China, Canada, France, Germany, Denmark, and Sweden combined (The Sentencing Project, 2020).

There is one crucial benefit of institutional corrections. Incarcerated individuals usually do not present a threat to public safety. However, mass incarceration and prison overcrowding have generated several negative outcomes, including racial bias and disparities. Researchers have found that harsh correctional policies and practices have fallen most heavily on African Americans and Hispanics (Guetzkow & Schoon, 2015). In fact, African Americans constitute more than 47% of the 2.1 million individuals incarcerated in the U.S. (Pettit & Gutierrez, 2018). Previous studies have also found that approximately one in three African Americans will experience incarceration at some point during their life (Bonczar, 2003), and that black men will spend approximately one-third of their lives in prison (Patterson & Wildeman, 2015).

Table 1. U.S. state and federal prison population, 1980–2020

Year	Number of People	Number Increase/Decrease	Percent Increase/Decrease
1980	315,974	N/A	N/A
1985	481,393	165,419	52.3
1990	739,549	258,156	53.6
1995	1,085,022	345,473	46.7
2000	1,334,174	249,152	22.9
2005	1,462,866	128,692	9.6
2010	1,552,669	89,803	6.1
2015	1,476,847	(75,822)	4.8
2020	1,311,100	(165,747)	11.2

(The Sentencing Project, 2020)

Family members of incarcerated minorities also experience significant collateral damage. For example, researchers have found that the children of African Americans who are incarcerated do worse in school and often exhibit behavioral problems (Wildeman, 2010). Furthermore, the wives or girlfriends of incarcerated African Americans often suffer from economic hardship and/or depression (Turney et al., 2012). Additionally, maternal incarceration often results in worse self-reported health, educational, and criminal justice outcomes for juveniles (Wildeman & Wang, 2017). Like non-incarcerated individuals, inmates frequently have chronic medical conditions. Unfortunately, the quality of healthcare for chronic medical conditions in correctional settings varies from one prison to the next and overcrowding usually decreases quality of care (Walmsley, 2005). Due to decreased quality of care, inmates are at a greater risk of developing infectious diseases, including HIV; chronic medical conditions, such as hypertension and diabetes; and substance use disorders (Wildeman & Wang, 2017). Mental health disorders are also prevalent in correctional settings, with approximately 25% of prison and jail detainees suffering from at least one psychiatric disorder (Appelbaum, 2011). Previous studies have also found that incarcerated individuals are at a greater risk of suicide (Huey & McNulty, 2005).

Overcrowding is also a major contributor to several problems, including reduced morale among correctional staff, increased levels of conflict and violence, and security difficulties. Mass incarceration also destroys social citizenship in three ways. First, incarceration creates barriers to "finding legal employment

Table 2. Total U.S. corrections population, 2019

	Number of People
Prison	1,380,427
Jail	745,200
Probation	3,602,213
Parole	873,712
Private prison	115,954
Total	6,717,506

(The Sentencing Project, 2020)

Table 3. International incarceration rates per 100,000 population, 2018

Country	Rate of Incarceration (Rounded to Nearest 10)
United States	660
El Salvador	620
Rwanda	460
Russia	380
Brazil	330
Australia	170
Spain	130
China	120
Canada	110
France	100
Germany	80
Denmark	60
Sweden	60
India	30

(The Sentencing Project, 2020)

by discouraging potential employers, interrupting employment history, eroding job skills, and undermining social connections to stable job opportunities" (Roberts, 2004, p. 1293). Second, neighborhoods where incarceration is concentrated are isolated from civic life, both internally and externally (Roberts, 2004). Third, incarceration denies citizenship through political disenfranchisement, or the loss of the right to vote. In the U.S., only Maine and Vermont had no laws regarding disenfranchisement. Meanwhile, 14 states do not allow inmates to vote, while the right to vote is denied to inmates and parolees in five states. Additionally, 15 states do not allow inmates, parolees, and/or probationers to vote. Finally, inmates, parolees, probationers, and ex-felons are prohibited from voting in 14 states (Travis et al., 2014).

As a result of state disenfranchisement policies, more than 6 million people were unable to vote in 2016 (The Sentencing Project, 2020). The rate of disenfranchisement in 2016 was nearly 2.5% for non-African Americans and more than 7% for African Americans (The Sentencing Project, 2020). There are also significant economic costs associated with mass incarceration and prison overcrowding, as budget allocations for the U.S. prison system have increased substantially when compared to other government services, including but not limited to education, transportation, and public assistance. According to the National Association of State Budget Officers, state expenditures on corrections were approximately $6.7 billion (The Sentencing Project, 2020). However, state expenditures increased to nearly $61 billion in 2018 (The Sentencing Project, 2020). In addition to significant economic and social costs, evidence regarding the deterrent effect of incarceration remains inconclusive. While some studies have found that prison modestly deters crime, many others argue that prison has little or no effect on crime and recidivism rates (Cochran et al., 2014).

SOLUTIONS AND RECOMMENDATIONS

Elements of Effective Community Corrections Programs

Because of the negative consequences caused by mass incarceration and prison overcrowding, the U.S. must return to the rehabilitative ideal prevalent during the early 1900s and increase its reliance on effective community corrections programs. Previous studies have identified several important components that, if implemented correctly, will likely increase the effectiveness of such programs. One of the most important components is the use of a validated risk and needs assessment to determine program placement. James (2015) states that risk and needs assessment tools usually "consist of a series of items used to collect data on behaviors and attitudes that research indicates are related to the risk of recidivism" (p. 2). The Risk-Needs-Responsivity (RNR) model serves as the primary framework for these assessment tools. The RNR model consists of three main elements. First, the risk principle states that high-risk offenders should receive intensive treatment, while low-risk offenders should receive minimal intervention (James, 2015). Second, the needs principle asserts that programs/services should focus on addressing the needs of participants. The most effective programs are those that target the following eight criminogenic needs that are most predictive of criminal behavior: 1) anti-social attitudes, values, and beliefs; 2) anti-social associates; 3) anti-social personality pattern; 4) family and marital problems; 5) substance abuse; 6) education issues; 7) employment issues; and 8) lack of prosocial activities (Hamilton et al., 2017; Warren, 2009).

Finally, the responsivity principle states that treatment should be delivered in a manner that considers the ability and learning style of each program participant (James, 2015). The RNR model is summarized in Figure 1.

Figure 1. Three core principles of the risk-needs-responsivity model
(James, 2015)

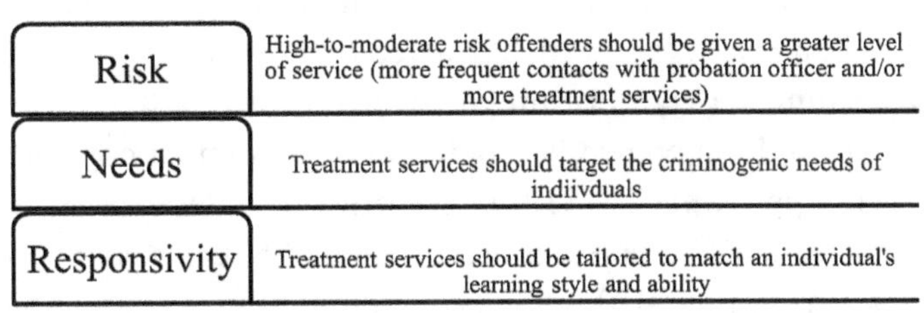

There are several validated assessment tools that are consistent with the RNR model, including the Level of Service/Risk, Need, Responsivity (LS/RNR), COMPAS Risk and Needs Assessment System, Ohio Risk Assessment System (ORAS), Structured Assessment of Violence Risk in Youth (SAVRY), and Rapid Risk Assessment for Sexual Offense Recidivism (RRASOR). In addition to using a risk and needs assessment, effective programs must provide participants with comprehensive evidence-based treatment services. Researchers have identified several elements of such services. For example, participants must be able to actively participate in their interventions (Simpson, 2004). Similarly, programs should provide family members with opportunities to participate in the interventions. Taylor (2016) found that higher levels of social and emotional support were associated with reductions in recidivism.

Effective programs should also strive to motivate the participant to change (Simpson, 2004). To accomplish this, programs must utilize four techniques. First and foremost, staff members must combine their enforcement and supervision responsibilities with instruction and modeling of prosocial behavior (Vera Institute of Justice, 2013). Second, program staff should assist participants with setting treatment goals that are both feasible and compatible with public safety goals and should provide each participant with regular updates regarding their treatment progress (Friedman et al., 2007). Third, programs should develop and implement graduated incentives and sanctions policies to improve program retention and participant success. Relatedly, staff should apply a variety of tangible and social rewards, including verbal praise, letters of commendation or certificates of achievement, gift cards, and/or the removal of a sanction. Sanctions should include verbal warnings, extra duties, and/or loss of privileges. Effective programs ensure that the application of rewards outweighs sanctions by at least 4:1 (Vera Institute of Justice, 2013).

Finally, effective programs provide continuous care as the participant moves through the criminal justice system and emphasize quality of treatment rather than the number of participants served (Friedman et al., 2007). The National Institute on Drug Abuse (NIDA) has identified several additional elements of effective programs that are specific to substance abuse treatment. For example, the NIDA (2016) asserts that effective substance abuse intervention and treatment programs target all forms of substance abuse, including tobacco, alcohol, and inhalant abuse. Furthermore, effective programs utilize skills training to increase social competency, reinforce attitudes against drug use, and help children resist drug use (NIDA, 2016). Staff characteristics also impact program effectiveness. Effective programs: 1) hire and retain experienced and qualified treatment staff; 2) provide initial and regular ongoing training; and 3) provide clinical supervision to improve service delivery skills (Makarios et al., 2016).

Benefits of Community Corrections

There are several benefits of community corrections programs. First, participation in community-based programs is substantially cheaper than incarceration. During Fiscal Year (FY) 2010, the prison population in Arizona was approximately 38,000, which equated to more than $897 million in expenditures, or approximately $14,000 per inmate (Vera Institute of Justice, 2013). Alternatively, the state of Arizona expended approximately $12 million on nearly 8,000 individuals under community supervision during FY 2010, which equated to approximately $1,600 per offender (Vera Institute of Justice, 2013). The cost savings are higher in some states. For example, the state of Maine spent approximately $93 million on roughly 1,900 inmates during FY 2010, which equated to approximately $48,000 per inmate. The same year, Maine paid approximately $8.8 million on 7,300 community corrections participants, which equated to roughly $1,200 per participant (Vera Institute of Justice, 2013). The cost savings of successful community corrections programs are even more substantial when considering the revolving door effect. When ex-offenders are returned to the community without substance use and mental health treatment, employment, and education, they frequently reoffend and are reincarcerated.

Previous studies have found that a majority of inmates suffer from one or more substance use disorders, and prisons and jails often provide ineffective substance abuse treatment (McLellan, 2017). By providing substance abuse treatment, community corrections programs may assist users with modifying their self-conceptions, learning techniques of change, and increasing self-efficacy (Bahr et al., 2010). Community corrections programs can also provide mental health treatment to individuals, which is particularly important due to the fact that it is common for inmates and newly released offenders to be dually diagnosed with substance use and mental health disorders (DeMatteo et al., 2013). These programs can also provide participants with employment and housing assistance. Full-time employment may help provide structure for newly released inmates, thereby restricting criminal opportunities (Bahr et al., 2010). Rather than utilizing a one-size-fits-all approach, community corrections programs can target substance abuse, mental health disorders, employment and housing issues, and other specific risk factors that contribute to criminal behavior. Because of this, community corrections programs are more effective at reducing recidivism than are prisons and jails (DeMatteo et al., 2013; Lipsey, 2009).

Disadvantages of Community Corrections

Nevertheless, there are several disadvantages of community corrections. Individuals and organizations often encounter numerous obstacles when attempting to implement effective community corrections programs, particularly when the programs provide substance abuse services. For example, probation officers and other criminal justice practitioners frequently rely on limited criteria when determining the need for treatment (Farabee et al., 1999). Similarly, many individuals are excluded from treatment due to factors unrelated to substance abuse, including individuals who have committed sexual or violent offenses (Farabee et al., 1999). Validated risk and needs assessments should be used when determining the need for treatment. These assessments are discussed in greater detail below. Programs also frequently struggle with recruiting, training, and retaining credentialed treatment staff (Farabee et al., 1999). This is especially true for programs located in rural areas. Fortunately, the utilization of technology-assisted addiction and mental health treatment services may minimize the issues experienced by programs in rural areas.

Probation and parole officers are often faced with a variety of factors outside their control that further impact the effectiveness of community corrections. For example, offenders are often sentenced to probation or placed on parole for long terms (Vera Institute of Justice, 2013). Similarly, offenders placed under community supervision are frequently responsible for community service obligations, fines, and fees that probation and parole officers are expected to monitor and enforce (Vera Institute of Justice, 2013). These standardized, one-size-fits-all conditions, which are set by judges and/or parole boards, are not conducive to effective treatment (Vera Institute of Justice, 2013). Additionally, offenders under community supervision are frequently incarcerated for violating their rules of probation or parole, which further contributes to the revolving door effect (Vera Institute of Justice, 2013). Furthermore, judges frequently require offenders with substance use disorders to remain abstinent during their supervision, which ignores the fact that recovery is a lifelong process that usually involves relapsing (Vera Institute of Justice, 2013).

RECOMMENDATIONS FOR FUTURE RESEARCH

Future research should focus on three primary areas. First, researchers should continue to assess the impact of incarceration and other types of sanctions on crime and recidivism rates from the perspective of the deterrence theory. As indicated above, research regarding the deterrent effect of punishment has produced inconsistent results. While some studies suggest that more severe punishments are more effective at deterring crime, others argue that such punishments increase criminal behavior. Future studies may further support the need for effective community corrections programs. Second, more research is needed about the impact of family involvement on the rehabilitation and recovery processes. Such studies may aid the identification and implementation of important program components and best practices. Third, researchers should dedicate a substantial amount of time and effort to evaluating the effectiveness of existing community corrections programs. One option for evaluating effectiveness is the evidence-based Correctional Program Checklist (CPC) developed by the University of Cincinnati.

The CPC is divided into two primary components. The first component, capacity, can be used to determine whether or not a program has the necessary leadership and development, staff, and quality assurance capabilities to deliver evidence-based services to participants (Vito & Higgins, 2015). Alternatively, the content component can be used to assess the extent to which the program is meeting the principles of the RNR model and providing evidence-based services to participants (Vito & Higgins, 2015). There are two primary advantages of the CPC assessment. First, researchers have found that the elements of the CPC are linked to decreases in recidivism (Vito & Higgins, 2015). Second, assessors are able to identify strengths and weaknesses of the program and provide recommendations to staff members that may assist with improving program effectiveness (Vito & Higgins, 2015). Researchers should actively disseminate future findings to criminal justice practitioners, policymakers, and the public in an effort to inform policy and practice.

CONCLUSION

The theories of retribution, deterrence, incapacitation, restorative justice, rehabilitation, reentry, and early intervention have all played a role in shaping America's correctional system. While the theory of rehabilitation was the dominant framework in the early 1900s, the rehabilitative ideal fell under attack in the 1970s, shifting the focus to deterrence and incapacitation. Severe sentencing laws, such as mandatory minimum and three-strikes sentencing, and more severe punishments for juveniles, sex offenders, and drug-related offenses caused a substantial increase in the incarceration rate. Mass incarceration in the U.S. has generated several negative consequences, including but not limited to significant economic and social costs, racial bias and disparities, collateral damage for family members and communities, and prison overcrowding. The use of community corrections programs as an alternative to sentencing may be beneficial in two ways. First, participation in community corrections programs is usually more cost effective than incarceration. Second, by providing individualized services to participants, community corrections programs are often more effective at reducing crime and recidivism.

However, community corrections programs must implement several key components to effectively reduce crime and recidivism rates. First, programs must use a validated risk and needs assessment when determining program placement. Second, participants should be provided with a variety of evidence-based treatment services, particularly those that target substance use and mental health disorders. Third, programs should focus on behavior modification through treatment goal setting and progress tracking, as well as the development and implementation of graduated incentives and sanctions policies. Finally, programs should strive to hire and retain qualified treatment staff and provide staff members with initial and ongoing training and clinical supervision. Future research should focus on: 1) analyzing the deterrent effect of incarceration and other types of sanctions; 2) assessing the impact of family involvement on program participants' recovery and rehabilitation; and 3) conducting program evaluations on existing community corrections programs using the CPC assessment tool to identify best practices.

REFERENCES

Appelbaum, P. S. (2011). Lost in the crowd: Prison mental health care, overcrowding, and the courts. *Law & Psychiatry*, *62*(10), 1121–1123. PMID:21969635

Bahr, S. J., Harris, L., Fisher, J. K., & Armstrong, A. H. (2010). Successful reentry: What differentiates successful and unsuccessful parolees? *International Journal of Offender Therapy and Comparative Criminology*, *54*(5), 667–692. doi:10.1177/0306624X09342435 PMID:19638473

Blumstein, A. (2011). Bringing down the U.S. prison population. *The Prison Journal*, *91*(3), 125–265. doi:10.1177/0032885511415218

Bonczar, T. P. (2003). *Prevalence of imprisonment in the U.S. population, 1974–2001*. U.S. Department of Justice, Bureau of Justice Statistics.

Cadora, E. (2014). How certain schemes to end mass incarceration can fail. *The Annals of the American Academy of Political and Social Science*, *651*(1), 277–285. doi:10.1177/0002716213503786

Cochran, J. C., Mears, D. P., & Bales, W. D. (2014). Assessing the effectiveness of correctional sanctions. *Journal of Quantitative Criminology*, *30*(2), 317–347. doi:10.100710940-013-9205-2

Cullen, F. T., & Jonson, C. L. (2016). *Correctional theory: Context and consequences* (2nd ed.). SAGE.

DeMatteo, D., LaDuke, C., Locklair, B. R., & Heilbrun, K. (2013). Community-based alternatives for justice-involved individuals with severe mental illness: Diversion, problem-solving courts, and reentry. *Journal of Criminal Justice*, *41*(2), 64–71. doi:10.1016/j.jcrimjus.2012.09.002

Farabee, D., Prendergast, M., Cartier, J., Wexler, H., Knight, K., & Anglin, D. (1999). Barriers to implementing effective drug treatment programs. *The Prison Journal*, *79*(2), 150–162. doi:10.1177/0032885599079002002

Friedmann, P. D., Taxman, F. S., & Henderson, C. E. (2007). Evidence-based treatment practices for drug-involved adults in the criminal justice system. *Journal of Substance Abuse Treatment*, *32*(3), 267–277. doi:10.1016/j.jsat.2006.12.020 PMID:17383551

Gottschalk, M. (2016). *Caught: The prison state and the lockdown of American politics*. Princeton University Press.

Guetzkow, J., & Schoon, E. (2015). If you build it, they will fill it: The consequences of prison overcrowding litigation. *Law & Society Review*, *49*(2), 401–432. doi:10.1111/lasr.12140

Hamilton, Z., Campagna, M., Tollefsbol, E., Van Wormer, J., & Barnoski, R. (2017). A more consistent application of the RNR model: The strong-R needs assessment. *Criminal Justice and Behavior*, *44*(2), 261–292. doi:10.1177/0093854816678032

Huey, M. P., & McNulty, T. L. (2005). Institutional conditions and prison suicide: Conditional effects of deprivation and overcrowding. *The Prison Journal*, *85*(4), 490–514. doi:10.1177/0032885505282258

James, N. (2015). *Risk and needs assessment in the criminal justice system*. Congressional Research Service.

Kang-Brown, J., Montagnet, C., & Heiss, J. (2021). *People in jail and prison in 2020*. Vera Institute of Justice.

Langan, P. A., & Levin, D. J. (2002). *Recidivism of prisoners released in 1994*. U.S. Department of Justice, Bureau of Justice Statistics. doi:10.1525/fsr.2002.15.1.58

Lee, H.-W. (2017). Taking deterrence seriously: The wide-scope deterrence theory of punishment. *Criminal Justice Ethics*, *36*(1), 2–24. doi:10.1080/0731129X.2017.1298879

Lipsey, M. W. (2009). The primary factors that characterize effective interventions with juvenile offenders: A meta-analytic overview. *Victims & Offenders: An International Journal of Evidence-Based Research, Policy & Practice*, *4*(2), 124–147.

Loughran, T. A., Pogarsky, G., Piquero, A. R., & Paternoster, R. (2012). Re-examining the functional form of the certainty effect in deterrence theory. *Justice Quarterly*, *29*(5), 712–741. doi:10.1080/07418825.2011.583931

Makarios, M., Lovins, L., Latessa, E., & Smith, P. (2016). Staff quality and treatment effectiveness: An examination of the relationship between staff factors and the effectiveness of correctional programs. *Justice Quarterly*, *33*(2), 348–367. doi:10.1080/07418825.2014.924546

Martinson, R. (1974). What works? Questions and answers about prison reform. *The Public Interest*, *35*, 22–54.

McLellan, A. T. (2017). Substance misuse and substance use disorders: Why do they matter in healthcare? *Transactions of the American Clinical and Climatological Association*, *128*, 112–130. PMID:28790493

Nagin, D. S. (2013). Deterrence in the twenty-first century. *Crime and Justice*, *42*(1), 199–263. doi:10.1086/670398

National Institute on Drug Abuse (NIDA). (2016). *Understanding drug abuse and addiction: What science says*. https://www.drugabuse.gov/publications/teaching-addiction-science/understanding-drug-abuse-addiction-what-science-says

Patterson, E. J., & Wildeman, C. (2015). Mass imprisonment and the life course revisited: Cumulative years spent imprisoned and marked for working-age black and white men. *Social Science Research*, *53*, 325–337. doi:10.1016/j.ssresearch.2015.06.011 PMID:26188457

Pettit, B., & Gutierrez, C. (2018). Mass incarceration and racial inequality. *American Journal of Economics and Sociology*, *77*(3–4), 1153–1182. doi:10.1111/ajes.12241

Roberts, D. E. (2004). The social and moral cost of mass incarceration in African American communities. *Stanford Law Review*, *56*(5), 1271–1305.

Sabol, W. J., & Couture, H. (2008). *Prison inmates at midyear 2007*. U.S. Department of Justice, Office of Justice Programs. doi:10.1037/e456192008-001

Siegfried, M. L. (2001). The promises and problematics of reentry court. *Criminal Justice Studies*, *14*(2–3), 201–219.

Simpson, D. D. (2004). A conceptual framework for drug treatment process and outcomes. *Journal of Substance Abuse Treatment, 27*(2), 99–121. doi:10.1016/j.jsat.2004.06.001 PMID:15450644

Taylor, C. J. (2016). The family's role in the reintegration of formerly incarcerated individuals: The direct effects of emotional support. *The Prison Journal, 96*(3), 331–354. doi:10.1177/0032885516635085

The Sentencing Project. (2020). *Trends in U.S. corrections*. https://www.sentencingproject.org/wp-content/uploads/2020/08/Trends-in-US-Corrections.pdf

Travis, J., Western, B., & Redburn, S. (2014). *The growth of incarceration in the United States: Exploring causes and consequences*. The National Academies Press.

Turney, K., Schnittker, J., & Wildeman, C. (2012). Those they leave behind: Paternal incarceration and maternal instrumental support. *Journal of Marriage and Family, 74*(5), 1149–1165. doi:10.1111/j.1741-3737.2012.00998.x

Vera Institute of Justice. (2013). *The potential of community corrections to improve safety and reduce incarceration*. Center on Sentencing and Corrections.

Vito, G. F., & Higgins, G. E. (2015). *Practical program evaluation for criminal justice*. Elsevier.

Walmsley, R. (2005). Prison health care and the extent of prison overcrowding. *International Journal of Prisoner Health, 1*(1), 9–12.

Warren, R. K. (2009). Evidence-based sentencing: The application of principles of evidence based practice to state sentencing practice and policy. *University of San Francisco Law Review. University of San Francisco. School of Law, 43*(3), 585–634.

Wildeman, C. (2010). Paternal incarceration and children's physically aggressive behaviors: Evidence from the Fragile Families and Child Wellbeing Study. *Social Forces, 89*(1), 285–309. doi:10.1353of.2010.0055

Wildeman, C., & Wang, E. A. (2017). Mass incarceration, public health, and widening inequality in the USA. *Lancet, 389*(10077), 1464–1474. doi:10.1016/S0140-6736(17)30259-3 PMID:28402828

Wright, V. (2010). *Deterrence in criminal justice: Evaluating certainty vs. severity of punishment*. The Sentencing Project. https://www.sentencingproject.org/wp-content/uploads/2016/01/Deterrence-in-Criminal-Justice.pdf

ADDITIONAL READING

Allison, S., Tarun, B., & Fuller, D. A. (2017). Mass incarceration and severe mental illness in the USA. *Lancet, 390*(10089), 25. doi:10.1016/S0140-6736(17)31479-4 PMID:28677552

Blair, L., Sullivan, C. C., Lux, J., Thielo, A. J., & Gormsen, L. (2016). Measuring drug court adherence to the what works literature: The creation of the Evidence-Based Correctional Program Checklist–Drug Court. *International Journal of Offender Therapy and Comparative Criminology, 60*(2), 165–188. doi:10.1177/0306624X14549950 PMID:25192736

Brinkley-Rubinstein, L., Zaller, N., Martino, S., Cloud, D. H., McCauley, E., Heise, A., & Seal, D. (2018). Criminal justice continuum for opioid users at risk of overdose. *Addictive Behaviors*, *86*, 104–110. doi:10.1016/j.addbeh.2018.02.024 PMID:29544869

Brown, T. N., Bell, M. L., & Patterson, E. J. (2016). Imprisoned by empathy: Familial incarceration and psychological distress among African American Men in the National Survey of American Life. *Journal of Health and Social Behavior*, *57*(2), 240–256. doi:10.1177/0022146516645924 PMID:27257267

Carmichael, J. T., & Burgos, G. (2012). Sentencing juvenile offenders to life in prison: The political sociology of juvenile punishment. *American Journal of Criminal Justice*, *37*(4), 602–629. doi:10.100712103-011-9135-1

Chuang, E., & Wells, R. (2010). The role of inter-agency collaboration in facilitating receipt of behavioral health services for youth involved with child welfare and juvenile justice. *Children and Youth Services Review*, *32*(12), 1814–1822. doi:10.1016/j.childyouth.2010.08.002 PMID:21076622

Comartin, E. B., Kernsmith, P. D., & Kernsmith, R. M. (2009). Sanctions for sex offenders: Fear and public policy. *Journal of Offender Rehabilitation*, *48*(7), 605–619. doi:10.1080/10509670903196066

Dodge, K. A., & Mandel, A. D. (2012). Building evidence for evidence-based policy making. *Criminology & Public Policy*, *11*(3), 525–534. doi:10.1111/j.1745-9133.2012.00828.x PMID:23956700

Dowden, C., & Andrews, D. A. (2003). Does family intervention work for delinquents? Results of a meta-analysis. *Canadian Journal of Criminology and Criminal Justice*, *45*(3), 327–342. doi:10.3138/cjccj.45.3.327

Duriez, S. A., Sullivan, C., Latessa, E. J., & Lovins, L. B. (2017). The evolution of correctional program assessment in the age of evidence-based practices. *Corrections: Policy, Practice and Research*, *3*(2), 119–136. doi:10.1080/23774657.2017.1343104

Garland, B., Wodahl, E., & Cota, L. (2016). Measuring public support for prisoner reentry options. *International Journal of Offender Therapy and Comparative Criminology*, *60*(12), 1406–1424. doi:10.1177/0306624X15578438 PMID:25816814

Gendreau, P., French, S. A., & Gionet, A. (2004). What works (what doesn't work): The principles of effective correctional treatment. *Journal of Community Corrections*, *13*(3), 4–10.

Greenwood, P., & Turner, S. (2009). An overview of prevention and intervention programs for juvenile offenders. *Victims & Offenders*, *4*(4), 365–374. doi:10.1080/15564880903227438

Handtke, V., Bretschneider, W., Elger, B., & Wangmo, T. (2017). The collision of care and punishment: Aging prisoners' view on compassionate release. *Punishment & Society*, *19*(1), 5–22. doi:10.1177/1462474516644679

Jonson, C. L., & Cullen, F. T. (2015). Prisoner reentry programs. *Crime and Justice*, *44*(1), 517–575. doi:10.1086/681554

Kapp, S. A., Petr, C. G., Robbins, M. L., & Choi, J. J. (2013). Collaboration between community mental health and juvenile justice systems: Barriers and facilitators. *Child & Adolescent Social Work Journal*, *30*(6), 505–517. doi:10.100710560-013-0300-x

Kifer, M., Hemmens, C., & Stohr, M. K. (2003). The goals of corrections: Perspectives from the line. *Criminal Justice Review*, *28*(1), 47–69. doi:10.1177/073401680302800104

Kleck, G., Sever, B., Li, S., & Gertz, M. (2005). The missing link in general deterrence research. *Criminology*, *43*(3), 623–660. doi:10.1111/j.0011-1348.2005.00019.x

Latessa, E. J., & Holsinger, A. (1998). The importance of evaluating correctional programs: Assessing outcome and quality. *Corrections Management Quarterly*, *2*(4), 22–29.

Lawson, N. (2016). It's a man's prison: How the traditional incarceration model fails female offenders in Kansas. *The Kansas Journal of Law & Public Policy*, *25*(2), 273–279.

Lipsey, M. W., & Cullen, F. T. (2007). The effectiveness of correctional rehabilitation: A review of systematic reviews. *Annual Review of Law and Social Science*, *3*(1), 297–320. doi:10.1146/annurev.lawsocsci.3.081806.112833

Lowenkamp, C. T., Latessa, E. J., & Holsinger, A. M. (2006). The risk principle in action: What have we learned from 13,676 offenders and 97 correctional programs? *Crime and Delinquency*, *52*(1), 77–93. doi:10.1177/0011128705281747

Lowenkamp, C. T., Latessa, E. J., & Smith, P. (2006). Does correctional program quality really matter? The impact of adhering to the principles of effective intervention. *Criminology & Public Policy*, *5*(3), 575–594. doi:10.1111/j.1745-9133.2006.00388.x

Lynch, M. (2012). Theorizing the role of the "war on drugs" in U.S. punishment. *Theoretical Criminology*, *16*(2), 175–199. doi:10.1177/1362480612441700

MacKenzie, D. L. (2000). Evidence based corrections: Identifying what works. *Crime and Delinquency*, *46*(4), 457–461. doi:10.1177/0011128700046004003

MacKenzie, D. L. (2006). *What works in corrections: Reducing the criminal activities of offenders and delinquents*. Cambridge University Press. doi:10.1017/CBO9780511499470

Makarios, M., Lovins, L. B., Myer, A. J., & Latessa, E. (2019). Treatment integrity and recidivism among sex offenders: The relationship between CPC scores and program effectiveness. *Corrections: Policy, Practice and Research*, *4*(2), 112–125. doi:10.1080/23774657.2017.1389318

Marion, N. (2002). Effectiveness of community-based correctional programs: A case study. *The Prison Journal*, *82*(4), 478–497. doi:10.1177/003288550208200404

Martin, M. S., Dorken, S. K., Wamboldt, A. D., & Wootten, S. E. (2012). Stopping the revolving door: A meta-analysis on the effectiveness of interventions for criminally involved individuals with major mental disorders. *Law and Human Behavior*, *36*(1), 1–12. doi:10.1037/h0093963 PMID:22471380

Matthews, B., Hubbard, D. J., & Latessa, E. (2001). Making the next step: Using evaluability assessment to improve correctional programming. *The Prison Journal*, *81*(4), 454–472. doi:10.1177/0032885501081004003

Matthews, S. K., & Agnew, R. (2008). Extending deterrence theory: Do delinquent peers condition the relationship between perceptions of getting caught and offending? *Journal of Research in Crime and Delinquency*, *45*(2), 91–118. doi:10.1177/0022427807313702

Mauer, M. (2011). Addressing racial disparities in incarceration. *The Prison Journal*, *91*(3), 87S–101S. doi:10.1177/0032885511415227

McCaskill, C. (2008). Next steps in breaking the cycle of reoffending: A call for reentry courts. *Federal Sentencing Reporter*, *20*(5), 308–309. doi:10.1525/fsr.2008.20.5.308

McLellan, A. T., Arndt, I. O., Metzger, D. S., Woody, G. E., & O'Brien, C. P. (1993). The effects of psychosocial services in substance abuse treatment. *Journal of the American Medical Association*, *269*(15), 1953–1959. doi:10.1001/jama.1993.03500150065028 PMID:8385230

Mears, D. P., & Cochran, J. C. (2018). Progressively tougher sanctioning and recidivism: Assessing the effects of different types of sanctions. *Journal of Research in Crime and Delinquency*, *55*(2), 194–241. doi:10.1177/0022427817739338

Miller, E. J. (2007). The therapeutic effects of managerial reentry courts. *Federal Sentencing Reporter*, *20*(2), 127–135. doi:10.1525/fsr.2007.20.2.127

Morgan, R. D., Flora, D. B., Kroner, D. G., Mills, J. F., Varghese, F., & Steffan, J. S. (2012). Treating offenders with mental illness: A research synthesis. *Law and Human Behavior*, *36*(1), 37–50. doi:10.1037/h0093964 PMID:22471384

Nellis, A. (2016). *The color of justice: Racial and ethnic disparity in state prisons*. The Sentencing Project.

O'Farrell, T. J. (1993). *Treating alcohol problems: Marital and family interventions*. The Guilford Press.

Phelps, M. S. (2011). Rehabilitation in the punitive era: The gap between rhetoric and reality in U.S. prison programs. *Law & Society Review*, *45*(1), 33–68. doi:10.1111/j.1540-5893.2011.00427.x PMID:24014890

Pitts, J. A., Griffin, H. III, & Johnson, W. W. (2014). Contemporary prison overcrowding: Short-term fixes to a perpetual problem. *Contemporary Justice Review: Issues in Criminal, Social, and Restorative Justice*, *17*(1), 124–139. doi:10.1080/10282580.2014.883844

Prendergast, M. L. (2011). Issues in defining and applying evidence-based practices: Criteria for treatment of criminal-justice involved clients. *Journal of Psychoactive Drugs*, *43*(1), 10–18. doi:10.1080/02791072.2011.601984 PMID:22185035

Raphael, S. (2009). Explaining the rise in U.S. incarceration rates. *Criminology & Public Policy*, *8*(1), 87–95. doi:10.1111/j.1745-9133.2009.00550.x

Schneider, A. L., & Ervin, L. (1990). Specific deterrence, rational choice, and decision heuristics: Applications in juvenile justice. *Social Science Quarterly*, *71*(3), 585–601.

Skeem, J. L., Manchak, S., & Peterson, J. K. (2011). Correctional policy for offenders with mental illness: Creating a new paradigm for recidivism reduction. *Law and Human Behavior*, *35*(2), 110–126. doi:10.100710979-010-9223-7 PMID:20390443

Smith, P., Gendreau, P., & Swatz, K. (2009). Validating the principles of effective intervention: A systematic review of the contributions of meta-analysis in the field of corrections. *Victims & Offenders*, *4*(2), 148–169. doi:10.1080/15564880802612581

Spence, D. H., & Haas, S. M. (2014). *Predictors of client success in day report centers: Successful program completion and its relationship to recidivism*. West Virginia Office of Research and Strategic Planning.

Terry, K. J. (2015). Sex offender laws in the United States: Smart policy or disproportionate sanctions? *International Journal of Comparative and Applied Criminal Justice*, *39*(2), 113–127. doi:10.1080/01924036.2014.973048

Wylie, L. E., Knutson, A. K., & Greene, E. (2018). Extraordinary and compelling: The use of compassionate release laws in the United States. *Psychology, Public Policy, and Law*, *24*(2), 216–234. doi:10.1037/law0000161

KEY TERMS AND DEFINITIONS

Collective Incapacitation: The use of traditional sentencing policies or strategies to incapacitate offenders who fall within certain categories of offenses, such as those who commit murder.

Deterrence: A correctional theory that asserts that individuals can be deterred from criminal behavior through certain, swift, and severe punishment.

Early Intervention: A correctional theory that emphasizes the need to intervene with at-risk children to prevent them from engaging in criminal and/or delinquent behavior.

Reentry: A correctional theory that argues that the primary goal of correctional institutions is to prepare offenders for successful reentry into society, while the goal of community corrections programs is to prevent individuals from reentering the criminal justice system.

Rehabilitation: A correctional theory that argues that individual factors cause crime, and reoffending can be reduced by providing effective treatment services that target these factors.

Restorative Justice: A correctional theory that asserts that the primary goal of corrections is to reverse the harm caused by crime and restore the offender, their victims, and the community.

Retribution: A correctional theory that argues that the primary purpose of the U.S. correctional system is to get even with offenders through punishment.

Revolving Door: The tendency of newly released inmates to re-enter the traditional criminal justice system after committing new crimes.

Selective Incapacitation: A type of incapacitation that occurs when criminal justice practitioners consider individual factors, such as the number of previous offenses, when sentencing offenders.

Chapter 10
Overview of Correctional Reform in India:
A "Different" Approach to Offender Rehabilitation

Divya Dubey
https://orcid.org/0000-0002-3003-301X
Amity Institute of Behavioural and Allied Sciences, Amity University, India

Vedika Agarwal
The University of Manchester, UK

ABSTRACT

Today, every prison around the world requires a correctional programme so that rehabilitation and reintegration of offenders can be done successfully. Correctional reforms is a serious issue and has been taken seriously even internationally. In India, many attempts have been made to improve the condition of prisons and prisoners, but little changes have been seen at the root-level. There is a scope of modifications in the correctional reforms to meet the present-day needs of the criminal justice system. The chapter will give an overview of the correctional reforms in Indian prisons and after reviewing the existing literature will attempt to identify the limitations of the correctional programs which need to be addressed for effective rehabilitation and reformation of prisoners. Lastly, the chapter will conclude with a number of suggestions and with a comprehensive model for rehabilitation.

INTRODUCTION

The correctional system of any nation is deeply rooted in history and tradition and represents societal attitudes formed by changing legal, ethical, and societal cultural norms. The inception of the idea of prison reform can be attributed to two factors- recidivism and the prison system's failure of effectively rehabilitating prisoners (O'Brien, 1995). The term 'Reform' is derived from the word "reformo" in Latin, which refers to changing or amending what is wrong and unacceptable.

DOI: 10.4018/978-1-7998-6884-2.ch010

This chapter will focus on the correctional reforms concerned with rehabilitation, and reintegration of the prisoners and attempt to identify the gap for effective rehabilitation of prisoners and skillful training to the prison staff, proper and efficient reform for juveniles, women, and adult offenders to minimize the re-offending rate and efficient functioning of the prisons in India.

In the history of the "reformation and rehabilitation" of offenders in India, numerous committees have been formed to effectively rehabilitate and reintegrate offenders. Sable (2020) in his paper Yerwada Jail visit discussed the report of the Indian Jail Reform Committee (1919-1920) involved in reforming the Indian prison which is as follows:

The Pakwasa committee, 1949 suggested a system of utilizing prisoners as "labor" without any vigilance over them. This is when the system of wages for prisoners' labor was introduced in India. They also introduced the system wherein the prisoners who adhered to the rules and regulations of the prison and did not violate the norms of the prison and showed exemplary behavior in the prison were rewarded by reducing their prison sentence (Ahmed, 2016). This was the big step towards prisoners' rehabilitation and reformation. Lalli (2019) in his paper attitude to Prison reforms discussed the historical background of Prison Reforms which states that in 1951 the Government of India invited Dr. W.C. Reckless, an expert in the field of correctional reforms of offenders from the United States, for a study on Indian prison administration. Dr. W.C. Reckless recommended that prisons should be transformed into reformation centers and outdated prison manuals should also be updated (Ahmed, 2016). The recommendations given by Dr. W.C. Reckless were approved during the 8th conference of the Inspector General of Prisons held in 1952. In 1957 the Government of India appointed the All-India Jail Committee and in 1960 All India Jail Committee submitted their report.

Thereafter, in 1980 the Indian government established a committee under the chairmanship of Justice AN. Mulla. The prime aim of this committee was to rehabilitate the prisoners. The Mulla committee gave numerous recommendations and some of the most important recommendations from the Mulla committee included that prisoners should get access to proper clothing, food, and sanitation. Prison staff should be trained and organized and people who were still under trial should be kept separate from the convicted prisoners. The committee also suggested that the trial period should be reduced, and the courts should come to a decision at the earliest and bail provision should be made available for undertrials to reduce the prison population. The Mulla committee also recommended that the Government should provide financial resources to prisoners. (Secretariat & Delhi, 2014).

Another committee, Justice V.R. Krishna Iyer Committee, 1987 was appointed to understand the situation of women prisoners in India. Recommendations that were made by Krishna Iyer Committee were that the Government of India should recruit more women in the police force to deal with issues related to women prisoners and child offenders (Model Prison Manual, 2003).

The committees also recognized that prisons could disrupt and damage many factors which enable an individual to desist from crime. Imprisonment can harden criminal attitudes, enhance criminal identity, and remove individuals from positive cultures and networks, disrupting their employment, accommodation, and family support. Therefore, safe, decent, and rehabilitative prisons cannot only mitigate these factors (and their cost to society) but provide a better foundation for rehabilitative success. A rehabilitative culture is beneficial for the lives of prison staff and prisoners in the establishment and for reducing re-offending (O'Brien, Marshall, & Karthaus, 2014).

Training of prisoners in various skills in the prison institutions has been given great attention by the Prison Department of Government of India and facilitated further by the Bureau of Research and Development which monitors the functioning of the prisons and provides funds for enhancing the existing resources inside the respective prison (Sanyal, 2019).

Several programs have been introduced in prisons to enable the offenders to meet the challenges of the outer world. These programs help them to develop skills that give a positive direction to their life and prove to be a source of employment upon release from prison (Khan, 1990). Furthermore, offenders are engaged in meaningful activities while in prisons and this reduces their indulgence in problematic behavior even while serving their sentence. Sanyal (2019) posits that the correctional system has shifted its focus from punitive measures to behavior modification ideology where several prosocial behaviors are taught to the offenders so that they can successfully be reintegrated into mainstream society.

The correctional method aims to reform and rehabilitate offenders irrespective of the nature of their offense. "*Prison is first a punishment - it removes the liberty of offenders, forcing them to comply with a structured, disciplined and tough regime where everyday choices that are usually taken for granted are removed*' (Ministry of Justice, 2010a: 6). Yet, to achieve the goal of reducing reoffending: '*We need a tough but intelligent Criminal Justice System that punishes people properly when they break the law, but also supports them so they don't commit a crime in the future* (Ministry of Justice Report, (2013:5). The modern goals of the correction system are to reform and rehabilitate the offenders along with punishing them for their wrongdoing.

Significant advancements have been made in the correctional system across the globe to maintain the rights of the prisoners and to modify their maladaptive behavior so that they can be successfully reintegrated into society. Vocational skills training is provided to the prisoners and regular changes are made to these life skill programs to meet the needs of the prisoners. Few NGOs have also introduced some programs like Meditation, Counselling, Vipassana, have also been introduced to curb negative feelings and leading offenders towards holistic development in the central prisons of India (Sanyal, 2019). However, there is still scope for further improvements and changes in the correctional reforms to reduce recidivism and for effective reformation of prisoners (Dhanuka & Lamba, 2020).

LITERATURE REVIEW

This section will review previous literature on prison reforms and prisoner conditions in Indian prisons. Through this section the authors attempt to give a brief outline of the various challenges present in the Indian prison reforms and rehabilitation of inmates by reviewing existing literature.

According to Chowdhury (2002), the prison law evolved into a reformative law aimed at addressing the problems with the existing prison administration in India. The author urged for some suitable reforms to improve prison administration in India. By analyzing various prison laws in India, the author indicated that prison laws developed during the British colonisation era had a different perspective and did not align with correctional penological thinking and neither aimed at reform. This paper only evaluates those prison laws that contribute the least towards the reformation of inmates. As a result, he categorically criticized the Prison Act of 1894, Prisoners Act of 1900, and West Bengal prison code as being insufficient, and called for their revision.

In India, inmate reformation is heavily reliant upon the role of NGOs in conducting various correctional programs according to Doin and Andres (2013). Prison transparency can be achieved through the work of NGOs in prisons and therefore also complying to international laws. Primary objective in prisons is to protect the human dignity of inmates and prevent any abuse they may be subject to, in addition to maintaining decent living conditions for them. Prisoners being treated humanely and having their basic needs met is imperative for effective reformation of inmates (O'Brien, Marshall, & Karthaus, 2014).

According to Kumar (2013) where he posits an idea that "human element" should be present in prison reform. The chapter also explains how the existing poor conditions violate Article 21 of fundamental rights. Prisons do not have proper food culture, sometimes there is no breakfast. Bad and unhygienic food inside the prison results in many health-related problems amongst inmates. Skipping breakfast and long fasting hours has many ill effects on the physical as well on the mental health of the prisoners. Therefore, prison reforms need a change so as to maintain the proper food culture inside the prison.

In addition, Fazal (2008) also conducts an analytical study about the health conditions of the inmates in Indian prisons. This study concluded that the number of inmates suffering from mental disorder, trauma and diseases are more prevalent than in the general population. There is also an increase rate of suicide amongst the prison population in India reflecting the deteriorating mental health of the inmates. Therefore, rehabilitative culture and psychological aid should be made accessible to the prison population.

Assessment done by Mitra and Pati (2011) highlighted the importance of prison reforms in India. This study confirmed that rights and the respect of the prisoners should be protected by introducing a more reformative approach to the penal system. They were proponents of the scientific way to the problem of criminal behavior and its consequences. The authors proposed that it is important to socialize offenders and teach them socially approved habits and norms so as to ensure their successful rehabilitation as a contributing member of the society. The paper also strongly suggested that protection of human rights is an integral part of prison reforms. Hence, reformation should be taken seriously by the prison administration and good and moral values should be inculcated in the prisoners.

Furthermore, M. Viji (2015) discusses the various issues existing in Indian prisons. The article referred to the National Human Rights Commission (NHRC) (1993-94) annual report about jail conditions in India. The common issues that are present in prisons are overcrowding, lack of proper sanitation, poor medical facilities, inadequate light, and food in many of the prisons of the country. There is also a severe lack of psychological aid and effective correctional programs in Indian prisons. Hence the commission has strongly recommended that the prison system is in dire need of reform. M. Viji (2015) states that these poor conditions are still prevalent in prisons in India. Therefore, there is an urgent need for improvement and reform policy changes in order to meet the modern aims of the prison system and to protect the fundamental rights of the inmates.

REHABILITATION / CORRECTIONAL REFORMS IN INDIAN PRISON

This section will explore the various correctional programs present in the Indian prisons, in particular life skills programs that aim to make the prisoners learn new skills and be engaged in meaningful activities. Reformations have been made in the arena of correction all around the world to maintain the rights of the prisoners and successfully reintegrate them into society and help them lead a dignified life. Because of the importance of skills in society, vocational skills programs are continuously revised. In addition, with the aid of psychological techniques, meditation and counseling, an effort is made to improve the offender's personality.

Bell (2002) asserts that criminals do not suddenly stop engaging in criminal activity as a result of imprisonment. They continue to commit crimes while incarcerated and these are not confined within the prison walls. Criminal activity may even increase upon incarceration. Prisons no doubt harden criminal attitudes and have become training grounds for the new inmates. Inmates test their criminal capacities against the corrections department and the community regularly.

Several programmes are present in Indian prisons such as educational programmes wherein one can complete their basic education, as well as vocational programmes and training in various skills are provided to increase their likelihood of employment in the future. Wage earning and Gratuity schemes and incentives are also used to reduce the financial burden on the convicts.

The correctional programmes have been introduced to bring positive change to the prisoners. Correctional programs bring about attitudinal change amongst prisoners. Correctional reformation should consider prisoners' needs to be effective (Tannenbaum, 1938). The experience of imprisonment leads the prisoners' identity to be diminished and they often feel lost and are subjected to disrespect and stigma. Imprisonment has a negative psychological impact and has also been equated to a traumatic experience (Haney, 2003). Therefore, correctional reforms are essential and should be implemented in prisons to not only maintain the mental health of offenders but also to reduce recidivism.

Correctional programs aim to bring about positive attitude change and equip the offenders with skills that will help them secure employment after release and become financially independent. In India, the jail administration provides training to the prisoners in accordance with their interests, skill, and aptitude so that they can relieve themselves of some of the financial burdens while learning new skills (Sanyal, 2019).

There is currently a more prominent accentuation on behavior modification, treatment, restoration, and mental development of offenders. The main aim is to prevent crime and reintegration of offenders into society. The reform comprises five primary components Vipassana, wellbeing, proficiency, social, and sports exercises (Department of Tihar Prisons, 2020).

Tihar Jail, New Delhi, one of the largest prison complexes in the world. It includes a population of 15561 against a total capacity of 10033. 13666 males and 362 females for under trials and 13 Male detainees, as of 30 September 2020. Tihar prison is known for its long history of reformation programs along with the latest correctional philosophy (Department of Tihar Prisons, 2020). Many correctional programmes such as educational programmes, spiritual programmes, vocational programmes, recreational activities are held where prisoners involve themselves in games or sports activities within the prison. Inter-jails, as well as Inter-ward sports competitions, are organized which boosts the prisoners' interest in sports and thereby physical fitness. Sports are organized in all prisons during winter sports festivals, which are generally referred to as "Tihar Olympics." Some cultural functions called 'Ethnic Tihar' are also organized from time to time where music, art, painting, qawwali, singing, dancing, are presented by the inmates. Sometimes, eminent personalities in the arena of sports and culture are also called to motivate the prisoners to take part in the competitions, which also improves the prisoners' mental and physical health; they also induce an interest in culture and moral values (Department of Tihar Prisons, 2020). Both religious and national festivals within the prisons are celebrated by all. The national flag is hoisted in all jails on Republic Day and Independence Day. All holy festivals are also celebrated. This is a major opportunity that allows the prison administration to express "We Care" to the inmates (Department of Tihar Prisons, 2020).

Educational programs are also conducted in prisons in India. Formal and adult education arrangements have been made for prisoners. Educational services are taken care of with the help of government support as well as NGOs' participation. Indira Gandhi National Open University (IGNOU), New Delhi, and the National Institute of Open Schooling (NIOS), Delhi provide Tihar Prison with education in which approximately 2640 and 1900 inmates are enrolled (Department of Tihar Prisons, 2020). Computer training is also available in Tihar prison for inmates (Department of Tihar Prisons, 2020). In Tihar Jail, the most important feature of the education system is that trained inmates willingly teach less educated inmates. This way one inmate helps the other inmate and develops a sense of helping each other which helps them grow with good conduct.

Many of the inmates who joined the 'Reformation by Education' course have been rehabilitated successfully. The government is responsible for the spending on tuition for Indira Gandhi National Open University (IGNOU) / Global Open School Institute (NIOS) courses. The study material like the notebooks and other stationery are also provided to the inmates for educational purposes by the jail administration.

Educational programs are a critical aspect of the Correctional programs of the Prison Department. The educational program is structured at multiple levels for distinct groups of prisoners such as illiterates, semi-literates, literates for those who would like to complete higher education. IGNOU from which a prisoner can pursue his studies and is offered and without specifying the place of test, i.e., prison, he is issued a certificate/degree for that course. Providing both formal and informal education is an essential component of the everyday life of prisoners. The Ministry of Human Resource Development's Department of Adult Education provides qualified prisoners with training to allow them to teach less educated and illiterate prisoners. The educational programmes in the prisons also help prisoners who are serving a short term by educating them to a level where they can print their name (Nargis, 2019).

Rehabilitation of prisoners was started in Indian prisons primarily because of the difficulties that are faced by the prisoners' post-release. Both for convicts and under-trials, a program for teaching different trades was launched in the prisons. This program involves the manufacturing of pen, bookbinding, manure making, screen printing, envelope making, tailoring, and cutting, shoemaking, which not only contributed to the learning of a new skill but also provided the prisoners with monetary benefits while in prison. The Social Welfare Department of Delhi Govt. provides loans to the inmates for setting up self-employed units, after their release from prison for successful rehabilitation (The Department of Tihar jail, 2020).

Regular exercises like Asans, Pranayam, Dhyan, Upasana, Yoga and Meditation also work as a correctional program inside the premises which inculcate the values, morals, discipline, and aid the inmates in developing a different approach towards life and changing their worldview. To bring a positive change in the aptitude of the prisoner, Yoga, and meditation classes are held to strengthen the mind and these programs have been started by various NGOs. These programs not only help the inmates but also the staff members of the prison to help them in releasing their negative energies and inoculates patience within them enabling them to tackle any demanding situations. Many centers within the prisons have been opened to impart moral education, counseling, and techniques of meditation to the inmates. (The Department of Tihar Prisons, 2020)

Creative Art Therapy also serves as a correctional program for the inmates inside the prison, it is psychotherapeutic and can be used in different settings and work as a reformatory process in the prisons (The Department of Tihar Prisons, 2020). It helps to express, channelize, and ventilate the feelings especially for prisoners who have tremendous anger, aggression, frustration, sense of helplessness, hopelessness, and emotional problems by encouraging and promoting creative art. Creative art also helps them in releasing their hidden emotions and realize their worth and bring a positive desire of improving themselves.

Societal participation in conducting reformation or rehabilitation for the prisoners by various NGOs, professors from renowned institutes such as IITs, psychiatrists, psychologists, teachers of various educational institutions are helping prisoners to reform. The presence of NGOs is primarily focused on the fields of schooling, vocational training, and therapy. Apart from formal education, classes in various languages are also held inside the prison. Today the correction system itself has seen many changes and there has been a shift from deterrence to rehabilitation and reintegration (The Department of Tihar Prisons, 2020).

Vipassana has been embraced as a prison reform in Tihar Jail. The key aim in implementing correctional reforms is to change the focus from custodial to restorative methodology. This noteworthy advancement has started a more human approach in managing offenders.

Sanyal (2019) has mentioned in her book "Rehabilitation of the Adult Prisoners in the Country" that for successful reintegration back into society Sri Ravi Shanker has started a project in the prison that will provide vocational training to the prisoners so that they successfully assimilate back into the society and earn their livelihood. One such project is SRIJAN that was started in Tihar Jail and had engaged offenders in activities like paper bag making, diaries making, which were then sold across Art of Living centers in India. The profits that they made were deposited in a bank account and given to them upon their release.

However, while assessing correctional programmes, it must also be ascertained that the people who are part of various correctional programmes are benefiting from them or not. The programs should also be allocated to the prisoners based on their interest as well as after assessing their attitude and various other psychological needs.

Thus, the conclusive statement is that while ensuring correctional programmes are being successfully implemented inside the prisons, the prison department should also ensure that identification and classification of prisoners are done for undertaking various training and making reformation a success.

REHABILITATION/ CORRECTIONAL POLICIES IN INDIA

Prison Management is an overly complex process. Prison management not only involves the implementation of various Acts, Rules, and processes but also requires the knowledge of psychology and human management. Most of India's prisons were constructed during the British colonization period. To date prison management is still governed by the Prisons Act of 1894, which has become entirely outdated. The field of prison management has seen many changes in various developed countries of the world; however, India has not been able to bring about the required changes yet. (Bureau of Police Research and Development, 2019). The ultimate goal of the Prison Administration is the reformation of offenders and humanization of prisoners. The following statement of Mahatma Gandhi encapsulates the essence of rehabilitation and reformation of offenders.

"Crime is the outcome of a diseased mind and jail must have an environment of a hospital for treatment and care."

The various Guidelines of the Supreme Court of India, the reports of different Prison Reform Committees, the Standard Minimum Rules for the Care of Prisoners, the Directives provided by the National Human Rights Commission (NHRC) and State Human Rights Commissions (SHRC), describe the urgent need to reframe new prison management policies and methodologies. (Bureau of Police Research & Development, 2019).

Emphasis was given to the reformist and human nature of prison administration. These also lead to the formation of the Reformative theory of punishment. Reformation theory is also known as rehabilitative sentencing. This theory criticizes all kinds of corporal punishment. This approach focuses on "reforming the offender as an individual so that they can once again become part of society and comply with society's laws and regulations" (Priya, 2014). The reformation theory proposes that the attention should be shifted from crime and the effects of punishment to the individual offender and their personality. (Priya,

2014) Reformation theory also supports parole and probation as the best measures to get offenders back to society as a reformed person. The reformative approach has been proven to be beneficial for juvenile delinquents, women as well as first-time offenders. However, recidivists and hardcore offenders are not associated favorably with the reformist policy.

The main aim of the theory is to rehabilitate the prisoners in penal institutions to transform them into law-abiding citizens. It focuses on the human approach of offenders inside the prison. It suggests that an idle mind could be a dangerous mind, so engaging prisoners at work, education, or at vocational activities where they can learn the skills to successfully reintegrate themselves into the outer world in society after their release is essential.

The rehabilitation policies of India have been going through changes and modifications for a decade now. In the 5th National conference (2016) on prison reform, the Government of India announced an Rs. 4000 crore package for prison reforms as part of the National Prison Policy being implemented by the center (Sanyal, 2019). This will redefine prisons as detention homes where the focus will be on the reformation and reintegration of prisoners.

According to Delhi Prison Rules, 2018 it has been mentioned that state governments will be urged to auction detainment facilities present in "prime regions" to produce assets to make current structures somewhere else. These structures will have cells with padded beds and clean toilets, close circuit TV cameras, video-conferencing offices, and space for yoga, sports, and extracurricular exercises. The arrangement incorporates building 200 penitentiaries to add to the 1,300 that exist in the nation. The government has set up committees to investigate the matter and offer a remedy. The reports given by Justice Mulla Committee Report on Prison Reforms (1982-83) and the Justice Krishna Iyer Committee on Women Prisoners (1986-87) have given a broad view of what problems are faced in Indian jails and recommended various measures. The Bureau of Police Research and Development (BPRD) has issued the latest draft of National Policy on Prison Reforms and Correctional Administration, 2007. The draft strategy incorporates recommendations for some much-needed developments to the prison act of 1894. This includes the introduction of reintegration and rehabilitation programs and the arrangement of officials to provide legitimate guidance to detainees. The draft also recommended setting up a research and development wing and providing monetary help to NGOs working for the rehabilitation of detainees and community-based treatment. Raghavan, (2008) stated that it is not the jail structures, however, what goes on inside them, that needs a change.

One of the policies for prisoners' reformation is that educational opportunities should be provided to the prisoners. Education of prisoners is considered important to change their faulty thinking, their perception towards life and also helps in reducing recidivism. In the present day, the jail manual states that every detainee should be given a program of schooling which will help the cycle of his socialization and restoration. To obtain these objectives properly trained staff and the facilities such as classrooms and libraries should also be provided inside the prison.

Other recommendations included adolescents should be given a chance to attend a regular school where they can continue receiving their formal education. The school should be a government-affiliated school, which is run by the Education Department of the State. The relevant resources such as trained teachers and study material required for successful learning of the juveniles should be provided. The staff recruited to impart education to adolescents in the prison should be paid well to motivate the staff for maintaining their interest in imparting their knowledge to them. In prisons in India, the school has classes for primary level, secondary and senior secondary.

Vocational training and work culture in all jails in India is looked at with a positive viewpoint. The new manual makes it necessary for all the states to have an advisory group to supervise the requirements and the interest of the detainees. The advisory group is also responsible for training the prisoners in skills of their choice, which will also in turn help them in earning their livelihood. Prison administration is also planning to provide these prisoners with the raw material so that they can engage in the work, even under-trial volunteers can be associated with the factories as proposed in the new manual.

Provisions for post-release care should be made available for effective rehabilitation and to reduce recidivism. Aftercare and follow up service is also an essential part of the rehabilitation process. Offenders should be able to seek help when they need it. For instance, support should be available for ex-convicts in case they require help with gaining employment or need a place to stay.

Rehabilitation Schemes of Different Countries

This section will summarize the Rehabilitation Model of different countries as discussed in the book "Rehabilitation of the Adult Prisoners in the country" written by Dr. Sanyal, a comprehensive projection of the features of rehabilitation schemes in other countries. This is done to bring attention to how other countries all around the globe are working towards the common goal, rehabilitation of prisoners, and how correctional reform has now become the primary aim of the Criminal Justice system. The countries are taking it seriously and trying to curb down the graph of recidivism.

Table 1. Recent changes in the correctional reforms in various countries

1	Japan	Shimane Asahi Rehabilitation Program, the first correctional facility in an Asian country, started in Japan to direct the prisoners towards a healthy lifestyle to reduce reoffending and self-harm tendencies in them (Leighton,2014).
2	Hong Kong	The Department of Correctional Services maintains a rehabilitation unit that makes suggestions to the courts on the suitability of prisoners in one of the four types of prisoner centers for incarceration. It also advises on job programs for pre-release. Effective applicants in Hong Kong could be released immediately from jail for supervision or allowed to go out to work and live in a supervisory hostel. (Chung,1999)
3	California	California focuses on the rehabilitation of prisoners. With states under constant economic stress and data showing that most prisoners are rearrested within 3 years of release, the need for reform is recognized by policymakers. There is now widespread consensus that it is far from a solution for all crimes to lock up and mostly neglect criminals (Sanyal. 2019). The administration released the study "The Future of California Corrections" in April 2012 to upgrade the prison system. The study highlighted the improvement in the classification system of inmates to fit inmates into the most suitable housing conditions, facilitating more rehabilitative services. In contrast to the previous workload change model, a new funding model called uniform staffing for prisons has now been adopted. The paradigm of programming in jails has been diversion programs, reentry centers, and reentry facilities. (California Department of Corrections and Rehabilitation, 2021)
4	United Kingdom	As part of its program of reform offenders and reducing re-offending, the Government has in the last few years conducted several wide-ranging reviews of rehabilitation initiatives, work regimes operating within the prison estate, and of the role of custody. These reviews have proposed reforms to sentencing policy, the prison regime, and the management of offenders inside and outside prison. (Ministry of Justice, 2010).
5	Germany	The German Penal system is based on a few core principles: reintegration and rehabilitation of offenders, the principle of normalization (wherein life in prison will resemble general living conditions outside the prison as much as possible), and the principle of damage reduction (prison authorities will attempt to mitigate the damaging consequences of imprisonment) (Sanyal, 2019)

The above table presents that the prison administration has started taking interest in rehabilitation and reintegration of prisoners to prevent recidivism and started working for the welfare of the offenders so that they can start a new life with a new perspective.

LIMITATIONS

Next, the authors will demonstrate that even though there are a few correctional reforms in place, there still exists a need for the criminal justice system to assess, evaluate and take affirmative steps for effective rehabilitation of prisoners. This section will focus on the deplorable conditions present in the prisons and how that is leading to human rights issues for them.

In numerous public forums, prison management and prisoner rehabilitation have been a subject of considerable discussion and sharp criticism. In recent years, the Supreme Court of India has dealt heavily with the inhumane and degrading conditions in prisons. The problems of the dilapidated correctional facilities, overcrowding, and congestion, increasing numbers of prisoners under trial, the inadequacy of prison personnel, lack of adequate care and treatment of prisoners, have drawn the attention of the press and social activists. The plight of prisoners has emerged as a crucial issue of public policy with growing advocacy for the defense of human rights in varied backgrounds (Bureau of Police Research & Development, 2003). The main pain of incarceration from the psychological viewpoint is the isolation from children and the eventual loss of personal contacts with family members, apart from the deprivation of freedom and security. The most significant feeling that continually haunts their minds is their future. After their release from jail, they are overly concerned about where to go. The prisoners are wary that their family members will not accept them on their return due to social stigma and various family norms.

Despite the provisions in jail manuals, another significant point is that jail authorities often fail to provide food, clothing, and essential things for the survival of inmates, since most jails are overcrowded and lack basic facilities.

In addition to the modern-day problems present in the Indian prisons, the British government had implemented the infamous 'Indian Prison Act' in 1894. There are many gaps in the Prison Act of 1894, such as the act allowing for corporal punishment in instances where a prison crime has been committed. Actions such as 'willful defiance' to prison rules, the use of language threatening or intimidating unethical or indecent conduct, and 'feeling sickness' constitute a prison offense under this act. The Act leaves the control to the Jail Superintendent to grant such a sentence. Furthermore, the Act does not specify how to assess these offenses (Report on the National Consultation on Prison Reform, 2010).

As a response to this act, the Indian government formed a few jail reform committees to provide suggestions regarding improving the conditions in the prisons. The National Human Rights Commission (NHRC) was formed in 1993 and many other organizations at the state level were also created to make 'Jail reform'.

Nevertheless, jails constitute a crucial area of concern for human rights. In a civilized society, a person in detention should not be reduced to the status of a non-person, and the prison system must therefore provide conditions consistent with human dignity and conducive to social mainstreaming (Viji: 2015). Prisoners are still human beings who have human rights even though they have been imprisoned. Mahatma Gandhi, the father of our nation, also considered prisons to be a temple. He believed that prisons should function as reform centres, provide prisoners with certain skills, and impart moral values (Dr. Sarma, 2017). Gandhi said, 'Hate the crime, not the criminal.' He used his time very well in prison studying new languages, reading the scriptures, discussing problems with fellow prisoners, and, above all, discussing issues related to moral education.

The conditions of prisoners in several states in India are now improving due to the rapid establishment of the Jail Reforms committee. A prison reform bill was suggested by the National Human Rights Commission in 1996. In 1998, the proposed bill was circulated to the states, several of which came out with new legislation. One such state is Rajasthan, which included in its 2001 Rajasthan Prisons Act a chapter on the rights and duties of prisoners. Similar attempts have been made in Madhya Pradesh to achieve 100 percent literacy among prisoners in some selected prisons. (Borah, 2018)

However, there is hardly any systematic work to continue reformation and rehabilitation after the offenders are released on bail or acquittal. The community needs to be involved in the rehabilitation program of correctional facilities because the rehabilitation of an offender becomes easy when there is community involvement **(Bedi**, 1983**).** After all, rehabilitation of prisoners will only take place if the community organizations are involved and support ex-offenders upon release from prison.

Figure 1. Problems faced by Prison reforms in India

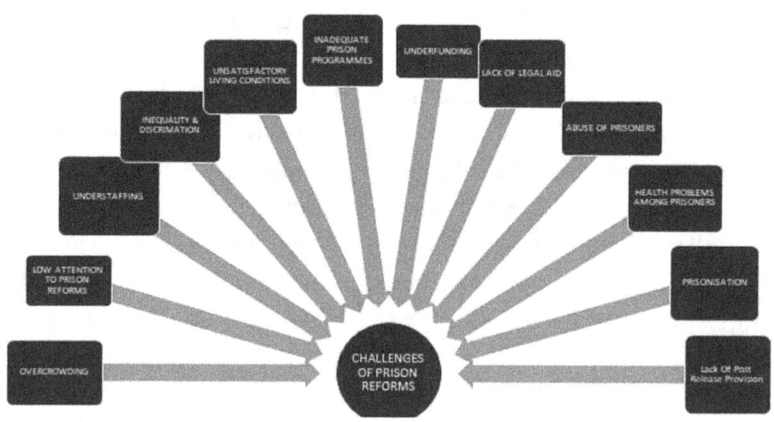

PRISON REFORMS AND COVID-19

According to the World Prison Brief database, India ranks 5th concerning prison population after the United States, China, Brazil, and Russia. Therefore, to curtail the spread of Covid-19, on March 16, 2020, the Supreme Court after analysing the situation of transmission of COVID-19 to prison inmates, prison staff, families of prisoners, and lawyers who were coming into the prison from outside, directed States and Union territories to submit steps which they would take to prevent the spread of the pandemic among prisoners and juveniles. On March 23, 2020, it was suggested that the prisoners who are convicted/charged with 7 years or less could be given parole or interim bail.

Tihar jail, the largest prison in the country, disclosed a plan to release 3,000 inmates (not hardened criminals) on parole after being directed by the supreme court to identify and understand which categories of prisoners could be released on a temporary basis to control the spread of COVID-19. Similarly, Maharashtra had released over 5,000 inmates and made COVID-19 screening mandatory for all the new prisoners. (Mallapur, 2020)

Furthermore, the Delhi government had also taken the step on the same line and asked the Delhi High Court to amend their rules to ensure that prisoners who had served a one-year sentence, and those who were undertrial and had been in jail for 3-months were to be released on parole/ furlough in case of specific offenses. After analyzing all the above issues and amended policies, it can be concluded that less dangerous prisoners were released to avoid overpopulation in prisons and to prevent the spread of COVID-19. (Mallapur, 2020)

Similarly, other countries around the world had also taken steps to prevent the spread of Covid-19 in prisons. According to the Business Insider report on March 17, 2020, Iran had released 85, 000 inmates temporarily to prevent the spread of COVID-19. The Los Angeles Times reported on March 20, 2020, that countries of California had released inmates in fear of the spread of the virus, reducing inmates by 6% over 3 weeks. As per The New York Times on March 23, 2020, 1,000 prisoners had been removed from prisons in New Jersey.

As per the newspaper, The Hindu reported that in India, violence, and clashes had broken out between inmates and police at one of the central correctional centers in Kolkata because prisoners were not allowed to meet their families till March 31 due to social distancing rule that was implemented across every prison of the country due to the prevalence of COVID-19 in the nation.

In response to the Apex court, many states had implemented screening, testing, quarantine facilities, testing, isolation wards for prisoners. Supply of masks, limiting outsiders, suspension of activities inside the prison for the offenders as a precautionary measure to avoid the spread of COVID-19.

As far as correctional programs are concerned inside the prison, it is lagging until vaccinations are not given to the prisoners and till the time they are not habituated to the do's and don'ts of the pandemic situation as in wearing of masks, social distancing, cleaning of hands and proper sanitization of prison from time to time. Proper training to the correctional and prison staff should be given to handling the current critical situation. There is also a need to think about alternative ways of reformation of prisoners and their families. Proper usage of idle time of prisoners should also be kept in mind so that they do not get involved in frequent fights and violence. The prison administration has realized that there is a dire need to focus on the problems existing in the prisons and the needs of the prisoners should be taken into consideration before any other pandemic-like situation arises again. (Mallapur, 2020)

RECOMMENDATION FOR PRISON CORRECTIONAL REFORMS

In addition to the aforementioned programs, the prison administration should also divert their attention towards creating a rehabilitative culture (refer to Fig. 2) inside the prisons. Rehabilitative culture depends on leadership and strong staff engagement (Bennett & Shuker, 2010). The core staff team needs to be actively engaged and have meaningful involvement in an establishment and everyday interactions with prisoners should be motivational and support learning whenever the opportunity arises. Realistic encouragement can show someone that they are accepted and believed in, and this increases the chance of being successfully rehabilitated (Farrall & Maruna 2004). Rehabilitative prison culture is one where all the staff and service users agree that the purpose is to enable service users to turn around their lives and desist from future offending. A rehabilitative prison is primarily safe, decent, and secure; in addition, it provides constant and consistent formal/informal opportunities to enable individuals to make positive changes to how they think, feel and behave.

Figure 2. Rehabilitative culture

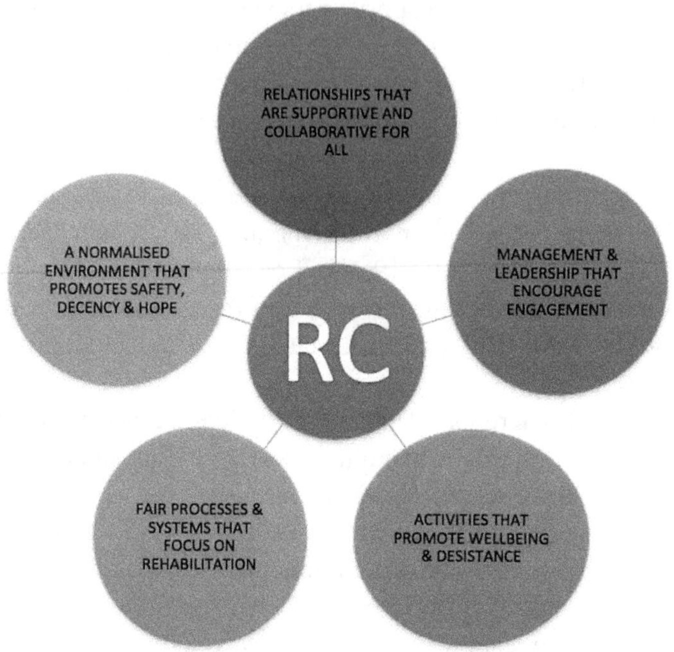

The prison system has three core functions – to punish, to protect, and to rehabilitate – which it is charged with undertaking humanely and transparently. Prisons serve well their basic function of incarcerating offenders, implementing the punishment handed down by courts. The prison system's role of protecting the public is in part met through giving communities respite for some time. However, the prison population in India has grown by a staggering 71% (Dhanuka & Lamba, 2020). Overpopulation (due to a high number of undertrials in the prison population, NCRB, 2017), is one of the major shortcomings that hinder the correctional reformation in the prison in addition to a shortage of staff (the prison staff ratio at the national level in India was 7 inmates per staff in all jails, NCRB, 2017), lack of training and absence of essential services that hampers the reformative efforts of the prison officials (Dhanuka & Lamba, 2020). But just as the prison population has increased, so has the awareness that the system operates too much like a revolving door; challenging how effective our present strategy is in providing longer-term public safety and recovery (O'Brien, Marshall & Karthaus, 2014).

There is existing research on correctional reform however, they rarely provide solutions for the identified gap between effective rehabilitation of prisoners. Most previous research highlights the various shortcomings of the correctional reforms, focusing on the basic needs of the prisoners. Thus, there is little emphasis given on the Human rights violations faced by the inmates, and in this section, the authors will attempt to give an integrative framework that draws from previous research, to mitigate these issues and for effective rehabilitation. Mohan (2008) states that many reforms are required for the effective functioning of the Indian law and justice system, and prison reformation is one of the most important. Research in the field also recognizes that several issues need urgent attention for effective correctional reformation to take place. The researchers argue that the physical structure of the prison, condition of the prisoners, training, and reorientation of prison personnel, and better correctional administration and management are a few of the grave problems that require to be addressed (Sanyal, 2019). Also, an integrative multidisciplinary team should be appointed in the prison system in India for meeting all the needs of the prisoners and in turn for reducing recidivism and effective reformation.

Figure 3. A rehabilitative culture in prisons is beneficial for both the prison staff as well as the prisoners and for reducing reoffending
Source: *O'Brien, Marshall & Karthaus, 2014.*

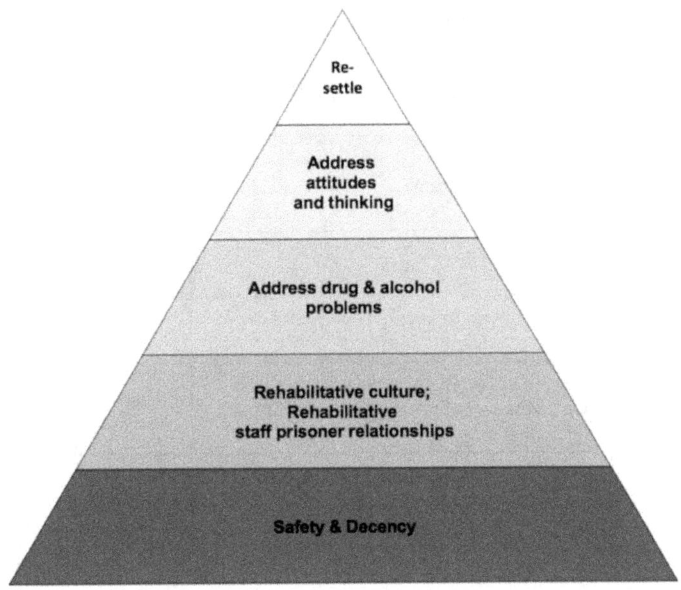

There are also some important recommendations given by the Justice Amitava Roy committee to provide solutions for the failure of prison reforms. The committee suggests that to overcome the issue of overcrowding, Special Fast-Track courts should be set up to deal with petty offenses. It also recommends that legal aid should be given to every prisoner and for that to happen, the lawyer-to-prisoner ratio should be at least one lawyer for every 30 prisoners. To compensate for understaffing it also proposes the Supreme Court fill the vacant positions in the prisons. Suggestions also included things like videoconferencing to be used for trial purposes, to allow for the prisoners to make a free call to their family in their first week in prison. There is a need for exploring alternative punishments. (Prison Reforms in India, 2020)

The authors' emphasis would be on giving comprehensive solutions to the various issues faced by the prisoners in India. Researchers also recognize that psychological support is an important aspect to be considered that affects the reformation and reintegration of offenders. Research also asserts that prisons are becoming breeding grounds for offenders due to the lack of proper correctional reforms in Indian prisons (Palakkappillil & Prasanna, 2017). This shows that there is a need to explore and evaluate the effectiveness of the existing correctional programmes and try to identify the scope for modifications and make the programmes more effective.

The authors suggest that the Criminal Propensity Scale by Dr. Shubhra Sanyal - which is an Indian adaptation of the Eysenck personality questionnaire which measures Psychoticism, Neuroticism, and Extraversion should be used in all central and state prisons of India. This scale can tell about the mental condition (state of the mind) of the offender to be released from prison and tells about the criminal propensity which can help in designing the rehabilitation program for the offender according to his responses.

Dr. Sanyal has explained in her manual of Criminal Propensity Scale, 2018 that high criminal propensity behavior with high social desirability inside the prison are less prone to rehabilitation than the ones with low criminal propensity and low social desirability. This is the first measure of its kind to be adapted and used in Indian settings. This scale will help the correctional department to segregate offenders with high propensity and in turn aid in determining the course of rehabilitation. It will also be useful in determining the types of vocational skills programs to implement and what reformative traits to be taught to the inmates. In the after-care program, ex-convicts' responses to criminal propensity will help decide the degree of their rehabilitation. (Sanyal, 2018).

Table 2. Criminal Propensity Scale outcomes

Criminal Propensity	Social Desirability	Bars	Intervention
High	High	Red bar, further treatment is needed (Low chances of rehabilitation)	Vocational programmes, sports, and games are needed.
Medium	Medium	Yellow bar, criminal tendencies, a habit of faking (chances of rehabilitation is low but higher than red)	Intense counseling, meditation, yoga, religious classes should be given.
Low	Low	The green bar, fit to be release	Counseling, other persuasive techniques can be used so that the person moves away from delusion to self-persecution.

The authors argue that the rehabilitation of prisoners will be effective only if the offenders are given appropriate vocational training so that they are employed after release. The educational facilities and vocational programmes should be updated to meet the demands of the ever-changing society. This will enable the offenders to gain relevant skills for gaining employment after release and lead an independent life. Srivastava (1977) states that once a prisoner is assured that he will be respected and lead a dignified life after release, he would believe in the rehabilitative purpose of the prison system.

Furthermore, prisoners should be given support even after release from prison and provisions should be put in effect so that they can easily access psychological or any other support that they require for leading an independent and dignified life. This will help in reducing recidivism. The correctional work nowadays seems to suffer a lot and responsibilities are lying more on the family and the society rather than the prison administration. So, there is a need to psycho-educate the family and society. This is also crucial as prisoners will face challenges once released from prison as well. Psychological interventions should be offered for the offenders as well as their families.

CONCLUSION

The chapter concludes with a summary, a balanced assessment of the contribution of the correctional framework in prisons in India, and a roadmap for future directions. For successful rehabilitation and reformation of prisoners, there should be several provisions added to the correctional reformation programs. The correctional reforms include vocational training and aid the offenders to become skillful and gain employment after release from the prisons. Such correctional programmes help the offenders in their identity formation and provide them a sense of dignity and respect once they get reintegrated back into society. Correctional programmes are humane and provide opportunities for the prisoners to engage in work which helps them to overcome their maladaptive pattern of behavior and adopt positive and skillful behavior. Furthermore, psychological interventions should also be a part of the correctional programmes. Although the Indian Judiciary has emphasized progressive judicial interventions on reform, still more needs to be done to incorporate the necessary reforms and their implementation.

Above all, the aim of the prison reform should not only be limited to upgrading the correctional reform and to make the prisoners' life more independent but making prisoners more humane and sensible should be the priority of such reforms.

Figure 4. An integrative solution

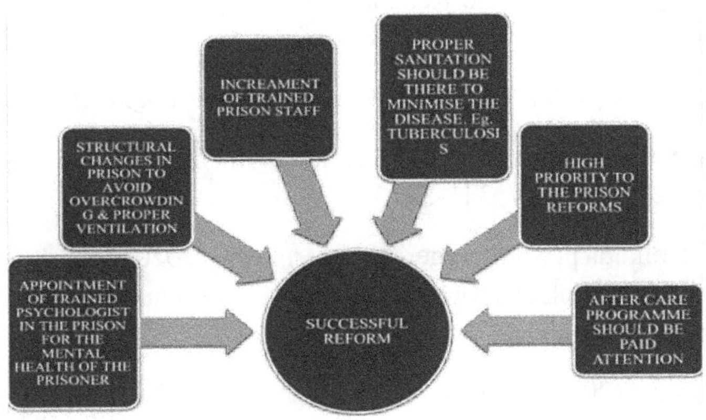

ACKNOWLEDGMENT

Researchers received no specific grant from any funding agency in the public, commercial or not-for-profit sectors.

REFERENCES

Ahmed, M. R. (2016). *After-care and rehabilitation of released prisoners: An Indian perspective*. Paper presented at 5th National Conference of Heads of Prisons of States & UTs on Prison Reforms, Convention Centre, NDCC, New Delhi, India.

Ahmed, Z. (2016). Jail reforms in India: A study of Indian jail reform committees. *International Journal of Multidisciplinary Education and Research*, *1*(3).

Bedi, M. S. (1983). Public participation in the rehabilitation and reintegration of offenders. *Indian Journal of Criminology*, *12*(1).

Bennett, P., & Shuker, R. (2010). Improving prisoner-staff relationships: Exporting Gredon's good practice. *The Howard Journal of Crime and Justice, 49*(5).

Borah, K. (2018). Jail administration in India: A review of Indian jail reform. *International Journal of Humanities and Social Sciences Research, 4*(2).

Bureau of Police, Research, and Development. (2003). Model prison manual for the superintendence and management of prisons in India. Ministry of Home Affairs, Government of India.

Bureau of Police, Research & Development. (2019). *Review and Implementation of Rules and Process for the Internal Management of Prisons and Prisoners*. https://bprd.nic.in/WriteReadData/userfiles/file/201907030915286643694ReviewandImplementationofRulesand-MM-08.pdf

Bureau of Police Research and Development. (2003). For the superintendents and management of prisons in India, Ministry of Home Affairs Government of India New Delhi. *Chapter-IV, 3*, 44.

California Department of Corrections and Rehabilitation. (2021). *After Prison Reforms*. https://www.cdcr.ca.gov/rehabilitation/programs/after-prison-programs/

Chowdhury, N. (2002). *Indian prison laws and correction of prisoners*. Deep & Deep.

Chung, W. M. (1999). Treatment programmes for offenders run by the Hong Kong correctional services. *UNAFEI Resource Material Series, 54*, 341-347.

Coronavirus: Curbs at Kolkata prison trigger violent clash. (2020, March 22). *The Hindu*. https://www.thehindu.com/news/cities/kolkata/coronavirus-curbs-at-kolkata-prison-trigger-violent-clash/article31132352.ece?homepage=true

Department of Tihar Prisons. (2020). *Reformation*. Government of NCT. http://tte.delhigovt.nic.in/wps/wcm/connect/lib_centraljail/Central+Jail/Home/Reformationv

Department of Tihar Prisons. (2020). *Psychological effects of vipassana on Tihar jail inmates*. Government of NCT. https://www.vridhamma.org/research/Psychological-Effects-of-Vipassana-on-Tihar-Jail-Inmate

Dhanuka, M., & Lamba, S. (2020). Analysis: India's prison system needs urgent reform. *Hindustan Times*.

Doin & Andres. (2013). *Working paper series on prison reform; civil society and prison: The 'invisible bars' challenge*. UNODC.

Dolan, M. (2020, March 20). California releases more jail inmates amid coronavirus crisis. *Los Angeles Times*. https://www.latimes.com/california/story/2020-03-20/california-releases-more-jail-inmates-amid-coronavirus-crisis

Farrell, S., & Maruna, S. (2004). Desistance focused criminal justice policy research: Introduction to a special issue on desistance from crime and public policy. *Howard Journal of Criminal Justice, 43*(4), 358–367. doi:10.1111/j.1468-2311.2004.00335.x

Fazal, S. (2008). *The health of prisoners*. New Century Publications.

Form, I. S. (2018). *Prison Reforms in India*. https://blog.forumias.com/prison-reforms/

Government of NCT. (2018). *Delhi Prison Rules*. http://tte.delhigovt.nic.in/wps/wcm/connect/ad693e00479000078773c72dd8755fce/Jail+manual+2018.pdf?MOD=AJPERES&lmod=-820682994&CACHEID=ad693e00479000078773c72dd8755fce

Haney, C. (2003). The psychological impact of incarceration: Implications for post-prison adjustment. *Prisoners once removed: The impact of Incarceration and Reentry on Children, Families, and Communities, 33*(66). https://www.cdcr.ca.gov/about-cdcr/strategic plan/

Khan, M. Z. (1990). *Work by jail inmates*. Inter-India Publications.

Kumar, S. (2013). Semi-private prison management in India. *Journal of Centre for Reforms, Development and Justice, 1*(3).

Lalli, U. (2000). Attitude to prison reforms: An empirical survey. *Indian Journal, 1*(1), 32.

Laws, D. R., & Ward, T. (2011). *Desistance and sexual offending: Alternatives to throwing away the keys*. The Guilford Press.

Leighton, P. (2014). A model prison for the next 50 years: The high-tech, public- private Shimane Asahi Rehabilitation Centre. *Justice Policy Journal, 11*(1).

Losel, F. (2010). *What works in offender rehabilitation: A global perspective* [Conference presentation]. 12th Annual Conference of the International Corrections and Prisons Association.

Mallapur, C. (2020, March 26). Coronavirus pandemic: India should wake up to the need for prison reforms. *Scroll.in*. https://scroll.in/article/957202/coronavirus-pandemic-india-should-wake-up-to-the-need-for-prison-reforms

Miller, J. M. (Ed.). (2009). *21st century criminology: A reference handbook*. Sage.

Ministry of Justice. (2010). *Breaking the cycle: Effective punishment, rehabilitation and sentencing of offenders*. The Stationery Office.

Ministry of Justice Report. (2010a). The Government of the United Kingdom.

Ministry of Justice Report. (2013). The Government of the United Kingdom.

Mohan, V., & Thakur, P. (2008) Modernizing prisons. *Times of India*.

Mohanty & Hazary. (1990). *Indian prison system*. Ashish Publishing House.

Nargis, S. (2019). Prisoners, their rights and reformation. *International Journal of Engineering and Management Research, 9*(4), 1–5. Advance online publication. doi:10.31033/ijemr.9.4.1

National Crime Records Bureau. (2017). *Prison statistics India*. Ministry of Home Affairs.

O'Brien, P. (1995). The prison on the continent: Europe 1865-1965. In N. Morris & D. Rothman (Eds.), *The Oxford history of prisons: The practise of punishment in western society* (pp. 178–201). Oxford University Press.

O'Brien, R., Karthaus, R., & Marshall, J. (2014). *RSA Transitions: Building a Rehabilitative Culture*. Academic Press.

Palakkappillil, J., & Prasanna, C. K. (2017). Criminality among youth and recidivism. *The Journal of Development Practice*, 3.

Pati, A. K., & Mitra, S. (2011). *Crime and correctional administration. MSW paper-12*. Netaji Subhas Open University.

Payne, A. (2020, March 17). Iran has released 85,000 prisoners in an emergency bid to stop the spread of the coronavirus. *Business Insider.* https://www.businessinsider.in/politics/news/iran-has-released-85000-prisoners-in-an-emergency-bid-to-stop-the-spread-of-the-coronavirus/articleshow/74674415.cms

Priya, T. (2014). *Reformative theory of punishment*. Acadamike Law Journal Knowledge Centre.

Raghavan, V. (2008). Prison reforms and some fundamentals. *The Hindu*. https://www.thehinducentre.com/the-arena/current-issues/article9805239.ece

Report on the National Consultation on Prison Reform. (2010). New Delhi: Academic Press.

Sable, V. (2020). *Yerwada Jail Visit- Prison Reforms in India*. Academic Press.

Sanyal, S. (2019). *Rehabilitation of the adult prisoners in the country*. New Delhi Publishers.

Srivastava, S. P. (1977). *The Indian prison community*. Pustak Kendra.

Tannenbaum, F. (1938). *Crime and community*. Columbia University Press. doi:10.7312/tann90782

Tully, T. (2020, March 23). 1,000 Inmates will be released from N.J. jails to curb coronavirus Risk. *The New York Times.* https://www.nytimes.com/2020/03/23/nyregion/coronavirus-nj-inmates-release.html

Viji. M. (2015). Human rights women prisoners and prison reforms in India- A Study. *AMIERJ*, *4*(2).

Ward, T., & Laws, D. R. (2010). Desistance from sex offending: Motivating change, enriching practise. *International Journal of Forensic Mental Health*, *9*(1), 11–23. doi:10.1080/14999011003791598

ADDITIONAL READING

Dirkzwager, A., & Kruttschnitt, C. (2012). Prisoners' perception of correctional officers' behavior in English and Dutch prisons. *Journal of Criminal Justice*, *40*(5), 404–412. doi:10.1016/j.jcrimjus.2012.06.004

Meena, N. (2019). *Correctional methods for rehabilitation of offenders in India*- Dissertation, National Law University, Delhi.

Nargis, S. (2019). Prisoners their rights and reformation. *International Journal of Engineering and Management Research*, *9*(4), 1–5. Advance online publication. doi:10.31033/ijemr.9.4.1

Sanyal, S. (2000). An assessment of the criminal propensity among prisoners in the Indian jails. SSRN *Electronic Journal.* doi:10.2139srn.3246935

Sanyal, S. (2019). *Rehabilitation of the adult prisoner in the country*. New Delhi Publishers.

KEY TERMS AND DEFINITIONS

Correctional Programs: Correctional programs are organised interventions that target predisposing factors directly linked to criminal conduct to lessen reoffending.

Criminal Propensity: It is the tendency of an individual to be inclined towards criminal behavior i.e., criminals show high on Psychoticism, Neuroticism and Extraversion and low on Social desirability on Criminal Propensity Scale.

Prison Reforms: Prison reform is an attempt to upgrade the condition inside prisons, to make the correctional programmes more effective for the offenders who are detained behind the bars, and to introduce the alternative of incarceration and to focus on the reintegration and rehabilitation of prisoners back to the society.

Recidivism: It can be defined as relapse of a convicted offender to offending behaviour. In other words, due to many factors such as financial deprivation, lack of support system, an offender might reoffend post release from prison. The act of reengaging in criminal behaviour after release is known as recidivism.

Reformation: Reformation is an improvement of the existing prison culture for the betterment of the offenders who are incarcerated or are behind the bars.

Rehabilitation: It is a transition of the offender from prison community to free community. It is a process of restoring offenders and helping them to grow and change and help mitigate the various environmental factors that led to engage in offending behaviour.

Rehabilitative Culture: An organisation or company is said to have rehabilitative culture when it allows its members to think about their futures with hope. It helps them to plan for a new lifestyle and prepare for it. It gives chances to modify their behaviours and attitudes and to try new identities. In rehabilitative culture people are appreciated for their charitable deeds.

Reintegration: It is the process of restoration of the offender successfully to the society. It is done through the introduction of various correctional and vocational programmes inside the prison which helps them assimilate back to the society successfully.

Social Desirability: It is a tendency of a person to respond in a manner that is more socially acceptable than their true self. It is generally done to project themselves in a more positive and socially approved light to avoid any kind of judgement or negative perception.

Work Programs: Work programmes are the programmes that help the offender in finding a job after his release from prison. These programmes help the prisoners in restoring their financial stability, to regain their lost identity and support them to reintegrate in the mainstream after release.

Chapter 11
The Transient State of Habitually Convicted Criminal Offenders

Kenny Hendrickson
University of the Virgin Islands, US Virgin Islands

Kula A. Francis
University of the Virgin Islands, US Virgin Islands

ABSTRACT

Globally, at least half of the released prisoner population will return to incarceration before the end of their first year in society. Going against generally accepted notions, deliberation should be given to the existence of transience in habitual recidivists' or habitual convicted criminal offenders' (HCCOs') life course. The HCCO is habitually, chronically, or serially recidivistic (above the average recorded number of arrests and imprisonment, i.e., anything above or equal to five). Furthermore, transience can be considered as junctures of socio-cognitive unsteadiness, impermanence, and inconstancy that leads to the uncoupling of positive bonds within human and environmental relationships. Accordingly, this chapter discusses two outlooks of the transient state of HCCO: the habitual prisoner revolving door syndrome and habitual transient life course disconnect. Finally, this work concludes by promoting the reentry and rehabilitation of convicted criminal offenders based on conditions of productive law-abiding citizenship.

INTRODUCTION

Globally, the average rates of criminal recidivism are as high as 60%, with the US peaking at 77% (Sumpter, 2020; Yukhnenko, Sridhar, & Fazel, 2019; BJS, 2015). Criminal recidivism can be best described as a "relapse of criminal behavior, which can include a range of outcomes, including re-arrest, reconviction, and reimprisonment (Fazel & Wolf, 2015, p. 1)." Byrne, Pattavina and Taxman (2015) confirmed that the rate of incarceration is steadily increasing annually across the world due in part to recidivism. Yukhnenko, Sridhar, and Fazel (2019) asserted that released prisoners are more at risk of

DOI: 10.4018/978-1-7998-6884-2.ch011

criminal recidivism, than convicted criminal offenders serving non-custodial sentences. Moreover, the current recidivism research aptly advances growing criminal re-convictions and re-incarcerations at a community-level (Jacobs & Skeem, 2021, Grubb, 2020). However, empirical data and research on the recurring individual-level recidivism (within a fixed period) are limited.

To study recurring individual-level recidivism, attention must be given to the plight of habitual convicted criminal offenders (HCCOs). Based on the writings of Capek (2017), habitual can be defined as a habit, pattern of intentional behaviors, developed and solidified through repetitive situations and frequency of occurrence. Thus, HCCOs are chronically or serially recidivistic (habit). A concern must also be given to the existence of perpetual psycho-social transience in the HCCO life course. Conservatively, transient offending has been described as committing "five or fewer offenses in a year (Weatherburn & Baker, 1999, p. 7)." For HCCO, their transient state is continuous, cyclical, and counteractive to reformative attempts. In this frame, transience can also be considered as socio-cognitive unsteadiness, impermanence and inconstancy that lead to the uncoupling of positive bonds within human and environmental relationships.

The main intent of this chapter is to stimulate academic, scholarly, socio-political and practitioner dialogs on the transient state of HCCOs. This work offers ideas and insight on the topic supported by literary evidence. This chapter is sectioned into two main inquiries pertaining to HCCO's transience. The first section of the chapter discusses the habitual prisoner revolving door syndrome and the missteps of prisoner reentry efforts. Prisoner reentry is normally defined as the process of leaving incarceration and returning to society (Matthew & Abrams, 2020). However, this section proposes prisoner reentry to encompass returning of HCCOs into criminal justice system and incarceration. The second section considers a proposed existence of habitual transient disconnect within the HCCO life course. Habitual transient disconnect can be described as progressive hyper-individualized dissociative resistance, socio-cognitive debonding and disengagement from the normality of citizenship. As a constructive conclusion, this work promotes idea of productive law-abiding citizenship as a means of encouraging desistance or breaking the cycle of habitual convicted criminal offending.

Habitual Prisoner Revolving Door Syndrome

As opposed to the 'fresh start' of prisoner reentry, habitual convicted criminal offenders (HCCOs) can best be regarded as habitual prisoners. The habitual prisoner's life course is largely shaped by a cycle of continuous imprisonment. As a result, there are three main categories of habitual prisoners: non-professional, professional and the institutionalized (Rao, 2012). The habitual non-professional prisoners are criminal offenders that have continued lapses into crime due to their surroundings and/or psycho-physical defect (Rao, 2012, p. 402). The professional habitual prisoners are career criminal offenders. The career criminal continually commit crime for monetary gains. The habitual professional prisoners accept incarceration as a normal risk to their profession. The last type of habitual prisoners are individuals, who are "prisonized," or institutionalized to prison life (SpearIt, 2011, p. 132). Broadly, the unaffected released habitual prisoner will revert, revisit, and recommit to their old ways of living (criminality and incarceration) (Lattimore, Steffey, & Visher, 2010). Thus, the numerous costly, repetitive, and "rehabilitative" internments in correctional facilities for the habitual prisoner could be considered periods for the development of estranged and hardened "super" criminals, and even worse, the cultivation of a permanence to imprisonment (Baillargeon et al., 2009).

For the released habitual prisoner, the time between prisoner reentry and incarceration can be considered as a period of psycho-social transience. It is possible that within psychological transient state, the individual's core prisoner identity will remain intact and be utilized as a beacon to find balance. Correspondingly, social transience is circumstantial, and an unsteady state caused by "a complex set of normative and operating principles embodied in historical structures, systems and practices, become replaced by another unknown set, which makes this period for very ambiguous and uncertain (Alas, Ennulo & Türnpuu, 2006, p. 272)." Many scholars like Travis and Visher (2005), consider reentry, probation, and recidivism as the parameters of prisoners' cyclical transient state of the revolving door prison syndrome. Petersilia (1999) observed that reentry "becoming a predictable (and increasingly short) transition on the prison-to-parole and back-to-prison revolving door cycle (p. 484)." The revolving prison door is deemed as a backward and forward fluctuations between "structural impediments to successful reentry" due to the individual's criminal convictions, resulting in imprisonment and recidivism (2008, p. 152). Weaver et al., (2012) wrote "the re-imprisoning of offenders following breach of overly onerous conditions, whilst disrupting any ongoing and promising interventions with those individuals in the community, will only serve to prolong the revolving prison door syndrome (p.95)."

Understanding the transience experienced by habitual prisoners dictates, shedding light on the inner workings of the prisoner revolving door syndrome (Harding et al., 2017). Comparisons can be drawn from the mechanics of an actual revolving door system to best understand the predicament of the habitual prisoner. An actual revolving door system has one entry and a centralized vertical shaft that hold multiple doors, often referred to as wings. These wings create forward rotating spaces or free-standing vestibules that allow for more persons to enter and exit buildings at the same time without the need of separate entry points. Imagine being stuck continuously circling in an actual revolving door until the point of dizziness, confusion, and disorientation. Once released, any individual would be disconnected from the building which they are attempting to go in or leave as well as displaced from the outside world. It would take some time for bearings of the situation and some form of normalcy to be regained.

What if the individual did not have a good bearing with the outside world to begin with? What if their normalcy gravitated with being inside the building? As illustrated in figure 1, the above actual revolving door scenario aptly applied to depict the cyclical transience of the habitual prisoner. The habitual prisoner's life course (wings) within prisoner revolving door syndrome turns into concerns with the influence of psycho-social centripetal (pull of personal challenges and difficulties) as well as centrifugal (push of criminality, conviction, and incarceration) forces. These conditions create acceleration that is continuous and unidirectional, curved towards prison reentries. Harding et al., (2017) contended that the duration of imprisonment creates a "higher risk for future offending (p. 11106)." Eventually, the prison system becomes a natural habitat for the habitual prisoner. In fact, Fry (1952) believed that HCCOs can only be truly studied in the prison setting because they have spent more time incarcerated than in the outside world. Burtch, Rane and Lindfiled (1999) cautioned of the dangers of the prison "revolving door syndrome" habituating offenders to institutional life of the criminal justice system (p. 378).

Unresponsively, criminal justice and public efforts to stop prison revolving door focus only on conditions at figurative entry point (prisoner reentry into society and prison) rather than the internal, habitual, socio-cognitive, and cyclical transience. As depicted in figure 1, the prisoner entries can be counted as moments of interchange between the prison system and personal as well as communal freedoms. Moreover, Criminal Justice researchers believe that the prisoner entries are affixed with *gateway barriers* (as seen in figure 1) made up of societal instabilities. Societal instabilities are naturally occurring uncertainties, imbalances, and breakdown within society's political, economic, psychological, social,

Figure 1. Chronicle of the prison revolving door

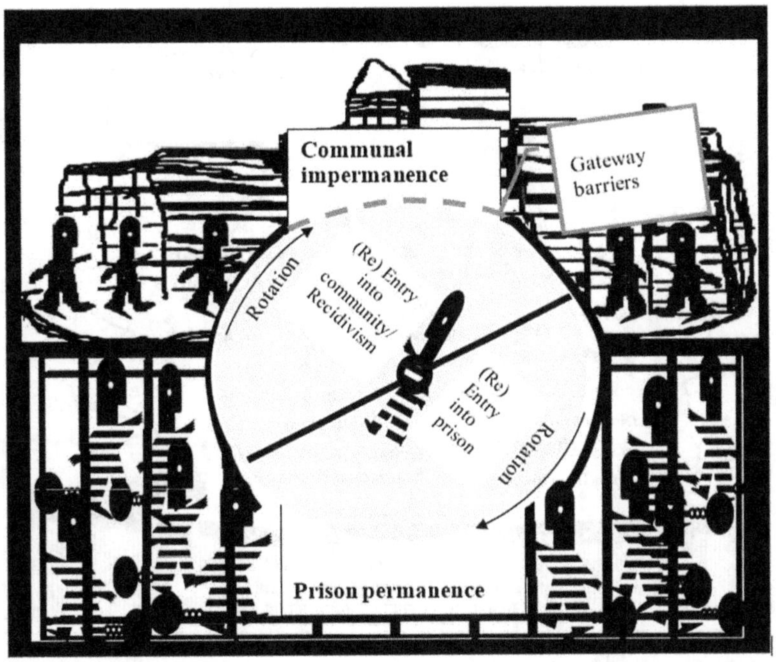

cultural, physical landscape. Rydberg and Grommons (2016); Burnett (2010, p. 663) and Lin, (2010) have contended that the overall disappointment of prisoners transitioning from reentry to recidivism are based on the experienced incarceration, the substantial correctional restrictions, and surveillances, as well as contending with social instabilities, such as poverty, vagrancy, prejudice, and redundancy.

In this token, gateway barriers are positioned as the cause for criminal intent, 'gumming up' the rehabilitative impact of imprisonment, and societal dissociation. Reisig et al., (2007) asserted that social constructed barriers eliminate breaking out of patterns within the prison revolving door syndrome. Barriers such as financial difficulties, family issues, illnesses, and disabilities (e.g., physical or mental), abuse (e.g., drug or sexual) and discriminatory barricades based on age, history, race, class, sexuality, and gender are also used to justify criminality and mass-incarceration as well as recidivism (Morani et al., 2011). Thus, gateway barriers are paraded by rehabilitative justice paradigms as social inter-personal restrictors to societal acclimatization. Leong (2006) along with Berg and Huebner (2011) have ascribed gateway barriers as societal miscarriages in providing equality/fairness, opportunities (e.g., work and housing) and the restrictions to socio-political rights. The finding of new gateway barriers ensures a superfluous public promotion of 'opening community resource faucets,' which results in the development of "resource drainage conundrum," as illustrated in figure 2.

Additionally, efforts in prisoner reentry and recidivism purportedly necessitates the development of prisoners' 'human potential,' anthropomorphizing the prisoners' afflictions, and expunging the trauma of criminal victimization from society's collective memory. The intention is to create acceptance and understanding for the criminal offender's plight. Interestingly, prisoners are also now being treated as dissatisfied customers rather than convicted prisoners. They are making demands on the justice system and victimized society. Auge-Dickhut, Koye, and Liebetrau (2015) satirically compared this occurrence to terrorists being considered and treated as victims or "dissatisfied customers (p. 127)." As the 'customer

Figure 2. Opened faucets and resource drainage of prisoner reentry

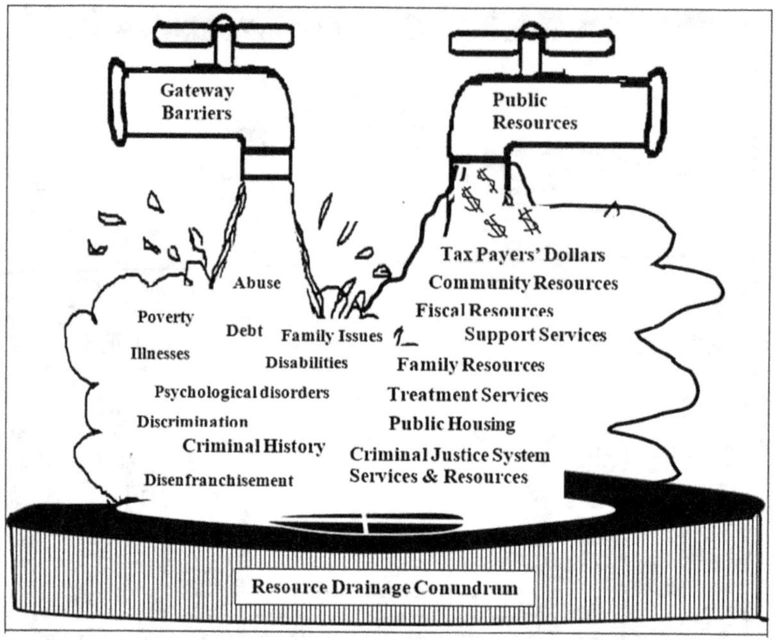

is always right,' the fault thus lies with society and not with the convicted criminal. From this perspective, recidivism would be considered prisoners as "permanently dissatisfied, but due to high barriers they cannot switch" their life course easily (2015, p. 127). These depictions signify the terms to which the efficacy of current justice, correctional and reintegration values are being challenged in favor of the demands for fairness, satisfaction, and accessibility for the convicted criminal offender.

Thanks to research on societal gateway barriers, a 'Kumbaya' motif cascades the discussion on the justice system, especially regarding the prisoner revolving door syndrome. Scholars along with activists are hyping the *unburdening* of prisoners from the weighty responsibility of *change* along with the *consequences* of their past criminality. In their discussion on the communal burden of increased background checks (since 9/11), Love and Frazier (2006) contended the need for convicted criminals to escape their past to ensure "heroic efforts to turn their lives around" (p. 50). Thus, there is an outbreak of social constructions that manipulate the ideals of justice. Constructs, such as the victimless crimes; societal elitism/white supremacy (repression by the man); prisons as industrial complexes, school to prison pipelines; racist drug laws and affluenza/spoiled brat defense, are being used to dispute responsibility to the criminality of offenses and lessening the retributive penalization. Time and resources are also being expended by politicians and special interest groups to find technicalities, pretexts, and loopholes to decriminalize offenses, such as prostitution and illegal drug use. Prisoner reentry initiatives have become efforts to decrease the prison population, without dealing with the problems of criminal offense(s).

While reform of the criminal justice system is needed, should criminal offenders be given openings to escape from taking responsibility or punishment for criminal acts? Should criminal offenders be allowed to monopolize psychological diagnoses, or the seemingly exaggerated excuse of a wealthy and/or privileged decadence to obtain a get out of jail card? Scholars like, Raine (2013) considered committing criminal offense as a psychological disorder, in much the same way as depression, anxiety, and schizophrenia. Glenn and Raine (2014) contended that the current laws pertaining to responsibility needs revised based on psychological disorders. Through psychological diagnosis, conviction and repeat criminal offense are publicly staged as a lack of free will and/or disagreements of social culpability, instead of acts of intentional choice. Furthermore, empathy for the psychological diagnosis of the convicted criminal offender/prisoner leads to a removal of ownership of criminal actions. This sits at the foreground of current socio-political concerns.

These socio-political fabrications of criminal offenses create an over-flowing reservoir of transient prisoners' gateway barriers and unfair insistence upon the inclusion of civic engagement in sharing the many growing responsibilities of each new trend to prisoner integration (Chunn & Menzies, 2006). Nonetheless, there has been no genuine consideration on a clear endgame or cost-benefit analysis to the mounting rehabilitative interventions. Schrag and Scotchmer (1997) pointed out that trying to find exogenous factors to criminality is "doomed to disappointment" as it is a "mutually reinforcing" and opportunistic activity (p. 325). There is also an unpredictability in isolating clear exponents to prison reintegration and a sizable variance in their manifestation in the lives of prisoners. Released prisoners attempting to reenter are left to 'roll the dice' as it relates to public involvement and the 'piping' of recognized gateway barriers.

The paradigms and social efforts that spotlight gateway barriers found within the prison revolving door syndrome contain an "inattentional blindness." Blumstein and Beck (2005) acknowledged the inherent transience of reentry as a point to which prisoners will either progress to full liberty from their communities or recommit to prison life. Based on this all or nothing argument, perhaps this is the reason prisoner advocates and criminal justice scholars focus on efforts in treating issues related to preparing prisoners for release. However, dealing with societal gateway barriers or setbacks for convicted criminal offenders becomes more like battling a mythical hydra (as depicted in figure 3). No matter the number of reentry setbacks that justice efforts endeavor to address, there will always be hordes of other obstacles that will continue to sprout up. Unlike Greek mythology, there are no fabled Herculean heroes or quick fixes to the labor of integrating convicted criminal offenders. As a 'Pandora's Box or a "can of worms," the consequence of contending with prisoner reentry barriers/setbacks is the over-burdening of an already besieged government and the exploitation of depleting community resources. Especially in the case of the habitual prisoner, whose life course is filled with perpetual obstacles, failed reentries, continual recidivism, and likelihood of prison permanence.

Habitual Transient Disconnect

Unlike the views presented in the first section on the habitual prisoner revolving door syndrome, the next section in this chapter targets going beyond the parameters of the habitual prisoner. Hence, the habitual convicted criminal offender's (HCCO's) life course encompasses patterns of living within society, re-occurring criminality and perpetual interfaces within criminal justice system (i.e., arrest, convictions, charges, and incarceration). The crossroads of deviant acts, noncompliance, along with the number of prisoner reentries not only mark episodes of foreseeable re-offenses and internment within a system of mass incarceration, but also the sequential waves of detachment or *transient disconnect* from normality of law-abiding citizenship. The HCCO's transient disconnect signifies an admixture of hyper-individualism, social debonding, dissociation from society, social bond enthalpy and criminality. Walther (2012) wrote the normality of law-abiding citizenship reflects legitimacy of residents and their duties, responsibilities as well as collective claims and demands. Normality of law-abiding citizenship

Figure 3. Recidivistic reentry setbacks model

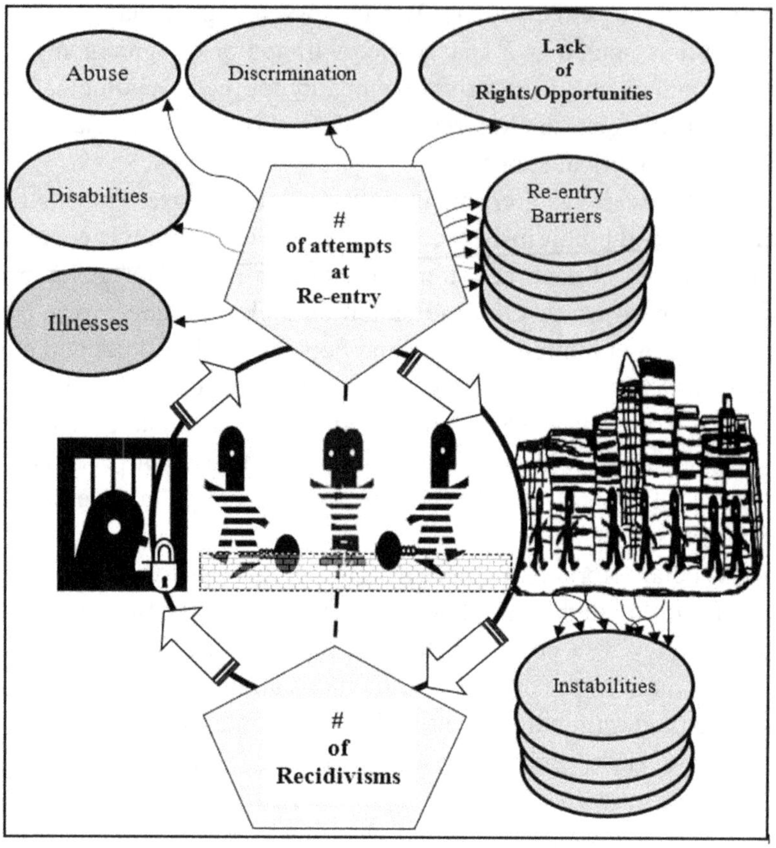

also regulates the goals and activities of citizens. Inspirationally, the normality of law-abiding citizenship "is our agreement to receive rights and privileges from the community and, in so doing, to pay for them through our willingness to live within certain boundaries and act in the interest of the whole (Block, 1998, p. 89)." Block also noted that law abiding citizenship requires concerns for the well-being, public accountability and more importantly connectedness of the community (1998, p. 89). Moreover, connectedness of citizenry requires the forming of societal bonds derived from structured and peaceable relationships, communication, culture, more importantly observance and conformity to the laws. Societal bonding also requires inclusion, acceptance and the possibilities of equality, prosperity, safety, and well-being for all societal inhabitants (Gilbert, 2007). Giacalone, Paul, and Jurkiewicz (2005) noted that the true law-abiding citizenship centers on societal obligations and "belongingness" rather than individual entitlement and materialism.

The HCCO's perpetual life-course transience signifies anomic junctures from normality of law-abiding citizenship. Merton's views of deviance in an anomic society reflects anomic junctures for HCCO as exacerbations of societal strain caused entitlement and materialism, the inability to achieve culturally defined aspirations and the dissociative inability or refusal to communally confirm (Featherstone & Deflem, 2003). Additionally, the transition from 'citizen to offender' is not simply a loss of social standing. It is also hyper-individualization that generates misgivings, resentments and utter contempt towards society that can be found in recidivists. Hoyle and Slater (2001) recognized that hyper-individualism "undermine a sense of trust, norms of cooperation, and expectations for reciprocity and mutual obligation (p. 791)." Thus, criminal offender disconnect provides a marker for the expression of hyper-individualized 'social debonding' as well as dissociation from the societal obligations and expectancies of an ideal citizen (as depicted in figure 4).

Importantly, Gordon (2004) offered meaningful insight on social debonding. Gordon (2004) described social debonding as a disruption of personal functioning and communal existence that signifies the physiological, psychological and/or 'socio-cultural cracks' or discontinuities, mismatches and incongruities within the community structures. Gordon's ideas of social debonding focused on the weight of the threat to victim's welfare. Mboka (2013) also argued that this lack of normalized social connection between the offender and their victims result in empathy deficits. Thus, there is a bounding equivalence to the social debonding of victimization and a socio-cultural dissociation experienced by offender.

Figure 4. Social debonding and dissociation

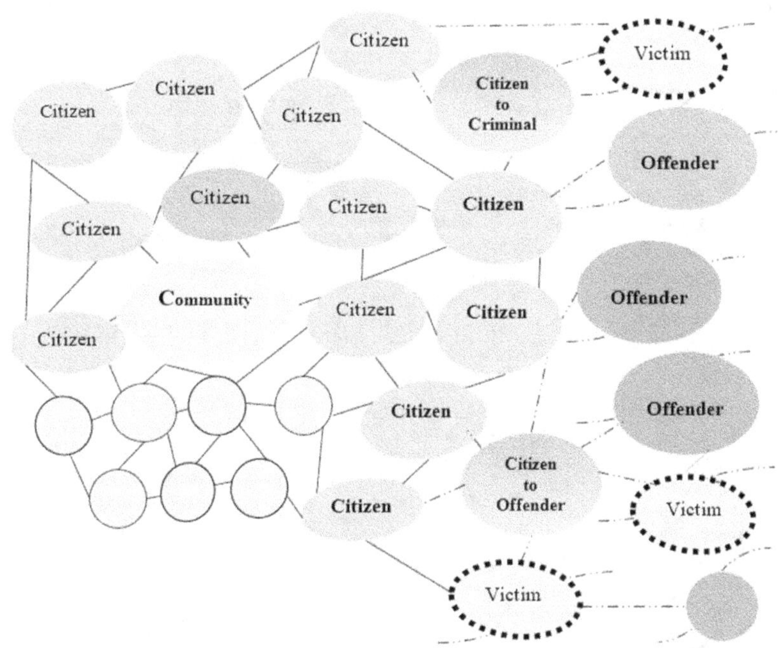

Socio-cultural dissociation is a cognitive 'freeing up of space' given to considerations of citizenship (responsibilities, constraints, and communal empathy) (Cloke & Milbourne, 2012). Aspects of dissociation are concerned with powerlessness, normlessness, and marginalized status (Asaro, 1972). It is also the "inability to achieve belonging, integration or even sometimes interaction" (Cloke & Milbourne, 2012, p. 270). As a result, dissociated individuals act upon society in attempts to achieve some form of societal connection on their terms, (Krishnamurti, 1992). Regrettably, like the "square peg in a round hole" analogy, their antisocial temperament is displayed through a hyper-connectivity of offenses (i.e., violation, infractions, transgressions, and volatile force). Freeman (2009) tendered that "when, however, crime came to be seen as an offense against the social order, the criminal was seen as being outside of society and inherently different from its other members" (p. 137). Accordingly, the impetus to habitual convicted criminal offenders' social debonding and dissociative resistance to society is disconnect.

Valliere (2007) considered criminal offenders as lacking any internal barriers that prevent deviant action. Although Valliere intended to describe a very specific type of offender, her delineation truly speaks to the disconnect found in HCCO. Her manifestation of criminality showcased a self-indulgence and overall indifference that allowed for the voidance of customary societal expectations of citizenry (moral and ethical beliefs) and a disregard for consequences. Especially for the more hardened professional criminal offender, this abandonment of their citizenry allows them to devalue the rights of others as well as seek gratification and/or attention for their actions (Lozano et al., 2011). Jointly, Moffitt's work on persistent offending identified a maladaptive life trajectory that is stable across time, but unresponsive to diverse as well as changing circumstances within society (1993, p. 685). The catalyst to persistent offending is not social conditions, but rather degrees in individual disconnecting with the standards of society. Thus, the transient disconnect is depicted as the cycloidal or looping curve to the cycle of HCCO (as seen in figure 5):

Figure 5. HCCO life course

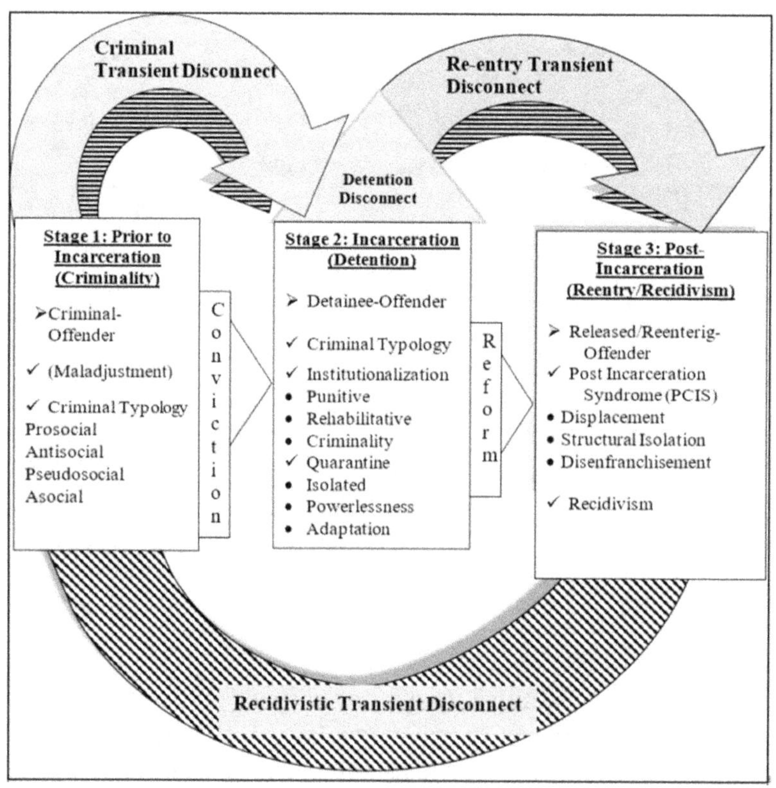

Transient disconnect can be determined in terms of social bond enthalpy. The social bond enthalpy is the intrinsic drive (e.g., levels of discontent and disregard) that causes enough de-cohesion or dissociation to prompt lawbreaking within an individual. It is expressed by autonomous contempt that entirely liberates the offender from the confines and constraints of citizenry such as societal structures, culturally constructive traditions (i.e., spiritual, moral, and ethical norms) and legitimacy. Transient disconnect can also be viewed as both a socio-cultural and psychological opposition and intolerance to values, norms, responsibilities, and common social expectations. Individuals beset by offender disconnect become maladjusted to society, leading to anti-social and adverse predilections. The consequence of these maladjustments is criminality patterns that indicate points disconnect for the more noticeable and persistent offenders' life cycle. Thus, consideration of transient disconnect must be able to examine the habituality of criminality, conviction, imprisonment, and recidivism. As seen visually in figure 5, to conceptualize the trajectory of habitual transient disconnects within sequences of HCCO's life course include the following segments: prior to incarceration, incarceration, and post incarceration. This landscape also provides the scope necessary for classifying the advancing phases of disconnect found in the life-course of persistent recidivist (Criminality, Detention, Reentry/Recidivism).

Prior to Incarceration: Criminality

As seen in figure 4, the criminal offender disconnect is the initial and primary social debonding and de-cohesion which results in a preliminary 'fracture' or detachment between an individual and the community. This primary disconnect is wide enough to elicit criminal behavior(s) and effects such as social instability, nonconformity, and rejection. The criminal offender disconnect deepens the resentment between the individual and their community. The communal dilemmas become unsurmountable as will the prime disconnect will expand from a minor 'fracture' to a complete social discontinuity in law abiding citizenry. The psycho-social expression of the prime disconnect is the committing counter-cultural or deviant response. Established on societal laws, severe deviant behaviors that are detriments to society or which causes major societal disruptions are considered criminal offenses or felonious acts. For this reason, criminal behaviors are partially, if not fully, determinants of the degrees of the offender's maladjustment but can also function as indicators of the depths of disconnect between the individual and society.

A "mashup" of the offender disconnects ideology and the categorization found in Schrag's *Typology of Criminality* (1961) was applied in this work to create a classification of the initial (prior to incarceration) primary criminal offender disconnect. While Schrag's typology may seem like a dated choice, it provides a practical heuristic in classifying criminal offenders. A classification of offender disconnect with an inclusion of Schrag's typology also considers specific norms and experiences, such as community and family background, criminal career, institutional role (Gibbons & Garrity, 1959). For this purpose, validity consistent with criminality, the core offender disconnect has been identified by the following terms: prosocial; antisocial; pseudo-social and asocial. Schrag identified the first degree of criminality as prosocial. Prosocial offenders derived 'disconnect' is inclusive of their awareness of social norms, and relationship with the broader community (i.e., family, friends, and civilian associates). The prosocial offender will decide to become indifferent or detached upon instances of singular or extenuating circumstances. Schrag (1961, p. 12) maintained that prosocial offenses may be brutal and destructive, but these wrong doings are one time and situational.

Subsequently, prosocial offenders often experience levels of guilt and remorse for their actions. The second degree of social disconnect is antisocial. Antisocial offenders are alarmingly disconnected from societal laws. Even though, 'family' ties are strongly kept as critical, their detachment is fueled by an irreverence and defiance of formal and legitimate authority. Schrag (1961, p. 12) identified them as "highly recidivistic." He also contended that their criminality starts earlier in life and progress in stages of delinquency, minor theft, then capping off with antagonistic law-breaking such as larceny and homicide.

The third degree of offender disconnect is pseudosocial. Pseudosocial offenders appear to have normal connections with the legitimate and illegitimate segments of society. Conversely, these connections are a ploy for exploitation. Pseudosocial offenders are cunning, logical, and possess enough social skills to appear abide with environmental protocols for periods of time. These offenders will shift allegiance to gain the advantage. Their warped discernment of morality and ethics allows a strategic utilization of conflicts and contradictions within social structures to fulfill their agendas. Rooted in profitability, pseudosocial criminal careers include embezzlement, defrauding, forgery, and conning. Lastly, Schrag (1961) considered the worst case of offender disconnect to be asocial. Asocial offenders severely detach from the basic social prescriptions of humanity. The asocial disconnect are based on corrupted notions of legitimacy and illegitimacy. This disconnect emancipates offenders from morality and boundaries set by social laws and relations. Asocial offenders are rash, careless and unplanned in nature. Asocial criminal careers contain a multiplicity of violence that range from assault and rape to various homicides, such as serial killing.

Incarceration: Detention

Once incarcerated, the convicted criminal's current institutionalized predicament is layered with their history of criminality, maladjustments, and/or previous periods of incarceration will continue the gestation of offender disconnect. Thus, incarceration becomes an incubation period for offender disconnects as it offers a juncture of forced institutionalized powerlessness. In relation to the offender's transition from criminal to prisoner, there is a realized incapacity to control over their existence while incarcerated. Through internalized structural domination and strategic rehabilitative measures of quarantining, specific forms of punitive dissociation (e.g., limiting, exclusion or elimination of privileges and closefisted security supervision) and compulsory activities, a defined prescribed trajectory of release is provided to the prisoner (Martin et al., 2012).

Supporters for incarceration may consider this period a "hopeful" *turning point* to changing the overall prisoner's life course. Adams (1977) identified that adversative prisoners to disciplinary measures exhibit signs of societal maladjustment. The correctional setting creates for the prisoner, occasion to dissociate from the efforts of institutionalized subjugation. Institutionalization offers a nothingness or bare existence for the prisoner (John, 2018). The atmosphere of institutionalized powerlessness creates for the prisoner, an awareness of the meaninglessness and self-estrangement from the larger social order. Additionally, the informal landscape of the correctional setting can strengthen the offender disconnect by creating an illusion of normality based on an enforced "prison code." The prisoner code fosters a normative orientation to a perceived hegemonic masculinity (toughness, social distance, and insensitivity), whether within male or female prisons, which is aligned with the length of detention and criminal record. The informal prison code designates social position within the correctional institution. This will augment the complexity and depth of offender disconnect and maladjustment within the penal population.

Unlike outer societal expectations, the cycle of transient disconnects and resulting criminality is respected, rewarded, and accepted by the growing transient populations of 'the imprisoned' that reside within the correctional system. Petit and Western (2004) supported this contention by asserting that incarceration is a more "tangible" turning point of persistent offending as status is gained by the magnitude of the offender's criminality and social dissociation. This acquired positioning will feed the offender disconnect and intern "diminish life chances" for the prisoner as well create "an attenuated form of citizenship (Petit & Western, 2004, p. 155)." For the prisoner, disconnect from society and adaptation to the correctional life becomes a tempered mode of survival that largely endorses a *façade* of enforced obedience to the formal and informal empowered. The disconnected prisoner will also resort to coercion, deception, misconduct, and withdrawal as defense measures against societal abandonment and the unwritten 'prison code' found within the correctional environment. Despite the fact the correctional setting attempts to rehabilitate, Thomas and Zaitzow (2006, p. 243) recognized that many cases of institutionalized incarceration "may be insufficient to motivate any significant personal transformation" as the basis of justice is isolation.

Post-Incarceration (PIC): Reentry/Recidivism

For the released prisoner, rehabilitative reentry strategies that center only on showcasing the need for monitoring, punitive reinforcement (i.e., three strike law) and health care intervention and treatment as well as other community services attempt to solve the difficulties of prison revolving door syndrome. These approaches place the burden of success on public efforts and stress the provision of beneficiary and economic opportunities. They are superficial in ensuring a feasible standardized reintegration strategy. The prisoner reentry strategies do not provide any assurance to deterring re-offenses. The reality of post-incarceration, especially for the persistent offender, is a continued nurturing of an already fermented disconnect.

Studies on post incarceration syndrome (PICS) have brought attention to the detachment experienced by prisoners upon released (van Willigenburg, 2020). While not a DSM-V diagnosis, PICS can be considered as symptoms that are caused by the trauma and the long-term effects of prolonged incarceration (2020, p. 171). Liem and Kunst characterized PICS as "re-experiencing, avoidance, hyper arousal and emotional numbing (2013, p. 1)." Additionally, their discussion on post-incarceration trauma offered context for disconnect found in PICS. Liem and Kunst (2013) described PICS disconnect as the creation of a "prison mask" to hideaway "permanent and unbridgeable" social distance and mistrust (p. 3). PICS disconnect exposes the dehumanizing consequence of prisoners losing control of their existence, capability to relate to external society, sense of time and a balance rationality. PICS disconnect also identifies the continued confinement the prison experience even after release. PICS disconnect is an expression of the released prisoner resilience against the outside world's pressures to confirm. If untreated the resonance of criminal- and detention- offender disconnect will create for the post incarcerated offender an inability to manage the issues related to phase displacement, structural isolation, and disenfranchisement (Gavin, 2020).

Phase displacement describes the effects of the 'time-losses by the convicted criminal offender as it relates to the outer world. This experience is both a temporal and socio-cultural lag. The reentering prisoner must deal with sensations of being 'steps-behind' the ordinary citizen. Phase displacement is formed from significant economic, technological, and social progression that occurred during their time of internment. Unable to catch up with society, a socio-temporal mismatch between the prisoner and the rest of society. For the persistent offender, the disconnect exposes the point at which past or brand-new patterns of criminality will surface (Delisi et al., 2011).

Another, contextual prompter overlaying the offender disconnect is social dilemma of structural isolation. It is both descriptor and primary dissociative trigger. Unlike the inconstancy of societal setbacks, the isolation experienced by the post-incarcerated is a state of exasperation based on a paucity of defined infrastructural stratification of citizenry. In her essay, *Money and Mass Incarceration*, Gottschalk (2009, p. 107) underscored the permanent flaw found in the societal social structures is a prescribed socio-cultural and economic segregations. Wacquant (2010) found linkage between the social change found within PICS disconnect and a continued lack of viable accessibility to socio-economic structures within specific strata (i.e., class, caste, and political systems/affiliations). The 'returning' offender will fall within the crumbling tiers of 'second class citizenry,' and therefore be plagued with the accompanying social dilemmas (Edgely, 2017; DeJarnatt, 2013). Congruently, the aggravated offenders will have little regard for and choose to abandon recognized weak societal structures and expectations of subsistence.

Convincingly, not only is the displaced offender attempting to be brought up to date, while contending with past social dilemmas, but they also suffer from disenfranchisement. Disenfranchisement is an instance of socio-political and socio-economic quarantine if not exile because of a criminal offenders' previous criminality, convictions and disconnect. This societal separation is purported to be the main cause of hardship, poor social standing as well as ineligibilities for common opportunities such as employment and improved housing for released convicted criminal offenders. In this instance, such structural rejection and isolation, could be used to demonstrate society's unwillingness to reconnect with the offender. The collateral damage of this incident is a substantiation of offender disconnect. It speaks to the query of most disenfranchised, 'why try to fight to be an upright citizen in a society that is unaccepting and inaccessible?' It also signifies a "in good faith" demand for prisoners to be given rights (civic, social and politics), residential privileges and legitimacy without any sureties of upholding the duties and responsibilities of law-abiding citizens.

For the HCCO, periods of post-incarceration not only continue to structure the depths of disconnect, but open avenues for new maladjustments and more expressive patterns of criminality during phases of recidivism. The HCCO's recidivistic disconnect is nurtured by the feelings of loss opportunities and a perceived absence of societal forgiveness, acceptance, and affirmation. The typology used to classify the initial criminal offender disconnect (primary and detention) can be used in the case of recidivistic disconnect (as illustrated in figure 4). Recidivistic offender disconnect can be considered as the culmination of the experienced discontinuity in the individual's life course. With each revolution in the HCCO life-course, it will become more of an immutable nexus to cyclic rigidity.

CONCLUSION

At a symposium on crime, Weatherburn and Baker (1999) asserted that transient offenders prominently contribute to criminal problems. Weatherburn and Baker (1999) only examined the plight of transient offenders based on juvenile delinquency and intermittent criminality (five or fewer offenses in a year). From these perspectives, criminal offending and transience will decay over time due to proper rehabilitation and/or aging out. However, the global rates of recidivism remain very high. The primary goal of this chapter was to bring attention to the existence of transience within the life course of habitual convicted criminal offenders (HCCO). For the HCCO, transience can be considered as continuous, and cyclical socio-cognitive unsteadiness, displacement, (settled permanence of) impermanence. HCCO transience is also junctures of uncoupling of human and environmental relationships, which is aligned with habitual criminality and incarceration. Although attention in this chapter began with a deliberation of HCCOs' transience within the revolving doors of prison systems; the over-hyped excuses of circumstantial gateway barriers and the prescribed prisoner 'victimization' by society should not be perpetuated.

A greater consideration must be given to habitual transient disconnects (continuous dissociative and socio-cognitive resistance, disengagement and debonding). Transient disconnects found within the life-stages of HCCOs are sparked by an adversative sense of hyper-individualism (undermines reciprocity, mutual obligations, and civic duty). Wikström and Sampson (2003) remarked that "interactions between individual characteristics and community contexts in producing criminal acts and shaping pathways in crime are poorly misunderstood" (p. 120). Wikström and Sampson (2003) also believed that much can be learned from a unified individual and environmental contextualizing of convicted criminal offender pathway. Similarly, Samenow (1984) referred to crime as being individualized and exemplifying of personal irresponsibility, rather than being environmental in origin. Samenow (1984) also saw futility in focusing on forces outside of the criminal offender. Tame (1998) contended that habits are not over-powering compulsions and, "what causes criminal activity is simply the freely chosen actions of individuals, and the ideas they develop about themselves, others and the world at large (p. 6)."

Global treatment of habitual transient disconnects should not solely be rooted in attempts to resolve habitual criminality or reduce the size of prison populations. Instead, the treatment of habitual transient disconnects must focus on scientifically unraveling the individualized, transitive, and dissociative socio-cognitive impermanence and disengagement from a community and from the idealism of productive law-abiding citizenship. Breaking the cycle of transient disconnect within the HCCOs' life course must involve concerns on freedom (individual and communal), civil rights, accountability, and empirically supported strategies for producing communal permanence based on habitual compliance and commitment to being productive law-abiding citizens. Values of productive law-abiding citizenship entails obedience of the laws, civic engagement, communitarianism, self-sacrifice for the greater communal good and full participation in the production of commonwealth.

Shaping resiliency based on habitual compliance and commitment to productive law-abiding citizenship could form an essential buffering capacity to combat HCCO disconnect. Productive law-abiding citizenship would also create needed turning point(s) to establish strong and positive social bonds as well as the encouragement of a constructive self-actualization regardless of communal and societal adversity. However, productive law-abiding citizenship also requires repealing or amending laws that discriminate, stigmatize, or impede moral societal connections. In addition, offender management programs instituted that utilize strategies of achieving productive law-abiding citizenship (i.e., Missouri's Parallel Universe program), have not been adequately and scientifically validated (Jonson & Cullen, 2015, p. 240). Therefore, investigation must be conducted to empirically prove that productive law-abiding citizenship strategies and approaches contain crucial predictors of successful prisoner rehabilitation and reentry, in addition to resolving the transient state of HCCO.

REFERENCES

Adams, T. C. (1977). Characteristics of state prisoners who demonstrate severe adjustment problems. *Journal of Clinical Psychology*, *33*(4), 1100–1103. doi:10.1002/1097-4679(197710)33:4<1100::AID-JCLP2270330439>3.0.CO;2-L PMID:925166

Alas, R., Ennulo, J., & Türnpuu, L. (2006). Managerial values in the institutional context. *Journal of Business Ethics*, *65*(3), 269–278. doi:10.100710551-005-5494-1

Asaro, J. M. (1972). Youth peer effect on scholastic performance and the development of predictive instrument of achievement. *Rural Sociology in the South: 1972 Proceedings*, *25*(2), 59–61. files.eric.ed.gov/fulltext/ED068213.pdf#page=79

Auge-Dickhut, S., Koye, B., & Liebetrau, A. (2015). *Customer value generation in banking: The Zurich model of customer-centricity*. Springer.

Baillargeon, J., Binswanger, I., Penn, J., Williams, B., & Murray, O. (2009). Psychiatric disorders and repeat incarcerations: The revolving prison door. *The American Journal of Psychiatry*, *166*(1), 103–109. doi:10.1176/appi.ajp.2008.08030416 PMID:19047321

Berg, M. T., & Huebner, B. M. (2011). Reentry and the ties that bind: An examination of social ties, employment, and recidivism. *Justice Quarterly*, *28*(2), 382–410. doi:10.1080/07418825.2010.498383

BJS. (2015). *Recidivism of Prisoners Released in 30 states in 2005: Patterns from 2005 to 2010*. Retrieved from http://www.bjs.gov/index.cfm?ty=pbdetail&iid=4986

Block, P. (1998). From leadership to citizenship. *Insights on leadership: Service, stewardship, spirit, and servant-leadership*, 87-95. Retrieved from beyondthecourse.co.nz/wp-content/uploads/From_Leadership_to_Citizenship.pdf

Blumstein, A., & Beck, A. J. (2005). Reentry as a transient state between liberty and recommitment. In J. Travis & C. Visher (Eds.), *Prisoner reentry and crime in America*. Cambridge University Press. doi:10.1017/CBO9780511813580.003

Burnett, R. (2010). The will and the ways to becoming an ex-offender. *International Journal of Offender Therapy and Comparative Criminology*, *54*(5), 663–666. doi:10.1177/0306624X10383845 PMID:20852061

Burtch, B., Rane, C., & Lindfield, S. (1999). The expanding prison. *Manitoba Law Journal*, *26*(3), 375–380. themanitobalawjournal.com/wp-content/uploads/articles/MLJ_26.3/Book%20Review%20The%20Expanding%20Prison.pdf

Byrne, J. M., Pattavina, A., & Taxman, F. S. (2015). International trends in prison upsizing and downsizing: In search of evidence of a global rehabilitation revolution. *Victims & Offenders*, *10*(4), 420–451. doi:10.1080/15564886.2015.1078186

Čapek, J. (2017). Habit and freedom in Merleau-Ponty and Ricoeur. *The Journal of Speculative Philosophy*, *31*(3), 432–443. doi:10.5325/jspecphil.31.3.0432

Chunn, D. E., & Menzies, R. (2006). "So, what does all of this have to do with criminology?" Surviving the restructuring of the discipline in the twenty-first century. *Canadian Journal of Criminology and Criminal Justice*, *48*(5), 663–680. doi:10.3138/cjccj.48.5.663

Cloke, P., & Milbourne, P. (2012). *International perspectives on rural homelessness*. Routledge.

DeJarnattD. (2013). Criminal records create a second-class citizenry: Changing the way adult convictions are vacated in Washington state. Seattle *Journal for Social Justice*. https://ssrn.com/abstract=2342791 doi:10.2139srn.2342791

Delisi, M., Kosloski, A. E., Drury, A. J., Vaughn, M. G., Beaver, K. M., Trulson, C. R., & Wright, J. P. (2011). Never desisters: A descriptive study of the life-course persistent offender. In Criminology Theory: A Life-Course Approach. Boston, MA: Jones & Bartlett.

Edgely, M. (2010). Criminals and (second-class) citizenship: Twenty-first century attainder? *Griffith Law Review*, *19*(3), 403–437. doi:10.1080/10383441.2010.10854683

Fazel, S., & Wolf, A. (2015). A systematic review of criminal recidivism rates worldwide: Current difficulties and recommendations for best practice. *PLoS One*, *10*(6), e0130390. doi:10.1371/journal.pone.0130390 PMID:26086423

Featherstone, R., & Deflem, M. (2003). Anomie and strain: Context and consequences of Merton's two theories. *Sociological Inquiry*, *73*(4), 471–489. doi:10.1111/1475-682X.00067

Fry, M. (1952). The habitual prisoner. *The Modern Law Review*, *15*(2), 155–159. doi:10.1111/j.1468-2230.1952.tb00229.x

Gavin, P. (2020). Irish ex-prisoner reflections on their psychological wellbeing whilst in prison in England and Wales. *Advancing Corrections Journal*, *9*(1), 101–118.

Giacalone, R. A., Paul, K., & Jurkiewicz, C. L. (2005). A preliminary investigation into the role of positive psychology in consumer sensitivity to corporate social performance. *Journal of Business Ethics*, *58*(4), 295–305. doi:10.100710551-004-5970-z

Gibbons, D., & Garrity, D. (1959). Some suggestions for the development of etiological and treatment theory in criminology. *Social Forces*, *38*(1), 51–58. doi:10.2307/2574016

Gilbert, E. (2007). Leaky borders and solid citizens: Governing security, prosperity, and quality of life in a North American partnership. *Antipode*, *39*(1), 77–98. doi:10.1111/j.1467-8330.2007.00507.x

Glenn, A. L., & Raine, A. (2014). Neurocriminology: Implications for the punishment, prediction, and prevention of criminal behaviour. *Nature Reviews. Neuroscience*, *15*(1), 54–63. doi:10.1038/nrn3640 PMID:24326688

Gordon, R. (2004). The social system as site of disaster impact and resource for recovery. *Australian Journal of Emergency Management, 19*(4), 16-22.

Gottschalk, M. (2009). Money and mass incarceration: The bad, the mad, and penal reform. *Criminology & Public Policy*, *8*(1), 97–109. doi:10.1111/j.1745-9133.2009.00547.x

Grubb, J. A. (2020). *Who goes to prison and why? Examining inmate characteristics and offense types. In Handbook on American Prisons*. Routledge.

Harding, D. J., Morenoff, J. D., Nguyen, A. P., & Bushway, S. D. (2017). Short-and long-term effects of imprisonment on future felony convictions and prison admissions. *Proceedings of the National Academy of Sciences of the United States of America, 114*(42), 11103–11108. doi:10.1073/pnas.1701544114 PMID:28973924

Hoyle, J. R., & Slater, R. O. (2001). Love, happiness, and America's schools: The role of educational leadership in the 21st century. *Phi Delta Kappan*, *82*(10), 790–794. doi:10.1177/003172170108201017

Jacobs, L. A., & Skeem, J. L. (2021). Neighborhood risk factors for recidivism: For whom do they matter? *American Journal of Community Psychology*, *67*(1-2), 103–115. doi:10.1002/ajcp.12463 PMID:32960992

Jonson, C. L., & Cullen, F. T. (2015). Prisoner reentry programs. *Crime and Justice*, *44*(1), 517–575. doi:10.1086/681554

Konkel, R. H., & Daquin, J. C. (2020). From the streets to prison and back: An examination of continuity of behaviors among offenders. *Corrections: Policy, Practice and Research*, 1–22. doi:10.1080/23774657.2020.1808116

Krishnamurti, J. (1992). *Social responsibility*. Krishnamurti Foundation of America.

Lattimore, P. K., Steffey, D. M., & Visher, C. A. (2010). Prisoner reentry in the first decade of the twenty-first century. *Victims & Offenders*, *5*(3), 253–267. doi:10.1080/15564886.2010.485907

LeBel, T. P., Burnett, R., Maruna, S., & Bushway, S. (2008). The chicken and egg' of subjective and social factors in desistance from crime. *European Journal of Criminology*, *5*(2), 131–159. doi:10.1177/1477370807087640

LeongN. (2006). Felon reenfranchisement: Political implications and potential for individual rehabilitative benefits. *Available at* SSRN 977280. doi:10.2139srn.977280

Liem, M., & Kunst, M. (2013). Is there a recognizable post-incarceration syndrome among released "lifers"? *International Journal of Law and Psychiatry*, *36*(3), 333–337. doi:10.1016/j.ijlp.2013.04.012 PMID:23642320

Love, M. C., & Frazier, A. (2006). Certificates of rehabilitation and other forms of relief from the collateral consequences of conviction: a survey of state laws. In ABA Commission on Effective Criminal Sanctions (Ed.), Second Chances in the Criminal Justice System: Alternatives to Incarceration and Reentry Strategies. Washington, DC: American Bar Association.

Lozano, A. T. R., Morgan, R. D., Murray, D. D., & Varghese, F. (2011). Prison tattoos as a reflection of the criminal lifestyle. *International Journal of Offender Therapy and Comparative Criminology*, *55*(4), 509–529. doi:10.1177/0306624X10370829 PMID:20508085

Martin, M. S., Dorken, S. K., Wamboldt, A. D., & Wootten, S. E. (2012). Stopping the revolving door: A meta-analysis on the effectiveness of interventions for criminally involved individuals with major mental disorders. *Law and Human Behavior*, *36*(1), 1–12. doi:10.1037/h0093963 PMID:22471380

Matthew, M., & Abrams, L. S. (2020). Practically emotional: Young men's perspectives on what works in reentry programs. *Journal of Social Service Research*, *46*(5), 658–670. doi:10.1080/01488376.2019.1617225

Mboka, A. K. (2013). Overview of the Arizona juvenile justice system. *Kriminologija & socijalna integracija: časopis za kriminologiju, penologiju i poremećaje u ponašanju, 20*(2), 73-87.

Moffitt, T. E. (1993). Adolescence-limited and life-course-persistent antisocial behavior: A developmental taxonomy. *Psychological Review*, *100*(4), 674–701. doi:10.1037/0033-295X.100.4.674 PMID:8255953

Morani, N. M., Wikoff, N., Linhorst, D. M., & Bratton, S. (2011). A description of the self-identified needs, service expenditures, and social outcomes of participants of a prisoner-reentry program. *The Prison Journal*, *91*(3), 347–365. doi:10.1177/0032885511409896

Petersilia, J. (1999). Parole and prisoner reentry in the United States. *Crime and Justice*, *26*, 479–529. doi:10.1086/449302

Petit, B., & Western, B. (2004). Mass imprisonment and the life course: Race and class inequality in U.S. incarceration. *American Sociological Review*, *69*(2), 151–169. doi:10.1177/000312240406900201

Raine, A. (2013). *The psychopathology of crime: Criminal behavior as a clinical disorder*. Elsevier.

Rao, R. J. (2012). Conscientious: A relevant personality factor in criminal behavior. *International Journal of Multidisciplinary Educational Research*, *1*(2), 398–409. http://www.ijmer.in/pdf/volume1-issue2-2012/398-409.pdf

Reisig, M. D., Bales, W., Hay, C., & Wang, X. (2007). The effect of racial inequality on black male recidivism. *Justice Quarterly*, *24*(3), 3408–3434. doi:10.1080/07418820701485387

Rydberg, J., & Grommon, E. (2016). A multimethod examination of the dynamics of recidivism during reentry. *Corrections: Policy, Practice and Research*, *1*(1), 40–60. doi:10.1080/23774657.2016.1105660

Samenow, S. E. (1984). *Inside the criminal mind*. Random House.

Schrag, C. (1961). Preliminary criminal typology. *Pacific Sociological Review*, *4*(1), 11–16. doi:10.2307/1388481

Schrag, J., & Scotchmer, S. (1997). The self-reinforcing nature of crime. *International Review of Law and Economics*, *17*(3), 325–335. doi:10.1016/S0144-8188(97)00025-2

SpearIt. (2011). Gender violence in prison & hyper-masculinities in the hood: Cycles of destructive masculinity. Washington University of Law & Policy, 37(5), 89-147.

Sumpter, C. (2020). Realising violent extremist risk assessments in Indonesia: Simplify and collaborate. *Journal for Deradicalization*, (22), 97–121.

Tame. (1998). *Freedom, responsibility, and justice: The criminology of the 'New Right.'* Retrieved from http://www2.libertarian.co.uk/sites/default/lanotepdf/legan030.pdf

Thomas, J., & Zaitzow, B. H. (2006). Conning or conversion? The role of religion in prison coping. *The Prison Journal*, *86*(2), 242–259. doi:10.1177/0032885506287952

Travis, J., & Visher, C. (Eds.). (2005). *Prisoner reentry and crime in America*. Cambridge University Press. doi:10.1017/CBO9780511813580

Valliere, V. (2007). Understanding the non-stranger rapist. *The Voice, 1*(11), 1-6. http://www.ncdsv.org/images/NDAA_UnderstandingNonstrangerRapist_TheVoice_vol_1_no_11_2007.pdf

van Willigenburg, T. (2020). Moral Injury, post-incarceration syndrome and religious coping behind bars. In S. Sremac & I. Jindra (Eds.), *Lived religion, conversion and recovery*. Palgrave Studies in Lived Religion and Societal Challenges. Palgrave Macmillan. doi:10.1007/978-3-030-40682-0_8

Wacquant, L. (2010). Prisoner reentry as myth and ceremony. *Dialectical Anthropology*, *34*(4), 605–620. doi:10.100710624-010-9215-5

Walther, A. (2012). *Participation or non-participation? Getting beyond dichotomies by applying an ideology-critical, a comparative and a biographical perspective. In Youth Participation in Europe: Beyond Discourses, Practices and Realities*. Policy Press.

Weatherburn, D., & Baker, J. (1999). Preventing crime and violence among transient and persistent offenders. In *3rd National Outlook Symposium on Crime in Australia, Mapping the Boundaries of Australia's Criminal Justice System*. The Australian Institute of Criminology. https://citeseerx.ist.psu.edu/viewdoc/download?doi=10.1.1.515.1328&rep=rep1&type=pdf

Weaver, B., Tata, C., Munro, M., & Barry, M. (2012). The failure of recall to prison: Early release, front-door and back-door sentencing and the revolving prison door in Scotland. *European Journal of Probation*, *4*(1), 85–98. doi:10.1177/206622031200400108

Weisberg, R. (2014). Meanings and measures of recidivism. *Southern California Law Review*, *87*(3), 785–804.

Wikström, P. O. H., & Sampson, R. J. (2003). Social mechanisms of community influences on crime and pathways in criminality. *Causes of conduct disorder and juvenile delinquency*, 118-148. Retrieved from http://www.pads.ac.uk/Documents/Social_mechanisms_of_community_influences_on_crime_and_pathways_in_criminality.pdf

YukhnenkoD.SridharS.FazelS. (2019). A systematic review of criminal recidivism rates worldwide: 3-year update. *Welcome Open Research*, *4*(28). doi:10.12688/wellcomeopenres.14970

ADDITIONAL READING

Alehegn, T., & Mentor, D. (2019). Mobile learning for social change: Democratizing education and civic engagement. In *Civic engagement and politics: Concepts, methodologies, tools, and applications* (pp. 412–426). IGI Global. doi:10.4018/978-1-5225-7669-3.ch020

Anestis, J. C., & Carbonell, J. L. (2014). Stopping the revolving door: Effectiveness of mental health court in reducing recidivism by mentally ill offenders. *Psychiatric Services (Washington, D.C.)*, *65*(9), 1105–1112. doi:10.1176/appi.ps.201300305 PMID:24881521

Gannon, T. A., Olver, M. E., Mallion, J. S., & James, M. (2019). Does specialized psychological treatment for offending reduce recidivism? A meta-analysis examining staff and program variables as predictors of treatment effectiveness. *Clinical Psychology Review*, *73*, 101752. doi:10.1016/j.cpr.2019.101752 PMID:31476514

Jung, J., Goel, S., & Skeem, J. (2020). The limits of human predictions of recidivism. *Science Advances*, *6*(7), eaaz0652. doi:10.1126ciadv.aaz0652 PMID:32110737

Prescott, J. J., Pyle, B., & Starr, S. B. (2019). Understanding violent-crime recidivism. *The Notre Dame Law Review*, *95*, 1643.

Tollenaar, N., & Van Der Heijden, P. G. (2019). Optimizing predictive performance of criminal recidivism models using registration data with binary and survival outcomes. *PLoS One*, *14*(3), e0213245. doi:10.1371/journal.pone.0213245 PMID:30849094

Trood, M. D., Spivak, B. L., & Ogloff, J. R. (2021). A systematic review and meta-analysis of the effects of judicial supervision on recidivism and well-being factors of criminal offenders. *Journal of Criminal Justice*, *74*, 101796. doi:10.1016/j.jcrimjus.2021.101796

Chapter 12
Procedural Justice and the Power of the Judge in the Courtroom:
A Comparison Between Africa and the West

Allan T. Moore
https://orcid.org/0000-0002-3202-0079
University of the West of Scotland, UK

ABSTRACT

In this chapter, the author conducts a critical analysis and comparison of laws and practices that legitimise discretionary power in the courtroom from a selection of global north and south jurisdictions. The specific offence of contempt of court in facie curiae is the central focus, where the use of full judicial autonomy, summary, and arbitrary hearings have survived now well into the 21st century. The research conducted shows that there is a global problem with significant overreach of power by members of the judiciary in nearly all jurisdictions investigated. In some cases, this could be viewed as being extreme enough in its overreach to justify being described as abuse of power. Further evidence is presented showing little by way of accountability being held against those judges who misuse their discretionary powers in the courtroom. Recommendations are that there should be reform or development of practice through both judicial training and proportionate disciplinary action where overreach is proven to have occurred in order to minimise future overreaches of power.

INTRODUCTION

Article four of the Code of Judicial Conduct for South African Judges (1994) on judicial independence shows best the complex and competing functions of the judge in the courtroom, exemplifying why some judges might find maintaining the correct balance of upholding neutrality whilst simultaneously using powers a difficult task. Section (a) sets out that a judge must "uphold the independence and integrity of the judiciary and the authority of the courts", followed by (b) that he or she must "maintain an indepen-

DOI: 10.4018/978-1-7998-6884-2.ch012

dence of mind in the performance of judicial duties". Initially these might seem to be quite straightforward and standard expectations, however the potential conflicts begin to emerge when examining note (i) which requires that "A judge acts fearlessly and according to his or her conscience because a judge is only accountable to the law" and later in note (iv) that judicial independence "…does not justify judicial misbehaviour and does not provide an excuse for failing to perform judicial functions with due diligence or for otherwise acting contrary to this Code."

So, on one hand there is the requirement to remain neutral and independent, and with diligence and care, whilst on the other there is the fact that the judge is tasked with being the custodian of the law and given significant powers to act 'fearlessly' and using their own subjective good conscience, all under the threat of being potentially accused of judicial misconduct should they get things wrong in this regard. Given the discussed provisions then, and the fact that there are similar expectations and consequences in jurisdictions around the world, key questions emerge that are the central focus of this chapter:

1. What are the discretionary powers that a judge has in acting 'according to his or her conscience' when in the courtroom?
2. When using the powers in question, does it appear that judges are always remaining neutral and independent as professional expectation and obligation would demand?
3. Are judges always using their powers legitimately or are there examples where there is significant overreach of power to the point that judges might be acting outside of the law?
4. What are the consequences for judges and other affected people if there is such an overreach of power in the courtroom?

In addition to these questions, another main aim of this chapter is to compare both in law and in practice the same issues in jurisdictions in the westernised / global north context on one hand, and in jurisdictions in Africa, the largest continent in the global south, on the other. There have been several past academic studies conducted examining the power of the judge from different perspectives, focusing on different individual jurisdictions. For example, it may be possible to draw conclusions from an examination of the actions of judges related to different individual offences or sentencing practices which can be reframed as evidence of how judges have used their discretionary powers, or in some cases may be argued to have overreached beyond what their powers legally permit. Several sources have made claims that judges are less susceptible to external influence than the general public, however past research has shown this not to be the case. In one such study, Hausegger and Haynie made the explicit assertion that "Judges are affected by their policy preferences, and decisions are made that benefit those preferences." (2003, p. 635) on their evaluation of the comparison of two jurisdictions, one in the North (Canada) and one in the South (South Africa). They further asserted that "Judging is a political behavior that exhibits similar actions affected by similar influences" (2003, p. 654), interpreted to mean that the authors' belief is that judges are not individually making neutral law-based decisions, rather their decisions are influenced by their own internalised beliefs and ideologies.

In backing up the assertion, the authors conducted rigorous quantitative research techniques, eventually concluding that:

Using comparable measures of dependent and independent variables, we find that chief justices in both Canada and South Africa do not assign their colleagues randomly. In both countries, policy preferences have an impact on those decisions... when panels concern salient issues, both Canadian and South African chief justices appoint judges closer to them more often. (Hausegger & Haynie, 2003, pp. 654-655)

In this context then, it is interesting that the research indicates no significant difference in practice, rather the fact that in both jurisdictions, senior judges have the ability to use their power to indirectly influence the outcomes of cases through ensuring that their own political preferences and wider ideological beliefs are reflected in the outcomes of key cases. It is important then to understand that whilst the objective is to compare and where relevant to contrast, this first source indicates clear comparability, where each country is equally weak in protection of objectivity, rather than either jurisdiction having any clear strength over the other in this regard. Further examples will be cited throughout this chapter to enable valid conclusions to be drawn, based upon analysis of a selection of countries from the global north and south.

BACKGROUND

On discussing the intricacies of a professional in the exercise of his or her duties, Soeharno highlights what can be understood to be one of the problems with the nature of any profession where an individual has a high degree of autonomy combined with power over another person:

The difference between the police officer and the accountant is that more is left to the discretion of the individual police officer and thus to his professional character. This difference between compliance and discretion shows something about the nature of professional character: there are limits on one hand, but professional autonomy on the other. This also shows in the nature of violations. While a violation of a clear norm is usually understood as binary, not meeting the standards of prudence is a rather gradual matter. (Soeharno, 2016, p. 31)

It can be observed then that not all professions have the same level of autonomy, rather this is dependent on the combination of the strictness of the rules and regulations they are obliged to follow, and the level of scrutiny they might be subject to in the course of their duties. In the context of Soeharno's final sentence above, it could be argued that whereas the matters an accountant is involved in have limited discretion due to the strictness of financial regulation, the role of the judge in the courtroom on the other hand includes a wide range of discretionary powers. As most lay individuals, whether participants in the courtroom or external observers, will not have specialist legal or procedural knowledge that would be required in order to genuinely understand if a judge has exceeded their discretionary limits, the effect is that whilst it is easy to locate much of the frequent *general* critique made by members of the public related to judgments passed on the basis of general morality or dissatisfaction with the result, there is little by way of detailed public criticism related to identifiable *specific* conduct or processes alleging that a judge has fallen foul of any kind of legal breach.

Soeharno is clear in his analysis of the role of the judge that the requirements are not about *moral* character – again the question might be how one would create an acceptable universal set of moral norms? Instead, the suitability for the role should be based on *professional* character. Soeharno outlines that:

To be of the right professional character means that the professional rightly takes into account in his actions the values and ideals that are connected with the institution. The selection and assessment of these values and ideals in specific actions is a prudent activity. It is not just about having the right intention or aim, but also about having the ability to mediate professional values and rules with the concrete situation, with an idea of general well-being in view. By continually searching for the optimal way to act, the professional character of the actor increases in quality. He then becomes able to act optimally in future situations. (Soeharno, 2016, pp. 39-40)

Herein lies the problem that there is a significant body of evidence as shown throughout this chapter that several judges appear to either lack the ability to or have overlooked the professional character requirement to balance those professional values and rules with the concrete situation they are faced with. Instead, there are several examples of either unnecessary demonstrations of personal power, or what could be described as an overreach of the actual professional autonomy held, as shown by successful appeals against some arbitrary judgments and sentences that have been handed down.

Barak similarly analyses the issues of judicial discretion and the power of the judge. He summarises the considerations that a judge should be making prior to exercising such discretion that might be controversial, setting out that:

Of course, the power to choose – judicial discretion – is never absolute. It is always subject to procedural limitations (such as fairness) and substantive limitations (such as reasonability, coherency, consistency, and rationality) ... When does exercising judicial discretion advance the role of a judge, and when does it depart from the proper path? (Barak, 2008, p. xiv)

Using Barak's examples of fairness of procedure, and substantive considerations of whether the actions can be deemed to be reasonable, coherent, consistent, and rational, perhaps in the future it may be possible to embark on a larger project of producing a matrix that lists all countries around the globe and how they perform under each of these headings. Such an exercise would be of use to see the true scale of judicial use of power worldwide. It would be easy though to become fixated on the numbers of cases involved, when importantly Stewart explains that the problem is not so much about the scale of the problem of judicial abuse of power, rather what is of the greatest importance is the effect that even isolated cases of abuse of power might have, writing that:

...while the number of judicial misconduct cases may be relatively small and isolated, the magnitude of those cases may have far-reaching repercussions for members of the judicial branch. Such judicial misconduct calls into question a judge's impartiality, dependability, or capacity to conduct official business. Moreover, such conduct reflects dis-favorably on the judiciary as a whole. (Stewart, 2003, p. 465)

Whereas most cases pass through the courtroom without controversy or issue, as explained by Stewart, all that it takes is for one case of significant abuse of power or overreach to gain exposure in either academic or public discourse to have potentially dramatic effects on perceptions on the professionality of the judiciary. This is a heavy burden for individual judges to carry, but also an important and ever-present reminder that judges cannot allow their full professionalism to slip even for a moment and must always align their considerations and actions with those principles of fairness, reasonableness, coherency, consistency, and rationality as explained by Barak previously. Such considerations present a strong argument as to why judges ought to act with genuine restraint even in those areas where historically they have had high levels of discretion to impose arbitrary punishment, such as when faced with potential prevarication, perjury, or contempt in the face of the court.

Stewart argues that judges' interpretation of their own powers must go beyond simply being technically correct, outlining that there are wider considerations that potentially could have the effect of legitimising or delegitimising such powers in the eyes of the general population:

The impact of a judicial decision on the liberty and property of ordinary citizens can be profound. Such extraordinary power is tolerable in a democracy solely because judges speak only at the behest of reason and the law... such an arrangement requires more than judges having a subjective belief that our decisions are in fact rendered fairly impartially or that we believe this of our colleagues. Our power requires an objective analysis; a reasonable person should find that our decisions appear to be fair and impartial as well. (Stewart, 2003, pp. 465-466)

This is a complex argument to make and one that would be difficult to formulate as any sort of enforceable mechanism or rule, especially where the judge's decision in question is found to be *technically* legal or within the range of discretion permitted. However, it is another clear explanation as to why a judge should be cautious to avoid a rush to judgment, when the effect of poor consideration of issues beyond the technical could result in their judgment being viewed as unfair or disproportionate use of power, as the reasonable person tends to evaluate the *overall* context beyond simply the technicalities of the law in isolation. Strengthening this perspective, Himma presents the argument that the judgment of law was founded historically upon the idea of decisions being based on the combined factors of law and morality, and that it was for the judge to make the decision on what behaviour could be deemed moral or immoral:

According to classical naturalism, the overlap of the content of law and morality is not a matter of contingent fact; rather, it is part of the very concept of law that its content conform to certain moral requirements. (Himma, 1999, p. 71)

If this view were to be accepted in a contemporary society or legal system, it carries the potential danger of the judge having the power to impose his or her own subjective moral standards on a case before them, when more frequently it is contemporarily understood that it is not the place of the courts to adopt any moral stance on laws passed by the legislature.

Dworkin in this regard presents the argument that that the use of power through judicial discretion is a necessary component of legal decision making if a judiciary is to be able to function properly:

[I]f someone's case is not clearly covered by such a rule . . . then that case cannot be decided by 'applying the law.' It must be decided by some official, like a judge, 'exercising his discretion,' which means reaching beyond the law for some other sort of standard to guide him in manufacturing a fresh legal rule or supplementing an old one. (Dworkin, 1977, p. 17)

The problem in many developed legal systems however, is that if the intention is to create such a new legal rule or precedent case, then (legislature aside) this is usually only within the powers of the highest court in a jurisdiction's judicial hierarchy, and to use such a power to establish a new legal rule would be deemed to be an illegitimate overreach of power if carried out by any court or individual judge elsewhere in the hierarchy in question.

A complex perspective related to Dworkin is put forward by Himma, who interprets Dworkin's overall philosophy as being that:

Dworkin believed that the validity of legal principles, unlike the validity of legal rules, cannot be explained in terms of official acts; for legal principles are valid by virtue of public and professional acceptance and not by virtue of formal promulgation. (Himma, 1999, p. 82)

In other words, Himma (1999) is interpreting that the rationale may be such that professional and public morals, if held by the majority, can collectively be asserted to be at least of equal value as purely legal rules are in their applicability to the consideration of matters in a court case. He explains this with relation to the concept of a murderer staking an inheritance claim from their victim's estate as per the *Riggs* case in the USA (Stewart, 1999, p. 79). At the time of the case there was no legal rule prohibiting such a claim, however the judge took the extraordinary decision of denying the claim on the basis that it was so obviously *morally* wrong for such a claim to be honored. The argument stemming from this then, is that the power of the judge should not be restricted to simply the legal rules, rather legitimate power might include a combination of legal rules and the inherent fairness or unfairness that such a strict adherence to those rules would result in when considering proportionality or natural law. This is complicated, as whilst the merits of the argument founded on that case are difficult to argue against – few would argue that a murderer ought to benefit from their own crime – there would be other cases where the morality would not be so clear cut and where there may be validity found in competing viewpoints. Summarised then, the question would be, if such an approach to judicial decision making were to be allowed, who draws the line in terms of what morality is definite and unequivocal, and what morality is deemed open to question? This may be an impossible question to answer in any conclusive sense.

Stewart sets out perhaps the best all-round explanation of the standing of a judge within the courtroom when he explains that:

A hallmark of the judiciary has been its historical posture of neutrality and impartiality toward litigants and the disputes they bring to the courts for resolution. Ascendance to the bench therefore represents more than a mere cloak of power; it also suggests a symbolic and practical detachment of the judge from his or her prior role as a partisan advocate. Once the oath of office has been taken, a judge represents something larger than himself or herself; a judge symbolically represents the very objectivity necessary for our democratic system of governance to function properly. (Stewart, 2003, p. 477)

Stewart is therefore arguing that the concepts of neutrality and objectivity, taking the 'self' and as far as is possible the notion of subjectivity out of the judge's actions, are crucial if the judiciary are to retain true legitimacy in the powers they have been entrusted with. In this context then, it becomes difficult to legitimise any arbitrary process whereby the judge adopts the position as witness, prosecutor, and judge in his or her own cause. Such a process or stance fatally undermines those necessary neutral and objective stances when remittance to a neutral third party is always possible. This is important when considering the judge taking punitive action against persons present in court for a variety of reasons including when confronted with a potential contempt in the face of the court.

CONTEMPT OF COURT

Contempt of court is an offence the by its nature requires a judge to use both discretion and power. Perhaps the most clear and concise definition of the offence originates from Lord President Clyde in the Scottish case of *Johnson v Grant* (1923) when he stated that,

The offence consists in interfering with the administration of the law; in impeding and perverting the course of justice... (Johnson v Grant, 1923, pp. 502-503)

Clyde goes on to discuss the common misconception and issue that

The currency of the phrase is particularly regrettable... It is not the dignity of the Court which is offended – a petty and misleading view of the issues involved – it is the fundamental supremacy of the law which is challenged. (Johnson v Grant, 1923, p. 503)

On analysis of these words, what Lord President Clyde was discussing nearly a century ago included an assertion that there are flaws at even the most basic level in contempt law, specifically regarding the title of the law itself. It is apparent that there was and indeed remains some confusion over what the purpose of contempt of court as a law is intended to be. Clyde was of the opinion that contempt of court was not intended to be read in the context of an insult to a particular Judge in their courtroom (although that particular action may in fact result in contempt being held) – it is not literally the moral judgment of 'contempt of the court' that is the issue. The fundamental issue instead is that the administration of justice and smooth running of the legal process should not be interfered with, and that it is that interference, undermining or damaging the legal process, which should be held to be 'contempt of court.'

Considering Clyde's clarification, it is then unhelpful when it becomes apparent that definitions still given by authors in some contemporary textbooks are fundamentally incorrect, or at least lack explanation of the correct context in their given definition of the offence of contempt of court, resulting in a realistic potential for confusion. For example, in 'A Fingertip Guide to Criminal Law' (1999), Harper and Hamilton provide a definition that:

Contempt of court is conduct offending against the dignity or authority of a court within or outwith its precincts. (Harper and Hamilton, 1999, p. 60)

The chapter within Harper's text then continues to list cases that contextualize their definition, where individuals have been successfully held in contempt due to their offending the dignity of the court (*John Allan*, 1826; *Young v Lees*, 1998; *Robert Clark or Williamson*, 1829), falling foul of exactly the misinterpretation that Lord President Clyde had highlighted over seventy years prior, whilst providing none of the necessary commentary to highlight that fundamentally, whatever the act that is deemed to constitute contempt, there must be some element of a *serious* and *substantial* interference with the administration of justice (see Contempt of Court Act 1981, UK), and that personal insult in isolation, regardless of personal afront or degrading nature, might not necessarily be legitimately held to be an actionable contempt of court. This is only one example of many texts that misinterpret the definition of contempt of court, however it is an example of the justification for a wider scale analysis of an area where judges have the potential to overreach beyond their legitimately held powers deliberately or unintentionally.

Contempt of court *in facie curiae*, the term being in Latin as many key aspects of legal terminology still are, meaning simply 'in the face of the court'; is the most controversial of the branches of the catch-all category of offences of contempt of court. It is a problematic area of law for several reasons, including the large volume of cases where clear misuse / abuse of power by the judge is present.

Complications emerge when the rules and principles associated with both common law contempt, and statutory contempt are examined in detail. In several common law jurisdictions, as evidenced within this chapter, the legal basis for contempt contains the requirement for the *mens rea* of *intention* to be proven by the prosecution through a fair hearing in order for any criminal finding or sanction to be legitimately applied. Some other countries contain provision for the requisite *mens rea* to be one or other of either *willful* or *excessively careless* conduct (see Muirhead v Douglas, 1979) in whatever act or omission has resulted in a finding of contempt. This requirement for *mens rea* to be established by the prosecution has clear implications on legal rights and safeguards for the defense, as well as on both burden and standard of proof that must be satisfied by the prosecution, leaving several areas as having potential for deliberate or inadvertent incorrect application of judicial power should those essential elements be left unaddressed.

Further problems emerge when considering the question of *objectivity* vs *subjectivity* in matters of contempt *in facie curiae*. This can be explained best by consideration of the question of; when do an individual's undesirable words or actions move beyond simply offending the dignity of the individual judge, which ought not to be actionable in avoiding the judge being seen to be acting in his or her own cause, to becoming something that is truly interfering with the administration of justice in that *serious* and *substantial* manner as required by the law, and then justifying judicial intervention? In other words, the question of when things move beyond subjective disapproval with an individual's conduct to becoming something that objectively speaking would be regarded as a true interference with the administration of justice or legal process that could not be handled without recourse to criminalization of the person responsible.

Often regarded as the seminal academic text about contempt of court, 'The History of Contempt of Court – The Form of Trial and the Mode of Punishment' was authored by *Sir John C. Fox* in 1927. Despite the end of *Pax Britannica* in 1914, at the time of writing there was little by way of varied international comparison for analysis since through the building of the British Empire, British colonial thinking, and jurisprudence had been imposed on several nations and regions which prior to colonization had their own independent judicial systems. This intervention of the British resulted in legal impacts that are still being felt today as will be shown later in this chapter when analysis is carried out of various jurisdictions around the world including former British colonies, many of whom still draw upon either current or in some cases outdated British case law and institutional writers as authorities when making decisions related to current cases. One area of Fox's discussion that must be criticised is when he examines in detail the justification for the use of the summary procedure for contempt *in facie curiae* that:

The modern practice of proceeding summarily to the punishment of contempt of court has been the subject of comment and protest, but the practice is founded upon immemorial usage, has, since the eighteenth century, been generally assumed or has not been expressly questioned by the court. (Fox, 1927, p. 3)

Fox is asserting that the criticisms of the practicing of summary and arbitrary punishment are flawed for the reason that the criticisers are operating on a misconception that the use of the process is only based on ancient tradition, and not on fundamentally sound grounds. He then moves on to spend several chapters examining this concept, particularly looking to the words emanating from parliament, prior existing cases, and legal doctrines. Of particular relevance, Fox looks to the case of *The King v Almon* from 1765. In his analysis of the Almon case, Fox quotes Wilmot's words relating to the summary procedure and contempt:

I have examined very carefully to see if I could find out any vestiges or traces of its introduction but can find none. It is as ancient as any other part of the common law; there is no priority or posteriority to be discovered about it and therefore (it) cannot be said to invade the common law, but to act in an alliance and friendly conjunction with every other provision which the wisdom of our ancestors has established for the general good of society... truth compels me to say that the mode of proceedings... stands upon the very same foundation and basis that trials by juries do – immemorial usage and practice. (Wilmot, 1765, p. 254)

And so, Justice Wilmot's words, relied upon by cases cited by Fox, are unambiguous in that the justification given for the summary process is that the 'wisdom of our ancestors' should not be questioned should its origins be unknown yet clearly ancient. Such a conclusion is so clearly illogical, based on vague and spurious grounds, and would be contemporarily inappropriate to use as an underpinning rationale for an applicable legal doctrine that is still in use today.

Looking in more depth at Wilmot's judgment in *Almon* then, Fox in his justification of Wilmot's words notes that:

The learned judge (Wilmot) argues that... libelling a judge in his judicial capacity is so punishable (summarily)... he points out that by our constitution the King is the fountain of justice and that he delegates his power to the Judges. Wilmot contends that arraignment of the justice of the judges is arraigning the King's justice; that it is an impeachment of his wisdom in the choice of his judges; that is excites dissatisfaction with judicial determinations and indisposes the minds of people to obey them; and this is the most fatal obstruction of justice and calls for a more immediate redress than any other obstruction... The Judges are not vindicating their own cause but the cause of the public. The advantage of a (summary) trial is pointed out. On (summary trial) the party can acquit himself by his own oath, whereas a jury may convict him on false evidence. (Fox, 1927, p. 9)

In analysing Fox's explanation and justification here, there are several flaws in the logic as presented. Firstly, it cannot be legitimately argued that a criticism of an individual judge is a criticism of the Monarch or the State's choice of judge, as over any period after appointment, an individual may go through any number of evolutions in terms of professional and personal circumstances, maturity, political leanings, and other personal characteristics. Personality and life circumstances do not remain static in the same context as they might have been at the time of any appointment having been made. There is no arguable link between the choice of a candidate based on their past experience and what their actions might be in the future, good or bad, desirable or undesirable. Such an assertion by Wilmot and affirmed by Fox would give the judiciary a complete immunity from criticism even in the face of undeniable *de facto* misconduct, and as such to maintain the integrity of the judiciary it *must* be open to criticism and to changing circumstances where these are necessary. This much is indisputable. The *only* legitimate question and debate to be had in this regard relates to the appropriate or inappropriate nature and form of any criticism, not over the appropriateness of legitimate criticism as an isolated concept, which is the unsustainable implication stemming from Wilmot and Fox's interpretations.

Secondly, Fox's discussion of judicial criticism 'exciting the dissatisfaction' of the people and 'indisposing their minds to obey judicial determinations' is never expanded upon or justified with reference to any example where this can be shown to have been the case – it is an unsubstantiated and arguably stereotypical assumption of the masses in both cases, and one which is demonstrably untrue given the trend in a great many jurisdictions in recent decades in removing the offence of *scandalizing the court* altogether from previously standing contempt of court laws.

Thirdly, the assertion that the judge is *never* vindicating their own cause, but *always* that of the public interest has two linked issues; firstly that there are a large number of decided cases, some of which will be discussed within this chapter, where that is simply not the case and are on record as such; and secondly there is an inferred blanket assumption in adopting the stance in question that a utilitarianist jurisprudential approach to tackling contempt of court (punishment for the greater good) is the sole valid approach, which is very much open to challenge.

Finally, the qualification of Wilmot's words by Fox relating to the benefits of the summary procedure are unjustifiable in the context they are used, as whilst there are of course potential benefits and drawbacks of any judicial process, summary and solemn alike, the simplistic justification given by Fox that a jury could simply get it wrong would by his same logic then be a criticism of literally *any* trial by jury, not just in cases of contempt of court. Neither does Fox reflect on the fundamentally important and specific point raised by the defendant in the original Almon case that the judge would "exercise the province of party, judge, evidence and jury" (Fox, 1927, p. 7) which was the crux of the whole case, rather Fox sweeps it under the carpet with the broader idea that a judge is effectively infallible and beyond reproach. The problem with this, is that Fox's perspective is factually flawed as has been demonstrated.

Thankfully, there has been at least some degree of progress towards a recognition that arbitrary findings and summary disposal for contempt of court may be inappropriate in contemporary legal systems as Gordon argues that:

The court should exercise its power to punish on the spot with great discretion and should always allow the "accused" an opportunity to explain his behaviour. It is common practice for judges to order persons guilty of contempt... to be detained until the end of the day or of the trial, and then to deal with them, thus giving them a chance to explain or purge their contempt. (Gordon, 2001, p. 750)

This discussion then appears to ask judges to pause or hesitate prior to making a summary finding of contempt or rushing to judgment and sentence in all but the most unusual of cases rather than act in the heat of the moment and risk making the wrong decision or potentially overreaching on their discretionary powers.

DISCUSSION AND CASES RELATED TO THE WEST / GLOBAL NORTH

Beginning the discussion with England & Wales, where the offence of contempt of court is said to have originated, there is a peculiarity in that some aspects of contempt of court are technically classed as criminal, whilst others are classed as civil. It would be accurate to then highlight that the potential for confusion is high related to what type of process and judicial power is permissible for each different potentially contemptuous act or omission. However, in reality this could be viewed as being at least to some extent a moot point. When discussing the potential for those accused of a contempt that is classed as civil to receive those same safeguards that an individual would have were he accused of a criminal act, Miller highlights the case of *Re Bramblevale Ltd* (1969), in which Lord Denning in his judgment noted that the offence is of criminal character (the potential to receive a custodial sentence in all cases regardless of whether or not it is technically classed as criminal or civil in nature) and so *must* be proven beyond reasonable doubt in all cases, with further corroborating evidence to prove contempt beyond the single opinion of the judge required (*Bramblevale*: 1063). The question of whether Lord Denning's statement is in fact a precedent to be followed though appears to still be in question, as although Miller notes that it "is now firmly settled that the criminal standard of beyond reasonable doubt applies" (Miller, 2000, p. 47), he then also goes on to highlight the case of *West Oxfordshire District Council v Beratec Ltd.* (The Times, 1986), decided nineteen years after *Bramblevale* where the lesser standard of the balance of probabilities was applied, also noting that this has been the standard applied in "at least one subsequent case" (Miller, 2000, p. 47). As such, the choice of Miller's words regarding settled law might be under question. Helpfully, Miller compares the situation to that within other western jurisdictions, noting that Canada adopts the standard of beyond reasonable doubt, whereas the United States of America appears to decide on the standard to be adopted similarly to England and Wales, based on the perceived appropriateness in the specific case in question. Miller eventually concludes that:

...it must be acknowledged that the dividing line between the two forms of contempt has never been drawn with precision, a position which is not helped by the apparent recognition of a hybrid comprised of a contempt which 'savours of criminality'. In particular there are certain grey areas in which the type of contempt involved either is or has been unclear. (Miller, 2000, p. 60-61)

Miller points to opinions from figures such as Sir John Donaldson who has asserted regarding separate civil and criminal contempt that "Whatever the value of this classification in earlier times, I venture to think that it now tends to mislead rather than assist" (*Attorney General v Newspaper Publishing PLC*, 1987, p. 276). In concluding the section then, Miller states that although there is a loose attempt to categorise contempt of court as either civil or criminal in England and Wales, that "the classification of the proceedings under national law is relevant, but not determinative of the issue" (Miller, 2000, p. 68), and that account of other factors including decisions from the European Court of Human Rights could not be ignored by the judiciary, if the judiciary should be challenged on the issue.

Moving on to consider the United States of America, and in looking to the case of *Mayberry v Pennsylvania* (1971), where the defendant repeatedly insulted the presiding judge, labelling him a 'fool', a 'tyrannical old dog', and other similar insults (being clear, these were simply insults and not accompanied by threats), the judge made a summary finding of contempt and sentenced Mayberry to the stunning total of twenty-two years' imprisonment. Both the finding and the sentence were overturned on appeal with the appeal court judging that the initial trial judge had been acting in his own cause, going well beyond any possible legitimate discretionary power he might have had; the subjective personal insults could not be described as having *seriously* interfered with the administration of justice as a finding of contempt of court required, and the judge ought to have applied reasonable professional restraint rather than acting in anger as he did. So how might it be the case that the initial trial judge believed he was acting within his powers? One possible answer might come from the lack of settled law on what can and cannot constitute contempt of court in the USA, with contrasting definitions found within different official sources and authorities.

In the USA contempt of court is a federal offence, and is defined in the Justice manual as:

...an act of disobedience or disrespect towards the judicial branch of the government, or an interference with its orderly process. It is an offense against a court of justice or a person to whom the judicial functions of the sovereignty have been delegated. (United States Department of Justice, 2020, Title 9-39.000)

Again, as with several other jurisdictions, there is a suggestion that words or actions that are purely *disrespectful* may be classed as contempt in their own right without any requirement that the administration of justice is compromised. However, it appears that the given definition is not fully settled when looking to other official authoritative sources. In the United States Code, it reads that the scope of contempt of court is more limited than is suggested in the Justice manual, and this further definition may render the legitimacy of the power to act against behavior that is disrespectful alone more debatable. In the code, the offence is defined more precisely as being:

(1) *Misbehavior of any person in its presence or so near thereto as to obstruct the administration of justice;*
(2) *Misbehavior of any of its officers in their official transactions;*
(3) Disobedience or resistance to its lawful writ, process, order, rule, decree, or command. (United States Code – Power of Court, 2018, p. 401)

Using this second definition then, it ought to at least be arguable by a person accused, that conduct which is purely disrespectful but does not fundamentally obstruct the administration of justice should not be classed as contempt of court. This interpretation is then backed up with further qualifications found within the appeal case of *United States v. McGainey* (1994) where it is noted by Circuit Judge Silberman that there are four specific elements that all must be satisfied for an individual to be held in contempt *in facie curiae*:

These elements are misbehavior of a person, in or near to the presence of the court, which obstructs the administration of justice, and which is committed with the required degree of criminal intent. (McGainey, p. 684)

So, in a further development, Judge Silberman is asserting that unlike in the first two definitions noted where *mens rea* is omitted from those given definitions, in his opinion proof of *mens rea* would be a clear requirement. In relation to the case under consideration then, and to demonstrate the rules then being used in practice Judge Silberman applied the circumstances:

Judge Robinson found that appellant did make the threatening gesture. He concluded that the government witnesses were credible and thought there were inconsistencies and discrepancies in appellant's testimony. The court held that in the context of a major drug trial in progress and considering the content of Nelson's testimony and Mrs. Williams' statements to appellant, appellant's conduct constituted misbehavior in the court's presence with the intent to threaten or intimidate the witness. In doing so it was noted that the appellant's conduct had satisfied all the necessary criteria to be classed as contempt of court. (McGainey, p. 684)

Despite the logical and clear rules set out in this case however, and perhaps due to the previously discussed ambiguity and inconsistency, it might come as no surprise that there have still been some highly questionable judgments in the USA. In particular, there is an affirmed notion found in *United States v. Griffin* (1996) that due to a judge having to take the time during an ongoing case to consider whether an action is interfering with the administration of justice, automatically means that the action *is* interfering with the administration of justice. The major flaw with this approach is of course that it clearly contradicts the regulation noted in the previously discussed United States Code. Using the logic in this case, literally any disruption to proceedings could be classed as contempt regardless of the existence or otherwise of any *truly* prejudicial effect on the administration of justice.

As criticised elsewhere there appears to be evidence of at least isolated examples where abuse of the summary procedure for contempt can be found. In the appeal case of *F.T.C. v. Trudeau* (2010) it was noted that the appellant had been called by a judge to a criminal contempt hearing based on several 'hate' emails received by the judge, apparently at the request of Mr Trudeau who on his own radio show had criticised the same judge for an earlier ruling. On conducting a summary contempt hearing the judge immediately found the appellant to be in contempt and sentenced him to thirty days in prison. On appeal however, the appeal court judges decided that:

The use of the summary contempt power is proper only for charges of misconduct, in open court, in the presence of the judge, which disturbs the court's business, where all of the essential elements of the misconduct are under the eye of the court, are actually observed by the court, and where immediate punishment is essential to prevent `demoralization of the court's authority' before the public. (Trudeau, p. 386)

As such, to be within the law the case ought to have been referred to a prosecutor for consideration and then, if necessary, the accused should have been prosecuted before a jury for determination. And so related to the USA, there is evidence of potential miscarriages of justice happening through misuse or abuse of power by a judge that would only come to light should the individual accused of contempt lodge an appeal to a court further up the hierarchy for further determination.

It does appear however at that point at least, that there is some consistency in the USA in the recognition of the issue of the professional requirement to be restrained when the matter is appealed to more senior courts. Stewart (2003) highlights the case of *re Jones*, where a fight broke out between two judges in Louisiana, and explains that:

The incident attracted local and national attention for several weeks and even served as the brunt of jokes from various comedians.... The Louisiana Supreme Court concluded that "widespread knowledge of the incident could only serve to stigmatize the fourth circuit... in the minds of persons waiting to be interviewed... employees... as well as citizens who read about it in the newspaper or saw it on the television." The Louisiana Supreme Court suspended Judge Jones without pay for thirty days on the grounds that he failed to restrain his temper in the course of performing his judicial duty. (Stewart, 2003, p. 470)

So, whilst the context in *re jones* might have been two judges fighting, the overarching consideration that the Supreme Court had was in the importance of judges being restrained in their personal behaviour when discharging their judicial duty. Several other of the cases highlighted in this chapter would appear *prima facie* to contain elements of judges with similar failures to act with appropriate restraint in the performance of their professional duties.

The problem does remain however, that judges in lower courts do still appear to act significantly beyond their powers, relying on the matter being brought to the attention of a higher court for scrutiny before the overreach is discovered and confirmed. Stewart highlights the case of *re Hoague*, in which a judge had personally witnessed a vehicle being driven on the road in a manner he subjectively perceived to be 'reckless and erratic'. The judge wrote a personal letter on official court stationary, which took the tone of an official court document summoning the driver to his courtroom on threat of both prosecution and seizure of the driver's vehicle. When the driver, arguably tricked into appearing in the courtroom, was present, Judge Hoague stated "You can say whatever you want, but at this point in time you had probably best shut your mouth until I'm finished talking" (Stewart, 2003, p. 472). It is quite astonishing with such a deceptive and arguably fraudulent abuse of power that the result of this judicial misconduct hearing was for Judge Hoague to be:

...disciplined for misuse of judicial office and suspended for six months, with the suspension stayed on the condition that he did not violate the Ohio Code of Judicial Conduct again. (Stewart, 2003, p. 472)

Such a lenient disciplinary result for such a serious abuse of power is quite simply not justifiable. That a judge in this context should only receive effectively a suspended sentence with no immediate effect whatsoever is a decision that could be argued to have the effect of reducing the credibility of the professionalism of the judiciary in the mind of the reasonable ordinary person. A further argument could be presented that such a lenient sanction could reasonably be perceived as the judiciary looking after its own personnel in a potentially corrupt fashion.

Moving from the USA to Canada then, the criminal law is almost entirely codified, with actionable offences being found split between the criminal code (1985) and within Federal statutes. Perhaps somewhat oddly then, some aspects of contempt of court such as *in facie curiae* are effectively the only criminal offences in the country which are still decided on a purely common law basis.

The superior courts in Canada are viewed as having an inherent power to punish contempt of court, and whilst changes could theoretically be made to the jurisdiction of the courts in this area, they would require a constitutional amendment as clarified within *MacMillan Bloedel Ltd. v. Simpson* (1995) where the judges in the case explained relating to their own powers that:

Although the inherent jurisdiction of superior courts is difficult to define, there is no doubt that the power to punish for all forms of contempt is within that jurisdiction. The rule of law requires a judicial system that can ensure that its orders are enforced, and its process respected... To remove the power to punish contempt... would maim the institution which is at the heart of our judicial system. Such an alteration is impermissible in Canada in the absence of a constitutional amendment. (MacMillan Bloedel, p. 3)

Whilst the argument for the necessity to punish behaviour that might be regarded as contempt of court is of course sound, in rebuttal to their argument however, questions still remain over why such a process must involve a summary / arbitrary procedure, and whether or not it is truly entirely appropriate for the judge in the court to carry the potential role of witness, prosecutor and judge simultaneously, or whether their decisions in this regard should be open to wider scrutiny through a requirement to refer potential contempt on to a different judge to deal with appropriately from a neutral position. No substance at even a minimal level is provided that might substantiate why such a process of referral would 'maim' the judiciary.

In terms of a Canadian definition of contempt of court *in facie curiae*, the Law Reform Commission of Canada began a lengthy process with the intention of reforming the law in this area in 1977, with the working paper eventually leading to a report in 1982 (Muldoon et al., 1982). Part of the major problem however with the 1982 report is that there is no overarching definition given for the offence in Canada. The only definitions given are the listing of specific acts that are viewed as being contemptuous in nature. As highlighted within the report when discussing confusion regarding the offence amongst ordinary citizens:

Can citizens really be blamed, though, for not being familiar with an offence which is not defined by statute, and whose rules are essentially contained within case law? The Commission is of the view that... a precise definition of them, will make it possible to dispel this impression (negative criticism of the offence), at least partially, by 'demystifying' certain concepts and explaining clearly the rationale for having the offences. (Muldoon et al., 1982, p. 5)

Perhaps bizarrely then, given the explicit acknowledgement of the issue, and as already mentioned, there is no attempt then made to define the overarching offence of contempt of court; instead, the is a simple list of offences is outlined as being:

- *obstruction of justice*
- *disruption of judicial proceedings*
- *defiance of judicial authority*
- *affront to judicial authority*
- *interference with judicial proceedings (sub judice)* (Muldoon et al., 1982, p. 21)

One is left to wonder why the offence as per the report was left so vaguely defined, and one point, admittedly conjecture, might be that the judiciary as the main stakeholder may not have found the thought of their powers being limited in this regard to be desirable. It is useful to look though at some of the extended discussion of the potential named offences listed as that discussion does give an insight into the minds of those proposing the updates in question. When covering disruption of judicial proceedings for example, discussion of avoiding the use of power to hold an individual in contempt for behaviour that might be insulting or offensive though with no true effect on the administration is enlightening:

...the offence of disruption of judicial proceedings must not be charged, firstly, to turn harmless or careless acts of discourtesy into criminal offences. In the vast majority of cases, a warning from the bench will be sufficient to restore order... Only serious misconduct... should be declared a criminal offence. (Muldoon et al., 1982, p. 22)

Looking to the detail of this point then, the inclusion of the term *harmless* indicates that there is an understanding that although technically briefly disruptive, many acts may not in fact cause any notable or lasting *harm* or effects beyond personally hurt feeling, and do not in fact have any *substantial* effect on the administration of justice. The use of the term *careless* and the argument surrounding it would also preclude any possibility of strict liability being applicable, as there would have to be consideration given to the state of mind of the individual accused of contempt. In other words, the argument presented would result in an absolute requirement for *mens rea* to be established in all cases of potential contempt of court.

The 1982 report did in fact progress to become a draft Bill in 1984, attempting to codify and clarify the law of contempt based on the report's findings and recommendations. This was very much a step toward potentially positive reform. However, when there was a change in Canadian political administration whilst the Bill was making its way through the different legislative stages, the Bill was shelved indefinitely, and no further attempt to date has been made to attempt any reform in the area. As such, the laws relating to contempt of court in Canada remain vague, poorly defined, and inconsistent with all other criminal laws in the country, leaving judges with an unsatisfactorily wide discretion in terms of how they can apply their powers, including the ongoing use of the summary procedure some four decades after the country was on the verge of abolishing it.

Although the country of Latvia might not spring immediately to mind as an obvious next choice for discussion, on the issue of potential misuse of power in the context of contempt of court, Latvia was a major talking point in the early part of the twenty-first century. In the case of *Zaicevs v. Latvia* (2001), Vasilijs Zaicevs was a solicitor working for a non-governmental organisation that had the remit "…to protect the rights of retired, disabled and less well-off persons and other vulnerable categories." (*Zaicevs*, p. 6) He accompanied one of his clients to a District Court to collect a record of a hearing held a few days earlier and had visited the office of the judge who had been responsible for the case. The judge did not allow a copy of the record to be given and asked that Zaicevs and his client leave the office immediately. After having left, the judge immediately filed a report that:

Mr Zaicevs burst into my office without permission, disturbing me at my work, and rudely demanded information to which he was not entitled, thus acting in flagrant breach of the rules [of conduct] within the precincts of a court and displaying a lack of respect. Vasilijs Zaicevs thereby infringed Article 201-39 of the Regulatory Offences Code. The offending party is unable to offer an explanation, having left the premises. (Zaicevs, p. 8)

Under the provisions mentioned by the judge, he was filing a motion for Zaicevs to be held in contempt of court, which is defined under Article 201-39 of the Latvian Regulatory Offences Code as being:

Contempt of court in the form of refusal on the part of a witness, victim or civil party or [their] representatives, a legal representative, expert, specialist, interpreter or participant in a civil case, or any other person, to comply with the orders of the presiding judge by failing to observe the rules during the hearing or by any conduct displaying flagrant disregard for the rules governing the hearing or the court, shall be punishable by a fine of two hundred and fifty latis or a period of administrative detention of up to fifteen days. (Zaicevs, p. 22)

To further justify the reasoning for his seeking a hearing for contempt of court, the judge also sent an explanatory note to the acting president of the court in the following terms:

On 20 July 2000, at around 11.30 a.m., I was working in my office ..., preparing a judgment in another case. The door of the office opened suddenly and Vasilijs Zaicevs and [Ņ.L.] burst in without permission.

In flagrant breach of the secrecy of deliberations, Vasilijs Zaicevs demanded, rudely and in a loud voice, that I provide him with a copy of the record in the case of [Ņ.L.]. I explained calmly that it was not our practice to provide copies of records. Vasilijs Zaicevs began shouting more loudly, demanding that

[N.L.'s] supposed rights be respected. He waved his mobile phone around and threatened to call the public prosecutor's office. As the two [visitors] refused to leave the office, I stood up and went towards the registry office in order to summon a security officer.

Zaicevs' conduct demonstrated a gross lack of respect for the court, in flagrant breach of the rules [of conduct] applicable within the precincts of a court: he not only addressed me in an impolite tone, but also issued threats, entered a judge's office without permission and breached the secrecy of deliberations. (Zaicevs, p. 9)

A similar account of the situation to that of the judge was given by a member of the court registry department who had been present throughout the incident.

Contextually it may be of some value to understand that the Latvian Administrative Procedure Law, enacted in 2004 and having not been amended from its prior iteration in this section give explicit requirements in sections 138 and 139 that in simple matters the minutes of court sitting must be signed no later than three days after the hearing, and in complex matters no more than five days (S.138), and participants involved in the hearing then have a further three days in order to identify and request changes to be made to the record (S.139), As such, it appears that Zaicevs was both entitled to receive the minutes in question, and indeed had a pressing and time-sensitive reason for wanting to acquire these. The question might be legitimately asked if the judge then, at least to some extent, might have contributed to the situation through the apparent failure to meet these strict legal obligations.

In any case, and regardless of this point, Zaicevs was ordered to appear at the District Court for a hearing to determine if he had been in contempt of court but did not attend. A few days later, he was representing a different client at the same court and after those proceedings he was given a summons for a contempt hearing into his earlier actions. Zaicevs then asked for permission to see copies of the documents containing evidence relating to the accusation against him but was refused by the acting President of the court. At this point, Zaicevs then wrote a letter of complaint regarding the refusal of access to information pertaining to his case to both the public prosecutor's office and the Latvian Minister of Justice. He was finally given access to the seven documents relating to his case, but only on the same day as that of his hearing. Perhaps on recognition of the inherent unfairness in being expected to prepare a defence at so little notice, the contempt hearing was postponed for two days.

When the hearing took place, Zaicevs contested the submitted written account of what the judge had alleged to have taken place. He requested that the judge should be summoned to give testimony in court but was told that there was no such provision that gave an individual accused of contempt the right to make such a demand. At the end of the hearing, predictably, Zaicevs was held in contempt and sentenced to three days imprisonment, in Latvia classed as *'administrative detention'* (*Zaicevs*, p. 16). This was based solely on the written accounts of the situation from the original judge and member of registry, and without Zaicevs having had the opportunity in court to test the evidence. In addition, Zaicevs on indicating his intention to appeal discovered that in the words of Article 279 of the Latvian Regulatory Offences Code it explicitly stated that "Any order given by a judge of the court… imposing a penalty for a regulatory offence shall be final and shall not be amenable to appeal…" (*Zaicevs*, p. 22) As a result, Zaicevs was imprisoned for the three days prescribed, with no opportunity to contest the decision.

In light then of a Latvian Constitutional Court judgment a few months later in which the lack of right of appeal in administrative matters where the offence can be declared comparable to a criminal offence, was declared to be incompatible with Article 6 of the European Convention on Human Rights

(ECHR), Zaicevs launched an appeal to the European Court of Human Rights (ECtHR). The Bench in the ECtHR examined Protocol No.7 related to Article 2 (the right of appeal in criminal proceedings) of the Convention, and in particular to its explanatory notes where it is clarified that:

Paragraph 2 of the article permits exceptions to this right of review by a higher tribunal:

- for offences of a minor character, as prescribed by law....

...When deciding whether an offence is of a minor character, an important criterion is the question of whether the offence is punishable by imprisonment or not. (Protocol No.7 ECHR, pp. 20-21)

Based on this then, the decision of the Bench of the ECtHR was simple and clear when they judged that:

Having regard to the aim of Article 2 and the nature of the guarantees for which it provides, the Court is satisfied that an offence for which the law prescribes a custodial sentence as the main punishment cannot be described as "minor" within the meaning of the second paragraph of that Article. As to the classification of the offence in national law, the Court has already pointed out that this has only a relative value. The exception invoked by the Government is therefore not applicable in the present case. (Zaicevs, p. 55)

Without making any judgment then on the substantive issue as to whether or not the actual conduct by Zaicevs might or might not constitute a contempt, the ECtHR did clarify that if a contempt of court is penalised by way of a 'criminal' sanction such as imprisonment, then regardless of the criminal or civil classification of the offence in any particular jurisdiction, for appeals purposes at least it *must* be treated in the same way as a criminal offence in all procedural circumstances.

In some of the final words of the ECtHR judgment, the wording makes it extremely clear as to how seriously they viewed the situation when they emphasised that:

However, this does nothing to alter the situation of the applicant, who was exposed to the full effects of the provision in question and therefore continues to be a "victim" of the alleged violation. (Zaicevs, p. 56)

It seems then that the judiciary and individual judges in some jurisdictions may take the matter of contempt, and by association the liberty of their citizens altogether too lightly in categorising and then attempting to defend their conduct in such a situation as that in the case of Zaicevs. There appeared to be several problematic areas in which Zaicevs had been genuinely compromised by the unlawful misuse of power by the judge and wider judiciary on one hand, and unlawful removal of legal safeguards that should have been lawfully granted to the accused on the other. Latvia has since amended their laws to allow for appeals in such matters, however it should not be the case that an individual who has suffered at the hands of such an obvious misuse or abuse of power must rely upon taking such extreme action as referring a matter to an international court to have such an obviously unfair use of power declared as such.

DISCUSSION AND CASES RELATED TO THE GLOBAL SOUTH / AFRICA

Perhaps unsurprisingly given the colonial history of much of the African continent, the early development of summary and arbitrary punishment by African courts for use against citizens for the offence of contempt of court can be found to have overtly and explicitly racist and colonial rationalisation. In the case of *Rex v Thomas Horatius Jackson*, the first reported case of contempt of court in Nigeria from 1925, the Chief Justice in the case relied on a passage found in an earlier British case from 1899 in which emphasis is made of the need for summary justice to follow potential contempt, though in limited circumstances which exclude the judge vindicating his or her own cause. Such qualifications and exceptions appear initially to be sensible. However, the passage takes a sinister turn when discussing the now generally accepted obsolescence of the need to punish for scandalising the court when it then notes:

But it must be considered that in small colonies, mainly of coloured populations, the enforcement in proper cases of contempt of court for attacks on the court may be absolutely necessary to preserve in such a community the dignity of and respect for the court. (Lord Morris, para. 1899)

In other words, the system of common law established by British rule in this regard explicitly set out that there should be one rule of relaxation for those of European or white descent, and a harsher, more punitive rule on the same issue for local indigenous populations grounded in precise notions of racial superiority. In that 1925 case, not only did Chief Justice Combe not dissent from the prior opinion, instead he declared that he did not accept that scandalising the court was obsolete and that matters could proceed on that basis. He declared that,

If he was satisfied that the circulation of the newspaper in question was mainly confined to the intelligent section of the community, he would have left the matter to public opinion. But unfortunately, the paper was widely read by the masses, whose confidence in the independence and justice of the court could be undermined... The sentence was therefore upheld. (Rewane, 1957, p. 175)

In this judgment then, no explicit reference was made to colonising and indigenous population, though the clear intention to consider some sections of society to be beyond reproach, with others highly corruptible, along with the inferences in the terms 'intelligent section' and 'masses' is almost certainly referring to segregation along those colonial lines.

Interestingly, Rewane in conducting some comparative analysis, noted the Kenyan case of *Rex v John Sylvanus Rathbone and others*, which had itself relied upon a judgment from Sierra Leone that had set out "In this country every court of record is the sole judge and exclusive judge of what amounts to a contempt of court." (*Rainy v Sierra Leone*, 1853) This could be argued to be the most extreme of positions to take in that it views each individual court as having its own inherent power to determine whether an individual should be summarily punished for contempt regardless of any existing jurisprudence or precedent relating to the matter. At the time, such a viewpoint in terms of the almost unlimited power of the judge was perhaps not as unusual as it might be deemed in contemporary times.

Having examined historical case law and legal opinion within the jurisdictions of Nigeria, Kenya and Sierra Leone then, the next issue to ascertain is if the law and associated powers of the judge have developed or progressed substantially since those times in the nineteenth and twentieth centuries.

In consideration of Nigeria, perhaps the most powerful of examples on how the law has developed in this regard can be found from examination of the transcript from the 2010 appeal case of the *Federal Republic of Nigeria v Joe Brown Akubueze*, where the Supreme Court set aside an earlier conviction and sentence for contempt of court after they judged that the appellant had not received a fair trial. In the earlier first instance case, the accused had been accused of the illegal importation of heroin into Nigeria and had not given any testimony in the early part of the trial. However, during the course of the trial, his counsel had been "harassed out of the proceedings" (*Akubueze*, p. 4), and the accused was ordered to secure new counsel within seven days, whilst he was remanded in prison custody, and in reality, was given no opportunity to source alternative counsel. Regardless, the court continued the trial despite the lack of counsel, and at its conclusion the accused was found guilty, sentenced to life and with a total of over a hundred-year sentence with hard labour. Unsurprisingly, upon conviction the accused was dissatisfied and appealed the verdict and sentence. That initial appeal was successful, and an order was made for a retrial. The prosecution, disagreeing made a further appeal leading to the specific case under analysis.

The appeal judges, on examining the detail of the initial proceedings noted that the lawyer for the accused had been initially held in contempt for what appeared to be a perfectly reasonable line of questioning of a witness, who he then argued was attempting to prevaricate. He had asked for the court's protection to intervene and compel the witness to answer the questions put to him. Instead, the judge made the extraordinary decision that it was the defence counsel himself who was delaying proceedings, stating:

The record here shows the deliberate attempt of defence counsel to delay these proceedings and to frustrate this trial. This is most unbecoming and unethical behaviour from a legal practitioner who is an officer of the court. For this contempt shown to this proceedings counsel is to be remanded forthwith till tomorrow when he will show cause why he should not be punished for said contempt. (Akubueze, pp. 8-9)

In other words, with no delay, option to present a case or defence, and no opportunity for representations (since the opportunity the next day was effectively to provide mitigation as to sentence), the judge found the defence counsel guilty of contempt, with an initial short custodial sentence. This threat from the judge effectively coerced the defence counsel into making an apology at that short hearing, where the judge then discharged the contempt finding, but on further threat that the contempt would be reinstated if he were to "repeat this bad behaviour in court" (*Akubueze*, p. 9). Understandably, at that point the counsel asked to be recused altogether from the case as he felt he could no longer provide a strong defence for his client under the conditions and was granted the request. It was through this combination of factors that the appeal court felt the first instance court judge herself had effectively harassed the defence counsel out of the case, leaving the accused in the position of lacking formal representation. The appeal court judged that:

...it was the tribunal that deliberately harassed and hounded out Mr. Etudo, learned counsel for the respondent. It would be unreasonable for Mr. Etudo to continue in the unfortunate situation in which he found himself. After all, his reputation and career were on the line... I do not for one minute see what Mr. Etudo did to warrant the invocation of contempt charge. Interference with his independent examination of a witness and his asking for court's protection is diametrically averse to civilized notion of fair trial. A fortiori if the counsel, as herein, is threatened with punishment for doing his lawful duty. What the trial judge did in this case, to say the least, is unconscionable of her function of holding an even keel or balance. The bludgeoning of counsel by the tribunal had its desired effect. The conduct of the tribunal was not only unfair; it was exceedingly high handed and therefore deprecated. (Akubueze, pp. 10-11)

As such, the Supreme court could not have been clearer in their reasoned judgment that the judge in the first instance court had been incorrect, using significantly damning reference to her deliberate (i.e., intentional) actions and the bludgeoning effects of her actions. Importantly then, the Supreme court turned its attention specifically to the powers of the judge, clarifying that:

Perhaps I need to remind the learned trial judge that invocation of the power to punish for contempt as done by her in this case, in the prevailing circumstance, is an unwarranted exhibition of raw and naked judicial power. I repeat that such is highly deprecated. It should have been avoided in the first instance. After all, the rationale for contempt is the need to vindicate the dignity of the court as an institution and, thereby, protect it from denigration and ensure due administration of justice. It is not to bolster the power, dignity, and ego of the judge as an individual. Worse, by such an unwarranted exhibition of naked judicial power which put counsel and his client in fear of the tribunal, an important trammel of fair hearing had been eroded. (Akubueze, p. 12)

In the context of Nigeria then, it is clear that the application of the law by the judiciary in this area has progressed considerably from how it stood in the earlier examined twentieth century cases, or at least for any judges who might continue misuse their power in an inappropriately arbitrary or summary manner, such overreaches will be corrected by a superior court when discovered. As an important note however, based on the evidence of this recent case law, it may be the case that some individual judges continue misuse their power until an overreach comes to light as it did in *Akubuese*.

A further important consideration here is that in Nigeria there appears to be a discrepancy between the case law on one hand, and written statute on the other. In *Akubuese*, and in other cases (see Chief Dibia v. Chief Ezigwe (1998) 9 NWLR 564), a specific rationale is repeated that powers of contempt exist to protect the *dignity* and *honour* of the court, whereas in Chapter 14 Section 133 of the Nigerian Criminal Code Act, on the subject of contempt of court the consistently used term throughout is *disrespect* shown toward the court, with no mention in any section of the terms *dignity* and / or *honour*. This is somewhat surprising in that to be enforceable; laws are generally required to be written in clear, precise, and consistent terms, something that is not the case on examination of the Nigerian context. With a lack of such clarity, it is perhaps unsurprising that some judges might derive their own meaning and relevance of application, reasonably so or otherwise.

In Kenya, the country initially did not rely upon any specific contempt laws, rather the courts applied foreign jurisprudence until 1967, when officially as per Section 5 of the Kenyan Judicature Act 1967 the country officially adopted the English provisions verbatim being one of the United Kingdom's most important colonial jurisdictions. This remained the case until very recently when Kenya finally enacted their own national legal instrument, the Contempt of Court Act 2016, which came into force in January 2017. The objectives of the now updated law are set out in section three, which similar to the application set out in Nigeria notes in S.3(a) that it is to "uphold the dignity and authority of the court", as well as four further key objectives which give the courts a wide range of circumstances in which they have the power to make decisions on potentially contemptuous actions. Somewhat surprisingly, when the global trend as previously noted has been to remove notions of scandalizing the court in favour of the ability of people to scrutinise the court and its decisions in the name of transparency, Kenya through its 2016 Act, instead, in S4. (b)(i) has reaffirmed that this is viewed as criminal contempt. Perhaps even more surprisingly, S7. (1) sets the default position as being that "An offence of contempt of court shall be tried summarily and the court shall keep a record of the proceedings", and whilst provision is made in S7. (2) for transfer of proceedings to an independent procedure, this is very much noted as a secondary consideration to the summary one. Even more confusing then, is that S7(3) outlines that these proceedings "shall not take away the right of any person to a fair trial" which does not align with the default summary procedure set out in subsection one, which *de facto* is an inherently unfair procedure from the outset.

This unfairness can be explained clearly from the perspective that the Act itself explicitly sets out in S10. (1) that the only type of contempt to which strict liability (the lack of requirement to establish *mens rea*) is applied is for publication related contempt of court, whereas all other forms of contempt, including contempt in the face of the court requires proof of *mens rea* that the conduct in question was carried out wilfully. With the requirement for proof of *mens rea*, it is incompatible with fair trial principles for the burden of proof to then be placed upon the accused to *disprove* the presence of *mens rea*, rather the burden of establishing *mens rea* must rest upon the prosecution for the process to be deemed fair in line with those universal fair trial requirements.

The theoretical unfairness of the current law is further established when examining the procedural rules, as Part IV of the Act on Contempt of Court proceedings, S25. (a) sets out that the accused person will be informed in writing of the contempt they have been charged with, before continuing in S25. (b) to allow them the opportunity to then present a defence. No provision is set out to require that *mens rea* is proven by the prosecution, and no guidance is included to ensure that the burden on the prosecution to prove that *mens rea* must be discharged, despite the explicit requirement for *mens rea* having already been established. Overall, it would be difficult to contend that the current laws are fit for purpose in this context, or that they provide sufficient guidance on when it would truly be appropriate for Kenyan judges to use their powers in a legitimate manner. Instead, these laws appear to be significantly open to allowing such judicial overreaches to continue through some of the substantive content, as well as the poor construction of the legislation in a technical sense.

In consideration of the above, it is unsurprising that the revised laws on contempt in Kenya have had to be tested and clarified through the courts themselves, and in 2018 the Kenyan Supreme Court was faced with a case that raised questions on when actions that heavily criticised the Kenyan judiciary might be legitimately classed as being contempt of court. In *Republic of Kenya v Ahmad Abolfathi Mohammed & another*, the court was tasked with examining:

...scenarios of conduct bordering on contempt, which this Court must signal, reprimand, and for the future, prescribe lines to be adhered to by any Advocate canvassing his or her client's case. (Mohammed & another, 2018, para. [1])

It is here that caution must be taken then as with any international comparative study where there may be differences between what a law says on paper on one hand, and how it is actually applied in practice on the other. In this context, the issue is what is set out in writing within the 2016 Act, compared to what the Kenyan courts are actually doing in terms of use of discretionary power on the other. In the case in question, it could be legitimately held that the specific comments made by the subject of the proceedings were some of the most disparaging that could possibly be made about the court. For example:

This Court is exercising illegitimate political power without any lawful jurisdiction over the respondents. Moreover, this case is a clear instance where the Court is acting as a surrogate of the State to legitimize the illegal and unlawful detention of the respondent (Mohammed & another, para. [2](i))

...we wish to state in the most emphatic manner that the Court is biased against the respondents, lacks impartiality, and the very minimum ingredient of independence from the State and its agents in this case is absent... (Mohammed & another, para. [2](ii))

This Court is a jurisprudential train wreck!!! It is incoherent. It is unpersuasive. It is unfaithful to the Constitution and is churning out constitutional interpretations that are at best, counterfeit. (Mohammed & another, para. [2](iii))

In summary, the various statements that were made allege illegitimate use of power, lack of independence, political bias, and effectively fraudulent behaviour. Scarcely could a more serious set of allegations be viewed as striking harder at the core ethics to which a judiciary must be held to and the potential effects that such allegations might have on both the institution and its individual judges. And yet the Supreme court, showed significant restraint in describing them as merely "conduct bordering on contempt" (*Mohammed & another*: para. [1]) as noted above. Indeed, the court did not overlook the various allegations, describing them as "a mode of address deliberately chosen, even though studiously insolent and impertinent, condescending and offensive" (*Mohammed & another*, para. [3]). It should not be a surprise then, that the court established that there was the possibility of a finding of contempt of court by denoting that "he was evincing wilful disrespect for the authority of the Court, conducting himself in a manner certainly calculated to lower the dignity of the Court" (*Mohammed & another*, para. [4]). The court's description of the conduct contains the specific wording necessary in order to make a finding of contempt, whether defined by the 2016 Act (using the term wilful *disrespect*), or from the case law (in discussion of the lowered *dignity* of the court). However, unexpectedly perhaps given the specifically constructed wording used by the court, the ruling continues to explain that "We may draw example from the law relating to contempt - even though we are not applying it in this instance" (*Mohammed & another*, para. [19]) before setting out hypothetical circumstances in which an individual might find themselves in contempt and effectively establishing a jurisprudence to be followed in future cases "signalling lines of caution and prescribing governing principles for future situations" (*Mohammed & another*, para. [24]).

It appears to be the case in *Mohammed & another*, that the court understood the difficulties with the lack of clarity and precision if the 2016 Act, and so rather than apply a law which lacked certainty, instead the Supreme Court took the opportunity to establish a more focused jurisprudence that could be followed from that point on, rather than risk a potential misuse of power or overreach by applying an approach that was not in place at the time the conduct in the case before them had taken place. In other words, the judiciary were careful to avoid such an overreach, even if their actions may have been in clear good faith. This is a commendable and appropriately restrained position to have adopted until the necessary clarity was provided and avoided any potential allegation of an of abuse of power.

To establish what the future Kenyan approach to contempt of court should be, the Supreme Court conduced an examination of similar provisions for punishment of different forms of misconduct in the court in several different sources of law, including Kenya's Advocates Act, Supreme Court Act, and further examples of case law. The court then gave its carefully reasoned judgment that:

We thus, in this instance, make it plain that counsel shall not engage in such course of conduct as is depicted in this ruling, and any default in that regard, in the future, shall occasion contempt-of-court proceedings, with the inevitable consequences, and if not, then appropriate sanctions for contempt in the face of the Court. (Mohammed & another, para. [29])

Considering the judgment then, although it is clearly the case that the underpinning legislation is poorly constructed and contradictory, this is not a fault of the judiciary, rather the responsibility of the legislature. The judiciary have shown clear restraint and a caution to guard against any potential deliberate or unintentional misuse of power. Instead, the top of the Kenyan court hierarchy has sought to establish a clear jurisprudence to adopt even when faced with the most potentially inflammatory examples of what in most jurisdictions would be regarded as being a clear case of contempt of court. As the publication of this ruling only took place in March 2019, it remains to be seen how these powers will be used in practice in the future, or if there will be consistency of approach or further discrepancies in individual cases.

For Sierra Leone, the Local Courts Act 2011 sets out in S.47 what constitutes contempt of court, with the provisions concise and on initial examination also appearing precise in nature. There are, however, still some issue when subject to significant scrutiny. The safeguard against undue power overreach appears to be in place at first reading, with a more stringent *mens rea* requirement than that in either Nigeria or Kenya; the requirement for *intention* to be shown relating to any insult (S.47(a)) or interruption (S.47(b)) of the court. *Intention* is a significantly more difficult *mens rea* to prove and is unusual in contempt proceedings where most jurisdictions instead rely on conduct only having to be *wilful* in nature. However, there are two major criticisms that can be made of Sierra Leone's provisions. Firstly, the only procedure explicitly noted for contempt of court is the summary procedure which has already been heavily criticised in terms of its legitimacy, and secondly, reference is made to a potential means of exculpation for an accuse where there is lawful excuse for the possible contempt, but no guidance or examples are given anywhere in the legislation as to what such a lawful excuse might be in this context.

As evidenced in the Kenyan context, to establish the reality of the way in which power is used in practice however, it is crucial again to look at what is actually happening in the Sierra Leone courts to gain clarity on how those courts are in fact using their powers. Unfortunately, in this regard, there is comparatively little to draw on as very few cases of contempt appear to have been transcribed and made publicly accessible. One case of note, though pre-dating the discussed legislation, is the *Attorney General and Another v Dr. Will*, a Supreme Court case from 2000. Here, an experienced defence counsel (Dr Jabbi) during the course of a case where he was defending his client (Dr Will) in, had sent a letter to the Supreme Court of Sierra Leone, and whilst the contents of the letter have not been transcribed, it is clear on reading the account given in the contempt hearing that it contained a number of potentially damaging and / or insulting statements related to the court and judges within it. The summary proceedings for contempt were then applied, with the opening paragraphs of the transcribed hearing asking for Dr Jabbi "to show cause why the contents thereof should not be deemed to be contemptuous of the Court" (*Attorney General and Another v Dr. Will*, 2000, p. 1), in other words that the burden of proof is immediately placed on the defence in the case, with the presumption being in favour of a guilty finding, unless the court could be persuaded otherwise. Dr Jabbi gave a lengthy explanation setting out several points that, by law, ought to have resulted in deliberation and response by the multi-judge panel. For example, clearly trying to negate the requisite *mens rea*, Dr Jabbi argued that:

...the letter was not by any stretch of the imagination intended to be contemptuous. I have profoundest respect not only for the Supreme Court of Sierra Leone but for every member individually and personally of the Supreme Court of Sierra Leone and indeed for all Courts, Justices, and officers of the Judiciary of Sierra Leone. Far be it from me to ever contemplate the contempt towards any of the officers of the Court. I have not consciously or intentionally done so in the said letter of 15th March... (Dr. Will, 2000, pp. 1-2)

Such a statement in defence should, if following a fair process, have required a substantive analysis and justification of the already inferred *mens rea* of *intention*, as the establishment of that *mens rea* is necessary as has been clarified under S47. (a) of the underpinning legislation when the contempt relates to insults as noted previously. Without having established that *mens rea*, a finding of contempt in this regard should not stand. Dr Jabbi continued to make an impassioned plea for any potential contempt to be purged, and indeed suggested an alternative resolution to the issue, stating:

I did not intend to be contemptuous towards this Court. I very much regret that the said letter has given that effect... And I unreservedly withdraw the parts of the letter that have given that effect... I respectfully urge your Lordships to accept my unreserved apologies for it and to also accept my plea that it be totally withdrawn and effaced both from the records end your memories. (Dr. Will, 2000, p. 2)

Such a course of action has been implemented in the past in other jurisdictions, where an unreserved apology related to potential contempt of court has been deemed purge any inflammatory or insulting statements, with them then removed from the record, and this could have been a chosen course of action by the judiciary here. However, this was not to be the case. In fact, a further statement by Dr Jabbi should again have resulted in a substantive legal discussion when he then effectively pled guilty to an offence that does not exist when he made the admission:

My Lords, on the basis of my acceptance of the offset, of the letter as unintentionally amounting to a contempt and on the basis of my unreserved acceptance of that effect and the parts of the letter and on the basis of my apology and undertaking I urge your Lordships to graciously treat the contempt as purged. (Dr. Will, 2000, p. 2)

So, whilst Dr Jabbi was effectively tendering the equivalent to a guilty plea related to the accusation of contempt, in the terms that he did this should categorically not have been accepted by the panel. To reaffirm the crucial factor here, the requirement for *mens rea* of *intention* to be proven in the context of insult is absolute, and without the existence of such intention, the matter cannot be legally regarded as contempt of court under the laws of Sierra Leone. The discussion that did not, but should then have then taken place between the judges in the case in order for any finding of contempt to validated can be summarised thus:

1. Is there a potentially *prima facie* case of contempt of court?
2. Can the court legally accept the guilty plea to an *unintentional* contempt?
3. Can the necessary *mens rea* of *intention* be inferred, with consideration given to the representations of the accused?

In answer to each of these, although it has not been possible to examine the letter in question, the answer is yes to question one, given the in-depth discussions from the contempt hearing. For question two, the answer is an unequivocal no. There is no basis in the laws of Sierra Leone to depart from the underpinning requirement for intention to be established. This is a clear and unambiguous requirement where the potentially contemptuous conduct is through insulting the judge or court. The professional and legal responsibility of the judges in this case therefore would have been to outline in their judgment explicitly why it was their belief that *intention* could be inferred from the facts regardless of Dr Jabbi's protestations to the contrary. So, whilst such an inference might have been possible, that crucial fact still must be explicitly justified. On the record however, the entirety of the judgment reads:

The Court by a unanimous verdict finds you guilty of contempt of this Court. Do you have anything to say before sentence? (Dr. Will, 2000, p. 2)

This is an unacceptable conclusion to the case, where although it is possible that the panel discussed the issue of *mens rea* in private deliberation, there is no evidence on record to suggest that this was the case. Dr Jabbi was sentenced to one day of imprisonment. With the lack of legal justification given then, it would appear that this may have been a case of overreach of power. It must be repeated, that the publicly available case law in the context of Sierra Leone in this area is extremely limited, making generalisation difficult, and so whilst it is difficult to draw conclusions relating to the country as a whole, the only indication that can be drawn is that there are at least isolated examples where there may be similar problems with overreach as have been seen elsewhere. This does lead on to one useful recommendation made at the conclusion of this chapter however, that further research is carried out in Sierra Leone in order to be able to show with transparency how judges in the courtroom are using their powers when they might take exception to any criticism of their actions.

Going beyond the three initial jurisdictions of Nigeria, Kenya, and Sierra Leone, and considering the difficulties faced with the analysis of Sierra Leone in particular, a further global south jurisdiction has been selected for analysis. Considering South Africa then, the definition for contempt of court *in facie curiae* is derived from the case of *Jerold Taitz* (1980) which set out that it would be contempt:

...when a person by word or conduct willfully violates or attempts to violate the dignity, repute or authority of the court or interferes in the administration of justice, in and during the sitting of court (Jerold Taitz, 1980, p. 61)

The inclusion of the term *willfully* here, as with several of the other cases discussed throughout the chapter, infers the necessity for *mens rea* being established prior to a finding of contempt, which, as discussed previously with regard to other jurisdictions, should require that the court only uses any potential summary process with restraint, however again as with those other jurisdictions, the South African judiciary have been clear in their attempted justification for the use of the summary procedure. For example, in the case of *S v Samaria* (2011) the judge noted that:

To proceed with the summary proceedings... it clearly is required that the court itself must be a witness to the act of contempt. As such, the actus reus, relied upon must have been completed, whilst the court is in sitting and where the court is itself a witness, to such an extent that if the conduct is viewed objectively, in the absence of an explanation, that it can be concluded beyond reasonable doubt that the conduct constitutes contempt of court in facie curiae. (S v Samaria, 2011, para. 12)

The rationale here is problematic in that what is being asserted is that:

1. The judge or judges must have *subjectively* viewed the conduct in question;

With the purpose of being able to confidently assert that;

2. They are convinced that if viewed *objectively* it would be said beyond doubt that the matters should be regarded as contempt of court.

The logical response to this is that it could only be deemed reasonable to conclude that a matter viewed *subjectively* can also be viewed similarly through an *objective* lens if there has been an opportunity to assess such an assertion by requiring others independent of the issue, to give informed opinion on the matter. Any claim that the opinion of an intrinsically linked individual should be viewed as objective would require significant further explicit justification to deduce logical validity. Further to this, no consideration is given within the rationale from *Samaria* to how the matter of *mens rea* should be addressed, rather the justification given is much more akin to a strict liability approach being adopted, which would by definition be an overreach of the legitimate power of the judge.

Unsurprisingly then given the flawed rationale presented in *Samaria*, there have been criticisms within South Africa similar to those that have been highlighted elsewhere. Heamington Mhlongo in examining some of the case law argues that:

It is submitted that the summary procedure violates the right to be tried by an independent and impartial tribunal; the right to legal representation and the right to be given the opportunity to prepare for trial as contained in the South African Constitution Act 108 of 1996. (Mhlongo, 2003, p. 78)

Returning to a point raised previously, it is apparent that even today when important conflicts of law are raised there is a tendency within several African countries to look to English or wider UK authorities for answers. *Mhlongo* in his discussion quotes Lord Denning, who when commenting on the nature of contempt in 1968 claimed that:

...we will never use this jurisdiction as a means to uphold our own dignity. That must rest on surer foundations. Nor will we use it to suppress those that speak against us. We do not fear criticism, nor do we resent it. For there is something more important at stake. It is no less than freedom of speech itself. It is the right of every man, in parliament or out of it, in the press or in broadcast, to make fair comment, even outspoken comment on matters of public interest. Those who comment can deal faithfully with all that is done in a court of justice. They can say we are mistaken, and our decisions are erroneous, whether they are subject to appeal or not. All we would ask is that those who criticise us will remember that, from the nature of our office, we cannot reply to their criticisms. (Lord Denning in R v Metropolitan Police Commissioner, ex parte Blackburn (No 2), 1968, p. 320)

Scarcely could there be any stronger a statement against the imposition of scandalizing the court as a category of contempt, nor any stronger a statement that could be used in arguing that in holding those who make public comment against the decisions of the court in contempt is a difficult stance to continue to attempt to justify.

Mhlongo concludes by stating based on the areas discussed that the summary procedure should be abolished in order that the alleged contemnor is given time to prepare a defence as they would be allowed for any other criminal or quasi-criminal offence, and that the use of the summary procedure itself is a disruption to the substantive case during which the potentially contemptuous conduct arose. In other words, the argument is that frequently the use of the summary procedure for contempt of court is a greater interference with the administration of justice than whatever the subject of the alleged contempt might have been, and in reality, the summary procedure is little more than an inappropriate symbolic demonstration of judicial power that is highly problematic in a legal sense.

Further strength can be given to this perspective with brief examination of one final jurisdiction. Contempt of court is defined within the Ethiopian Criminal Code as being:

(1) *Whoever, in the course of a judicial inquiry, proceeding or hearing,*
   (a) *In any manner insults, holds up to ridicule, threatens or disturbs the Court or a judge in the discharge of his duty;* or
   (b) *In any other manner disturbs the activities of the Court, is punishable with simple imprisonment not exceeding one year, or fine not exceeding three thousand Birr*

The Court may deal with the crime summarily. (The Criminal Code of The Federal Democratic Republic of Ethiopia, 2004, Art. 449)

Nigusse (2013) argues though relating to (1)(a) that "…not every act of insolence is considered as contempt of court under Ethiopian law" (p. 10), and when examining the definition in more detail, argues that:

While there are some words which are obviously insulting, others may not but would be held to be so according to the tone and manner in which they are said. For example, a court may be insulted by the most innocent words uttered in a particular manner or tone. Thus, whether or not the language used amounts to be insulting the court is a question of fact that needs to be proved. (Nigusse, 2013, p. 10)

The broad point that Nigusse is therefore arguing is that in many cases there might be a broader context relevant to explore than simply what might have been said or done, and that the only way of this being discovered fully would be through an appropriately objective procedure in order that a full objective consideration can be given to the matter. Nigusse continues a balanced analysis and concludes that:

The summary procedure used to punish in facie curiae contempt of court can limit the accused's right to a fair trial. At the same time, the citizen's right to freedom of expression can be limited in punishing the crime of ex facie curiae contempt of court [scandalizing the court] …the point is that before limiting the rights of the citizen it is necessary to test how and when such limitations can be justified. (Nigusse, 2013, p. 30)

Nigusse stops short of calling for the summary procedure to be removed altogether but emphasises that the judiciary must accept that despite rhetoric presented to the contrary, there are *de facto* restrictions stemming from the existing provisions as well as the procedure invoked relating both to freedom of expression (through imposition of the offence of scandalizing the court), and right to a fair trial. He is arguing that if the judiciary intend to continue using such a summary procedure, then, that judges in individual cases must as a matter of professional responsibility explicitly consider whether the use of power in a manner that results in such a restriction of rights is truly the only possible recourse, or if the matter could be dealt with in any other way that would allow those rights to still be respected as far as possible.

CONCLUSION AND RECOMMENDATIONS

From examination of everything included in this chapter, certain conclusions can be drawn, though care must be taken to explain that whilst the examples have been presented in an accurate manner, it is important not to over-generalise, since perhaps one the biggest problems with this area of criminal justice is that only a small proportion of cases where judges use their discretionary powers in cases such as those of contempt of court are either published or reported on. This makes scrutiny of the judiciary in this area exceedingly difficult to achieve, and as such a recommendation is that all cases involving the use of summary hearings or use of judicial power in such a way should be recorded, transcribed, and published in full to ensure clear transparency and the ability for overreach of power to be easily identified, ensuring that miscarriages of justice are kept to a minimum.

Reflecting on each of the questions set at the outset of the chapter, the first question will be addressed toward the end of this section. Reflecting initially on the second question; if it appears that judges are maintaining the necessary neutrality and independence at all times as demanded through professional expectation; and from the selection of cases analysed covering multiple jurisdictions in this chapter, the answer has to be no. Whilst there is no suggestion of either systemic or institutional level problems with overreach or abuse of power, especially given the tendency for courts further up the hierarchy to identify and appropriately deal with cases of overreach, there are too many identified cases to argue that this isn't at least a notable and ongoing problem that requires serious attention. A recommendation would be for continuous professional development training for all judges, repeated at a reasonable interval to be determined, to reinforce to judges their obligations to remain neutral, independent, and objective, and to take care when using their discretionary powers.

In returning to question three and whether there are examples of overreach where judges are acting outside of what is legally permitted, there is a problem. It is apparent that cases are almost exclusively only coming to light or being reported when a dubious finding of contempt has been made, custodial sentence given, which has then been *appealed*. Whilst it *is* positive to note that regardless of the jurisdiction there does seem to be consistency in recognising when the power of the judge has been misused once a case has been *appealed*, the further problem is equally as clear and consistent in that a question is left open as to how many similar cases of misuse of power have occurred in first instance cases that have not been discovered or documented due to *no appeal* being lodged. As a matter of urgency, a requirement for full recording and reporting of all cases of contempt of court would provide clarity moving forward and might act as a deterrent against the rogue or hasty judge from acting without full consideration for the consequences a potential overreach of power. This is a recommendation which should not be overlooked if a judiciary is serious about avoiding miscarriages of justice.

There are further serious concerns in terms of overreach or misuse of power that often are still not recognised or discussed during even the successful appeals cases highlighted that must be reiterated. Whilst consistently across all jurisdictions analysed there is a clear and explicit legal requirement for *mens rea* to be proven for a finding of contempt to be made, it is overly concerning that in all the jurisdictions examined without exception there is truly little to no consideration of *mens rea* actually having to be evidenced during whatever procedure is invoked. The fact that the requirement for *mens rea* imposes a positive obligation on a prosecution to lead evidence to prove the existence of that *mens rea*, should be no different to the same requirement for *mens rea* in any other action by an accused which carries criminal hallmarks. This means that the burden of proof *must* remain with the prosecution in all cases without exception, and this burden *cannot* be reversed on to the accused at the outset of a hearing as is currently the case in so many jurisdictions. Yet in the majority of cases discussed, effectively the summary procedure invoked and still frequently defended by the judiciary in nearly every jurisdiction continues with such a *de facto* unlawful reversal of burden. The summary procedure is almost perfectly aligned with principles of strict liability where proof of *mens rea* is not required, however the insurmountable problem is that in all the jurisdictions examined, there is a clear and explicit *mens rea* requirement which is continually being breached. Whilst an argument could be made, though still tenuous, to support the summary procedure where the *mens rea* is that of *wilful* conduct and could therefore be inferred, there is no valid argument that can be presented to support such a summary procedure where the *mens rea* requires *intention* to be proven. This relatively simple legal reality is often completely ignored when the judiciaries of multiple jurisdictions have discussed the issue of the summary process. The only conclusion that can reasonably be drawn is that where *mens rea* is a requirement for a finding of contempt to be made, the ongoing use of the summary procedure is in itself an overreach or misuse of power. Unlike the conclusions related to question two, for question three this is categorised as a systemic problem or legal anomaly.

Question four asked what the consequences were for judges and other affected people when there is a clear overreach of power in the courtroom. This question can be answered in two ways; when the overreach is not discovered; and when the overreach is challenged, and it is agreed that power was in fact misused. On the first part, when there is such an overreach and a judgment of contempt is made illegitimately, this can have several effects on an individual. If made against a lay person this can include deprivation of liberty or false imprisonment, or potentially loss of money where a financial penalty has been ordered. For a lawyer, this can have significant professional implications. On the other hand, there are no material effect on the judge under the circumstance that the overreach remains undiscovered.

On the second part, where there is an appeal and the higher court accepts that there was such an overreach, in some cases this does not have the ability to mitigate the harm caused to an individual who may have already completed the full custodial sentence that was ordered in the first instance. This has been the case in several examples discussed in this chapter. In terms of any effects on the judge or judges in question then, this is open to interpretation. Whilst some examples have identified quite damning words on record spoken regarding the conduct of the judges in question by superior members of the judiciary, comparatively little by way of any truly disciplinary action has been established that might be proportionate to those damning words. For example, in the *re Hoague* case in USA, the judge who had intentionally abused his power to threaten a road user in a personal vendetta, there was in effect no punishment at all – a six-month suspension that would *only* come into effect if he broke the judicial code again has no substantial or immediate effect for what in many other professions would be a clear example of gross misconduct resulting in immediate termination of employment. Likewise, in the Nigerian case of *Akubueze*, the record of the appeal case shows the displeasure of the appeal court and strongly worded criticism of the initial trial judge, yet there is no record of *any* sanction being made against the judge in question. So, whilst there might not be impunity from criticism, there does appear on the face of the evidence to be either a tendency toward self-protection in an institutional sense, or at the very least a reluctance to truly punish misuse or abuse of power that in other contexts or professions would likely be dealt with much more severely. This lack of proportionate disciplinary action appears to be the case regardless of whether the overreach of power was through genuine oversight or driven by subjective malice, and in itself could be argued to be damaging to the reputation of multiple judiciaries around the world.

Whilst the first question set at the outset, on what discretionary powers the judge has, is addressed throughout the chapter through the examination of each jurisdiction on the subject of contempt of court specifically, there are further discretionary powers that could also be discussed in the same amount of detail. In an earlier draft of this chapter, there sections were written on the powers of sentencing, particularly related to capital punishment, which initial research suggested have had a similarly problematic history of overreach or misuse of power. As such, a further recommendation is to expand the research in this area to take account of all other areas of identifiable judicial discretion where the potential exists for overreach of powers to occur.

On the subject of the comparative approach taken in writing this chapter, and as with any comparative study, there are questions of to what extent conclusions and recommendations can be understood to have general application. Having looked to examples of England & Wales, USA, Canada, and Latvia from the western or global north context, and Nigeria, Kenya, Sierra Leone, South Africa and Ethiopia from the African global south perspective, although there are historical differences that have led to the current situation, some of which being problematic in themselves, there is comparatively little difference in a contemporary sense in terms of underpinning theoretical approaches or procedures invoked by any of the countries in question. This is of benefit as it ensures the validity of the comparative analysis conducted which might not have been the case if there were several material differences uncovered. On the contrary, the validity of the findings should be seen to retain a high level of validity where the contexts for analysis contain little by way of meaningful variation. This means that on all the conclusions and recommendations above, these should be taken to be universal in nature, with the recommendations being made for all jurisdictions rather than any one in particular.

Some further conclusions can be drawn at least to an extent that judiciaries in Africa appear to retain a slightly higher level of importance and focus on terms of any challenge to the personal dignity or respect of the individual judge either in the courtroom or outside of it. There has been a tendency to retain the offence of scandalizing the court in some cases where the general global trend has been to remove it in favour of the ability for the media and public to scrutinise and criticise decisions of the judiciary. This is not to say that the issue has been ignored in the global south, indeed there has been explicit discussion of the contemporary position on scandalizing the court, and a perspective and rationale given when this has been raised. The laws in place surrounding offences of contempt of court do in some cases still retain the traditional hallmarks of dignity and respect being explicitly protected, where the jurisprudence in the global north has at least in theory moved more toward the requirement for challenges being to the administration of justice rather than any personal affront suffered by the individual judge.

It cannot be concluded with certainty why this slight difference might be the case; however, one reason might be that both underpinning legal theory and criminal procedure in many African jurisdictions are frequently still based on historic British and particularly English law. In several examples identified, African cases from the twenty-first century are still reliant on and quoting English or Scottish cases and institutional writers from the nineteenth and early twentieth century in their reasoning. There does appear to be a reluctance to break from tradition, even when that tradition is arguably colonial, or even racist, in nature. Decolonising the curriculum is frequently a point of discussion in the education sector, and perhaps now is the time to examine in a meaningful way whether it is time to also explore decolonisation of the law more fully.

REFERENCES

Barak, A. (2008). *The judge in a democracy*. Princeton University Press.

Dworkin, R. M. (1977). *Taking rights seriously*. Harvard University Press.

Fox, J. C. (1927). *The history of contempt of court – The form of trial and the mode of punishment*. Clarendon Press.

Gordon, G. H. (2001). *The criminal law of Scotland* (3rd ed., Vol. 2Green & Son Ltd.

Harper, R. J., & Hamilton, P. (1999). A fingertip guide to criminal Law (4th ed.). Butterworths.

Hausegger, L., & Haynie, S. (2003). Judicial decision-making and the use of panels in the Canadian Supreme Court and the South African appellate division. *Law & Society Review*, *37*(3), 635–657. doi:10.1111/1540-5893.3703006

Himma, K. E. (1999). Judicial discretion and the concept of law. *Oxford Journal of Legal Studies*, *19*(1), 71–82. doi:10.1093/ojls/19.1.71

Mhlongo, H. (2003). Criminal law: From the law reports: The place of criminal contempt in an open and democratic society in the light of in re Chinamasa 2001 SA 902 (ZSC). *Codicillus, South Africa*, *44*(1), 75–79.

Miller, C. J. (2000). *Contempt of court* (3rd ed.). Oxford University Press.

Nigusse, D. G. (2013). *Contempt of court: A comparative study between South Africa and Ethiopia. Open Science Repository Law*.

Rewane, O. N. (1957). Contempt of court in Nigerian criminal law. *Journal of African Law*, *1*(3), 172–185. doi:10.1017/S0021855300002266

Soeharno, J. (2016). *The integrity of the judge: A philosophical inquiry*. Routledge. doi:10.4324/9781315556697

Stewart, C. E. (2003). Abuse of power and judicial misconduct: A reflection on contemporary ethical issues facing judges. *University of St. Thomas Law Journal*, *1*(1), 464–479.

APPENDIX: ADDITIONAL RESOURCES

Reports

Report number 17 on Contempt of Court, Law Reform Commission of Canada, 1982
Working Paper No. 20, Contempt of Court, Law Reform Commission of Canada 1977, pp.23–24

Cases

Attorney General and Another v Dr. Will (SC.MISC.APP. 6/99) [2000] SLSC 8
Attorney General v Newspaper Publishing PLC [1987] QB 1
Chief Dibia v. Chief Ezigwe (1998) 9 NWLR 564
Federal Republic of Nigeria v Joe Brown Akubueze (2010) LCN/3943 (SC)
F.T.C. v. Trudeau 606 F 3d 382 (7th Cir 2010)
In re Hoague, Off. Disciplinary Counsel, 725 N.E. 2d 1108 Ohio (2000)
In re Jones, 800. So. 2d 828 (2001)
Jerold Taitz (1980) 4 SACC 60
John Allan 1826 Shaw 172
Johnson v Grant 1923 SLT 501
MacMillan Bloedel Ltd. v. Simpson 1995 CanLII 57 (SCC)
Mayberry v Pennsylvania 400 US 455 (1971)
Muirhead v Douglas 1979 SLT (Notes) 17
R v Commissioner of Police of the Metropolis, Ex parte Blackburn [1968] 2 Q.B. 118
Rainy v Sierra Leone (1853) 8 Moo. P.C.C. 47
Re Bramblevale Ltd [1969] 3 All ER 1062
Republic (of Kenya) v Ahmad Abolfathi Mohammed & another Cr. App. No. 2 of 2018
Rex v John Sylvanus Rathbone and others (1945) 21, Kenya L.R., Part II, 15
Rex v Thomas Horatius Jackson (1925) 6 N.L.R. 49
Riggs v Palmer, 22 NE 188, 191 (1889)
Robert Clark or Williamson 1829 Shaw 215
S v Samaria ((P) 1760/2010) [2011] NAHC 20
The King v Almon 1765, reported in 1802 within Wilmot's Opinions and Judgments, Notes, 243
United States v. Griffin 84 F 3d 820 (7th Cir 1996)
United States v. McGainey 37 F 3d 682 (DC Cir 1994)
West Oxfordshire District Council v Beratec Ltd, The Times, 30th October 1986
Young v Lees 1998 SCCR 558
Zaicevs v. Latvia, Application no. 65022/01 ECtHR

Legislation / Regulations

Code of Judicial Conduct 1994 (South Africa)
Contempt of Court Act 1981 (United Kingdom)
Contempt of Court Act 2016 (Kenya)

Criminal Code 1985 (Canada)
Criminal Code of the Federal Democratic Republic of Ethiopia, Proclamation No.414/2004
Justice Manual 2020, United States Department of Justice
Kenyan Judicature Act 1967
Latvian Administrative Procedure Law 2004
Latvian Regulatory Offences Code
Local Courts Act 2011 (Sierre Leone)
Nigerian Criminal Code Act 1990
United States Code, Office of the Law Revision Counsel of the United States House of Representatives, 1947

Chapter 13
Culture, Ethnicity, and Hate Crimes:
A Comparative Analysis of Preventive Laws Between India and the USA

Debarati Halder
Parul Institute of Law, Parul University, India

Dhananjay Bhati
Karnavati University, India

ABSTRACT

Traditionally, India is a multilingual, multi-religious, and multicultural country. Ingression of different races in India has brought in different personal laws. Similar to India, the US also has a multiracial, religious, linguistic, and cultural society. The country also has similar experiences of hate crimes, especially from the perspectives of racial violence. This chapter aims to research the hate crime preventive laws in the US and India to find the best solutions from both jurisdictions.

INTRODUCTION

India, the largest democracy in the world is a country with multilingual, multi religious and multicultural population. Different races have co-existed in India since time immemorial. The rich anthropological history of India would show that Aryans and Dravidians had developed their own distinct socio-legal cultures since ancient times (Naqvi, Ibrar, & Bangash, 2011; Bhawuk, 2012). The Vedas, ancient scripts, the great epics of Ramayana and Mahabharata may show the existence of class-based distinction and discrimination. (Witzel, 1999). Simultaneously these ancient scripts may also show the existence of law and order and policing system which would control social and moral crimes. The system gave way to customary laws related to inheritance, marriages and further social divisions based on caste and sub caste (Halder, & Jaishankar, 2008). The criminal justice system got moulded according to the demands of the new ruling dynasties and the class and caste based social system. This reflected in the

DOI: 10.4018/978-1-7998-6884-2.ch013

mediaeval period as well. The invasion of non-Hindu rulers, especially the Muslims, further introduced new systems of policing, courts and restitution of justice (Thilagaraj, 2013). This period saw shifting of leniency towards non-Hindu victims and stricter sentences for non-Muslim accused (Blake, 1979). However, several Muslim rulers from different dynasties including the Mughals tried to bring in uniform criminal procedural laws for their subjects irrespective of their religion, caste, and creed. But this was made possible only during the British colonial rule when the entire Indian peninsula was brought under single ruler, i.e., the British Empire. The British rulers created several laws including the Indian Penal Code, Criminal Procedural laws etc., which introduced and recognised several existing and new offences including offences against the property, against human body, against the State etc. Punishment policies were changed according to the British colonial understanding. As such, whereas certain general criminal offences like murder, culpable homicide etc., or burglary etc received the traditional penological understanding, more power was given to the agents of the government, i.e., the police to act in an arbitrary manner especially to non- Europeans and non-Christians (Lal, 1999). This gradual shifting of protective *legal* veil to the ruling community since ancient times had given rise to ethnic group clashes and further division among people depending upon the religious and cultural practices. In 1947 India got independence from the colonial rulers and the independent Indian government created a unique constitution which upheld certain rights including right to equality and right to practice one's religious and cultural practices etc as prime fundamental rights (Lal, 1999).

The Indian Penal Code was reformed to shred the colonial nature and was made uniform to all, irrespective of class, caste, religion, language ethnic background etc. But socio-political reasons along with the socio-cultural diversity continued to create hate crimes in India and for curbing the same, the Indian parliament had to create specific legislations. Some of these extended the scope to curb ethnic clashes, some had been created to address crimes generating from socio-economic diversities and some had been enacted to curb hate crimes targeting gender. These were done keeping in consideration the existence of right to equality and freedom of speech which have been considered as prime fundamental rights under the Indian constitution. There had been several amendments to the constitution of India for suiting the needs of specific rights of people including the selection of judges to the higher judiciary which would maintain proper balance and impartiality in hearing cases affecting the rights of people from different socio-economic-lingual-religious groups. However, in certain cases the execution of these laws could not successfully restrict escalation of hate crimes. But considering the socio-religious-cultural diversity, it may be seen that the laws could in general control the aggressive mind-sets of separatists which could have easily influenced minds of people especially those who belong to religious-socio-economically politically and culturally minority groups.

Unlike India, USA has grown into country with a multi-cultural-lingual-socio-religious society since 18th century onwards. The country may not have a history of ancient legal scripts which laid the base for personal laws but has a deep colonial past like India. (Kramer, 2002). US is neither free from hate crimes. Colonial past, slave trade, economic recessions, and huge flow of immigrants in the USA post-world war for job opportunities and better living conditions created conditions for escalation of hate crimes. (Coester, 2008). The US constitution upholds right to equality, fair trial, and freedom of speech and right to practice own religious and cultural practices. The US constitution was created in the 18th century and there had been a gradual improvement in the understanding of rights including civil rights from a holistic perspective (Gressman, 1952). However, irrespective of the existence of constitutional guarantees and laws to curb hate crimes including racial crimes, crimes against gender etc, these crimes have existed and are growing (Considine, 2017). After the 9/11 attack, Islamophobia had reached new heights Considine, 2017). Hate crimes targeting people of colour had extended to Asians and African migrant workers, tourists, and visitors (Considine, 2017). However, the hate crime laws had been partially successful in creating deterrence for the perpetrators and promises for restitution of justice for victims.

As both India and US have multilingual, multi-cultural- religious-racial societies with socio-economic disparities, it is necessary to compare the anti-hate crime laws to understand how both countries have ensured basic rights and freedoms while curbing hate crimes including racial violence. Both India and US have history of politicising hate crimes (Levin, & Rabrenovic, 2001). It may be argued that the laws for curbing hate crimes may have been customised for protecting the interest of a particular stakeholder who may be influential to initiate the hate crimes. But looking at the constitutional protection to the fundamental and human rights, it would be pertinent to note that the laws and the execution of the same may not be permitted to go overboard the constitutional mandates. This chapter restricts its discussion with the critical analysis of the laws of both the countries that are enacted and are being used to curb the hate crimes. The first part being the introduction, the second part discusses on the constitutional mandates and hate crime curbing laws of India. The third part discusses on the major hate crime curbing laws of the US. The fourth part is the conclusion.

CONSTITUTIONAL MANDATES AND HATE CRIMES CURBING LAWS IN INDIA

The term "Hate crime" was first coined in United States in the late 1970's for the intent of collecting hate crime statistics by US Department of Justice (Chambliss,2011). The Organization on Security and Co-operation in Europe (OSCE) defines hate crimes as the criminal acts which are perpetrated with a bias motive (OSCE, 2009). The reason these crimes are often quoted as "bias-motivated crimes" is due to the reason that these crimes are perpetrated and targeted to a particular social group due to disparities in culture, religious practices, ethnicity, and customs. Hate crime is not defined anywhere under the present Indian law as a legal offence but it is often construed as a criminal act which occurs when a perpetrator targets a victim or particular social group having distinct cultural practices. Such bias-motivated attack does not only undermine victim's right but the social structure as whole which makes it more heinous than many other severe offences.

In India, hate crime or 'prejudice-motivated violence' has not been a new phenomenon. The country has had a long and tortuous history of sectarian mass violence (Engineer,1997; Varshney, 2002). Tracing back the history, the country was born in the congregation of the tragic partition in 1947 that led to over two million deaths (Pandey, 2009). Since then, there have been epic incidents of hate crimes in the name of 'communal riots' resulting to many deaths involving mob attacking of different caste and religious minorities. The Indian culture is broadly divided into a combination of various religions having different customs and practices. Moreover, different group of communities have different modes of communication due to which a minority individual or group of individuals are targeted based on their language, religious practices, and the customs they follow. There may be offences motivated by biasness but still may not fit into it to be categorize as hate crime unless the victim was attacked due to differences in religious practices, ethnicity, customs, and protected characteristics of one race to another. The biasness can also be relevant due to perpetrator's personal reasons such as prejudice, resentment, jealousy, hostility, intolerance, or a turbulent emotional state of hate not corresponding to biasness due to social identity or background. Hate crimes are thus delegated or entirely spurred by the apparent or genuine social personality of the person in question. In contemporary times, the incidents such as honor kill

(Halder & Jaishankar, 2017) in the name of love-jihad, cow-vigilantism in the name of mob-lynching, discrimination and derogatory speeches which incites hatred towards other and lead violence, caste-based killing for fulfilling as a majority with higher social status and other factors are the examples of hate crimes in India.

India is a multi-cultural and multi-religious state. Being a secular country, the states are divided into many different culture and religious practices. Since the very formations of country after the partition in 1947, the incidents related to hate crimes are majorly based on religions, castes, and gender. Due to different religious ideologies and practices, there is often evidence of sectarian mass violence which involves hate crimes such as lynching and hate speeches directed by one community to the other. The reasons behind religious persecution are mainly based on cow vigilante violence and religion-based processions which still the country is facing too. After the post-British era, there is an unprecedented growth seen in religious-based violence including anti-Sikh riots of 1984, Gujarat riots of 2002, and Muzzafarnagar riots of 2013. The National Crime Record Bureau (NCRB) reported highest number of communal violence cases between the years 2014 to 2016 (Kancharla, 2019). Caste based discrimination has also been evident in the Indian history of hate crimes apart from religious-based crimes. The Indian caste system is hierarchically separated into four different *varna*s, including the *Brahmins* that are clerics and otherworldly educators, then the *Kshatriyas* that are mainly the warriors, following the *Vaishyas,* that are traders and business communities and *Shudras* that are considered as the lowest class consisting of workers including slaves. The caste system encompasses a complex ordering of social groups on the basis of ritual purity. Apart from these four classifications, there is a fifth class which is outside the *varna* framework and comprise of those known as "untouchables" or *Dalits*; they are frequently appointed assignments also ceremonially contaminating to justify consideration inside the conventional Varna framework (Embree, 1988; Kolenda,1978; Srinivas, 1966). The notion of caste-based violence was perhaps an affirmation of reality that the Constitution of India has not explicitly addressed the historical wrong of untouchability since its commencement by affirming all practices of discrimination based on caste-based or gender-based untouchability as constitutionally illegitimate.

The major cases of hate crimes in India are on Dalits mainly due to their pronounced historical social status as 'untouchables." The Amnesty India's hate crime tracker has recorded a total of 181 incidents of alleged hate crimes only in the first quarter of 2019 only, steepest rise since 2016 (Special correspondent,2019). Over two-thirds of the victims were targeted because they were *Dalits*, while 40 of them were suffered on account of their Muslim Identity. The recent reports of the National Crime Record Bureau also suggest that India's rate of hate crimes are alarmingly increasing every year majorly based on caste and religious biasness, followed by gender-based biases. There are several instances where people with different sexual orientation are harassed by attackers based on their gender and sexuality. However, the inciting problem is that the National Crime Records Bureau (NCRB) only records the biased attacks based on gender and not based on the sexual orientation, which makes it even more difficult to even trace the exact number of victims (Bhat, 2018).

CONSTITUTIONAL PROVISIONS AND LEGISLATIONS GOVERNING VARIOUS HATE CRIMES IN INDIA

Examining the present situation of hate crimes in India, through statistics and sources, it is evident that hate crimes have the capability to not only violate the rights guaranteed by the state but international human rights too. The ruthless attacks on human dignity have undermined the individual rights enshrined under the constitution of India by virtue of being born as an Indian citizen. Following the records, the data shows how in the last few years hate crimes have increased at an alarming rate and has questioned the law and order of the country pertinently. The ideas of Justice, Liberty, Equality, Fraternity; the basic features of the Constitution of India have been defeated by commencement of the same. Hate crimes are the direct violation of fundamental rights enshrined under the Part III of the Constitution of India. Hate crimes does not only violate an individual's right to life with dignity but also violates the right to equality and non-discrimination

Article 14 of the Indian Constitution envisages two principles, "equality before the laws' and "equal protection of the laws" (Bhat, 2018). The article clearly unites the position that every citizen in India is equal before the law and the law is ought to treat everyone equally. However, equal protection of laws has not been justified in case of hate crimes incidents. Hate crimes are the acts that violate the right to equality of an individual and later question the national framework of real 'equal protection of the laws.

Hate crimes also violate the ethos of Article 15 and Article 17 of the Constitution of India which furthers the very intent of Article 14. Articles 15 of the Indian Constitution abolish any kind of discrimination on the grounds of religion, caste, race, sex, and place of birth or any of them. Furthermore, Article 17 expressly prohibits the evil of untouchability and makes it a punishable offence." However, the current data still shows that minorities in India are majorly targeted based on their religion, caste, and gender identity. The inhumane attacks on a person's dignity have violated these fundamental principles of law. Hate crimes puts a chilling effect on free speech and expression which is guaranteed under Article 19 of the Constitution of India, which guarantees freedom of speech and expression to all citizens. in the case of Jamuna Prasad v. Lachhi Ram (1954), the apex court in India held that rights of free speech and expression are natural and inherent in the status of the citizens of a country. However, various sources suggest how minorities are afraid of exercising their rights of free speech and expression due to oppression and attacks on the ground of sexual orientation. It simply suggests how in the absence of proper law, even these basic rights enshrined by the Constitution are being crushed.

Fundamental rights are the highest rights in India which are guaranteed to all citizens. Being India a democratic and secular country, the state is bound to protect and infringement of the same is justifiable before the courts. One of the most important rights in the Indian Constitution is Article 21, which declares the real objective and value of right to life and personal liberty. On multiple occasions, Article 21 of the Indian Constitution has been comprehended by the Indian Judiciary as the most essential right of a human. As in the landmark case of Kharak Singh v. State of Uttar Pradesh (1963), the Supreme Court concisely interpreted the scope of the term *'life'* as something more than mere animal existence. Subsequently, the Court in Ashok (Dr) v. Union of India (1997) held that the rights under Article 21 include all aspects dignified existence of living. The rights enshrined under Article 14, 19 and 21 forms the 'golden triangle' and these three rights must be read together to understand the inherent meaning of right to life. However, due to hate crimes the right to life and personal liberty has been violated and the value of life is getting minimalized by the perpetrators merely in the name of exercising their rights.

Although the offence of hate crimes is nowhere expressly mentioned under the Indian Penal Code, 1908 and other penal laws, various provisions relating to anti-hate crime are mentioned such as offences against public tranquility that are amongst 'unlawful assembly' under section 141 and 'rioting' under section 146 of the Code. The Code also penalizes any activity which promotes enmity among diverse groups under Section 153A, which discusses about penalty for promoting enmity between distinct groups on grounds of religion, race, place of birth, residence, language, etc., and doing acts prejudicial to maintains of harmony and Section 153B which discusses about penalty for imputations, assertions prejudicial to national integration. Among many forms of hate Crimes, hate speech including Online Hate Speech under Information Technology Act, 2000 is prohibited in India which is based upon caste, creed, colour and ethnicity. Again, hate speech is not a per-se crime however, there are many provisions under the Indian Penal Code and Code of Criminal Procedure, 1973 (CrPC) which put limitations on freedom of speech and expression. Further, The Representation of People Act of 1931 (RPA) forbids corrupt practices and demonstrations which can harm the sanctity of fair elections. The Section 123(3) of the Act restricts any practices which may cause disdain or ill will between people for the sake of religion, race, station, or language. The Scheduled Castes and the Scheduled Tribes (Prevention of Atrocities) Act of 1989 (popularly known as Atrocities Act) has been acknowledged as an apt provision which protects the marginalized and weaker groups of sections of society from potential discrimination in the name of colour, creed, caste, and profession. This Act is framed to prevent atrocities against SC's and ST's but does not include hate crimes as a separate control discipline appealing punishment for perpetrating the same. However, in the light of rising hate crimes especially against Dalits, this provision has been used as hate crime preventive mechanism.

It must also be noted that Indian judiciary has also taken responsibility in curbing hate crimes by providing justice to the needy when the state machineries and laws fail to prevent or control such crimes against humanity, the role of Judiciary comes into play to protect the people and enforce the rights of the victims. In Union of India v. Sankulchand Himmatlal Seth (1977), Justice Untawali recalled the Indian judiciary as a *"watching tower above all the big structures of the other limbs of the state from which it keeps a watch like a sentinel on the functions of the other limbs."* It is therefore, upon Judiciary to keep any eye on things which needs urgent attention and pass necessary guidelines for the solution of the same. The Supreme Court in Tehseen S. Poonawalla v. Union of India (2018) largely discussed on lynching describing it as *'an affront to the rule of law and to the exalted values of the Constitution itself'*. The court while stating on hate crime observed that, *"hate crimes as a product of intolerance, ideological dominance and prejudice ought not to be tolerated; lest it results in a reign of terror."* The court in this notable case on hate crimes also passed certain guidelines under three heads: preventive measures, remedial measures, and punitive measures through direction of state. It is pertinent to note that this was the landmark case where the court for the first time finally recommended the legislature to create a separate offence for lynching and provide adequate punishment for the same as to instill a sense of fear in the minds of people. However, as the role of Judiciary being limited to guide the state and to narrate the law, the immediate steps still have not been initiated to make legislation for the same. Considering the nature of hate crimes and its related complexities in India, there is an urgent need for incorporating hate crimes in criminal codes to recognize them really as hate 'crime.'

ANALYSIS OF ANTI-HATE CRIME LAWS OF THE US

Americans like Indians enjoy equal protection of laws irrespective of colour, race, and gender etc. The 14th Amendment to the US constitution mandates that the no one should be discriminated when it comes to the equal protection of laws in relation to the core fundamental rights guaranteed by the US constitution which dates to 18th century. Equal protection clause relates to the protection against arbitrary action by the government to the racial minority group. This also extends its scope to provide right to access justice, social welfare mechanism by all. Several researchers have shown that white supremacists have resisted people from non-white communities to access education, proper livelihood and right to residence in white dominant areas (Kennedy, 1993; McMurtry, Findling et al., 2019; Umaña-Taylor, 2016; Giulietti, Tonin, & Vlassopoulos, 2019). There had been incidences on religion-based violence as well especially after 9/11 (Chandrasekhar, 2003). As such Muslims and Afro Asian people in the US have been violently targeted. One of the earliest laws addressing such racial violence in the US is the 18 U.S. Code S 245, especially subsection (b). For the purpose of this chapter, it would be pertinent to discuss this provision in detail. USC S245 specifically speak about federally protected activities and penalises those who violate the said Section. A minute analysis of Ss(b) of U.S. Code S 245 would show the following activities which are federally protected: namely, voting, campaigning for a specific political ideology/party or person, activity as a poll watcher, any other authorised election official, participating and/enjoying any state governed/administered benefits, services, privileges etc., enjoying state funded financial facilities, right to access justice, right to be defended, right to work in the courts in different capacity including as a juror, right to employment in government as well as private sectors, right to join any labour organisation, right to travel, right to buy and sale properties, stay in properties either bought by the individual/s, or rented on a long term basis or rented for short term basis, getting engaged in interstate commerce which are permitted by law, right to entertainment including right to enter in to movie theatres, right to consume food according own choice from any public shops etc.

In short, S. 245(B) USC 18 protects all activities that have been guaranteed by the US constitution as well as by the Universal Declaration of Human Rights especially through several conventions and declarations including International Covenant on civil and political rights, international covenant on socio-economic cultural rights etc. This section penalises any person who wilfully interferes or threatens to interfere with the above-mentioned activities because of race, colour, ethnicity, national origin, religion etc., of the victim. The section indicates that the act of interference with the federally protected acts would attract the punishment for fine and/or imprisonment for maximum to one year. In case of bodily injury resulting from such interference and/or threatening to use firearms, explosives etc, the imprisonment sentence would be enhanced to maximum ten years and in case of kidnapping, sexual assault including that of aggravated nature, death etc resulting due to such interference, the punishment would extend to life term or even death penalty. This section extends its scope for abetment and attempt to commit the offences as well. The statute very clearly mentions that the right to free speech and right to peaceful assembly would not be applicable here when the said acts are done with an intention to interfere with the federally protected activities. Interestingly even though the US constitution has expanded the scope of free speech rights through First amendment guarantees, the said right is restricted in cases where it falls within the meaning of S,245(B) of USC 18. This provision has been used in several cases in recent times: for example, consider the case of El Paso Walmart supercentre mass shooting case in August 2019: the 21-year Crusius allegedly opened fire in the Walmart causing death to 23 individuals and injuring many more (BBC,2019). It seemed to be a planned attack against the Hispanics who (according to the accused) had invaded Texas and caused "cultural and ethnic replacements". The accused had released a statement on internet on this before he went ahead for mass shooting. He was charged for hate crimes, using firearms for interfering with federally protected activities and also for causing death under the S. 245(B) USC 18. Consider again the case of a 31-year-old man from Florida who was arrested under the same provision for racially motivated hate propaganda through his social media account against a candidate for a local city council election (Department of Justice, 2019). The charges were fixed mainly fixed for his hate campaign and threats targeted to the victim.

Interestingly, even though First amendment guarantees of the US constitution provides a wide range of rights to express one's opinion which may include sharing hateful message as well, the rights get restricted when the freedom of speech and expression is used for sharing hate campaigns within the meaning of S,245 USC 18. Further S.247 of the USC 18 is also noteworthy in this regard which prohibits intentional damage to religious property and causing obstruction for religious practices. This provision indicates that heavy fines and jail terms may be awarded in case of bodily injury and death due to such damage and obstructions. The religious property in this section includes all sorts of properties which facilitate religious practices. In 2009, the scope of the hate crime laws in the US were extended to include hateful activities targeting individuals because of the victim's gender and gender orientation. The Matthew Shepard and James Byrd, Jr. Hate Crimes Prevention Act of 2009, S249 USC 18 therefore prescribes punishment for causing bodily injury or death, attempting to and abetment to cause such injuries etc., for hate crimes motivated by gender and/or gender orientation of the victim/s.

While these prominent federal hate crime laws are being used to address hate crimes in the US, there have been incidences of racial discrimination and police atrocities. On numerous occasions, police had stopped, detained, and used force to search people of colour (Halder, 2020). Racial minority people had always remained a soft target for police when it comes to suspect and apprehend probable offenders. However, several reports have also suggested that police officers who had illegally detained and used force on racial minority people have been charged and prosecuted. This biasness has existed since long and it has also impacted on the proper execution of laws.

CONCLUSION

When compared with Indian laws addressing hate crimes it may be seen that the US federal laws addressing hate crimes have been framed in a more focussed and uniform way. But the laws in India have been developed considering the circumstances especially keeping in mind about racial, religious, linguistic intolerance and violence caused due to wilful causing of bodily injury, deaths, vandalism affecting properties etc. Further, the hate speech laws in both the countries differ due to the multiple vernacular languages that may be used in India and the different sentiments and ideologies of people basing on their religion, caste, creed, political ideologies, traditional customs, language, culture etc. As such, what may be considered as hate speech in India, may not be considered as hate speech in the US. This has directly impacted on the internet speech rights. During the pandemic in 2020 spanning over to first part of 2021, these authors have observed several occasions where social media platforms have been targeted by the Indian government for their negligence to consider communal hate speech as prohibited contents. Resultant in last weeks of February 2021, the government of India came out with Information Technology (Intermediary Guidelines and Digital Media Ethics Code) Rules, 2021 which makes the web companies hosted in foreign countries (mostly in the US) personally liable for not taking action on contents which may fall within the category of hate speech, riotous, disrupting the internal peace and security of India etc. It cannot be accepted that hate crimes and hate speech may go hand in hand especially with the growth of internet-based communication system. Hence it has become necessary for nation states to contribute more for development of universal understanding on hate crimes through platforms like Institutes of the UN Crime Prevention and Criminal Justice Programme Network (PNI) which may further help the countries to develop hate crime preventive laws and execute the same according to the global standards of tolerance, justice, and peacebuilding capacities.

REFERENCES

Ainslie, E. (1988). *Sources of Indian tradition: From the beginnings to 1800*. Columbia University Press.

Asghar Ali Engineer (Ed.). (1997). Communal riots in post-independence India (2nd ed.). University Press.

Ashutosh Varshney. (2002). *Ethnic conflict and civic life: Hindus and Muslims in India*. Yale University Press.

BBC. (2019). *Texas Walmart shooting: El Paso attack 'domestic terrorism'*. https://www.bbc.com/news/world-us-canada-49226573

Bhawuk, D. P. (2012). India and the culture of peace: Beyond ethnic, religious, and other conflicts. In *Handbook of ethnic conflict* (pp. 137–174). Springer. doi:10.1007/978-1-4614-0448-4_7

Blake, S. P. (1979). The patrimonial-bureaucratic empire of the Mughals. *The Journal of Asian Studies, 39*(1), 77–94. doi:10.2307/2053505

Chambliss, W. J. (2011). *Crime and criminal behaviour*. Academic Press.

Chandrasekhar, C. A. (2003). Flying while brown: Federal civil rights remedies to post-9/11 airline racial profiling of South Asians. *Asian LJ, 10*, 215.

Coester, M. (2008). Hate crime. *Victimisation surveys in Germany*, 46.

Considine, C. (2017). The racialization of Islam in the United States: Islamophobia, hate crimes, and "flying while brown.". *Religions, 8*(9), 165. doi:10.3390/rel8090165

Department of Justice. (2019). *Florida man arrested for making racially motivated threats in interference with election in Charlottesville and cyberstalking*. Published in https://www.justice.gov/opa/pr/florida-man-arrested-making-racially-motivated-threats-interference-election-charlottesville

Giulietti, C., Tonin, M., & Vlassopoulos, M. (2019). Racial discrimination in local public services: A field experiment in the United States. *Journal of the European Economic Association, 17*(1), 165–204. doi:10.1093/jeea/jvx045 PMID:32161517

Gressman, E. (1952). The unhappy history of civil rights legislation. *Michigan Law Review, 50*(8), 1323–1358. doi:10.2307/1284416

Gyanendra Pandey. (2001). *Remembering partition: Violence, nationalism, and history in India*. Cambridge University Press.

HalderD. (2020) *Stop, search, frisk and detain: A comparative analysis of police power between India, UK, and US* (Draft paper unpublished). https://ssrn.com/abstract=3722731 doi:10.2139srn.3722731

Halder, D., & Jaishankar, K. (2008). Property rights of Hindu women: A critical review of succession laws of ancient, medieval, and modern India. *Journal of Law and Religion, 24*, 101-122.

Halder, D., & Jaishankar, K. (2017). Love marriages, inter-caste violence, and therapeutic jurisprudential approach of the courts in India. In D. Halder & K. Jaishankar (Eds.), *Therapeutic jurisprudence and overcoming violence against women* (pp. 30–42). IGI Global. doi:10.4018/978-1-5225-2472-4.ch003

Kancharla, B. (2009). *The intriguing case of data on 'communal incidents' in India.* https://factly.in/the-intriguing-case-of-data-on-communal-incidents-in-india/

Kennedy, R. (1993). State, criminal law, and racial discrimination: A comment. *Harvard Law Review, 107*(6), 1255. doi:10.2307/1341843

Kolenda, P. (1978). *Caste in contemporary India: Beyond organic solidarity.* Benjamin/Cumming Publishing Co.

Kramer, P. A. (2002). Empires, exceptions, and Anglo-Saxons: Race and rule between the British and United States empires, 1880–1910. *The Journal of American History, 88*(4), 1315–1353. doi:10.2307/2700600

Lal, V. (1999). Everyday crime, native mendacity, and the cultural psychology of justice in colonial India. *Studies in History, 15*(1), 145–166. doi:10.1177/025764309901500105 PMID:22452024

Levin, J., & Rabrenovic, G. (2001). *Hate crimes and ethnic conflict: An introduction.* Academic Press.

McMurtry, C. L., Findling, M. G., Casey, L. S., Blendon, R. J., Benson, J. M., Sayde, J. M., & Miller, C. (2019). Discrimination in the United States: Experiences of Asian Americans. *Health Services Research, 54*(S2), 1419–1430. doi:10.1111/1475-6773.13225 PMID:31657465

Mohsin, A. B. (2018). The case for collecting hate crimes data in India. Law & Policy Brief, 4(9).

Naqvi, R. H., Ibrar, M., & Bangash, S. (2011). Cultural history of Indian subcontinent; with special reference to arts and music. *JL & Soc'y, 41*, 37.

OSCE. (2009). *Decision No. 9/09 on combating hate crimes.* https://www.osce.org/cio/40695

Special Correspondent. (2019). *Amnesty report: Hate crimes rose sharply the first half of 2019.* Published in https://www.thehindu.com/news/national/amnesty-report-hate-crimes-rose-sharply-the-first-half-of-2019/article29598191.ece

Srinivas, M. N. (1966). *Caste: Its twentieth century avatar.* Viking.

Thilagaraj, R. (2013). Criminal justice system in India. In *Handbook of Asian criminology* (pp. 199–211). Springer. doi:10.1007/978-1-4614-5218-8_13

Umaña-Taylor, A. J. (2016). A post-racial society in which ethnic-racial discrimination still exists and has significant consequences for youths' adjustment. *Current Directions in Psychological Science, 25*(2), 111–118. doi:10.1177/0963721415627858

Witzel, M. (1999). *Aryan and non-Aryan names in Vedic India: Data for the linguistic situation, c. 1900-500 BC.* http://crossasia-repository.ub.uni-heidelberg.de/112/1/AryanandnonAryan_1999.pdf

Chapter 14
Charge Sheet to Charging:
A Comparative Analysis of Case Management by Police and Prosecution Between India and the UK With Special Reference to Cybercrime

Debarati Halder
Parul Institute of Law, Parul University, India

ABSTRACT

Police and prosecution are the two essential elements in criminal justice systems, especially for justice delivery to the victims as well as for the accused. Cybercrimes targeting women have remained a menace for the victims, police, and prosecution for over a decade now in India and the UK. This chapter aims to research on the comparative analysis of relationship of police and prosecution for case management with special reference to cybercrimes against women cases between UK and India to find positive solutions for restitution of justice in such cases.

INTRODUCTION

Women victims of online harassments may not get justice due to several reasons. These may include slow reporting, slow process of investigation, and lack of cooperation from the victims, internet platforms, and other criminal justice stakeholders, especially when it is related to cross border criminal activities (Halder & Jaishankar, 2011). It is widely accepted among researchers that women often do not report cybercrime victimisation to the police in many jurisdictions (Saha et al., 2019) because either they may not be empowered to reach out to the police with their cases, or the police may not be aware of the patterns of victimisation, consequences of the same, and impact of the same on the victims. By saying that they are not empowered, this author emphasises two points: (i) such women may not be empowered to physically reach out to the police or to the courts with their complaints. Their right to speech and expression, and right to information may be extremely limited. Hence, even if they are victimised online,

DOI: 10.4018/978-1-7998-6884-2.ch014

they may not be able to report the same. They may remain perpetual victims because of socio-economic political oppression (Halder & Jaishankar, 2012), (ii) Such women may not be digitally empowered, and they may come to know about their victimisation from different sources. However, they may not be aware as how to access the respective digital platforms to report the harassment and victimisation (Halder & Jaishankar, 2014). There may be different patterns of cyber victimisation of women. For instance, some may be interpersonal, some may be organised crimes, and some may be victimless crimes.

These may include victimisation by way of unauthorised access to the data, devices or networks, cyberstalking, cyberbullying, and trolling, revenge porn, and non-consensual image sharing, voyeurism, etc. Many of the aforementioned criminal activities may or may not be recognised by domestic laws. In the event that such criminal activities are not recognised, the victims may face severe challenges from the police as they may be refused any legal recourse. This had been the situation for victimisation by way of sextortion, revenge porn, cyber-gender bullying, trolling, cyber-flashing etc., in several jurisdictions, including countries like India, Sri Lanka, Bangladesh etc. In the US, Canada, Australia, and some European Union countries, the criminal laws have been expanded to include some of the above-mentioned criminal activities. However, internationally, the situation has not improved much since the late 1990s or in the early 2000s. There is a clear process which may lead one to understand how the occurrence of criminal activities, including cybercrime cases, may be approached by the criminal justice system. This includes the process shown in Figure 1.

Figure 1.

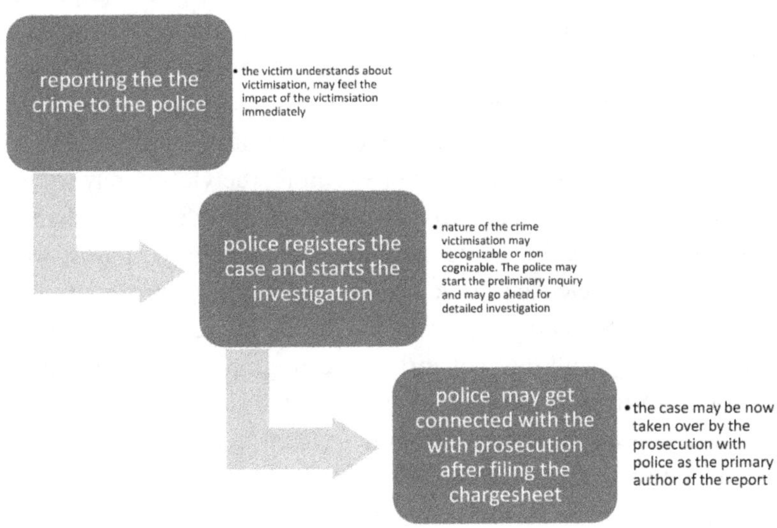

The above flow chart illustrates the general process whereby the police may receive the case details from the victim, document the same, and go forward with the investigation as what happened and how it happened. The police will search for any digital footprints, profile the modus operandi, review the outcome of the offence, including whether the outcomes involved significant monetary loss, property loss, bodily injury, or death; or whether the outcome of the case was minor, or had affected a specific class of people.

Before going into a detailed investigation, the police may also go forth with a preliminary investigation to better understand the nature of the offence before deciding whether the same may require further investigation. At this stage, the police may decide that the case is trivial and therefore, not worthy of further investigation (Citron, 2009). This generally happens in cybercrime victimisation cases where, due to lack of awareness regarding the recent trends of cybercrimes or regarding the laws addressing the same, the officer in charge may be reluctant to accept the case for further investigation (Forouzan et al., 2018)). In certain cases, the victims, especially when the victim is a woman, withdraws the complaint for any number of reasons. This may include fear of re-victimisation by the perpetrator who may become angry and revengeful, fear of sudden public exposure, or reluctance to give the necessary time needed to successfully prosecute the case (Halder & Jaishankar, 2011). The various reasons for not proceeding with the investigation must be documented by the police and must be forwarded to the court. Once the charge sheet is provided to the prosecution, the prosecution may further investigate the entire case based on the documents and evidence provided by the police, and in certain common law countries like the UK and US, the prosecution may require the police to gather stronger, more compelling evidence. In certain civil law countries, prosecution may even direct the police to delve deeper during the investigation (Tonry, 2012), which are intended to strengthen the prosecution's case. In any criminal matter, it may be seen that the defendant may never have an opportunity to defend his rights in accordance with the Universal Declaration of Human Rights. (Wilson, 2014). Unlike physical criminal offences, investigation and prosecution in cybercrime cases may require specialized expertise in evidence collection. The officers must understand the nature of the case, layers of platforms on which the crimes may have been committed, the liability (if any) of the service providers, layers of digital footprints, etc.

Defendants may hire lawyers who may be knowledgeable and experienced in cybercrimes, and in turn, they may swiftly shift the burden on others including the investigating officers, the victims and /or any other third parties in defending their clients. Such situations may arise when the investigating officer may not be aware of how to preserve the digital evidence. Such situations may also arise when the victim herself tries to deal directly with the perpetrator. For example, the victim may try to engage the hackers by trying to persuade them to take down the offensive content (Halder, & Jaishankar, 2015). There are separate provisions for addressing cybercrimes including cybercrimes against women in the UK and India which are followed by the police and judiciary for investigating, prosecuting, and sentencing purposes. Many of these laws have been amended over the in relation to criminal advancements in identity theft, cyberbullying and trolling, stalking, voyeurism, pornography (including extreme pornography). Both countries store this information in comprehensive databases to showcase the sheer numbers of cybercrime cases which have been reported to the police (Gabriel & Hemblade, 2019). And yet, there is no singular answer to the question as why there are less convictions for cybercrime cases. This chapter aims to answer this question through a comparative analysis of the police-prosecutorial relationship in dealing with criminal cases, especially cybercrime cases targeting women victims.

Indian criminal procedural laws have been framed based on British colonial criminal procedural systems which favoured a deep connection between police, prosecution, and judiciary. However, Chapters 12 (information to the police and their powers to investigate) and 16(commencement of the proceedings) under the Criminal Procedure Code, 1973, India would show that the modern criminal procedure code makes a clear distinction between the powers of the police and the prosecutors and makes the police answerable to the judicial magistrate rather than to the prosecution. The system in UK in this regard is different. The Police and CPS relations would show that once the police submit the investigation reports in the form of charge sheet to the directorate of the prosecution, the formal procedure for a pretrial hearing may start in which the defendant may have to face the prosecution first and not the magistrate (The Crown Prosecution Service, 2018). The entire fate of the case may depend on this. There are certain common patterns of cybercrimes against women which may have seen more reporting in both the jurisdictions and may have been addressed in a better way by the police and the prosecution in both the countries. In the next segment of this chapter, I discuss the positive and negative aspects of such sorts of case managements. Here, I will also discuss on whether this type of case management may prove to be beneficial for the victims. In the conclusion, I will offer certain findings and suggestions as how the situation may improve in both the countries for the benefit of women at large.

CASE MANAGEMENT BY POLICE AND PROSECUTION UNDER INDIAN CRIMINAL PROCEDURE CODE

The Indian policing system for criminal case management largely depends on Criminal Procedure Code, 1973 which has a colonial past. This provision was originally created in 1861, amended in 1882, and then further amended for suiting the purpose of criminal procedures of an independent India in 1973. As such, the code provides wide-ranging powers to the police for conducting an investigation, which must be unfettered (Puducherry Police, n.d). An investigation by police will include taking the testimony of victims and witnesses, conducting search and seizure protocols, and preparing an evidence log of the confiscated items. The investigating officer may be assisted by forensic experts with collecting and preserving the evidence for trial purposes.

There are no hard and fast rules as far as taking directions from the prosecution. S.173 of the Criminal Procedure Code mandates that after completion of the investigation, the police must make a file of the case, or the charge sheet, that must be completed within a maximum 90 days for capital punishment cases or those in which imprisonment for life or for a term of not less than 10years is possible. In other cases, the charge sheet needs to be completed within a maximum period of 60 days. However, S.167 (5) of the Criminal Procedure Code further states that the judicial magistrate may have the power to release the offender if the investigation is not finished within the stipulated time. Hence, if the police fail to file the charge sheet within this specified time frame, and the case is a bailable offence, the judicial magistrate needs to release the individual on bail if the accused had furnished the bail. But in summary trials, S.167(5) of the Criminal Procedure Code indicates that after the completion of the time frame of 6 months for filing the charge sheet, if the police fail to do so, the magistrate may have the power to stop the investigation, unless the investigating officer petitioned the court requesting that further time is needed for the completion of the case. During this stage of preparing the charge sheet, police officers in India generally do not consult the prosecutor. On the other hand, the investigating officer would need to provide reports on the stages of the investigation directly to the magistrate. However, this does not mean that the magistrate takes the role of investigating magistrate as they do in the civil and inquisitorial systems.

India follows a mixed system that includes a unitary and federal government system. While some powers for governance and administration are with the central government, some power for governance and administration remain with the states. The police administration falls within the scope of the state administration in India. (Ray, 1978). India has a directorate of prosecution which is managed by the state and each state may appoint officials for the directorate of prosecution. This is evident in S.25A of the Criminal Procedure Code which states as follows:

1. *"The State Government may establish a Directorate of Prosecution consisting of a Director of Prosecution and as many Deputy Directors of Prosecution as it thinks fit.*
2. *A person shall be eligible to be appointed as a Director of Prosecution or a Deputy Director of Prosecution, only if he has been in practice as an advocate for not less than ten years and such appointment shall be made with the concurrence of the Chief Justice of the High Court.*
3. *The Head of the Directorate of Prosecution shall be the Director of Prosecution, who shall function under the administrative control of the Head of the Home Department in the State.*
4. *Every Deputy Director of Prosecution shall be subordinate to the Director of Prosecution.*
5. *Every Public Prosecutor, Additional Public Prosecutor and Special Public Prosecutor appointed by the State Government under Sub-Section (1), or as the case may be, Sub-Section (8), of section 24 to conduct cases in the High Court shall be subordinate to the Director of Prosecution.*
6. *Every Public Prosecutor, Additional Public Prosecutor and Special Public Prosecutor appointed by the State Government under Sub-Section (3), or as the case may be, Sub-Section (8), of section 24 to conduct cases in District Courts and every Assistant Public Prosecutor appointed under Sub-Section (1) of section 25 shall be subordinate to the Deputy Director of Prosecution.*
7. *The powers and functions of the Director of Prosecution and the Deputy Directors of Prosecution and the areas for which each of the Deputy Directors of Prosecution have been appointed shall be such as the State 8. Government may, by notification, specify.*
   The provisions of this section shall not apply to the Advocate General for the State while performing the functions of a Public Prosecutor."

Even though the powers and function of the prosecutor includes prosecuting the cases and advising the police in relation to the charge sheet. It should be noted that the prosecutors in India do direct the police nor do the police frame the charge sheet for the best interest of the prosecution and the victims that they are representing, which typically occurs in several common law countries, including the UK or USA.

Prosecutors in India do not have power to restrict the defendants from being tried by the magistrates. Further, India does not have a jury system. Hence, no defendant may claim to be tried by the juries. However, as has been mentioned in S.6 of the Criminal Procedure Code (which discusses about the classes of criminal courts in India), the trial court system is divided in several categories depending upon the jurisdiction: this is mainly related to the gravity of the offences, and the punishments prescribed by the statutes for such offences. As such, the highest trial court is session's court which may try any offence authorised by law including offences with the most significant punishments, including capital punishment, life imprisonment, and imprisonment for more ten years. There is also the assistant session's court which may try offences for which the prescribed punishment is limited to a maximum of no more than ten years imprisonment. Below this court is the chief judicial magistrate's court which may try offences in which the conviction calls for no more than seven years of imprisonment.

Next, are the courts of judicial magistrate - class I, which can try offences that dictate imprisonment for three years and /or fines up to Rs. 10,000. The lowest level of courts in this rank is the judicial magistrate's court of class II, which can try offences with maximum imprisonment up to one year and / or fines up to the limit of Rs. 5000. Apart from these, there are executive magistrate courts, which may be managed by senior bureaucrats who hold the position of district magistrates. In some cases, the state government may also appoint police commissioners as executive magistrates. These executive magistrates are not judicial magistrates and their powers as magistrates are limited when compared with the powers of the judicial magistrates who are appointed for the courts above mentioned.

Further, there are several other special courts for specific cases including juvenile offences and sexual offences against children, family matters, terrorism-related cases, drugs, and narcotics-related cases etc. These special courts are generally hold the rank of session's courts. Each of the above-mentioned courts may have different levels of prosecuting officers. For example, public prosecutors may have to manage the cases in the session's courts and the assistant public prosecutors may be given the charge of cases that may be dealt with by judicial magistrates other than session's judges and chief judicial magistrates. This has been discussed on S.25 of the Criminal Procedure Code, which discusses about Assistant public prosecutors and states as follows:

1. "*The State Government shall appoint in every district one or more Assistant public Prosecutors for conducting prosecutions in the Courts of Magistrates.*
    1A. *The Central Government may appoint one or more Assistant Public Prosecutors for the purpose of conducting any case or class of cases in the Courts of Magistrates.*
2. *Save as otherwise provided in Sub-Section (3), no police officer shall be eligible to be appointed as an Assistant Public Prosecutor.*
3. *Where no Assistant Public Prosecutor is available for the purposes of any particular case, the District Magistrate may appoint any other person to be the Assistant Public Prosecutor in charge of that case;*
   Provided that a police officer shall not be so appointed—
    (a) *if he has taken any part in the investigation into the offence with respect to which the accused is being prosecuted;* or
    (b) *if he is below the rank of Inspector.*"

Cybercrimes against women may be of various types. These may include offences of sexual and non-sexual nature. These may also include offences facilitated through information and digital communication technology as well as computer-assisted offline crimes. As such, the offences may include offences related to cyberbullying, trolling, cyber stalking, economic crimes including dating scams, unauthorised access to data, devices, non-consensual image sharing, voyeurism, revenge pornography, and sharing sexually explicit materials. Even though India has a specific statute, i.e., Information Technology Act 2000 (amended in 2008), which is dedicated to addressing ecommerce crimes, cyberterrorism, and certain types of cybercrimes, this law does not include any specific language for crimes against women.

This, however, has been addressed in the Indian Penal Code which was amended by Criminal Law Amendment Act 2013. However, except for a few categories of criminal activities including cyberstalking and voyeurism, this provision does not address other specific categories of cybercrimes against women. As such, there is confusion about the gravity of certain types of offences. For example, revenge porn is not recognised by any law as a criminal offence even though this is loosely related to voyeurism. Further, depending on the modus operandi and the consequences of the offence, the police may tend to book the offences based on different laws that may or may not address the problem of the victim.

Since most of the cases fall under the category of criminal cases, they are mostly dealt with by the above-mentioned criminal courts. These cases may be bailable or non bailable, cognizable or non-cognizable. When the police start an investigation into such cases, they may have to face two major challenges, namely: (a) cooperation of the victims and the online platforms where the crime may have taken place, and (b) jurisdictional issues. In the former case, victims may lodge the complaints, but may not further provide necessary evidence including the screenshots, information related to the digital profiles of the offenders, that may be helpful for the investigation of the offence.

Even after decades of education and awareness, this author has observed that several women who are victims of cybercrimes in India have withdrawn their complaints at the initial stage because lodging a formal complaint with the police may invoke secondary victimisation at the hands of the criminal justice system, along with certain social taboos. This has given way to another larger problem. Some police officers may never have come across any cybercrime complaints from women during the careers; therefore, when they do come across such complaints, they either refuse to take the complaints because they may not fully understand the nature of the complaint. Or, if the said offence is not recognised under Indian law, the police officer may not know how to proceed, therefore, training is essential. When officers get transferred from their respective offices which may have been designated for handling cybercrimes cases, the new officers may need additional training, which may delay the entire operation of investigation, preparation of charge sheet, and taking the case to the trial.

Non-cooperation from the websites is another challenge that the police officer may confront when investigating a cybercrime. There may be various reasons for not revealing the actual identity, IP address, and geolocation of the offender by the companies. This may include not agreeing that the content is offensive and/or the anonymity of the offender. This may be compounded by jurisdictional issues. If the accused is situated in a foreign country, the entire investigation may come to an abrupt halt because the officers may not proceed unless there are formal communications with the officers and the courts of that country. The external affairs ministry may be involved in processing the letter of rogatory from one court in India to the foreign court. Bilateral treaties between the concerned countries play a huge role in investigating and prosecuting these cases. Although, most of the cybercrimes targeting women are not considered as significant unless they have graver consequences like human trafficking or a homicide.

Because of the legal protocols prescribed by the criminal procedure code, public prosecutors or assistant public prosecutors will be able to review the case in its entirety after the charge sheet is submitted to the magistrate. Given the above discussion regarding the challenges faced by the police, this stage of initiation of trials may arise only in limited cases. However, even in such stages, the prosecutor may have limited opportunity to interact with the police. Only when the magistrate may need to enquire about the details of the prosecution witnesses, the prosecutor may ask the police officer to bring forward more evidence for the prosecution.

A perfect coupling of the police and the prosecution may be seen from the stage of examination of the witnesses where the prosecutor (and the defence) may seek for adjournments for bringing in better evidence and supporting the case with better legal analysis. Indian prosecutors are generally not allowed to withdraw the case as S.321 of the Criminal Procedure Code indicates that withdrawal is not allowed unless there are proper reasons that are accepted by the magistrate. However, in some rare cases, prosecutors may withdraw if they do not have sufficient support for a successful prosecution. This may include proper time to get ready for the trial and/or sufficient evidence. Prosecutors do not have the legal power to interact with the defendants during the pre-trial procedures like what may happen in several common law countries. Even if the case results in a summons case trial which are held for petty to less serious offences, or summary trial, the prosecutor may not be able to persuade the defendant to accept a guilty plea without the case going before the magistrate. However, this is not the case for cybercrimes targeting children, especially child pornography cases, phishing cases, or cases involving unauthorised access to computer data, which may not necessarily include cases of cybercrimes against women. In most of these cases, the prosecutor may successfully prove the responsibility of the defendant with proper interpretation of the laws based on the evidence produced by the police to the magistrate while submitting the charge sheet and based on evidence that may be called for during the trial. For cybercrimes targeting women, prosecutors may not be able to collect the necessary evidence - either for the mismanagement of the digital evidence by the victims or the police, or due to the lack of cooperation from the victims.

However, this does not necessarily mean that the scenario is bleak in India. There is an emerging group of prosecutors who are well trained in handling cybercrime cases. Even though they may not be allowed to guide the investigating officer in preparing the charge sheet, they can conduct trials with the available evidence, and may also get the police to bring additional evidence for supporting the prosecution during the trial. For example, the 2018 case of State of West Bengal vs Animesh Boxi (2017) Based on the charge sheet submitted to the magistrate of first class in the Midnapore district of West Bengal, the prosecution was able to successfully prove the charges against the defendant charged with the sexual assault of a woman, voyeurism, stalking (including cyber stalking), and conveying/uploading sexually explicit contents on cyber platforms. However, this is just one of the rare examples where the prosecution could win because the prosecutor was well trained, and the victim and the police cooperated with the prosecution.

CASE MANAGEMENT BY POLICE AND PROSECUTION UNDER THE UK LAWS

The case management system in the UK is completely different than the Indian system. In the UK, prosecutors have more power in deciding about the fate of the defendants regarding trial by the juries. While Indian criminal procedure code has divided the cases into three categories for the purpose of trial (namely warrant, summon and summary cases and trials), in the UK the cases are divided as indictable-only offences, either way offences or summary offences. While the judicial magistrate holds the ultimate power in deciding the fate of the defendant, the prosecutor may work with the police much earlier than what takes place in the Indian criminal justice system. The case details are submitted to the prosecution first for better cooperation between the police and prosecutor. In the UK, the prosecutors and the police may have a better relationship than in India. This is evident from certain guidelines including guidelines related to police and crown prosecution guidelines, the code for Crown Prosecutors, social media –guidelines on prosecuting cases involving communications sent via social media (Crown and Prosecution Services, 2018). The investigating officer must go ahead for collecting the evidence for reported cybercrimes targeted against women as per the Police and Evidence Act, 1984 (Pace Act). The social media –guidelines on prosecuting cases involving communications sent via social media have mentioned about online crimes targeting women and children, which includes virtual mobbing, revenge pornography, cyberstalking, criminal intimidation, cyberbullying, online defamation, and publishing information which may disclose the identity of the complainant of sexual offences etc. While the investigative powers of the police remain unfettered, the police have the liberty to consult with the prosecutor about proceeding in gather further evidence. The charging decisions rests on the police (after the completion of the investigation) and the prosecution (before taking the case to the trial). The prosecutor's decision to prosecute as stated in clause 3.1 of the Crown prosecution Code is as follows:

In more serious or complex cases, prosecutors decide whether a person should be charged with a criminal offence and, if so, what that offence should be. Prosecutors may also advise on or authorise out-of-court disposals as an alternative to prosecution. They make their decisions in accordance with this Code, the

DPP's Guidance on Charging and any relevant legal guidance or policy. The police apply the same principles in deciding whether to start criminal proceedings against a person in those cases for which they are responsible.

The Code of Crown Prosecutors emphasise on Full code test, and threshold test, based on which the prosecutors may decide to go ahead with the prosecution. Full code test is explained as below:

The Full Code Test has two stages: (i) the evidential stage; followed by (ii) the public interest stage......... The Full Code Test should be applied:

when all outstanding reasonable lines of inquiry have been pursued; or

prior to the investigation being completed, if the prosecutor is satisfied that any further evidence or material is unlikely to affect the application of the Full Code Test, whether in favour of or against a prosecution.

Threshold test on the other hand needs to pass five conditions for charging: these are as follows:

"Reasonable ground for suspecting that the person to be charged has committed an offence.

Further evidence can be obtained to provide realistic prospect of conviction.

The seriousness or the circumstance of the case justifies the making of an immediate charging decision.

There are continuing substantial grounds to object to bail in accordance with the Bail Act 1976 and in all the circumstances of the case it is proper to do so.

It is in the public interest to charge the suspect".

It is only when that the five conditions are fulfilled, the criminal justice machinery may go ahead for charging. In the absence of above, the victim may be guided to avail other measures including initiating private suits which may or may not be a hybrid legal process including civil and criminal laws for restoration of justice.

CONCLUSION AND SUGGESTION

The above discussions may show that the English criminal procedural systems may provide better facilities for the police and prosecutors to frame the charges against the accused which may be beneficial for the victim justice. But this system is not beyond criticism as some critics have pointed out that the rights of the accused are hugely suppressed. Given the fact that on virtual platforms a person may be posed as an accused if another uses his virtual identity to commit crimes, the rights of the former to prove his innocence may be lesser in the current set up. But in such cases the police and the prosecution must rely heavily on analysis of digital footprints left by the real accused as well as the other person who may have been posed as an accused by the former. In India on the other hand, cases of online harassment against women may not be given due justice because the police may not consult with the prosecutor at the pre-trial stage. Resultant the time for the trial may be longer especially when the prosecutor may have knowledge regarding information technology laws.

In some cases where the prosecutors are not well trained in handling the digital evidence and the cybercrime cases, the defendants may escape the clutches of the law swiftly. Indian law makers may consider introducing rules for improving the police-prosecution relationship to improve the case management situation related to cybercrimes cases. India has recently introduced Information Technology (Intermediary Guidelines and Digital Media Ethics Code) Rules, 2021 which enhances the responsibility of the websites. As discussed above, this is another addition to the array of legislations criminalising certain cyber offences. This may not be fruitful if the criminal justice organisation stays unconnected for application of such rules and regulations.

RECOMMENDATIONS

As the above discussion may show, prosecution in UK has the responsibility of charging an offender after critical evaluation of the evidence. In India, this is a magisterial job under S.228 of the Criminal Procedure Code. Unlike the Indian criminal procedure code which is the main guiding statute for conducting the criminal cases in India, there are several guidelines available in the UK issued on Code for Crown Prosecution, crown prosecution and police relationships, social media crime prosecution, etc., which may not only provide a clear guideline as how to handle the criminal matters by the prosecutor and the police including the cybercrime cases.

The cybercrime prosecution guidelines and social media –guidelines on prosecuting cases involving communications sent via social media lay down different types of cybercrimes that may happen against women and children predominantly other than financial crimes. These documents also lay down the legal provisions which are best applicable for prosecuting such offences. These may help the police to understand how to proceed for investigation of such offences and how to carry forward the case with the prosecutors. Women victims may not always report cybercrimes to the police. But once reported, the police may proceed with the investigation in a better way than what may happen in India because the legal provisions related to collection, preserving of evidence and burden of proving the same are time tested in the UK. These provisions along with the specific criminal laws addressing several categories of online criminal activities make it easier for the police and prosecution to understand how to proceed with cases and manage the cases before the actual trial commences since the prosecutors are the authorities for charging and they have the power to decide whether to send a case for trial or whether to go ahead with out of court disposal of the case. As such, the prosecutors may have wider scope to investigate the case details and the evidence collected by the police, which may prevent the escalation of the victimisation for the victims.

Pre-trial proceedings and the role of the prosecutors are heavily criticised from the perspective of rights of the accused (especially from the perspective of right to be tried by the magistrate and juries (Myers, 2017). In this regard, mention must be made for prosecutorial power to object for bail and emphasise on no contact and prohibitory orders that may impose on the accused. India does not have any such rules where the magistrate may impose no contact orders while the accused is released on bail or where such order may be imposed after the accused may be released after a simple imprisonment. This notion of no contact order is impliedly included in the order for bail and monitoring order on the probation officers post release from judicial custody. But due to absence of an expressed legislative provision, the accused may go ahead for contacting the offender for meting out more harassment as a revenge.

In Indian criminal legal set up, this may be considered as a second offence by the same accused. But this may not deter the accused from re-victimising the victim. While in the UK the prosecution may press for no contact order while allowing the case for magisterial decision, the prosecution generally considers the probability even before the accused may apply for bail. This may prevent the accused from accessing the digital communication technology for re-victimising the victim.

REFERENCES

Citron, D. K. (2009). Law's expressive value in combating cyber gender harassment. *Michigan Law Review*, *108*, 373.

Forouzan, H., Jahankhani, H., & McCarthy, J. (2018). An examination into the level of training, education, and awareness among frontline police officers in tackling cybercrime within the Metropolitan Police Service. *Cyber Criminology*, 307-323.

Gabriel, H., & Hemblade, H. (2019). *FEMICIDE cyber-crimes against women & Girls* (vol. 11). http://femicide-watch.org/sites/default/files/FemicideVolXI.pdf

Halder, D., & Jaishankar, K. (2011). Cyber gender harassment and secondary victimization: A comparative analysis of the United States, the UK, and India. *Victims & Offenders*, *6*(4), 386–398.

Halder, D., & Jaishankar, K. (2012). *Cyber Crime and the victimization of women: Laws, rights, and regulations*. IGI Global. doi:10.4018/978-1-60960-830-9

Halder, D., & Jaishankar, K. (2014). Online victimization of Andaman Jarawa tribal women: An analysis of the 'human safari.' *British Journal of Criminology*, *54*(4), 673-688.

Halder, D., & Jaishankar, K. (2015). Irrational coping theory and positive criminology: A framework to protect victims of cyber-crime. In N. Ronel & D. Segev (Eds.), *Positive criminology* (pp. 276–291). Routledge. doi:10.4324/9781315796536-20

Harkin, D., Whelan, C., & Chang, L. (2018). The challenges facing specialist police cyber- crime units: An empirical analysis. *Police Practice and Research*, *19*(6), 519–536.

Myers, N. M. (2017). Eroding the presumption of innocence: Pre-trial detention and the use of conditional release on bail. *British Journal of Criminology*, *57*(3), 664–683.

Puducherry Police. (n.d.). *Powers of police to arrest, procedure of arrest, and documentation of arrest*. https://police.py.gov.in/Police%20manual/Chapter%20PDF/CHAPTER%2038%20C%20Powers%20of%20Police%20to%20arrest,%20procedure%20of%20arrest,%20and%20documentatio.pdf

Ray, A. (1978). Police administration and centre-state relations in India. *The Indian Journal of Public Administration*, *24*(1), 38–44.

Saha, T., & Srivastava, A. (2014). Indian women at risk in the cyber space: A conceptual model of reasons of victimization. *International Journal of Cyber Criminology*, *8*(1).

The Crown Prosecution Service. (2018). *Police and CPS relations*. https://www.cps.gov.uk/legal-guidance/police-and-cps-relations

Tonry, M. (2012). Prosecutors and politics in comparative perspective. *Crime and Justice*, *41*(1), 1–33.

van de Weijer, S. G., Leukfeldt, R., & Bernasco, W. (2019). Determinants of reporting cybercrime: A comparison between identity theft, consumer fraud, and hacking. *European Journal of Criminology*, *16*(4), 486–508.

Wall, D. S. (2015). The Internet as a conduit for criminal activity. *Information Technology and the Criminal Justice System*, 77-98.

Wilson, L. A. (2014). The rights of victims vs the rights of the accused: Striking a balance between the rights of victims and accused persons in the international criminal justice setting. *UW Austl. L. Rev.*, *38*, 152.

Chapter 15
Homelessness, Mental Health Afflictions, Problematic Substance Use, and Associated Criminality:
A Transformative Justice Resolution

Jayesh D'Souza
UCLA Extension, USA

ABSTRACT

Homelessness and related community ailments have plagued society for a number of years, and governments have found it difficult to get these under control. The sheer number of homeless with mental health afflictions and problematic substance use problems leaves no doubt about the need for a stronger, more urgent government response. Community ailments such as these have led to increased crime rates and incarcerations and overcrowded prisons without a lasting solution in sight. This chapter uses the transformative justice model, with the expectation it produces better results than current models, by examining the source of homelessness, mental health afflictions, and problematic substance use and their bi-directional relationship with crime. This inter-jurisdictional study compares the current situations in the state of California and the province of Ontario, which have a high percent of homeless populations. It proves that special attention to vulnerable populations such as racialized groups, the socioeconomically disadvantaged, and youth is warranted.

INTRODUCTION

In 2019, San Francisco resident Paneez Kosarian was attacked by a man outside her condominium building because, in his mind, he was attempting to "save her from robots." Media reports differ on whether he had problematic substance use or mental health afflictions, but they concur that he had no known address; he was homeless. Incidents such as these have led to growing public sentiment against the homeless, those

DOI: 10.4018/978-1-7998-6884-2.ch015

with mental resistance health afflictions and those who suffer from problematic substance use. Backlash in the form of to building navigation centers and tent encampments in residential areas, due to the spurt in crime committed by the homeless, has garnered increasing attention to vulnerable populations in California. According to one report, almost half of the homeless population in the United States is in California where rising house prices and astronomical rents have locked many out of the housing and rental market. Research studies suggest that homelessness is intrinsically linked to problematic substance use and mental health afflictions (McDonagh, 2011; Piat et al., 2015; Fuller, 2019).

The situation is no different across the border in Ontario, Canada's most populous province. Brad Chapman, a 43-year-old father found himself homeless, and in and out of jail due to a drug dependency, until his death on the streets of Toronto (Boisvert, 2018). His case helped substantiate research findings that long-term homelessness impacts the well-being of individuals due to problematic substance use, cognitive impairments, chronic illness, and mental health problems. This and other similar incidents put focus on treatment services and the increased need for interventions for these individuals. This was also significant in another context: it sparked interest in the relationship between psychoactive substance use and crime and the impact on the criminal justice system (Berenbaumm, 2019).

In line with this trend, cities within California and Ontario are witnessing an increase in crime driven by poverty, homelessness, mental health afflictions and problematic substance use and putting immense pressure on limited resources allocated to the criminal justice systems. This chapter studies these community ailments, evaluates governments' performance in addressing them and identifies crime-reduction outcomes using the transformative justice approach. These encompass proper discharge planning, reintegration, housing assistance, social supports, employment, training, and education. Finally, it provides recommendations for state/provincial government policy shifts in keeping with the transformative justice theme of this chapter.

RETRIBUTIVE, RESTORATIVE OR TRANSFORMATIVE JUSTICE?

There is a good reason homelessness and associated mental health afflictions and problematic substance use are associated with criminogenic behavior. The Institute of Fiscal Studies and Democracy (2018) explains that jurisdictions deal with the symptoms of homelessness but not the underlying issues also known as the feeder roots of homelessness. Groups of people such as those in foster care, military veterans, prisoners, and discharges from hospitals have all experienced serious life disruptions only to find themselves at a point where desolation intersects with criminality. In its attempt to address this criminality, the chapter reviews the merit of three approaches to justice as follows and finds that the transformative justice model is most suitable from a criminal justice reform perspective.

Retributive Justice

The retributive approach to justice asserts that criminals must be punished for their actions and has its foundations in the philosophies of Georg Hegel (1942), Immanuel Kant (1956) and Herbert Morris (1968). Ezorsky (1972) contends that moral balance is the centerpiece of retributive justice where a criminal act is countered with retaliatory punishment of equal magnitude and where punishment restores the unfair advantage a person has gained in society by failing to exercise what another has exercised: self-control and self-restraint. Norval Morris (1974) argues that while the victim's desire for punishing the perpetrators may impede any immediate hopes for peace, reconciliation may be achieved in the long run by limiting retributivism.

Restorative Justice

Quinney and Wildeman (1991) discuss moving from retributive justice to a peace-making resolution of conflict. McCold (1995) and Bazemore (1998) explain restorative justice as an approach that seeks to repair the relationship between the victim, transgressor, and community. It involves the transgressor showing remorse about wronging the victim and the victim achieving a sense of vindication when the transgressor understands the pain caused to the victim. Justice can be achieved by securing a balance between institutional control, and self-regulation and self-discipline. Reintegration can be achieved by mending social relationships through programs such as victim restitution, offender accountability and victim-offender remediation. Harris (2004), Lofton (2004), and Daly (2000) outline the limitations of restorative justice in that it does not take into consideration conditions that influence a person's actions such as socio-economic background and while it is more beneficial than conventional courthouse justice, it does not necessarily result in healing in societies where racial and ethnic inequalities exist.

Transformative Justice

Transformative justice came into prominence through the writings of Ruth Morris (1999), a Canadian Quaker, who believed that fractured urban settings could not only be restored but transformed. She attributed the high population of minorities in the penal system to unemployment, job discrimination, housing discrimination and racist attacks which she termed "structural injustices." Morris advocated the abolishment of the current penal system which she saw as ineffective due to the high incarceration rates, recidivism, and cost of maintenance. Her recommendations included probation, bail supervision, Victim Offender Reconciliation Programs (VORP) and community service work orders which she felt were more-cost effective alternatives to prison terms that she described as "caging." She also suggested housing alternatives that provide a safe, living environment for the incarcerated and treatment programs for justice-involved individuals with mental health and substance use problems (Morris, 2000).

Transformative justice can manifest itself in different forms. Barak (2014) provides tangible solutions to transform justice-involved individuals including prison-to-community life skills training, technical courses like gardening, cooking, cleaning and maintenance, and sanction-to-solution programs that combine reconciliation and restitution conducted at therapy-halfway houses. Soothill (2010) and Zoellick (2018) propose several alternative-to-incarceration remedies including treatment for addiction-related offences, family-related interventions that will help those in the system build relationships with their families, and social programs that cater to the psychological development and transformation of justice-involved individuals. Whitehouse and Fitzgerald (2020) advise that individuals can return to society as law-abiding citizens through programs that "nourish fusion with prosocial groups and values and defuse offenders from toxic groups". The rationale is that those who demonstrate the inclination to develop prosocial fused relationships while in the system will certainly have the ability to build prosocial fusion families outside it.

COMMUNITY AILMENTS AND CRIMINALITY: THE ESSENTIAL QUESTIONS

Ruth Morris' philosophy forms the basis of this chapter as it provides treatment and not punishment as the basis for a policy discourse on homelessness, mental health afflictions and problematic substance use in relation to crime. The opinions from experts on possible solutions for community ailments, the government's performance in addressing these issues and performance indicators to measure progress are presented as the chapter progresses. The study adopted the constructivist paradigm in developing a research design. Mertens (2019) and Dickson et al. (2016) maintain that this paradigm is useful for studies that assume that knowledge is a socially constructed phenomenon and that a researcher can best gain insights about a situation from those who have direct experience with that situation. Another assumption of this type of research design is that reality is subjective and based on the individual perspectives of the study's participants (Mertens, 2019).

This study revolves around qualitative research where, under the assumptions of the constructivist paradigm, participants were interviewed to understand their perspective on the subject under study. Interviews took place between February 1, 2020, and April 30, 2020, over the telephone and employed a semi-structured format using open-ended questions after all ethical and consent and procedures were complied with. Magaldi and Berler (2020) describe semi-structured interviews as exploratory in nature that are commonly used in qualitative research studies in the social sciences. These interviews focus on a core topic but are structured to foster discovery by permitting the interview to follow topical trajectories as the conversation unfolds. Respondents were encouraged to express their thoughts and requested to respond to follow-up questions related to the focal points of this study. Interviews were conducted until insights from the responses became repetitive.

Experts' opinions shed light on the cause-effect relationship between crime and homelessness, mental health afflictions, and problematic substance use. These experts were also asked to evaluate the government's performance in addressing these societal ailments and for their opinions on performance improvement and metrics. The study solicited ten participants for their views, five with related work experience in California and the other five in Ontario. They are:

Ms. Amber Kellen (Ontario) directs evaluations on the social impacts of community issues and develops initiatives and partnerships to address them. Her published research covers problematic substance use, homelessness, and the criminal justice system.

Ms. Maggie Merritt (California) serves in an advisory capacity on brain health issues to several statewide commissions working closely with government officials and legislators.

Dr. John Weekes (Ontario) is a social scientist recognized for his contributions to humanitarian corrections and whose experience covers the areas of forensic psychology and addictions, and psychiatry and behavioural neurosciences.

Dr. Douglas Polcin's (California) expertise extends to treatments for drug and alcohol related problems for which he has received several grants.

Ms. Laurie Monsebraaten (Ontario) is a long-time journalist covering topics from social justice to poverty.

Dr. Maya Buenaventura (California) is an attorney who has worked with low-income families and conducted research on interventions for individuals in the criminal-justice system and the homeless.

Dr. Lori Regenstreif (Ontario) is a medical doctor and the co-founder of a shelter health network who has also assisted patients in mental health diversion programs.

Mr. Drew Soderborg and Mr. Luke Koushmaro (California) are state bureaucrats who impart non-partisan advice on public safety policy issues, specifically, community corrections and rehabilitation programs.
Mr. Jean-Philippe Crête (Ontario) is a provincial bureaucrat and part-time criminal justice instructor.
Mr. Brandon Martin (California) researches state and local criminal justice reform and corrections policy for a nonpartisan policy think tank.

These experts are also referred to as interviewees and study participants throughout the course of this study. Their responses have been kept anonymous to protect confidentiality. The study purports to answer the following questions with the help of their responses:

1. Is the transformative justice model a good fit for criminal justice-involved individuals with experiences of homelessness, mental health afflictions and problematic substance use?
2. Is there expert consensus on remedial policy options and programmatic solutions for criminal justice-involved individuals with experiences of homelessness, mental health afflictions and problematic substance use?
3. Are there differences in government approaches in addressing ailments experienced by criminal justice-involved individuals in the United States and Canada, particularly, California and Ontario?

In evaluating the results of this study, the process of international benchmarking was deployed where relevant criminal justice practices adopted by the state government of California and the provincial government of Ontario were compared. Several reports and articles were reviewed to support or refute interviewee responses. A thorough data analysis helped to inductively draw conclusions and provide recommendations for changes to the current system.

CRITICAL THEMES IN CURRENT PRACTICES

The experts interviewed from this study were from diverse professional backgrounds and included lawyers, doctors, journalists, bureaucrats, and community service managers. They were chosen after random online searches for experts in California and Ontario revealed that they were the best fit for this study. A content analysis of primary and secondary data was manually conducted to identify links between the findings of the interviews and the literature review and draw generalizations. This yielded an understanding of the circumstances surrounding populations suffering from homelessness, mental health afflictions and problematic substance use, the shortcomings of government approaches in addressing these problems and improvements needed to achieve positive outcomes. The ensuing discussion sheds light on these:

Justice-Involved Individuals Should Not Be Treated as Criminals Without Understanding Their Social Conditions

Homelessness

Study participants generally agreed that homelessness has been needlessly criminalized considering the circumstances that led to it. These include lack of shelters and access to services, difficulty in securing employment and housing, and problematic substance use. The homeless are highly likely to get misdemeanors for sleeping on the sidewalk or urinating in public. One of the interviewees detailed the plight of the homeless, "They do not have private space. They live in public space and must face the consequences arising out of it. They have no money to pay fines and indulge in petty crime to pay for addictions. Their conviction histories prevent landlords from renting out to them. The government should get rid of legislation that criminalizes homelessness. Much of the problem is at the roots as with the child welfare system. If there is an incident at the foster care home, the police are called, and the involved individual has a criminal record coming out of foster care at the age of 18 (Interview, Ontario expert)." Another interviewee affirmed these sentiments, "These people are victims of the system. Those with mental health issues and the homeless have been criminalized. It started with Ronald Regan's closure of asylums which created prisons and homelessness. People with mental health issues should not be sent to jail. They are not cared for and should not be treated the same way as cancer (Interview, California expert)."

The experts explicated the link between homelessness and criminal activity as symptoms of a bigger problem which is poverty. Their comments made clear that these are people who have not had financial support in early life and now find themselves without adequate housing or basic needs. Homelessness is a strong factor linked to crime that is not as much recognized or given importance. It is the driving force behind criminal activity and is related to a person's upbringing and circumstances. The homeless indulge in petty crimes because they do not have a place to stay and nothing to eat. One of the interviewees suggested that poor people purposely get busted to spend winter in prison because they do not want to freeze out in the cold, "Apartments are being turned to condominiums and re-gentrification is making it harder for people to find housing. In some cases, prisons are more of a safe haven than the streets (Interview, Ontario expert)." An interviewee suggested housing where people are required to be alcohol and drug free could mitigate the problem more than shelters, "Homelessness is a result of high rates of inequality in terms of financial resources. San Francisco has homeless shelters, but this has no impact on reducing crime rates (Interview, California expert)."

Anecdotal evidence reveals that the stigma associated with homelessness results in the homeless shunning assistance like supportive housing. California and Ontario have engaged in public awareness campaigns to counter stigma and renaming homeless shelters has been suggested as an option (Ferguson, 2018). Criminalization has hit the homeless hard in both jurisdictions. Resulting arrests or warrants give landlords a reason to reject housing applications while fines drain the homeless of already scarce resources. An example of the futility of criminalization of homelessness is Ontario's *Safe Street Act* which cost Toronto police almost $1 million in implementation costs to hand out $4 million in tickets between 2000 and 2010, almost all of which was never paid because the fines of $60 to $500 per ticket were too high and beyond the means of the ticketed (Monsebraaten, 2015). Evidence shows that youth and racialized group populations have suffered the most from criminalization of the homeless. Youth homelessness is a result of childhoods confined to foster homes and a product of child protection and justice systems that are dependent on punishment rather than rehabilitation. Criminalization of traumatized youth, unreasonable bail conditions and poorly trained group care and corrections personnel result in youth, especially Black and Indigenous youth, ending up on the streets (Treleaven, 2019). The literature also reveals that homeless racialized groups have been impacted by past evictions, criminal records, and the inability to pay security deposits when landlords do not accept housing vouchers. (Wiltz, 2019). Risk-averse conditions imposed by bail courts also add to the problem. These individuals often have trouble persuading the courts that they will abide by their bail conditions and even if they are released on bail, they end of up breaching bail conditions due to lack of a permanent address (Housing, Health, and Justice Community of Interest, 2019).

Mental Health Afflictions

Most study participants concurred that those with mental health afflictions find it difficult to conform to laws and there is a need to fight stigma that comes with these afflictions, especially, for those who have had brushes with the law so they can seek help. One of the participants claimed that 60% of those in the California state prison system have mental health afflictions while another put this figure at 30% in Ontario's corrections facilities. One of the interviewees asserted that deinstitutionalization in the 1960s was a strong negative factor for these high figures. Interviewees also agreed that this cohort had trouble coping with society. This resulted in them finding themselves on the wrong side of the law as a result of acts of petty theft, public disruption, and other low-level crime. Thus, the necessity of getting them into treatment because untreated mental health conditions could lead to addictions which could resulted in the afflicted flouting the law, "These people are victims not perpetrators. Studies have shown the connection between autism and crime and how steadying those with autism would reduce criminal incidents (Interview, California expert)."

One of the experts held that mental health afflictions not only resulted in petty crime but major incidents like mass shootings. There is stigma and discrimination against this client population but what makes it worse is the fact that it is politically unpopular to support people who have criminal backgrounds, "Words like 'offender' are pejorative (Interview, Ontario expert)". Another participant, with an outlier opinion, expounded that mental health is not a strong influence on criminality and is more a stereotype, "Someone with a mental condition might be taken advantage of to rob a store. The mental health connection to criminal justice waxes and wanes. It is difficult to know which causes which due to minimal populations. There are other aspects to criminal activity besides mental health. Some facets of mental health conditions may contribute to criminal activity as seen when the courts declare an individual to be not criminally responsible due to the individual's mental health (Interview, Ontario expert)."

California and Ontario have made attempts to reduce the stigma and discrimination against those with mental health conditions through legislation but a large section of the afflicted population in both jurisdictions go untreated (Jeffe, 1987). It would benefit both governments to take note of studies that showed treatment, along with reducing stigma and discrimination associated with mental health afflictions, can result in higher tax collections and economic benefits for governments and produce a high return on the dollar (Ashwood et al., 2017). Another common experience for both jurisdictions was the unintended consequences of deinstitutionalization which attempted to integrate the mentally ill into the community. It resulted in fewer psychiatric facilities for afflicted individuals and increased their interactions with the police leading some to label prisons as "de facto mental institutions" (Picard, 2017). The policy of confining those with mental health afflictions to solitary confinement in prisons has also garnered attention, especially in Ontario. Such was the case of Christina Jahn who was forced into segregation for more than 200 days at a local detention center in Ontario despite suffering from schizophrenia and breast cancer. The outcome of *Jahn v. the Ontario Ministry of Community Safety and Correction Services* forced governments to rethink segregation practices for those with pre-existing mental health conditions (Miller & Crawford, 2018).

At this point, it might be suitable to comment on the impact of deinstitutionalization in the United States and Canada which resulted in mental health services being delivered by community-based agencies and clinics. Its original intention was to integrate those with mental afflictions with rest of society, but these individuals continued to be marginalized and isolated. Padwa et al. (2016) explain the problems which made it onerous for these individuals to cope, "Medication side effects made it difficult to function independently; in spite of disability welfare subsidies, they continued to live in isolation from the mainstream community; and placement in supported work settings lowered their confidence and led to demoralizing episodes of inactivity" (p. 242). This was compounded by the fact that community-based mental health clinics did not meet the medical requirements of deinstitutionalized patients. The issues faced by these institutions were the same as those that plague community-based mental health systems today including a shortfall of funding. The individuals that bore the consequences of the inadequacies of the new system were the ones who were suffering the most. They ended up being frequently hospitalized, admitted to nursing homes, incarcerated or homeless (Padwa et al., 2016).

Problematic Substance Use

Experts provided valuable insight into the relationship between problematic substance use and criminal activity. The perception was that there is a significant relationship between the two as often the substances consumed are illegal and offenders have a compulsion to finance their habit. Hence, problematic substance use is a driver of crime, according to many of the study participants, who observed that help is not always forthcoming to vulnerable individuals because they incite fear. One of the interviewees delved deeper into the subject stating that problematic substance use is a strong criminogenic factor, and that the severity of the crime is correlated to the extent of addiction, "Alcohol-related crime is extinctive, that is, it is associated with violence and destruction. Drug-related crime is acquisitive crime and involves acquiring money for drugs through robbery, theft and fraud (Interview, Ontario expert)."

An interviewee seconded this opinion and philosophized that problematic substance use leads to desperation just like hunger and the poorer someone is, the more likely the time in prison. Alcohol leads to violent crime like assault, domestic abuse, and impaired driving. Stimulants, like methamphetamine, result in behaviors that lead to incarceration due to violent crime. Opioids are associated with trafficking and prostitution. Due to their addictive nature, fewer legal opioids are being prescribed and for shorter periods of time due to their addictive nature, one of the experts revealed. Another interviewee expressed frustration that many in the system lack access to health care providers and social workers. Hence, they self-medicate. To escape drug tests, some switch to hard drugs for which they are not tested, thus, exacerbating the problem. Several interviewees were in favor of publicly funded interventions and drug decriminalization where simple possession of drugs would no longer be a crime and users could get help for their addictions.

Just as is the case with mental health, those with problematic substance use are quite often stigmatized. A study in Ontario is one of a few to conclude that this stigma exists even among health care practitioners treating problematic substance users and educational anti-stigma interventions are required to change their attitudes (Giliauskas & Gogolishvili, 2018). The numbers also show a link between addictions and justice-involved individuals. Those with problematic substance use have high incarceration rates and high overdose rates a year after being released from prison (Groot et al., 2016). Random drug testing at California prisons showed that drug use is a problem because it produced a ten percent failure rate among inmates (Raphael et al., 2017). These statistics inform us that those in the criminal justice system need support and treating them as criminals will not help them overcome their addictions. Besides eliminating the stigma surrounding and ending the criminalization of homelessness, mental health afflictions and problematic substance use, governments must institute profound changes to programs and policies some of which are explored below.

The Government Must Enhance Service Provision and Provide the Right Service to the Right People at the Right Time

Housing

The perceptions of the experts on the state/provincial government's performance in addressing homelessness and associated criminality were mostly negative. The tone was one of frustration owing to the fact that homelessness is not a government priority and so much more could be done to address the problem. Cutbacks in funding and changing government priorities have seen a drop in the number of individuals benefitting from local housing programs. In addition to this, minimum wage raises opposed by the government act as a disincentive for people to work. When high costs of living erode their earnings, they start relying more on social assistance. Experts outlined these and other issues with government policies and programs such as lack of discharge planning, over-incarceration, lack of affordable housing and ineffective rent control regulations that lead to homelessness. With regard to discharge planning, some interviewees stressed that those individuals released from custody or remand have no access to social services, "Screening is done at time of release but there is no tracking system for where these people go after being released. There is no proper long-term discharge planning. The government must build transitional housing for those released. In a big city like Toronto, there are only 30 safe beds (also known as crisis support beds) around the city which allow a 30-day maximum stay. It was very difficult to get people into these as they do not accept advance reservations. In one instance of poor planning, those released from one of the city's detention centers, must travel way outside the city by public transit to reach the shelter (Interview, Ontario expert)."

Study participants proposed a course of action for the government to consider helping these vulnerable individuals. This comprised of reforms to tackle affordable housing and social issues such as poverty and disabilities, and income support for basic necessities, such as food and shelter, to help people stay on their feet, "The lack of provision of the basics needed to survive leads to more serious issues because crime is connected to poverty. With reforms such as housing benefits, criminal justice costs will go down. A basic or liveable income will lighten the burden on government criminal justice budgets (Interview, Ontario expert)." One of the interviewees asserted that permanent and transitional housing is only a start and the government should find solutions that assist tenants with eviction proceedings, provide short-term loans to pay rent arrears and build modular housing. It should also permit developers to bypass building rules and offer environmental regulation waivers. Finally, the government should intervene to increase permanent housing retention, address racial disparities in public housing evictions and engage in better case management. These measures, according to the experts, will help governments to enhance current performance. One of the study participants felt that the government is already making a strong attempt to address the problem, but housing affordability issues continue to persist. The expert suggested how government can better shape policy, "The government should be asking questions like how to keep people out of prison, do they have a place to stay and are there employment opportunities for them (Interview, California expert)."

In California and Ontario, where a large proportion of the homeless population is unemployed, the state/provincial governments must realign priorities to build lasting solutions, "California can't arrest its way out of the housing crisis...Those efforts [housing initiatives] are much more cost-effective than anything involving the very expensive criminal justice system... (Flory, 2020)." These solutions could be in the form of permanent supportive housing, affordable housing or the evidence-based Housing

First program that provides participants not only with long-term housing but also wrap-around services which address the mental health and substance dependency needs of participants (O'Grady & Lafleur, 2016). Table 1 provides a summary of stakeholder group recommendations to address homelessness and improve housing availability.

Table 1. Stakeholder Recommendations for Addressing Homelessness and Housing to Reduce Incarceration Rates and Assist Justice-Involved Individuals

Recommendation	Stakeholder Group
• Invest in discharge planning (for housing, employment, and social services). • Adopt rent-geared-to-income housing policies. • Provide housing protection for those who enter short-term custodial services.	John Howard Society
• Make "no-fault" evictions illegal and ensure compliance with and enforcement of the law.	Advocacy Center for Tenants Ontario
• Prohibit rent gouging committed through vacancy decontrol. • Commit to investment in community housing repair. • Conduct data tracking for rental buildings.	Association of Municipalities Ontario

Source: 1. Effective Just and Humane a Case for Client Centered Collaboration, John Howard Society and Wellesley Institute, May 2012.
2. Submission to the Standing Committee on General Government on Bill 124, Rental Fairness Act, 2017, Advocacy Center for Tenants Ontario.
3. Fixing the Housing Affordability Crisis: Municipal Recommendations for Housing in Ontario, Association of Municipalities Ontario.

There have also been calls for changes to administrative practices and social policy reform. A report by the California Legislative Analyst's Office (LAO) commented on a recent $1 billion pledge announcement by the state government to fight homelessness. The LAO's report indicated that throwing money at the problem is a worthless endeavor. Instead, the government must draft specific action plans and coordinate with stakeholders in determining how to put these funds to use (Morales et al., 2020). Improvements could also be made to the Ontario government's policies. In one example, those on social assistance in the province presently have any additional income like child support or part-time work, capped and clawed-back by the government if the amount exceeds this cap. This policy should be abolished so poor families can build personal savings for housing (Noble, 2015).

Mental Health Afflictions

Just like for homelessness, government performance in addressing mental health afflictions fell below the expectations of the experts interviewed for this study. Some of these experts were of the perception that the political affiliation of the government in power is a key determinant of its policies towards mental health affliction, "Some governments have been impressive in terms of being innovation-driven and supporting evidence-based public policy solutions for mental health. Other governments' decisions are ideologically-driven rather than empirically-based (Interview, Ontario expert)." Some interviewees rued the fact that government funding announcements for mental health are of low priority even though mental health assessments are of vital importance in treating mental health conditions. One of the interviewees was of the opinion that lack of funding results in growing waiting lists for treatment and rehabilitation services, "It is important to start treatment early before the situation gets out of hand. Government action should encompass development of a tracking system, increased budgets and reduced waiting lists (Interview, Ontario expert)." Another study participant agreed with this explaining that funding is also important for hiring more psychologists and mental health workers to meet the needs of patients.

While one of the interviewees identified some positives in current systems such as providing timely access to treatment services to prisoners and handling urgent referrals efficiently, other interviewees raised questions about gaps in the current systems. One of them observed that even though the police are trained to deal with the mentally afflicted as first responders and diversion programs are in place, the government's policies and practices are reactionary rather than proactive. Another study participant expressed full confidence in the police handling the mentally afflicted but referenced the main problem as keeping those with mental health afflictions on their medications after they are released from prison. This view was supported by some of the other participants one of whom suggested that governments focus on the long-term needs of those with mental health conditions and get the private sector involved in the process, "Amazon, in 2017, made billion in profits but paid truly little in taxes. Companies don't contribute to the well-being of society (Interview, California expert)." Besides all of this, it is imperative for the government to boost legislative efforts, as one of the experts stated, with regard to private insurance coverage for mental health and to amend the *Mental Health Services Act* to cover: 1) the mentally ill and homeless, 2) the mentally ill and criminal system violators, and 3) at-risk youth.

A research review uncovered the potential to reform the current systems in California and Ontario. California's mental health agenda is founded on the *Mental Health Services Act (MHSA),* but the government realized the need to build on this because of the present number of homeless individuals with mental health afflictions. The cornerstone of the new proposals is reforming legal and bureaucratic requirements for involuntary treatment what some might consider a reversal of the *Lanterman-Petris-Short (LPS) Act* which advocated deinstitutionalization and has resulted in those who need treatment ending up homeless on the streets (Wiener, 2020). Ontario would also benefit from these reforms to its *Mental Health Act* as a significant proportion of its homeless also suffer from mental health afflictions (Wellesley Institute, 2017). Other considerations for improvement are: 1) Both California and Ontario offer diversion programs through mental health courts but there are questions about the procedure for determining who qualifies to be diverted to a mental health court and if legal representation for justice-involved individuals from racialized communities is adequately provided, 2) In California, state prison inmates have recourse to evidence-based treatment and integration programs (California Department of Corrections and Rehabilitation, 2020) but a report on the issue indicated that those with mental health afflictions would be better served if the state substituted prison sentences with timely treatment (Graves, 2020), and 3) Ontario has received scathing criticism for its health care model in prisons being reactionary and lacking "continuity and transition of care into community services (John Howard Society of Ontario, 2016)."

Problematic Substance Use

Like with mental health, programs for problematic substance use have exhibited shortcomings in both California and Ontario. According to the experts interviewed for this study, current government programs have fallen short of creating a lasting impact on justice-involved individuals and lack sufficient reduction strategies. In fact, the experts favored that problematic substance use be framed as a health care problem and not a criminal justice one. One of the experts elaborated that, first and foremost, a more comprehensive response that includes alternative options for care and rehabilitation was needed because a medical environment is more suited to those with problematic substance use than jails, "While drug courts support these individuals, the government needs to go further by developing fully-funded diversion and re-entry programs because weak integration programs lead to higher rates of recidivism. These individuals need care until they properly reintegrate (Interview, Ontario expert)."

With regard to those in the criminal justice system, experts stressed that measures should be implemented for treatment as well as relapse prevention. Some acknowledged the need for harm reduction programs, overdose prevention education, the establishment of meeting places where problematic drug users can seek help from doctors, nurses and other medical staff members, and sober houses, "The United States incarcerates more people in the world than any other country. Taking criminal justice resources and allocating them to community support would be helpful (Interview, California expert)." A further development of the system currently in place could help address problematic substance use more effectively. For one, both California and Ontario have experienced many overdoses in their prisons; body scanners to detect drugs smuggled into prisons have proven to be ineffective for reasons such as lack of training on how to read x-rays (Cook, 2019). Significant areas that need attention include the inadequate number of medical staff members, lack of education on how to deal with problematic substance users and inadequate naloxone training for corrections officers. Implementation efforts should incorporate the establishment of overdose prevention sites in prisons where inmates consume drugs under medical supervision and long-term treatment of problematic substance users to reduce the cost of crime and increase social and economic benefits to society. (Krebs et al., 2017).

The interviewees produced contrasting perceptions of the effectiveness of the systems in California and Ontario. One of the interviewees hailed California's CalAim model as suitable for other governments to follow. CalAim is a program directed at improving health outcomes in the state by identifying and managing individual risk, adopting a whole person care approach, and taking into account social determinants of an individual's health care problems (California Department of Health Care Services, 2020). Another interviewee was critical of Ontario's model, "In Australia, comprehensive programs have seen crime numbers fall. The provincial government has taken a lot away from public health. Programs have been defunded including funding for youth detention centers. Fetal alcohol victims are not going to school and are working full-time with no support. The government has even pulled funding from schools (Interview, Ontario expert)." This contrasts with the Canadian federal government which, one of the interviewees propounded, "is well recognized as having the strongest infrastructure for treatment services in the world and is a leader in rehabilitative corrections (Interview, Ontario expert)."

A literature review resulted in interesting facts about problematic substance use and the criminal justice system in California which has important implications for other states and provinces. The state has a large population that is addicted to opioids and many of its homeless suffer from problematic substance use. The state offers several programs ranging from cognitive-behavioral interventions, evidence-based programs, time-limited re-entry services for inmates (California Department of Corrections and Rehabilitation, 2020) to drug courts which emphasize treatment over incarceration. These courts helped lower recidivism rates but were impacted by the introduction of Proposition 47 which re-classified certain drug crimes from felonies to misdemeanors to reduce the number of prosecutions (Bird, 2018). There have been calls for this proposition to be amended as it undermines the rehabilitation of justice-involved individuals with problematic substance use.

Table 2 encapsulates key expert recommendations for governments to be successful in fighting homelessness, mental health afflictions and problematic substance use.

Table 2. Experts' Policy Recommendations to Address Homelessness, Mental Health Afflictions and Problematic Substance Use

Community Ailment	Expert Policy Advice
Homelessness	• Build affordable and permanent/transitional housing. • Provide support for basic needs and a basic income to address poverty/disabilities. • Assist tenants with eviction proceedings, short-term loan programs to pay rent arrears and modular housing. • Permit developers to bypass building rules and offer environmental regulation waivers. • Increase permanent housing retention, address racial disparities in public housing evictions and engage in better case management.
Mental Health Afflictions	• Adopt a pro-active approach instead of a reactionary one. • Institute proper procedures for determining who might be diverted to a mental health court and if legal representation for justice-involved individuals from racialized communities is adequately provided. • Increase mental health budgets, reduce waiting lists, hire more psychologists and mental health workers, and develop a tracking system for service provision. • Focus on long-term recovery and keep patients on medications after they are released from prison. • Ensure the private sector contributes its fair share to the well-being of society. • Strengthen legislation to include private sector insurance coverage and make current legislation more inclusive of different types of problems associated with mental health and different segments of society.
Problematic Substance Use	• Treat it as a health care problem and incorporate alternative options for care and rehabilitation instead of prison. • Establish harm reduction programs, overdose prevention education and overdose prevention sites for prisons with a focus on long-term treatment to prevent relapses. • Develop a comprehensive model to encompass fully funded diversion and re-entry programs and sober houses. • Staff prisons with members from the medical community based on need, provide training to corrections personnel such as naloxone dispensation and x-ray training to prevent drugs from being smuggled into prisons. • Advance evidence to influence public policy.

As governments make progress towards program objectives, it becomes imperative for them to develop and expand tracking systems to capture relevant data to measure success rates. An evaluation of these efforts is presented next.

Data Tracking is Vital for Performance Management but Current Systems Measuring Outcomes Do Not Pass Muster

Housing

Data tracking systems are important to assess if policy changes are effective and if programs are meeting their objectives. In view of this, study participants proposed a transformation in data tracking and performance management for homelessness and housing. An expert endorsed the creation of a Homeless Management Information System where the government can keep track of the number of shelters, the number of evictions, especially, among racialized communities and the number of homeless cases diverted through homeless courts. The expert also stated the importance of conducting randomized control trials to find out which programs work best, developing performance indicators and monitoring outcomes. As part of this effort, the government should have a tracking system for fines and tickets issued to the homeless and work towards reducing these over a period. Some of the experts spoke in favor of collecting crime-based metrics like the number of homeless in proportion to the number of crimes committed by them and the number of court cases involving the homeless against the homeless count. One of the participants catechized, "How do you define criminal activity? Parse out cannabis use. Parse out criminal activity related to poverty. Parse out criminal activity related to obtaining food. How many people are able to make ends meet? (Interview, Ontario expert)" Another study participant felt that that it would be quite challenging to quantify data when addressing the homelessness problem in relation to criminal activity.

There are both positives and negatives on action taken by California and Ontario when it comes to measuring government performance pertaining to homelessness and housing. The government of California has committed to developing a homelessness tracking system that collects statewide local information with the goal of analyzing homelessness data against state homelessness programs to test for their effectiveness (Douglas, 2020). An assessment of Ontario's performance management system concluded that there are several data collection gaps in provincial housing administration pertaining to wait-lists, outcome-based performance measures and individual programs (Advocacy Center for Tenants Ontario, 2019).

Mental Health Afflictions

Several study participants voiced their support for enhancements to the current performance management system for mental health afflictions in California and Ontario. They put forward for consideration a number of indicators including: 1) those that help in advancing evidence to influence mental health public policy, 2) those that track health conditions such as axis 1 diagnoses, developmental delay, attention deficit hyperactivity disorder and fetal alcohol syndrome in justice-involved individuals, 3) the percentage of the prison population with mental health afflictions being assigned to the appropriate professional for treatment, the percentage of those being kept in segregation and the percentage of those actually getting the services they need, and 4) changes in the rate of incarcerations and re-arrests as a result of services provided.

The governments of California and Ontario are currently involved in developing forensic mental health indicators in their respective jurisdictions. California has a Mental Health Tracking System (MHTS) where all inmate-patient information is monitored including the inmate's history of afflictions, medication history and other treatment information, and suicide risk data (California Correctional Health Care Services, 2009). Ontario is in the process of building a standardized performance measurement framework for mental health afflictions and problematic substance use, in consultation with stakeholders, which will measure emergency department visits and hospitalizations, wait times for health services, awareness of service availability, and early problem identification and intervention for youth (Government of Ontario, 2020).

Problematic Substance Use

Interviewees connoted that the performance measures listed below would help governments address problematic substance use and crime:

- Indicators such as the percentage of problematic substance users, percentage of drug use populations and the number of places for needle exchanges.

- Indicators such as the number of individuals who survive because of rehabilitation, the number of overdoses, the number of cases where a safe supply of drugs that are not toxic are provided and the number of safe injection sites.
- Indicators such as the percentage of people who get connected to drug courts.
- Indicators such as number of individuals with problematic substance use matched against arrest and conviction data over time.
- Indications such as the quantity and quality of reduction strategies like injection sites, harm reduction programs, needle-exchange programs, and the use of epidemiology-related indicators (frequency and patterns).
- The ability to keep problematic substance users as a part of society and not isolate them.
- Success in ensuring treatments is evidence-based, utilize resources effectively and cost-effectively.

To facilitate this, interviewees opined that governments should have a system that exclusively keeps track of data connected to problematic substance use and take measures to see trends go down. They should also maintain research units to track data and monitor trends where data capturing and monitoring teams: 1) work closely with the police, 2) follow through once a justice-involved individual is released, 3) monitor the adherence to drug prevention policies by engaging in surveillance and monitoring, and 4) work in partnership with academic and research institutes.

Additionally, study participants expressed the need for jurisdictions to conduct an evaluation of programs to see if they are working and if they are worth the investment as these programs can be costly. Suggested criteria against which program evaluations should be conducted are: 1) recidivism rate which is the rate at which prisoners released re-enter the criminal justice system, 2) fidelity which answers the question: is program design and delivery in line with pre-stated objectives?, 3) cost-effectiveness analyses to ascertain if programs are financially viable, and iv) subjectivity which is about services being provided based on the needs of the individual.

Ontario's efforts in establishing performance metrics for problematic substance use have already been mentioned in the previous section. California tracks inmate data for problematic substance use rehabilitation but according to a report by the Legislative Analyst's Office, quantitative metrics like the number of rehabilitation program hours lodged and the number of inmates achieving educational benchmarks are insufficient. The report recommends more detailed measures such as the amount of time spent on waitlists, participation rates in programs that meet inmates' needs, the rates at which they are progressing towards rehabilitation, the percentage of inmates released without all their needs being met and the quality of delivery of rehabilitative services (Taylor, 2017). While this section shows that governments lag in performance management efforts, the next section addresses how this can be improved with the help of a program logic model.

CONSTRUCTING A LOGIC MODEL FOR TRANSFORMATIVE JUSTICE

This section portrays findings from the literature review and interview participants' views through a single illustration using a logic model. This model can be traced back to one first used by the U.S. Agency for International Development in the 1960s for depicting the flow of resources and processes towards the achievement of outputs, outcomes, and impacts (McEwan & Bigelow, 1997). Logic models provide clarity to a program's purpose through the schematic representation of a service delivery mechanism that benefits individuals, groups, and communities (Montague, 2000). They assist in i) mapping out complex cause-effect relationships, ii) facilitating planning by simplifying logical connections, and iii) evaluating program contributions through a performance measurement system (Chen et al., 2018). Table 3 presents a logic model for transformative justice.

Logic models can be collaborative where different levels in the organization join forces to achieve the same outputs, outcomes and impacts and also cross-sectoral where organizations integrate ideas and actions about the utilization of resources and processes towards attaining a common objective (Poon et al., 2012). There are also temporal logic models that allow for the incorporation of periodic updates as programs change over time. This aids in monitoring the evolution of the model and increasing its flexibility, responsiveness, and sustainability (den Heyer, 2002). These are options for the transformative justice logic model presented above. The next section provides a pathway for the achievement of these outputs, outcomes, and impacts.

SOLUTIONS AND RECOMMENDATIONS FOR ADDRESSING COMMUNITY AILMENTS

There were three criminal justice approaches initially considered for this study. Retributive justice provides the optics of a system that is serious about fighting crime. In an "eye for an eye" world, it punishes those who have been found guilty of transgressing the law (Hegel,1942; Kant, 1956; Morris, 1968; Ezorsky, 1972; & Morris, 1974). Restorative justice is a conciliatory approach between justice-involved individuals and their victims, but it stops short of diagnosing the reasons for unlawful behavior and tracking progress towards systemic improvements (Quinney & Wildeman, 1991; McCold, 1995; Bazemore, 1998; Daly, 2000; Harris, 2004; & Lofton, 2004). That role belongs to the transformative justice model where the circumstances of the justice-involved individual are considered, services are provided to the individual to prevent the transgression from recurring and performance indicators are used as milestones to improve service provision (Morris, 1999; Morris, 2000). Based on interviews with experts, it can be concluded that his model is the best fit for this study as expert recommendations are centered around its principles. It is also worth mentioning that although this is a case study of state/provincial government policies in California and Ontario, the lessons from this study could possibly be applied to other states and provinces but this cannot be stated definitively due to the small sample size. The discussion that ensues provides the salient points of the study's findings and the next steps for action from a transformative justice perspective.

End Mass Criminalization

The relationship between homelessness, mental health afflictions, problematic substance use and the criminal justice system is bi-directional as determined by this study. It is, therefore, important to address community ailment concerns and fix problems within the criminal justice system concurrently. A crucial step regarding the latter was taken when the Supreme Court denied an attempt by American cities to prosecute the homeless who slept in public spaces (Wolf & Woodyard, 2019). This gave hope to anti-mass criminalization efforts that minor, non-violent offences such as panhandling could also be decriminalized. Besides ending mass criminalization, attempts must be made to prevent discrimination. There have been calls to strengthen human rights protections for those with police records to prevent

Table 3. A Program Logic Model for Transformative Justice

A Transformative Justice-Based Program Logic Model			
Inputs	**Activities**	**Outputs**	**Outcomes**
• Investment in the provision of housing and treatment facilities. • Proactive planning that focuses on prevention. • Advanced Management. Information Systems • Partnerships with the private sector. • Partnerships with the police. • Partnerships with academic institutions and research institutes.	• Eliminate barriers to access to employment and housing, increase the minimum wage and provide basic income support. • End mass criminalization, reform the criminal code for misdemeanor charges against the homeless and decriminalize drugs. • Expand alternatives to prison terms including probation, bail supervision, Victim Offender Reconciliation Programs (VORP) and community service work orders. • Reform risk-averse conditions imposed by bail courts. • Provide incentives for those on social assistance to save for housing and eliminate disincentives. • Reform legal and bureaucratic requirements for involuntary treatment. • Monitor inmates' history of afflictions, medication history and suicide risk data. Advance evidence to influence policies, programs, and services in correctional facilities. • Consult with stakeholders on how to direct funds to areas of need. • Ensure program design and delivery is in line with pre-stated objectives, the most cost-effective options are pursued, and services are being provided to the right individuals.	• Number of programs that provide long-term social services to those who are released from custody or remand. • Number of housing alternatives, shelters and treatment programs and amount of time spent on waitlists. • Number of publicly funded interventions for mental health afflictions in justice-involved individuals. • Number of harm reduction strategies including the provision of a safer supply of non-toxic drugs and safe injection sites. • Number of drug prevention programs and places for needle exchanges. • Number of follow-ups through surveillance-based transition programs once a justice-involved individual is released. • Percentage of the prison population with mental health afflictions being assigned to the appropriate professional for treatment, the percentage of those being kept in segregation and the percentage of those actually getting the services they need. • Participation rates in programs that meet inmates' rehabilitative needs, the rates at which inmates are progressing towards rehabilitation, the percentage of inmates released without all their rehabilitative needs being met and the quality of delivery of rehabilitative services.	• Reduction in the number of fines and tickets issued to the homeless. • Reduction in the number of evictions especially among youth/racialized communities and the number of homeless cases diverted through homeless courts. • Reduction of the impact of past evictions and criminal records on access to services. • Increase in the rate of awareness of service availability for mental health afflictions for early problem identification and intervention particularly for youth/racialized communities and decrease in emergency department visits and hospitalizations. • Decrease in the percentage of problematic substance use population with arrest and conviction records and an increase in the percentage of people who get connected to drug courts. • Increase in the number of individuals who survive problematic substance use because of rehabilitation services and a decrease in the number of overdose cases. • Reduction of the number of criminal cases that result from individuals making ends meet. • Reduction in the number of court cases involving the homeless and the proportion of crimes committed by them against the number of homeless. • Decrease in the rate of incarcerations and re-arrests as a result of treatment services provided.
Assumptions		**Impacts**	
• Government commitment to transformative justice reform. • Prioritization of social welfare programs by the government.		• Lower incarceration rates, rates of recidivism and cost of prison maintenance. • Vulnerable individuals are treated as part of society and not isolated. • Higher tax collections for government and economic benefits for society.	

discrimination in employment and housing. An advocacy group proposes promoting reparative justice, decriminalizing drugs, ending over-policing particularly in areas of color, reducing and expunging of drug sentences for minor offences, and reducing stigma associated with justice-involved individuals with minor drug records (Drug Policy Alliance, 2020).

Identify and Remedy the Root Cause of the Problem

There was an overwhelming agreement among the experts interviewed that poverty was the underlying cause of homelessness and related mental health and addiction problems. Studies have also noted socioeconomic status and child welfare failures as among the leading cause of youth homelessness (Kouyoumdjian et al., 2016). One of the experts interviewed advocated the need for a basic income policy for the poor and vocational guidance for the incarcerated to help them find their way, "There has been no adult to guide them ever in their lives and someone needs to help them to find themselves (Interview, Ontario expert)." Some governments have already introduced basic income to compensate for the dwindling social safety net in modern societies (Keegan, 2018). Another expert was in favor of a mechanism by which the police worked with health care workers to assist those who come in conflict with the law, "Efforts must be made to find alternatives to incarceration along with committing to housing and mental health support, reducing poverty, and supporting non-profit organizations that collaborate with people in custody (Interview, Ontario expert)."

Enforce Prevention, Promotion, and Early Intervention Practices

Reviewed literature supports the argument that prevention, promotion and early intervention pay off. Governments must take a proactive approach to ensure that people have recourse to programs before becoming at risk, "The justice system should not be seen as the first viable access point for treatment (John Howard Society of Ontario, 2015)." Just as importantly, governments must find a way to eliminate the barriers to early intervention. Long wait times for services negatively affect early intervention especially among youth and the impact is experienced over their lifetimes. Also, early diversion programs should be made mandatory for those who are at high risk for future involvement with the justice system. Pre-charge diversion programs should be offered to youth as an alternative to entering the prison system for minor crimes (Public Safety Canada, 1998). Within the realm of promotion and early prevention, governments should strengthen their efforts to reduce the stigma surrounding homelessness, mental health afflictions and problematic substance use, "With information comes awareness and understanding, with the goal of reducing the stigma that prevents people from seeking the help they need (Victoria News, 2020)."

Prioritize Innovative and Evidence-Based Solutions

Homelessness, mental health afflictions and problematic drug use demand a distinct set of actions for overcoming problems with each. With the failure of policy tools such as rent control and affordable housing, governments are constantly exploring different avenues to fight homelessness. Recommendations for state/provincial governments include taking legal action against cities that fail to reduce homeless rates, appointing a homelessness czar to coordinate initiatives in their respective jurisdictions in what has been described as a fragmented system, providing effective case management services to the homelessness to increase housing stability and diverting a percentage of sales or income tax revenues to pay for housing initiatives (Levin, 2020). Evidence-based interventions from eviction moratoriums and support for survivors of intimate partner violence to landlord mediation have worked successfully in European jurisdictions. Governments should endeavor to improve access to 1) legal services through community legal clinics for those facing eviction, 2) financial services in the form of rent banks, energy assistance payments and credit counselling agencies (Homeless Hub, 2020), 3) educational services on tenant rights, such as relocation payments, in cases of displacement (Poppe, 2018), and 4) program services like homeless courts that allow people to get rid of debt from tickets, and possibly a police record for "homelessness" crimes through community work (Goldberg, 2016). Governments should also find a way to encourage innovative solutions such as modular housing which are prefabricated units that can be built quickly and used as supportive housing (Brenner, 2019). Finally, governments must seize the opportunity to streamline regulations that would result in lowering development and construction costs without compromising consumer safety and protection (Homeless Hub, 2020).

While cognitive-behavioral intervention programs have already been rolled out in prisons, newer approaches like trauma-informed care are being introduced there. This involves staff members helping mental health-afflicted inmates, who may have a history of physical, emotional, or sexual abuse, with coping mechanisms to prevent re-traumatization. Outpatient competency restoration administered to justice-involved individuals through outpatient community mental health systems is effective, less costly than inpatient treatments and poses no threat to citizen safety (Stringer, 2019). It should be noted that some studies, namely, Peterson et al. (2014) and Manchak and Morgan (2018) evince the connection between mental health attributes and crime as insubstantial and lay emphasis on other factors such as early-onset criminality and antisocial personality disorder as stronger links between the two variables. With this in mind, Wilson and Draine (2006) and Van Horn et al. (2019) suggest behavioral health interventions or correctional interventions that manage and control these traits in justice-involved individuals rather than address mental health issues.

Research studies indicate that individuals, who've had brushes with the law, suffer high death rates post-incarceration from preventable causes such as accidental drug overdoses. Sober houses offer a housing option for those individuals battling problematic substance use. These offer an alcohol- and drug-free living environment, and a 12-step self-help program. Reviews have conveyed a positive message about sober houses because they have helped a high percentage of participants reduce or stop problematic use of substances and have created improvements in their lives through increased employment, fewer psychiatric symptoms, and fewer arrests. Sober houses can not only serve as a conduit to reintegration but an alternative to incarceration (Polcin et al., 2010; Bauer et al., 2016; Stein et al., 2017).

Expand Diversion, Reentry, and Reintegration Programs

While prison programs have proved to have a positive outcome on the behaviors of justice-involved individuals, study participants felt that long-term programs are generally lacking. This has resulted in these individuals again finding themselves in conflict with the law resulting in the overcrowding of prisons (Aborn et al., 1999). A study by psychologist, Dr. Harry K. Wexler, revealed an almost 50 percentage point drop-in recidivism rates among prisoners involved in the prison's drug treatment program which included aftercare. Results such as these should compel governments to mandate gradual prisoner release through the issuance of temporary absence passes to facilitate prisoner assimilation into the community (American Psychological Association, 2004). An expert interviewed for this study opined that corrections services should focus as much on the post-incarceration phase as the custody phase, "The system needs to focus on reintegration and leverage knowledge brokers just like the Canadian Center on Substance Use and Addiction, an arms-length agency created to shape social policy around addictions (Interview, Ontario expert)." These knowledge brokers collaborate with community partners to gather data that better informs the delivery and impact of evidence-based solutions for addictions (Canadian Center on Substance Use and Addiction, 2020). Discharge planning should begin right after incarceration till after the individual's re-entry into society and incorporate an assessment of local capacity for services like community-based support systems, transportation, government identification, healthcare, employment, education, housing, financial resources, food, and clothing to enable reintegration (Backer et al., 2007). One of the study participants rued the lack of proper discharge planning and continuity of care, "There should be discharge planning funding for community safety. Too many individuals are kept in pre-charge custody (around 70%) and even 1-2% of those in immigration detention are being held with these individuals. This needs to change (Interview, Ontario expert)." When it comes to reentry programs, there have been calls for patient navigators who could assist the reentry population at specially established health homes to meet their health care and social service needs (Davis et al., 2011).

Engage in Performance Management

This study found that governments' data tracking and performance measurement efforts could be considered moderate at best. Most study participants called for metrics pertaining to the factors leading to homelessness, mental health afflictions and problematic substance use, suitability of services being provided to these individuals and the circumstances that lead to reincarceration. Monitoring data such as the percentage of income vulnerable populations spend on housing, the impact of police record checks (for convictions and non-convictions) on employment, the linkage of people who experience imprisonment to high-quality primary care and the geographic distribution of reintegration facilities relative to the concentration of parolees would help shape future social and criminal justice policy (John Howard Society of Ontario, 2018; Kouyoumdjian et al., 2019; James, 2015). There should also be special indicators, for those segments of the population most susceptible like racialized groups, single mothers, and immigrants from certain countries, that track data such as retention in housing, reductions in length of homeless episodes, and recurrences of mental health afflictions and problematic substance use to truly evaluate the effectiveness of programs (Canadian Mental Health Association, 2010). One of the main findings of this study is the impact of homelessness, mental health afflictions and problematic substance use on youth. Therefore, there should be distinct indicators to monitor the quality of service provided by children's home/aid societies to address the foster care needs of children, high school graduation rates, completion of employment-related skills training programs and workforce readiness through career planning (Guirguis-Younger et al., 2014). Information should also be collected to measure stability and recovery from trauma such as participation of youth in interventions, participation in daily activities and coping skills, reductions in problematic substance use, ability to manage mental health afflictions, control over impulses and self-esteem, "We need indicators sufficiently sensitive to reflect youth's gradual disengagement from the streets, and their increasing connection to the community and relationships with non-homeless peers,…" (Hollywood Homeless Youth Partnership, 2013, p. 4). What has proven to help youth are early intervention programs as evidenced by the Geelong Project in Australia. It involves population screening of at-risk youth, follows a family-centered approach in supporting these youth and engages family workers and school well-being staff members to respond to their needs (MacKenzie & Meessen, 2019). Australia's Reconnect services program caters to Indigenous youth and young people experiencing mental health afflictions by working towards improving their connection to their work, educational and community environments (Australian Department of Social Services, 2020). At the local level, a plan to improve the well-being of the Indigenous population in Calgary serves as a model for other jurisdictions. Its central theme involves the provision of cultural supports including indigenous-specific programs run by staff members with indigenous-awareness training. Other supports included in the plan were employment/training, addictions support, and affordable housing and transportation (Aboriginal Standing Committee on Housing and Homelessness, 2012). Figure 1 charts the policy options for building a transformative justice model as discussed in this study.

Figure 1. Actionable Policy Options for Addressing Community Ailments

A best practices portal through which different levels of government can indulge in program knowledge exchange can benefit vulnerable populations not to mention those that are justice involved. This chapter concludes with a summary on how best to improve the lives of those with lived experiences of homelessness, mental health afflictions and problematic substance abuse, reduce incidence of them coming in conflict with the law and help them take advantage of suitable rehabilitation programs to avoid recidivism.

CONCLUSION

The comparison of the problem-solving approaches between California and Ontario revealed that these depend on the ideology of the government in power. As evidenced in the primary and secondary data, 1) liberal governments actively fund services while conservative ones cut funding to services for the homeless, the mentally afflicted and problematic substance users who come into conflict with the law, 2) governments irrespective of ideology could perform better in addressing these community ailments and 3) governments must develop policies to address the feeder roots of the problem. In relation to the last point, one of the interviewees commented, "To find a solution, you have to look at what led to the problem. Holistic defense is less likely to result in crime (Interview, California expert)." The concept of holistic defense is based on the principles of transformative justice where the facts of the case and the life circumstances that have resulted in an individual's involvement with the justice system are considered when resolving the case (Anderson et al., 2019). Moreover, ending mass criminalization, addressing poverty and other root causes, enforcing prevention, promotion, and early intervention policies, prioritizing innovation and evidence-based solutions, expanding diversion, reentry, and reintegration programs, and engaging in effective performance management could lead to better results in meeting the goals of transformative justice. These policy levers could also produce long-term effects that complement stigmatization reframing and de-framing strategies in countering stigma associated with vulnerable populations. The timing is perfect to build on the foundations of transformative justice in California, Ontario, and other jurisdictions because statistics reveal that retributive and restorative justice philosophies have not been successful in addressing community needs. Under this, the aforementioned recommendations could form part of a criminal justice and social framework that foster a deeper discussion on how to build sustainable communities, help formulate concrete strategies that better the outcomes for the homeless, mentally afflicted, and problematic substance users and lay the groundwork for criminal justice reform.

This research received no specific grant from any funding agency in the public, commercial, or not-for-profit sectors.

REFERENCES

Aboriginal Standing Committee on Housing and Homelessness. (2012). *Plan to end aboriginal homelessness in Calgary*. Ethics of Development in a Global Environment. https://calgaryhomeless.com/content/uploads/Aboriginal-Plan-2012.pdf

Aborn, J., van den Toorn, A., Hockin, J., Jordon, S., Nayvelt, M., & Finkelstein, M. (1999, July 26). *The California prison and rehabilitation system*. http://web.stanford.edu/class/e297c/poverty_prejudice/citypoverty/c

Adom, D., Yeboah, A., & Anrakh, K. (2016). Constructivism philosophical paradigm: Implication for research, teaching and learning. *Global Journal of Arts Humanities and Social Sciences*, *4*(10), 1–9.

Advocacy Center for Tenants Ontario. (2019, November). *We can't wait: Preserving our affordable rental housing in Ontario*. https://www.acto.ca/production/wp-

American Psychological Association. (2004, March 23). *Inmate drug abuse treatment slows prison's revolving door*. https://www.apa.org/research/action/aftercare

Anderson, J., Buenaventura, M., & Heaton, P. (2019, January). The effects of holistic defense on criminal justice outcomes. *Harvard Law Review, 123*(3), 820–893.

Ashwood, J. S., Briscombe, B., Collins, R. L., Wong, E. C., Eberhart, N. K., Cerully, J., May, L., Roth, B., & Burnam, M. A. (2017). Investment in social marketing campaign to reduce stigma and discrimination associated with mental illness yields positive economic benefits to California. *Rand Health Quarterly, 6*(2), 5.

Australian Department of Social Services. (2020). *Housing Support.* https://www.dss.gov.au/housing-support/programmes-services/homelessness

Backer, T. E., Howard, E. A., & Moran, G. E. (2007). The role of effective discharge planning in preventing homelessness. *The Journal of Primary Prevention, 28*, 229–243.

Barak, M. (2014). Re-imagining punishment: An exercise in "intersectional criminal justice.". *Laws, 3*(4), 693–705.

Barker, J., Humphries, P., McArthur, M., & Thomson, L. (2012). *Literature Review: Effective interventions for working with young people who are homeless or at risk of homelessness.* Australian Department of Families, Housing, Community Services and Indigenous Affairs. https://www.dss.gov.au/sites/default/files/documents/06_2012/literature_review.pdf

Bauer, L. K., Brody, J. K., León, C., & Baggett, T. P. (2016). Characteristics of homeless adults who died of drug overdose: A retrospective record review. *Journal of Health Care for the Poor and Underserved, 27*(2), 846–859. https://doi.org/10.1353/hpu.2016.0075

Bazemore, G. (1998). Restorative justice and earned redemption: Communities, victims, and offender reintegration. *The American Behavioral Scientist, 41*(6), 768–813.

Berenbaumm, E. (2019, April). *Homeless and health outcomes: What are the associations?* Public Health Ontario, Queen's Printer for Ontario. https://www.publichealthontario.ca/-/media/documents/e/2019/eb-homelessness-health.pdf?la=en

Bird, M., Lofstrom, M., Martin, B., Raphael, S., & Nguyen, V. (2018, June). *The impact of proposition 47 on crime and recidivism.* The Public Policy Institute of California. https://www.ppic.org/wp-content/uploads/r_0618mbr.pdf

Boisvert, N. (2018, November). *Police didn't do enough to help homeless man overdosing on opiates, inquest hears.* CBC News. https://www.cbc.ca/news/canada/toronto/brad-chapman-inquest-day-1-1.4921265

Brenner, J. (2019, October). *New modular housing model tackles affordable housing crisis In Los Angeles.* Forbes. https://www.forbes.com/sites/juliabrenner/2019/10/30/new-modular-housing-model-tackles-affordable-housing-crisis-in-los-angeles/

California Correctional Health Care Services. (2009). *Mental health services delivery system:* Program guide overview. https://www.clearinghouse.net/chDocs/public/PC-CA-0002-0012.pdf

California Department of Corrections and Rehabilitation. (2020, January). *CDCR and CCHCS unveil expanded priorities through renewed mission and vision statements*. https://www.cdcr.ca.gov/news/2020/01/08/cdcr-and-cchcs-unveil-expanded-priorities-through-renewed-mission-and-vision-statements/

California Department of Corrections and Rehabilitation. (2020). *Mental health program (MHP)*. https://www.cdcr.ca.gov/dhcs/mental-health-program/

California Department of Health Care Services. (2020). *California advancing and innovating Medi-Cal*. https://www.dhcs.ca.gov/provgovpart/Pages/CalAIM.aspx

Canadian Center on Substance Use and Addiction. (2020). *Knowledge Broker*. https://www.ccsa.ca/knowledge-broker

Canadian Mental Health Association. (2010, November). *Submission to Honourable Jay C. Hope, Deputy Minister – Correctional Services, Ministry of Community Safety and Correctional Services Accessibility Roundtable*. https://ontario.cmha.ca/documents/submission-to-honourable-jay-c-hope-deputy-minister/

Chen, H., Pan, H., Morosanu, L. & Turner, N. (2018). Using logic models and the action model/change model schema in planning the learning community program: A comparative case study. *Canadian Journal of Program Evaluation, 33*(1), 49–68. doi:10.3138/cjpe.42116

Cook, S. (2019, May). *Suspected drug overdoses at Ontario correctional facility lead to death, hospitalization*. The Globe and Mail. https://www.theglobeandmail.com/canada/toronto/article-suspected-drug-overdoses-at-ontario-correctional-facility-lead-to/

Daly, K. (2000). Restorative justice in diverse and unequal societies. *Law in Context (Bundoora, Vic.), 7*(1), 167–190.

Davis, L., Williams, M., Derose, K., Steinberg, P., Nicosia, N., Overton, A., Miyashiro, L., Turner, S., Fain, T., & Williams, E. (2011). *Understanding the public health implications of prisoner reentry in California: State-of-the-state report*. RAND Corporation. https://www.rand.org/pubs/monographs/MG1165.html

den Heyer, M. (2002). The Temporal logic model concept. *The Canadian Journal of Program Evaluation, 17*(2), 27–47.

Douglas, T. (2020, February). *Newsom: Unified data system will help state track progress on homelessness*. Techwire. https://www.techwire.net/news/newsom-unified-homeless-data-system-will-help-state-track-progress.html

Drug Policy Alliance. (2020). *Mass incarceration and criminalization*. https://www.drugpolicy.org/issues/mass-criminalization

Ezorsky, G. (1972, March). Retributive justice. *Canadian Journal of Philosophy, 1*(3), 365–368.

Ferguson, A. (2018). City looks to rename homeless services; 'shelter' to be phased out. *CityNews*. https://toronto.citynews.ca/2018/02/25/city-looks-rename-homeless-services-shelter-phased/

Flory, J. (2020, February). *Arresting people who are homeless will make a bad problem worse.* CalMatters. https://calmatters.org/commentary/arresting-homeless-people-will-make-a-bad-problem-worse/

Fuller, T. (2019, October 21). As homelessness surges in California, so does a backlash. *The New York Times*, p. A1.

Giliauskas, D., & Gogolishvili, D. (2018, October). *Interventions to reduce stigma among health care providers who work with substance users.* Ontario HIV Treatment Network. https://www.ohtn.on.ca/rapid-response-interventions-to-reduce-stigma-among-health-care-providers-working-with-substance-users/

Goldberg, E. (2016, April 19). *Homeless court removes housing, job barriers for people on the streets.* Huffington Post. https://www.huffingtonpost.ca/entry/homeless-court-removes-housing-job-barriers-for-people-on-the-streets_n_57155088e4b0060ccda414cb?ri18n=true

Government of Ontario. (2020). *Roadmap to wellness: A plan to build Ontario's mental health and addictions system.* https://www.ontario.ca/page/roadmap-wellness-plan-build-ontarios-mental-health-and-addictions-system

Graves, S. (2020, March). *Many Californians in prisons and jails have mental health needs.* California Budget and Policy Center. https://calbudgetcenter.org/resources/prisons-and-jails-have-mental-health-needs/

Groot, E., Kouyoumdjian, F. G., Kiefer, L., Madadi, P., Gross, J., Prevost, B., Jhirad, R., Huyer, D., Snowdon, V., & Persaud, N. (2016). Drug toxicity deaths after release from incarceration in Ontario, 2006-2013: Review of Coroner's Cases. *PLoS One, 11*(7), e0157512. https://doi.org/10.1371/journal.pone.0157512

Guirguis-Younger, M., McNeil, R., & Hwang, S. W. (Eds.). (2014). *Homelessness & health in Canada.* University of Ottawa Press.

Harris, M. K. (2004). An expansive, transformative view of restorative justice. *Contemporary Justice Review, 7*(1), 117–141.

Hegel, G. W. F. (1942). *The philosophy of right* (T. Knox, Trans.). Oxford University Press.

Hollywood Homeless Youth Partnership. (2013, January). Measuring success in housing programs for homeless youth: The need for youth-specific performance measures. *Policy Brief.*

Homeless Hub. (2020). *Regulatory barriers to affordable housing.* https://www.homelesshub.ca/resource/regulatory-barriers-affordable-housing

Homeless Hub. (2020). *Solutions: Supporting communities to prevent and end homelessness.* https://www.homelesshub.ca/solutions/prevention

Housing, Health, and Justice Community of Interest. (2019, February). *Closed quarters: Challenges and opportunities in stabilizing housing and mental health across the justice sector.* https://www.eenet.ca/ClosedQuarters

James, N. (2015, January 12). *Offender reentry: Correctional statistics, reintegration into the community, and recidivism.* Congressional Research Service, 7-5700.

Jeffe, S. B. (1987, March 22). *California: Good aims, bad results.* L.A. Times. https://www.latimes.com/archives/la-xpm-1987-03-22-op-14759-story.html

John Howard Society of Ontario. (2015, August). *Unlocking change: Decriminalizing mental health issues in Ontario.* http://www.johnhoward.on.ca/wp-content/uploads/2015/07/Unlocking-Change-Final-August-2015.pdf

John Howard Society of Ontario. (2016, April). *Fractured care: Public health opportunities in Ontario's correctional institutions.* John Howard Society of Ontario. https://johnhoward.on.ca/wp-content/uploads/2016/04/Fractured-Care-Final.pdf

John Howard Society of Ontario. (2018, February). *The invisible burden: Police records and the barriers to employment in Toronto.* https://policerecordhub.ca/wp-content/uploads/2018/02/The-Invisible-Burden-Report-FINAL.pdf

Kant, I. (1956). *Critique of practical reason* (L. W. Beck, Trans.). Macmillan Publishing Co.

Keegan, M. (2018, June 27). *Benefit or burden? The cities trying out universal basic income.* The Guardian. https://www.theguardian.com/cities/2018/jun/27/benefit-or-burden-the-cities-trying-out-universal-basic-income

Kouyoumdjian, F., Kim, M., Kiran, T., Cheng, S., Fung, K., Orkin, A., Kendall, C., Green, S., Matheson, F., & Kiefer, L. (2019, October). Attachment to primary care and team-based primary care. *Canadian Family Physician Medecin de Famille Canadien, 65*(10), e433–e442.

Kouyoumdjian, F., Schuler, A., Matheson, F., & Hwang, S. W. (2016, March). Health status of prisoners in Canada: Narrative review. *Canadian Family Physician Medecin de Famille Canadien, 62*(3), 215–222.

Krebs, E., Urada, D., Evans, E., Huang, D., Hser, Y., & Nosyk, B. (2017, May). The costs of crime during and after publicly funded treatment for opioid use disorders: A population-level study for the state of California. *Addiction (Abingdon, England), 112*(5), 838–851.

Levin, M. (2020, January). *You've just been named California's homelessness czar — what's your first move?* CalMatters. https://calmatters.org/housing/2020/01/california-homelessness-czar-options-ratings-cost-efficiency/

Lofton, B. P. (2004). Does restorative justice challenge systemic injustices? In Critical issues in restorative justice (pp. 377-385). Criminal Justice Press and Willan Publishing.

MacKenzie, D., & Meessen, S. (2019, October). *Intervening early to prevent youth homelessness: Lessons from the Geelong project.* Child Family Community Australia. https://aifs.gov.au/cfca/webinars/intervening-early-prevent-youth-homelessness-lessons-geelong-project

Magaldi, D., & Berler, M. (2020). Semi-structured interviews. In V. Zeigler-Hill & T. K. Shackelford (Eds.), *Encyclopedia of personality and individual differences.* Springer.

Manchak, S. M., & Morgan, R. D. (2018). Offenders with mental illness in prison. In J. Wooldredge & P. Smith (Eds.), *The Oxford handbook of prisons and imprisonment* (pp. 1–26). Oxford University Press.

McCold, P. (1995, March 31). *Restorative justice: The role of the community.* Paper presented to the Academy of Criminal Justice Sciences Annual Conference, Boston, MA.

McDonagh, T. (2011). *Tackling homelessness and exclusion: Understanding complex lives.* https://www.jrf.org.uk/sites/default/files/jrf/migrated/files/homelessness-exclusion-services-summary.pdf

McEwan, K., & Bigelow, D. (1997). Using a logic model to focus health services on population health goals. *The Canadian Journal of Program Evaluation, 12*(1), 167–174.

Mertens, D. M. (2019). *Research and evaluation in education and psychology. In Integrating Diversity With Quantitative, Qualitative, and Mixed Methods.* Sage Publishing.

Miller, J., & Crawford, B. (2018). *Ontario human rights tribunal orders province to stop segregating mentally ill inmates.* Ottawa Citizen. https://ottawacitizen.com/news/local-news/ontario-human-rights-tribunal-orders-province-to-stop-segregating-mentally-ill-inmates/

Monsebraaten, L. (2015). *Toronto legal clinic helps homeless fight unpayable 'nuisance' tickets.* Toronto Star. https://www.thestar.com/news/gta/2015/03/09/toronto-legal-clinic-helps-homeless-fight-unpayable-nuisance-tickets.html

Montague, S. (2000). Focusing on inputs, outputs, and outcomes: Are international approaches to performance management really so different? *The Canadian Journal of Program Evaluation, 15*(1), 139–148.

Morales, L., Barocio, J., Short, A. & Hashida, C. (2020, February). *The 2020-21 budget: The governor's homelessness plan.* California Legislative Analyst's Office.

Morris, H. (1968). Persons and punishment. *The Monist, 52*(4), 475–501. doi:10.5840/monist196852436

Morris, N. (1974, May). The future of imprisonment: Toward a punitive philosophy. *Michigan Law Review, 72*(6), 1161–1180.

Morris, N. (1974). The future of imprisonment: Toward a punitive philosophy. *Michigan Law Review, 72*(6), 1161–1180. doi:10.2307/1287619

Morris, R. (1999, September 13). *Why transformative justice?* Paper presented at Reconciling and Restoring Relationships-A Responsibility for All Christians. ICCPPC World Congress, Mexico City.

Morris, R. (2000). *Stories of transformative justice.* Canadian Scholars' Press Inc.

Noble, A. (2015). *Beyond housing first: A holistic response to family homelessness in Canada.* Raising The Roof. https://www.homelesshub.ca/resource/beyond-housing-first-holistic-response-family-homelessness-canada

O'Grady, W., & Lafleur, R. (2016, November). *Reintegration in Ontario: Practices, priorities, and effective models.* John Howard Society of Ontario. https://johnhoward.on.ca/wp-content/uploads/2016/11/Reintegration-in-Ontario-Final.pdf

Padwa, H., Meldrum, M., Friedman, J. R., & Braslow, J. T. (2016). A mental health system in recovery: The era of deinstitutionalisation in California. In D. Kritsotaki, V. Long, & M. Smith (Eds.), *Deinstitutionalisation and after: Post-war psychiatry in the western world* (pp. 241–265). Palgrave Macmillan.

Peterson, J. K., Kennealy, P., Skeem, J., Bray, B., & Zvonkovic, A. (2014). How often and how consistently do symptoms directly precede criminal behavior among offenders with mental illness? *Law and Human Behavior*, *38*(5), 439–449.

Piat, M., Polvere, L., Kirst, M., Voronka, J., Zabkiewicz, D., Plante, M., Isaak, C., Nolin, D., Nelson, G., & Goering, P. (2014). Pathways into homelessness: Understanding how both individual and structural factors contribute to and sustain homelessness in Canada. *Urban Studies (Edinburgh, Scotland)*, *52*(10), 2366–2382.

Picard, A. (2017, June 1). *The mentally ill are sick. So why do we put them in jail.* TVO Current Affairs. https://www.tvo.org/article/the-mentally-ill-are-sick-so-why-do-we-put-them-in-jail

Polcin, D., Korcha, R., Bond, J., & Galloway, G. (2010). What did we learn from our study on sober living houses and where do we go from here? *Journal of Psychoactive Drugs*, *42*(4), 425–433.

Poon, B., Leung, J. W., Louie, A., & Dios, C. V. (2012). The key functions of collaborative logic modelling: Insights from the British Columbia early childhood dental programs. *The Canadian Journal of Program Evaluation*, *27*, 87–102.

Poppe, B. (2018, March). *Unlocking doors to homelessness prevention: Solutions for preventing homelessness and eviction.* Eviction and Homelessness Prevention Research Project. https://static1.squarespace.com/static/59e4bd08d7bdce1e8a5b15bb/t/5ac2302d03ce648731d78cfd/1522675761270/Eviction++Homelessness+Prevention+Research+Report_FINAL_33018.pdf

Public Safety Canada. (1998, January). *Adult offender diversion programs.* https://www.publicsafety.gc.ca/cnt/rsrcs/pblctns/ffndr-dvrsn/index-en.aspx

Quinney, R., & Wildeman, J. (1991). *The problem of crime: A peace and social justice perspective.* Mayfield Pub Co Publication.

Raphael, S., Loftstrom, M., & Martin, B. (2017, April). *The effects of California's enhanced drug and contraband interdiction program on drug abuse and inmate misconduct in California's prisons.* California Department of Corrections and Rehabilitation Policy Briefing. https://nicic.gov/effects-california-s-enhanced-drug-and-contraband-interdiction-program-drug-abuse-and-inmate

Soothill, K. (2010). Sex offender recidivism. *Crime and Justice*, *39*, 145.

Stein, M. D., Flori, J. N., Risi, M. M., Conti, M. T., Anderson, B. J., & Bailey, G. L. (2017). Overdose history is associated with post-detoxification treatment preference for persons with opioid use disorder. *Substance abuse*, *38*(4), 389–393. https://doi.org/10.1080/08897077.2017.1353570

Stringer, H. (2019, March). Improving mental health for inmates. *American Psychological Association*, *50*(3), 46.

Taylor, M. (2017, December 6). *Improving in-prison rehabilitation programs.* California Legislative Analyst's Office. https://lao.ca.gov/Publications/Report/3720

The Institute of Fiscal Studies and Democracy. (2018). *Ending homelessness: A summary of proceedings.* No. 18003. https://ifsd.ca/web/default/files/Presentations/Reports/18003%20-%20Homelessness%20Symposium%20-%20Summary%20of%20Proceedings%20-%2029%20March%202018.pdf

Treleaven, S. (2019). Life after foster care in Canada. *Maclean's*. https://www.macleans.ca/society/life-after-foster-care-in-canada/

Unrau, Y. (1993). A program logic model approach to conceptualizing social service programs. *The Canadian Journal of Program Evaluation*, *8*(1), 117–134.

Van Horn, S. A., Morgan, R. D., Brusman-Lovins, L., Littlefield, A. K., Hunter, J. T., Gigax, G., & Ridley, K. (2019). Changing lives and changing outcomes: "What works" in an intervention for justice-involved persons with mental illness. *Psychological Services*, *16*(4), 693–700. https://doi.org/10.1037/ser0000248

Victoria News. (2020, April 20). *We're in it together: Mental health in greater Victoria.* Black Press Media. https://www.vicnews.com/community/were-in-it-together-mental-health-in-greater-victoria/

Wellesley Institute. (2017, November). *Supportive housing for Ontario.* Wellesley Institute Policy Brief. https://www.wellesleyinstitute.com/wp-content/uploads/2017/11/Wellesley-Brief-Ontario-Supportive-Housing-1.pdf

Whitehouse, H., & Fitzgerald, R. (2020). Fusion and reform: The potential for identity fusion to reduce recidivism and improve reintegration. *Anthropology in Action*, *27*(1).

Wiener, J. (2020, March 5). *Newsom's to-do list on mental health.* https://www.newsreview.com/sacramento/newsoms-to-do-list-on-mental/content?oid=29844024

Wilson, A. B., & Draine, J. (2006). Collaborations between criminal justice and mental health systems for prisoner reentry. *Psychiatric Services (Washington, D.C.)*, *57*(6), 875–878.

Wiltz, T. (2019). *A pileup of inequities: Why people of color are hit hardest by homelessness.* The Pew Charitable Trusts. https://www.pewtrusts.org/en/research-and-analysis/blogs/stateline/2019/03/29/a-pileup-of-inequities-why-people-of-color-are-hit-hardest-by-homelessness

Wolf, R., & Woodyard, C. (2019, December 16). Supreme Court refuses to consider cities' efforts to prosecute the homeless for sleeping outside. *USA Today.* https://www.usatoday.com/story/news/politics/2019/12/16/homeless-supreme-court-living-street-crime/4403793002/

Zoellick, J. C. (2018). Lock them up! Lock them up? A critique of the prison mosaic. Futures: The *Journal of Policy. Planning and Futures Studies*, *101*, 1–9.

ADDITIONAL READING

Britton, P., & Pilnik, L. (2018). Preventing homelessness for system-involved youth. *Juvenile & Family Court Journal*, *69*(1), 19–33. doi:10.1111/jfcj.12107

Capeheart, M. (2020). Toward transformative justice. In *Social Justice* (pp. 87–114). Rutgers University Press., doi:10.36019/9781978806894-006

Crowley, M., & Jones, D. (2017). A framework for valuing investments in a nurturing society: Opportunities for prevention research. *Clinical Child and Family Psychology Review*, *20*(1), 87–103. doi:10.100710567-017-0228-3 PMID:28247294

Graham, H., & White, R. (2015). *Innovative justice*. Routledge.

Parsons, A. (2018). *From asylum to prison: Deinstitutionalization and the rise of mass incarceration after 1945*. The University of North Carolina Press. doi:10.5149/northcarolina/9781469640631.001.0001

Ross, K., & Muro, D. (2020). Possibilities of prison-based restorative justice: Transformation beyond recidivism. *Contemporary Justice Review, 23*(3), 291–313. doi:10.1080/10282580.2020.1783258

West, G., & Morris, R. (2000). The case for penal abolition. In The Case for Penal Abolition. Canadian Scholars' Press and Women's Press.

KEY TERMS AND DEFINITIONS

Community Service Work Order: This is a decree issued by a court that allows individuals who come in contact with the law to perform unpaid work for their communities in lieu of incarceration for a specific period.

Deinstitutionalization: A government program that resulted in mental health patients being switched from psychiatric hospitals to mental health clinics for treatment with the hope that community care will promote integration.

Discharge Planning: The process of transitioning care for individuals once they leave a correctional institution to which they have been confined often carried out by a social worker or a case manager.

Evidence-Based Policy: The concept of adopting and implementing policies that have empirically proved to be successful as a result of the evaluations of past programs.

Homeless Court: A court set up to care for the homeless that focuses on treatment and rehabilitation for minor offences rather than punishment (incarceration).

Incarceration: The result of a decision by the courts to confine an individual to corrections as a result of the individual being in conflict with the law.

Intervention: A strategy that is deployed for the purpose of changing the behavior or the health status of individuals usually through educational programs.

Recidivism: The probability that those who have come into conflict with the law will do so again after their release from corrections.

Reentry and Reintegration: The moment a person is released from a correctional facility and enters into and assimilates with society through residence, education, or employment.

Victim Offender Reconciliation Programs: A program through which victims of crime meet with those who have wronged them to make them understand the impact of their actions and achieve reconciliation.

Chapter 16
From Victim to Criminality:
Understanding Sex Trafficking Within the Walls of Sex Work – Victimization of Victims of Commercial Sexual Exploitation

Vipin Vijay Nair
O. P. Jindal Global University, India

Sandra Anil Varkey
https://orcid.org/0000-0001-5576-6909
O. P. Jindal Global University, India

ABSTRACT

Trafficking of persons, primarily women and children, is one of the growing social dilemmas concerning global society today. Not only is human trafficking a highly sensitive and polarizing subject, but it is also considered a common norm in many countries. Many women recruited into commercial sex work are coerced into the profession exploiting their financial and economic condition but continue to work in the profession to survive through easy money. The chapter focuses on a theoretical framework for understanding the victimization of female sex workers. It also reflects various lacuna in the present criminal justice system and law enforcement mechanism in criminalizing victims within the sex work industry. The chapter narrates the voices of commercial sex workers in India over the prejudices and criminalization by various laws and regulations towards their consensual sex work. The chapter recommends sensitization training and awareness amongst various stakeholders of the criminal justice system.

INTRODUCTION

Trafficking of persons, primarily women, and children, is one of the growing social dilemmas concerning global society today. Not only is human trafficking an extremely sensitive and polarizing subject, but it is also considered a common norm in many countries. The United Nations Protocol to Prevent, Suppress and Punish Trafficking of Persons, Especially Women and Children of 2000 (further, "The

DOI: 10.4018/978-1-7998-6884-2.ch016

UN Protocol"), Article 3, has defined trafficking to include inter alia, "*any recruitment, transportation, purchase, sale or harboring of persons, by threat, force, fraud or violence.... for exploitation which includes prostitution, or for holding such person in forced labor or slavery-like practices*." (United Nations Protocol to Prevent, Suppress, and Punish Trafficking of Persons, 2000).

Sex trafficking is intrinsically linked with the practice and prevalence of commercial sexual exploitation across states. The UN Protocol states that sex-trafficking is a prima facie violation of basic human rights, including the inherent right to autonomy and freedom from sexual violence. Despite, such international principles, the report submitted by the International Labour Organization (ILO) in 2012, reflected that the global commercial sex trade practices buy and sell close to 20.9 million children and adults into commercial sexual servitude every year. (International Labour Office, 2012) Women and girl children are considered most vulnerable in this practice and constitute 98% of the total sex trafficking victims. (International Labour Office, 2012).

This commercial practice of buying and selling often operates in the realm of the economic principles of demand and supply reducing women and girls, to mere market commodities. This trend is reflected in The Global Report on Trafficking in Persons launched by the United Nations Office on Drugs and Crimes (UNODC) which consistently states that most victims of global human trafficking are women and girls who are trafficked for sexual exploitation most of whom who were still minors when forced into prostitution. (Global Report on Trafficking in Persons, 2016). Further, the report released by the UNODC recorded a staggering number of 25,000 reported cases of human trafficking, with three-fourth of the victims being trafficked for sexual exploitation primarily in Asia, Europe, and America. (Global Report on Trafficking in Persons, 2016). Apart from sexual exploitation, various other reports have also recorded the prevalence of sexual slavery where victims are abducted and exposed to sexual abuse while held in captivity (Bernard & Durham, 2014, p. 428).

The UN Report, 2018 on Trafficking of Person, attempted to paint a holistic picture of the socio-demographic pattern of trafficking around the world. In Western and Southern Europe, the report reflected that out of 5,500 victims of human trafficking were detected across 18 countries in the region, 66% of them were trafficked for sexual exploitation. (United Nations Office on Drugs and Crime, 2018). Similarly, in the Central and South-Eastern Europe Region, an estimate of 4 out of every 5 trafficked victims was a woman and out of 1382 victims detected across 14 countries in this region, 70% was sold into the commercials sex market. (United Nations Office on Drugs and Crime, 2018). In Eastern Europe and Central Asia as well, most of the trafficking victims were women with 55% of them (out of 599 detected victims across six countries) were trafficked for sex trade and exploitation. (United Nations Office on Drugs and Crime, 2018). Finally, in the South Asian region, including India, 59% of the total victims (1,099 victims detected) were female with 50% of them (out of 641 victims across four countries), being trafficked for sexual exploitation. (United Nations Office on Drugs and Crime, 2018). As reflected in the data, most human trafficking victims across most nations are women who are trafficked for the sole purpose of sexual exploitation, and commercial sex work without their conscious consent to enter this field. The data portrays a horrifying representation of the gravity and magnitude of human trafficking for commercial sex work across the world, despite the international community frowning upon this practice. Further, since the question of whether female sex work is legal, does not have a uniform concrete answer which exemplifies the taboo, ignorance, and lack of attention received by this crime and the sex workers consequently are forced to live and work in deplorable conditions.

This chapter attempts to address the concerns surrounding commercial sex practices and the victimization of sex workers, with a primal focus on the Indian scenario

THEORIES OF CAUSATION

The theoretical literature about commercial sexual exploitation and sex work is debated by scholars at both the macro-level and the micro-level. The former school of thought analyses the influence of the macro-economic systems in the economy such as the existent legal framework, criminal status of those who are directly involved in the sex trade and those who facilitate sex trade, to decipher the cause of sexual exploitation and sex work at a structural level. *Alternatively,* micro-level theories review the victimization of individuals and their entry and exit to the field of sexual exploitation. This chapter will focus on the legal, philosophical, and political perspectives of sexual exploitation and sex work on the premise of a few macro and micro-level indicators.

Macro Theories of Causation: Feminist Approach

A substantive portion of explanatory theories referring to violence and exploitation against women stem from feminist studies. These theories endorse a wide and transdisciplinary view that attempts decrypt the experience and roles of individuals, on the grounds of gender (Miriam, 2005, p.14). Feminist theories have gained seminal importance in sexual crimes including intimate partner violence and global institutional degradation and oppression of women. In the context of sexual exploitation and sex work, however, feminist studies aim to understand whether women, under any circumstance, will voluntarily engage in the commercial sex trade in return for monetary compensation (Wilson & Butler, 2014).

Within the overarching feminist approach to sex work, theorists and scholars are further divided into Neo-Abolitionists and Sex Positivists.

Neo-Abolitionists

Modern-day Neo-abolitionist theory concerning sexual exploitation is grounded on the studies of *Radical and Marxist Feminism.* Concisely, Neo abolitionist theories conclusively dictate that the existing societal structures are inherently patriarchal (Loue, 2001). As such, violent behavior against women is an act of social control premised on institutional sexism and a structural trend of dominance by men (Dobash & Dobash, 1979). Sexual exploitation, therefore, is deemed to be a result of predominant male privilege, as men presume their inherent right to control and abuse women.

Within radical feminism, theorists highlight the historical practice of sexism in society ranging from negating a woman's access to education, public life, and many labor markets (Loue, 2001) In this backdrop, the commercialization of sex is presumed to be an act of perpetuating male dominance over women by glorifying the inequalities between male and female. Radical feminism, therefore, conclusively terms all forms of sex trading as oppressive and an act of a patriarchal system (Weitzer, 2007, p.457).

Marxist's theories subscribe to a similar ideology by stating that, *"sexuality is to feminism what work is to Marxism, that which is one's own, yet taken away"* (MacKinnon, 1989). The theory contends that the existence of capitalism presupposes the oppression of women, as women will constantly be economically dependent on men in a patriarchal society.

The Neo-Abolitionist theories have, however, been attacked owing to their absolutist approach by focusing solely on sexually abused women by negating women's autonomy to choose the profession of their choice (Wolken, 2004, p.409). The theory is argued to categories all women who are involved in commercial sex practices as victims of a patriarchal society, thereby diluting the theories of feminism about a woman's autonomy of choice (Fitzgerald & Munro, 2012, p.183). As a response to the criticisms raised against this approach of equating all forms of the sex trade as a result of coercion and fraud, new forms of pro-sex theories began appearing in the debate of voluntary sex commercialization and sex work.

Sex-Positivists

Sex-positivists purport a pro-sex theory and emphasis on the autonomous authority women inherit in choosing their profession, including sex work. The theory identifies sex-labor with liberalism while arguing that women should inherit the agency and autonomy to decide their trade interests. (Almodavar, 1999, p.119). As such, from the perspective of sex positivists, what is deemed as intimate and private is a subjective concern that varies from one woman to another, and any form of pre-conveyed notion which dictates a woman's choice of professions is deemed to be patriarchal and oppressive (Gerassi, 2015, p.94). By recognizing commercial sexual activities as a form of reputable labor, this theory purported that the sex trade ought to be regulated and normalized on par with other professions.

However, pro-sex perspectives have faced staggering amounts of criticisms from various schools of literature. One primal contention to the presumption of consensual involvement of sex work by women is the concern that sex positivism ignores the astounding rates of sexual abuse and history of sexual assaults, primarily stemming from the lack of alternative economic opportunities for women (Hughes, 2005, p.5). On the moral and religious perspective, debates suggest that the commodification of trust as an economic product sold in sex markets is detrimental to the moral culture on a national and international level (Weitzer, 2007).

Therefore, though the theory of sex-positive is seemingly progressive and in-tune with a substantial portion of feminist studies, statistical, moral, and religious contentions continue to plague this philosophical approach of understanding commercial sex work.

Micro Theories of Causation: Critical Victimization

Unlike the extensive debates in the macro-theories of causation, micro-theoretical studies in concern suffer from a dearth of academic and scholarly inputs. The available discussions, however, attempted to analyze the entry to and exit from sex work and sexual exploitation. This part of the book will discuss some of the recognized theories of causation from a micro perspective.

Theory of Entry Into Sexual Exploitation

First, the life course theory is a primal explanation that tries to analyze one's entry into sex work, by purporting that the impact of every experience, including victimization, is directly influenced by the childhood and adolescent life stages of the concerned person (Reid, 2012, p.268). These impacts travel back to the victim's childhood and indicators of harmful social control processes during that time i.e., the need for acceptance and love. The theory argues that such influences instill in the child a desire for a better life and is attracted to the fast cash that accommodates sex work, thereby facilitating the girl's entry into commercial sex work. (Reid, 2012)

Second, the theory of social control highlighted the correlation between a girl and the ideals of conventional society. This bond is argued, to push girls to delinquent behavior. Further, the *prima facie* benefits of the street economy coupled with the difficulty of being accepted in the formal economy are believed to influence such girls into exploring the sex trade. (Gerassi, 2015, p.94)

Third, the structural - choice theory of victimization into commercial sex, examines the lifestyle routine of individuals with the risk of entry into the sex trade. It was found that households with low income and abusive nature, and the lack of other alternative economic options often encourages young women to enter into this field. (Gerassi, 2015, p.94)

In addition to these theories, discussions also relate to addiction studies and substance abuse, where it was found that women and young girls are often subject to substance use before their sexual exploitation (Farley & Barken, 1998, p.43). In this regard, a cross-sectional study was conducted among 237 prostitutions and 407 comparison women to analyze the sequence, timing, and frequency of substance usage among prostitutes. The study revealed that an estimate of 66% of surveyed prostitutes have consumed drugs before entering into the field, while 18% of them initiated drug use along with prostitution and another 17% used drugs after their entry. (Potterat et al., 1998, p.339). The study forwarded that early subjection to substance abuse is a non-ignorable element concerning a girl's entry into sexual exploitation.

Theories of Exit From Sexual Exploitation

Similar to entry theories, there is a lacuna of literature and discussion about a women's exit from sexual exploitation and sex work. One recognized model, identified as the "Breakaway Model," hypothesis a tipping point in everyone's life, wherein the cumulative negative experience of the trade will eventually result in any exit from the practice (Månsson & Hedin, 1999, p.17). The model suggests that an alteration of a woman's social network and worldview will influence the exit from prostitution.

Another influential model is the "Typology of Transition" concept, wherein four ideologies of exit from commercial sex work are envisioned. These stages include (i) a re-creationary method of exit wherein the woman experience a life-altering experience which triggers their exit, (ii) gradual transition from sex work, wherein the women seek aid from formal support services to exit the commercial market, (iii) a natural and intrinsic need to exit the practice begins developing in the woman and (iv) women continuously shuffle from commercial sex work, treatment centers, and criminal justice bodies (Sanders, 2007).

Therefore, a women's exit from the commercial sex trade can be influenced by a plethora of reasons and experiences ranging from her attitude, believes, intentions, and the surrounding environment.

The Broken Window Theory

Another interesting and prominent theory about the causation of sexual exploitation is the broken window theory. The theory purports that the prominent signals of crime, anti-social behavioral patterns, and other civil and political disorders encourage further crime in society. The theory was discussed by criminologists' James Q. Wilson and George L. Kelling, who in their article proposed that policing and containing minor offenses in the society such as loitering and graffiti, will reduce more heinous crimes. (Kelling & Wilson, 1982). This was premised on the principles that "*If a window in a building is broken and left not repaired, all of the windows will soon be broken*" (Kelling & Wilson, 1982, at 31) The theory is, therefore, an assumption on the correlation between the appearance of society and the subsequent level of disorder in the society. (Samahra, 2012)

The theory proposed three factors that instigate crime in society. *First,* the existence of social norms in a community and the need to conform to such norms. *Second,* the lack of routine and efficient monitoring of crimes in society, and *third,* the social singling and subsequent signal crimes (Harcourt, 1998, p.29; Samaha, 2012, p.1563). As such, the theory is built on the principle that the surrounding environment communicates to the people and therefore, a disordered environment is assumed to send indicators that criminal behavior in the particular community is less detected or is less likely to be noticed. Consequently, the deterioration of order in a community commences from this concept of a 'broken window' i.e., less supervision and correction of crimes in the area, and this practice alters the way people behave in communal spaces. (Harcourt, 1998) In simple terms, if one broken window is left ignored and unprepared, it will facilitate other broken windows which will eventually break down the communal order in society.

To illustrate, in the late 80's period, the city of New York witnessed severe crime rates and violence (Claidière, 2016). George Kelling, the co-author of the article which introduced the broken window theory ("The Broken Window"), was employed to the position of a consultant to mitigate the problems of the New York City Transit Authority. (Claidière, 2016). Kelling saw the awful conditions of the subway stations and ordered to clean the graffiti on the walls daily. The continues clearing of the walls eventually led to a decrease of graffiti being painted on the walls. (Claidière, 2016). Consequently, the police personnel also began implementing measures to create a "zero-tolerance" policy for graffiti painting with an easier procedure to arrest the culprits. With the stricter enforcement policies, eventually, the crimes occurring in subway stations such as fare evasion, urination, etc., substantially reduced. (Claidière, 2016). This was cited as one of the most efficient examples of the functioning of the theory, where minor signs of disorder in the society including graffiti painting and dirty streets were strictly penalized, which eventually led to a fall in crime rate. Therefore, the thesis of the theory, which assumes that petty crimes and disorderly behavior in society will trigger more such behavior causing an epidemic effect, was reinstated through this example.

The Broken Window Theory addresses prostitution and commercial sex within the concept of communal disorder, by consistently categorizing prostitutes as a variable of, and an element of communal disorder (Harcourt, 1998, p.291). Typically, an ideal society is assumed to consist of "decent citizens" and "criminal and disorderly people." (Wilson & Kelling, 1982). The latter category of people is believed to be inclusive of disreputable folk including drunks, addicts, and prostitutes, and are generally termed as outsiders to the society. (Wilson & Kelling, 1982) Therefore, the theory categorically separates people into disorderly and orderly individuals and attempts to deter crime and sexual exploitation in society by aesthetically promoting the ideals of sobriety, orderliness, law enforcement, and cleanliness in the society.

THE INDIAN PERSPECTIVE

Slavery is defined as, situations where "*one human effectively "owns" another, so the former can exploit the latter in any form*" (University for peace, human rights reference handbook, 2003). Consequently, the buying and selling of women and girls for sexual exploitation, at the very least, is akin to slavery.

Despite this notion, the Indian commercial sex work industry has over 3 million women who are either working voluntarily or are under-aged or have been coerced into selling their bodies. (Ministry of Women and Child Development, 2008). The data collected reflects that 35.47% of the total sex workers in India, entered the industry before the age of 18. (Ministry of Women and Child Development, 2008) In 2012, the Human Rights Watch (HRW) estimated a higher number of 15 million sex workers in the country. (Human Rights Watch, 2012). In recent times, per the National Crime Record Bureau (NCRB) report of 2019, there were 5900 cases of human trafficking reported in 2017, 5788 cases in

2018, and a significant increase of 6616 cases in 2019. The data also reflected that the Indian state of Rajasthan witnessed the highest number of cases of minors being trafficked i.e., 653 cases. A perusal of the data revealed that sex trafficking and commercial sale for prostitution was the primal reason for human trafficking and the state of Maharashtra reported 946 such cases only in 2019. (National Crime Records Bureau, 2019).

This commercial exchange of women in the country and their forced confinement within sex brothels, their inhuman work environment, exploitation by brothel owners, pimps, and the like has been reported several times by both HRW and other non-governmental organizations. However, the lives of such women are dominated by the brothel operators, and the victims are denied the right to even refuse any customer. This lack of power often leads to sex workers being highly prone to sexually transmitted diseases.

The reasons for the entry of women into commercial sex work in the country are similar to those discussed in the theoretical studies analyzed in the previous section. A review of numerous studies that focused particularly on the Indian scenario revealed that most women and children are trafficked across the country and are pushed into the industry either through coercion, force, or deceit. (Jorden et al., 2013, p.359). Further, owing to the financial constraints and rural poverty, many Indian families tend to sell their girl children into the industry in return for monetary security. (Jorden et al., 2013, p.359). However, in addition to the commonly understood reasons for entry into sex work, the Indian system further has certain unique features that push women into the industry involuntarily and voluntarily. As a consequence of this plagued thinking, economic options, and status of women in the country are significantly lower when compared to men.

Social and Cultural Practices

The Indian historic culture and the popular manifestations therein, tend to reduce women to mere commodities. An ideal woman as per Indian standards can be found in the ancient Manu Scripts of 200 BC which states that "*by a young girl, by a young woman, or even by an aged one, nothing must be done independently, even in her own house*". (Mazumdar & Mazumdar, 2004, p. 393). Developing from the traditions, women in the country are generally reduced to merely a wife, a mother, and a homemaker. (Mazumdar & Mazumdar, 2004, p. 393). In rural regions, 'bride burning or sathi,' is an accepted social practice where the widowed woman will burn herself on her husband's funeral fire, to signify that her purpose has ended. (Nangia, 1997, p.643)

With the advent of Independence, women were granted equal legal status on par with men, and legislations were formulated that banned the practice of sathi and protected women from oppression, harassment, and mistreatment. However, women in the country are still arguably in vulnerable positions owing to the embedded patriarchal notions and a cultural sanction that allows men to dominate women. (Swain et al., 2011, p. 357). Though there has been significant development in women's rights over the recent years, the social stigma surrounding a widowed woman, the low social status of women, and her economic and social vulnerability push her to find a place in prostitution even today.

The Devadasi System

In addition to cultural notions, Indian religious practices sanction the prostitution of women through the *Devadasi system.* This practice is present even today, despite the seemingly progressive and democratic development in the country. The *Devadasi* ritual is a practice through which young girls (aged five to six) primarily from the lower caste, Dalits, (Who are Dalits,2014) are "married" to Yellamma, a Hindu Goddess figure. (Shingal, 2015, p.107). Consequent to the ritual, the girls are viewed as "female slaves of God" and are used by higher-caste men for sexual purposes. (Hyun Jin Lee, 2011, p.1).

Today, the *Devadasi* practice is intertwined with poverty and economic necessity. Though the ritual of "marriage" remains largely the same, modern-day practices of *Devdasi's* are almost solely restricted to sex work, prostitution and exploitation and do not include the ancient practices of temple worshiping. (Shingal, 2015, p.107). Simply put, the system is now an institutional outlet for the commercial sale of girl children, under the pretense of religion and tradition, in return for sufficient monetary compensation. The intrinsic link between religion and sexual exploitation leads to thousands of women being transitioned into Devadasis annually. (Dalrymple 2008). Recent studies reflect that there is an estimate of 44,000 to 2,50,000 *devadasi's* in India today. (Th Hindu, 2006). In addition to being an underground tradition practiced primarily in the states of Karnataka, Andhra Pradesh, and Maharashtra, the International Labour Organization in its studies found that the *Devadasi* system is also exploited as a cover for trafficking women into commercial sex work. (UN General Assembly, 2012).

On the legal front, the Indian Legislature has attempted to ban the practice back in 1924, through Section 371 and 373 of the Indian Penal Code 1860, to make all acts of dedicating girls for commercial sex work, even in the name of religion or tradition, illegal. Following this, multiple states have enacted domestic statutes including the Bombay (Devadasi) Protection Act, 1934, the Madras (Devadasi) Protection Act, 1947, and the Maharashtra Devadasi (Abolition of Dedication) Bill, 2005, all of which cumulatively aim at declaring the practice *prima facie* unlawful, even if done with the consent of the girl. However, despite arguably stringent legislation, religious pressure, economic background, poverty, tradition, and coercion continue to push girls into this practice. The legal system has, therefore, failed to deliver effective results in curbing the so-called *religious prostitution (Vishal v Union of India,* 1990) and the practice continues to act as a significant causal reason for female prostitution in the country.

Poverty and Lack of Economic Alternatives

Financial constraints, cultural limitations, lack of education, and the low status of women in the country cumulatively limit the available economic options for women in India. (Mohindra, Haddas, & Narayana, 2012). As a consequence of this, only 20.5% of women in the country are engaged in employment in the organized sector. (Ministry of Statistics and Programme Implementation, Government of India, 2014) Even if employed, the treatment of women continues to be discriminatory. The average salary for women employees is only Rs.428.66. per day in rural areas and Rs. 609.7 per day in urban areas, when compared Rs. 550 per day for men in rural areas, and Rs. 805.52 per day for men in urban areas. (Ministry of Statistics and Programme Implementation, Government of India, 2014). Further, the average literacy rate of women is only 53.7% as opposed to 75.3% educated men, reflecting a 21.6% gap between men and women. (Ministry of Statistics and Programme Implementation, Government of India, 2014). Recent reports of 2019 further reveal that, women in the country collectively earn 19% less than men i.e., where men earn Rs. 242.49, women only earn Rs. 196.3, reflecting the heinous gender pay gap in the country (Bhattacharyya, 2019).

The contribution of women in the formal economy is, therefore, limited and below potential, particularly in comparison to men causing financial constraints in women-run families owing to which they turn to the sex trade as a viable and efficient alternative.

To study the tryst with informal labor markets and sex work, a survey of 3000 commercial sex workers in India was conducted. (Sahni & Shankar, 2013). The survey sample first attempted to distinguish between sex workers who were formally employed in the labor market and others who directly entered sex work to locate their reasons for engaging in this particular trade. The records first revealed that out of 3000 women, 1488 women were employed before entering into the commercial sex trade, while 1158 women entered directly. (Sahni & Shankar, 2013). With the women who were formally employed, the survey further reported that most of them were engaged in informal activities and faced similar salary disparities as discussed above. Additionally, 70% of the respondents hailed from poverty-ridden backgrounds (with most women having incomes amounting only to Rs. 500-1000 per month), and there was a high rate of illiteracy among the women. (Sahni & Shankar, 2013). Similarly, 57.68% of women who entered the sex trade directly were also from rural areas, with 59.9% of them having poor incomes. 47.8 of these women received no schooling experience or educational background. In both categories of sex workers, the age category of women was between 19-22 years. (Sahni & Shankar, 2013). Consequently, the inherent gender disadvantage of women concerning the labor market, coupled with the low social status and low educational qualifications influenced such women to enter the commercial sex market.

Even in the formal sector women employees are discriminated against based on their sex. Women who engage in the sex trade, who was earlier employed in the formal sector, often cite instances where their work experiences have been coercive, exploitative, without adequate remuneration, and sometimes they were even expected to deliver sexual favors in return for work. (Sahni & Shankar, 2013). For most unskilled and unemployed women, therefore, the commercial sex market is a viable and flexible alternative that provides them with substantial economic independence and financial stability. (Sahni & Shankar, 2013, p.33). Further, the sex trade enabled them to provide for their family and gain autonomy and over their bodies. (Morgan, 2009, p. 364).

In conclusion, for most women, entering the sex market is part of an economic decision based on their experiences in the labor market, salary disparity, lack of job security, or lack of adequate income to feed their families. Sex work, therefore, allowed such women to become economically independent. To illustrate, 63% of females who have been engaged in various jobs, earn up to Rs. 1000 per month, while close to 68% of sex workers earn an average of Rs. 5000 per month. Women's entry into sex work cannot be analyzed in isolation as is intrinsically linked with their economic status, gender, and the discrimination faced in other employment options. Therefore, economic desperation and coercion are the seemingly underlying premise based on which Indian women are trafficked into or voluntarily engage with commercial sex work.

THE LIMP IN THE INDIAN LEGAL FRAMEWORK

Despite a considerable number of women being engaged in commercial sex work, voluntarily and otherwise, India lacks a comprehensive legal framework for their protection from sexual exploitation and trafficking. The country follows an abolitionist perspective and attempts to forward a regressive and detrimental treatment towards women who engage in soliciting and the sex trade. As a result of this flawed approach, many women in the country live within the bounds of contemporary slavery after being tricked, sold, or otherwise forced into prostitution from which they are barred from escaping.

International Legal Perspective

Multiple legislations and international conventions explicitly bar all forms of slavery and trafficking around the world. Under article 4 of the Universal Declaration of Human Rights, all forms of female slavery are prohibited, including the slave trade. Similarly, Article 8 the International Covenant on Civil and Political Rights (CPPR), also prohibits slavery. This right has received the status of *jus cogens* i.e., it is part of the International Customary Law, which is binding on all states. (Cook, 2003, p.97). Further, the CPPR also prohibits all forms of slavery and the slave trade under Article 8(1) and Article 8(2).

Recently, the Human Rights Committee attempted to implement the CPPR rights by directing all states to submit reports stating the measures taken to implement the international principles and prevent human trafficking within and across borders. (United Nations High Commissioner for Refugees, 2000.), The concern of human trafficking has also been significantly addressed in the Council of Europe Convention on Action against Trafficking in Human Beings.

Indian Legal Framework

In the Indian national legal framework, the principles related to commercial sex work and trafficking are dissected into various legislations.

First, the primal law of the land, the Constitution of India, 1950 guarantees to all persons the right to life (Article 21), freedom (Article 19), right to equality (Article 14) and constitutional remedies on par with international human rights norms. Under Article 23, all persons are endowed with the fundamental right to be protected from all forms of exploitation and explicitly prohibits all forms of trafficking and forced labor. Any such offense under his Article is eligible for punishment per Article 23(2).

Second, the Indian Penal Code, 1860, criminalizes prostitution. However, these provisions (Section 372 and 373) are restricted to children rendering older women ineligible for protection under these sections. The code also criminalizes trading minors in the country or outside for sex work, and procreation of minor girls in scattered provisions. However, the laws related to prostitution are vague, and limited under the Code, particularly for older women.

Per contra, the code attempts to socially shun commercial sex workers by codifying that sex workers can be charged for causing 'public nuisance' under Section 290 or for 'obscene conduct under Section 294. The justice system, therefore, often invokes the Code to persecute commercial sex workers for public indecency or nuisance making them victims of trafficking but also convicts under the legal framework. Despite these regulations, as per the National AIDS Control Programme report (2007-2012), there are over 80,000 commercial sex workers in India with most of them entering the industry when they were below 18 years of age (National Aids Control Organization, 2012).

Third, India is a signatory to the Convention for the Suppression of the Traffic in Persons and the Exploitation of Prostitution of Others, 1949. This treaty was consequently implemented as part of the domestic legal system through the Suppression of Immoral Traffic in Women and Girls, 1956 ("SITA") which was later renamed as the Immoral Traffic (Prevention) Act, 1956 as it stands today. Per this Act, commercial sex workers are permitted to practice their profession within a private sphere through public solicitation activities that are deemed illegal. Indian laws differentiate between prostitution and consensual, voluntary selling of one's body in return for financial gratification. While the latter is permissible in law, "prostitution" as defined under Section 2(f) of the Immoral Trafficking Act, 1956, refers to sexual exploitation of any person for business activities and is termed as illegal. Therefore, sexual activities occurring in public spheres and organized prostitution including brothels and pimping are categorized as illegal activities. The Act further codifies multiple offenses including, operating a brothel, making a livelihood from the money earned from commercial sex, detaining persons for sex work even with consent, to target individuals who work in the sex trade.

The Indian Act, however, deviates from the purpose and principles behind the Trafficking Convention. While the convention prohibits all forms of punishment against victims of prostitution with a clear objective of punishing only those who facilitate, entice and exchange women for prostitution and sex work, the Indian Act has a trend of discriminatory against the victims by treating them as offenders and punishing them for immoral acts. (Misra et al., 2000, p.88). This is in direct contravention to the principles enshrined under the Convention which aimed to disincentives all forms of sexual exploitation by protecting the victims.

The Act also places immense power upon the police force to conduct 'raid and rescue' operations as per their will, which allows the officials to easily invoke these provisions to prosecute commercial sex workers. (Shetye, 2018, p.70). The Act further criminalizes the operating of a brothel near any public place, disallows adults from living off the earnings of sex workers even if it's an economic necessity, and empowers the police to search any suspected brothels, etc.

A perusal of the legislative framework reveals two failures of the Indian system. The first prominent failure is the lack of efficiency in the existing laws. This is evident from the horrifying number of women and girls who continue to be trafficked for sex purposes in India. As per newspaper reports, India had an estimate of 38,503 women who were trafficked from 2011-2019 (Khan, 2020). Further, the infamous areas such as the "red-light district" of Mumbai and Kolkata, continues to house several brothels with the flourishing commercial sex trade (Khan, 2020). Owing to the lack of legislative clarity, awareness, and proof, many of the victims are denied rescue and rehabilitation offers from the concerned authorities and continue to engage in the sex trade to make means for a living. Therefore, thousands of females continue to be forced to work in sexual slavery (Miko & Park, 2001) with most of the victims being young girls of the age 10 -14, (Jubilee Action, 2002) particularly those who are marginalized by caste or living in socio-economic desperation.

The second failure is the lack of statutes, policies, and legal framework which provides explicit protection to, and upliftment of sex workers. Though the Act allows for private solicitation, there is no codified legal standards, safeguards, or initiatives to protect the lives of the sex workers, which leaves them vulnerable and enslaved in this field of work, without legal or social protection. (Human Rights Watch, 1996) Apart from the constitutional guarantees available to all citizens, no legislation addresses the unique problems of brothels, sex trade, and private solicitation or address any specific responsibilities and obligations of those who engage in sex work, and those who hire women for commercial sex. *Alternatively,* the laws merely attempt to provide forums through which officials can punish the sex workers, despite them being victims to the vicious cycle of poverty, economic constraint, social stigmatization, and commercial sex work.

The Judicial Response

The Indian adjudicatory body, though known for its judicial activism, has been heavily biased against commercial sex workers and the large-scale atrocities the segment faces. One of the primary contentions regarding the statute was the constitutional validity of Section 20 of the SITA, which authorized the magistrate to remove any women who are deemed to be a prostitute from any place in its jurisdiction, including her home. The magistrate could further, prohibit the woman/girl from re-entering the jurisdiction. The provision was challenged through various parties and PIL's and finally, the concern reached the Supreme Court as being a violation of Article 14 of the Constitution in *State of Uttar Pradesh v Kaushaliya,* 1963. However, the five-judge bench of the Apex Court blatantly discriminated against and reduce the status of women engaged in sex work and prostitutes owing to their prejudices. By holding that Section 20 is not violative of anyone's right to equality, the judges unanimously seem to opine that the problem of prostitution, is the very reason for prostitutes and the this is an inherent social evil. Prostitutes were further deemed to be inferior, and lower in societal status when compared to other women, merely due to their profession. Regardless of whether they were coerced into, forced into, or voluntarily entered sex work, the court opined that only the suppression, deportation, and removal of prostitutes will solve the problem in any society. The justices, therefore, failed to uphold the principles of the Convention which India claims to have incorporated in the statute, to protect the victims of sex trafficking and commercial sexual abuse from any form of prosecution. Rather, the judgment asserted that the prostitutes themselves are the offenders, while completely negating the active role of perpetrators, brothel owners, and pimps who facilitate the industry.

Following this judgment, the court in *Begum v State,* 1962 addressed the crux of the problem of prostitution and sex trade in the country. The judgment deviated from the regressive trend in the earlier case, to opine that the State ought to create alternatives for sex workers to earn a livelihood rather than prosecuting them. However, the judgment merely remained on paper. The court failed to suggest any alternatives for women employed sex trade and did not address the need to codify stricter penal laws for those who benefit from or facilitate commercial sex work.

Even in recent cases, the courts have continued their prejudice towards prostitutes and the social destruction they cause to human civilization. In the case of *Upendra Baxi and Lotika Sarkar v State of Uttar Pradesh,* 1981, the deplorable conditions of a 'Protective Homes' in Agra which housed 100-125 women, was addressed. For 16 years, the Supreme Court noted blatant abuse in the homes, but never initiated a concrete response, and did not take any material action, in favor of the victims. During the case, 19 inmates disappeared from such homes and their traces were unknown, however, the judges did not take implement any discourse to ensure that the inmates ought not to live in degrading and inhumane conditions. Finally, Justice PN Bhagwati was vehemently prejudicial to prostitutes by stating that minor girls ought not to stay in such homes with "hardened prostitutes". By viewing prostitutes as derogatory characters, and a social disturbance, the Hon'ble Justice negated the possibility that they were also victims in the society who have accepted the heinous living conditions in the Homes and opted for prostitution to make livelihood due to lack of other economic alternatives. The case was eventually transferred to National Human Rights Commission which is merely a statutory authority with recommendatory powers, and the Apex Court blatantly failed to use its constitutional powers to proceed with the victims of the commercial sex trade (Rejmi, 2006).

Finally, in the case of *Gaurav Jain v Union of India,* 1997, Justice Ramaswamy employed a comparatively pro-victim approach and analyzed the gamut of concerns about the commercial sex industry in the country including socio-economic issues, human rights, and violation of constitutional principles. He further went on to address the derogatory and exploitative treatment taken by the police personnel on the victims of prostitution by noting that the women engaged in the professions are generally poor, and illiterate who is the ideal target group for the police nexus. However, the judgment once again failed to implement the existing constitutional schema for the protection of victims, rather, the judge merely ordered rescuing and rehabilitation programs. (Rejmi, 2006) Though this is a positive step in comparison to the previous judgments, the court did not dwell into the imminent need to deter human trafficking, particularly concerning women and children for the sex trade. Now in society, swift implementation of rigorous punishment for those who facilitate sex trade, market women and girls, and benefit from trafficking for prostitution should be of prime importance.

Further, the judge also termed prostitutes as "fallen women", which entails a perspective that they are less than, or in lower social status when compared to other women which reinstate the core problem of the Indian judicial body of viewing prostitutes and commercial sex workers as derogatory humans in the society. (Rejmi, 2006)

The Supreme Court has, therefore, failed to address the inhumane, deplorable, and violent condition of prostitution objectively and effectively in the country. (Rejmi, 2006) The core problem of trafficking has been ignored, and most judgments tend to focus on the victims themselves being the offenders. The blame and burden of causing social disturbance through prostitution are placed on the prostitutes themselves, who are the, however, the vulnerable target of this criminal nexus, while the facilitators of prostitution and those who reap benefits from this system are ignored by the judicial lens. This prejudicial treatment furthers the already existing bias towards commercial sex workers, which worsens their living conditions and strips them of their chance to attain constitutional protection.

VOICE OF COMMERCIAL SEX WORKERS IN INDIA

With the existence of a broken legal system, a prejudicial judicial body, and the derogatory status of commercial sex workers in the country, one can guess the plight of such women and children in the country. Despite being stripped of their rights, justice, and health, the victims of this vicious socio-economic cycle are further subject to heinous forms of sexual exploitation, torture, and slavery-like living conditions in the country. The following part will aim at exploring anecdotes of persons engaged in commercial sex work in the country.

Humans of Bombay is a social media platform where many Indian persons share their life stories, experiences, and insights. One particularly interesting feed was the story of Nillu, a young woman who was saved from a sex brothel. (Nair, 2017). In her narratives, she reveals that she was born an orphan and was subsequently raped by "a uniformed man," in Nepal who also impregnated her. At the early age of 15, she was forced to be a mother and a rape victim. She states that she was then sold for INR 1,00,000 to a brothel, and then again for INR 60,000 to a man who demanded sexual favors. (Nair, 2017). Her life in the brothels of Mumbai was characterized by years of alcoholism, deplorable living conditions, and providing sexual favors to drunk men. Though she was eventually saved by Purnata, an organization that helps victims of trafficking, she clarifies that she voluntarily chose to enter the sex trade and continue for nine years as it was the only economic option available to her to feed her child. (Nair, 2017) Her story reflects the underlying theme of this chapter, which attempts to highlight how desperation, poverty, and lack of economic alternatives force young women to enter the commercial sex trade.

As discussed in earlier sections, even if engaged in formal employment, women are treated in a derogatory manner and often reduced to mere sex objects for the gratification of men. For most women, sex work is generally their last resort to earn a living. As highlighted in the narratives of many sex workers in the city of Kolkata, women who were earlier engaged in construction work were forced to provide sexual acts if they wanted to retain their job, women who were working as housemaids were harassed by the men in the houses they visited, and women employed elsewhere were chosen for daily tasks only if they were willing to return sexual compensation. (Sinha, 2014, p.234). Another narrative by a 31-year-old sex worker in Kolkata, illustrated how she was earlier engaged in a medical job, sales jobs and as a cook, but the common experience of being harassed, bullied, and forced into sexual favors propelled her to choose the line of commercial sex work to achieve autonomy over her body. (Sinha, 2014, p.234). As such, irrespective of a woman's educational background, cultural upbringing, or economic status, the discriminated treatment inflicted on women in all fields of work, compels them to believe that engaging in commercial sex work is the only viable economic alternative that enables them to retain control over their lives and body.

The story of Chithra, a woman born in a lower-caste, poverty-ridden family in Bihar, is another bizarre narrative of how a woman's socio-economic status forces her into this profession. (Sinha, 1999, p.67). After her father had incurred debt from a moneylender for the marriage of her elder sisters, Pramod (a go-between who made living out of trafficking), promised Chitra's father that he would give her decent employment and pay all the father's debts. Believing the false promises, the 14-year-old Chithra went with Pramod who sold her to a pimp for $600. (Sinha, 1999, p.67) Eventually, Chithra was forced to solicit men and was told to charge higher wages as she was a young virgin. She eventually found a place in prostitution. Though she attempted to escape several times, however, eventually she realized that the area she lived in was guarded by a well-recognized gang of pimps and goons, and her life was stuck inside the walls of the brothel. (Sinha, 1999, p.67)

The above stories reflect the failure of the Indian legal and political system to cater to the needs of the victims of the sex trade in the country. Women like Chithra and others, suffer in their daily lives to earn a meager livelihood for themselves. Further, in many cases, there have been instances where the police personnel have raided brothels at odd times and arrested and convicted everyone in such brothels when they fail to find some specific person. As such, many times the wrong accused is charge-sheeted and even when the victim in such cases supports the prosecution case and her trafficking, she does not receive any monetary compensation. (Sinha, 1999).

As evident from the anecdotes, women are usually forced into the sex trade through illegal trafficking and are rendered victims of a form of structural violence that includes poverty, sexism, cultural pressure, social stigma, and male dominance. In addition to this, sex workers are often denied the right to request contraceptives or protection during sexual activities to prevent the spread of sexually transmitted diseases. By denying women access to the most basic human right to live, as envisioned under Article 21, India has continued to take a blind eye to the issue and has failed to address the severity of the atrocious condition of the commercial sex trade and the victims involved.

A HUMAN RIGHTS APPROACH TO PROSTITUTION

Legal models of targeting commercial sex work are generally categorized into complete prohibition, partial legalization, social-control legal frameworks, and pro-work legislation. (Sagade & Forster, 2018, p.34) Keeping in lieu of the sex - positivists theory, and the right of women to choose the profession of her choice, while also balancing this right with the socio-economic condition of sex work in India, this chapter attempts to forward the well-recognized human rights perspective to the commercial sex trade as a viable alternative in India. i.e., partial decriminalization of prostitution along with a pro-work framework.

The first essential initiative under this model is to inflict harsh punishments for all those who are involved in facilitating the sex trade in the country. (Overs & Loff, 2013). Structured penal provisions ought to be drafted specifically to target those who trade women, force women and children into sex work, and use under-aged girls in the sex industry. This policy measure will be on par with the International Labour Organization's Convention, which mandates all member parties to *"suppress the use of forced or compulsory labor in all its forms within the shortest possible period"* under Article 1(1), and the Convention on the Rights of Child which requires the member states to *"protect every child from exploitation"*, per Article 24. By implementing the stricter and structured regulations, India will be able to curb the number of women and children who are forced into commercial sex work and protect this vulnerable category from living in such deplorable conditions.

The second initiative is to enable and legalize the voluntary sex trade of adult women. (Sagade & Forster, 2018). Presently, commercial sex work is taboo in society, it is viewed as an unethical, immoral, and social evil that is rarely discussed in communities. To mitigate this perspective, sex work ought to be openly discussed as a professional woman voluntarily choose. This discussion will push the policymakers and judiciary to change their biased attitude towards sex workers and formulate adequate guidelines for women's protection against harassment and exploitation within the sex work industry (Sagade & Forster, 2018).

Further, in India, sex work is usually restricted to shady, underground businesses that are governed by bribery, blackmail, abuse, and dominance. (Sagade &Forster, 2018) As a result of this, the brutality and harassment inflicted on the sex workers from officials including the police, are often left unchallenged, and prostitutes rarely raise concerns regarding violations by brother's managers or clients. (Kotiswaram, 2014). In the present system, sex workers are prone to sexual abuse, exploitation, and dominance from pimps, brothel owners, and even the police. (Kotiswaram, 2014). Decriminalization of voluntary sex work can, therefore, mitigate this concern and promote safe sex practices in the industry.

This hybrid model, therefore, will dilute the conceptualization that sex workers are vulnerable victims in dire need of rescue, as the industry is inherently coercive and unjustified. (Cavalieri, 2011, p.1409). Though India has a complex employment framework, where no specific legislation is concerting minimal protection of women, the commercial sex industry forwarded by the voice of Indian sex workers, require immediate attention by the policy framers.

SUGGESTIONS FOR THE INDIAN LEGAL FRAMEWORK

Similar to the hybrid model, the Indian legal framework in theory, has legalized private and voluntary commercial sex work, while also penalizing acts of human trafficking for the purposes of sex work. However, the system continues to lack a codified set of civil liberties, rights, and safety measures available to sex workers. Further, despite being a lawful trade, commercial sex work and prostitution is heavily stigmatized in the country causing such acts to function underground, as women are reluctant in being publicly acknowledged as a sex worker as they will either be forced into medical check-ups, or described in derogatory terms, or send to compulsory rehabilitation centers, and sometimes even prison. Therefore, the concerns of the sex workers are ignored, buried, and neglected which increases the vulnerability and harassment in the profession. To improve this abusive situation, the author forwards the following suggestions for the improvement of the legal and political schema in the country.

Amendments to the Immoral (Trafficking) Prevention Act, 1956

The *Immoral (Trafficking) Prevention Act, 1956,* legalizes the act of private commercial sex. However, the Act requires certain modifications to ensure protection to sex workers. *Firstly,* per Section 3 of the Act the act of keeping brothels or allowing premises to be used as a brothel is penalized. This creates a contradiction in the vision to legalize of commercial sex trade. The lack of an institutional system where voluntary sex workers can reside, practice their profession, and built a reputable recognition will force such workers to reside in shady, underground, and improperly constructed premises. This situation will further, decrease the quality of the lives of sex workers and their living conditions as such, the Act ought to ideally allow commercial brothels which may be subject to proper regulations and inspections. *Second,* Section 4 of the Act prescribes punishment for living off the earning gained from prostitution. This negates the validity, and legality of the profession and further undermines the status of the work as sex workers will be denied the opportunity to economically support their families through their earning. Finally, public laws including "causing public nuisance," ought to not be inflicted on sex workers and unlawfully utilized to harass the without proper regulation and supervision. Repealing or altering the usage of these laws will, therefore, enable consenting adults to trade sex freely and institutionally under efficient regulations.

Implement Specific Legislations to Address Sexual Harassment of Sex Workers in their Workplace

Legislations similar to the *Sexual Harassment of Women at Workplace (Prevention Prohibition and Redressal) Act, 2013,* should be extended to, or implemented for sex workers in their premise of work. Their area of work, the acts which equate to sexual harassment, the available authorities and means to seek redressal along with specific penal sanctions, compensation and other remedies should be laid down in the Act with reference to sex work. This will ensure that all related workers and employers will take preventive measures against all forms of harassment, forceful sexual exploitation and other forms of coercion which are likely to happen in sex trade. Similar to the Prevention of Sexual Harassment Act, any instance of harassment in sex trade should be addressed through a complaint mechanism and the brothel owner should be authorized to initiate criminal proceedings against the offender under the Indian Penal Code.

Increase the Participation of Sex Workers in Policy Making

Sex workers should be afforded the opportunity and recognition to collectively voice their concerns, needs, demands and the problems they face in their workplace. This will enable organizations and the legislature, to draft laws and implement policies which are relevant and required by the vulnerable community. The same should be made aware to the police personnel, law enforcement agencies and the general public to disseminate knowledge about the commercial sex market and prostitution which will increase sensitivity and cooperation among authorities and the public, which will subsequently reduce the social stigma and prejudicial thinking related to prostitution.

Effective Implementation of Policies

To ensure the effected implementation of policies, the judiciary and the legal system should address the concerns pertaining the sex work industry by either spreading awareness regarding the available human rights instruments which can be used by aggrieved sex workers to approach the justice system, or the courts ought to take *suo moto* actions to report the violent acts against sex workers by state and non-state actors. Further, the sex workers should be protected against unwarranted and unnecessary arrests by police personnel, and from harassment and insensitive attitude from other authorities. When interacting with the justice system, the confidentiality of sex workers should be protected, and the authorities should be properly skilled and equipped to address cases of sexual harassment, exploitation, and abuse. Further, free legal service by trained legal personnel and advocates should be made available to sex workers to ensure that they have adequate access to the justice system to attain redressal and compensation when their rights have been violated.

CONCLUSION

The chapter attempted to critically analyze the plight of commercial sex workers in India through the lens of their causes of entry to the industry, judicial and legislative response, and anecdotal evidence. The general theme of the paper suggests that women sex workers in the country, are blatantly denied their basic rights and subject to heinous working conditions and inhuman living environments.

Women engaged in commercial sex-work are rightly entitled to constitutional protection and their right to live with dignity. These rights include the right to political representation, equality before the law, and freedom from sexual exploitation. However, as witnessed in the Chapter, India fails to adequately uphold these rights concerning sex workers by considering them as an inherent social evil. Therefore, there is an inherent need for the nation to adopt a holistic step towards recognizing the rights of sex workers and the State to intervene in matters for the regulation, participation, and protection of sex workers. Further, the author urges the country to abolish the gender stereotypical notions of female chastity and the notions of a patriarchal society to protect these victims from social shunning and expulsion from societies. The need of the hour is, therefore, to implement an effective and efficient justice system guided by the police personnel and laws to mitigate the injustices faced by women and children who fell prey to this commercial market. By creating awareness pertaining to the commercial sex trade, fighting the stigmatization related to prostitution and commercial sex work, and incorporating the suggestions made for an effective legislation and law enforcement mechanism, the author attempts to make an immediate call for action to uplift the commercial sex work industry and bring it in par with the reputation, and protection received by all other professions.

REFERENCES

Almodovar, N. (1999). For their own good: The results of the prostitution laws as enforced by cops. *Politician and Judges. Hastings Women's L.J., 10*, 119. https://repository.uchastings.edu/hwlj/vol10/iss1/7

Bernard, V., & Durham, H. (2014). Sexual violence in armed conflict: From breaking silence to breaking the cycle. *International Review of the Red Cross*, *96*(894), 427–434. doi:10.1017/S1816383115000442

Bhattacharyya, R. (2019, March 7). *Gender pay gap high in India: Men get paid Rs 242 every hour, women earn Rs 46 less*. The Economic Times. https://economictimes.indiatimes.com/magazines/panache/gender-pay-gap-still-high-women-in-india-earn-19-pc-less-than-men-report/articleshow/68302223.cms

Cavalieri, S. (2011). Between victim and agent: A third-way feminist account of trafficking for sex work. *Indiana Law Journal (Indianapolis, Ind.)*, *86*(4), 1409–1458.

Claidière, N. (2016, November 10). *Experimental evidence for the Broken Window Theory*. International Cognition and Culture Institute. http://cognitionandculture.net/blogs/nicolas-claidires-blog/experimental-evidence-for-the-broken-window-theory/

Convention for the Suppression of the Traffic in Persons and the Exploitation of the Prostitution of Others. Dec. 2, 1949, 96 U.N.T.S. 271, G.A. Res. 317 (IV), (entered into force July 25, 1951) India acceded to the Trafficking Convention on January 9, *1953*, http://untreaty.un.org/ENGLISH/bible/englishinternetbible/parti/chapterVil/treatyl 1.asp

Cook, R. H. (2003). Dynamic content: The strategic contingency of international law. *Duke Journal of Comparative and International Law, 14*(1), 97–98. https://scholarship.law.duke.edu/djcil/vol14/iss1/3

Dalrymple, W. (2008, June 19). *Serving the goddess*. The New Yorker. https://www.newyorker.com/magazine/2008/08/04/serving-the-goddess

Exploratory review of route-specific, gendered, and age-graded dynamics of exploitation: Applying life course theory to victimization in sex trafficking in North America. (n.d.). *Aggression and Violent Behavior, 17(*3), 257–271. doi:10.1016/j.avb.2012.02.005

Farley, M., & Barken, H. (1998). Prostitution, violence, and posttraumatic stress disorder. *Women & Health*, *27*(3), 37–49. doi:10.1300/J013v27n03_03 PMID:9698636

Fitzgerald, S. A., & Munro, V. E. (2012). Sex work and regulation of vulnerability(ies): Introduction. *Feminist Legal Studies*, *20*(3), 183–188. doi:10.100710691-012-9212-y

Gerassi, L. (2015). Heated debate: Theoretical perspectives of sexual exploitation and sex work. *Journal of Sociology and Social Welfare*, *42*(4), 79–100. https://www.ncbi.nlm.nih.gov/pmc/articles/PMC4730391/ PMID:26834302

Harcourt, B. (1998). Reflecting on the Subject: A critique of the social influence conception of deterrence, the broken windows theory, and order-maintenance policing New York style. *Michigan Law Review*, *97*(2), 291–389. doi:10.2307/1290289

Hughes, D. M. (2005). The demand for sex trafficking. *Women's Studies Program, University of Rhode Island, 26*, 5. https://www.academia.edu/3415676/The_Demand_for_Victims_of_Sex_Trafficking

Hyun, J. L. (2011). Temple prostitutes: Devadasi practice and human trafficking in India. *Regent Journal of International Law*, *1*, 2.

National Aids Control Organisation. (2012). *The National AIDS Control Programme Phase III. (2007-2012).* http://www.naco.gov.in/sites/default/files/NACP%20III%20-

International Labour Office (ILO). (2012). *ILO Global Estimate of Forced Labour.* https://www.ilo.org/wcmsp5/groups/public/---ed_norm/---declaration/documents/publication/wcms_182004.pdf

Jordan, J., Patel, B., & Rapp, L. (2013). Domestic minor sex trafficking: A social work perspective on misidentification, victims, buyers, traffickers, treatment, and reform of current practice. *Journal of Human Behavior in the Social Environment, 23*(3), 356–369. doi:10.1080/10911359.2013.764198

Kelling, G. L., & Wilson, J. Q. (1982, March). Broken windows. *The Atlantic.* https://www.theatlantic.com/magazine/archive/1982/03/broken-windows/304465/

Khan, F. (2020, February 18). *India had 38,503 victims of trafficking in 2011-19. Only 77 have got compensation.* The Print. https://theprint.in/india/india-had-38503-victims-of-trafficking-in-2011-19-only-77-have-got-compensation/365761/

Kotiswaran, P. (2014). Beyond the allures of criminalisation: Rethinking the regulation of sex work in India. *Criminology & Criminal Justice, 14*(5), 565–579. doi:10.1177/1748895814542533

MacKinnon, C. A. (1982). Feminism, Marxism, method and the state, An agenda for theory. *Feminist Theory, 7*(3), 515–544.

Månsson, S.-A., & Hedin, U.-C. (1999). Breaking the Matthew effect - on women leaving prostitution. *International Journal of Social Welfare, 8*(1), 67–77. doi:10.1111/1468-2397.00063

Mazumdar, S., & Mazumdar, S. (2004). Religion and place attachment: A study of sacred places. *Journal of Environmental Psychology, 24*(3), 385–397. doi:10.1016/j.jenvp.2004.08.005

Miko, F. T., & Park, G. (2001). *Trafficking in women and children: The U.S. and international response.* Congressional Research Service. https://www.everycrsreport.com/files/20010801_RL30545_18350f9e73685f6041b54b4f929553d7088849d9.pdf

Ministry of Statistics and Programme Implementation, Government of India. (2014). *Participation in Economy.* http://mospi.nic.in/sites/default/files/reports_and_publication/cso_social_statices_division/Chapter_4_2014.pdf

Miriam, K. (2005). Stopping the traffic in women: Power, agency, and abolition in feminist debates over sex-trafficking. *Journal of Social Philosophy, 36*(1), 1–17. doi:10.1111/j.1467-9833.2005.00254.x

Misra, G., Mahal, A., & Shah, R. (2000). Protecting the rights of sex workers: The Indian experience. *Health and Human Rights, 5*(1), 88. doi:10.2307/4065224 PMID:11154525

Mohindra, K. S., Haddad, S., & Narayana, D. (2012). Debt, shame, and survival: Becoming and living as widows in rural Kerala, India. *BMC International Health and Human Rights, 12*(1), 28. doi:10.1186/1472-698X-12-28 PMID:23126457

Morgan, A. (2009). Sex at the margins: Migration, labour markets, and the rescue industry. *Journal of Social Policy, 38*(2), 364–365. doi:10.1017/S0047279408002900

Nangia, A. (1997). The tragedy of bride burning in India: How should the law address it. *Brooklyn Journal of International Law, 22*(3), 637-694. https://brooklynworks.brooklaw.edu/bjil/vol22/iss3/4

Navsarjan Trust. (2014). *Who are the Dalits?* https://navsarjantrust.org/who-are-dalits/

Policing prostitution in India: An examination of field experiences at Mumbai. (n.d.). *International Journal of Criminal Justice Sciences, 13*(1), 68–76. doi:10.5281/zenodo.1403388

Potterat, J. J., Rothenberg, R. B., Muth, S. Q., Darrow, W. W., & Phillips-Plummer, L. (1998). Pathways to prostitution: The chronology of sexual and drug abuse milestones. *Journal of Sex Research, 35*(4), 333–340. https://doi.org/10.1080/00224499809551951

Sagade, J., & Forster, C. (2018). Recognising the human rights of female sex workers in India: Moving from prohibition to decriminalisation and a pro-work model. *Indian Journal of Gender Studies, 25*(1), 26–46. https://doi.org/10.1177/0971521517738450

Sahni, R., & Shankar, V. K. (2013, February). *Sex work and its linkages with informal labour markets in India: Findings from the first pan-India survey of female sex workers* (No. 416). Institute of Development Studies. https://onlinelibrary.wiley.com/doi/pdfdirect/10.1111/j.2040-0209.2013.00416.x

Samaha, A. (2012). Regulation for the sake of appearance. *Harvard Law Review, 125*, 1563. https://harvardlawreview.org/2012/05/regulation-for-the-sake-of-appearance/

Shingal, A. (2015). The devadasi system: Temple prostitution in India. *UCLA Women's Law Journal, 22*(1), 107. https://escholarship.org/uc/item/37z853br

Sinha, M. (1999). Sex, structural violence, and AIDS: Case studies of Indian prostitutes. *Women's Studies Quarterly, 27*(1/2), 65–72. https://www.jstor.org/stable/40003399

Sinha, S. (2014). Reasons for women's entry into sex work: A case study of Kolkata, India. *Sexuality & Culture, 19*(1), 216–235. doi:10.100712119-014-9256-z

Swain, S. N., Saggurti, N., Battala, M., Verma, R. K., & Jain, A. K. (2011). Experience of violence and adverse reproductive health outcomes, HIV risks among mobile female sex workers in India. *BMC Public Health, 11*(1), 357. https://doi.org/10.1186/1471-2458-11-357

The Hindu. (2006, January 30). *Project combat launched to eradicate "Devadasi" system.* https://www.thehindu.com/archive/print/2006/01/30/

United Nations High Commissioner for Refugees. (2000). *Refworld | CCPR General Comment No. 28: Article 3 (The Equality of Rights Between Men and Women).* https://www.refworld.org/docid/45139c9b4.html

United Nations Office on Drugs and Crime. (2018). *Global report on trafficking in persons.* United Nations Publication. https://www.unodc.org/documents/data-and-analysis/glotip/2018/GLOTiP_2018_BOOK_web_small.pdf

Weitzer, R. (2007). The social construction of sex trafficking: Ideology and institutionalization of a moral crusade. *Politics & Society, 35*(3), 447–475. https://doi.org/10.1177/0032329207304319

Wilson, B., & Butler, L. D. (2014). Running a gauntlet: A review of victimization and violence in the pre-entry, post-entry, and peri-/post-exit periods of commercial sexual exploitation. *Psychological Trauma: Theory, Research, Practice, and Policy*, *6*(5), 494–504. https://doi.org/10.1037/a0032977

Wolken, C. L. (2004). Feminist Legal theory and human trafficking in the United States: Towards a new framework. *University of Maryland Law Journal of Race, 6*(2), 407–437. https://digitalcommons.law.umaryland.edu/rrgc/vol6/iss2/9/

Chapter 17
Centers for the Investigative Interviewing of Children in Turkey

Huseyin Batman
Ankara University, Turkey

ABSTRACT

Conducting interviews with witnesses and suspects is a core function of policing across the world. Child sexual abuse is broadly described as any sexual activity involving a child where consent is not or cannot be given. Child sexual abuse differs from other types of childhood victimization in that there is usually no witness apart from the victim and the accused and often no physical evidence. This chapter aims to summarize the components that play important role during the investigative interviewing of children. In addition to that, the role of the interviewers, interview aids, cognitive interview, risks of repeated interviewing of children, and effects of child sexual abuse on children will be outlined. This chapter will also give information about the child interviewing centers that are still being used actively in Turkey.

INTRODUCTION

In recent years, sexual abuse has become a universal problem that affects the whole world's agenda and causes psychological and negative consequences in the short and long term (Karakartal, 2020, p.145). Child sexual abuse can be considered also a public health problem with a global prevalence estimated at 11.8%, or 118 per 1000 children (Stoltenborgh et al., 2011 as cited in Sumampouw et al., 2020, p.170). More and more often, children are becoming involved in the legal system to provide courtroom testimony, especially in sexual abuse cases (Ceci & Bruck, 1993). For instance, in the United States, the number and the rate of victims have fluctuated between 2014 and 2018. Comparing the national rounded number of victims from 2014 (675,000) to the national rounded number of victims in 2018 (678.000) shows an increase of 0.4 percent (Child Maltreatment, 2018, p.ii).

In Turkey, according to statistics of the Ministry of Justice 650 children are sent to courthouses due to child sexual abuse cases each month (Child Sexual Abuse Report, 2016). The actual prevalence of

DOI: 10.4018/978-1-7998-6884-2.ch017

sexual abuse is more difficult to document accurately, because few victims disclose such abuse for various reasons, including fear, guilt, repression, and shame (Finkelhor, 1979; Russell, 1983; Schultz, 1973 as cited in Palmer et al.,1999, p.230). Child sexual abuse is broadly described as any sexual activity involving a child where consent is not or cannot be given (Dominguez, Nelke, & Perry 2001, p.202, as cited in Horwath, 2010, p. 143). Child sexual abuse is not only harmful to the child, jeopardizing child safety and well-being; it is also a crime (Faller, 2015, p.37).

Historically, in many countries children have been regarded by legal practitioners and other concerned professionals as unreliable eyewitnesses. Indeed, before the 1980s, children were believed to be poor witnesses, prone to making things up, highly suggestible, and not able to distinguish fantasy from reality in essence, second-class witnesses (Holliday et al., 2014, p.119). However, recent psychological research has shown that children are capable of reporting previously experienced events in a meaningful and accurate manner (Sattar, 2000, p.9). Malloy, Wright, and Skagerberg (2012, p.105) allege that even young children can provide the police with invaluable information if they are interviewed appropriately.

Investigative interviewing is a broader term an interrogation, describing fair, dualistic, and open-minded communication to obtain accurate and reliable information carried out within a framework of national and international law (Holmberg, 2014, p.146). Any investigative interview with a witness aims is to elicit the most accurate and detailed account of an alleged offense in a manner that does not place undue stress on the interviewee (Milne & Bull, 1999 as cited in Wright, Powell, Ridge - Damien, 2007, p.395). The most crucial step in a child sexual abuse case is to get the testimony of the child (Polat, 2017, p.110). Children are usually the only eyewitness of these traumatic events (Brubacher et al., 2013). Only 5% of the perpetrators of child sexual abuse and %o1 of incest cases can be found (Child Sexual Abuse Report, 2016). Timing of the interview is very important to get the right information from children (Güler et al., 2016, p.100). Children should be interviewed as early as possible, because the longer the delay between an experience and the initial interview, the more likely it is that children will forget the experience and consequently be vulnerable to suggestive influences. Increased delay is especially a problem in sexual abuse cases (Gitlin & Pezdek, 2009, p.74). Children also should be informed about the aim and the duration of the interview (Atılgan, Yağcıoğlu, & Çavdar, 2014, p.13). Interviewees need guidance, for most of them, an interview about sexual abuse is a possibly frightening experience (Faller, 2015, p.41). They should also have a right to say "I don't know" during the interview (Ermağan, 2015 as cited in Çağlar and Türk, 2020, p.14), because children may not know all the answer to the questions.

It is really difficult to determine the reasons why some children are more susceptible to abuse than others. Several factors may put children at risk of sexual victimization. The primary reason is social isolation. "Children who are left alone, are unsupervised, and who do not have the physical presence of numerous friends and neighbors are more likely to be abused (Sgroi, 1982; Finkelhor, 1984)." In addition to that mother also plays an important role in the child's vulnerability. Research show that a mother "who is absent, who is not close to her child emotionally, who is sexually punitive or religiously fanatic, who never finished high school, or who keeps herself isolated is more likely to have a child who will be abused" (Sgroi, 1982; James and Nasjleti, 1983; Finkelhor, 1984 as cited in Tower, 1999, p.126). Moreover, children who have handicaps (physical limitations or emotional disturbances) are particularly vulnerable to victimization (Young, 1982 as cited in Tower, 1999, p.127). This chapter aims to give information about important components of an interview with children, discuss the risks of multiple interviews and effects of child sexual abuse on child. Also, it aims to summarize the development of investigative interviewing of children in Turkey.

INTERVIEW WITH CHILDREN

Lamb, Malloy and La Rooy (2011, p.15) noted that children are often a crucial source of information about the offenses in which they have been involved as victims or witnesses. The main aim of an investigation is to answer two primary questions: i) What happened (if anything did happen, ii) Who did it? (Milne & Bull, 2008, p.8). In 1990, the Court of Appeal (for England and Wales) ruled that children of any age could provide evidence in criminal trials if the judge deemed the child "to possess sufficient intelligence to justify the reception of the evidence and understand the duty of speaking the truth (Peterson, 2001, p.16)." Child sexual abuse differs from other types of childhood victimization in that there are usually no witnesses apart from the victim and the accused and often no physical evidence. Therefore, children must tell someone about it (Bussey, 2009, p.212). When children witness a crime, they may be asked to describe and identify the persons involved in the event. The information provided by the child witnesses may be used to narrow the search for the suspect and eventually to select foils for the line up identification task (Pozzulo, 2007, p.283). During the interview; age of child, development level and the effects of the trauma should be taken into consideration (Kırımsoy et al., 2013, p.98). Children with disabilities are also especially vulnerable to abuse (Westcott, 1991). Children with learning disabilities may need extra time spent on getting to know a person; therefore, rapport is also obligatory for a successful interview with them (Bull, 1995 as cited in Milne, 1999, p.173). Questions should be kept as simple and concrete as possible (Milne, 1999, p.174). The United Nations Convention on the Rights of the Child (1990) and the Council of Europe's Convention on the Protection of Children against Sexual Exploitation and Sexual Abuse (2007) mandate that special care is provided to child witnesses during the legal process (Quas & Sumaroka, 2011, p.329). Similarly in Turkey, special care has been given to children who have been abused sexually (Mağdur et al., 2021).

DIFFICULTIES OF INTERVIEWING CHILDREN

Children are arguably the most criminally victimized people in society (Finkelhor, 2008, p.3). Assessing children suspected of being sexually maltreated is not easy, and over the years the issue of how sexual abuse should be assessed and diagnosed has evoked much debate (Gumpert, 2007, p.251). In The US Department of Health & Services (2010) found that in 80% of the cases the abuser is a parent; in 38% of the cases the abuser is the mother; in 19% the father and 18% both of them. In the remaining 25% of the cases the abusers were mothers acting in concert with another abuser (an abuser unknown to the victim, male relative, or stepfather) (Odeljan, Butorac, & Bailey, 2015, p.1). Therefore children may be motivated to keep information secret or deny that they were abused because they wish to protect familiar perpetrators, especially family members (Orbach & Shiloach, 2007, p.116). In addition to that, children may be reluctant to talk with an unfamiliar interviewer about sensitive or embarrassing issues, such as socially proscribed forms of intimate touching or to acknowledge "coercive, repeated abuse" that can instill high levels of fear, shame, and mistrust (Orbach & Shiloach, 2007, p.116). Some children have also fear of harm by the abuser, fear of rejection by the family, fear of disbelief, fear of the reaction of social environment, fear of family break up and fear of embarrassment (Westcott & Davies, 2014, p.249).

Apart from all of that, children compared with adults, are more suggestible and their accounts of events less accurate and detailed (Blandon & Pezdek, 2009, p.70). Children speeches about the events tend to be short and lacking in much detail. Communication with them can be difficult to follow because of their inconsistencies in enunciation and they sometimes use words of which they have little understanding (Howitt, 2009, p.354). Also, children may fail to understand the questions (Holliday, Brainerd & Reyna, 2008, p.93). Young children (3-6) are unlikely to be aware of the differences between the legal interview and normal conversations with parents (Bourg et al., 1999, p.64). It can be said that all these difficulties make the role of the interviewer very important. Interviewers need to become competent in building rapport and communicating with children using appropriate questions (Stewart et al., 2011, p.199).

THE IMPORTANCE OF INTERVIEWER

Specialized skills are required when interviewing children in a forensic context (Powell et al., 2010 as cited in Sumampouw et al., 2020, p.170). The forensic interviewer is seen as a fact-finder, objectively accumulating details of legal relevance and documenting children's statements verbatim, if possible. He or she is supportive but remains neutral to the veracity of the information provided and abstains from a relationship that could unduly influence children's reports (Saywitz & Camparo, 2009, p.114). Forensic interviewers must be familiar with current interview methodology and the supporting literature (Stewart et al., 2011, p.200). Some interview factors which may affect children's eyewitness accuracy and resistance to misinformation have been identified. For instance; the types of questions asked, frequency of the questions that are asked, the types of information about which children are interviewed and the interview context play an important role during the interview (Eisen et al., 1999, p.33). Establishing rapport with a child can be considered as a crucial step in an investigative interview and should precede and discussion of suspected child abuse (Hershkowitz, 2011, p.109). Interviewers should build rapport with witnesses because it helps to facilitate disclosure and maximizes informativeness (Lamb & Garretson, 2003, p.158). In addition to that, interviewers need to know about memory processes to be able to interview appropriately, as such knowledge will help interviewers to develop appropriate strategies to obtain the maximum quantity of information from an interviewee without jeopardizing the quality of the information gained (Milne & Bull, 2008, p.9).

Interview Aids

Researchers have explored alternative techniques aimed at facilitating more complete recall (Lamb et al., 2008, p.43). When witnesses or victims encounter difficulty remembering persons or events, they may be asked to examine props, drawings, or photographs to facilitate memory (David & Loftus, 2007, p.217). The use of prop items relevant to the event in question (e.g., real items, scale models, toys, photographs) may increase the similarity between the vent and the retrieval condition (interview), thereby enhancing recall by providing reminders of the event (Tulving & Thompson, 1973), or providing opportunities for children to overcome linguistic deficits by demonstrating rather than, or as well as, telling what they remember (Pipe, Gee, & Wilson, 1993 as cited in Lamb et al., 2008, p.47).

Drawings can also be used in forensic interviews as a means of enhancing children's accounts. Drawings have been used in two different ways:

1. As direct communicative aids whereby children draw and talk about what they have experienced (Butler, Gross, & Hayne, 1995; Gross & Hayne, 1998, 1999; Salmon, Roncolato, & Gleitzman, 2003; Wesson & Salmon, 2001 as cited in Lamb et al., 2008, p.45).

2. They may help children generate retrieval cues for further recall (Butler et al., 1995). Drawing may also reduce the social demand characteristics of the interview by increasing rapport, increasing the child's comfort level, and prolonging the interview so that children have more opportunity to retrieve and report information (Gross & Hayne, 1998; Salmon et al., 2003 as cited in Lamb et al., 2008, p.45). After drawing, children should be encouraged to speak about their drawn pictures (Atılgan, Yağcıoğlu, & Çavdar, 2014, p.56).

Police forces worldwide retain collections of photographs of persons convicted of serious offenses, indexed by offense, gender, and age (Davies, 1996, p.245). Using photographs may decrease some of the difficulties associated with other props. Unlike toys and dolls, photographs are defined by being representations of other things and thus may facilitate recall of information by reminding children of details they may not otherwise spontaneously report (Brown, 2011, p.230). Consideration must be given to what aids are used, the timing and manner in which they are introduced into the interview, and the developmental capacities of the children (Brown, 2011, p.229).

COGNITIVE INTERVIEW

The cognitive interview (CI) is an effective eyewitness memory tool (Radvansky, 2011, p. 269). It was developed by using psychological theories of memory to extract as much accurate information as possible from the willing interviewee (Shawyer, Milne, & Bull, 2009, p. 32). The first published paper on the use of the CI with children appeared in 1988. In this pilot study Ed Geiselman and Padilla found that children interviewed with a CI recalled 21% more correct information than did other children (Milne & Bull, 1999, p.137). Milne and Bull (1996) provide evidence that the cognitive interview is effective for children with a learning disability (Gudjonsson, 1999, p.69). The original cognitive interview involved four instructions; these required the witness to:

1. mentally reconstructing the environmental and personal context in existence at the time of the event,
2. reporting everything, even partial information,
3. recounting the sequence of events in a variety of orders;
4. reporting the events from a variety of perspectives (Saywitz & Camparo, 2009, p.109).

The cognitive interview takes more time to administer than the standard interview. However, given the amount of extra work that might be required without that information the costs well worth it (Radvansky, 2011, p.269). However, Fisher and Geiselman (1992) recognized that the CI did not have sufficient structure for practical use, and that police officers questioning skills were often inadequate for the task of interviewing. Consequently, they developed an Enhanced Cognitive Interview (ECI) using further psychological knowledge from the fields of memory research and communication skills, which they presented in the form of an interviewing handbook (Fisher & Geiselman, 1992 as cited in Clarke, 2005, p.33).

REPEATED INTERVIEWING OF CHILDREN

In a forensic environment, children are usually interviewed more than once (Quas & Sumaroka, 2011). Some authorities estimate that the average child witness may be questioned 12 times during an investigation (Whitcombe, 1992), this figure may be an underestimate if one considers the number of times that parents, friends, or mental health professionals may also question these children (Ceci, Bruck, & Battin, 2000, p.178). According to research that was carried out by the Ministry of Justice in Turkey, children approximately have to tell what happens 17 times to authorities in the forensic process (Bağ & Alşen, 2016). According to Ceci and Bruck (1995), repeated interviewing may *contaminate children's reports* (Santtila, Korkman & Sandnabba, 2004, p.22). Laboratory research suggests that repeated requests for information within an interview may signal to a child that their earlier answer was incorrect. Also, young children especially, are prone to change their answers when questioned repeatedly (Holliday et al., 2012, p.121). Interviewing children more than once by several people may cause psychological problems (Polat, 2015). Repeated interviewing is also associated with baleful effects. First, as interviews are repeated, so is the length of time between the original event and the interview; this allows for the weakening of the original memory trace, and as a result of this weakening, more intrusions can infiltrate the memory system (Ceci & Bruck, 1995, p.108).

However, several steps have been taken nationally and internationally to ensure that multiple interviews do not occur, for instance in the United Kingdom, the Memorandum of Good Practice for interviewing children in criminal cases warns against interviewing a child more than once unless there is a good reason for doing so (Home Office, 1992). Similarly in Turkey, there are some measures to protect children from being interviewed more than once. According to the Turkish Criminal Procedure Code (236/1); "A child or the victim who has suffered psychological damages from the committed crime, shall be heard only one time in relation to investigation or prosecution of the committed crime. Cases which pose a necessity with respect to revealing the factual truth are exceptions (Turkish Criminal Procedure Code, 2009, p.240)."

EFFECTS OF CHILD SEXUAL ABUSE ON CHILD

Child sexual abuse is a serious public health problem which, in the majority of cases, interferes in the adequate development of those who suffer from it and has negative repercussions on the physical and psychological condition of the victim. The experience of child sexual abuse can be considered an extreme situation which, as described by Lazarus and Folkman (1984), usually results in an elevated level of stress and unease in most individuals (Beltran, 2009, p.135). The nature and dynamics of sexual abuse and sexually abusive relationships are often traumatic. When sexual abuse occurs in childhood it can hinder normal social growth and be a cause of many different psychosocial problems (Maltz, 2002 as cited in Hall & Hall, 2011, p.2).

Childhood sexual abuse has been correlated with higher levels of depression, guilt, shame, self-blame, eating disorders, somatic concerns, anxiety, dissociative patterns, repression, denial, sexual problems, relationship problems and trauma. The psychological effects of child sexual abuse often occur irrespective of the particular extent of trauma the child experienced during the abuse. With respect to trauma, the American Psychiatric Association's Diagnostic and Statistical Manual, Fifth Edition (DSM-5), classify the trigger to Post Traumatic Stress Disorder (PTSD) as exposure to actual or threatened death, serious injury or sexual violation (Sinanan, 2015, p.1).

The most common diagnosis given to children who have documented histories of sexual abuse is posttraumatic stress disorder (PTSD) (Berliner & Elliott, 2002; Kendall-Tackett, Williams, & Finkelhor, 1993; McLeer et al., 1998; Putnam, 2003; Ruggiero, McLeer, & Dixon, 2000). PTSD symptom clusters include avoidance and/or numbing behaviours, hyperarousal symtoms, and experiencing parts of the trauma (Goodyear-Brown, Fath & Myers, 2012, p.14).

CHILD INTERVIEW CENTERS IN TURKEY

The first step to establish a special place for interviewing children in Turkey began with the High Education Committee Law in 1981 (article/7). This law allows universities to establish Child Protection Center in university hospitals (Humanistik Büro, 2014). Child Protection Centers were also a part of the "Children First Project" that was signed between Turkey and UNICEF. By this project, it was targeted to increase the capacity of institutions that aim to protect children from neglect and exploitation (Kök, 2019, p.93). The first Child Protection Center established in 1998 in İzmir province in Dr.Behçet Uz Child Hospital (Bağ & Alşen, 2016, p.10). Child Protection Center is still in service and its mission is to check if there is any child exploitation case such as physical, sexual exploitation or neglect (Hümanistik Büro, 2014). Child Protection Centers consist of some specialist medical doctors such as Child Psychiatrist, Forensic Medicine Psychiatrist, Child Surgery, Child Health Specialist and Social Worker or Psychologist (Dağlı & İnanıcı, 2011).

The second step that was taken in Turkey was Child Monitoring Centers (CMC) which was built in 2012 by a legal arrangement (circular:2012/20). The mission of the Child Monitoring Center is to deal only with child sexual exploitation cases. The Ministry of Health organized training for the staff of these centers in 2010. Interview rooms were placed in big state hospitals, especially on a different floor or building. These centers help the referral of children to necessary hospital clinics such as forensic examination unit, child psychiatry clinic, etc (Bayün & Dinçer, 2013, p.92). It can be considered as a big reform for Turkey to establish these centers out of police stations and noisy corridors of courthouses. Child Monitoring Center Team has five members; forensic interviewer, family interviewer, representatives from the Ministry of Family Labour and Social Services, nurse and medical doctor. Child Monitoring Centers are used for multi-purposes, such as front interview, family interview, forensic interview, forensic examination, child health examination and social work assessment (Bağ & Alşen, 2016, p.11). Child Monitorıng Centers help children to give a testimony to a public prosecutor and a lawyer via an interviewer in a specially designed room. Children are protected from repeated interviews and being retraumatized by this interview model (Kök, 2019, p.97).

The third step that was taken to interview children in Turkey is Child-Friendly Interview Rooms. The main goal of the Child-Friendly Interview Room is described as enabling child protection through principles of interviewing children in a friendly environment by experienced staff. According to the standards, the interview is carried out by a judge in the presence of a psychologist/social worker. Other persons (prosecutor, advocate, accused, private complainant) are present in a separate room and can participate in the interview via a communication system, two-side mirror and/or live broadcast of the interview (Ümit, Çavdar, & Yağcıoğlu, 2014, p.27). Child-Friendly Interview Rooms are a part of the Justice for Children Project that was developed between Unicef and the Ministry of Justice. It consists of three parts such as i) waiting room, ii) interviewing room, and iii) monitoring room. Interviews are carried out not only with sexually abused children but also with eye witnesses, children driven into crime, a victim of domestic violence and the other vulnerable groups. These rooms are formed in courthouses. It aims to allow children to give their testimony without seeing the perpetrators and protect them from other threats that may face in law courts. There are 96 child-friendly interview rooms in 73 different provinces according to statistics of the Ministry of Justice (Mağdur Hakları Daire Başkanlığı, 2021). There are two cameras in the interview room, the first one shows all parts of the room, the second one focuses only on the face of a child. There is also a microphone which allows communicating between interviewer and judge also to hear the answer of the child. All communication is being followed by National Judicial System (UYAP) and Voice and Scene Information System (SEGBIS). Interviewers use interview aids such as anatomic toys, paper, and pencils to facilitate the interview with the child (Türk, 2017, p.24).

CONCLUSION

Child sexual abuse is one of the most known global problems that affect millions of children, it cuts across boundaries of race, culture, class, and religion. The investigation of many child sexual abuse cases starts with an investigative interview of a child. Child sexual abuse differs from the other type of crime, because in many child sexual abuse cases there is no medical and physical evidence also the only source of information is usually the child who is the victim of the crime. An investigative interview aims to know what happened and if there is a criminal who did it.

Turkey has been making big efforts to allow children to give their testimony in an appropriate room with educated interviewers. Child Protection Center, Child Monitoring Center and Child-Friendly Interview Room (AGO) models are still active and have been used extensively. However, there is still a lot of work to do which requires mutual efforts. Developed countries should be open to cooperation and help. Protecting children from crime and criminals can not be left to chance.

REFERENCES

Atılgan, Ü. E., Yağcıoğlu, S., & Çavdar, Y. (2014). Çocuklarla adli görüşme odaları. İhtiyaçları, İyi Uygulama Örnekleri ve Çocuklarla Adli Görüşme Standartları. *Journal of Law and Human Behaviour.*, *38*, 171–180.

Bağ, Ö., & Alşen, S. (2016). Çocuğun cinsel istismarının değerlendirilmesinde yeni model: Çocuk İzlem Merkezleri. *Izmir Dr. Behçet Uz Çocuk Hastanesi Dergisi*, *6*(1), 9–14. doi:10.5222/buchd.2016.009

Bayün, S., & Dinçer, C. N. (2013*). Çocuk İzlem Merkezi. Hukuk Gündemi Dergisi, 2013/2*. Retrieved on 24.04.2021. http://www.ankarabarosu.org.tr/siteler/ankarabarosu/hgdmakale/2013-2/23.pdf

Blandon-Gitlin, I., & Pezdek, K. (2009). Children's memory in forensic contexts: Suggestibility, false memory, and individual differences. In B. L. Bottoms, C. J. Najdowski, & G. S. Goodman (Eds.), *Children as victims, witnesses, and offenders: Psychological science and the law* (pp. 57–80). Guilford.

Bourg, W., Broderick, R., Flagor, R., Kelly, M. D., Ervin, L. D., & Butler, J. (1999). *A Child Interviewer's guidebook*. Sage.

Brown, D. (2011). The use of supplementary techniques in forensic interviews with children. In E. M. Lamb, D. J. La Rooy, & L. C. Katz (Eds.), *Children's testimony: A handbook of psychological resarch and forensic practices* (pp. 217–250). Wiley. doi:10.1002/9781119998495.ch12

Brubacher, P.S., Malloy, C.L., Lamb, E.M., & Roberts, P.K. (2013). How do interviewers and children discuss individual occurrences of alleged repeated abuse in forensic interviews? *Applied Cognitive Psychology*. 443-450. doi:10.1002/acp.2920

Bussey, K. (2009). An international perspective on child witnesses. In L. B. Bottoms, J. C. Najdowski, & S. G. Goodman (Eds.), *Children as victims, witnesses and offenders, Psychological Science and Law* (pp. 209–232). The Guildford Press.

Çağlar, E. E., & Türk, T. (2019). İstismara Maruz Kalan Çocuklarla Adli Görüşme: Nichd Protokolü Önerisi. *TAAD*, *38*, 393–412.

Ceci, J. S., & Bruck, M. (1995). *Jeopardy in the courtroom: A scientific analysis of children's testimony*. American Psychological Association. doi:10.1037/10180-000

Ceci, J. S., Bruck, M., & Battin, B. D. (2000). The suggestibility of children's testimony. In F. D. Bjorklund (Ed.), *False Memory Creation In Children and Adults* (pp. 169–202). Lawrence Erlbaum.

Child, S. A. R. (2016). *Şiddeti Önleme ve Rehabilitasyon Derneği. Acıbadem Üniversitesi Suç ve Şiddetle Mücadele Uygulama ve Araştırma Merkezi*. Erişim Adresi: https://www.imdat.org/kopyas%C4%B1-grooming

Child Maltreatment. 29'th Year of Reporting. (2018). Department of Health & Human Services-USA. Washington: ACF.

Clarke, C. (2005). *A national evaluation of PEACE investigative interviewing* (Unpublished PhD thesis). Institute of Criminal Justice Studies. The University of Portsmouth.

Dağlı, T., & İnanıcı, M.A. (2011). *Hastane temelli çocuk koruma merkezleri için başvuru kitabı ihmal ve istismara uğrayan çocuğa bütüncül yaklaşım*. Ankara: Fersa Ofset Matbaacılık.

Davies, M. G. (1996). Children's identification evidence. In L. S. Sporer, S. R. Malpass, & G. Koehnken (Eds.), *In psychological issues in eyewitness identification* (pp. 233–258). Lawrence Erlbaum.

Davis, D., & Loftus, E.F. (2007). *Internal and external sources of information in adult witness memory*. Researchgate.

Faller, K. C. (2015). Forty years of forensic interviewing of children suspected of sexual abuse, 1974-2014: Historical benchmarks. *Journal of Social Sciences.*, *4*, 34–65.

Gitlin, B. I., & Pezdek, K. (2009). Children's memory in forensic contexts. In L. B. Bottoms, J. C. Najdowski, & S. G. Goodman (Eds.), *Children as victims, witnesses and Offenders: Psychological science and law* (pp. 57–80). The Guildford Press.

Goodyear-Brown, P., Fath, A., & Myers, L. (2012). Child sSexual Abuse. In P. Goodyear-Brown (Ed.), *Handbook of child sexual abuse: Identification, assessment, and treatment* (pp. 1–28). John Wiley & Sons.

Great Britain Home Office. (1992). *Memorandum of Good Practice on Video Recorded Interviews with Child Witnesses For Criminal Proceedings*. London: HMSO.

Gudjohnsson, G. (1999). Testimony from persons with mental disorders. In H. A. Armstrong, E. Shepherd, & D. Wolchover (Eds.), Analysing witness testimony (pp. 62–75). London: Blackstone.

Güler, G., Yıldırım, V., Kütük, Ö. M., & Toros, F. (2016). Adli Psikiyatrik Değerlendirme ve Çocuk ile İletişim. *Adli Tıp Bülteni.*, *2*, 98–106.

Gumpert, H. C. (2007). Clinical and organizational perspectives on denial and delayed disclosure. In E. M. Pipe, E. M. Lamb, Y. Orbach, & C. A. Cederborg (Eds.), *Child sexual abuse: Disclosure, delay and denial* (pp. 251–264). Taylor & Francis.

Hall, M., & Hall, J. (2011). *The long term effects of child sexual abuse*. Retrieved from, https://www.counseling.org/docs/disaster-and-trauma_sexual-abuse/long-term-effects-of-childhood-sexual-abuse.pdf?sfvrsn=2

Hershkowitz, I. (2011). Rapport Building in Investigative Interviews of Children. In *Children's Testimony: A Handbook of Psychological Research and Forensic Practice* (pp. 109–128). John Wiley & Sons Ltd.

Holliday, E. R., Brainerd, J. C., & Reyna, F. V. (2008). Interviewing Vulnerable Witness. In G. Davies & C. Hollin (Eds.), *Forensic psychology* (pp. 87–112). John Wiley.

Holliday, E. R., Humphries, E. H., Brainerd, J. C., & Reyna, F. V. (2012). Interviewing vulnerable witnesses. In G. Davies & A. Beech (Eds.), *Forensic psychology: Crime, justice, law, interventions* (pp. 115–134). John Wiley & Sons Ltd.

Holliday, R. E., Humphries, J. E., Brainerd, C. J., & Reyna, V. F. (2014). Eyewitness Evidence. In G. Davies & A. Beech (Eds.), *Forensic Psychology: Crime Justice Law Interventions* (2nd ed., pp. 115–134). John Wiley & Sons Ltd.

Holmberg, U. (2014). Interviewing suspects. In G. Davies & A. Beech (Eds.), *Forensic psychology: Crime justice law interventions* (pp. 135–150). John Wiley.

Horvath, H. A. M. (2010). Child victims of sexual abuse. In M. J. Brown & A. E. Campbell (Eds.), *The cambridge handbook of forensic psychology* (pp. 143–152). Cambridge University Press.

Howitt, D. (2009). *Introduction to forensic & criminal psychology* (3rd ed.). Pearson Education Ltd.

Hümanistik, B. (2014). *Türkiye'de çocuk koruma ve önleme sistemleri haritası*. http://www.cocukkorumaharitasi.info/dosyadepo/kitap.pdf

Karakartal, D. (2020). Çocuk Cinsel İstismarının Önlenmesinde Cinsel Eğitimin Önemi. *International Journal of Humanities and Education.*, *13*, 145–156.

Kırımsoy, E., Acar, H., Yokuş Sevük, H., Kaynak, H., Aydın, M., Antakyalıoğlu, Ş., Özdemir, U., Mutlu, Y., & Baykara Acar, Y. (2013). *Çocuk Adalet Sistemi Çalışanları Eğitim Programı:Kolaylaştırıcılar için Vaka Temelli Eğitim Kitabı*. Retrieved on: 19.02.2021. https://www.unicef.org/turkey/media/5466/file/VAKA%20TEMELL%C4%B0%20E%C4%9E%C4%B0T%C4%B0M%20K%C4%B0TABI%20_%20Kas%C4%B1m%202013.pdf

Kök, H. (2019). *Türkiye'de Cinsel İstismara Uğrayan Çocuklara Yönelik Hizmet ve Uygulamaların Değerlendirilmesi: Bir Model Önerisi* (Unpublished PhD Thesis). Hacettepe Üniversitesi.

Lamb, E. M., & Garretson, E. M. (2003). The effects of interviewer and child gender on the informativeness of alleged child sexual abuse victims in forensic interviews. *Law and Human Behavior, 27*, 157–171.

Lamb, E. M., Hershkowitz, I., Orbach, Y., & Esplin, W. P. (2008). *Tell me what happened: Structured investigative interviews of child victims and witness*. John Wiley & Sons Ltd.

Lamb, E. M., Malloy, C. L., & Rooy, J. D. (2011). Setting realistic expectations: Developmental characteristics, capacities and limitations. In E. M. Lamb, J. D. La Rooy, C. L. Malloy, & C. Katz (Eds.), *Children's testimony: A handbook of psychological research and forensic practice* (2nd ed., pp. 15–48). John Wiley & Sons Ltd.

Mağdur Hakları Daire Başkanlığı. (2021). *AGO Nedir?* Retrieved on: 25.04.2021. https://magdur.adalet.gov.tr/Home//SayfaDetay/agonedir

Malloy, C. L., Wright, B. D., & Skagerberg, M. E. (2012). In G. Davies & A. Beech (Eds.), *Forensic psychology: Crime justice, law, interventions* (pp. 99–114). John Wiley & Sons Ltd.

Milne, R., & Bull, R. (1999). *Investigative interviewing psychology and practice*. John Wiley & Sons Ltd.

Milne, R., & Bull, R. (2008). *Interviewing victims of crime, including children and people with intellectual disabilities*. Researchgate.

Odeljan, R., Butorac, K., & Bailey, A. (2015). *Investigative interview with children*. Research Gate.

Orbach, Y., & Shiloach, H. (2007). Reluctant disclosures of child sexual abuse. In E. M. Pipe, E. M. Lamb, Y. Orbach, & C. A. Cederborg (Eds.), *Child sexual abuse: Disclosure, delay and denial* (pp. 115–134). Taylor & Francis Group.

Palmer, L. K., Frantz, C. E., Armsworth, M. W., Swank, P., Copley, J. V., & Bush, G. A. (1999). Neuropsychological sequelae of chronically psychologically traumatized children: Specific findings in memory and higher cognitive functions. In L. M. Williams & V. L. Banyard (Eds.), *Trauma & memory* (pp. 229–244). Sage Publications, Inc.

Paterson, B. (2001). *Improving children's eyewitness memory: Cognitive and social considerations* (Unpublished PhD dissertation). University of Portsmouth.

Polat, O. (2015). Tüm Boyutlarıyla Pedofili. *Adli Tıp Bülteni., 1*, 60–70.

Polat, O. (2017). *Tüm boyutlarıyla çocuk istismarı*. Seçkin.

Pozzulo, D. J. (2007). Person description and identification by child witnesses. In L. C. R. Lindsay, F. D. Ross, D. J. Read, & P. M. Toglia (Eds.), (pp. 283–308). The handbook of eyewitness psychology. Lawrence Erlbaum Pub.

Quas, A. J., & Sumaroka, M. (2011). Consequences of legal involvement on child victims of maltreatment. In E. M. Lamb, L. J. D. Rooy, C. L. Malloy, & C. Katz (Eds.), *Children's testimony: A handbook of psychological research and forensic practices* (pp. 323–350). John Wiley & Sons Ltd.

Radvansky, G. A. (2011). *Human memory*. Routledge.

Santtila, P., Korkman, J., & Sandnabba, K. (2004). Effects of interview phase, repeated interviewing, presence of a support serson and anatomically detailed dolls on child sexual abuse interviews. *Psychology, Crime & Law*, *10*, 21–35.

Sattar, R. G. (2000). *The interviewing and preparation of child witnesses for legal purposes* (Unpublished PhD dissertation). University of Portsmouth.

Saywitz, J. K., & Camparo, B. L. (2009). Contemporary child forensic interviewing: Evolving consensus and innovation over 25 years. In L. B. Bottoms, J. C. Najdowski, & S. G. Goodman (Eds.), *Children as victims, witnesses and offenders, Psychological science and law* (pp. 102–127). The Guildford Press.

Shawyer, A., Milne, B., & Bull, R. (2009). Investigative interviewing in the UK. In T. Williamson, B. Milne, & P. S. Savage (Eds.), *International developments in investigative interviewing* (pp. 24–38). Willan Pub.

Sinanan, N.A. (2015). Trauma and treatment of child sexual abuse. *Journal of Trauma & Treatment*, 1-5. doi:. doi:10.4172/2167-1222.S4-024

Sumampouw, N. E. J., Otgaar, H., La Rooy, D., & Ruiter, C. (2020). The quality of forensic child interviewing in child sexual abuse cases in Indonesia. *Journal of Police and Criminal Psychology*, *35*, 170–181.

Turkish Criminal Procedure Code. (2009). Retrieved on 22.04.2021. https://www.legislationline.org/download/id/4257/file/Turkey_CPC_2009_en.pdf

Ümit, E., Çavdar, Y., & Yağcıoğlu, S. (2014). *Interview rooms for children: Needs, examples of best practices and standards for child friendly interview*. Summary Report. https://www.unicef.org/turkey/en/reports/judicial-interview-room

Westcott, H. (1991). The abuse of disabled children: A review of the literature. *Child: Care, Health and Development*, *17*(4), 243–258.

Westcott, H. L., & Davies, G. (2014). Safeguarding witnesses. In G. Davies & A. Beech (Eds.), *Forensic psychology: Crime justice law interventions* (pp. 247–264). John Wiley.

Wright, R., Powell, M. B., & Ridge-Damien, T. (2007). What criteria do police officers' use to measure the success of an interview with a child witness? *Psychology, Crime & Law*, *13*(4), 395–404.

Compilation of References

Aboriginal Standing Committee on Housing and Homelessness. (2012). *Plan to end aboriginal homelessness in Calgary.* Ethics of Development in a Global Environment. https://calgaryhomeless.com/content/uploads/Aboriginal-Plan-2012.pdf

Aborn, J., van den Toorn, A., Hockin, J., Jordon, S., Nayvelt, M., & Finkelstein, M. (1999, July 26). *The California prison and rehabilitation system.* http://web.stanford.edu/class/e297c/poverty_prejudice/citypoverty/c

Abrams, D. S., Bertrand, M., & Mullainathan, S. (2012). Do judges vary in their treatment of race? *The Journal of Legal Studies, 41*(2), 347–383. doi:10.1086/666006

Adams, I., & Mastracci, S. (2017). Visibility is a trap: The ethics of police body-worn cameras and control. *Administrative Theory & Praxis, 39*(4), 313–328. doi:10.1080/10841806.2017.1381482

Adams, R. E., Rohe, W. M., & Arcury, T. A. (2002). Implementing community-oriented policing: Organizational change and street officer attitudes. *Crime and Delinquency, 48*(3), 399–430. doi:10.1177/0011128702048003003

Adams, T. C. (1977). Characteristics of state prisoners who demonstrate severe adjustment problems. *Journal of Clinical Psychology, 33*(4), 1100–1103. doi:10.1002/1097-4679(197710)33:4<1100::AID-JCLP2270330439>3.0.CO;2-L PMID:925166

Adedoyin, C., Robinson, M., Clayton, D. M., Moore, S., Jones-Eversley, S., Crosby, S., & Boamah, D. A. (2018). A synergy of contemporary activism to address police maltreatment of Black males: An intersectional analysis. *Journal of Human Behavior in the Social Environment, 28*(8), 1078–1090. doi:10.1080/10911359.2018.1513886

Adom, D., Yeboah, A., & Anrakh, K. (2016). Constructivism philosophical paradigm: Implication for research, teaching and learning. *Global Journal of Arts Humanities and Social Sciences, 4*(10), 1–9.

Advancement Project. (2005). Education on lockdown: The school to jailhouse track. Washington, DC: Author.

Advocacy Center for Tenants Ontario. (2019, November). *We can't wait: Preserving our affordable rental housing in Ontario.* https://www.acto.ca/production/wp-

Agbiboa, D. E. (2013). Corruption and economic crime in Nigeria: Social and economic perspectives. *African Security Review, 22*(1), 47–66. doi:10.1080/10246029.2012.736869

Agwanwo, D. E. (2014). State policing and police efficiency in Nigeria. *Research on Humanities and Social Sciences, 4*(5), 165–173.

Ahmed, M. R. (2016). *After-care and rehabilitation of released prisoners: An Indian perspective.* Paper presented at 5th National Conference of Heads of Prisons of States & UTs on Prison Reforms, Convention Centre, NDCC, New Delhi, India.

Ahmed, Z. (2016). Jail reforms in India: A study of Indian jail reform committees. *International Journal of Multidisciplinary Education and Research*, *1*(3).

Ainslie, E. (1988). *Sources of Indian tradition: From the beginnings to 1800*. Columbia University Press.

Akinyemi, A. (2016). *Police seizes 19 vehicles from ex-IG Solomon Arase*. https://www.naij.com/1019651-scandal-nigeria-police-force-seizes-19-vehicles-ex-ig-solomonarase.html

Akubo, A. (2015). Institutional Decay and Corrupt/Unethical Practices: Problems and Prospects for the Police Force in Nigeria. *IOSR Journal of Humanities and Social Science*, *20*(8), 66–72.

Alao, B., & Adeyemi, O. (2019). Ethics and governance of the Nigeria police force: A study of the Lagos state police command (2015-2016). *Global Scientific Journal*, *7*(2).

Alas, R., Ennulo, J., & Türnpuu, L. (2006). Managerial values in the institutional context. *Journal of Business Ethics*, *65*(3), 269–278. doi:10.100710551-005-5494-1

Albright, S. & Denq, F. (1996). Employer attitudes toward hiring ex-offenders. *Prison Journal, 76*(2).

Alemika, E. E. (2018). Why has police reform failed to produce reformed police in Nigeria? In O. Owen (Ed.), Police reform in Nigeria: The devolution debate. Monograph Series No.30, CLEEN Foundation.

Alemika, E. E. (2018). The constraints of rights-based policing in Africa. In E.E. M. R. Alemika & S. Howell (Eds.), *Policing reform in Africa: moving towards a rights-based approach in a climate of terrorism, insurgency, and serious violent crime* (pp. 14–43). APCOF.

Alemika, E. E., & Chukwuma, I. (2000). *Police-community violence in Nigeria*. Centre for Law Enforcement Education and National Human Rights Commission.

Alexander, M. (2010). *The new Jim Crow: Mass incarcerations in the age of color blindness*. New Press.

Alike, E. (2020, December 1). Insecurity: Governors are frustrated, almost helpless. *This Day*. https://www.thisdaylive.com/index.php/2020/12/01

Allard, P. (2002). *Life sentences: Denying welfare benefits to women convicted of drug offenses*. The Sentencing Project.

Allen, A. (2012). Ethics in correctional and forensic psychology: Getting the balance right. *Australian Psychologist*, *48*(1), 47–56. doi:10.1111/j.1742-9544.2012.00079.x

Allen, T. T., & Parker, M. M. (2013). Police officers and their perceived relationship with urban communities: Does living in the community influence police decisions? *Social Development Issues*, *35*(3), 82–95.

Allwell, R. (2020). *End SARS: The Movement against Police Brutality in Nigeria* (Vol. 33). Harvard Law School.

Almodovar, N. (1999). For their own good: The results of the prostitution laws as enforced by cops. *Politician and Judges. Hastings Women's L.J., 10*, 119. https://repository.uchastings.edu/hwlj/vol10/iss1/7

Alper, M., & Durose, M. R. (2018). *2018 update on prison recidivism: A 9-year follow-up period (2005-2014)*. US. Department of Justice NCJ 250975. https://www.bjs.gov/content/pub/pdf/18upr9yfup0514.pdf

American Psychological Association Services, Inc. (2021). *The pathway from Exclusionary discipline to the school to prison pipeline*. https://www.apa.org/advocacy/health-disparities/discipline-facts.pdf

American Psychological Association. (2004, March 23). *Inmate drug abuse treatment slows prison's revolving door.* https://www.apa.org/research/action/aftercare

Amnesty International. (2020). *Nigeria: Time to end impunity, torture and other Violations by special anti-robbery squad (SARS).* https://www.justice.gov/eoir/page/file/1290111/download

Anderson, J., Buenaventura, M., & Heaton, P. (2019, January). The effects of holistic defense on criminal justice outcomes. *Harvard Law Review, 123*(3), 820–893.

Andrews, D. A. (2006). Enhancing adherence to risk-need-responsivity: Making quality a matter of policy. *Criminology & Public Policy, 5*(3), 595–602. doi:10.1111/j.1745-9133.2006.00394.x

Andrews, D. A. (2012). The risk-need-responsivity (RNR) model of correctional assessment and treatment. In J. A. Dvoskin, J. L. Skeem, R. W. Novaco, & K. S. Douglas (Eds.), *Using Social Science to Reduce Violent Offending* (pp. 127–156). Oxford University Press, Inc.

Annie E. Casey Foundation. (2011). *No place for kids: The case for reducing juvenile incarceration.* Author.

Antrobus, E., Bradford, B., Murphy, K., & Sargeant, E. (2015). Community Norms, Procedural Justice, and the Public's Perceptions of Police Legitimacy. *Journal of Contemporary Criminal Justice, 31*(2), 151–170. doi:10.1177/1043986214568840

Appelbaum, P. S. (2011). Lost in the crowd: Prison mental health care, overcrowding, and the courts. *Law & Psychiatry, 62*(10), 1121–1123. PMID:21969635

Aremu, A., Pakes, F., & Johnston, L. (2011). The moderating effect of emotional intelligence on the reduction of corruption in the Nigerian Police. *Police Practice and Research, 12*(3), 195–208. doi:10.1080/15614263.2010.536724

Aremu, O. (2014). *Policing and terrorism: Challenges and issues in intelligence.* Stirling-Horden Publishers.

Ariel, B. (2017). Police body cameras in large police departments. *The Journal of Criminal Law & Criminology, 106*(4), 729–768.

Ariel, B., Farrar, W., & Sutherland, A. (2015). The effect of police body-worn cameras on use of force and citizens' complaints against the police: A randomized controlled trial. *Journal of Quantitative Criminology, 31*(3), 509–535. doi:10.100710940-014-9236-3

Ariel, B., Sutherland, A., Henstock, D., Young, J., Drover, P., Sykes, J., Megicks, S., & Henderson, R. (2016). Report: increases in police use of force in the presence of body-worn cameras are driven by officer discretion: A protocol-based subgroup analysis of ten randomized experiments. *Journal of Experimental Criminology, 12*(3), 453–463. doi:10.100711292-016-9261-3

Armstead, D. R. (2019). Attitudes of black Americans towards police misconduct in an urban area (Order No. 13858102). Available from Dissertations & Theses @ Walden University; ProQuest Dissertations & Theses Global. *Social Sciences*, 2315248494.

Arvidson, J. (2019). The utility and efficacy of cognitive behavioral interventions in the arena of corrections. An overview and appeal to the field of probation. *Forensic Scholars Today, 4*(4), 1-11. https://1q5krviw73e3rlh854lufacx-wpengine.netdna-ssl.com/wp-content/uploads/2019/04/FST-4.4-Utility-and-Efficacy-of-Cognitive-Behavioral-Interventions.pdf

Asaro, J. M. (1972). Youth peer effect on scholastic performance and the development of predictive instrument of achievement. *Rural Sociology in the South: 1972 Proceedings, 25*(2), 59–61. files.eric.ed.gov/fulltext/ED068213.pdf#page=79

Asghar Ali Engineer (Ed.). (1997). Communal riots in post-independence India (2nd ed.). University Press.

Ashutosh Varshney. (2002). *Ethnic conflict and civic life: Hindus and Muslims in India.* Yale University Press.

Ashwood, J. S., Briscombe, B., Collins, R. L., Wong, E. C., Eberhart, N. K., Cerully, J., May, L., Roth, B., & Burnam, M. A. (2017). Investment in social marketing campaign to reduce stigma and discrimination associated with mental illness yields positive economic benefits to California. *Rand Health Quarterly*, *6*(2), 5.

Atılgan, Ü. E., Yağcıoğlu, S., & Çavdar, Y. (2014). Çocuklarla adli görüşme odaları. İhtiyaçları, İyi Uygulama Örnekleri ve Çocuklarla Adli Görüşme Standartları. *Journal of Law and Human Behaviour.*, *38*, 171–180.

Audu, A. M. (2016). *Community policing: Exploring the police/community relationship for crime control in Nigeria.* https://livrepository.liverpool.ac.uk/3002254/1/200817963

Auge-Dickhut, S., Koye, B., & Liebetrau, A. (2015). *Customer value generation in banking: The Zurich model of customer-centricity*. Springer.

Aurand, A., Emmanuel, D., Yentel, D., Errico, E., & Pang, M. (2017). *Out of reach 2017: The high cost of housing.* National Low Income Housing Coalition. Retrieved from http://nlihc.org/sites/default/files/oor/OOR_2017.pdf

Australian Department of Social Services. (2020). *Housing Support.* https://www.dss.gov.au/housing-support/programmes-services/homelessness

Ayer, R. V. (1995). The prison crisis: An essay on social and political foundations of criminal justice policy. *Public Administration Quarterly*, *19*(1), 42–50. http://www.jstor.org/stable/40861644

Azad, A., Crawford, E., & Kaila, H. (2018). *Conflict and violence in Nigeria: Results from the north east, north central, and south south zones*. Washington, DC: World Bank Group.

Backer, T. E., Howard, E. A., & Moran, G. E. (2007). The role of effective discharge planning in preventing homelessness. *The Journal of Primary Prevention*, *28*, 229–243.

Badcock, M., & Altmann, E. (2020 February 21). Police evidence lost in Stuart hack attack; six suspected drug dealers walk free. *WPTV West Palm Beach News*. https://www.wptv.com/news/local-news/stuart/police-evidence-lost-in-stuart-hack-attack-six-suspected-drug-dealers-walk-free

Bağ, Ö., & Alşen, S. (2016). Çocuğun cinsel istismarının değerlendirilmesinde yeni model: Çocuk İzlem Merkezleri. *Izmir Dr. Behçet Uz Çocuk Hastanesi Dergisi*, *6*(1), 9–14. doi:10.5222/buchd.2016.009

Bahr, S. J., Armstrong, A. H., Gibbs, B. G., Harris, P. E., & Fisher, J. K. (2005). The reentry process: How parolees adjust to release from prison. *Fathering*, *3*(3), 243–265. doi:10.3149/fth.0303.243

Bahr, S. J., Harris, L., Fisher, J. K., & Armstrong, A. H. (2010). Successful reentry: What differentiates successful and unsuccessful parolees? *International Journal of Offender Therapy and Comparative Criminology*, *54*(5), 667–692. doi:10.1177/0306624X09342435 PMID:19638473

Baillargeon, J., Binswanger, I., Penn, J., Williams, B., & Murray, O. (2009). Psychiatric disorders and repeat incarcerations: The revolving prison door. *The American Journal of Psychiatry*, *166*(1), 103–109. doi:10.1176/appi.ajp.2008.08030416 PMID:19047321

Baker, B. (2008). Community policing in Freetown, Sierra Leone: Foreign import or local solution? *Journal of Intervention and State Building*, *2*(1), 23-42.

Baker, B. (2002). Living with non-state policing in South Africa: The issues and dilemmas. *The Journal of Modern African Studies*, *1*(40), 29–53. doi:10.1017/S0022278X01003809

Baldry, E. (2010). Women in transition: From prison to . . .. *Current Issues in Criminal Justice, 22*(2), 253–267. doi:10.1080/10345329.2010.12035885

Banks, D., Hendrix, J., Hickman, M., & Kychelhahn, T. (2019). National sources of law enforcement employment data. U.S. Department of Justice, Office of Justice Programs. Bureau of justice Statistics. NCJ 249681.

Banner, S. (2002). *The death penalty: An American history*. Harvard University Press.

Barak, A. (2008). *The judge in a democracy*. Princeton University Press.

Barak, M. (2014). Re-imagining punishment: An exercise in "intersectional criminal justice.". *Laws, 3*(4), 693–705.

Barker, J., Humphries, P., McArthur, M., & Thomson, L. (2012). *Literature Review: Effective interventions for working with young people who are homeless or at risk of homelessness*. Australian Department of Families, Housing, Community Services and Indigenous Affairs. https://www.dss.gov.au/sites/default/files/documents/06_2012/literature_review.pdf

Barta, T. (2008). Sorry, and not sorry, in Australia: How the apology to the Stolen Generations buried a history of genocide. *Journal of Genocide Research, 10*(2), 201–214. doi:10.1080/14623520802065438

Bauer, L. K., Brody, J. K., León, C., & Baggett, T. P. (2016). Characteristics of homeless adults who died of drug overdose: A retrospective record review. *Journal of Health Care for the Poor and Underserved, 27*(2), 846–859. https://doi.org/10.1353/hpu.2016.0075

Bayün, S., & Dinçer, C. N. (2013*). Çocuk İzlem Merkezi. Hukuk Gündemi Dergisi, 2013/2*. Retrieved on 24.04.2021. http://www.ankarabarosu.org.tr/siteler/ankarabarosu/hgdmakale/2013-2/23.pdf

Bazemore, G. (1998). Restorative justice and earned redemption: Communities, victims, and offender reintegration. *The American Behavioral Scientist, 41*(6), 768–813.

BBC News Africa. (2020). *Coronavirus: Security forces kill more Nigerians than Covid-19*. https://www.bbc.com/news/world-africa-52317196

BBC. (2019). *Texas Walmart shooting: El Paso attack 'domestic terrorism'*. https://www.bbc.com/news/world-us-canada-49226573

Bedi, M. S. (1983). Public participation in the rehabilitation and reintegration of offenders. *Indian Journal of Criminology, 12*(1).

Bellin, J., & Pemberton, S. (2019). Policing the admissibility of body camera evidence. *Fordham Law Review, 87*(4), 1425–1457.

Bennett, P., & Shuker, R. (2010). Improving prisoner-staff relationships: Exporting Gredon's good practice. *The Howard Journal of Crime and Justice, 49*(5).

Bensen, E. (2003). Rehabilitate or punish? Psychologists are not only providing treatment to prisoners; they're also contributing to debate over the nature of prison itself. *APA Monitor, 34*(7). https://www.apa.org/monitor/julaug03/rehab

Bent-Goodley, T., & Smith, C. M. (2017). An African-centered approach to community policing. *Journal of Human Behavior in the Social Environment, 27*(1/2), 92–99. doi:10.1080/10911359.2016.1266856

Berenbaumm, E. (2019, April). *Homeless and health outcomes: What are the associations?* Public Health Ontario, Queen's Printer for Ontario. https://www.publichealthontario.ca/-/media/documents/e/2019/eb-homelessness-health.pdf?la=en

Berg, M. T., & Huebner, B. M. (2011). Reentry and the ties that bind: An examination of social ties, employment, and recidivism. *Justice Quarterly*, *28*(2), 382–410. doi:10.1080/07418825.2010.498383

Bernard, V., & Durham, H. (2014). Sexual violence in armed conflict: From breaking silence to breaking the cycle. *International Review of the Red Cross*, *96*(894), 427–434. doi:10.1017/S1816383115000442

Bhattacharyya, R. (2019, March 7). *Gender pay gap high in India: Men get paid Rs 242 every hour, women earn Rs 46 less*. The Economic Times. https://economictimes.indiatimes.com/magazines/panache/gender-pay-gap-still-high-women-in-india-earn-19-pc-less-than-men-report/articleshow/68302223.cms

Bhawuk, D. P. (2012). India and the culture of peace: Beyond ethnic, religious, and other conflicts. In *Handbook of ethnic conflict* (pp. 137–174). Springer. doi:10.1007/978-1-4614-0448-4_7

Bies, K. J. (2017). Let the sunshine in: Illuminating the powerful role police unions play in shielding officer misconduct. [vi]. *Stanford Law & Policy Review*, *28*(1), 109.

Bird, M., Lofstrom, M., Martin, B., Raphael, S., & Nguyen, V. (2018, June). *The impact of proposition 47 on crime and recidivism.* The Public Policy Institute of California. https://www.ppic.org/wp-content/uploads/r_0618mbr.pdf

Birzer, M. L., & Nolan, R. E. (2002). Learning strategies of selected urban police related to community policing. *Policing, 25*(2), 242. http://dx.doi.org.ezp.waldenulibrary.org/10.1108/13639510210429356

BJS. (2015). *Recidivism of Prisoners Released in 30 states in 2005: Patterns from 2005 to 2010.* Retrieved from http://www.bjs.gov/index.cfm?ty=pbdetail&iid=4986

Black, S. (2009). Security and the SRO. *The American School Board Journal, 196*(6), 30–31.

Blad, E., Kim, H. Y., Decker, S, Manzo, K. K., Maxwell, L. A., & Peerle, H. (2018). School shootings of 2018: What's behind the numbers? *Education Week.*

Blagden, N., Winder, B., & Hames, C. (2016). "They Treat Us Like Human Beings"-Experiencing a Therapeutic Sex Offenders Prison: Impact on Prisoners and Staff and Implications for Treatment. *International Journal of Offender Therapy and Comparative Criminology*, *60*(4), 371–296. doi:10.1177/0306624X14553227 PMID:25305193

Blake, S. P. (1979). The patrimonial-bureaucratic empire of the Mughals. *The Journal of Asian Studies*, *39*(1), 77–94. doi:10.2307/2053505

Blandon-Gitlin, I., & Pezdek, K. (2009). Children's memory in forensic contexts: Suggestibility, false memory, and individual differences. In B. L. Bottoms, C. J. Najdowski, & G. S. Goodman (Eds.), *Children as victims, witnesses, and offenders: Psychological science and the law* (pp. 57–80). Guilford.

Block, P. (1998). From leadership to citizenship. *Insights on leadership: Service, stewardship, spirit, and servant-leadership*, 87-95. Retrieved from beyondthecourse.co.nz/wp-content/uploads/From_Leadership_to_Citizenship.pdf

Blumstein, A. (2011). Bringing down the U.S. prison population. *The Prison Journal*, *91*(3), 125–265. doi:10.1177/0032885511415218

Blumstein, A. (2012). Crime and incarceration in the United States. In A. Dvoskin, J. L. Skeem, R. W. Novaco, & K. S. Douglas (Eds.), *Using social science to reduce violent offending* (pp. 3–30). Oxford University Press, Inc.

Blumstein, A., & Beck, A. J. (2005). Reentry as a transient state between liberty and recommitment. In J. Travis & C. Visher (Eds.), *Prisoner reentry and crime in America*. Cambridge University Press. doi:10.1017/CBO9780511813580.003

Boisvert, N. (2018, November). *Police didn't do enough to help homeless man overdosing on opiates, inquest hears.* CBC News. https://www.cbc.ca/news/canada/toronto/brad-chapman-inquest-day-1-1.4921265

Bonczar, T. P. (2003). *Prevalence of imprisonment in the U.S. population, 1974–2001.* U.S. Department of Justice, Bureau of Justice Statistics.

Bond, B. (2001). Principals and SROs: Defining roles. *Principal Leadership, 1*(8), 52–55.

Bonesteel, M. (2020, June 10). Athletes' petition calls for congress to end qualified immunity for police. *The Washington Post.* https://www.washingtonpost.com/sports/2020/06/10/athletes-petition-calls-congress-end-qualified-immunity-police/

Bonilla-Silva, E. (2001). *White supremacy and racism in the post-civil rights era.* Lynne Rienner Publishers.

Bonta, J., & Andrews, D. A. (2007). *Risk-Need-Responsivity Model for offender assessment and rehabilitation.* Retrieved from https://www.publicsafety.gc.ca/cnt/rsrcs/pblctns/rsk-nd-rspnsvty/rsk-nd-rspnsvty-eng.pdf

Borah, K. (2018). Jail administration in India: A review of Indian jail reform. *International Journal of Humanities and Social Sciences Research, 4*(2).

Bourg, W., Broderick, R., Flagor, R., Kelly, M. D., Ervin, L. D., & Butler, J. (1999). *A Child Interviewer's guidebook.* Sage.

Boyer, A., & Uchida, A. (2015). Incident between round Rock pd officers and student caught on camera. *KEYE TV.* https://cbsaustin.com/news/local/incident-between-round-rock-pd-officer-and-student-caught-on-camera

Bradford, B., Hohl, K., Jackson, J., & MacQueen, S. (2015). Obeying the Rules of the Road: Procedural Justice, Social Identity, and Normative Compliance. *Journal of Contemporary Criminal Justice, 31*(2), 171–191. doi:10.1177/1043986214568833

Braga, A., Coldren, J. R., Sousa, W., Rodriguez, D., & Alper, O. (2017). The benefits of body-worn cameras: New findings from a randomized controlled trial at the Las Vegas Metropolitan Police Department. *National Institute of Justice.* https://www.ncjrs.gov/pdffiles1/nij/grants/251416.pdf

Brave Heart, M. Y. H., Chase, J., Elkins, J., & Altschul, D. B. (2011). Historical trauma among indigenous peoples of the Americas: Concepts, research, and clinical considerations. *Journal of Psychoactive Drugs, 43*(4), 282–290. doi:10.1080/02791072.2011.628913 PMID:22400458

Brenner, J. (2019, October). *New modular housing model tackles affordable housing crisis In Los Angeles.* Forbes. https://www.forbes.com/sites/juliabrenner/2019/10/30/new-modular-housing-model-tackles-affordable-housing-crisis-in-los-angeles/

Brewer, R., & Grabosky, P. (2014). The unraveling of public security in the United States: The dark side of police–community co-production. *American Journal of Criminal Justice, 39*(1), 139–154. doi:10.100712103-012-9194-y

Brown, P. (2017 July 25). Seattle police union challenges new body camera requirement. *KUOW: Puget Sound Public Radio.* https://www.kuow.org/stories/seattle-police-union-challenges-new-body-camera-requirement

Brown, D. (2011). The use of supplementary techniques in forensic interviews with children. In E. M. Lamb, D. J. La Rooy, & L. C. Katz (Eds.), *Children's testimony: A handbook of psychological resarch and forensic practices* (pp. 217–250). Wiley. doi:10.1002/9781119998495.ch12

Brown, L. S. (2013). Treating the effects of psychological trauma. In G. Koocher, J. C. Norcross, & B. Greene (Eds.), *Psychologists' desk reference* (pp. 290–293). doi:10.1093/med:psych/9780199845491.003.0060

Brown, R., Novak, K., & Frank, J. (2009). Identifying variation in police officer behavior between juveniles and adults. *Journal of Criminal Justice*, *37*(2), 200–208. doi:10.1016/j.jcrimjus.2009.02.004

Brubacher, P.S., Malloy, C.L., Lamb, E.M., & Roberts, P.K. (2013). How do interviewers and children discuss individual occurrences of alleged repeated abuse in forensic interviews? *Applied Cognitive Psychology*. 443-450. doi:10.1002/acp.2920

Brunson, R. K. (2015). Focused deterrence and improved police–community relations: Unpacking the proverbial "black box.". *Criminology & Public Policy*, *14*(3), 507–514. doi:10.1111/1745-9133.12141

Bullock, K., & Bunce, A. (2020). 'The prison don't talk to you about getting out of prison' "On why prisons in England and Wales fail to rehabilitate prisoners. *Criminology & Criminal Justice*, *20*(1), 111–127. doi:10.1177/1748895818800743

Bureau of Justice (BJS). (2017). *Mental health problems of prison and jail inmates.* Bureau of Justice Statistics Special Report. Retrieved from https://www.bjs.gov/content/pub/pdf/mhppji.pdf

Bureau of Justice Assistance. (1994). *Understanding community policing: A framework for action monograph (NCJ 148457).* US Department of Justice.

Bureau of Police Research and Development. (2003). For the superintendents and management of prisons in India, Ministry of Home Affairs Government of India New Delhi. *Chapter-IV, 3*, 44.

Bureau of Police, Research & Development. (2019). *Review and Implementation of Rules and Process for the Internal Management of Prisons and Prisoners.* https://bprd.nic.in/WriteReadData/userfiles/file/201907030915286643694ReviewandImplementationofRulesand-MM-08.pdf

Bureau of Police, Research, and Development. (2003). Model prison manual for the superintendence and management of prisons in India. Ministry of Home Affairs, Government of India.

Burnett, R. (2010). The will and the ways to becoming an ex-offender. *International Journal of Offender Therapy and Comparative Criminology*, *54*(5), 663–666. doi:10.1177/0306624X10383845 PMID:20852061

Burrow, J. D., & Apel, R. (2008). Youth behavior, school structure, and student risk of victimization. *Justice Quarterly*, *25*(2), 349–380. doi:10.1080/07418820802025181

Burtch, B., Rane, C., & Lindfield, S. (1999). The expanding prison. *Manitoba Law Journal*, *26*(3), 375–380. themanitobalawjournal.com/wp-content/uploads/articles/MLJ_26.3/Book%20Review%20The%20Expanding%20Prison.pdf

Bush, C. L. (2020a). *Public perceptions of delays in the release of police body-worn camera footage* (Publication No. 8442) [Doctoral dissertation, Walden University]. Walden Dissertations and Doctoral Studies. https://scholarworks.waldenu.edu/dissertations/8442

Bush, C. L. (2020b). Public perceptions of delays in the release of police body-worn camera footage. *Journal of Social Change*, *13*(1), 1–17. doi:10.5590/JOSC.2020.13.1.01

Bussey, K. (2009). An international perspective on child witnesses. In L. B. Bottoms, J. C. Najdowski, & S. G. Goodman (Eds.), *Children as victims, witnesses and offenders, Psychological Science and Law* (pp. 209–232). The Guildford Press.

Byrne, J. M., Pattavina, A., & Taxman, F. S. (2015). International trends in prison upsizing and downsizing: In search of evidence of a global rehabilitation revolution. *Victims & Offenders*, *10*(4), 420–451. doi:10.1080/15564886.2015.1078186

Cadora, E. (2014). How certain schemes to end mass incarceration can fail. *The Annals of the American Academy of Political and Social Science*, *651*(1), 277–285. doi:10.1177/0002716213503786

Çağlar, E. E., & Türk, T. (2019). İstismara Maruz Kalan Çocuklarla Adli Görüşme: Nichd Protokolü Önerisi. *TAAD*, *38*, 393–412.

Cain, B. E., & Parker, B. (2020). The Uncertain Future of Felon Disenfranchisement. *Mo. L. Rev.*, *84*. Available at: https://scholarship.law.missouri.edu/mlr/vol84/iss4/4

Caldwell, M. (1956). Group Dynamics in the Prison Community. *Journal of Criminal Law and Criminology*, *46*(5), 648–657. doi:10.2307/1139377

California Correctional Health Care Services. (2009). *Mental health services delivery system:* Program guide overview. https://www.clearinghouse.net/chDocs/public/PC-CA-0002-0012.pdf

California Department of Corrections and Rehabilitation. (2020). *Mental health program (MHP).* https://www.cdcr.ca.gov/dhcs/mental-health-program/

California Department of Corrections and Rehabilitation. (2020, January). *CDCR and CCHCS unveil expanded priorities through renewed mission and vision statements.* https://www.cdcr.ca.gov/news/2020/01/08/cdcr-and-cchcs-unveil-expanded-priorities-through-renewed-mission-and-vision-statements/

California Department of Corrections and Rehabilitation. (2021). *After Prison Reforms.* https://www.cdcr.ca.gov/rehabilitation/programs/after-prison-programs/

California Department of Health Care Services. (2020). *California advancing and innovating Medi-Cal.* https://www.dhcs.ca.gov/provgovpart/Pages/CalAIM.aspx

Campbell, J. (2020). *Nigerians cry out against police brutality.* Council on Foreign Affairs.

Canadian Center on Substance Use and Addiction. (2020). *Knowledge Broker.* https://www.ccsa.ca/knowledge-broker

Canadian Mental Health Association. (2010, November). *Submission to Honourable Jay C. Hope, Deputy Minister – Correctional Services, Ministry of Community Safety and Correctional Services Accessibility Roundtable.* https://ontario.cmha.ca/documents/submission-to-honourable-jay-c-hope-deputy-minister/

Canady, M., James, B., & Nease, J. (2012). *To protect and educate: The school resources officer and the prevention of violence in schools.* National Association of School Resource Officers.

Canales, K. (2020 July 8). People are buying used police body cameras on eBay and other sites and discovering unencrypted footage of officers searching homes. *Business Insider.* https://www.businessinsider.com/used-police-body-cameras-sold-ebay-footage-surveillance-2020-7

Čapek, J. (2017). Habit and freedom in Merleau-Ponty and Ricoeur. *The Journal of Speculative Philosophy*, *31*(3), 432–443. doi:10.5325/jspecphil.31.3.0432

Carbado, D. W., & Rock, P. (2016). What exposes African Americans to police violence? *Harvard Civil Rights-Civil Liberties Law Review*, *51*(1), 159–187.

Carlos, H. (2019). Disqualifying immunity: How qualified immunity exacerbates police misconduct and why congress must destroy it. *Southern University Law Review. Southern University and A & M College. School of Law*, *46*(2), 283. doi:10.2139srn.3334586

Casey, J. (2010). Implementing community policing in different countries and cultures. *Pakistan Journal of Criminology*, *4*(2), 55–70.

Cavalieri, S. (2011). Between victim and agent: A third-way feminist account of trafficking for sex work. *Indiana Law Journal (Indianapolis, Ind.), 86*(4), 1409–1458.

Ceci, J. S., & Bruck, M. (1995). *Jeopardy in the courtroom: A scientific analysis of children's testimony*. American Psychological Association. doi:10.1037/10180-000

Ceci, J. S., Bruck, M., & Battin, B. D. (2000). The suggestibility of children's testimony. In F. D. Bjorklund (Ed.), *False Memory Creation In Children and Adults* (pp. 169–202). Lawrence Erlbaum.

Centers for Disease Control and Prevention. (2020). *Interim guidance on management of coronavirus disease 2019 (COVID-19) in correctional and detention facilities*. https://www.cdc.gov/coronavirus/2019-ncov/community/correction-detention/ guidance-correctional-detention.html

Cerda, M., Tracy, M., Messner, S. F., Vlahov, D., Tardiff, K., & Galea, S. (2009). Misdemeanor policing, physical disorder, and gun-related homicide: A spatial analytic test of "broken-windows" theory. *Epidemiology (Cambridge, Mass.), 20*(4), 533–541. doi:10.1097/EDE.0b013e3181a48a99 PMID:19525689

Chambliss, W. J. (2011). *Crime and criminal behaviour*. Academic Press.

Chandrasekhar, C. A. (2003). Flying while brown: Federal civil rights remedies to post-9/11 airline racial profiling of South Asians. *Asian LJ, 10*, 215.

Chappell, A. T., Monk-Turner, E., & Payne, B. K. (2011). Broken windows or window breakers: The influence of physical and social disorder on quality of life. *Justice Quarterly, 28*(3), 522–540. doi:10.1080/07418825.2010.526129

Chen, H., Pan, H., Morosanu, L. & Turner, N. (2018). Using logic models and the action model/change model schema in planning the learning community program: A comparative case study. *Canadian Journal of Program Evaluation, 33*(1), 49–68. doi:10.3138/cjpe.42116

Chermak, S., McGarrell, E., & Gruenewald, J. (2006). Media coverage of police misconduct and attitudes toward police. *Policing, 29*(2), 261–281. doi:10.1108/13639510610667664

Chiemelie, E. (2014). *Nigerian Police since 1960. THISDAY Newspaper.*

Child Maltreatment. 29'th Year of Reporting. (2018). Department of Health & Human Services-USA. Washington: ACF.

Child, S. A. R. (2016). *Şiddeti Önleme ve Rehabilitasyon Derneği. Acıbadem Üniversitesi Suç ve Şiddetle Mücadele Uygulama ve Araştırma Merkezi*. Erişim Adresi: https://www.imdat.org/kopyas%C4%B1-grooming

Children's Defense Fund. (2007). *America's cradle to prison pipeline*. CDF.

Chin, R. J., Schroedel, J., & Rowen, L. (2016). *Whose lives matter? The media's failure to cover police shootings of Native Americans*. Paper presented at the 58th Annual Conference of the Western Social Science Association Western Association of Social Science, Reno, NV.

Chowdhury, N. (2002). *Indian prison laws and correction of prisoners*. Deep & Deep.

Chung, W. M. (1999). Treatment programmes for offenders run by the Hong Kong correctional services. *UNAFEI Resource Material Series, 54*, 341-347.

Chunn, D. E., & Menzies, R. (2006). "So, what does all of this have to do with criminology?" Surviving the restructuring of the discipline in the twenty-first century. *Canadian Journal of Criminology and Criminal Justice, 48*(5), 663–680. doi:10.3138/cjccj.48.5.663

Citron, D. K. (2009). Law's expressive value in combating cyber gender harassment. *Michigan Law Review, 108*, 373.

Claidière, N. (2016, November 10). *Experimental evidence for the Broken Window Theory*. International Cognition and Culture Institute. http://cognitionandculture.net/blogs/nicolas-claidires-blog/experimental-evidence-for-the-broken-window-theory/

Clare, J., Henstock, D., McComb, C., Newland, R., & Barnes, G. C. (2019). The results of a randomized controlled trial of police body-worn video in Australia. *Journal of Experimental Criminology*. Advance online publication. doi:10.100711292-019-09387-w

Clarke, C. (2005). *A national evaluation of PEACE investigative interviewing* (Unpublished PhD thesis). Institute of Criminal Justice Studies. The University of Portsmouth.

Clark, S. (2011). The role of law enforcement in schools: The Virginia experience a practitioner report. *Directions for Youth Development, 129*(129), 89–101. doi:10.1002/yd.389 PMID:21491575

Cloke, P., & Milbourne, P. (2012). *International perspectives on rural homelessness*. Routledge.

Coates, T. N. (2015). The black family in the age of mass incarceration. *Atlantic (Boston, Mass.), 316*(3), 82.

Cochran, J. C., Mears, D. P., & Bales, W. D. (2014). Assessing the effectiveness of correctional sanctions. *Journal of Quantitative Criminology, 30*(2), 317–347. doi:10.100710940-013-9205-2

Coester, M. (2008). Hate crime. *Victimisation surveys in Germany*, 46.

Cohen, T. H., & Whetzel, J. (2014). The neglected "R" – responsivity and the federal offender. *Federal Probation Journal, 78*(2), 11 – 18. https://www.uscourts.gov/federal-probation-journal

Consella, R. (2003). Punishing dangerousness through preventive detention: Illustrating the institutional link between school and prison. *New Directions for Youth Development: Deconstructing the School-to-Prison Pipeline*, 63-65.

Considine, C. (2017). The racialization of Islam in the United States: Islamophobia, hate crimes, and "flying while brown.". *Religions, 8*(9), 165. doi:10.3390/rel8090165

Constitution of the Federal Republic of Nigeria. (1999). Federal Government of Nigeria.

Convention for the Suppression of the Traffic in Persons and the Exploitation of the Prostitution of Others. Dec. 2, 1949, 96 U.N.T.S. 271, G.A. Res. 317 (IV), (entered into force July 25, 1951) India acceded to the Trafficking Convention on January 9, *1953*, http://untreaty.un.org/ENGLISH/bible/englishinternetbible/parti/chapterVil/treatyl 1.asp

Cook, R. H. (2003). Dynamic content: The strategic contingency of international law. *Duke Journal of Comparative and International Law, 14*(1), 97–98. https://scholarship.law.duke.edu/djcil/vol14/iss1/3

Cook, S. (2019, May). *Suspected drug overdoses at Ontario correctional facility lead to death, hospitalization.* The Globe and Mail. https://www.theglobeandmail.com/canada/toronto/article-suspected-drug-overdoses-at-ontario-correctional-facility-lead-to/

Cooley, W., Bemiller, M., Jefferis, E., & Penix, R. (2019). Neighborhood by neighborhood: Community policing in a rust belt city. *Policing, 42*(2), 226-239. http://dx.doi.org.ezp.waldenulibrary.org/10.1108/PIJPSM-01-2018-0002

Coon, J. K., & Travis, L. F. III. (2012). The role of police in public schools: A comparison of principal and police reports of activities in schools. *Police Practice and Research, 13*(1), 15–30. doi:10.1080/15614263.2011.589570

Coquilhat, J. (2008). *Community Policing: An international Literature Review*. New Zealand Police.

Coronavirus: Curbs at Kolkata prison trigger violent clash. (2020, March 22). *The Hindu.* https://www.thehindu.com/news/cities/kolkata/coronavirus-curbs-at-kolkata-prison-trigger-violent-clash/article31132352.ece?homepage=true

Cortes, K., & Rogers, S. (2010). *Reentry Housing Options: The Policymakers' Guide.* Council of State Governments.

Crawford, C. & Burns, R. (2015). *Preventing school violence: Assessing armed guardians, school policy, and context.* Academic Press.

Crawford, C., & Burns, R. (2016). Reducing school violence considering school characteristics and the impact of law enforcement, school security, and environmental factors. *Policing, 39*(3), 455–477. doi:10.1108/PIJPSM-05-2016-0061

Criminal Justice Joint Inspection (CJJI). (2017). *An inspection of through the gate resettlement services for prisoners serving 12 months or more.* https://www.justiceinspectorates.gov.uk/cjji/wp-content/ uploads/sites/2/2017/06/Through-the-Gate-phase-2-report.pdf

Criminal Justice Training Council (CJTC). (2020). LEAB model body-worn camera policy. *State of Vermont Online.* https://vcjc.vermont.gov/content/leab-model-body-worn-camera-policy

Crow, M. S., Snyder, J. A., Crichlow, V. J., & Smykla, J. O. (2017). Community perceptions of police body-worn cameras: The impact of views on fairness, fear, performance, and privacy. *Criminal Justice and Behavior, 44*(4), 589–610. doi:10.1177/0093854816688037

Crunden, E. A. (2017). Dallas school police tased a 7-year-old, and then boy slammed a 12-year-old the next day. *ThinkProgress.* https://archive.thinkprogress.org/dallas-police-schools-violence-kids-fd6cd565a8c0/

Culhane, D. (2003). Their spirits live within us: Aboriginal women in Downtown Eastside Vancouver emerging into visibility. *American Indian Quarterly, 27*(3/4), 593–606. doi:10.1353/aiq.2004.0073

Culhane, S. E., Boman, J. H. IV, & Schweitzer, K. (2016). Public perceptions of the justifiability of police shootings: The role of body cameras in a pre- and post-Ferguson experiment. *Police Quarterly, 19*(3), 251–274. doi:10.1177/1098611116651403

Cullen, F. T., & Jonson, C. L. (2016). *Correctional theory: Context and consequences* (2nd ed.). SAGE.

D'Andrade, A. C., & Valdez, M. (2012). Reunifying from behind bars: A quantitative study of the relationship between parental incarceration, service use, and foster care reunification. *Social Work in Public Health, 27*(6), 616–636. doi:10.1080/19371918.2012.713294 PMID:22963161

Dağlı, T., & İnanıcı, M.A. (2011). *Hastane temelli çocuk koruma merkezleri için başvuru kitabı ihmal ve istismara uğrayan çocuğa bütüncül yaklaşım.* Ankara: Fersa Ofset Matbaacılık.

Dahler, D. (2020 March 9). Heart-warming birthday treat captured on police body cam. *CBS News.* https://www.cbsnews.com/news/body-cameras-capture-georgia-officers-act-of-kindness-2020-03-09/

Dalrymple, W. (2008, June 19). *Serving the goddess.* The New Yorker. https://www.newyorker.com/magazine/2008/08/04/serving-the-goddess

Daly, K. (2000). Restorative justice in diverse and unequal societies. *Law in Context (Bundoora, Vic.), 7*(1), 167–190.

Dandurand, Y., Christian, J., Murdoch, D., Brown, R. E., & Chin, V. (2008). *Conditional Release Violations, Suspensions and Revocations – A Comparative Analysis.* Vancouver: ICCLR. http://www.icclr.law.ubc.ca/files/books/Conditional%20Release%20Violations%20Final_English.pdf

Daniels, F. A. (2012). A Historical Survey of Amalgamation of the Northern and Southern police departments of Nigeria in 1930. *European Scientific Journal, 8*(18), 205–217.

Davies, M. G. (1996). Children's identification evidence. In L. S. Sporer, S. R. Malpass, & G. Koehnken (Eds.), *In psychological issues in eyewitness identification* (pp. 233–258). Lawrence Erlbaum.

Davis, D., & Loftus, E.F. (2007). *Internal and external sources of information in adult witness memory.* Researchgate.

Davis, L., Williams, M., Derose, K., Steinberg, P., Nicosia, N., Overton, A., Miyashiro, L., Turner, S., Fain, T., & Williams, E. (2011). *Understanding the public health implications of prisoner reentry in California: State-of-the-state report.* RAND Corporation. https://www.rand.org/pubs/monographs/MG1165.html

Davis, C., Bahr, S. J., & Ward, C. (2012). The process of offender reintegration: Perceptions of what helps prisoners reenter society. *Criminology & Criminal Justice, 13*(4), 446–469. doi:10.1177/1748895812454748

Davis, R. C., Ortiz, C. W., Euler, S., & Kuykendall, L. (2015). Revisiting "Measuring What Matters": Developing a Suite of Standardized Performance Measures for Policing. *Police Quarterly, 18*(4), 469–495. doi:10.1177/1098611115598990

Day, A., Bryan, J., Davey, L., & Casey, S. (2006). The process of change in offender rehabilitation programmes. *Psychology, Crime & Law, 12*(5), 473–487. doi:10.1080/10683160500151209

De Claire, K., & Dixon, L. (2015). The effects of prison visits from family members on prisoners' well-being, prison rule-breaking, and recidivism: A review of research since 1991. *Journal of Trauma Violence, and Abuse, 18*(2), 185–199. doi:10.1177/1524838015603209 PMID:26330175

De Claire, L., Dixon, L., & Larkin, M. (2019). How prisoners and their partners experience the maintenance of their relationship during a prison sentence. *Journal of Community & Applied Social Psychology, 30*(3), 293–306. Advance online publication. doi:10.1002/casp.2445

DeJarnattD. (2013). Criminal records create a second-class citizenry: Changing the way adult convictions are vacated in Washington state. Seattle *Journal for Social Justice.* https://ssrn.com/abstract=2342791 doi:10.2139srn.2342791

Delisi, M., Kosloski, A. E., Drury, A. J., Vaughn, M. G., Beaver, K. M., Trulson, C. R., & Wright, J. P. (2011). Never desisters: A descriptive study of the life-course persistent offender. In Criminology Theory: A Life-Course Approach. Boston, MA: Jones & Bartlett.

DeMatteo, D., LaDuke, C., Locklair, B. R., & Heilbrun, K. (2013). Community-based alternatives for justice-involved individuals with severe mental illness: Diversion, problem-solving courts, and reentry. *Journal of Criminal Justice, 41*(2), 64–71. doi:10.1016/j.jcrimjus.2012.09.002

Dempsy, J. S., & Forst, L. (2008). An Introduction to Policing (4th ed.). Academic Press.

den Heyer, M. (2002). The Temporal logic model concept. *The Canadian Journal of Program Evaluation, 17*(2), 27–47.

Department of Justice. (2019). *Florida man arrested for making racially motivated threats in interference with election in Charlottesville and cyberstalking.* Published in https://www.justice.gov/opa/pr/florida-man-arrested-making-racially-motivated-threats-interference-election-charlottesville

Department of Tihar Prisons. (2020). *Psychological effects of vipassana on Tihar jail inmates.* Government of NCT. https://www.vridhamma.org/research/Psychological-Effects-of-Vipassana-on-Tihar-Jail-Inmate

Department of Tihar Prisons. (2020). *Reformation.* Government of NCT. http://tte.delhigovt.nic.in/wps/wcm/connect/lib_centraljail/Central+Jail/Home/Reformationv

DeVan, K. (2016, September 22). Harrisburg Researchers Suggest Community Policing to Build Trust in Police States News Services. *Penn State News.* https:/link.gale.com

Dhanuka, M., & Lamba, S. (2020). Analysis: India's prison system needs urgent reform. *Hindustan Times*.

Dibie, R. (2007). Ethical Leadership, Social Responsibility and Corruption in Nigeria. *International Review of Politics and Development*, *5*(1), 1–42.

Dibie, R. (2014). *Public Administration Theory, Analysis and Application*. Babcock University Press.

Dickson, S. R., Polaschek, D. L. L., & Casey, A. R. (2013). Can the quality of high-risk violent prisoners' release plans predict recidivism following intensive rehabilitation? A comparison with risk assessment instruments. *Psychology, Crime & Law*, *19*(4), 371–389. doi:10.1080/1068316X.2011.640634

Diliberti, M., Jackson, M., Correa, S., & Padgett, Z. (2019). *Crime, Violence, Discipline, and Safety in U.S. Public Schools: Findings from the School Survey on Crime and Safety: 2017–18 (NCES 2019-061). U.S. Department of Education*. National Center for Education Statistics. https://nces.ed.gov/pubsearch

Doane, E., & Cumberland, D. M. (2018). Community policing: Using needs assessment to gain understanding before implementing. *Performance Improvement Quarterly*, *31*(2), 165–187. doi:10.1002/piq.21264

Dodge, M., & Pogrebin, M. (2001). Collateral costs of imprisonment for women: Complications of reintegration. *The Prison Journal*, *81*(1), 42–54. doi:10.1177/0032885501081001004

Doin & Andres. (2013). *Working paper series on prison reform; civil society and prison: The 'invisible bars' challenge.* UNODC.

Dolan, M. (2020, March 20). California releases more jail inmates amid coronavirus crisis. *Los Angeles Times*. https://www.latimes.com/california/story/2020-03-20/california-releases-more-jail-inmates-amid-coronavirus-crisis

Douglas, T. (2020, February). *Newsom: Unified data system will help state track progress on homelessness*. Techwire. https://www.techwire.net/news/newsom-unified-homeless-data-system-will-help-state-track-progress.html

Dowler, K., & Sparks, R. (2008). Victimization, contact with police, and neighborhood conditions: Reconsidering African American and Hispanic attitudes toward the police. *Police Practice and Research*, *9*(5), 395–415. doi:10.1080/15614260801980760

Drug Policy Alliance. (2020). *Mass incarceration and criminalization*. https://www.drugpolicy.org/issues/mass-criminalization

Du Bois, W. E. B. (2003). *Darkwater: Voices from within the veil*. Humanity Books.

Duxbury, L., & Bennell, C. (2019). *Police in schools: An evidence-based look at the use of school resource officers*. Routledge. doi:10.4324/9780429243905

Dworkin, R. M. (1977). *Taking rights seriously*. Harvard University Press.

Edgely, M. (2010). Criminals and (second-class) citizenship: Twenty-first century attainder? *Griffith Law Review*, *19*(3), 403–437. doi:10.1080/10383441.2010.10854683

Ellinghaus, K. (2006). Indigenous assimilation and absorption in the United States and Australia. *Pacific Historical Review*, *75*(4), 563–585. doi:10.1525/phr.2006.75.4.563

Esfahani, A., & Shahbazi, G. (2014). Workplace bullying in nursing: The case of Azerbaijan Province, Iran. *Iranian Journal of Nursing and Midwifery Research*, *19*(4), 409–415. http://ijnmr.mui.ac.ir/index.php/ijnm PMID:25183984

Esparza Flores, N. (2018). Contributing Factors to Mass Incarceration and Recidivism. *Themis: Research Journal of Justice Studies and Forensic Science, 6*(4). Retrieved from https://scholarworks.sjsu.edu/themis/vol6/iss1/4

Everett, R. S., & Wojtkiewicz, R. A. (2002). Difference, Disparity, and Race/Ethnic Bias in Federal Sentencing. *Journal of Quantitative Criminology, 18*(2), 189–211. doi:10.1023/A:1015258732676

Exploratory review of route-specific, gendered, and age-graded dynamics of exploitation: Applying life course theory to victimization in sex trafficking in North America. (n.d.). *Aggression and Violent Behavior, 17*(3), 257–271. doi:10.1016/j.avb.2012.02.005

Ezorsky, G. (1972, March). Retributive justice. *Canadian Journal of Philosophy, 1*(3), 365–368.

Faller, K. C. (2015). Forty years of forensic interviewing of children suspected of sexual abuse, 1974-2014: Historical benchmarks. *Journal of Social Sciences., 4*, 34–65.

Farabee, D., Prendergast, M., Cartier, J., Wexler, H., Knight, K., & Anglin, D. (1999). Barriers to implementing effective drug treatment programs. *The Prison Journal, 79*(2), 150–162. doi:10.1177/0032885599079002002

Farley, M., & Barken, H. (1998). Prostitution, violence, and posttraumatic stress disorder. *Women & Health, 27*(3), 37–49. doi:10.1300/J013v27n03_03 PMID:9698636

Farrell, S., & Maruna, S. (2004). Desistance focused criminal justice policy research: Introduction to a special issue on desistance from crime and public policy. *Howard Journal of Criminal Justice, 43*(4), 358–367. doi:10.1111/j.1468-2311.2004.00335.x

Fazal, S. (2008). *The health of prisoners*. New Century Publications.

Fazel, S., & Wolf, A. (2015). A systematic review of criminal recidivism rates worldwide: Current difficulties and recommendations for best practice. *PLoS One, 10*(6), e0130390. doi:10.1371/journal.pone.0130390 PMID:26086423

Feagin, J. R. (1991). The continuing significance of race: Antiblack discrimination in public places. *American Sociological Review, 56*(1), 101–116. doi:10.2307/2095676

Feagin, J. R. (2006). *Systemic racism: A theory of oppression*. Routledge.

Featherstone, R., & Deflem, M. (2003). Anomie and strain: Context and consequences of Merton's two theories. *Sociological Inquiry, 73*(4), 471–489. doi:10.1111/1475-682X.00067

Ferguson, A. (2018). City looks to rename homeless services; 'shelter' to be phased out. *CityNews*. https://toronto.citynews.ca/2018/02/25/city-looks-rename-homeless-services-shelter-phased/

Feucht, T., & Holt, T. (2016, September). Does cognitive behavioral therapy work in criminal justice? A new analysis from crimesolutions.gov (Report No. NCJ249825). *National Institute of Justice Journal, 277*, 10–17. http://nij.gov/journals/277/pages/crimesolutions-cbt.aspx

Finn, P., Shively, M., McDevitt, J., Lassiter, W., & Rich, T. (2005). *Comparison of program activities and lessons learned among 19 school resource officer (SRO) programs*. United States Department of Justice.

Fitzgerald, S. A., & Munro, V. E. (2012). Sex work and regulation of vulnerability(ies): Introduction. *Feminist Legal Studies, 20*(3), 183–188. doi:10.100710691-012-9212-y

Flaherty, J. (2020 December 1). Lawyer irked by deletion of Little Rock police footage. *Arkansas Democrat Gazette*. https://www.arkansasonline.com/news/2020/dec/01/lawyer-irked-by-deletion-of-police-footage/?news

Flory, J. (2020, February). *Arresting people who are homeless will make a bad problem worse.* CalMatters. https://calmatters.org/commentary/arresting-homeless-people-will-make-a-bad-problem-worse/

Ford, H. (2008). *Evaluating the operational effectiveness of west African female police officers' participation in peace support operations: The case of Ghana and Nigeria.* Kofi Anan International Peace keeping Training centre (KAIPTC) Occasional paper.

Form, I. S. (2018). *Prison Reforms in India.* https://blog.forumias.com/prison-reforms/

Forouzan, H., Jahankhani, H., & McCarthy, J. (2018). An examination into the level of training, education, and awareness among frontline police officers in tackling cybercrime within the Metropolitan Police Service. *Cyber Criminology*, 307-323.

Fox, J. C. (1927). *The history of contempt of court – The form of trial and the mode of punishment.* Clarendon Press.

Franke, I., Vogel, T., Eher, R., & Dudeck, M. (2019). Prison mental healthcare: Recent developments and future challenges. *Current Opinion in Psychiatry, 32*(4), 342–347. doi:10.1097/YCO.0000000000000504 PMID:30855296

Franklin, J. H. (2011). *From slavery to freedom: A history of African Americans.* McGraw-Hill/Connect Learn Succeed.

Friedmann, P. D., Taxman, F. S., & Henderson, C. E. (2007). Evidence-based treatment practices for drug-involved adults in the criminal justice system. *Journal of Substance Abuse Treatment, 32*(3), 267–277. doi:10.1016/j.jsat.2006.12.020 PMID:17383551

Fry, M. (1952). The habitual prisoner. *The Modern Law Review, 15*(2), 155–159. doi:10.1111/j.1468-2230.1952.tb00229.x

Fuller, T. (2019, October 21). As homelessness surges in California, so does a backlash. *The New York Times*, p. A1.

Gabriel, H., & Hemblade, H. (2019). *FEMICIDE cyber-crimes against women & Girls* (vol. 11). http://femicide-watch.org/sites/default/files/FemicideVolXI.pdf

Galassi, A., Mpofu, E., & Athanasou, J. (2015). Therapeutic Community Treatment of an Inmate Population with Substance Use Disorders: Post-Release Trends in Re-Arrest, Re-Incarceration, and Drug Misuse Relapse. *International Journal of Environmental Research and Public Health, 12*(6), 7059–7072. doi:10.3390/ijerph120607059 PMID:26103591

Garland, D. (2010). *Peculiar institution: American death penalty in an age of abolition.* Oxford University Press.

Gaub, J., & White, M. (2020). Open to interpretation: Confronting the challenges of understanding the current state of body-worn camera research. *American Journal of Criminal Justice, 45*(5), 899–913. doi:10.100712103-020-09518-4

Gau, J. M., & Brunson, R. K. (2015). Procedural Injustice, Lost Legitimacy, and Self-Help: Young Males' Adaptations to Perceived Unfairness in Urban Policing Tactics. *Journal of Contemporary Criminal Justice, 31*(2), 132–150. doi:10.1177/1043986214568841

Gau, J. M., & Pratt, T. C. (2010). Revisiting broken windows theory: Examining the sources of the discriminant validity of perceived disorder and crime. *Journal of Criminal Justice, 38*(4), 758–766. doi:10.1016/j.jcrimjus.2010.05.002

Gavin, P. (2020). Irish ex-prisoner reflections on their psychological wellbeing whilst in prison in England and Wales. *Advancing Corrections Journal, 9*(1), 101–118.

Geary, P. (2016). *The Right to Remain Silent: Police department adoption and deployment of social media* (Dissertation). Retrieved from ProQuest Dissertations & Theses Global. (UMI No. 10147470)

Gendreau, P., & Smith, P. (2012). Assessment and treatment strategies for correctional institutions. In J. A. Dvoskin, R. Skeem, W. Novaco, & K. S. Douglas (Eds.), Using social science to reduce violent offending (pp. 157 – 177). Oxford University Press, Inc.

Gerassi, L. (2015). Heated debate: Theoretical perspectives of sexual exploitation and sex work. *Journal of Sociology and Social Welfare*, *42*(4), 79–100. https://www.ncbi.nlm.nih.gov/pmc/articles/PMC4730391/ PMID:26834302

Geringer-Sameth, E. (2020 February 27). Initial report shows benefits and challenges of NYPD body camera program for police watchdog. *Gotham Gazette.* https://www.gothamgazette.com/city/9167-initial-report-shows-benefits-and-challenges-of-nypd-body-camera-program-for-watchdog-agency

Giacalone, R. A., Paul, K., & Jurkiewicz, C. L. (2005). A preliminary investigation into the role of positive psychology in consumer sensitivity to corporate social performance. *Journal of Business Ethics*, *58*(4), 295–305. doi:10.100710551-004-5970-z

Gibbons, D., & Garrity, D. (1959). Some suggestions for the development of etiological and treatment theory in criminology. *Social Forces*, *38*(1), 51–58. doi:10.2307/2574016

Gilbert, E. (2007). Leaky borders and solid citizens: Governing security, prosperity, and quality of life in a North American partnership. *Antipode*, *39*(1), 77–98. doi:10.1111/j.1467-8330.2007.00507.x

Giliauskas, D., & Gogolishvili, D. (2018, October). *Interventions to reduce stigma among health care providers who work with substance users.* Ontario HIV Treatment Network. https://www.ohtn.on.ca/rapid-response-interventions-to-reduce-stigma-among-health-care-providers-working-with-substance-users/

Gill, H., Meyer, J. P., Lee, K., Shin, K. H., & Yoon, C. Y. (2011). Affective and continuance commitment and their relations with deviant workplace behaviors in Korea. *Asia Pacific Journal of Management*, *28*(3), 595–607. doi:10.100710490-009-9165-0

Gitlin, B. I., & Pezdek, K. (2009). Children's memory in forensic contexts. In L. B. Bottoms, J. C. Najdowski, & S. G. Goodman (Eds.), *Children as victims, witnesses and Offenders: Psychological science and law* (pp. 57–80). The Guildford Press.

Giulietti, C., Tonin, M., & Vlassopoulos, M. (2019). Racial discrimination in local public services: A field experiment in the United States. *Journal of the European Economic Association*, *17*(1), 165–204. doi:10.1093/jeea/jvx045 PMID:32161517

Glenn, A. L., & Raine, A. (2014). Neurocriminology: Implications for the punishment, prediction, and prevention of criminal behaviour. *Nature Reviews. Neuroscience*, *15*(1), 54–63. doi:10.1038/nrn3640 PMID:24326688

Glick, B., & Prince, R. (2016). *Implementing successful cognitive behavioral interventions.* Civic Research Institute.

Gliha, L. (2019 October 25). Aurora PD says body cameras recorded but fell off during altercation with man who later died. *Fox 31 News, Denver.* https://kdvr.com/news/problem-solvers/family-of-man-who-died-after-altercation-with-aurora-first-responders-says-body-camera-footage-disgusting/

Goldberg, E. (2016, April 19). *Homeless court removes housing, job barriers for people on the streets.* Huffington Post. https://www.huffingtonpost.ca/entry/homeless-court-removes-housing-job-barriers-for-people-on-the-streets_n_57155088e4b0060ccda414cb?ri18n=true

Gonzales, A. R., & Cochran, D. Q. (2017). Police-worn body cameras: An antidote to the "Ferguson Effect"? *Missouri Law Review*, *82*(2), 299–337.

Goodyear-Brown, P., Fath, A., & Myers, L. (2012). Child sSexual Abuse. In P. Goodyear-Brown (Ed.), *Handbook of child sexual abuse: Identification, assessment, and treatment* (pp. 1–28). John Wiley & Sons.

Gordon, R. (2004). The social system as site of disaster impact and resource for recovery. *Australian Journal of Emergency Management, 19*(4), 16-22.

Gordon, G. H. (2001). *The criminal law of Scotland* (3rd ed., Vol. 2Green & Son Ltd.

Gottfredson, D. C., Crosse, S., Tang, Z., Bauer, E. L., Harmon, M. A., Hagen, C. A., & Greene, A. D. (2020). Effects of school resource officers on school crime and responses to school crime. *Criminology & Public Policy, 19*(3), 905–940. doi:10.1111/1745-9133.12512

Gottschalk, M. (2009). Money and mass incarceration: The bad, the mad, and penal reform. *Criminology & Public Policy, 8*(1), 97–109. doi:10.1111/j.1745-9133.2009.00547.x

Gottschalk, M. (2016). *Caught: The prison state and the lockdown of American politics*. Princeton University Press.

Government of NCT. (2018). *Delhi Prison Rules*. http://tte.delhigovt.nic.in/wps/wcm/connect/ad-693e00479000078773c72dd8755fce/Jail+manual+2018.pdf?MOD=AJPERES&lmod=-820682994&CACHEID=ad693e00479000078773c72dd8755fce

Government of Ontario. (2020). *Roadmap to wellness: A plan to build Ontario's mental health and addictions system.* https://www.ontario.ca/page/roadmap-wellness-plan-build-ontarios-mental-health-and-addictions-system

Graham, A., McManus, H., Cullen, F., Burton, V. Jr, & Jonson, C. (2019). Videos don't lie: African Americans support for body-worn cameras. *Criminal Justice Review, 44*(3), 1–20. doi:10.1177/0734016819846229

Graves, S. (2020, March). *Many Californians in prisons and jails have mental health needs.* California Budget and Policy Center. https://calbudgetcenter.org/resources/prisons-and-jails-have-mental-health-needs/

Graziano, L., Schuck, A., & Martin, C. (2010). Police misconduct, media coverage, and public perceptions of racial profiling: An experiment. *Justice Quarterly, 34*(2), 52–76. doi:10.1080/07418820902763046

Great Britain Home Office. (1992). *Memorandum of Good Practice on Video Recorded Interviews with Child Witnesses For Criminal Proceedings*. London: HMSO.

Gressman, E. (1952). The unhappy history of civil rights legislation. *Michigan Law Review, 50*(8), 1323–1358. doi:10.2307/1284416

Groenwald, H., & Peake, G. (2004). *Police reform through community-based policing: Philosophy and guidelines for implementation*. New York: Safer World and International Police Academy.

Groot, E., Kouyoumdjian, F. G., Kiefer, L., Madadi, P., Gross, J., Prevost, B., Jhirad, R., Huyer, D., Snowdon, V., & Persaud, N. (2016). Drug toxicity deaths after release from incarceration in Ontario, 2006-2013: Review of Coroner's Cases. *PLoS One, 11*(7), e0157512. https://doi.org/10.1371/journal.pone.0157512

Grubb, J. A. (2020). *Who goes to prison and why? Examining inmate characteristics and offense types. In Handbook on American Prisons*. Routledge.

Gudjohnsson, G. (1999). Testimony from persons with mental disorders. In H. A. Armstrong, E. Shepherd, & D. Wolchover (Eds.), Analysing witness testimony (pp. 62–75). London: Blackstone.

Guetzkow, J., & Schoon, E. (2015). If you build it, they will fill it: The consequences of prison overcrowding litigation. *Law & Society Review, 49*(2), 401–432. doi:10.1111/lasr.12140

Guirguis-Younger, M., McNeil, R., & Hwang, S. W. (Eds.). (2014). *Homelessness & health in Canada*. University of Ottawa Press.

Güler, G., Yıldırım, V., Kütük, Ö. M., & Toros, F. (2016). Adli Psikiyatrik Değerlendirme ve Çocuk ile İletişim. *Adli Tıp Bülteni., 2*, 98–106.

Gulleng, D.Y. (2016). Police recruitment patterns and professionalism: Implications for effective crime prevention and control in Nigeria. *African Journal of Modern Society*, *4*(2), 57-80.

Gumpert, H. C. (2007). Clinical and organizational perspectives on denial and delayed disclosure. In E. M. Pipe, E. M. Lamb, Y. Orbach, & C. A. Cederborg (Eds.), *Child sexual abuse: Disclosure, delay and denial* (pp. 251–264). Taylor & Francis.

Gundersen, K., & Svartdal, F. (2006). Aggression Replacement Training in Norway: Outcome evaluation of 11 Norwegian student projects. *Scandinavian Journal of Educational Research*, *50*(1), 63–81. doi:10.1080/00313830500372059

Gyanendra Pandey. (2001). *Remembering partition: Violence, nationalism, and history in India*. Cambridge University Press.

Hagan, B. O., Wang, E. A., Aminawung, J. A., Albizu-Garcia, C. E., Zaller, N., Nyamu, S., Shavit, S., Deluca, J., & Fox, A. D. (2018). History of Solitary Confinement Is Associated with Post-Traumatic Stress Disorder Symptoms among Individuals Recently Released from Prison. *Journal of Urban Health*, *95*(2), 141–148. doi:10.100711524-017-0138-1 PMID:28281161

Hairston, C. F. (2007). *Focus on Children with Incarcerated Parents: An Overview of the Research Literature*. Annie E. Casey Foundation.

Halder, D., & Jaishankar, K. (2008). Property rights of Hindu women: A critical review of succession laws of ancient, medieval, and modern India. *Journal of Law and Religion*, *24*, 101-122.

Halder, D., & Jaishankar, K. (2014). Online victimization of Andaman Jarawa tribal women: An analysis of the 'human safari.' *British Journal of Criminology*, *54*(4), 673-688.

HalderD. (2020) *Stop, search, frisk and detain: A comparative analysis of police power between India, UK, and US* (Draft paper unpublished). https://ssrn.com/abstract=3722731 doi:10.2139srn.3722731

Halder, D., & Jaishankar, K. (2011). Cyber gender harassment and secondary victimization: A comparative analysis of the United States, the UK, and India. *Victims & Offenders*, *6*(4), 386–398.

Halder, D., & Jaishankar, K. (2012). *Cyber Crime and the victimization of women: Laws, rights, and regulations*. IGI Global. doi:10.4018/978-1-60960-830-9

Halder, D., & Jaishankar, K. (2015). Irrational coping theory and positive criminology: A framework to protect victims of cyber-crime. In N. Ronel & D. Segev (Eds.), *Positive criminology* (pp. 276–291). Routledge. doi:10.4324/9781315796536-20

Halder, D., & Jaishankar, K. (2017). Love marriages, inter-caste violence, and therapeutic jurisprudential approach of the courts in India. In D. Halder & K. Jaishankar (Eds.), *Therapeutic jurisprudence and overcoming violence against women* (pp. 30–42). IGI Global. doi:10.4018/978-1-5225-2472-4.ch003

Hall, M., & Hall, J. (2011). *The long term effects of child sexual abuse.* Retrieved from, https://www.counseling.org/docs/disaster-and-trauma_sexual-abuse/long-term-effects-of-childhood-sexual-abuse.pdf?sfvrsn=2

Hamilton, Z., Campagna, M., Tollefsbol, E., Van Wormer, J., & Barnoski, R. (2017). A more consistent application of the RNR model: The strong-R needs assessment. *Criminal Justice and Behavior*, *44*(2), 261–292. doi:10.1177/0093854816678032

Haney, C. (2003). The psychological impact of incarceration: Implications for post-prison adjustment. *Prisoners once removed: The impact of Incarceration and Reentry on Children, Families, and Communities*, *33*(66). https://www.cdcr.ca.gov/about-cdcr/strategic plan/

Harcourt, B. (1998). Reflecting on the Subject: A critique of the social influence conception of deterrence, the broken windows theory, and order-maintenance policing New York style. *Michigan Law Review*, *97*(2), 291–389. doi:10.2307/1290289

Harding, D. J., Morenoff, J. D., Nguyen, A. P., & Bushway, S. D. (2017). Short-and long-term effects of imprisonment on future felony convictions and prison admissions. *Proceedings of the National Academy of Sciences of the United States of America*, *114*(42), 11103–11108. doi:10.1073/pnas.1701544114 PMID:28973924

Harkin, D., Whelan, C., & Chang, L. (2018). The challenges facing specialist police cyber- crime units: An empirical analysis. *Police Practice and Research*, *19*(6), 519–536.

Harper, R. J., & Hamilton, P. (1999). A fingertip guide to criminal Law (4th ed.). Butterworths.

Harris, M. K. (2004). An expansive, transformative view of restorative justice. *Contemporary Justice Review*, *7*(1), 117–141.

Hassell, K. D. (2016). Reducing police misconduct. In R. J. Burke (Ed.), *Stress in policing: Sources, consequences, and interventions* (pp. 220–236). Routledge. doi:10.4324/9781315611075-13

Hausegger, L., & Haynie, S. (2003). Judicial decision-making and the use of panels in the Canadian Supreme Court and the South African appellate division. *Law & Society Review*, *37*(3), 635–657. doi:10.1111/1540-5893.3703006

Heaviside, S., Rowand, C., William, C., & Farris, E. (1998). Violence and discipline problems in U.S. public schools: 1996-97. Department of Education, national Center for Education Statistics., NCES 98-030.

Hegel, G. W. F. (1942). *The philosophy of right* (T. Knox, Trans.). Oxford University Press.

Heitzeg, N. A. (2009). Education or incarceration: Zero tolerance policies and the school to prison pipeline. *The Forum of Public Policy*. https://eric.ed.gov/?id=EJ870076

Helgesen, E. (2011). Allotment of justice: How U. S. policy in Indian country perpetuates the victimization of American Indians. *University of Florida Journal of Law and Public Policy*, *22*(3), 441–472.

Hemmer, J. W. (2017). *Exploring police beliefs in community-oriented policing and community trust: A multiple case study* (Dissertation). ProQuest Dissertations & Theses Global. (1965399982)

Henstock, D., & Ariel, B. (2017). Testing the effects of police body-worn cameras on use of force during arrests: A randomised controlled trial in a large British police force. *European Journal of Criminology*, *14*(6), 720–750. doi:10.1177/1477370816686120

Hershkowitz, I. (2011). Rapport Building in Investigative Interviews of Children. In *Children's Testimony: A Handbook of Psychological Research and Forensic Practice* (pp. 109–128). John Wiley & Sons Ltd.

Higgins, E. M., Overstreet, S., Coffey, B., & Fisher, B. W. (2020). "Bridging the gap": School resource officers as bridge builders in the community policing era. *Journal of Crime and Justice*, *43*(4), 433–448. doi:10.1080/0735648X.2019.1704837

Hills, A. (2008). The dialectic of police reform in Nigeria. *The Journal of Modern African Studies*, *46*(2), 215–334. doi:10.1017/S0022278X08003200

Hills, A. (2012). Lost in translation: Why Nigeria's police don't implement democratic reforms. *The Royal Institute of International Affairs*, *88*(4), 740–755. doi:10.1111/j.1468-2346.2012.01099.x

Himma, K. E. (1999). Judicial discretion and the concept of law. *Oxford Journal of Legal Studies*, *19*(1), 71–82. doi:10.1093/ojls/19.1.71

Hindi, S. (2017 November 21). Body camera video: Officers asked suspect to drop knife more than 40 times. *The Coloradoan*. https://www.coloradoan.com/story/news/2017/11/21/police-body-camera-video-fatal-shooting-jeremy-holmes/884711001/

Hinds, L., & Murphy, K. (2007). Public satisfaction with police: Using procedural justice to improve police legitimacy. *Australian and New Zealand Journal of Criminology*, *40*(1), 27–42. doi:10.1375/acri.40.1.27

Hirschfield, P. (2009). another way out: The impact of juvenile arrest on high school dropout. *Sociology of Education*, *82*(4), 368–393. doi:10.1177/003804070908200404

Hlavka, H. R., Wheelock, D., & Cossyleon, J. E. (2016). Narratives of commitment: Looking for Work with a criminal record. *The Sociological Quarterly*, *56*(2), 213–236. doi:10.1111/tsq.12086

Hlavka, H., Wheelock, D., & Jones, R. (2015). Ex-offender accounts of successful re-entry from prison. *Journal of Offender Rehabilitation*, *54*(6), 426–428. doi:10.1080/10509674.2015.1057630

Hockenberry, S. (2014). *Juvenile in residential placement, 2011. U.S. Department of Justice. Office of Justice Programs.* Office of Juvenile Justice and Delinquency Prevention. https://ojjdp.ojp.gov/sites/g/files/xyckuh176/files/pubs/246826.pdf

Hogan, D. (1983a). The effectiveness of licensing: History, evidence, and recommendations. *Law and Human Behavior*, *7*(213), 117–138. doi:10.1007/BF01044517

Hogan, D. (1983b). Professional regulation: An introduction to the issue. *Law and Human Behavior*, *7*(213), 99–101. doi:10.1007/BF01044515

Holcombe, M. (2019 December 4). LAPD officer allegedly caught fondling corpse. *CNN*. https://www.cnn.com/2019/12/04/us/lapd-officer-fondle-corpse/index.html

Holliday, E. R., Brainerd, J. C., & Reyna, F. V. (2008). Interviewing Vulnerable Witness. In G. Davies & C. Hollin (Eds.), *Forensic psychology* (pp. 87–112). John Wiley.

Holliday, E. R., Humphries, E. H., Brainerd, J. C., & Reyna, F. V. (2012). Interviewing vulnerable witnesses. In G. Davies & A. Beech (Eds.), *Forensic psychology: Crime, justice, law, interventions* (pp. 115–134). John Wiley & Sons Ltd.

Holliday, R. E., Humphries, J. E., Brainerd, C. J., & Reyna, V. F. (2014). Eyewitness Evidence. In G. Davies & A. Beech (Eds.), *Forensic Psychology: Crime Justice Law Interventions* (2nd ed., pp. 115–134). John Wiley & Sons Ltd.

Hollywood Homeless Youth Partnership. (2013, January). Measuring success in housing programs for homeless youth: The need for youth-specific performance measures. *Policy Brief.*

Holmberg, U. (2014). Interviewing suspects. In G. Davies & A. Beech (Eds.), *Forensic psychology: Crime justice law interventions* (pp. 135–150). John Wiley.

Homeless Hub. (2020). *Regulatory barriers to affordable housing.* https://www.homelesshub.ca/resource/regulatory-barriers-affordable-housing

Homeless Hub. (2020). *Solutions: Supporting communities to prevent and end homelessness.* https://www.homelesshub.ca/solutions/prevention

Hong, S. (2017). Does increasing ethnic representativeness reduce police misconduct? *Public Administration Review*, *77*(2), 195–205. doi:10.1111/puar.12629

Horvath, H. A. M. (2010). Child victims of sexual abuse. In M. J. Brown & A. E. Campbell (Eds.), *The cambridge handbook of forensic psychology* (pp. 143–152). Cambridge University Press.

Housing, Health, and Justice Community of Interest. (2019, February). *Closed quarters: Challenges and opportunities in stabilizing housing and mental health across the justice sector.* https://www.eenet.ca/ClosedQuarters

Howells, K. (2004). Anger and Its Links to Violent Offending. *Psychiatry, Psychology and Law, 11*(2), 189–196. doi:10.1375/pplt.2004.11.2.189

Howitt, D. (2009). *Introduction to forensic & criminal psychology* (3rd ed.). Pearson Education Ltd.

Hoyle, J. R., & Slater, R. O. (2001). Love, happiness, and America's schools: The role of educational leadership in the 21st century. *Phi Delta Kappan, 82*(10), 790–794. doi:10.1177/003172170108201017

Huey, M. P., & McNulty, T. L. (2005). Institutional conditions and prison suicide: Conditional effects of deprivation and overcrowding. *The Prison Journal, 85*(4), 490–514. doi:10.1177/0032885505282258

Hughes, D. M. (2005). The demand for sex trafficking. *Women's Studies Program, University of Rhode Island, 26*, 5. https://www.academia.edu/3415676/The_Demand_for_Victims_of_Sex_Trafficking

Human Rights Watch. (2010). *Everyone is on the Game. Corruption and human right abuses by the Nigeria police force.* https://www.hrw.org/sites/default/files/reports/nigeria0810webwcover.pdf

Human Rights Watch. (2010). *Everyone's in on the Game Corruption and Human Rights Abuses by the Nigeria Police Force*. Available: http://www.hrw.org

Human Rights Watch. (2018). *Rest in Pieces: Police Torture and Deaths in Custody*. https://www.refworld.org/docid/45d2f62c2.html

Human Rights Watch. (2020). *Crackdown on police brutality protests*. Author.

Hümanistik, B. (2014). *Türkiye'de çocuk koruma ve önleme sistemleri haritası*. http://www.cocukkorumaharitasi.info/dosyadepo/kitap.pdf

Hunt, V. H., Taylor, M. A., Fitzgerald, B., Button, E. D., & Kerr, B. (2019). An examination of the characteristics and perceptions of school resource officers in rural and urban Oklahoma schools. *Journal of Rural Social Sciences, 34*(2), 1–25.

Hutson, H. R., Rice, P. L. Jr, Chana, J. K., Kyriacou, D. N., Chang, Y., & Miller, R. M. (2007). A review of police pursuit fatalities in the United States from 1982–2004. *Prehospital Emergency Care, 11*(3), 278–283. doi:10.1080/10903120701385414 PMID:17613900

Hyman, I. A., & Perone, D. C. (1998). The other side of school violence: Educator policies and practices that may contribute to student misbehavior. *Journal of School Psychology, 36*(1), 7–27. doi:10.1016/S0022-4405(97)87007-0

Hyun, J. L. (2011). Temple prostitutes: Devadasi practice and human trafficking in India. *Regent Journal of International Law, 1*, 2.

Ibietan, J., & Joshua, S. (2013). Ethics in the Nigerian Public Sector: A Discourse. *The Public Administration and Social Policies Review V, 1*(10).

Ikogho, J. (2006). *Police Companion and Public Guide*. Law View Consult.

Ikuteyijo, L. O. (2009). The challenges of community policing in Nigeria. *International Journal of Police Science & Management, 11*(3), 285–293. doi:10.1350/ijps.2009.11.3.130

International Crisis Group. (2018). *Stopping Nigeria's spiraling farmer-herder conflict*. https://www.crisisgroup.org/africa/west-africa/nigeria/262

International Labour Office (ILO). (2012). *ILO Global Estimate of Forced Labour*. https://www.ilo.org/wcmsp5/groups/public/---ed_norm/---declaration/documents/publication/wcms_182004.pdf

Iwarimie-Jaja, D. (2010). *Police and Policing in the Nigeria Political system.* Portharcourt: Pearl Publishers.

Jackman, T. (2016, September 16). Fraternal Order of Police union endorses Trump. *The Washington Post*. https://www.washingtonpost.com/news/true-crime/wp/2016/09/16/fraternal-order-of-police-union-endorses-trump/

Jackman, T. (2020 July 2). Federal body camera bill, inspired by Park Police killing of Bijan Ghaisar, included in House police reform package. *The Washington Post*. https://www.washingtonpost.com/crime-law/2020/06/09/federal-body-camera-bill-inspired-by-park-police-killing-bijan-ghaisar-included-house-police-reform-package/

Jackson, J. L., Sr. (2020, June 18). Police reform was never going to be easy—but now's the time. *The Washington Informer, 55*(36), 26. https://www.washingtoninformer.com/jesse-jackson-police-reform-was-never-going-to-be-easy-but-nows-the-time/

Jacobs, J. B., & Olitsky, E. (2004). Leadership and correctional reform. *Pace Law Review*, *24*(2), 477–496. https://digitalcommons.pace.edu

Jacobs, L. A., & Skeem, J. L. (2021). Neighborhood risk factors for recidivism: For whom do they matter? *American Journal of Community Psychology*, *67*(1-2), 103–115. doi:10.1002/ajcp.12463 PMID:32960992

James, N. (2015, January 12). *Offender reentry: Correctional statistics, reintegration into the community, and recidivism.* Congressional Research Service, 7-5700.

James, N. (2015). *Risk and needs assessment in the criminal justice system*. Congressional Research Service.

Jeffe, S. B. (1987, March 22). *California: Good aims, bad results*. L.A. Times. https://www.latimes.com/archives/la-xpm-1987-03-22-op-14759-story.html

Jenkins, M. J. (2016). Police support for community problem-solving and broken windows policing. *American Journal of Criminal Justice*, *41*(2), 220–235. doi:10.100712103-015-9302-x

Jennings, W. G., Khey, D. N., Maskaly, J., & Donner, C. M. (2011). Evaluating the relationship between law enforcement and school security measures and violent crime in schools. *Journal of Police Crisis Negotiations*, *11*(2), 109–124. doi:10.1080/15332586.2011.581511

Jennings, W. G., Lynch, M. D., & Fridell, L. A. (2015). Evaluating the impact of police officer body-worn cameras (BWCs) on response-to-resistance and serious external complaints: Evidence from the Orlando police department (OPD) experience utilizing a randomized controlled experiment. *Journal of Criminal Justice*, *43*(6), 480–486. doi:10.1016/j.jcrimjus.2015.10.003

Jew, C. L., Green, K. E., & Kroger, J. (1999). Development and validation of a measure of resiliency. *Measurement & Evaluation in Counseling & Development*, *32*(2), 75–89. doi:10.1080/07481756.1999.12068973

John Howard Society of Ontario. (2015, August). *Unlocking change: Decriminalizing mental health issues in Ontario.* http://www.johnhoward.on.ca/wp-content/uploads/2015/07/Unlocking-Change-Final-August-2015.pdf

John Howard Society of Ontario. (2016, April). *Fractured care: Public health opportunities in Ontario's correctional institutions.* John Howard Society of Ontario. https://johnhoward.on.ca/wp-content/uploads/2016/04/Fractured-Care-Final.pdf

John Howard Society of Ontario. (2018, February). *The invisible burden: Police records and the barriers to employment in Toronto*. https://policerecordhub.ca/wp-content/uploads/2018/02/The-Invisible-Burden-Report-FINAL.pdf

Johnson, K. (2020, June 10). Union: 'We don't want to protect bad cops'. *USA Today*, p. 3A. https:link.gale.com/apps/doc/A626234671/OVIC?u+minn4020&xid=4df20ec9

Johnson, R. (2014). Ethnoracial factors in the U.S. prison system: Forensic psychological realities of correctional officers. In Color Behind Bars (vol. 2). Praeger.

Johnson, I. (2013). Policing in contemporary Nigeria: Issues and challenges. *African Journal for the Psychological Study of Social Issues*, *16*(1), 71–77.

Johnson, L. M. (1999). School Violence: The effectiveness of a school resource officer program in a southern city. *Journal of Criminal Justice*, *27*(2), 173–192. doi:10.1016/S0047-2352(98)00049-X

Jonson, C. L., & Cullen, F. T. (2015). Prisoner reentry programs. *Crime and Justice*, *44*(1), 517–575. doi:10.1086/681554

Jordan, J., Patel, B., & Rapp, L. (2013). Domestic minor sex trafficking: A social work perspective on misidentification, victims, buyers, traffickers, treatment, and reform of current practice. *Journal of Human Behavior in the Social Environment*, *23*(3), 356–369. doi:10.1080/10911359.2013.764198

Kahn, K. B., & Martin, K. D. (2016). Policing and race: Disparate treatment, perceptions, and policy responses. *Social Issues and Policy Review*, *10*(1), 82–121. doi:10.1111ipr.12019

Kamalu, N. C., & Onveozili, E. C. (2018). A critical analysis of the 'broken windows' policing in New York city and its impact: Implications for the criminal justice system and the African American community. *African Journal of Criminology and Justice Studies: AJCJS*, *11*(1), 71–94.

Kancharla, B. (2009). *The intriguing case of data on 'communal incidents' in India*. https://factly.in/the-intriguing-case-of-data-on-communal-incidents-in-india/

Kang-Brown, J., Montagnet, C., & Heiss, J. (2021). *People in jail and prison in 2020*. Vera Institute of Justice.

Kant, I. (1956). *Critique of practical reason* (L. W. Beck, Trans.). Macmillan Publishing Co.

Karakartal, D. (2020). Çocuk Cinsel İstismarının Önlenmesinde Cinsel Eğitimin Önemi. *International Journal of Humanities and Education.*, *13*, 145–156.

Keegan, M. (2018, June 27). *Benefit or burden? The cities trying out universal basic income*. The Guardian. https://www.theguardian.com/cities/2018/jun/27/benefit-or-burden-the-cities-trying-out-universal-basic-income

Keene, D. E., Smoyer, A. B., & Blankenship, K. M. (2018). Stigma, housing, and identity after prison. *The Sociological Review*, *66*(4), 799–815. doi:10.1177/0038026118777447 PMID:32855574

Kelling, G. L., & Wilson, J. Q. (1982, March). Broken windows. *The Atlantic*. https://www.theatlantic.com/magazine/archive/1982/03/broken-windows/304465/

Kennedy, M. (2001). Teachers with a badge. *Security and Safety*, *4*, 36–38.

Kennedy, R. (1993). State, criminal law, and racial discrimination: A comment. *Harvard Law Review*, *107*(6), 1255. doi:10.2307/1341843

Kerley, K. R., & Benson, M. L. (2000). Does community-oriented policing help build stronger communities? *Police Quarterly*, *3*(1), 46–69. doi:10.1177/1098611100003001002

Kesten, K. L., Leavitt-Smith, E., Rau, D. R., Shelton, D., Zhnag, W., Wagner, J., & Trestman, R. L. (2012). Recidivism rates among mentally ill inmates: Impact of the Connecticut Offender Reentry Program. *Journal of Correctional Health Care*, *18*(1), 20–28. doi:10.1177/1078345811421117 PMID:22095006

Khan, F. (2020, February 18). *India had 38,503 victims of trafficking in 2011-19. Only 77 have got compensation.* The Print. https://theprint.in/india/india-had-38503-victims-of-trafficking-in-2011-19-only-77-have-got-compensation/365761/

Khan, M. Z. (1990). *Work by jail inmates.* Inter-India Publications.

Kindy, K. (2019, January 21). Some U.S. police departments dump body-warn camera programs amid high costs. *The Washington Post.* https://www.washingtonpost.com/national/some-us-police-departments-dump-body-camera-programs-amid-high-costs/2019/01/21/991f0e66-03ad-11e9-b6a9-0aa5c2fcc9e4_story.html

Kinner, S. A., Young, J. T., Snow, K., Southalan, L., Lopez-Acuña, D., Ferreira-Borges, C., & O'Moore, E. (2020). Prisons and custodial settings are part of a comprehensive response to COVID-19. *The Lancet. Public Health, 5*(4), e188–e189. doi:10.1016/S2468-2667(20)30058-X PMID:32197116

Kırımsoy, E., Acar, H., Yokuş Sevük, H., Kaynak, H., Aydın, M., Antakyalıoğlu, Ş., Özdemir, U., Mutlu, Y., & Baykara Acar, Y. (2013). *Çocuk Adalet Sistemi Çalışanları Eğitim Programı:Kolaylaştırıcılar için Vaka Temelli Eğitim Kitabı.* Retrieved on: 19.02.2021. https://www.unicef.org/turkey/media/5466/file/VAKA%20TEMELL%C4%B0%20E%C4%9E%C4%B0T%C4%B0M%20K%C4%B0TABI%20_%20Kas%C4%B1m%202013.pdf

Klinger, D. (2004). *Into the kill zone.* Jossey-Bass, Inc.

Klinker-Lockwood, S., Nally, J. M., & Ho, T. (2016). Race, education, employment, and recidivism among offenders in the United States: An exploration of complex issues in the Indianapolis metropolitan area. *International Journal of Criminal Justice Sciences, 11*(1), 57–74.

Kocorowski, J. (2020, August 29). *Melvin Gordon Reacts to Jacob Blake Shooting: 'It Just Shocked Me'.* https://www.si.com/college/wisconsin/football/melvin-gordon-kenosha-jacob-blake-Jake

Kök, H. (2019). *Türkiye'de Cinsel İstismara Uğrayan Çocuklara Yönelik Hizmet ve Uygulamaların Değerlendirilmesi: Bir Model Önerisi* (Unpublished PhD Thesis). Hacettepe Üniversitesi.

Kolenda, P. (1978). *Caste in contemporary India: Beyond organic solidarity.* Benjamin/Cumming Publishing Co.

Konkel, R. H., & Daquin, J. C. (2020). From the streets to prison and back: An examination of continuity of behaviors among offenders. *Corrections: Policy, Practice and Research*, 1–22. doi:10.1080/23774657.2020.1808116

Koslicki, W. M. (2019). Accountability or efficiency? Body-worn cameras as replicative technology. *Criminal Justice Review (Atlanta, Ga.), 44*(3), 356–368. doi:10.1177/0734016819856079

Koslicki, W. M., Makin, D. A., & Willits, D. (2020). When no one is watching: Evaluating the impact of body-worn cameras on use of force incidents. *Policing and Society, 30*(5), 1–14. doi:10.1080/10439463.2020.1765778

Kotiswaran, P. (2014). Beyond the allures of criminalisation: Rethinking the regulation of sex work in India. *Criminology & Criminal Justice, 14*(5), 565–579. doi:10.1177/1748895814542533

Kouyoumdjian, F., Kim, M., Kiran, T., Cheng, S., Fung, K., Orkin, A., Kendall, C., Green, S., Matheson, F., & Kiefer, L. (2019, October). Attachment to primary care and team-based primary care. *Canadian Family Physician Medecin de Famille Canadien, 65*(10), e433–e442.

Kouyoumdjian, F., Schuler, A., Matheson, F., & Hwang, S. W. (2016, March). Health status of prisoners in Canada: Narrative review. *Canadian Family Physician Medecin de Famille Canadien, 62*(3), 215–222.

Kramer, P. A. (2002). Empires, exceptions, and Anglo-Saxons: Race and rule between the British and United States empires, 1880–1910. *The Journal of American History, 88*(4), 1315–1353. doi:10.2307/2700600

Krebs, E., Urada, D., Evans, E., Huang, D., Hser, Y., & Nosyk, B. (2017, May). The costs of crime during and after publicly funded treatment for opioid use disorders: A population-level study for the state of California. *Addiction (Abingdon, England)*, *112*(5), 838–851.

Krishnamurti, J. (1992). *Social responsibility*. Krishnamurti Foundation of America.

Kumar, S. (2013). Semi-private prison management in India. *Journal of Centre for Reforms, Development and Justice*, *1*(3).

Ladapo, O. A. (2011). Effective investigations, a pivot to efficient criminal justice administration: Challenges in Nigeria. *African Journal of Criminology and Justice Studies*, *5*(1 &2), 79–94.

Lalli, U. (2000). Attitude to prison reforms: An empirical survey. *Indian Journal*, *1*(1), 32.

Lal, V. (1999). Everyday crime, native mendacity, and the cultural psychology of justice in colonial India. *Studies in History*, *15*(1), 145–166. doi:10.1177/025764309901500105 PMID:22452024

Lamb, E. M., & Garretson, E. M. (2003). The effects of interviewer and child gender on the informativeness of alleged child sexual abuse victims in forensic interviews. *Law and Human Behavior*, *27*, 157–171.

Lamb, E. M., Hershkowitz, I., Orbach, Y., & Esplin, W. P. (2008). *Tell me what happened: Structured investigative interviews of child victims and witness*. John Wiley & Sons Ltd.

Lamb, E. M., Malloy, C. L., & Rooy, J. D. (2011). Setting realistic expectations: Developmental characteristics, capacities and limitations. In E. M. Lamb, J. D. La Rooy, C. L. Malloy, & C. Katz (Eds.), *Children's testimony: A handbook of psychological research and forensic practice* (2nd ed., pp. 15–48). John Wiley & Sons Ltd.

Langan, P. A., & Levin, D. J. (2002). *Recidivism of prisoners released in 1994*. U.S. Department of Justice, Bureau of Justice Statistics. doi:10.1525/fsr.2002.15.1.58

Lange, K. (2019 October 19). A Carmel police body camera fell off at a critical moment. It's not all that rare. *Indianapolis Star*. https://www.indystar.com/story/news/local/hamilton-county/carmel/2020/10/19/carmel-police-axon-body-camera-fell-off-critical-moment/5941701002/

Lar, J. (2018). Policing actors, plural processes, and hybridization: Histories of everyday policing practice in central Nigeria. *Stability*, *7*(1), 1–15. doi:10.5334ta.605

Laswell, H. D. (1950). *World politics and personal insecurity*. Free Press.

Latessa, E. J. (2004). The challenge of change: Correctional programs and evidence-based practices. *Criminology & Public Policy*, *3*(4), 546–560. doi:10.1111/j.1745-9133.2004.tb00061.x

Lattimore, P. K., Steffey, D. M., & Visher, C. A. (2010). Prisoner reentry in the first decade of the twenty-first century. *Victims & Offenders*, *5*(3), 253–267. doi:10.1080/15564886.2010.485907

Lawrence, D. S., McClure, D., Malm, A., Lynch, M., & La Vigne, N. (2019). Activation of body-worn cameras: Variation by officer, over time, and by policing activity. *Criminal Justice Review*, *44*(3), 339–355. doi:10.1177/0734016819846228

Lawrence, R. (2007). *School crime and juvenile justice*. Oxford University Press.

Laws, D. R., & Ward, T. (2011). *Desistance and sexual offending: Alternatives to throwing away the keys*. The Guilford Press.

LeBel, T. P., Burnett, R., Maruna, S., & Bushway, S. (2008). The chicken and egg' of subjective and social factors in desistance from crime. *European Journal of Criminology*, *5*(2), 131–159. doi:10.1177/1477370807087640

Lee, T. (2016). Tennessee citizens police academies: Program and participant characteristics. *American Journal of Criminal Justice, 41*(2), 236–254.

Lee, H. D., Kim, D., Woo, Y., & Reyns, B. W. (2019). Determinants of citizen support for community-oriented policing. *Police Practice and Research, 20*(1), 34–47. doi:10.1080/15614263.2017.1396459

Lee, H.-W. (2017). Taking deterrence seriously: The wide-scope deterrence theory of punishment. *Criminal Justice Ethics, 36*(1), 2–24. doi:10.1080/0731129X.2017.1298879

Lee, J., Lim, H., & Lee, H. (2015). Differential social distance and confidence in the police. *International Journal of Police Science & Management, 17*(3), 147–154. doi:10.1177/1461355715596305

Leighton, P. (2014). A model prison for the next 50 years: The high-tech, public- private Shimane Asahi Rehabilitation Centre. *Justice Policy Journal, 11*(1).

LeongN. (2006). Felon reenfranchisement: Political implications and potential for individual rehabilitative benefits. *Available at* SSRN 977280. doi:10.2139srn.977280

Levin, J., & Rabrenovic, G. (2001). *Hate crimes and ethnic conflict: An introduction.* Academic Press.

Levin, M. (2020, January). *You've just been named California's homelessness czar— what's your first move?* CalMatters. https://calmatters.org/housing/2020/01/california-homelessness-czar-options-ratings-cost-efficiency/

Liederbach, J., Fritsch, E. J., Carter, D. L., & Bannister, A. (2008). Exploring the limits of collaboration in community policing: A direct comparison of police and citizen views. *Policing, 31*(2), 271-291. doi:http://dx.doi.org.ezp.waldenu-library.org/10.1108/13639510810878721

Liem, M., & Kunst, M. (2013). Is there a recognizable post-incarceration syndrome among released "lifers"? *International Journal of Law and Psychiatry, 36*(3), 333–337. doi:10.1016/j.ijlp.2013.04.012 PMID:23642320

Lindsay, R. (2019 July 8). Behind the body camera: The ethics, adoption, and impact of recording police interactions. *WNPR, Connecticut Public Radio Online.* https://www.wnpr.org/post/behind-body-camera-ethics-adoption-and-impact-recording-police-interactions

Lipsey, M. W. (2009). The primary factors that characterize effective interventions with juvenile offenders: A meta-analytic overview. *Victims & Offenders: An International Journal of Evidence-Based Research, Policy & Practice, 4*(2), 124–147.

Lizama, J., Matthews, V., & Reyes, S. (2014). What works? Short-term, in custody treatment programs [Policy Brief]. *Center for Public Policy.* http://cpp.fullerton.edu/pdf/What%20Works.pdf

Lofton, B. P. (2004). Does restorative justice challenge systemic injustices? In Critical issues in restorative justice (pp. 377-385). Criminal Justice Press and Willan Publishing.

Lombardo, R. M., & Donner, C. M. (2018). Can community policing increase residents' informal social control? Testing the impact of the Chicago Alternative Policing Strategy. *Police Practice and Research, 19*(5), 427–442. doi:10.1080/15614263.2017.1405265

Loo, C. (1993). An integrative-sequential model of treatment for PTSD: A case study of the Japanese American internment and redress. *Clinical Psychology Review, 13*, 89–117. doi:10.1016/0272-7358(93)90036-L

Losel, F. (2010). *What works in offender rehabilitation: A global perspective* [Conference presentation]. 12th Annual Conference of the International Corrections and Prisons Association.

Lou, M., & Griggs, B. (2019 February 27). A proposed Tennessee law would make it a felony for police officers to disable their body cams. *CNN.* https://www.cnn.com/2019/02/27/us/tennessee-body-cam-felony-trnd/index.html

Loughran, T. A., Pogarsky, G., Piquero, A. R., & Paternoster, R. (2012). Re-examining the functional form of the certainty effect in deterrence theory. *Justice Quarterly*, *29*(5), 712–741. doi:10.1080/07418825.2011.583931

Love, M. C., & Frazier, A. (2006). Certificates of rehabilitation and other forms of relief from the collateral consequences of conviction: a survey of state laws. In ABA Commission on Effective Criminal Sanctions (Ed.), Second Chances in the Criminal Justice System: Alternatives to Incarceration and Reentry Strategies. Washington, DC: American Bar Association.

Lozano, A. T. R., Morgan, R. D., Murray, D. D., & Varghese, F. (2011). Prison tattoos as a reflection of the criminal lifestyle. *International Journal of Offender Therapy and Comparative Criminology*, *55*(4), 509–529. doi:10.1177/0306624X10370829 PMID:20508085

Lum, C., Koper, C. S., Wilson, D. B., Stoltz, M., Goodier, M., Eggins, E., Higginson, A., & Mazerolle, L. (2020). Body-worn cameras' effects on police officers and citizen behavior: A systematic review. *Campbell Systematic Review, 16*(3).

Lum, C., Koper, C., Merola, L., Scherer, A., & Reioux, A. (2015). Existing and ongoing body worn camera research: knowledge gaps and opportunities. *Laura and John Arnold Foundation*. https://www.arnoldfoundation.org/wp-content/uploads/Phase-I-Report-Nov-28-2015-FINAL.pdf

Lum, C., Stoltz, M., Koper, C. S., & Scherer, J. A. (2019). Research on body-worn cameras: What we know, what we need to know. *Criminology & Public Policy*, *18*(1), 93–118. doi:10.1111/1745-9133.12412

Lumsden, E. (2017). How much is police brutality costing America? *University of Hawai'i Law Review*, *41*(1), 142–202.

Lurigio, A. J., Rollins, A., & Fallon, J. (2004). The effects of serious mental illness on offender reentry. *Federal Probation*, *68*(2), 45–52.

MacKenzie, D., & Meessen, S. (2019, October). *Intervening early to prevent youth homelessness: Lessons from the Geelong project.* Child Family Community Australia. https://aifs.gov.au/cfca/webinars/intervening-early-prevent-youth-homelessness-lessons-geelong-project

MacKinnon, C. A. (1982). Feminism, Marxism, method and the state, An agenda for theory. *Feminist Theory*, *7*(3), 515–544.

Magaldi, D., & Berler, M. (2020). Semi-structured interviews. In V. Zeigler-Hill & T. K. Shackelford (Eds.), *Encyclopedia of personality and individual differences*. Springer.

Mağdur Hakları Daire Başkanlığı. (2021). *AGO Nedir?* Retrieved on: 25.04.2021. https://magdur.adalet.gov.tr/Home//SayfaDetay/agonedir

Makarios, M., Lovins, L., Latessa, E., & Smith, P. (2016). Staff quality and treatment effectiveness: An examination of the relationship between staff factors and the effectiveness of correctional programs. *Justice Quarterly*, *33*(2), 348–367. doi:10.1080/07418825.2014.924546

Mallapur, C. (2020, March 26). Coronavirus pandemic: India should wake up to the need for prison reforms. *Scroll.in*. https://scroll.in/article/957202/coronavirus-pandemic-india-should-wake-up-to-the-need-for-prison-reforms

Malloy, C. L., Wright, B. D., & Skagerberg, M. E. (2012). In G. Davies & A. Beech (Eds.), *Forensic psychology: Crime justice, law, interventions* (pp. 99–114). John Wiley & Sons Ltd.

Malm, A. (2019). Promise of police body-worn cameras. *Criminology & Public Policy*, *18*(1), 119–130. doi:10.1111/1745-9133.12420

Malumfashi, S. (2020). Nigeria's SARS: A brief History of the anti-robbery squad. *Aljazeera*. Available at https://www.aljazeera.com/features/2020/10/22/sars-a-brief-history-of-a-rogue-unit

Manchak, S. M., & Morgan, R. D. (2018). Offenders with mental illness in prison. In J. Wooldredge & P. Smith (Eds.), *The Oxford handbook of prisons and imprisonment* (pp. 1–26). Oxford University Press.

Mandery, E. J. (1994). Qualified immunity or absolute impunity? the moral hazards of extending qualified immunity to lower-level public officials. *Harvard Journal of Law & Public Policy*, *17*(2), 479. https://ezp.waldenulibrary.org

Mangan, A., Thomas, R., Davies, A., & Gasper, R. (2018). The challenges of police–community collaboration: Identity manoeuvres and power struggles in a neighborhood-based meeting. *Public Management Review*, *20*(9), 1353–1373. doi:10.1080/14719037.2017.1383718

Manning, P. (2003). *Policing contingencies*. The University of Chicago Press. doi:10.7208/chicago/9780226503523.001.0001

Månsson, S.-A., & Hedin, U.-C. (1999). Breaking the Matthew effect - on women leaving prostitution. *International Journal of Social Welfare*, *8*(1), 67–77. doi:10.1111/1468-2397.00063

Marable, M. (1999). *Black Liberation in Conservative America*. South End Press.

Marlowe, D. B. (2020). The most carefully studied, yet least understood terms in the criminal justice lexicon: Risk, need, and responsivity. *Policy Research Associates, Inc.* https://www.prainc.com/risk-need-responsivity

Martin, M. S., Dorken, S. K., Wamboldt, A. D., & Wootten, S. E. (2012). Stopping the revolving door: A meta-analysis on the effectiveness of interventions for criminally involved individuals with major mental disorders. *Law and Human Behavior*, *36*(1), 1–12. doi:10.1037/h0093963 PMID:22471380

Martinson, R. (1974). What works? Questions and answers about prison reform. *The Public Interest*, *35*, 22–54.

Maruna, S. (2001). *Making good: How ex-convicts reform and rebuild their lives*. American Psychological Association. doi:10.1037/10430-000

Mateescu, A., Rosenblat, A., & Boyd, D. (2016). Dreams of accountability guaranteed surveillance: The promises and costs of body-worn cameras. *Surveillance & Society*, *14*(1), 122–127. doi:10.24908s.v14i1.6282

Matthew, M., & Abrams, L. S. (2020). Practically emotional: Young men's perspectives on what works in reentry programs. *Journal of Social Service Research*, *46*(5), 658–670. doi:10.1080/01488376.2019.1617225

Mawby, R. I. (1990). *Comparative policing issues: The British and American experience in international perspective*. Unwin Hyman Ltd.

Maxwell, N. (2020 July 15). Body cameras: What is different and what is the same. *Alamogordo Daily News*. https://www.alamogordonews.com/story/news/local/community/2020/07/15/local-law-enforcement-and-new-body-cam-rules/5441740002/

Mazumdar, S., & Mazumdar, S. (2004). Religion and place attachment: A study of sacred places. *Journal of Environmental Psychology*, *24*(3), 385–397. doi:10.1016/j.jenvp.2004.08.005

Mboka, A. K. (2013). Overview of the Arizona juvenile justice system. *Kriminologija & socijalna integracija: časopis za kriminologiju, penologiju i poremećaje u ponašanju*, *20*(2), 73-87.

McCamman, M., & Culhane, S. (2017). Police body cameras and us: Public perceptions of the justification of the police use of force in the body camera era. *Translational Issues in Psychological Science*, *3*(2), 167–175. doi:10.1037/tps0000117

McCarthy, M. M., Porter, L. E., Townsley, M., & Alpert, G. P. (2019). The effect of community-oriented policing on police use of force: Does community matter? *Policing*, *42*(4), 556–570. doi:10.1108/PIJPSM-10-2018-0148

McCold, P. (1995, March 31). *Restorative justice: The role of the community.* Paper presented to the Academy of Criminal Justice Sciences Annual Conference, Boston, MA.

McCorkle, R. C., & Miethe, T. D. (1998). The political and organizational response to gangs: An examination of a moral panic in Nevada. *Justice Quarterly, 15*(1), 41–64. doi:10.1080/07418829800093631

McCurdy, B. L., Empson, D. N., Knoster, T., Fluke, S. M., & Grant, C. A. (2019). School resource officers and school-wide PBIS: Considerations for training. *Revisiting School Failure: Alternative Education for Children and Youth, 4*(63), 317–324. doi:10.1080/1045988X.2019.1605970

McDaniel, J. (2001). *School resource officer: What we know, what we think we know, what we need to know.* https://files.nc.gov/ncdps/div/JJ/whatweknow.pdf

McDonagh, T. (2011). *Tackling homelessness and exclusion: Understanding complex lives.* https://www.jrf.org.uk/sites/default/files/jrf/migrated/files/homelessness-exclusion-services-summary.pdf

McEwan, K., & Bigelow, D. (1997). Using a logic model to focus health services on population health goals. *The Canadian Journal of Program Evaluation, 12*(1), 167–174.

McFarland, M. J., Taylor, J., McFarland, C. A. S., & Friedman, K. L. (2018). Perceived unfair treatment by police, race, and telomere length: A Nashville community-based sample of Black and white men. *Journal of Health and Social Behavior, 59*(4), 585–600. doi:10.1177/0022146518811144 PMID:30417689

McKay, T., Comfort, M., Lindquist, C., & Bir, A. (2016). If family matters: Supporting family relationships during incarceration and reentry. *Criminology & Public Policy, 15*(2), 529–542. doi:10.1111/1745-9133.12209

McKelvey, W. (2017 May 10). PA Senate approves police body camera bill the ACLU says restricts public access. *Penn Live Patriot News.* https://www.pennlive.com/politics/2017/05/police_body_cameras.html

McKenna, J.M., Martinez-Prather, K., & Bowman, S. W. (2014). The role of school-based law enforcement officer and how these roles are established: A qualitative study. *Criminal Justice Policy Review, 27*(4), 420–443. doi:10.1177/0887403414551001

McLellan, A. T. (2017). Substance misuse and substance use disorders: Why do they matter in healthcare? *Transactions of the American Clinical and Climatological Association, 128*, 112–130. PMID:28790493

McMenamin, D. (2020, August 25) *LeBron James says Black community 'terrified' of police conduct.* https://www.espn.com/nba/story/_/id/29735483/lebron-james-says-Black-community-terrified-result-police-conduct-Dave

McMurran, M. (2002). *Motivating offenders to change: a guide to enhancing engagement in therapy.* Wiley. doi:10.1002/9780470713471

McMurtry, C. L., Findling, M. G., Casey, L. S., Blendon, R. J., Benson, J. M., Sayde, J. M., & Miller, C. (2019). Discrimination in the United States: Experiences of Asian Americans. *Health Services Research, 54*(S2), 1419–1430. doi:10.1111/1475-6773.13225 PMID:31657465

Meck, S. (2018). Focusing the lens of justice: The implementation of police body cameras is a management right, not a mandatory subject of collective bargaining. *The Florida Bar Journal, 92*(4), 42–47.

Merola, L., Lum, C., Koper, C. S., & Scherer, A. (2016). *Body worn cameras and the courts: A national survey of state prosecutors (Report for the Laura and John Arnold Foundation).* Center for Evidence-Based Crime Policy, George Mason University. https://bja.ojp.gov/sites/g/files/xyckuh186/files/media/document/bwcprosecutors.pdf

Mertens, D. M. (2019). *Research and evaluation in education and psychology. In Integrating Diversity With Quantitative, Qualitative, and Mixed Methods*. Sage Publishing.

Metrick, B. (2019a July 1). Find out if your town's police officers wear body cameras: check here. *Penn-Live Patriot News*. https://www.pennlive.com/news/2019/07/does-your-local-police-department-have-body-cameras.html

Metrick, B. (2019b July 1). Police body cameras can help officers and suspects, so why don't more departments have them? *Penn-Live Patriot News*. https://www.pennlive.com/news/2019/07/why-dont-more-police-departments-have-body-cams-cost-is-the-biggest-but-not-the-only-reason.html

Mettler, S., & Sorelle, M. (2014). Policy feedback theory. In P. A. Sabatier & C. M. Weible (Eds.), *Theories of the policy process* (3rd ed., pp. 151–181). Westview Press.

Mhlongo, H. (2003). Criminal law: From the law reports: The place of criminal contempt in an open and democratic society in the light of in re Chinamasa 2001 SA 902 (ZSC). *Codicillus, South Africa*, *44*(1), 75–79.

Micucci, A. J., & Gomme, I. M. (2005). American police and subcultural support for the use of excessive force. *Journal of Criminal Justice*, *33*(5), 487–500. doi:10.1016/j.jcrimjus.2005.06.002

Miethe, T. D., Lieberman, J. D., Heen, M. S. J., & Sousa, W. H. (2019). Public attitudes about body-worn cameras in police work: A national study of the sources of their contextual variability. *Criminal Justice Review*, *44*(3), 263–283. doi:10.1177/0734016819846241

Miko, F. T., & Park, G. (2001). *Trafficking in women and children: The U.S. and international response*. Congressional Research Service. https://www.everycrsreport.com/files/20010801_RL30545_18350f9e73685f6041b54b4f929553d7088849d9.pdf

Millar, M., & Burke, L. (2012, July). Thinking beyond 'utility': Some comments on probation practice and training. *Howard Journal of Criminal Justice*, *51*(3), 317–330. doi:10.1111/j.1468-2311.2012.00711.x

Miller, J., & Crawford, B. (2018). *Ontario human rights tribunal orders province to stop segregating mentally ill inmates*. Ottawa Citizen. https://ottawacitizen.com/news/local-news/ontario-human-rights-tribunal-orders-province-to-stop-segregating-mentally-ill-inmates/

Miller, L., & Toliver, J. (2014). Implementing a body-worn camera program: recommendations and lessons learned. *US Department of Justice Online, Police Executive Research Forum*. https://www.justice.gov/iso/opa/resources/472014912134715246869.pdf

Miller, C. J. (2000). *Contempt of court* (3rd ed.). Oxford University Press.

Miller, J. M. (Ed.). (2009). *21st century criminology: A reference handbook*. Sage.

Miller, L. (2004). Good cop–bad cop: Problem officers, law enforcement culture, and strategies for success. *Journal of Police and Criminal Psychology*, *19*(2), 30–48. doi:10.1007/BF02813871

Miller, T. R., Lawrence, B. A., Carlson, N. N., Hendrie, D., Randall, S., Rockett, I. R. H., & Spicer, R. S. (2017). Perils of police action: A cautionary tale from U.S. data sets. *Injury Prevention*, *23*(1), 27–32. doi:10.1136/injuryprev-2016-042023 PMID:27457242

Miller, W., & Rollnick, S. (2002). *Motivational interviewing: Preparing people for change*. Guilford Press.

Milne, R., & Bull, R. (2008). *Interviewing victims of crime, including children and people with intellectual disabilities*. Researchgate.

Milne, R., & Bull, R. (1999). *Investigative interviewing psychology and practice*. John Wiley & Sons Ltd.

Ministry of Justice Report. (2010a). The Government of the United Kingdom.

Ministry of Justice Report. (2013). The Government of the United Kingdom.

Ministry of Justice. (2010). *Breaking the cycle: Effective punishment, rehabilitation and sentencing of offenders*. The Stationery Office.

Ministry of Justice. (2017). *Prison performance statistics 2016 to 2017*. Retrieved from https://www.gov.uk/government/statistics/prison-performance-statistics-2016-to-2017

Ministry of Statistics and Programme Implementation, Government of India. (2014). *Participation in Economy*. http://mospi.nic.in/sites/default/files/reports_and_publication/cso_social_statices_division/Chapter_4_2014.pdf

Minnesota Dept. of Corrections. (2011). *Effects of prison visitation on offender recidivism*. St. Paul, MN: Author. Retrieved from doc.state.mn.us/pages/files/large-files/Publications/11-11MNPrisonVisitationStudy.pdf

Miriam, K. (2005). Stopping the traffic in women: Power, agency, and abolition in feminist debates over sex-trafficking. *Journal of Social Philosophy*, *36*(1), 1–17. doi:10.1111/j.1467-9833.2005.00254.x

Misra, G., Mahal, A., & Shah, R. (2000). Protecting the rights of sex workers: The Indian experience. *Health and Human Rights*, *5*(1), 88. doi:10.2307/4065224 PMID:11154525

Mitchell, R. J., Ariel, B., Firpo, M. E., Fraiman, R., Castillo, F., Hyatt, J. M., Weinborn, C., & Brants Sabo, H. (2018). Measuring the effect of body-worn cameras on complaints in Latin America: The case of traffic police in Uruguay. *Policing*, *41*(4), 510–524. doi:10.1108/PIJPSM-01-2018-0004

Moffitt, T. E. (1993). Adolescence-limited and life-course-persistent antisocial behavior: A developmental taxonomy. *Psychological Review*, *100*(4), 674–701. doi:10.1037/0033-295X.100.4.674 PMID:8255953

Mohan, V., & Thakur, P. (2008) Modernizing prisons. *Times of India*.

Mohanty & Hazary. (1990). *Indian prison system*. Ashish Publishing House.

Mohindra, K. S., Haddad, S., & Narayana, D. (2012). Debt, shame, and survival: Becoming and living as widows in rural Kerala, India. *BMC International Health and Human Rights*, *12*(1), 28. doi:10.1186/1472-698X-12-28 PMID:23126457

Mohsin, A. B. (2018). The case for collecting hate crimes data in India. Law & Policy Brief, 4(9).

Monsebraaten, L. (2015). *Toronto legal clinic helps homeless fight unpayable 'nuisance' tickets*. Toronto Star. https://www.thestar.com/news/gta/2015/03/09/toronto-legal-clinic-helps-homeless-fight-unpayable-nuisance-tickets.html

Montague, S. (2000). Focusing on inputs, outputs, and outcomes: Are international approaches to performance management really so different? *The Canadian Journal of Program Evaluation*, *15*(1), 139–148.

Morabito, M. S. (2010). Understanding community policing as an innovation: Patterns of adoption. *Crime and Delinquency*, *56*(4), 564–587. doi:10.1177/0011128707311643

Morales, L., Barocio, J., Short, A. & Hashida, C. (2020, February). *The 2020-21 budget: The governor's homelessness plan*. California Legislative Analyst's Office.

Moran, D. (2012). Prisoner reintegration and the stigma of prison time inscribed on the body. *Punishment & Society*, *14*(5), 564–583. doi:10.1177/1462474512464008

Morani, N. M., Wikoff, N., Linhorst, D. M., & Bratton, S. (2011). A description of the self-identified needs, service expenditures, and social outcomes of participants of a prisoner-reentry program. *The Prison Journal*, *91*(3), 347–365. doi:10.1177/0032885511409896

Morenoff, J. D., & Harding, D. J. (2014). Incarceration, prison reentry, and communities. *Annual Review of Sociology, 40*(1), 411–429. doi:10.1146/annurev-soc-071811-145511 PMID:25400321

Morgan, A. (2009). Sex at the margins: Migration, labour markets, and the rescue industry. *Journal of Social Policy, 38*(2), 364–365. doi:10.1017/S0047279408002900

Morris, R. (1999, September 13). *Why transformative justice?* Paper presented at Reconciling and Restoring Relationships-A Responsibility for All Christians. ICCPPC World Congress, Mexico City.

Morris, H. (1968). Persons and punishment. *The Monist, 52*(4), 475–501. doi:10.5840/monist196852436

Morris, N. (1974, May). The future of imprisonment: Toward a punitive philosophy. *Michigan Law Review, 72*(6), 1161–1180.

Morris, R. (2000). *Stories of transformative justice*. Canadian Scholars' Press Inc.

Morton, D. (2018). Improving police transparency and accountability in violent encounters with African Americans. *Journal of African American Studies, 22*(1), 125–138. doi:10.100712111-018-9396-6

Mowen, T. J., & Visher, C. A. (2016). Changing the ties that bind: How incarceration impacts family relationships. *Criminology & Public Policy, 15*(2), 503–528. doi:10.1111/1745-9133.12207

Mowen, T., & Brent, J. (2016). School discipline as a turning point: The cumulative effect of suspension on arrest. *Journal of Research in Crime and Delinquency, 53*(5), 628–653. doi:10.1177/0022427816643135

Mrazek, P. J., & Mrazek, D. A. (1987). Resilience in child maltreatment victims: A conceptual exploration. *Child Abuse & Neglect, 11*(3), 357–366. doi:10.1016/0145-2134(87)90009-3 PMID:3676892

Muirhead, J., & Fortune, C. (2016). Yoga in prisons: A review of the literature. *Aggression and Violent Behavior, 28*, 57–63. doi:10.1016/j.avb.2016.03.013

Müller, N. (2020). *Nigeria's police work between international reform ideas and national security arrangements* (PRIF Working Papers, 48). Frankfurt am Main: Hessische Stiftung Friedens-und Konfliktforschung. https://nbnresolving.org/urn:nbn:de:0168-ssoar-69033-6

Murphy, E. (2016 October 14). Body cam catches groomsmen's dance practice after police respond to noise complaint. *ABC News*. https://abcnews.go.com/Lifestyle/body-cam-catches-groomsmens-dance-practice-police-respond/story?id=42810933

Murphy, F. (2011). Archives of sorrow: An exploration of Australia's Stolen Generations and their journey into the past. *History and Anthropology, 22*(4), 481–495. doi:10.1080/02757206.2011.626775

Murphy, K. (2015). Does procedural justice matter to youth? Comparing adults' and youths' willingness to collaborate with police. *Policing and Society, 25*(1), 53–76. doi:10.1080/10439463.2013.802786

Musu-Gillette, L., Zhang, A., Wang, K., Zhang, J., Kemp, J., Diliberti, M., & Oudekerk, B. A. (2018). *Indicators of school crime and safety: 2017 (NCES 2018-036/NCJ 251413)*. Washington, DC: National Center for Education Statistics, U.S. Department of Education, and Bureau of justice Statistics, Office of Justice Programs, U.S. Department of Justice.

Musu, L., Zhang, A., Wang, K., Zhang, J., & Oudekerk, B. A. (2019). *Indicators of school crime and safety: 2018 (NCES 2019-047/NCJ 252571)*. National Center for Education Statistics. U.S. Department of Education, and Bureau of Justice Statics, Office of Justice Programs, U.S. Department of Justice.

Myers, N. M. (2017). Eroding the presumption of innocence: Pre-trial detention and the use of conditional release on bail. *British Journal of Criminology, 57*(3), 664–683.

NAACP. (2005). *Interrupting the school to prison pipeline*. Washington, DC: NAACP.

Na, C., & Gottfredson, D. C. (2013). Police officers in schools: Effects on school crime and the processing of offending behaviors. *Justice Quarterly, 30*(4), 619–650. doi:10.1080/07418825.2011.615754

Nadozie, E. (2017, December 23). How I founded SARS in the Police- RTD CP Medinda. *Vanguard.* https://www.vanguardngr.com/2017/12/founded-sars-police-rtd-cp-midenda/

Nagata, D. K. (1993). *Legacy of injustice: Exploring the cross-generational impact of the Japanese American internment.* Plenum Press. doi:10.1007/978-1-4899-1118-6

Nagata, D. K. (1998). Intergenerational effects of the Japanese American internment. In Y. Danieli (Ed.), *International handbook of multigenerational legacies of trauma* (pp. 125–139). Plenum Press. doi:10.1007/978-1-4757-5567-1_8

Nagata, D. K., & Cheng, W. J. Y. (2003). Intergenerational communication of race-related trauma by Japanese American former internees. *The American Journal of Orthopsychiatry, 73*(3), 266–278. doi:10.1037/0002-9432.73.3.266 PMID:12921207

Nagata, D. K., Trierweiler, S. J., & Talbot, R. (1999). Long-term effects of internment during early childhood on third-generation Japanese Americans. *The American Journal of Orthopsychiatry, 69*(1), 19–29. doi:10.1037/h0080378 PMID:9990433

Nagin, D. S. (2013). Deterrence in the twenty-first century. *Crime and Justice, 42*(1), 199–263. doi:10.1086/670398

Najdowski, C. J., Bottoms, B. L., & Goff, P. A. (2015). Stereotype threat and racial differences in citizens' experiences of police encounters. *Law and Human Behavior, 39*(5), 463–477. doi:10.1037/lhb0000140 PMID:26030449

Nangia, A. (1997). The tragedy of bride burning in India: How should the law address it. *Brooklyn Journal of International Law, 22*(3), 637-694. https://brooklynworks.brooklaw.edu/bjil/vol22/iss3/4

Naqvi, R. H., Ibrar, M., & Bangash, S. (2011). Cultural history of Indian subcontinent; with special reference to arts and music. *JL & Soc'y, 41*, 37.

Nargis, S. (2019). Prisoners, their rights and reformation. *International Journal of Engineering and Management Research, 9*(4), 1–5. Advance online publication. doi:10.31033/ijemr.9.4.1

National Academies of Sciences, Engineering, and Medicine. (2018). Proactive policing: Effects on crime and communities. *The National Academies Press.* https://www.nap.edu/resource/24928/Race.pdf

National Aids Control Organisation. (2012). *The National AIDS Control Programme Phase III. (2007-2012).* http://www.naco.gov.in/sites/default/files/NACP%20III%20-

National Association of Drug Court Professionals (NADCP). (2020). *Treatment Courts.* https://www.nadcp.org

National Association of School Resource Officers. (2021). https://www.nasro.org/faq/

National Conference of State Legislators (NCSL). (2018). Body-worn-camera data. *NCSL Online.* https://www.ncsl.org/research/civil-and-criminal-justice/body-worn-cameras-interactive-graphic.aspx#/

National Crime Records Bureau. (2017). *Prison statistics India.* Ministry of Home Affairs.

National Institute of Education. (1978). *Violent schools – Safe schools: The safe school study report to congress.* U.S. Government Printing Office.

National Institute on Drug Abuse (NIDA). (2016). *Understanding drug abuse and addiction: What science says.* https://www.drugabuse.gov/publications/teaching-addiction-science/understanding-drug-abuse-addiction-what-science-says

Navsarjan Trust. (2014). *Who are the Dalits?* https://navsarjantrust.org/who-are-dalits/

Ndubuisi. J. M., and Olumide, K.O (2020). Assessment of the role of the Nigerian police force in the promotion and protection of human rights in Nigeria. *Annual Survey of International Comparative Law*, *23*(1), 19-30.

Nelson, L., & Lind, D. (2015). *The school to prison pipeline, explained.* The Policy Institute. https://www.justicepolicy.org/news/8775

Network on Police Reform in Nigeria. (2010). Criminal force: Torture, abuse, and extrajudicial killings by the Nigeria police force. New York: Open Society Justice Initiative.

Newman, L. (2018 August 11). Police bodycams can be hacked to doctor footage. *Wired.* https://www.wired.com/story/police-body-camera-vulnerabilities/

Nigeria Police Force (2020). *ICT Department.* NPF.

Nigerian Security Tracker –Council on Foreign Relations weekly update. (n.d.). https://www.cfr.org/nigeria/nigeria-security-tracker/p29483

Nigusse, D. G. (2013). *Contempt of court: A comparative study between South Africa and Ethiopia. Open Science Repository Law.*

Nix, J., Todak, N., & Tregle, B. (2020). Understanding body-worn-camera diffusion in U.S. policing. *Police Quarterly*, *23*(3), 396–422. doi:10.1177/1098611120917937

Nix, J., & Wolfe, S. E. (2015). The impact of negative publicity on police self-legitimacy. *Justice Quarterly*, *34*(1), 84–108. doi:10.1080/07418825.2015.1102954

Noble, A. (2015). *Beyond housing first: A holistic response to family homelessness in Canada.* Raising The Roof. https://www.homelesshub.ca/resource/beyond-housing-first-holistic-response-family-homelessness-canada

O'Brien, P. (1995). The prison on the continent: Europe 1865-1965. In N. Morris & D. Rothman (Eds.), *The Oxford history of prisons: The practise of punishment in western society* (pp. 178–201). Oxford University Press.

O'Grady, W., & Lafleur, R. (2016, November). *Reintegration in Ontario: Practices, priorities, and effective models.* John Howard Society of Ontario. https://johnhoward.on.ca/wp-content/uploads/2016/11/Reintegration-in-Ontario-Final.pdf

O'Brien, R., Karthaus, R., & Marshall, J. (2014). *RSA Transitions: Building a Rehabilitative Culture.* Academic Press.

Odeljan, R., Butorac, K., & Bailey, A. (2015). *Investigative interview with children.* Research Gate.

Odey, R. (2017). *Corruption, harassment, and injustice. Unlawful conduct of the Nigerian police towards civilians.* GRIN Verlag. https://www.grin.com/document/354593

Ojukwu, E. C. (2016). *Discovering the police: An excursion into police personality, powers, performance, and prudence.* Kraft Books Limited.

Okenyodo, O. (2016). Governance, accountability, and security in Nigeria. *Africa Security Brief, 31.*

Okey Ordu, G. E., & Nnam, M. U. (2017). Community policing in Nigeria: A critical analysis of current developments. *International Journal of Criminal Justice Sciences*, *12*(1), 83–97.

Okocha, C. (2020, August 26). Govs will not be responsible for funding of community policing, Says Akeredolu. *This Day.* https://www.thisdaylive.com/index.php/2020/08/26/

Oladipo, S. B. (2013). Ethnicity and marginalization within the Nigerian state: A case study of the Nigeria police force. *Research on Humanities and Social Sciences, 3*(1), 79–85.

Oloyede, F., & Elega, A. A. (2019) Exploring hashtag activism in Nigeria: A case of #Endsars campaign. In *Conference Proceeding: 5th In Communication and Media Studies (CRPC 2018).* https:// crcp.emu.edu.tr/Documents/Books/CRCP%202018%20Proceeding%20Book%20-%20Approved%20One

Olusegun, O. J. (2016). Community policing in south-west Nigeria: Finding a nexus between the police and the people. *Journal of Education and Practice, 7*(23), 29–35.

Oluwafifehan, O. (2019). *Protest against SARS in Nigeria.* Credit/opinionnigeria.com.

Omilana, T. (2019). Police abuse of power and limits of punishments. 17th April 2021: Twitter/NGR Senate. Police Act Cap., LFN 2004.

Onyeozili, E. C. (2005, April). Obstacles to effective policing in Nigeria. *African Journal of Criminology and Justice Studies, 1*(1).

Orbach, Y., & Shiloach, H. (2007). Reluctant disclosures of child sexual abuse. In E. M. Pipe, E. M. Lamb, Y. Orbach, & C. A. Cederborg (Eds.), *Child sexual abuse: Disclosure, delay and denial* (pp. 115–134). Taylor & Francis Group.

Oriola, T. (2020, October 20). General Buratai: Leave the army out of #EndSARS protest. *Premium Times.* https:// opinion.premiumtimesng.com

Ortiz, R. (2019 December 20). Fort Worth police officer who fatally shot Atatiana Jefferson indicted on murder charge. *NBC News.* https://www.nbcnews.com/news/us-news/fort-worth-police-officer-who-fatally-shot-atatiana-jefferson-indicted-n1105916

OSCE. (2009). *Decision No. 9/09 on combating hate crimes.* https://www.osce.org/cio/40695

Owen, O. (2018). Police reform in Nigeria: The devolution debate. Monograph Series. No 30, CLEEN Foundation.

Owens, C., & Finn, W. (2018). Body-worn video through the lens of a cluster randomized controlled trial in London: Implications for future research. *Policing. Journal of Policy Practice, 12*(1), 77–82.

Padwa, H., Meldrum, M., Friedman, J. R., & Braslow, J. T. (2016). A mental health system in recovery: The era of deinstitutionalisation in California. In D. Kritsotaki, V. Long, & M. Smith (Eds.), *Deinstitutionalisation and after: Post-war psychiatry in the western world* (pp. 241–265). Palgrave Macmillan.

Paez, R. A., & Dierenfeldtb, R. (2020). Community policing and youth offending: A comparison of large and small jurisdictions in the United States. *International Journal of Adolescence and Youth, 1*(25), 140–153. doi:10.1080/02673843.2019.1601115

Palakkappillil, J., & Prasanna, C. K. (2017). Criminality among youth and recidivism. *The Journal of Development Practice*, 3.

Palmater, P. (2016). Shining light on the dark places: Addressing police racism and sexualized violence against indigenous women and girls in the National Inquiry. *Canadian Journal of Women and the Law, 28*(2), 253–284. doi:10.3138/cjwl.28.2.253

Palmer, L. K., Frantz, C. E., Armsworth, M. W., Swank, P., Copley, J. V., & Bush, G. A. (1999). Neuropsychological sequelae of chronically psychologically traumatized children: Specific findings in memory and higher cognitive functions. In L. M. Williams & V. L. Banyard (Eds.), *Trauma & memory* (pp. 229–244). Sage Publications, Inc.

Patel, C. (2020). Tackling police racism. *The World Today, 76*(4), 12–15.

Paterson, B. (2001). *Improving children's eyewitness memory: Cognitive and social considerations* (Unpublished PhD dissertation). University of Portsmouth.

Pati, A. K., & Mitra, S. (2011). *Crime and correctional administration. MSW paper-12*. Netaji Subhas Open University.

Patterson, E. J., & Wildeman, C. (2015). Mass imprisonment and the life course revisited: Cumulative years spent imprisoned and marked for working-age black and white men. *Social Science Research*, *53*, 325–337. doi:10.1016/j.ssresearch.2015.06.011 PMID:26188457

Patterson, G. (2007). The role of police officers in elementary and secondary schools: Implications for police-school social work collaboration. *School Social Work Journal*, *31*(2), 82–99.

Patterson, J. (1995). Community policing: Learning the lessons of history. *FBI Law Enforcement Bulletin*, *64*(11), 5.

Payne, A. (2020, March 17). Iran has released 85,000 prisoners in an emergency bid to stop the spread of the coronavirus. *Business Insider*. https://www.businessinsider.in/politics/news/iran-has-released-85000-prisoners-in-an-emergency-bid-to-stop-the-spread-of-the-coronavirus/articleshow/74674415.cms

Pelfrey, W. V. Jr. (2004). The inchoate nature of community policing: Differences between community policing and traditional police officers. *Justice Quarterly*, *21*(3), 579–601. doi:10.1080/07418820400095911

Pelura, G. (2020). Note: Section 1983 & Qualified Immunity: Qualifying the death of due process and Americas Most Vulnerable Classes since 1871. Can it Be Fixed. *William & Mary Journal of Race, Gender, and Social Justice*, *26*, 749. https: advance-lexis.com.ezp.waldenulibary.org

Pennsylvania Commission on Crime and Delinquency (PCCD). (2020). Body-worn camera policy recommendations. *Pennsylvania Commission on Crime and Delinquency Online*. https://www.pccd.pa.gov/criminaljustice/advisory_boards/Documents/BWC%20Policy%20Recommendations%20Commission%20Approved.pdf

Pennsylvania District Attorneys Association (PDAA). (2018). Pennsylvania district attorneys issue best practices on body-worn cameras. *Pennsylvania District Attorneys Association Online*. https://www.pdaa.org/pennsylvania-district-attorneys-issue-best-practices-on-body-worn-cameras/

Pennsylvania Law Enforcement Accreditation Commission (PALEAC). (2020). LEAC Standards Manual. *LEAC Online*. https://pcpa.memberclicks.net/assets/docs/AccreditationDocuments/Standards%20Manual%20AUGUST%202020%20FINAL.pdf

Perez, N. M., Bromley, M., & Cochran, J. (2017). Organizational commitment among sheriffs' deputies during the shift to community-oriented policing. *Policing*, *40*(2), 321–355. doi:10.1108/PIJPSM-04-2016-0051

Perry, B. (2009). Impacts of disparate policing in Indian country. *Policing and Society*, *19*(3), 263–281. doi:10.1080/10439460902871348

Petersilia, J. (1999). Parole and prisoner reentry in the United States. *Crime and Justice*, *26*, 479–529. doi:10.1086/449302

Petersilia, J. (2003). *When prisoners come home: parole and prisoner reentry*. Oxford University Press.

Peterson, J. K., Kennealy, P., Skeem, J., Bray, B., & Zvonkovic, A. (2014). How often and how consistently do symptoms directly precede criminal behavior among offenders with mental illness? *Law and Human Behavior*, *38*(5), 439–449.

Petit, B., & Western, B. (2004). Mass imprisonment and the life course: Race and class inequality in U.S. incarceration. *American Sociological Review*, *69*(2), 151–169. doi:10.1177/000312240406900201

Petteruti, A. (2011). *Education under arrest: The case against schools*. Justice Policy Institute.

Pettit, B., & Gutierrez, C. (2018). Mass incarceration and racial inequality. *American Journal of Economics and Sociology, 77*(3–4), 1153–1182. doi:10.1111/ajes.12241

Peyton, K., Sierra-Arévalo, M., & Rand, D. (2019). A field experiment on community policing and police legitimacy. *Proceedings of the National Academy of Sciences of the United States of America, 116*(40), 19894–19898. doi:10.1073/pnas.1910157116 PMID:31527240

Phillips, L. A., & Spencer, W. M. (2013). The challenges of re-entry from prison to society. *Journal of Current Issues in Crime, Law, and Law Enforcement, 6*(2), 123–133.

Piat, M., Polvere, L., Kirst, M., Voronka, J., Zabkiewicz, D., Plante, M., Isaak, C., Nolin, D., Nelson, G., & Goering, P. (2014). Pathways into homelessness: Understanding how both individual and structural factors contribute to and sustain homelessness in Canada. *Urban Studies (Edinburgh, Scotland), 52*(10), 2366–2382.

Picard, A. (2017, June 1). *The mentally ill are sick. So why do we put them in jail.* TVO Current Affairs. https://www.tvo.org/article/the-mentally-ill-are-sick-so-why-do-we-put-them-in-jail

Polat, O. (2015). Tüm Boyutlarıyla Pedofili. *Adli Tıp Bülteni., 1*, 60–70.

Polat, O. (2017). *Tüm boyutlarıyla çocuk istismarı.* Seçkin.

Polcin, D., Korcha, R., Bond, J., & Galloway, G. (2010). What did we learn from our study on sober living houses and where do we go from here? *Journal of Psychoactive Drugs, 42*(4), 425–433.

Police Executive Research Forum (PERF). (2016). *Guiding principles on use of force.* https://www.policeforum.org/assets/30%20guiding%20principles.pdf

Police Executive Research Forum. (2018). Cost and benefits of body-worn camera deployments. *Police Executive Research Forum Online.* https://www.policeforum.org/assets/BWCCostBenefit.pdf

Policing prostitution in India: An examination of field experiences at Mumbai. (n.d.). *International Journal of Criminal Justice Sciences, 13*(1), 68–76. doi:10.5281/zenodo.1403388

Pontes, C. (2017). Can bad police officers be kept off the streets? giving control back to the police chiefs. *Journal of California Law Enforcement, 51*(2), 15–20. https://ezp.waldenulibrary.org/login?qurl=https%3A%2F%2Fwww.proquest.com%2Ftrade-journals%2Fcan-bad-police-officers-be-kept-off-streets%2Fdocview%2F1937605636%2Fse-2%3Faccountid%3D14872

Poon, B., Leung, J. W., Louie, A., & Dios, C. V. (2012). The key functions of collaborative logic modelling: Insights from the British Columbia early childhood dental programs. *The Canadian Journal of Program Evaluation, 27*, 87–102.

Poppe, B. (2018, March). *Unlocking doors to homelessness prevention: Solutions for preventing homelessness and eviction.* Eviction and Homelessness Prevention Research Project. https://static1.squarespace.com/static/59e4bd08d7bdce1e8a5b15bb/t/5ac2302d03ce648731d78cfd/1522675761270/Eviction++Homelessness+Prevention+Research+Report_FINAL_33018.pdf

Potterat, J. J., Rothenberg, R. B., Muth, S. Q., Darrow, W. W., & Phillips-Plummer, L. (1998). Pathways to prostitution: The chronology of sexual and drug abuse milestones. *Journal of Sex Research, 35*(4), 333–340. https://doi.org/10.1080/00224499809551951

Powell, T. (2017 June 27). Body-worn camera captures heart-warming moment police officer serenades elderly blind woman. *Evening Standard.* https://www.standard.co.uk/news/world/heartwarming-moment-police-officer-serenades-elderly-blind-woman-caught-on-bodycam-a3574226.html

Pozzulo, D. J. (2007). Person description and identification by child witnesses. In L. C. R. Lindsay, F. D. Ross, D. J. Read, & P. M. Toglia (Eds.), (pp. 283–308). The handbook of eyewitness psychology. Lawrence Erlbaum Pub.

Priya, T. (2014). *Reformative theory of punishment*. Acadamike Law Journal Knowledge Centre.

Public Safety Canada. (1998, January). *Adult offender diversion programs*. https://www.publicsafety.gc.ca/cnt/rsrcs/pblctns/ffndr-dvrsn/index-en.aspx

Puducherry Police. (n.d.). *Powers of police to arrest, procedure of arrest, and documentation of arrest*. https://police.py.gov.in/Police%20manual/Chapter%20PDF/CHAPTER%2038%20C%20Powers%20of%20Police%20to%20arrest,%20procedure%20of%20arrest,%20and%20documentatio.pdf

Quas, A. J., & Sumaroka, M. (2011). Consequences of legal involvement on child victims of maltreatment. In E. M. Lamb, L. J. D. Rooy, C. L. Malloy, & C. Katz (Eds.), *Children's testimony: A handbook of psychological research and forensic practices* (pp. 323–350). John Wiley & Sons Ltd.

Quinney, R., & Wildeman, J. (1991). *The problem of crime: A peace and social justice perspective*. Mayfield Pub Co Publication.

Quinn, R. C., & Hope, C. E., & Cryer-Couper, Q. R. (2019). Neighborhood cohesion and procedural justice in policing among Black adults: The moderating role of cultural race-related stress. *Journal of Community Psychology*. Advance online publication. doi:10/1002/jcop.22251

Radvansky, G. A. (2011). *Human memory*. Routledge.

Raghavan, V. (2008). Prison reforms and some fundamentals. *The Hindu*. https://www.thehinducentre.com/the-arena/current-issues/article9805239.ece

Raine, A. (2013). *The psychopathology of crime: Criminal behavior as a clinical disorder*. Elsevier.

Ramey, D. M. (2016). The influence of early school punishment and therapy/medication on social control experience during young adulthood. *Criminology*, *54*(1), 113–141. doi:10.1111/1745-9125.12095

Rao, R. J. (2012). Conscientious: A relevant personality factor in criminal behavior. *International Journal of Multidisciplinary Educational Research*, *1*(2), 398–409. http://www.ijmer.in/pdf/volume1-issue2-2012/398-409.pdf

Raphael, S., Loftstrom, M., & Martin, B. (2017, April). *The effects of California's enhanced drug and contraband interdiction program on drug abuse and inmate misconduct in California's prisons*. California Department of Corrections and Rehabilitation Policy Briefing. https://nicic.gov/effects-california-s-enhanced-drug-and-contraband-interdiction-program-drug-abuse-and-inmate

Ray, A. (1978). Police administration and centre-state relations in India. *The Indian Journal of Public Administration*, *24*(1), 38–44.

Ray, J. M. (Ed.). (2014). *Rethinking community policing*. LFB Scholarly Publishing.

Ready, J., & Young, J. (2020 October 1). The unfulfilled potential of police body cameras in the Era of Black lives matter. *Slate*. https://slate.com/technology/2020/10/black-lives-matter-police-body-cameras.html

Ready, J., & Young, J. (2015). The impact of on-officer video cameras on police-citizen contacts: Findings from a controlled experiment in Mesa, AZ. *Journal of Experimental Criminology*, *11*(3), 445–458. doi:10.100711292-015-9237-8

Reardon, C. M. (2013). Cell phone, police recording and the intersection of the first and fourth amendments. *Duke Law Journal*, *63*(3), 735–779.

Reaves, B. (2010). *Local police departments, 2007.* U.S. Department of Justice, Bureau of Justice Studies, Office of Justice Programs. https://www.bjs.gov/content/pub/pdf/lpd07.pdf

Reinwald, C. H. (2020). A one-two punch: How qualified immunity's double dose of reasonableness dooms excessive force claims in the fourth circuit. *North Carolina Law Review*, *98*(3), 665–687. https://scholarship.law.unc.edu/nclr/vol98/iss3/7

Reisig, M. D. (2010). Community and problem-oriented policing. *Crime and Justice*, *39*(1), 1–53. doi:10.1086/652384

Reisig, M. D., Bales, W., Hay, C., & Wang, X. (2007). The effect of racial inequality on black male recidivism. *Justice Quarterly*, *24*(3), 3408–3434. doi:10.1080/07418820701485387

Ren, L., Zhao, J., & He, N. (2019). Broken windows theory and citizen engagement. *Justice Quarterly*, *36*(1), 1–30. do i:10.1080/07418825.2017.1374434

Report on the National Consultation on Prison Reform. (2010). New Delhi: Academic Press.

Rewane, O. N. (1957). Contempt of court in Nigerian criminal law. *Journal of African Law*, *1*(3), 172–185. doi:10.1017/S0021855300002266

Richie, B. (2001). Challenges incarcerated women face as they return to their communities: Findings from life history interviews. *Crime and Delinquency*, *47*(3), 368–389. doi:10.1177/0011128701047003005

Rios, V. M. (2011). *Punished: Policing the Lives of Black and Latino Boys*. NYU Press.

Ritter, K., West, J., & Trotzer, J. (1987). Comparing family counseling and group counseling: An interview with George Gazda, James Hansen, and Alan Hovestadt. *Journal of Counseling and Development*, *65*(6), 295–300. doi:10.1002/j.1556-6676.1987.tb01289.x

Roberts, D. E. (2004). The social and moral cost of mass incarceration in African American communities. *Stanford Law Review*, *56*(5), 1271–1305.

Robinson, G., & McNeill, F. (2008). Exploring the dynamics of compliance with community penalties. *Theoretical Criminology*, *12*(4), 431–449. doi:10.1177/1362480608097151

Romanucci, A., Raveendran, B., & Burton, C. (2020, September). Confronting Qualified Immunity and the 'Reasonable 'Officer Standard. *Trial (Boston, Mass.)*, *56*(9), 24. https: links.gale.com

Ropes Berry, K., Kennedy, C., Lloyd, M., Veeh, C. A., & Tripodi, S. J. (2020). The Intersectional Effects of Race and Gender on Time to Reincarceration. *Justice Quarterly*, *37*(1), 132–160. doi:10.1080/07418825.2018.1524508

Rosenbaum, D. P., & Lurigio, A. J. (1994). Inside look at community policing reform: Definitions, organizational changes, and evaluation findings. *Crime and Delinquency*, *3*(40), 299–314. doi:10.1177/0011128794040003001

Ruddell, R., & May, D. C. (2011). Challenging our perceptions of rural policing: An examination of school resource officers in rural and urban Kentucky schools. *Journal of Anthropology and Sociology*, *1*(1), 1–14.

Rydberg, J., & Grommon, E. (2016). A multimethod examination of the dynamics of recidivism during reentry. *Corrections: Policy, Practice and Research*, *1*(1), 40–60. doi:10.1080/23774657.2016.1105660

Sable, V. (2020). *Yerwada Jail Visit- Prison Reforms in India.* Academic Press.

Sabol, W. J., & Couture, H. (2008). *Prison inmates at midyear 2007.* U.S. Department of Justice, Office of Justice Programs. doi:10.1037/e456192008-001

Sacharoff, L., & Lustbader, S. (2017). Who should own police body camera videos? *Washington University Law Review*, *95*(2), 269.

Sagade, J., & Forster, C. (2018). Recognising the human rights of female sex workers in India: Moving from prohibition to decriminalisation and a pro-work model. *Indian Journal of Gender Studies*, *25*(1), 26–46. https://doi.org/10.1177/0971521517738450

Saha, T., & Srivastava, A. (2014). Indian women at risk in the cyber space: A conceptual model of reasons of victimization. *International Journal of Cyber Criminology*, *8*(1).

Sahni, R., & Shankar, V. K. (2013, February). *Sex work and its linkages with informal labour markets in India: Findings from the first pan-India survey of female sex workers* (No. 416). Institute of Development Studies. https://onlinelibrary.wiley.com/doi/pdfdirect/10.1111/j.2040-0209.2013.00416.x

Samaha, A. (2012). Regulation for the sake of appearance. *Harvard Law Review*, *125*, 1563. https://harvardlawreview.org/2012/05/regulation-for-the-sake-of-appearance/

Samenow, S. E. (1984). *Inside the criminal mind.* Random House.

Sanchez-Meier, S., Johnston, F. E., & Vanhasselt, V. B. (2002). Multi-Family Group Therapy for Families of Incarcerated Felons. *Justice Quarterly*, *37*(1), 132–160. doi:10.1300/J189v01n02_04

Sandhu, A. (2017). 'I'm glad that was on camera': A case study of police officers' perceptions of cameras. *Policing and Society*, *29*(2), 223–235. doi:10.1080/10439463.2017.1285917

Santtila, P., Korkman, J., & Sandnabba, K. (2004). Effects of interview phase, repeated interviewing, presence of a support serson and anatomically detailed dolls on child sexual abuse interviews. *Psychology, Crime & Law*, *10*, 21–35.

Sanyal, S. (2019). *Rehabilitation of the adult prisoners in the country.* New Delhi Publishers.

Sarre, R., & Langos, C. (2014). Policing young people: Can the notion of police legitimacy play a role? *Journal of the Institute of Justice & International Studies*, *13*, 1–10.

Sattar, R. G. (2000). *The interviewing and preparation of child witnesses for legal purposes* (Unpublished PhD dissertation). University of Portsmouth.

Saulnier, A., Burke, K. C., & Bottoms, B. L. (2019). The effects of body-worn camera footage and eyewitness race on jurors' perceptions of police use of force. *Behavioral Sciences & the Law*, *37*(6), 732–750. doi:10.1002/bsl.2443 PMID:31997421

Saunders, J., & Kilmer, B. (2019). Changing the narrative: Police–community partnerships and racial reconciliation. *Justice Quarterly*, 1–25. doi:10.1080/07418825.2019.1568520

Saywitz, J. K., & Camparo, B. L. (2009). Contemporary child forensic interviewing: Evolving consensus and innovation over 25 years. In L. B. Bottoms, J. C. Najdowski, & S. G. Goodman (Eds.), *Children as victims, witnesses and offenders, Psychological science and law* (pp. 102–127). The Guildford Press.

Schaeffer, C. M., & Borduin, C. M. (1999). Mother-adolescent-sibling conflict in families of juvenile felons. *The Journal of Genetic Psychology*, *160*(1), 115–118. doi:10.1080/00221329909595386 PMID:10048216

Schindler, A. (2020 December 3). JSO: Dislodged police body cameras "'non-issue;'" public concerned about transparency. *ABC First Coast News*. https://www.firstcoastnews.com/article/news/local/dislodged-body-worn-cameras-hinder-transparency-but-are-not-tracked-by-jso/77-666a8644-0191-4c90-b40c-5a18d6f7c90e

Schrag, C. (1961). Preliminary criminal typology. *Pacific Sociological Review*, *4*(1), 11–16. doi:10.2307/1388481

Schrag, J., & Scotchmer, S. (1997). The self-reinforcing nature of crime. *International Review of Law and Economics*, *17*(3), 325–335. doi:10.1016/S0144-8188(97)00025-2

Schwartsz, M. (2015). *Policing and (in)security in fragile and conflict affected settings: A review of perspectives on policing in sub-Saharan Africa*. Knowledge Platform Security and Rule of Law, Global Centre on Cooperative Security.

Schwartz, J. C. (2020). After Qualified Immunity. *Columbia Law Review, 120*(2), 309–388.

Shawyer, A., Milne, B., & Bull, R. (2009). Investigative interviewing in the UK. In T. Williamson, B. Milne, & P. S. Savage (Eds.), *International developments in investigative interviewing* (pp. 24–38). Willan Pub.

Shingal, A. (2015). The devadasi system: Temple prostitution in India. *UCLA Women's Law Journal, 22*(1), 107. https://escholarship.org/uc/item/37z853br

Siegel, L. J. (2008). *Criminology: The core*. Thomas Higher Education.

Siegfried, M. L. (2001). The promises and problematics of reentry court. *Criminal Justice Studies, 14*(2–3), 201–219.

Simpson, D. D. (2004). A conceptual framework for drug treatment process and outcomes. *Journal of Substance Abuse Treatment, 27*(2), 99–121. doi:10.1016/j.jsat.2004.06.001 PMID:15450644

Sinanan, N.A. (2015). Trauma and treatment of child sexual abuse. *Journal of Trauma & Treatment*, 1-5. doi:. doi:10.4172/2167-1222.S4-024

Singh, A.A., Chung, Y. B., & Dean, J.K. (2006). Acculturation Level and Internalized Homophobia of Asian American Lesbian and Bisexual Women. *Journal of LGBTQ Issues in Counseling, 1*(2), 3-19. doi:10.1300/J462v01n02_02

Sinha, S. (2014). Reasons for women's entry into sex work: A case study of Kolkata, India. *Sexuality & Culture, 19*(1), 216–235. doi:10.100712119-014-9256-z

Sinha, M. (1999). Sex, structural violence, and AIDS: Case studies of Indian prostitutes. *Women's Studies Quarterly, 27*(1/2), 65–72. https://www.jstor.org/stable/40003399

Skinner-Osei, P., & Stepteau-Watson, D. (2018). A qualitative analysis of African American fathers' struggle with reentry, recidivism, and reunification after participation in re-entry programs. *Journal of Human Behavior in the Social Environment, 28*(2), 240–255. doi:10.1080/10911359.2017.1402724

Skogan, W. (2006). Advocate - The promise of community policing. In D. Weisburd & A. Braga (Eds.), *Police Innovations: Contrasting Perspectives* (pp. 27–43). Cambridge University Press. http://www.ncjrs.gov/policing/use139.htm

Skogan, W. G. (1994). The impact of community policing on neighborhood residents: A cross-site analysis. In D. P. Rosenbaum (Ed.), *The challenge of community policing: Testing the promises* (pp. 167–181). Sage. doi:10.4135/9781483327006.n9

Smith, B. (1998). Children in custody: 20-year trends in juvenile detention, correctional, and shelter facilities. *Crime and Delinquency, 44*(4), 526–543. doi:10.1177/0011128798044004004

Smykla, J. O., Crow, M. S., Crichlow, V. J., & Snyder, J. A. (2015). Police body-worn cameras: Perceptions of law enforcement leadership. *American Journal of Criminal Justice, 41*(3), 424–443. doi:10.100712103-015-9316-4

Snyder, H., & Sickmund, M. (2006). *Juvenile offenders and victims: 2006 national report. office of juvenile justice and delinquency prevention*. U.S. Department of Justice.

SO Panel. (2012). *Police Reform in Nigeria*. Civic Society Final Report.

Social Work Licensing Requirements. (2020). *Educational Requirements for a Social Work License*. https://socialworklicensure.org/articles/social-work-license-requirements/

Soeharno, J. (2016). *The integrity of the judge: A philosophical inquiry*. Routledge. doi:10.4324/9781315556697

Solis, J., Franco-Paredes, C., Henao-Martınez, A. F., Krsak, M., & Zimmer, S. M. (2020). Structural Vulnerability in the United States Revealed in Three Waves of Novel Coronavirus Disease (COVID-19). *The American Journal of Tropical Medicine and Hygiene*. Advance online publication. doi:10.4269/ajtmh.20-0391 PMID:32383432

Somerville, P. (2009). Understanding community policing. *Policing*, *32*(2), 261–277. doi:10.1108/13639510910958172

Soothill, K. (2010). Sex offender recidivism. *Crime and Justice*, *39*, 145.

Sousa, W. H., Miethe, T. D., & Sakiyama, M. (2018). Inconsistencies in public opinion of body-worn cameras on police: Transparency, trust, and improved Police–Citizen relationships. *Policing. Journal of Policy Practice*, *12*(1), 100–108.

Southall, A. (2020 November 30). Police body cameras cited as 'powerful tool' against stop-and-frisk abuses. *The New York Times*. https://www.nytimes.com/2020/11/30/nyregion/nypd-body-cameras.html

SpearIt. (2011). Gender violence in prison & hyper-masculinities in the hood: Cycles of destructive masculinity. Washington University of Law & Policy, 37(5), 89-147.

Special Correspondent. (2019). *Amnesty report: Hate crimes rose sharply the first half of 2019*. Published in https://www.thehindu.com/news/national/amnesty-report-hate-crimes-rose-sharply-the-first-half-of-2019/article29598191.ece

Srinivas, M. N. (1966). *Caste: Its twentieth century avatar*. Viking.

Srivastava, S. P. (1977). *The Indian prison community*. Pustak Kendra.

Staff, J. (2015). *State police to probe 'takedown' of student by officer that led to protest, arrests at Pawtucket school*. https://www.providencejournal.com/article/20151015/NEWS/151019570

Starr, S. B., & Rehavi, M. M. (2013). Mandatory sentencing and racial disparity: Assessing the role of prosecutors and the effects of booker. *The Yale Law Journal*, *123*(1), 2–80.

State of Vermont. (2020 June 23). Testimony provided to the house government operations and judiciary committees on S.B. 219 and S.B. 119. *State of Vermont Online*. https://legislature.vermont.gov/Documents/2020/WorkGroups/House%20Government%22Operations/Bills/S.219/Written%20Testimony/S.219~James%20Lyall~ACLU-VT%20Written%20Testimony~6-24-2020.pdf

Stein, M. D., Flori, J. N., Risi, M. M., Conti, M. T., Anderson, B. J., & Bailey, G. L. (2017). Overdose history is associated with post-detoxification treatment preference for persons with opioid use disorder. *Substance abuse*, *38*(4), 389–393. https://doi.org/10.1080/08897077.2017.1353570

Stelloh, T., & Conner, T. (2015). Video shows cop body-slamming high school girl in S.C. classroom. *NBC News*. https://www.nbcnews.com/news/us-news/video-apprears-show-cop-body-slamming-student-s-f-classroom-n451896

Stephens, D. W. (2011). *Police discipline: A case for change*. National Institute of Justice.

Stewart, C. E. (2003). Abuse of power and judicial misconduct: A reflection on contemporary ethical issues facing judges. *University of St. Thomas Law Journal*, *1*(1), 464–479.

Stolberg, S. G. (2015). A.C.L.U. sues over handcuffing of boy, 8, and girl, 9, in Kentucky school. *The New York Times*. https://www.nytimes.com/2015/08/04/us/aclu-sues-over-handcuffing-of-boy-8-and-girl-9-in-kentucky-school.html

Stone, U., Liddell, M., & Matinovic, M. (2017). Incarcerated mothers: Issues and barriers of regaining custody of children. *The Prison Journal*, *97*(3), 296–317. doi:10.1177/0032885517703957

Stringer, H. (2019, March). Improving mental health for inmates. *American Psychological Association*, *50*(3), 46.

Sue, D. W., Capodilupo, C. M., Torino, G. C., Bucceri, J. M., Holder, A. M. B., Nadal, K. L., & Esquilin, M. (2007). Racial microaggressions in everyday life: Implications for clinical practice. *The American Psychologist, 62*(4), 271–286. doi:10.1037/0003-066X.62.4.271 PMID:17516773

Sumampouw, N. E. J., Otgaar, H., La Rooy, D., & Ruiter, C. (2020). The quality of forensic child interviewing in child sexual abuse cases in Indonesia. *Journal of Police and Criminal Psychology, 35*, 170–181.

Sumpter, C. (2020). Realising violent extremist risk assessments in Indonesia: Simplify and collaborate. *Journal for Deradicalization*, (22), 97–121.

Sunshine, J., & Tyler, T. R. (2003). The role of procedural justice and legitimacy in shaping public support for policing. *Law & Society Review, 37*(3), 513–547. doi:10.1111/1540-5893.3703002

Surfin, J. (2019). *3 things to know: Cultural humility*. Hogg Foundation for Mental Health. https://hogg.utexas.edu/3-things-to-know-cultural-humility

Sutherland, A., Ariel, B., Farrar, W., & De Anda, R. (2017). Post-experimental follow-ups—Fade-out versus persistence effects: The Rialto police body-worn camera experiment four years on. *Journal of Criminal Justice, 53*, 110–116. doi:10.1016/j.jcrimjus.2017.09.008

Swain, S. N., Saggurti, N., Battala, M., Verma, R. K., & Jain, A. K. (2011). Experience of violence and adverse reproductive health outcomes, HIV risks among mobile female sex workers in India. *BMC Public Health, 11*(1), 357. https://doi.org/10.1186/1471-2458-11-357

Swartz, K., Osborne, D. L., Dawson-Edwards, C., & Higgins, G. E. (2016). Policing schools: Examining the impact of place management activities on school violence. *American Journal of Criminal Justice, 41*(3), 465–483. doi:10.100712103-015-9306-6

Taliferro, W., Pham, D., & Cielinski, A. (2016). *A look at trends, gaps, and opportunities in correctional education and training*. Retrieved from https://www.clasp.org/sites/default/files/public/resources-and-publications/publication-1/2016.10.27_fromincarcerationtoreentry.pdf

Tame. (1998). *Freedom, responsibility, and justice: The criminology of the 'New Right.'* Retrieved from http://www2.libertarian.co.uk/sites/default/lanotepdf/legan030.pdf

Tannenbaum, F. (1938). *Crime and community*. Columbia University Press. doi:10.7312/tann90782

Taylor, M. (2017, December 6). *Improving in-prison rehabilitation programs*. California Legislative Analyst's Office. https://lao.ca.gov/Publications/Report/3720

Taylor, C. J. (2016). The family's role in the reintegration of formerly incarcerated individuals: The direct effects of emotional support. *The Prison Journal, 96*(3), 331–354. doi:10.1177/0032885516635085

Taylor, E., & Lee, M. (2019). Off the record? Arrestee concerns about the manipulation, modification, and misrepresentation of police body-worn camera footage. *Surveillance & Society, 17*(3/4), 473–483. doi:10.24908s.v17i3/4.6550

Templeton, R. (1998). *Super scapegoating: Teen 'super predators' hype set state for draconian legislation*. FAIR.

Tews, M. J., & Stafford, K. (2020). Tattoos and perceptions of employment suitability in the hospitality industry. *Journal of Human Resources in Hospitality & Tourism, 19*(2), 148–167. doi:10.1080/15332845.2020.1702865

Texas Commission on Law Enforcement. (2013). *Contract information for Texas indecent school district police department*. Author.

The American Civil Liberties Union. (2008). *Locating the school-to-prison pipeline.* https://www.aclu.org/node/29079%C2%A0

The Crown Prosecution Service. (2018). *Police and CPS relations.* https://www.cps.gov.uk/legal-guidance/police-and-cps-relations

The Hindu. (2006, January 30). *Project combat launched to eradicate "Devadasi" system.* https://www.thehindu.com/archive/print/2006/01/30/

The Institute of Fiscal Studies and Democracy. (2018). *Ending homelessness: A summary of proceedings.* No. 18003. https://ifsd.ca/web/default/files/Presentations/Reports/18003%20-%20Homelessness%20Symposium%20-%20Summary%20of%20Proceedings%20-%2029%20March%202018.pdf

The Nigeria Police Force. (n.d.). Retrieved from www.npf.gov.ng

The Sentencing Project. (2020). *Trends in U.S. corrections.* https://www.sentencingproject.org/wp-content/uploads/2020/08/Trends-in-US-Corrections.pdf

Thilagaraj, R. (2013). Criminal justice system in India. In *Handbook of Asian criminology* (pp. 199–211). Springer. doi:10.1007/978-1-4614-5218-8_13

Thisday. (2020). *Akeredolu: Amotekun will not be subsumed under FG's community policing.* Academic Press.

Thomas, T. (2019 July 10). Lawrenceville police latest victims of cyberattack. *WSB-TV Atlanta News Online.* https://www.wsbtv.com/news/local/gwinnett-county/lawrenceville-police-the-latest-victims-of-cyber-attack/968533646/

Thomas, J., & Zaitzow, B. H. (2006). Conning or conversion? The role of religion in prison coping. *The Prison Journal, 86*(2), 242–259. doi:10.1177/0032885506287952

Thompson, A. (2020 December 2). All cops to wear cameras in NJ. *New Jersey Today.* https://njtoday.net/2020/12/02/all-cops-to-wear-cameras-in-nj/

Tillyer, M. S., Fisher, B. S., & Wilcox, P. (2011). The effects of school crime prevention on students' violent victimization, risk perception, and fear of crime: A multilevel opportunity perspective. *Justice Quarterly, 28*(2), 249–277. doi:10.1080/07418825.2010.493526

Tillyer, R. (2018). Assessing the impact of community-oriented policing on arrest. *Justice Quarterly, 35*(3), 526–555. doi:10.1080/07418825.2017.1327609

Timler, K., Brown, H., & Varcoe, C. (2019). Growing connection beyond prison walls: How a prison garden fosters rehabilitation and healing for incarcerated men. *Journal of Offender Rehabilitation, 58*(5), 444–463. doi:10.1080/10509674.2019.1615598

Todak, N., & Gaub, J. E. (2019). Predictors of police body-worn camera acceptance: Digging deeper into officers' perceptions. *Policing, 43*(2), 299–313. doi:10.1108/PIJPSM-06-2019-0085

Tonry, M. (2012). Prosecutors and politics in comparative perspective. *Crime and Justice, 41*(1), 1–33.

Toronto Police Service. (2016). Body-worn cameras: A report on the findings of the pilot project to test the value and feasibility of body-worn cameras for police officers in Toronto. *US Department of Justice, Bureau of Justice Administration Online.* https://bja.ojp.gov/sites/g/files/xyckuh186/files/media/document/tps-body-worn-camera-pilot-project-evaluation.pdf

Travis, J., & Visher, C. (Eds.). (2005). *Prisoner reentry and crime in America.* Cambridge University Press. doi:10.1017/CBO9780511813580

Travis, J., Western, B., & Redburn, S. (2014). *The growth of incarceration in the United States: Exploring causes and consequences.* The National Academies Press.

Treleaven, S. (2019). Life after foster care in Canada. *Maclean's.* https://www.macleans.ca/society/life-after-foster-care-in-canada/

Tremblay, M., & Sutherland, J. (2017). The effectiveness of parenting programs for incarcerated mothers: A systematic review. *Journal of Child and Family Studies, 26*(12), 3247–3265. doi:10.100710826-017-0900-8

Trojanowicz & Bucqueroux. (1998). *Community policing: How to get started* (2nd ed.). Alderson Publishing Co.

Trojanowicz, R. C., & Bucqueroux, B. (1994). Community policing: How to get started (1st ed.). Anderson.

Trump, K. S. (1998). Keeping the peace: What you should know about staffing a school security department. *The American School Board Journal, 185*(3), 31–35.

Tully, T. (2020, March 23). 1,000 Inmates will be released from N.J. jails to curb coronavirus Risk. *The New York Times.* https://www.nytimes.com/2020/03/23/nyregion/coronavirus-nj-inmates-release.html

Turkish Criminal Procedure Code. (2009). Retrieved on 22.04.2021. https://www.legislationline.org/download/id/4257/file/Turkey_CPC_2009_en.pdf

Turney, K., Schnittker, J., & Wildeman, C. (2012). Those they leave behind: Paternal incarceration and maternal instrumental support. *Journal of Marriage and Family, 74*(5), 1149–1165. doi:10.1111/j.1741-3737.2012.00998.x

Tyler, T. R. (1990). *Why people obey the law.* Yale University Press.

Tyler, T. R. (2004). Enhancing police legitimacy. *The Annals of the American Academy of Political and Social Science, 593*(1), 84–99. doi:10.1177/0002716203262627

Tyler, T. R., & Fagan, J. (2008). Why do people cooperate with the police? *Ohio State Journal of Criminal Law, 6*, 231–275.

U.S. Commission on Civil Rights. (2018). *Police use of force: An examination of modern policing practices.* https://www.usccr.gov/pubs/2018/11-15-Police-Force.pdf

U.S. Department of Education office for Civil Rights. (2018). *Civil rights data collections: School climate and safety. Data Snapshot: School Discipline.* https://www2.ed.gov/about/offices/list/ocr/docs/school-climate-and-safety.pdf

U.S. Department of Justice, Office of Community Oriented Policing Services (COPS). (2021). *Supporting Safe Schools.* https://cops.usdoj.gov/supportingsafeschools

U.S. Government Accountability Office. (2018). *K-12 education: Discipline disparities for black students, boys, and students with disabilities.* Report to Congressional Requesters. https://www.gao.gov/products/gao-18-258

Ukoji, V., Ayodokun, A., & Eze, V. (2019). *Nigeria watch: Eighth report on violence in Nigeria.* IFRA-Nigeria Working Paper Series, No 59.

Umaña-Taylor, A. J. (2016). A post-racial society in which ethnic-racial discrimination still exists and has significant consequences for youths' adjustment. *Current Directions in Psychological Science, 25*(2), 111–118. doi:10.1177/0963721415627858

Umeagbolesi & Ijeoma. (2013). Institutional decay and corrupt/unethical practices: Problems and prospects for the police force in Nigeria. *IOSR Journal of Humanities and Social Science., 20*(8), 66–72.

Ümit, E., Çavdar, Y., & Yağcıoğlu, S. (2014). *Interview rooms for children: Needs, examples of best practices and standards for child friendly interview.* Summary Report. https://www.unicef.org/turkey/en/reports/judicial-interview-room

United Nations High Commissioner for Refugees. (2000). *Refworld | CCPR General Comment No. 28: Article 3 (The Equality of Rights Between Men and Women).* https://www.refworld.org/docid/45139c9b4.html

United Nations Office on Drugs and Crime. (2018). *Global report on trafficking in persons.* United Nations Publication. https://www.unodc.org/documents/data-and-analysis/glotip/2018/GLOTiP_2018_BOOK_web_small.pdf

Unrau, Y. (1993). A program logic model approach to conceptualizing social service programs. *The Canadian Journal of Program Evaluation, 8*(1), 117–134.

Upturn and Leadership Conference on Civil and Human Rights (LCCHR). (2017). The body-worn camera scorecard. *Upturn and the Leadership Conference on Civil and Human Rights Online.* https://www.bwcscorecard.org/static/pdfs/LCCHR%20and%20Upturn%20-%20BWC%20Scorecard%20v.3.04.pdf

Valliere, V. (2007). Understanding the non-stranger rapist. *The Voice, 1*(11), 1-6. http://www.ncdsv.org/images/NDAA_UnderstandingNonstrangerRapist_TheVoice_vol_1_no_11_2007.pdf

van de Weijer, S. G., Leukfeldt, R., & Bernasco, W. (2019). Determinants of reporting cybercrime: A comparison between identity theft, consumer fraud, and hacking. *European Journal of Criminology, 16*(4), 486–508.

Van Horn, S. A., Morgan, R. D., Brusman-Lovins, L., Littlefield, A. K., Hunter, J. T., Gigax, G., & Ridley, K. (2019). Changing lives and changing outcomes: "What works" in an intervention for justice-involved persons with mental illness. *Psychological Services, 16*(4), 693–700. https://doi.org/10.1037/ser0000248

Van Ness, L. (2020 January 14). Body cameras may not be the easy answer everyone was looking for. *The Pew Charitable Trusts.* https://www.pewtrusts.org/en/research-and-analysis/blogs/stateline/2020/01/14/body-cameras-may-not-be-the-easy-answer-everyone-was-looking-for

van Willigenburg, T. (2020). Moral Injury, post-incarceration syndrome and religious coping behind bars. In S. Sremac & I. Jindra (Eds.), *Lived religion, conversion and recovery.* Palgrave Studies in Lived Religion and Societal Challenges. Palgrave Macmillan. doi:10.1007/978-3-030-40682-0_8

van Zyl Smit, D. (2018). Rehabilitation as a dominant idea in European prison law: Problems and prospects. *Romania Journal of Sociological Studies. New Series, 1*, 9–18.

Varn, K. (2020 August 12). Once reluctant, Pinellas sheriff exploring body cameras for deputies. *Tampa Bay Times.* https://www.tampabay.com/news/crime/2020/08/12/once-reluctant-pinellas-sheriff-exploring-body-cameras-for-deputies/

Vera Institute of Justice. (2013). *The potential of community corrections to improve safety and reduce incarceration.* Center on Sentencing and Corrections.

Victoria News. (2020, April 20). *We're in it together: Mental health in greater Victoria.* Black Press Media. https://www.vicnews.com/community/were-in-it-together-mental-health-in-greater-victoria/

Viji. M. (2015). Human rights women prisoners and prison reforms in India- A Study. *AMIERJ, 4*(2).

Vito, G. F., & Higgins, G. E. (2015). *Practical program evaluation for criminal justice.* Elsevier.

Wacquant, L. (2010). Prisoner reentry as myth and ceremony. *Dialectical Anthropology, 34*(4), 605–620. doi:10.100710624-010-9215-5

Wahl, R. (2017). No justice, no peace? The police, people of color, and the paradox of protecting human rights. *Human Rights Quarterly, 39*(4), 811-831. http://dx.doi.org.ezp.waldenulibrary.org/10.1353/hrq.2017.0050

Wald, S., Spohn, C., & MeLone, M. (2007). *The color of justice: Race, ethnicity, and crime in America* (4th ed.). Belmont, CA: Wadsworth.

Wald, S., & Losen, D. (2003). *Defining and re-directing a school to prison pipeline*. Harvard Civil Rights Project.

Wall, D. S. (2015). The Internet as a conduit for criminal activity. *Information Technology and the Criminal Justice System*, 77-98.

Walmsley, R. (2005). Prison health care and the extent of prison overcrowding. *International Journal of Prisoner Health*, *1*(1), 9–12.

Walmsley, R. (2016). *World Prison Population List* (11th ed.). International Centre for Prison Studies, Kings College. https://www.prisonstudies.org/sites/default/files/resources/downloads/world_prison_population_list_11th_edition_0.pdf

Walsh, W. F., & Vito, G. F. (2019). *Police leadership and administration: A 21st-century strategic approach*. Routledge.

Walters, G. (2011). Predicting recidivism with the psychological inventory of criminal thinking styles and Level of Service Inventory-Revised: Screening Version. *Law and Human Behavior*, *35*(3), 211–220. doi:10.100710979-010-9231-7 PMID:20464628

Walther, A. (2012). *Participation or non-participation? Getting beyond dichotomies by applying an ideology-critical, a comparative and a biographical perspective. In Youth Participation in Europe: Beyond Discourses, Practices and Realities*. Policy Press.

Ward, T. (2002). The management of risk and the design of good lives. *Australian Psychologist*, *37*(3), 172–179. doi:10.1080/00050060210001706846

Ward, T., Day, A., Howells, K., & Birgden, A. (2004). The multifactor offender readiness model. *Aggression and Violent Behavior*, *9*(6), 645–673. doi:10.1016/j.avb.2003.08.001

Ward, T., & Laws, D. R. (2010). Desistance from sex offending: Motivating change, enriching practise. *International Journal of Forensic Mental Health*, *9*(1), 11–23. doi:10.1080/14999011003791598

Warren, R. K. (2009). Evidence-based sentencing: The application of principles of evidence based practice to state sentencing practice and policy. *University of San Francisco Law Review. University of San Francisco. School of Law*, *43*(3), 585–634.

Watanbe, B. (2020 November 24). Critics wary as Everett OKs body camera program for police. *The Herald*. https://www.heraldnet.com/news/critics-wary-as-everett-oks-body-camera-program-for-police/

Wear, M. (2015, September 18). Hold police fraternities accountable. *USA Today*, p. 9A.

Weatherburn, D., & Baker, J. (1999). Preventing crime and violence among transient and persistent offenders. In *3rd National Outlook Symposium on Crime in Australia, Mapping the Boundaries of Australia's Criminal Justice System*. The Australian Institute of Criminology. https://citeseerx.ist.psu.edu/viewdoc/download?doi=10.1.1.515.1328&rep=rep1&type=pdf

Weaver, B., Tata, C., Munro, M., & Barry, M. (2012). The failure of recall to prison: Early release, front-door and back-door sentencing and the revolving prison door in Scotland. *European Journal of Probation*, *4*(1), 85–98. doi:10.1177/206622031200400108

Webb, V. J., & Katz, C. M. (1998). Citizen ratings of the importance of community policing activities. In *Community Policing: Contemporary Readings*. Waveland Press.

Wehrman, M. M., & De Angelis, J. (2011). Citizen willingness to participate in police–community partnerships: Exploring the influence of race and neighborhood context. *Police Quarterly*, *14*(1), 48–69. doi:10.1177/1098611110393134

Wei, F., Lee, J., & Kwan, H. K. (2016). Impact of active constructive leadership and passive corrective leadership on collective organizational commitment. *Leadership and Organizational Development Journal, 37*(7), 822 – 842. https://psycnet.apa.org/record/2016-57029-001

Weiler, S., & Cray, M. (2011). Police at school: A brief history and current status of school resources officers. *The Clearing House: A Journal of Educational Strategies, Issues and Ideas, 84*(4), 160–163. doi:10.1080/00098655.2011.564986

Weisberg, R. (2014). Meanings and measures of recidivism. *Southern California Law Review, 87*(3), 785–804.

Weitzer, R. (2007). The social construction of sex trafficking: Ideology and institutionalization of a moral crusade. *Politics & Society, 35*(3), 447–475. https://doi.org/10.1177/0032329207304319

Weitzer, R., & Tuch, S. A. (2004). Race and perception of police misconduct. *Social Problems, 51*(3), 305–325. doi:10.1525p.2004.51.3.305

Weitzer, R., Tuch, S. A., & Skogan, W. G. (2008). Police–community relations in a majority-black city. *Journal of Research in Crime and Delinquency, 45*(4), 398–428. doi:10.1177/0022427808322617

Wellesley Institute. (2017, November). *Supportive housing for Ontario.* Wellesley Institute Policy Brief. https://www.wellesleyinstitute.com/wp-content/uploads/2017/11/Wellesley-Brief-Ontario-Supportive-Housing-1.pdf

Welsh, B. C., Braga, A. A., & Bruinsma, G. J. (2015). Reimagining broken windows: From theory to policy. *Journal of Research in Crime and Delinquency, 52*(4), 447–463. doi:10.1177/0022427815581399

Westcott, H. (1991). The abuse of disabled children: A review of the literature. *Child: Care, Health and Development, 17*(4), 243–258.

Westcott, H. L., & Davies, G. (2014). Safeguarding witnesses. In G. Davies & A. Beech (Eds.), *Forensic psychology: Crime justice law interventions* (pp. 247–264). John Wiley.

Westcott, K. (2015). Race, criminalization, and historical trauma in the United States: Making the case for a new justice framework. *Traumatology, 21*(4), 273–284. doi:10.1037/trm0000048

Western, B., & Smith, N. (2018). Formerly Incarcerated Parents and Their Children. *Demography, 55*(3), 823–847. doi:10.100713524-018-0677-4 PMID:29770923

Whitehouse, H., & Fitzgerald, R. (2020). Fusion and reform: The potential for identity fusion to reduce recidivism and improve reintegration. *Anthropology in Action, 27*(1).

White, M. D. (2019). Translating the story on body-worn cameras. *Criminology & Public Policy, 18*(1), 89–91. doi:10.1111/1745-9133.12421

White, M. D., Todak, N., & Gaub, J. E. (2018). Examining body-worn camera integration and acceptance among police officers, citizens, and external stakeholders. *Criminology & Public Policy, 17*(3), 649–677. doi:10.1111/1745-9133.12376

Whitten, E. L. (2017). *A case study of the effects the current community policing models have on rural police leaders in the south-central United States* (Dissertation). ProQuest Dissertations & Theses Global. (1874980994)

Wiener, J. (2020, March 5). *Newsom's to-do list on mental health.* https://www.newsreview.com/sacramento/newsoms-to-do-list-on-mental/content?oid=29844024

Wiggins, O. (2020, October 1). As decision nears on reform proposals, Maryland lawmakers struggle over police "Bill of Rights." *The Washington Post.*

Wikström, P. O. H., & Sampson, R. J. (2003). Social mechanisms of community influences on crime and pathways in criminality. *Causes of conduct disorder and juvenile delinquency*, 118-148. Retrieved from http://www.pads.ac.uk/Documents/Social_mechanisms_of_community_influences_on_crime_and_pathways_in_criminality.pdf

Wildeman, C. (2010). Paternal incarceration and children's physically aggressive behaviors: Evidence from the Fragile Families and Child Wellbeing Study. *Social Forces*, *89*(1), 285–309. doi:10.1353of.2010.0055

Wildeman, C., & Wang, E. A. (2017). Mass incarceration, public health, and widening inequality in the USA. *Lancet*, *389*(10077), 1464–1474. doi:10.1016/S0140-6736(17)30259-3 PMID:28402828

Wilson, A. B., & Draine, J. (2006). Collaborations between criminal justice and mental health systems for prisoner reentry. *Psychiatric Services (Washington, D.C.)*, *57*(6), 875–878.

Wilson, B., & Butler, L. D. (2014). Running a gauntlet: A review of victimization and violence in the pre-entry, post-entry, and peri-/post-exit periods of commercial sexual exploitation. *Psychological Trauma: Theory, Research, Practice, and Policy*, *6*(5), 494–504. https://doi.org/10.1037/a0032977

Wilson, L. A. (2014). The rights of victims vs the rights of the accused: Striking a balance between the rights of victims and accused persons in the international criminal justice setting. *UW Austl. L. Rev.*, *38*, 152.

Wiltz, T. (2019). *A pileup of inequities: Why people of color are hit hardest by homelessness.* The Pew Charitable Trusts. https://www.pewtrusts.org/en/research-and-analysis/blogs/stateline/2019/03/29/a-pileup-of-inequities-why-people-of-color-are-hit-hardest-by-homelessness

Wisler, D.& Onwudiwe, I.D. (2007). *Community policing: A comparative view.* Academic Press.

Witzel, M. (1999). *Aryan and non-Aryan names in Vedic India: Data for the linguistic situation, c. 1900-500 BC.* http://crossasia-repository.ub.uni-heidelberg.de/112/1/AryanandnonAryan_1999.pdf

Wolf, R., & Woodyard, C. (2019, December 16). Supreme Court refuses to consider cities' efforts to prosecute the homeless for sleeping outside. *USA Today.* https://www.usatoday.com/story/news/politics/2019/12/16/homeless-supreme-court-living-street-crime/4403793002/

Wolken, C. L. (2004). Feminist Legal theory and human trafficking in the United States: Towards a new framework. *University of Maryland Law Journal of Race*, *6*(2), 407–437. https://digitalcommons.law.umaryland.edu/rrgc/vol6/iss2/9/

Woodward, S. (2016). The police killings no one is talking about. *In These Times.* Retrieved from: https://www.inthesetimes.com/features/native_american_police_killings_native_lives_matter.html

World Health Organization (WHO). (n.d.). *Mental health and prisons: Information sheet.* Retrieved from https://www.who.int/mental_health/policy/mh_in_prison.pdf

Wright, V. (2010). *Deterrence in criminal justice: Evaluating certainty vs. severity of punishment.* The Sentencing Project. https://www.sentencingproject.org/wp-content/uploads/2016/01/Deterrence-in-Criminal-Justice.pdf

Wright, R., Powell, M. B., & Ridge-Damien, T. (2007). What criteria do police officers' use to measure the success of an interview with a child witness? *Psychology, Crime & Law*, *13*(4), 395–404.

Wycoff, M. A., & Skogan, W. G. (1994). Community policing in Madison: An analysis of implementation and impact. In D. P. Rosenbaum (Ed.), *The challenge of community policing: Testing the promises* (pp. 75–91). Sage. doi:10.4135/9781483327006.n4

Xu, Y., Fiedler, M. L., & Flaming, K. H. (2005). Discovering the impact of community policing: The broken windows thesis, collective efficacy, and citizens' judgment. *Journal of Research in Crime and Delinquency*, *42*(2), 147–186.

Yang, S.-M. (2010). Assessing the spatial-temporal relationship between disorder and violence. *Journal of Quantitative Criminology*, *26*(1), 139–163. doi:10.100710940-009-9085-7

Yokum, D., Ravishankar, A., & Coppock, A. (2019). A randomized control trial evaluating the effects of police body-worn cameras. *Proceedings of the National Academy of Sciences - PNAS, 116*(21), 10329-10332. 10.1073/pnas.1814773116

YukhnenkoD.SridharS.FazelS. (2019). A systematic review of criminal recidivism rates worldwide: 3-year update. *Welcome Open Research, 4*(28), doi:10.12688/wellcomeopenres.14970.2

YukhnenkoD.SridharS.FazelS. (2019). A systematic review of criminal recidivism rates worldwide: 3-year update. *Welcome Open Research*, *4*(28). doi:10.12688/wellcomeopenres.14970

Zamoff, M. (2019). Assessing the impact of police body camera evidence on the litigation of excessive force cases. *Georgia Law Review (Athens, Ga.)*, *54*(1), 1–60.

Zoellick, J. C. (2018). Lock them up! Lock them up? A critique of the prison mosaic. Futures: The *Journal of Policy. Planning and Futures Studies*, *101*, 1–9.

About the Contributors

Michael Pittaro, PhD, is a 30-year criminal justice veteran, highly experienced in working with criminal offenders. Before pursuing a career in higher education, Dr. Pittaro worked in corrections administration; has served as the Executive Director of a county outpatient drug and alcohol facility; and as Executive Director of a county drug and alcohol prevention agency. Dr. Pittaro holds a BS in Criminal Justice; an MPA in Public Administration; and a PhD in criminal justice. Dr. Pittaro serves on three International Editorial Advisory Boards, including the International Journal of Criminal Justice Sciences, the International Journal of Cyber Criminology, and on the Academic Advisory Council / Journal with Karnavati University's United School of Law, India. He has also served for the past three years as a program committee member for the South Asian Society of Criminology and Victimology and as a federal grant peer reviewer for the United States Department of Justice and National Institute of Justice. He is a regular contributor to In Public Safety, Corrections One, and Psychology Today.

* * *

Adebowale Idowu Adeyeye holds a PhD in Peace Studies (South Africa); MA Peace and Development Studies, MSc, BSc, Political Science (Ilorin). His areas of interest are in Peace, Conflict and International Relations. He is a Lecturer and current Head, Department of Political Sciences, Osun State University, Osogbo, Nigeria. Adebowale Adeyeye has written widely on Conflicts, Insurgency and Terrorism strategies and Tactics in Africa and other areas including Democracy and Development.

Olugbemiga Samuel AFOLABI PhD is an Associate Professor of Political Science and Chair, Department of Political Science, Obafemi Awolowo University (OAU) Ile Ife Nigeria and a Research Fellow, Department of Politics, University of Johannesburg, South Africa. He has taught in several universities both at undergraduate and postgraduate levels within and outside Africa. His competence covers areas of study such as Electoral/Democratic Studies, Higher Education, Research Methodology, Decolonization/Post-colonial theories; Political Philosophy/Theory as well as Security and governance. Dr Afolabi is a recipient of many awards, grants and fellowships with publications in reputable journals.

Vedika Agarwal has completed her Masters of Science in Forensic Psychology and Mental Health at the University of Manchester, United Kingdom. A Psychology post-graduate with a strong background in mental health as well as core skills and understanding of forensic psychology and practice. She has experience working with special needs children, distressed young adults, delinquent young adults, adults suffering with various mental health problems. In her professional career, she has worked in Tihar Prison

Complex as a Psychological First Aid Responder and this has given her valuable insight into prison life. She conducted semi-structured interviews with inmates in a one-on-one setting and identified inmates posing suicidal tendencies. She was responsible for providing Psychological First Aid to the inmates who required it. During her work experience in Tihar prisons, she also leads and conducted various activities for inmates to improve their wellbeing. Vedika also assisted in rehabilitation efforts through counseling by a trained counselor of emotionally distressed high-risk inmates. She was vital in supporting inmates through their traumatic experiences and depressive episodes and also provided special guidance on drug abuse, suicidal, and self-harm tendencies. She has volunteered in various NGOs and mental health organizations. She has monitored and assessed children and young adults with mental health problems such as autism spectrum disorder, down syndrome, intellectual disabilities, or learning disabilities. She has experience working as a special educator and promotes positive interaction in the classroom by helping students focus on important concepts, and overall help the students to develop academic and social skills. In addition, she mentored and counseled underprivileged children and helped them to deal with everyday life problems. Furthermore, she dealt with socially backward, psychologically disturbed, and delinquent children and through the means of creativity and play therapy helped them resolve the difficulties that they faced in their lives and improve their mental wellbeing. She is compassionate and understands the circumstances and the mental state of the service users; in turn, helps them manage their symptoms by planning their future treatment plans. Her expertise lies in counseling and conducting integrative therapy techniques with children, young adults, and adults with various mental health problems. She specializes in the rehabilitation and reformation of prisoners and ex-convicts. She is also a research scholar and has successfully completed three research papers in the field of psychology and sociology. Few of her research articles have also been published in imminent psychology magazines. Her broad research interests are 'Understanding of the Criminal mind and the different Reformation Interventions used for offenders'. She is passionate and determined to help reform and rehabilitate ex-offenders and prisoners and understand the reasons behind the criminal behavior. She is a graduate member of the British Psychological Society and is also Forensic Psychology Aptitude and Caliber Test (F-PACT) certified.

Christopher L. Bush, PhD, is the founder of Crossing Over Consulting Services, an anger management consulting service that helps individuals manage their anger behavior through coaching. Before devoting his time working part-time with youth and adults with their anger, Dr. Christopher L. Bush self-published his first book, Crossing Over From your Personal Barriers. A self-help book that provides inspiration and motivation to individuals who are struggling with life choices and decisions. In addition, to the publication of his book, Dr. Christopher L. Bush has spoken at venues providing motivational speaking to audiences that included, ex-offenders, to homeless individuals, youth and young adults. Since completing his dissertation spring 2020, Dr. Christopher L. Bush has a published article (fall 2020) in the Journal of Social Change. In addition, upon completing his doctorate Dr. Bush has extended his dissertation to developing a training where law enforcement will engage in community policing training specifically with the black community called STR "I"VE (pronounced, I STRIVE). Dr. Christopher L. Bush is an adjunct professor at Allen County Community College providing instruction in Criminal Justice course work (Introduction to Criminal Justice, Law Enforcement Operations and Procedures and Criminal Investigations). In addition to being an adjunct professor, Dr. Christopher L. Bush full time work is in prevention science with the state of Kansas, where he over sees grants and contracts ensuring the work around prevention substance abuse and behavior health is a message shared across KS. His work efforts have awarded him with two high recognizable state achievements, the distinguish award for A notable event/achievement that is significant in scope, effort, or impact on government operations or service to citizens. Dr. Christopher L. Bush, also have been recognized for a meritorious award for execution of duties far beyond the service level commonly expected by the employees' customers that is of great benefit to, or reflects highly on, the agency or the state. Dr. Christopher L. Bush is a member of Kappa Alpha Psi Fraternity Inc., and Polemarch of the local chapter in Topeka, KS. In addition, he serves as the Undergraduate Chapter advisor for Kansas State University and Washburn University members of Kappa Alpha Psi Fraternity, Inc. He also serves as a member of the National Honor Society Leadership/ Criminal Justice and Walden University- Sigma Alpha Pi/Alpha Phi Sigma and a Member of the 2011 Greater Topeka Leadership. Dr. Christopher Bush resides in Topeka, KS with his wife and two sons.

Jayesh D'Souza, Ph.D., recently completed a Certificate in Sustainability at UCLA Extension. He has several public policy publications to his credit. His book, Terrorist Financing, Money Laundering, and Tax Evasion: Examining the Performance of Financial Intelligence Units has sold all over the world. His writings are based on several years of experience working in the public, consulting, and academic sectors.

Divya Dubey is pursuing her Doctorate in Forensic Psychology from Amity University, Lucknow campus, India. Presently, she is working as a Consultant in the department of Risk, threat and Response at Inspire Solutions, Dubai. She has completed her online professional diploma in Criminal Profiling and Crime Scene Analysis from The Forensic Criminology Institute Alaska, United States. On the recommendation of the Academy of Behavioral Profiling (ABP) Board of Examiners, the International Association of Forensic Criminologists (IAFC) awarded her the member status of DIPLOMAT (D-ABP). In 2009, she received her Masters in Clinical and Industrial Psychology, with a meritorious position from Lucknow University, India. In 2011, She completed her one year professional post graduate diploma in Forensic Psychology from Gujarat Forensic Sciences University, Gandhinagar, Gujarat, India where she got trained in number of tools used in detection of deception such as Polygraph, Layered voice analysis, Brain electrical oscillation signature profiling (BEOS). She also has a licence in operating Layered Voice Analysis (LVA 6.50) from Nemesysco, Israel. In 2011, She was hired as a Project Assistant in the Department of Cognitive and Brain Sciences at Indian Institute of Technology (IIT) Gandhinagar, Gujarat, India. She also worked as an intern in Sabarmati Jail, Ahmedabad in 2012, Gujarat and Tihar Jail, New Delhi, 2019 providing psychological first aid to offenders and also worked on their rehabilitation programme. She has also presented papers in International conferences and has also published her review papers on International Journals. In 2020, she has also published one of her chapters on "Psychological Impact of COVID-19" published by Royal Book Publishing. She is also working as an Editorial Board Member and Reviewer in one of the International Journals.

Scott Duncan, PhD, is an assistant professor of criminal justice at Bloomsburg University. He earned graduate degrees from Belmont University and the University of Cincinnati, and a Ph.D. from Nova Southeastern University in 2019. His research and teaching interests include criminal investigation, policing, and criminal intelligence.

Mary J. Flanegan is a veteran of the United States Marine Corps where she spent almost 16 years as a military policeman specializing in traffic accident investigation. Mary spent many years working for various Departments of Corrections at state levels as a probation – parole officer and as a case manager – counselor in prison systems. She holds a Bachelor of Science degree in Criminal Justice and Equine

Management from the University of Findlay in Findlay, Ohio. She obtained a Master of Science degree in Criminal Justice with specialties in Legal Aspects and Emergency Management from Saint Leo University in Saint Leo, Florida, and is currently completing the requirements for a Doctorate in Criminal Justice also from Saint Leo University. Mary is passionate about Criminal Justice reform focusing on reforms in policing and corrections. In her free time, she enjoys spending time with her rescue dogs.

Kula Francis, PhD, is an Associate Professor of Political Science in the College of Liberal Arts and Social Sciences at the University of the Virgin Islands. She holds a Doctorate of Philosophy in Urban Studies and Public Affairs from the University of Akron in Ohio. Her current research interests are social equity in public organizations, evaluation, international relations, history, politics, and public administration.

Hannah Geczi is currently a master's student in the School of Criminal Justice at the University of Cincinnati. She graduated with her B.A. in Criminal Justice from Bloomsburg University of Pennsylvania in 2020. Her research interests focus on policing and crime prevention.

Valene Gresham, PsyD is an assistant professor at the Chicago School of Professional Psychology as well as a clinical & forensic psychologist working in private practice and consulting in Paris, France. Dr. Gresham is also licensed and practicing in the UK.

Daskyes Gulleng, PhD, holds a PhD in Sociology (Criminology) from the University of Jos, Nigeria. He teaches Criminology and Security Studies in the same University. He is a researcher whose interest cuts across prison management and violence, human right and military involvement in internal security operations in Nigeria, formal and informal policing in rural communities and anti-corruption studies. He has published in both local and international journals in his research area.

Debarati Halder, LL.B, LL.M, Ph.D (Law) (NLSIU), is presently working as Professor of Law, Parul Institute of Law, Parul University, Gujarat, India. She is also the founder-Secretary of South Asian Society of Criminology and Victimology and Founder, Centre for Cyber victim counselling. She is also the member of board of Trustee at International Society of Therapeutic Jurisprudence.

Marty Allen Hatfield obtained a Bachelor of Science in Criminal Justice in 2015, Master of Science in Criminal Justice in 2016, Master of Arts in Intelligence Studies, and is currently pursuing a PhD in Criminal Justice at Liberty University. He is currently a Criminal Justice Program Manager with the Justice and Community Services Section of the Division of Administrative Services, where he is responsible for the management and oversight of several federal and state grant programs provided by the U.S. Department of Justice and the state of West Virginia including, but not limited to, the Community Corrections Grant Program, Justice Assistance Grant Program, Comprehensive Opioid, Stimulant, and Substance Abuse Program, National Criminal History Improvement Grant Program, and Paul Coverdell Forensic Science Improvement Grant Program.

Kenny Hendrickson, PhD, is an Associate Professor of Public Administration and Social Sciences, and the Director of the Master of Public Administration Program in the College of Liberal Arts and Social Sciences at the University of the Virgin Islands. He holds a Doctorate of Philosophy in Urban

Studies and Public Affairs from the University of Akron in Ohio. His current research interests are centered on organizational authenticity and care, workplace performativity, discretion and professional decision making.

Ronn Johnson, Ph.D., ABPP is a tenured full professor of psychiatry as well as the Associate Dean for Diversity and Inclusion at Creighton University School of Medicine. Concurrently, he is the lead clinical psychologist at the mental health clinic at the Nebraska-Western VA Healthcare System (NWI).

Sheri Jenkins Keenan, PhD, is the Coordinator of The Center for Community Criminology & Research and an Assistant Professor in the Department of Criminology & Criminal Justice at The University of Memphis. She holds a Ph.D. in Criminal Justice, Master of Science and Bachelor of Science in criminal justice, and a Bachelor of Arts in Sociology. Dr. Keenan has 14 years of experience in law enforcement and corrections. Her research interests focus on policing special populations with an emphasis on juveniles: delinquency, mental illness, school safety, gangs/threat groups, and juvenile justice program evaluation. Dr. Keenan's publications deal with such areas as K12 tracking, school violence, zero tolerance policies, nature and extent of mental health moving through the juvenile justice system, juvenile drug courts, transfer/waiver, bullying/cyber-bullying, gang violence, and rational choice theory. Keenan has an accomplished grant record, is a member of several state, regional, and national professional organizations, serves on numerous local advisory committees and boards, and is a state certified ACE trainer. Dr. Keenan is a LIFETIME member of SCJA.

Allan T. Moore, Ph.D., is a lecturer in criminology and criminal justice at the University of the West of Scotland, and formerly a lecturer in law. He has a number of central interests, including procedural justice, arbitrary punishment and detention, mass violence particularly in the areas of genocide, crimes against humanity, and terrorism. He has past published work on trends in the judiciary, the use of propaganda in preparation for genocide, reintegration of perpetrators of mass violence to mainstream society, and the role of the arts in peace and security strategies, as well as a range of other areas in the central fields of law and justice. Dr Moore has affiliation with several professional organisations, including membership of the International Association of Genocide Scholars, the Society of Legal Scholars, the British Institute in East Africa, and the Scottish Institute for Policing Research.

Derek Moore has a Master of Criminal Justice degree from Saint Leo University in Forensic Science and Behavioral Studies. He is currently active duty in the Marine Corps while finishing his Doctor of Criminal Justice Degree from Saint Leo University. His major interest includes topics in homeland security specifically human trafficking and cognitive behavioral therapy programs. He is an avid marathon runner and often travels the world to race in big events. He is retiring from the Marine Corps this fall to pursue a career field in criminal justice reform.

Jessica Mueller-Coyne, Psy.D is an adjunct professor in the department of psychology at San Diego State University (SDSU) and a lecturer in SDSU's Forensic Psychology Certificate program. She is also a licensed psychologist in California and a registered clinical psychologist in New Zealand. Dr. Mueller-Coyne is currently a clinical psychologist at the New Zealand Department of Corrections.

Vipin Vijay Nair, PhD, is currently working as an Assistant Professor (Criminology and Victimology) at Jindal Institute of Behavioural Sciences, O.P Jindal Global University. He was awarded his Doctorate in Behavioural Sciences from O. P. Jindal Global University and received his Master's in Criminology from LNJN National Institute of Criminology and Forensic Sciences, GGSIPU, where he was awarded the University Silver medal for his academic and research vigor. He has qualified UGC-NET lectureship (Criminology) in 2016 and was invited as a resource person at a two-day National Workshop on "Career Advancement in Criminology". He has been awarded the silver medal for Best Scientific Research paper at the 38th National Conference of Indian Society of Criminology in 2015. Nair has completed many academic and individual research projects and is actively pursuing research in the field of victimology and criminology, with active involvement in the Centre of Victimology and Psychological Studies and Centre for Criminology and Forensic Studies at Jindal Institute of Behavioural Sciences, JGU. He is dedicated to contributing inter-disciplinary work in the field of victimology and criminology by working on articles, essays, and research papers. He has presented in several International conferences across the globe. He is currently affiliated as member of few national and international organisations like World Society of Victimology, American Society of Criminology, British Society of Criminology, Indian Society of Criminology, Indian Criminology & Forensic Science Association, and others.

Olumide Omodunbi is a graduate of Political Science and International Relations of Osun State University, Osogbo, Nigeria. He holds a Master's of Science Degree in Political Science from Obafemi Awolowo University, Ile-Ife, Osun, Nigeria. Olumide currently works in the Department of Political Sciences, Osun State University as a Lecturer. His research interests includes Conflict, Security and Nigeria Government and Politics.

Sheryl Pelletier is an Adjunct Professor of criminal justice within the College of Education and Social Services at Saint Leo University. Sheryl is a current doctoral candidate in the Doctor of Criminal Justice program at Saint Leo University and also holds a Master of Science in criminal justice with a specialization in legal studies, a BS in criminal justice, and a post-baccalaureate certificate in paralegal studies. Her twenty-plus-year career working in the legal arena and approximately half of that time studying criminology brings a unique perspective to criminal justice analysis and reform. Her current research interest includes the impact of societal demands for change and their impact on judicial administration in the U.S. court system.

Sandra Anil Varkey is currently a legal scholar and researcher with a research interest in Criminology, Victimology, penology, and the Criminal Justice system.

Index

www.ingramcontent.com/pod-product-compliance
Lightning Source LLC
LaVergne TN
LVHW060406300926
849162LV00006B/1357
* 9 7 8 1 7 9 9 8 6 8 8 4 2 *